Enjoy!
Diana Lindsay
Ricardo AB-

RICARDO BRECEDA | ACCIDENTAL ARTIST

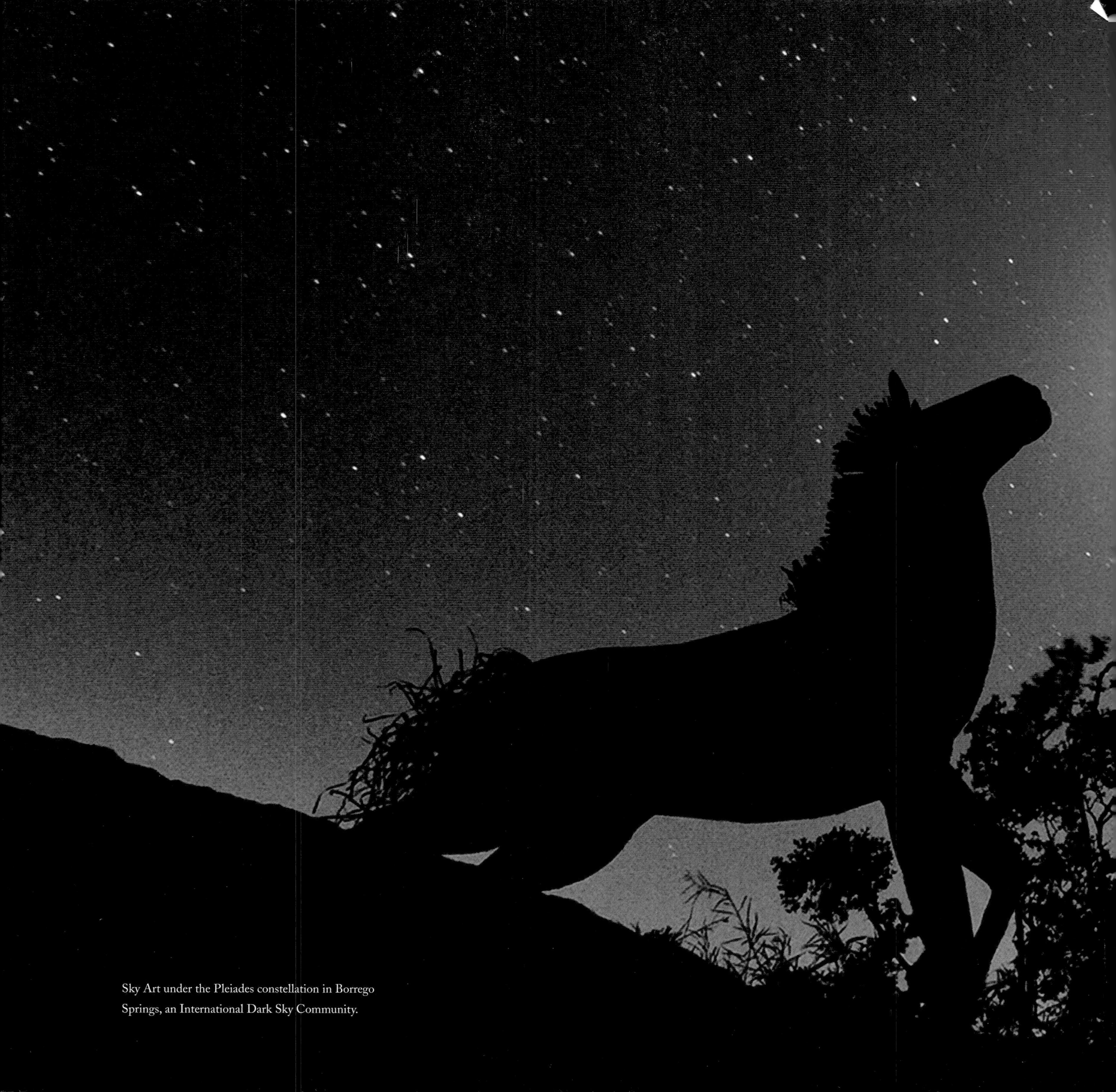

Sky Art under the Pleiades constellation in Borrego Springs, an International Dark Sky Community.

RICARDO BRECEDA

ACCIDENTAL ARTIST

DIANA LINDSAY

SUNBELT PUBLICATIONS
SAN DIEGO

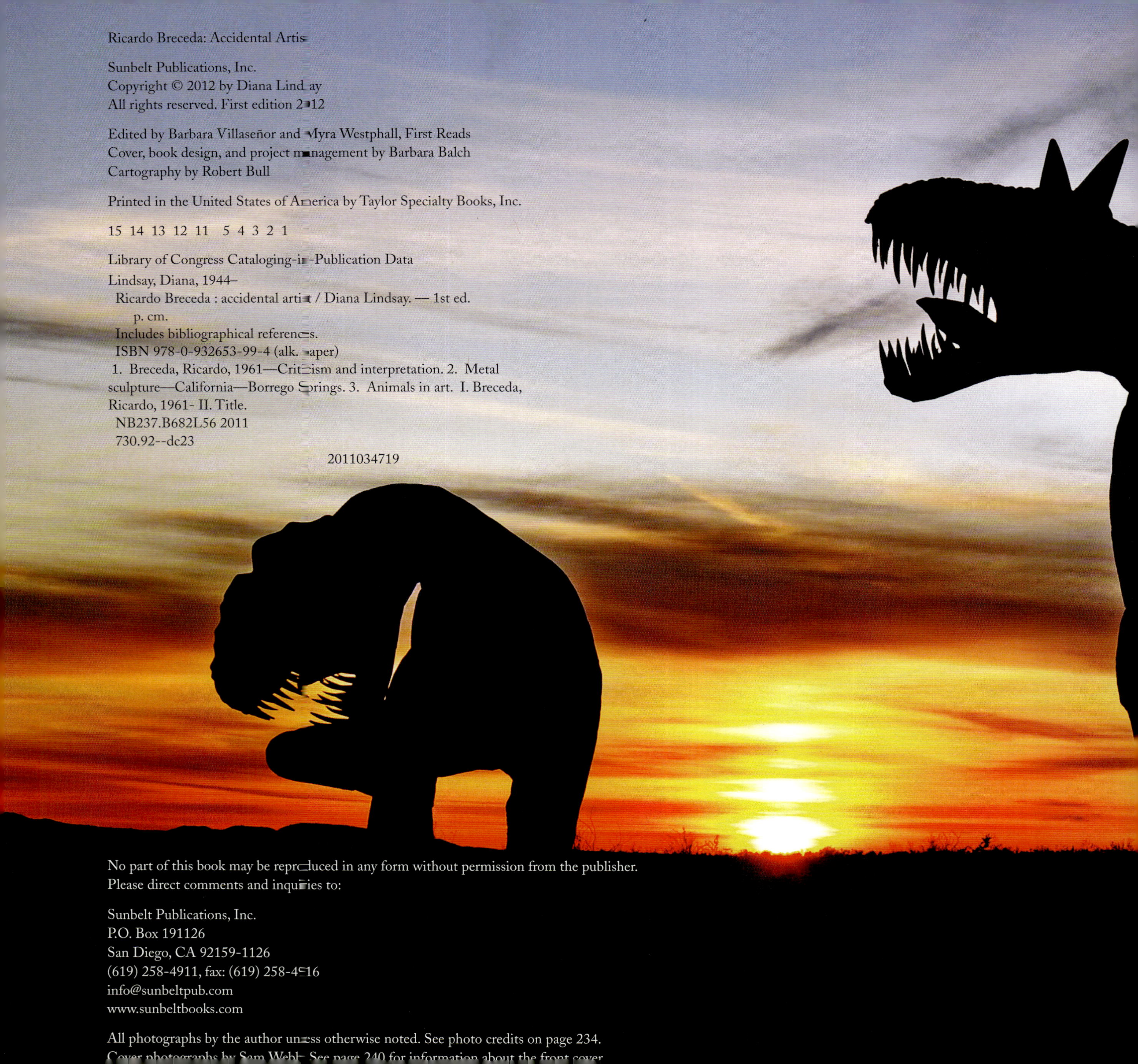

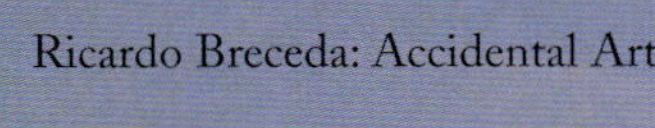

Ricardo Breceda: Accidental Artist

Sunbelt Publications, Inc.
 First edition 2012

Edited by Barbara Villaseñor and Myra Westphall, First Reads
Cover, book design, and project management by Barbara Balch
Cartography by Robert Bull

Printed in the United States of America by Taylor Specialty Books, Inc.

15 14 13 12 11 5 4 3 2 1

Library of Congress Cataloging-in-Publication Data

Lindsay, Diana, 1944–
Ricardo Breceda : accidental artist / Diana Lindsay. — 1st ed.
p. cm.
Includes bibliographical references.
ISBN 978-0-932653-99-4 (alk. paper)
1. Breceda, Ricardo, 1961—Criticism and interpretation. 2. Metal sculpture—California—Borrego Springs. 3. Animals in art. I. Breceda, Ricardo, 1961- II. Title.
NB237.B682L56 2011
730.92--dc23

2011034719

Please direct comments and inquiries to:

Sunbelt Publications, Inc.
P.O. Box 191126
San Diego, CA 92159-1126
(619) 258-4911, fax: (619) 258-4916
info@sunbeltpub.com
www.sunbeltbooks.com

All photographs by the author unless otherwise noted. See photo credits on page 234.
Cover photographs by Sam Webb. See page 240 for information about the front cover.

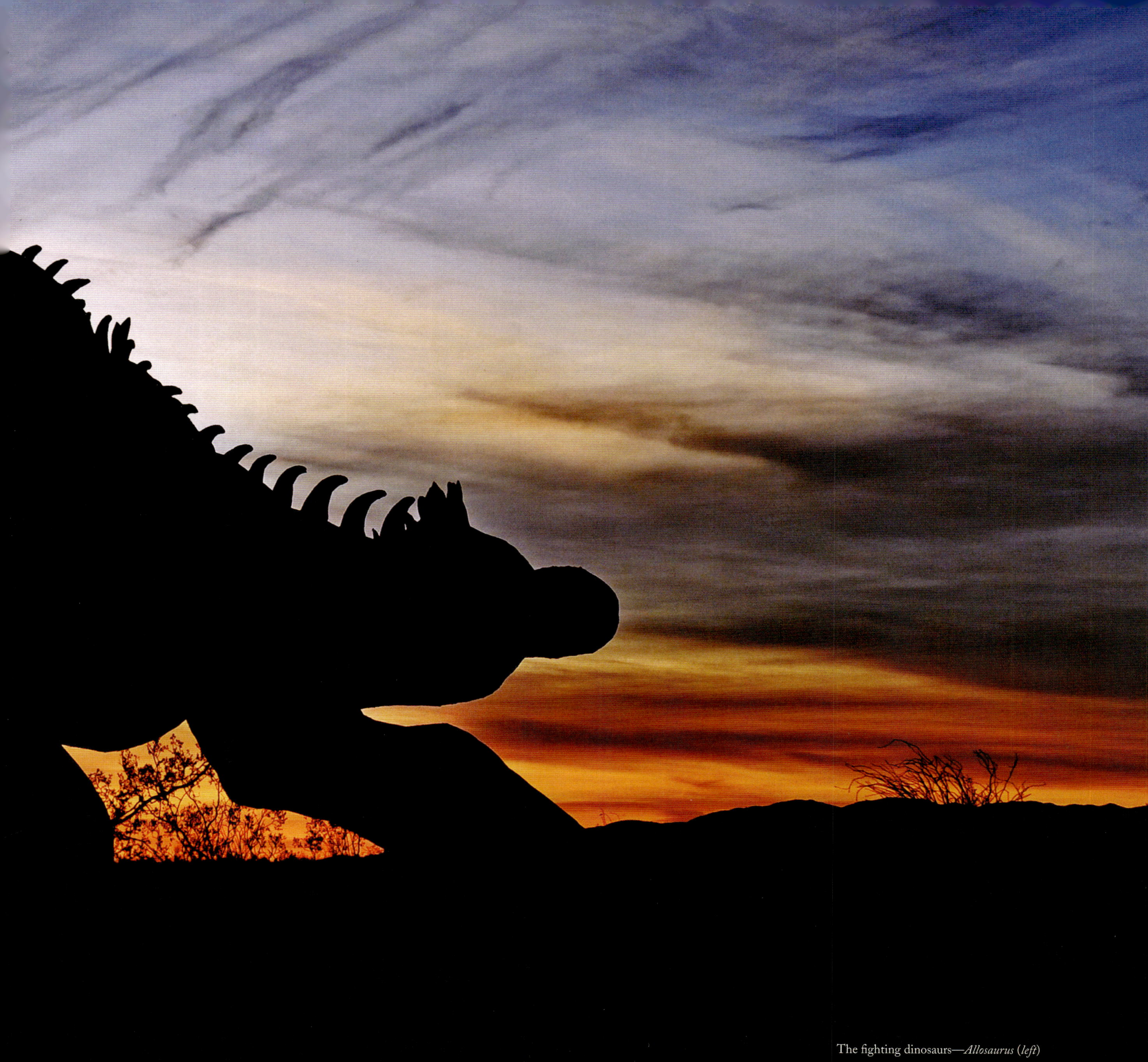

The fighting dinosaurs—*Allosaurus* (*left*) and *Carnotaurus* (*right*) —at sunrise.

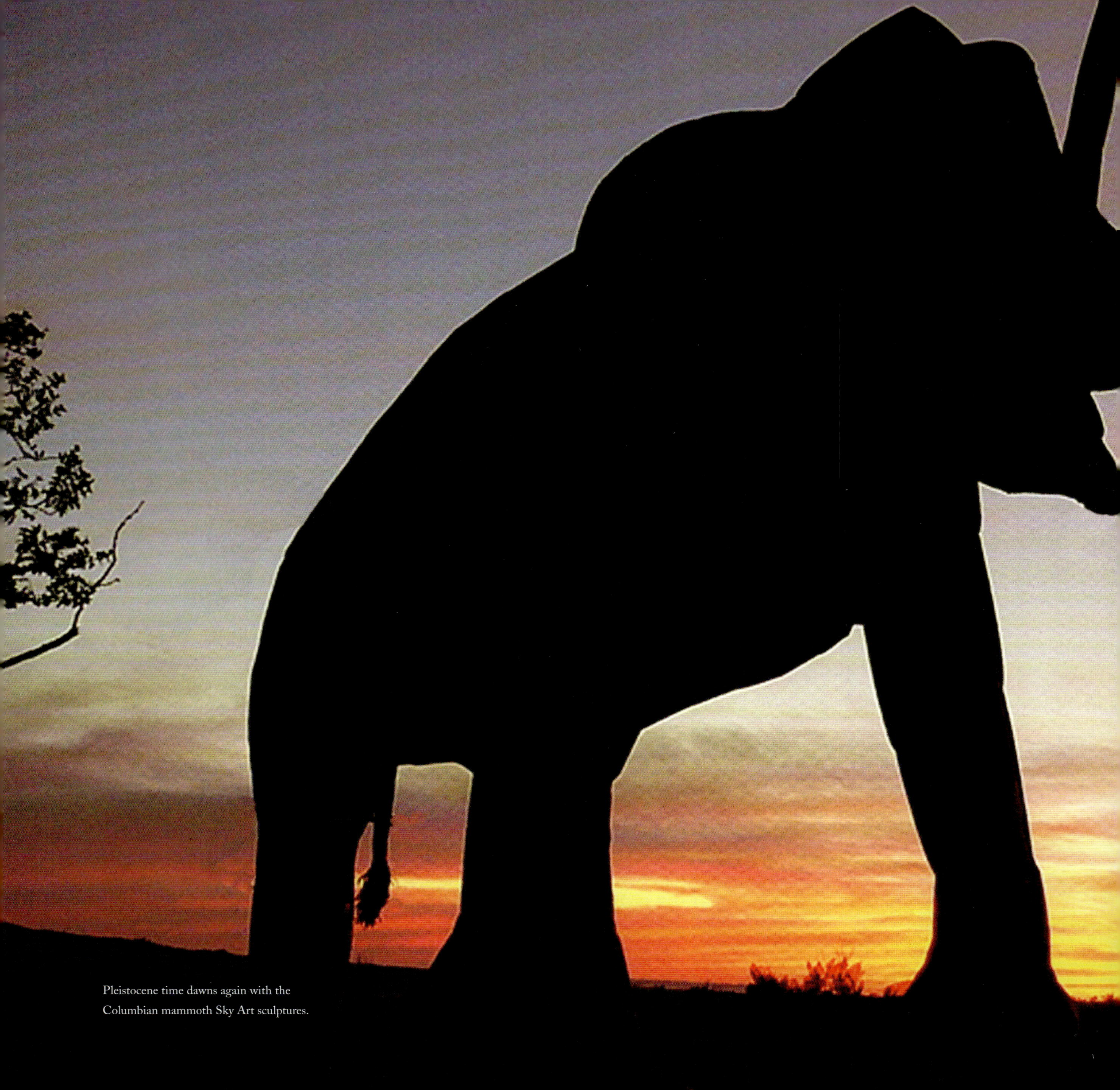

Pleistocene time dawns again with the
Columbian mammoth Sky Art sculptures.

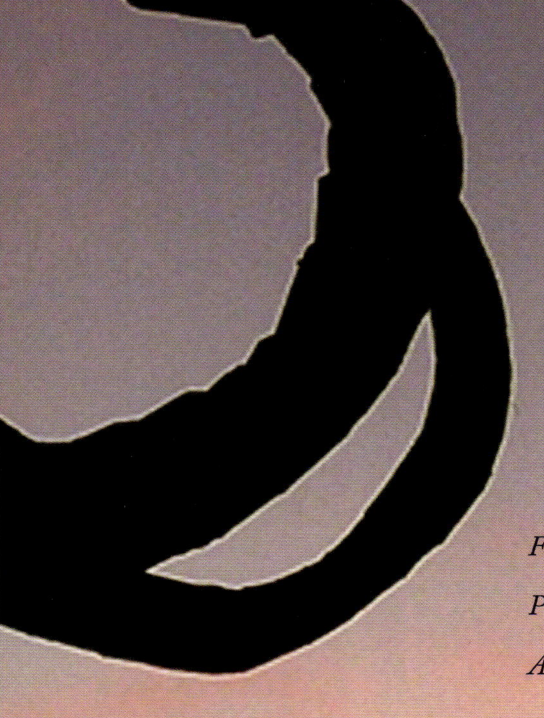

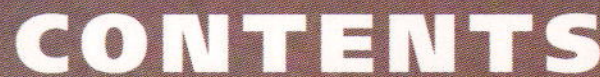

CONTENTS

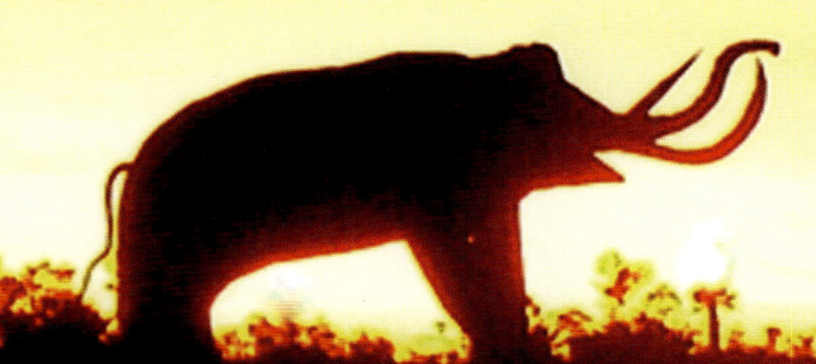

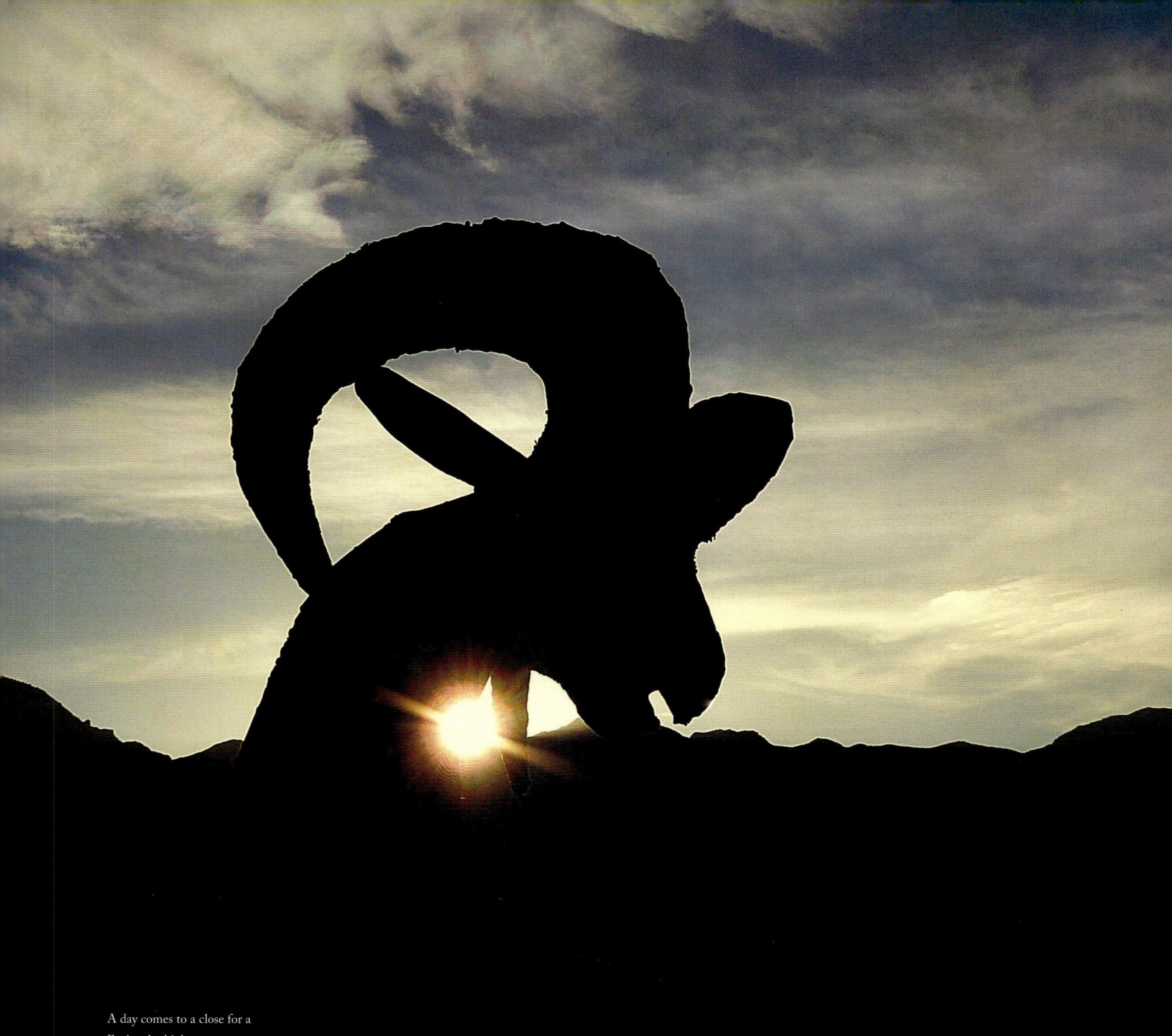

A day comes to a close for a Peninsular bighorn ram.

FOREWORD

For weeks, for months, I'd been hearing about this crazy-*loco* artist who does huge life-size metal sculptures of elephants, giraffes, and dinosaurs.

"Come on," said my friend Dennis. "Meet me at the 15 and 76 tomorrow morning and we'll drive up to see Ricardo. He just finished a couple of life-size mammoths for me."

"Okay, Dennis," I said. "I'll meet you there tomorrow morning."

It was a nice, peaceful drive north on Highway 76, which goes inland from Oceanside where I live.

"Is Ricardo Mexican?" I asked.

"Yes, of course, and for years I'd been seeing his metal sculptures off the side of the road when I'd drive by," Dennis said to me, "and they always looked pretty good. But then, recently, they got so good and realistic looking that I was amazed. So one day I gave myself extra time so I could stop and see more of his work. It was electrifying to meet the man. He was so full of passion for what he does. I haven't been able to stop smiling since."

Well, the moment we drove up to Ricardo's compound off of the 215, I'd, too, begun grinning—I just couldn't help it. I mean, it's every kid's dream to travel back in time and come face to face with gigantic mammoths and huge sloths. And all these metal sculptures looked so real and menacing. Then here came Ricardo himself to greet us. He, too, was all smiles and full of happy crazy*loco* energy.

We started talking in Spanish and gave each other a great big happy hug. He was immediately like family to me, full of joy and no hidden agenda.

The day we spent with Ricardo, we helped him transport the two new huge sculptures on a flatbed trailer and set them up out in the desert, and then turning them this way and that way, until they both looked totally natural. Then we got back on the highway, and drove by the sculptures like we were tourists and didn't know the mammoth and her baby were there—WHAT A SIGHT! WHAT A SURPRISE! TAKING US BACK MILLIONS OF YEARS! We were truly kids once again, and there are no borders or boundaries or time limitations between people who are having fun!

This is Ricardo Breceda! An artist full of passion! A Picasso who works with metal with the gusto of a child!

Drive out to Borrego and see for yourself! Take the kids. Take the grandparents! We all could use a little more awe and adventure in our lives!

Victor E. Villaseñor

P.S. Ricardo also made the mother *burro* and *burrito* that stand by the gate to our *rancho* in Oceanside, pulling an old cart. Thank you, Ricardo, *gracias* with all my heart and soul, for bringing such wonder and joy to the world!

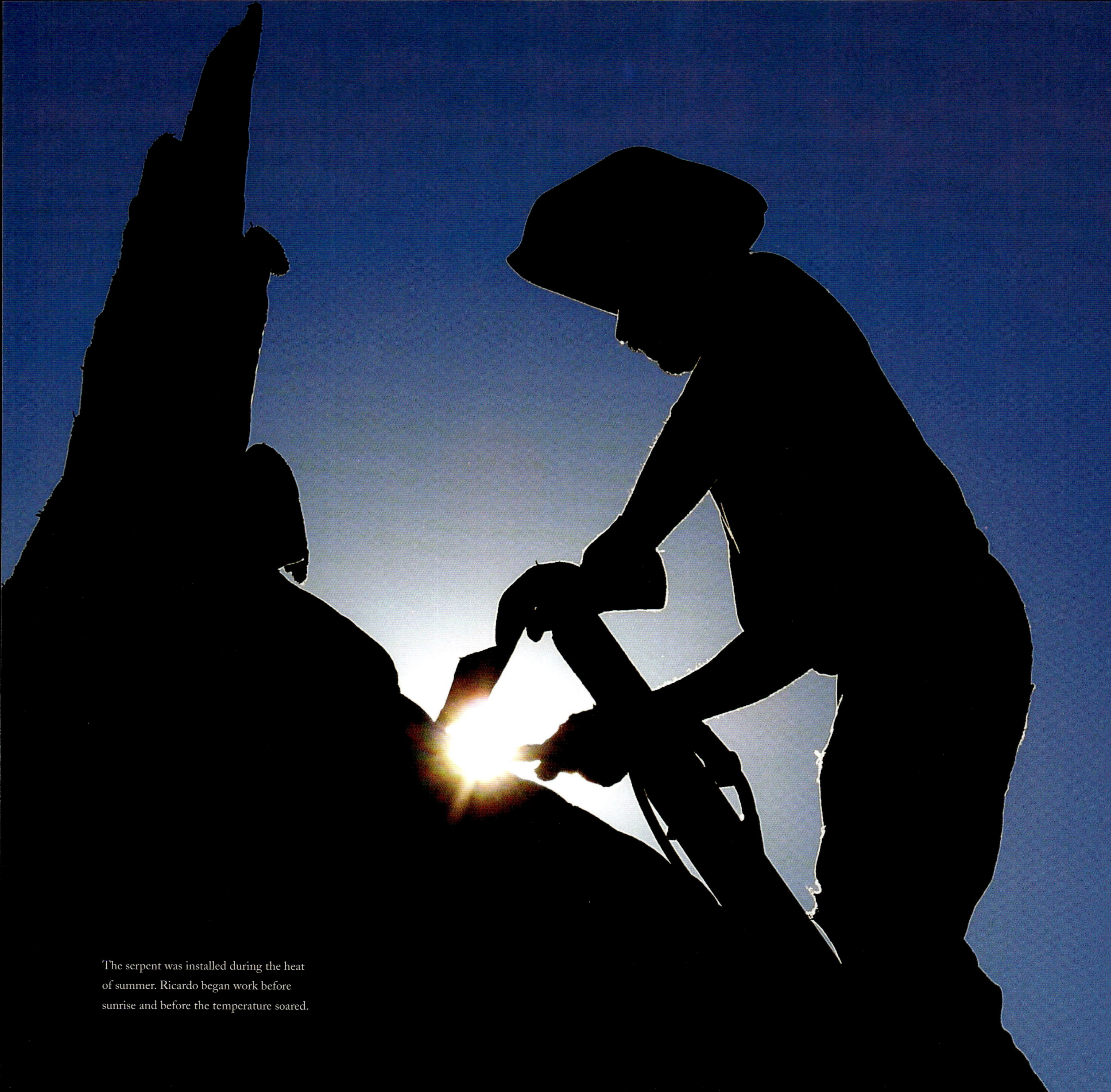

The serpent was installed during the heat of summer. Ricardo began work before sunrise and before the temperature soared.

PREFACE

When I was approached to research and write a book in three months, I thought it couldn't be done. Perhaps those same thoughts went through Ricardo Breceda's mind when his daughter, Lianna, asked him to make her a life-size dinosaur. His response to her request was to see it as a personal challenge. If his daughter wanted him to do that, he would figure out a way. Right from the beginning, I had something in common with Ricardo—I had been presented a challenge that looked nearly impossible, and I was determined to do it.

It was another challenge to get two strong-minded people with their own set of goals and timetables to agree on whose priorities were more important. It took a lot of cajoling and trust building to get Ricardo to make time for me and open up, and sharing a bottle of *cerveza* probably helped. I told him to think of me as *familia,* his *hermana gringa*. I assumed things would go much more smoothly after our "happy hour."

I was wrong. Ricardo is such a private person and used to getting his own way, I couldn't even arrange to get a professional photographer to come to his shop because he had moved it and would not tell me where it was located. He said he would eventually tell me when the time was right, but that was unsettling as my deadline was quickly looming. Finally, the time came for me to visit his shop, and I ended up taking the photographs myself, but only after we had traveled together to Durango, Mexico, and visited where he grew up.

We arrived in Durango minutes after the deputy chief of the state prison was assassinated. His truck had been riddled with bullets by alleged narco-traffickers. Viewing the truck as we drove by and seeing the *Federales* dressed in full military gear with masks on their faces, bulletproof vests, and submachine guns in their arms drove home the danger of living in Durango these days and was very unnerving.

In contrast, Ricardo's family could not have been more warm and welcoming. They eagerly answered all my questions about Ricardo's youth. It didn't take me long to figure out that Ricardo himself didn't care about dates and didn't save any paperwork, and that some details he gave me changed from one story to the next. Luckily, Ricardo's older sister Ernestina was able to provide dates and photographs that I needed. Ricardo's mother and father willingly shared information, as well as his brother Oscar and his sister Yolanda. Leonardo, Ricardo's nephew, graciously provided transportation while we were visiting, and both he and Oscar helped with translations.

Ricardo's family was also concerned for our safety, and they cautioned us to limit our daily trips to surrounding areas to daylight hours. The community where his family lives had just hired a twenty-four-hour security service to guard the

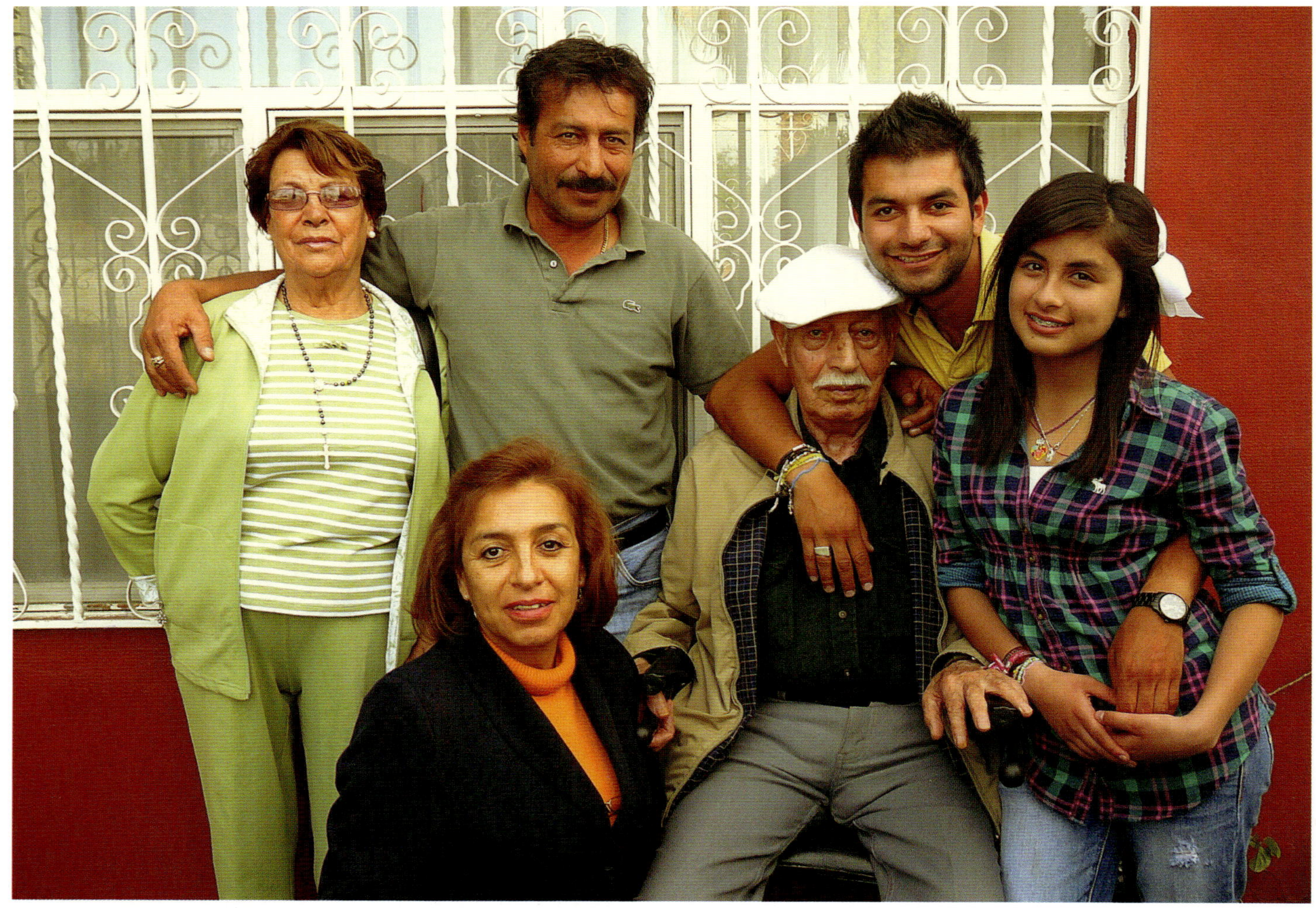

Ricardo and his family in Durango. *Clockwise from upper left*: Ricardo's mother Estela, Ricardo, Ricardo's nephew Leonardo, Ricardo's niece Beyonagi, Ricardo's father Celso, and Ricardo's sister Ernestina.

front entrance to the residential area. It was a real eye opener to the grim side of living in a cartel-infested country.

After we returned to California, Ricardo finally agreed to take me to his main shop, which is in Rosarito Beach, Baja California. His crew, including his right-hand man, "Porfirio" Sandoval Sanchez, endured my many questions and amiably tolerated my incessant photography as they worked on a section of a sculpture of gigantic proportions, a magical serpent.

With unrelenting passion, both Ricardo and I have prevailed, and each of us has met our separate artistic goals and deadlines. The culmination is this book, which recounts the vibrant life and art of Ricardo Breceda, an artist by accident, and a true genius.

Thanks for making time for me in your busy schedule, *hermano*. It was fun!

Diana Lindsay
May 1, 2011

A GUIDE TO THE PHOTOGRAPHS

The photographs of the sculptures in this book are arranged in three categories:

- FT: Sculptures inspired by science as presented in *Fossil Treasues of the Anza-Borrego Desert* (Chapters 1–3)
- HN: Sculptures inspired by historical events or natural features of the Anza-Borrego region (Chapter 4)
- WF: sculptures based on whim and fantasy (Chapter 5)

Within each of these categories, sculptures are listed by site, generally north to south. Interspersed among these are groups of photographs (identified below with an asterisk*) that pertain to chapter topics and the life and art of Ricardo Breceda.

For detailed information about each category and site, see the Appendix starting on page 215. Refer to the site location map on pages 228–229 to find the sculptures when visiting the Anza-Borrego area.

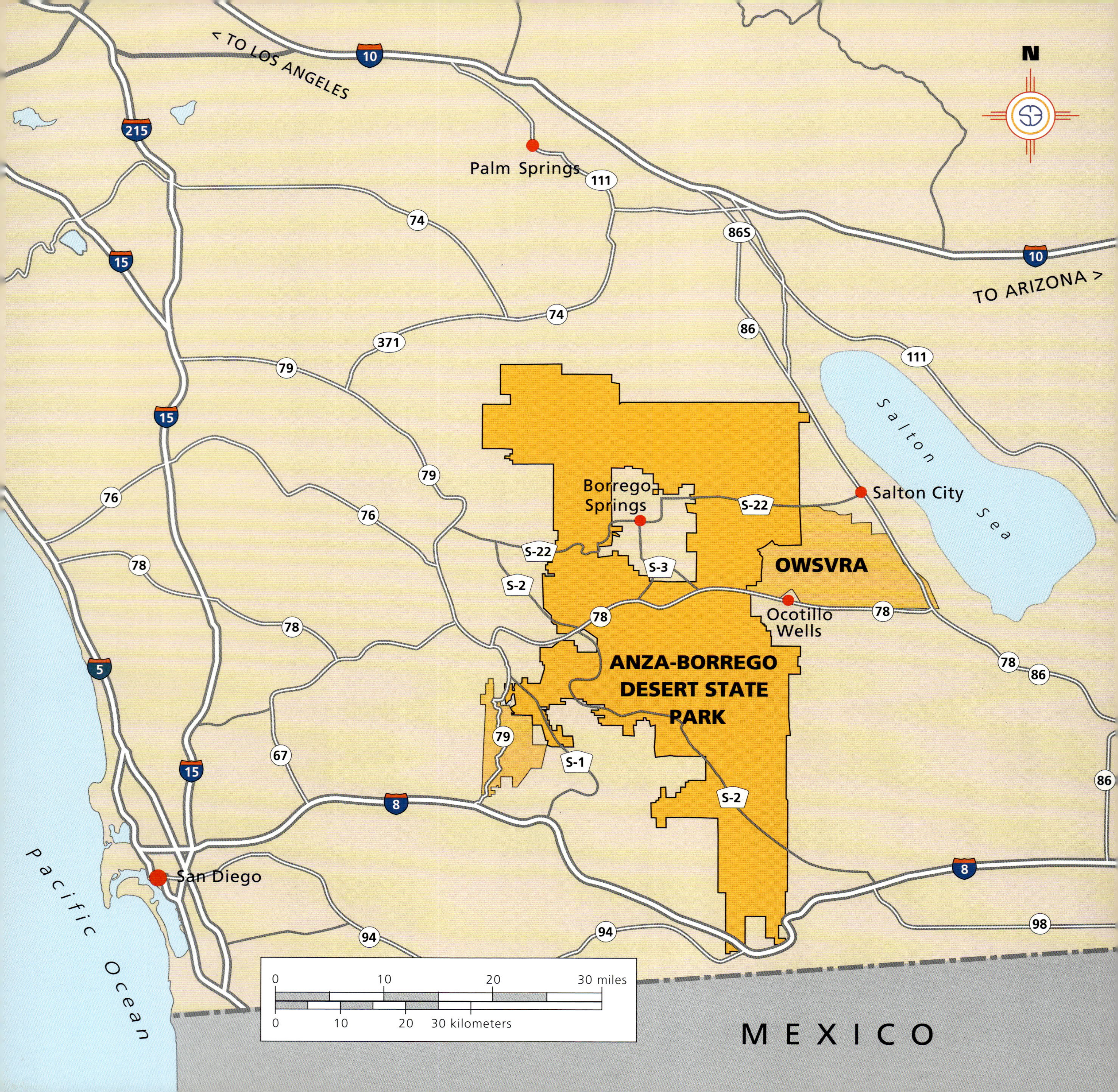

N
< TO LOS ANGELES
10
215
Palm Springs
111
74
86S
15
10
TO ARIZONA >
74
86
371
111
79
15
Salton Sea
79
Borrego Springs
Salton City
S-22
76
76
S-22
OWSVRA
78
S-3
S-2
Ocotillo Wells
78
78
78
78
86
ANZA-BORREGO DESERT STATE PARK
5
79
67
S-1
86
15
8
S-2
San Diego
8
Pacific Ocean
94
94
98
0
10
20
30 miles
0
10
20
30 kilometers
MEXICO

RICARDO BRECEDA | ACCIDENTAL ARTIST

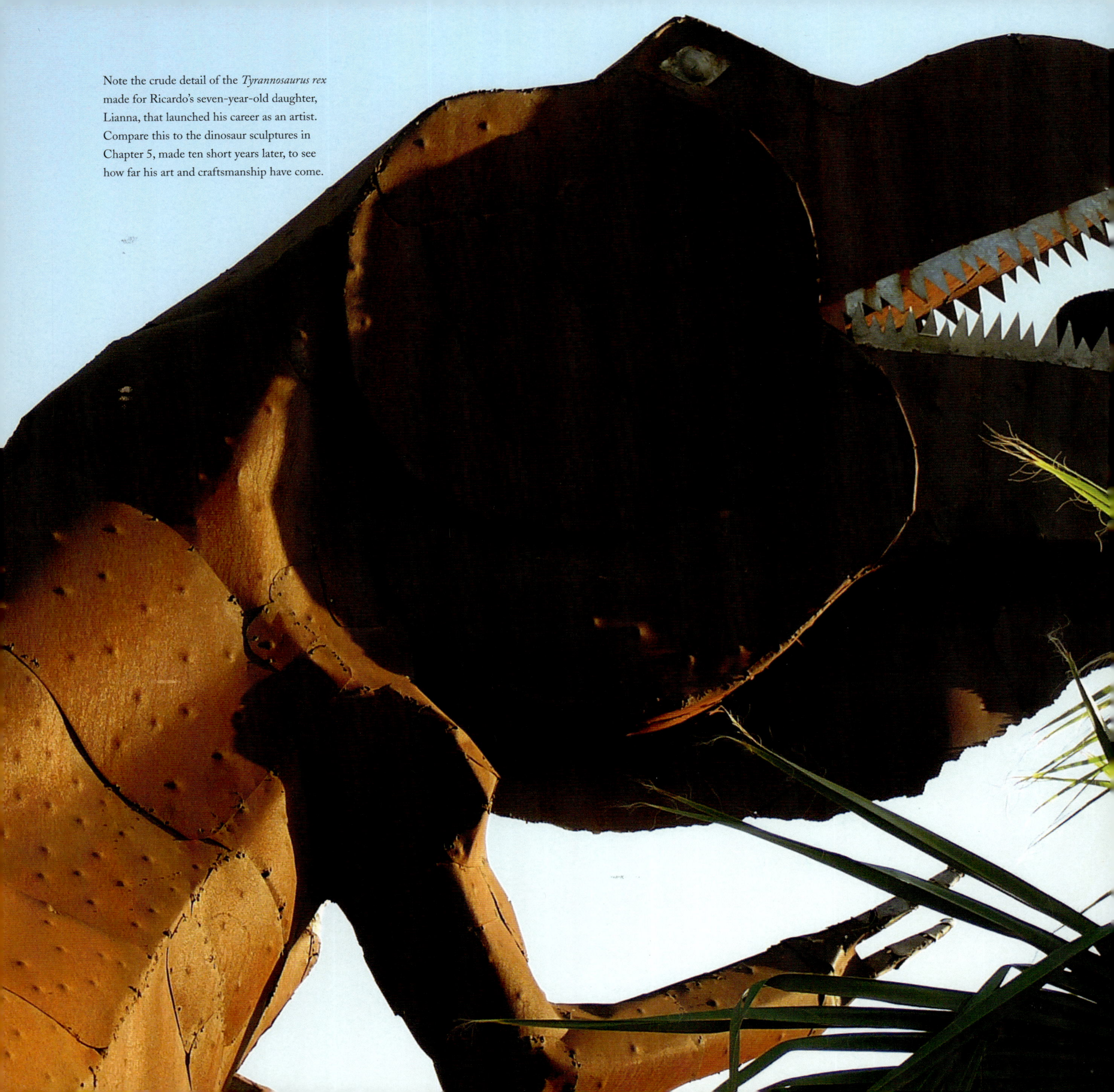

Note the crude detail of the *Tyrannosaurus rex* made for Ricardo's seven-year-old daughter, Lianna, that launched his career as an artist. Compare this to the dinosaur sculptures in Chapter 5, made ten short years later, to see how far his art and craftsmanship have come.

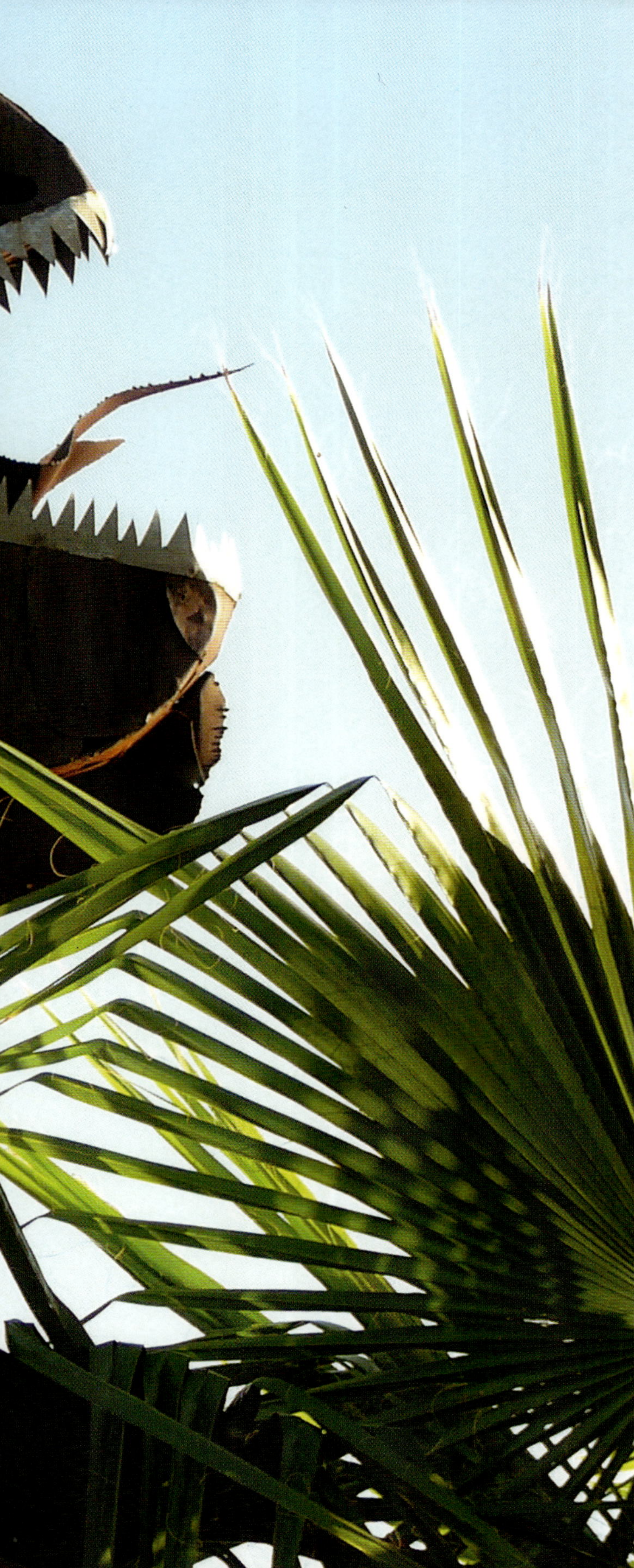

CHAPTER 1

THE BEGINNING

How does one become an artist? For Ricardo Arroyo Breceda, the answer is by accident—literally and figuratively.

Ricardo's seven-year-old daughter, Lianna, said, "Daddy, make me a life-size dinosaur like those in *Jurassic Park.*" With scrap metal, wire, and a welding machine, and with no formal art training whatsoever, Ricardo set out on a journey that went well beyond his daughter's request.

After a few months of trial and error and diligent perseverance, Ricardo presented her with a seventeen-foot-tall *Tyrannosaurus rex*, a life-size *Spinosaurus,* and a *Triceratops*. Although boxy and crude, these first sculptures delighted and amazed Lianna. In the process of creating this spectacular gift, his rewards were twofold: he affirmed that he would do anything to bring his child happiness and joy, and, at the same time, he discovered his hidden talent, a creative passion that would become his life's work.

As his awakened artistry grew and his collection of sculptures increased, he turned his talent into a business, selling individual pieces to passing motorists drawn to his sculpture garden when they caught sight of the metal menagerie leering at the speeding vehicles at the freeway fence.

Today, only ten short years later, Ricardo's rustic metal sculptures are installed in Australia, Canada, and Mexico, and in collections in the United States, including Maryland,

Arkansas, Idaho, New Mexico, Nevada, Arizona, and throughout California. His largest concentration of sculptures—129 to date—is scattered over a desert landscape surrounded by the magnificent Anza-Borrego Desert State Park in California. Located at Galleta Meadows in Borrego Springs, these intriguing statues give tribute to the Plio-Pleistocene animals that once roamed the valley and to the rich historical and natural features of this desert area. A collection of fanciful creatures are also installed there, including a serpent that is 350 feet long. Though they are exhibited on private property, the public is welcome to enjoy them "up close and personal."

Ricardo is a very gifted artist who only a decade ago gave little thought to art. His story is an inspiration of how self-confidence and focus on a task at hand, as well as love and passion, can lead to new opportunities and personal growth. Today Ricardo is a world-renowned artist in his field.

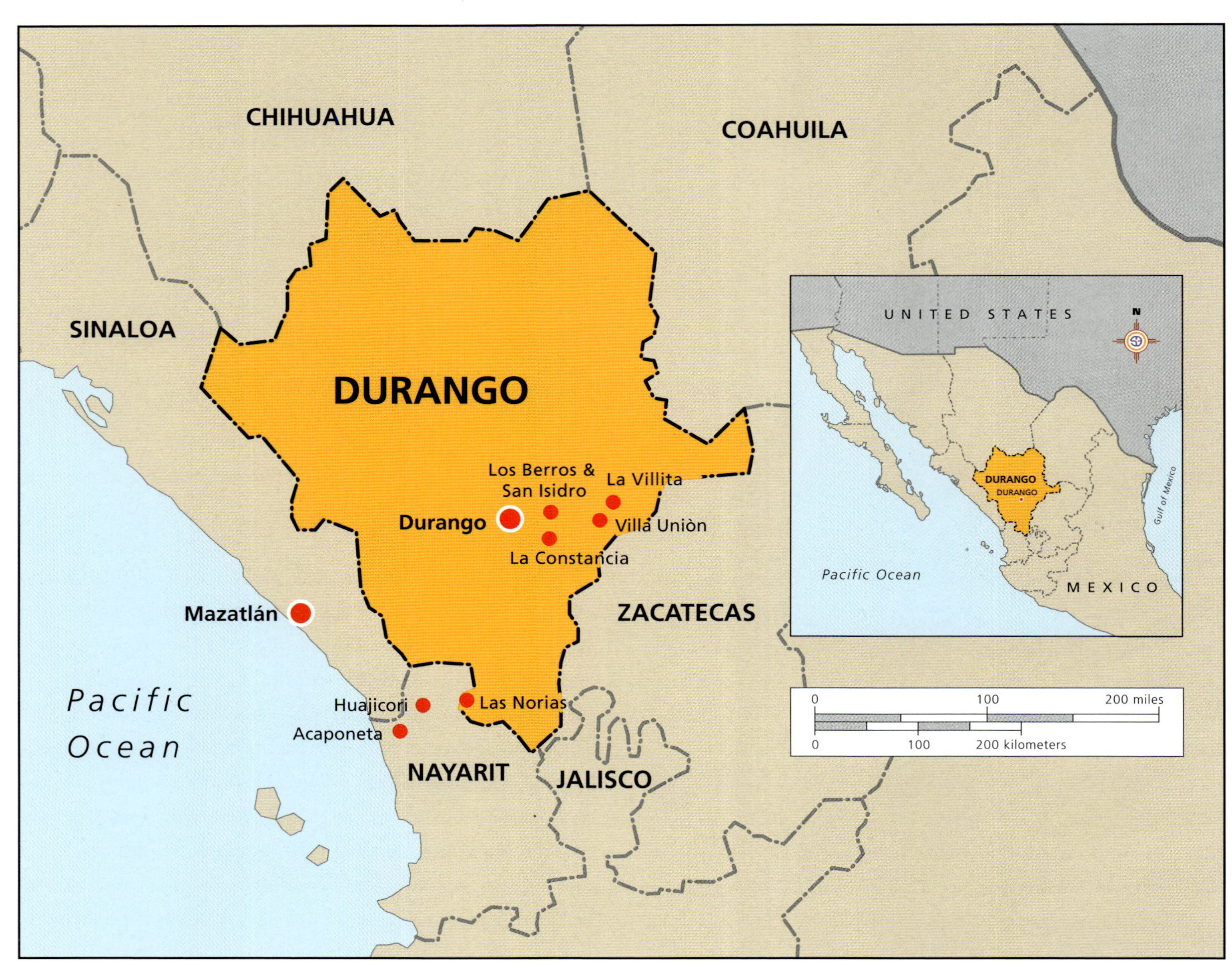

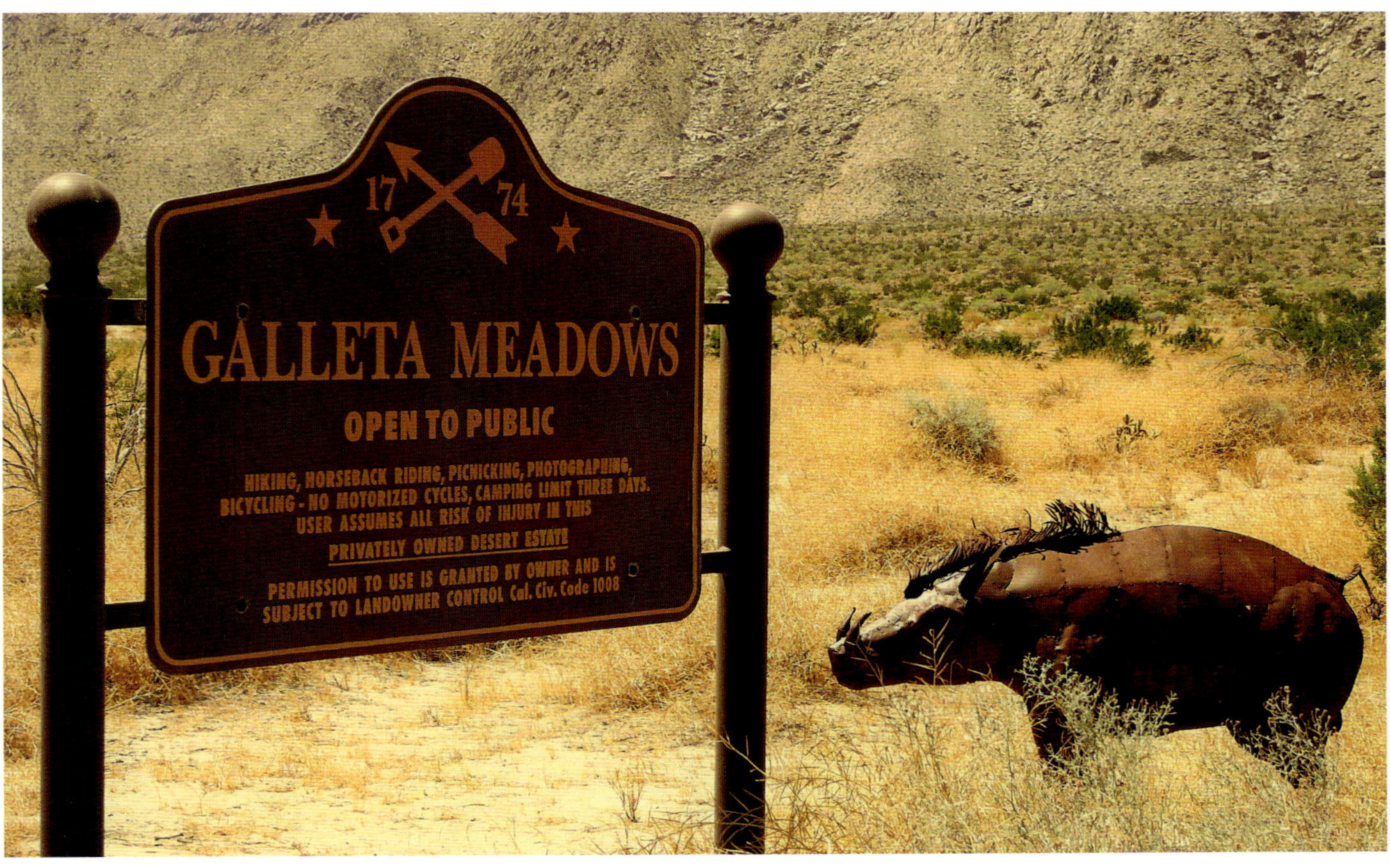

FT-1 Peccary Family. The peccary (*Playygonus* sp.) was one of the first fossils discovered in North America in the early 1800s. This creature roamed in the Anza-Borrego area from 3 million to 1.7 million years ago.

Ricardo's art has encouraged the development of other metal sculptors and the sale of their creations in the United States and along the Mexican border, but he alone has earned the title "The Picasso of Steel."

Even a Picasso had to start somewhere. For Ricardo, it all started in Durango, Mexico.

Durango lies almost at the heart of Mexico. It is a state that has a history of independence, but it has never been a place that offered an unconditional invitation for "outsiders" to settle. Fittingly, the state's symbol is the scorpion. Historically, it is a region of rebellion with a long record of bloody battles between the indigenous peoples and the Mexican government. Perhaps not surprisingly, Durango is also the birthplace of Pancho Villa, the famed Mexican revolutionary. Like the old American West, it was not a place for the fainthearted.

Durango is incredibly beautiful in its geographic diversity. Durango has it all—mountains to the west; vast, arid valleys to the east; and endless landscapes of stark, high desert backed by huge skies. Rivers and streams zigzag through the countryside, allowing for the survival of small settlements and villages made up of *ranchos*—some cattlemen and dairy

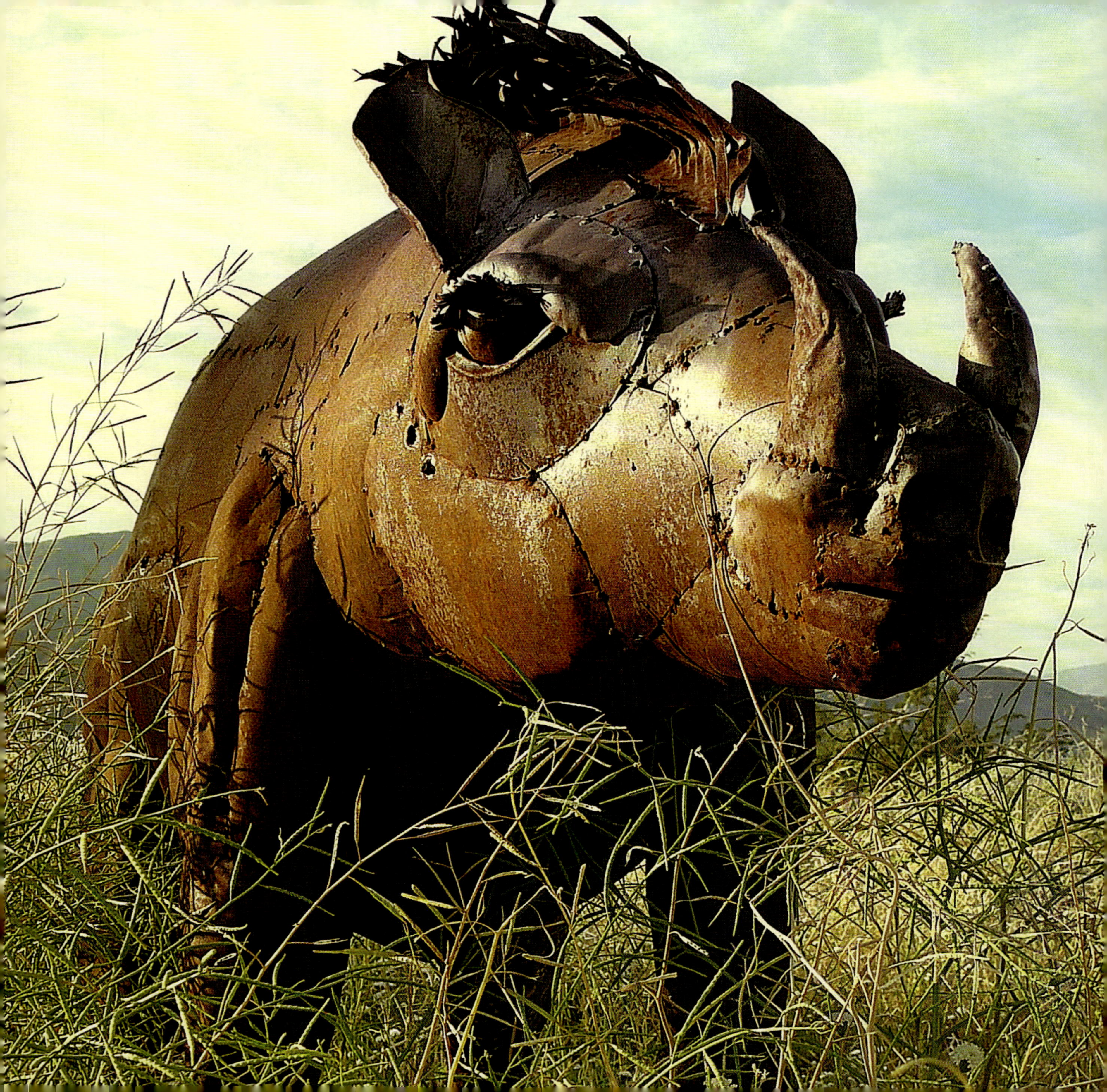

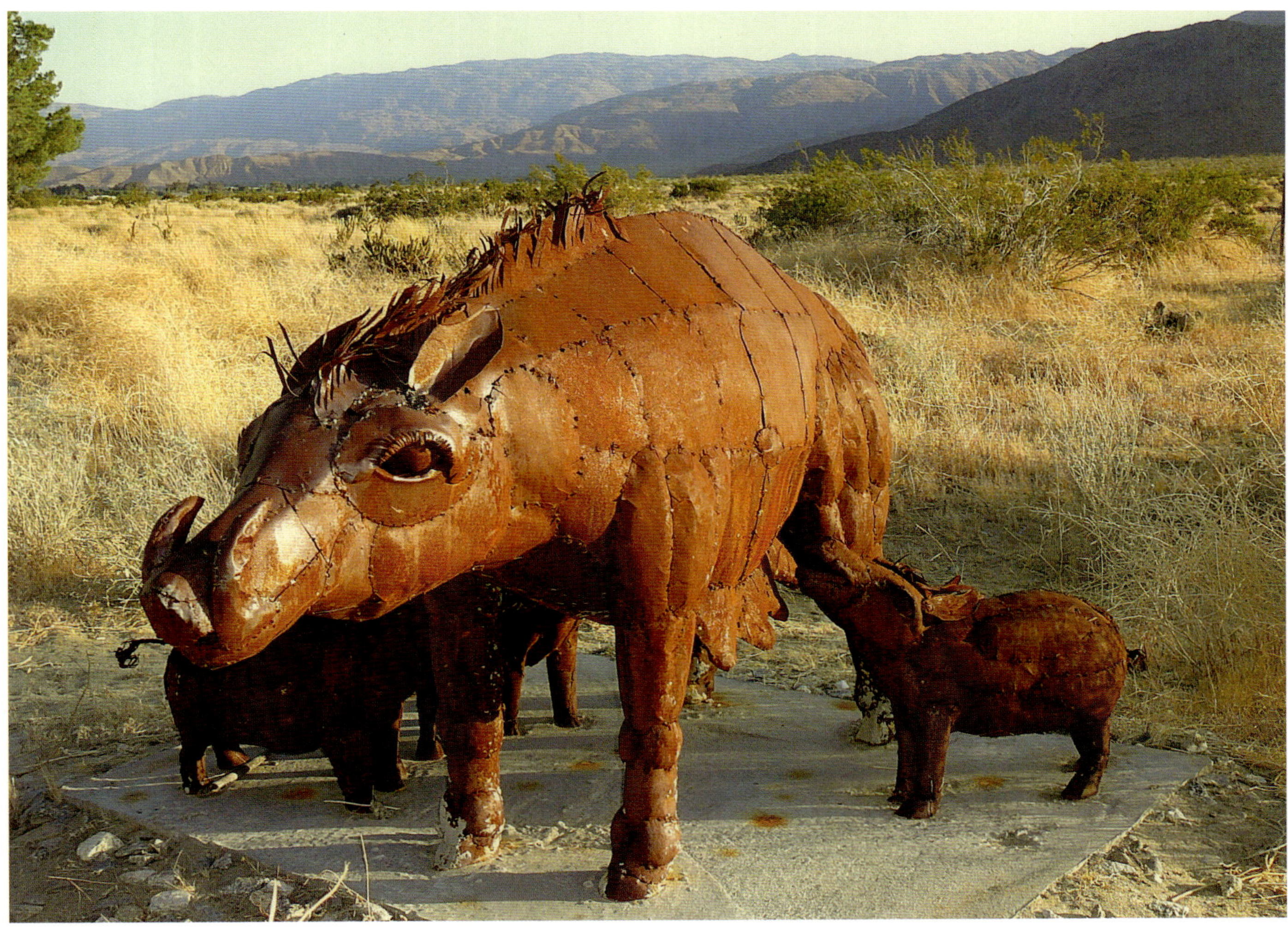

FT-1 Peccary Family. The peccary family (Tayassuidae) evolved almost entirely in North America and is closely related to Old World pigs (Suidae). Like their living relatives, they ate everything from leaves, seeds, and roots to worms, small vertebrates, and eggs.

farmers. A few towns and medium-size cities, the capital city of Durango being the largest and the commercial hub, are scattered across this enormous, landlocked state.

Because of its geographic beauty, during the middle and later part of the last century it became a popular location for many memorable Hollywood movies, such as *Bandido, The Magnificent Seven, The Sons of Katie Elder, True Grit, The Wild Bunch,* and *Chisum.* To have seen some of these movies gives the reader a glimpse of the broad scope of Durango's landscape.

The people who had the courage to come to Durango and make it their home were strong, independent, and determined to carve out a life for themselves and their families. It was into this beautiful, wild, and sometimes harsh and hostile land that the *familias,* the ancestors, of the accidental artist Ricardo Breceda settled.

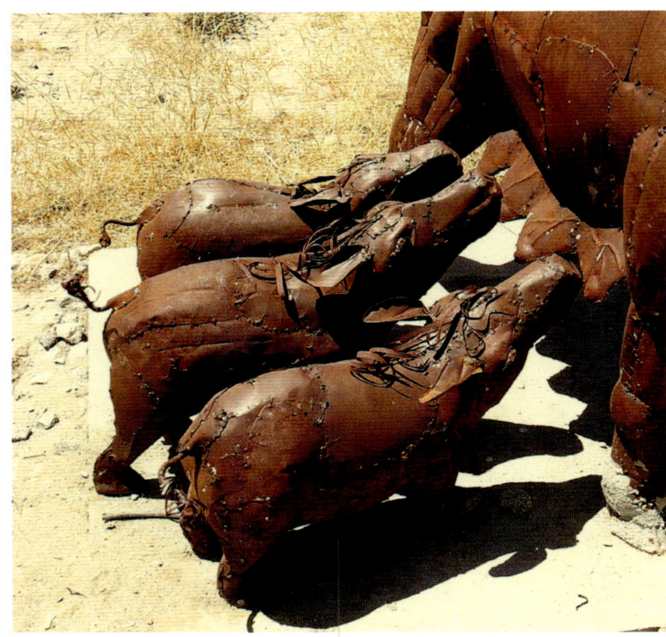

FT-1 Peccary Family. Peccaries today are found throughout the western hemisphere in a variety of habitats. In the Southwest, they are found in desert scrub and arid woodlands.

Ricardo's great-grandparents, Nicolás Arroyo and Juana Herrera, sometime before the turn of the last century, purchased a 250-acre ranch in La Villita, fifty miles east of the capital city of Durango, and raised their family there. They willed the ranch to their son Celso Arroyo Herrera and his wife, Wenselada Jaquez, who had four sons, one of whom was Celso Arroyo Jaquez, Ricardo's father. It was there on the ranch that Ricardo's father met the woman who would become his wife, Estela Breceda Barbosa.

One summer Estela came from Zacatecas to visit her married sister, who lived near La Villita. They went to the ranch to visit Ricardo's grandparents. Estela immediately fell in love with the young blue-eyed, light-skinned Celso, who had inherited his father's eye and skin color. Perhaps he reminded her of her own blue-eyed father, Luís Breceda Reyes. Estela's eyes and skin coloring were dark like those of her mother, Rita Barbosa Ayala. Most likely Spanish—or

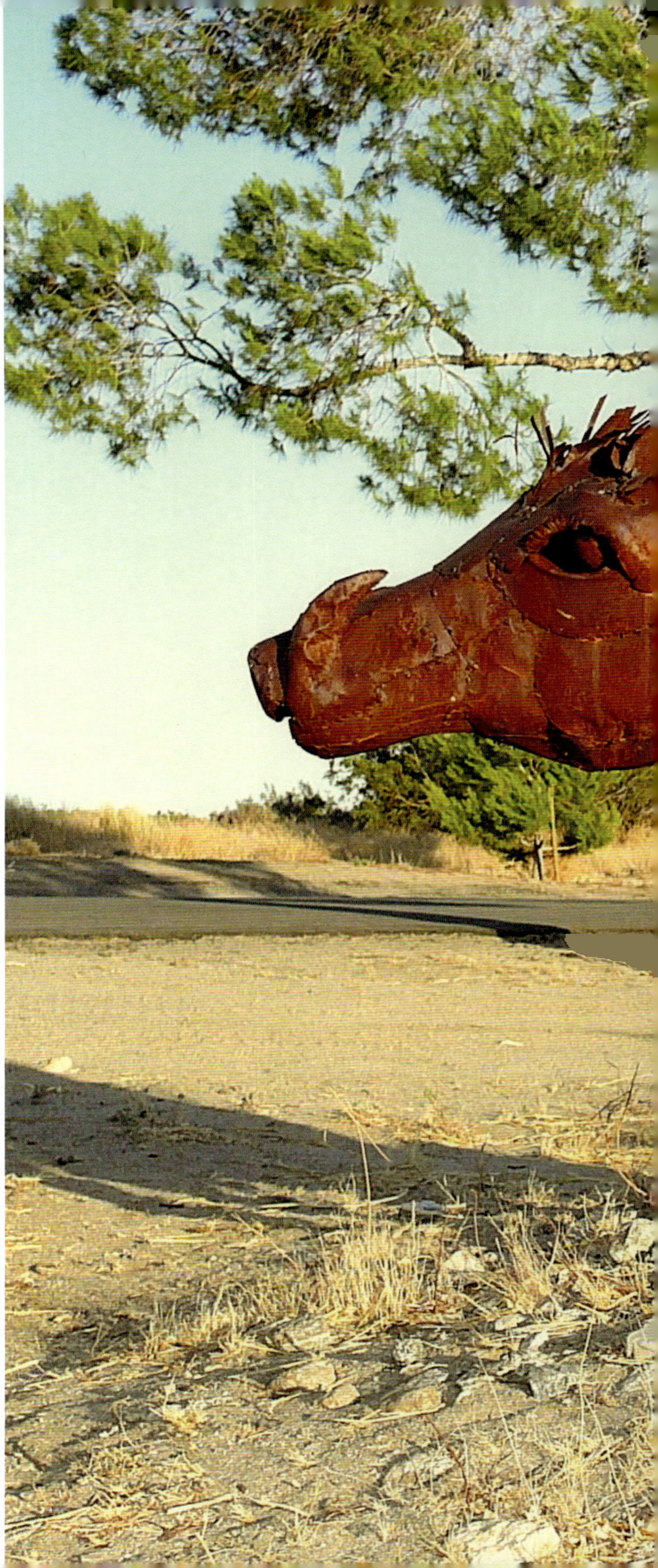

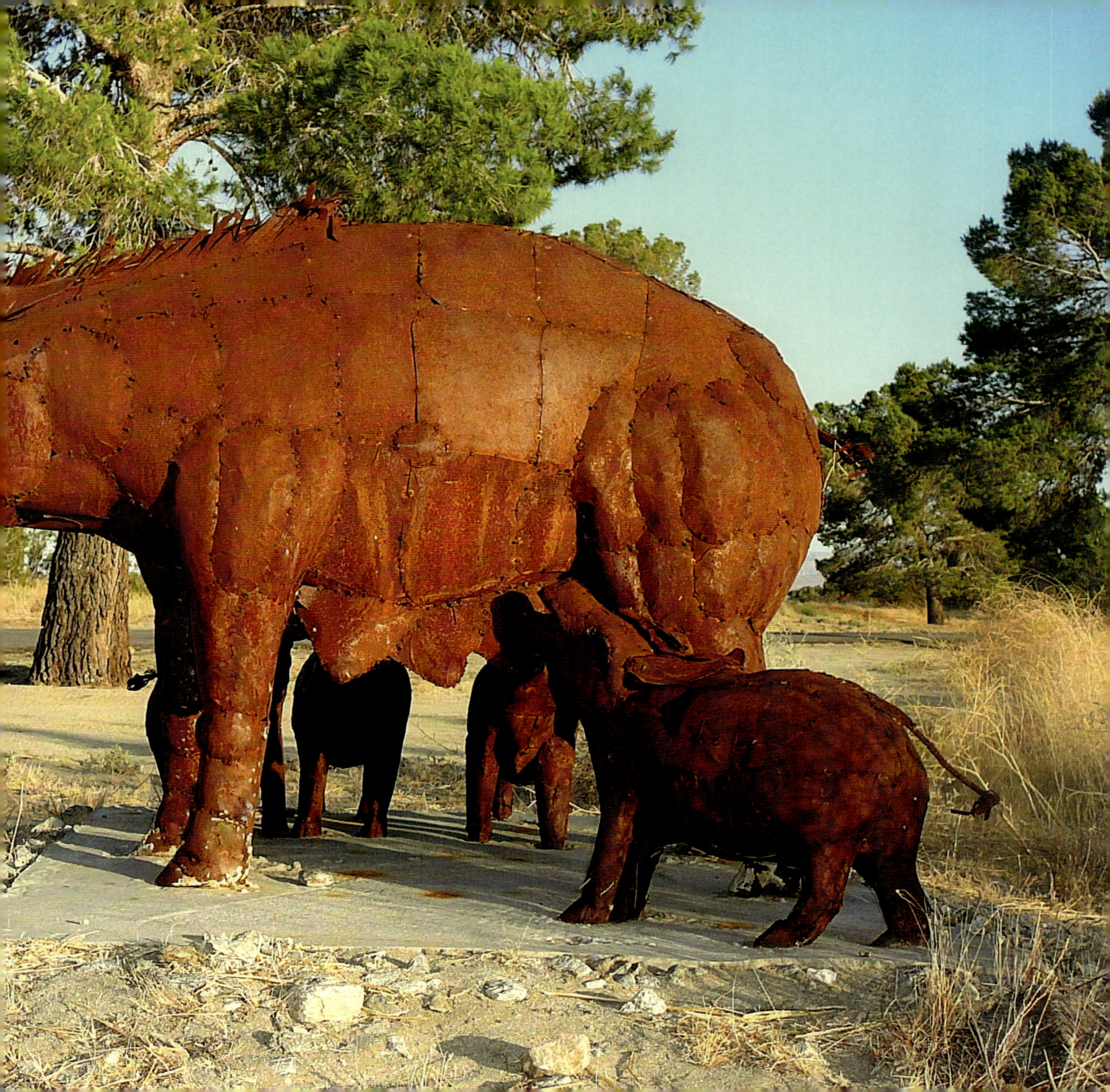

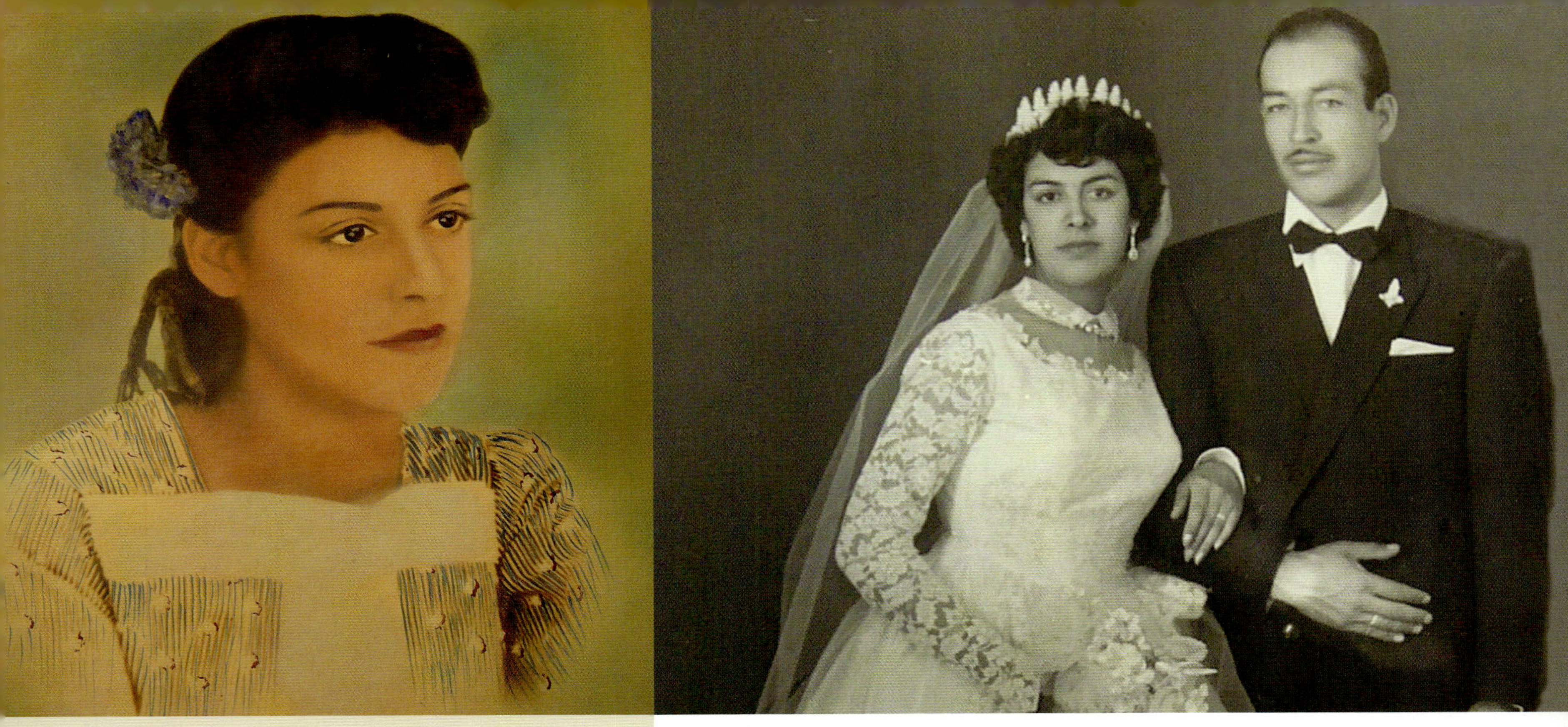

THE ARROYO BRECEDA FAMILY

Ricardo's parents, Estela Breceda Barbosa and Celso Arroyo Jaquez, were married in Durango, Mexico, in 1956. Together they raised eight children. Ricardo is the fourth child born to Estela and Celso and their oldest living son. Ricardo regularly visits his family in Mexico, and family members, in turn, make annual visits to the United States. Ricardo uses his mother's family name in the United States rather than his Mexican surname of Arroyo. *From left*: Estela as a young woman; Estela's and Celso's wedding picture; the Arroyo Breceda family name plate and address located at the front entrance to their home in Durango, Mexico; Celso as a young man.

possibly Portuguese or French—blood flowed through Estela's and Celso's veins. Estela and Celso represented the true lifeblood of Mexico—the mestizos or *los mezclados*—blending their European and indigenous genes to produce a wealth of colors and handsome features in their future children.

Celso and Estela were married on November 6, 1956. They began their life together in Villa Unión, a settlement near La Villita, and a year later their first son, Rafael, was born. More children were soon on the way: Ernestina, Yolanda, and, on December 28, 1961, Ricardo. The *familia* continued to grow with the births of Rodolfo, Estelita, Celso Luís, and finally, in 1968, Oscar.

When Ricardo's grandparents retired, they left the ranch to their sons and bought a house next door to Celso and Estela—Ricardo's parents' home. Celso bought out the interest in the ranch from his brothers and became the sole

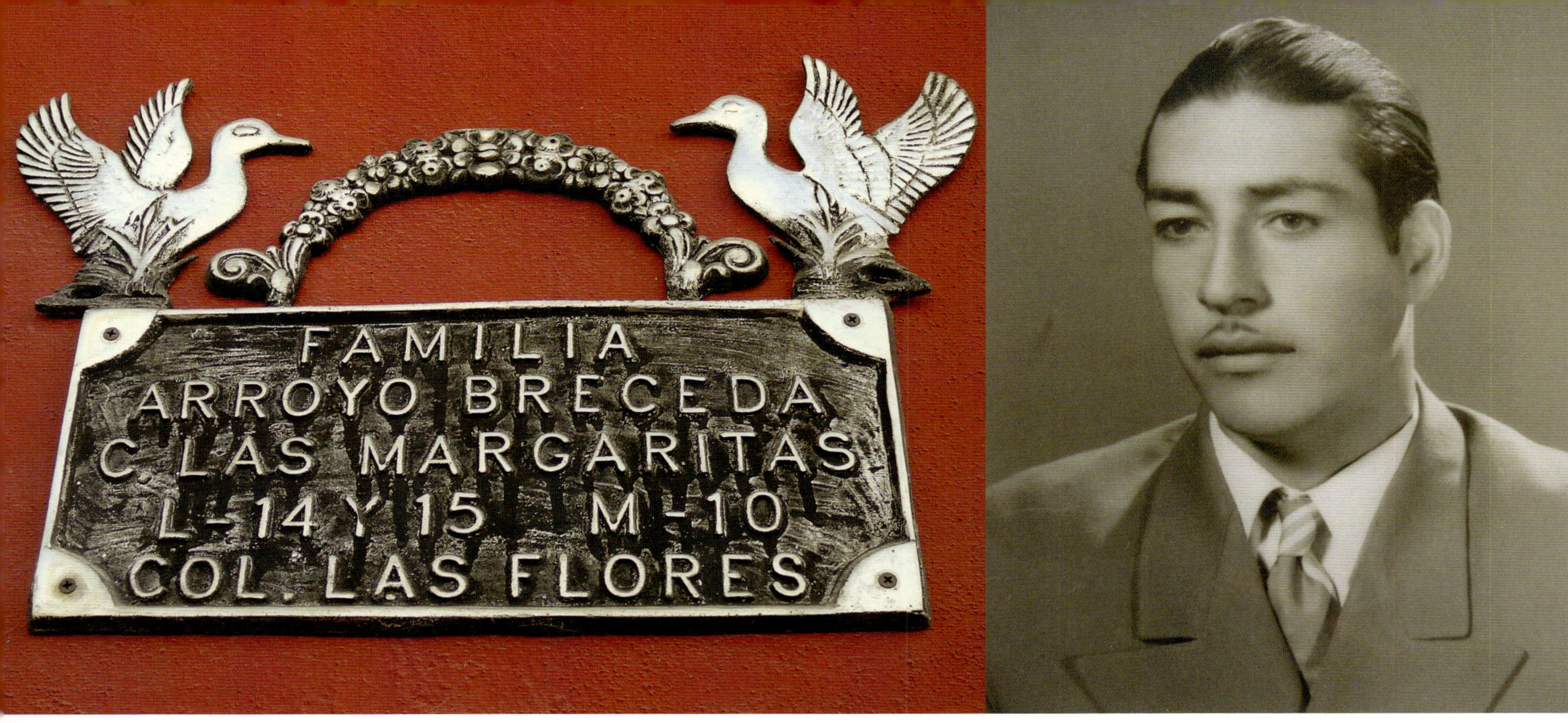

owner. He managed the ranch at La Villita while living in Villa Unión. He grew corn, beans, and alfalfa and hired help to harvest the crops. He also had sixty head of cattle.

Celso and Estela wanted the best for their children. Although neither one of them had more than three or four years of schooling, they recognized that a strong work ethic and a good education would be key for their children's success. By the time Oscar was born, Celso had just started working in the United States, hundreds of miles to the north, to earn extra money. He intended to provide well for his family and worked abroad for three years.

Ricardo's parents knew that they had produced a child of independent spirit and unique individuality. Ricardo was an imp, always pushing the limits, naturally curious and clever. He continually both entertained and frustrated his family with his growing stubbornness and determination.

"From the very beginning Ricardo was a little different," according to his mother, Estela. "He always took the initiative to learn new things. He was not intimidated by difficult tasks and would work on them until they were completed."

"I'll never forget how Ricardo, as a little boy, would deliberately break his toys just so he could spend hours trying to put them back together again! None of my other children did that," Estela said.

Ricardo exhibited tremendous self-assurance and personal strength as a child. "He felt that he could do anything and that nothing would stop him if he had a vision," Estela said. "I always thought these traits would bring him success." She also revealed that it wasn't always easy living with a child who was always striving to be better than anyone else.

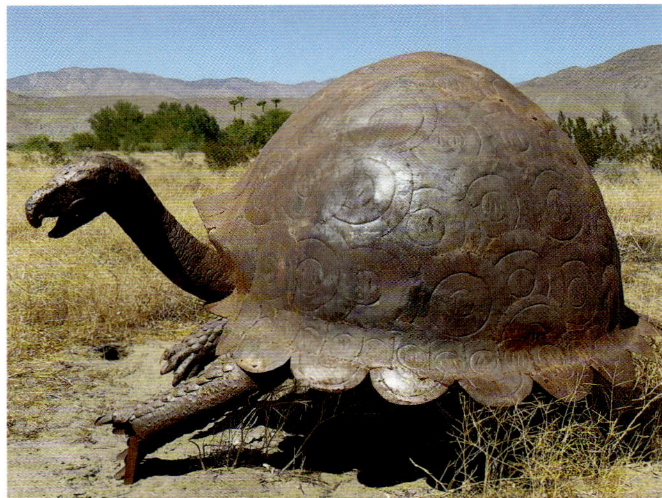

FT-2 Giant Tortoise. The presence of the non-burrowing giant tortoise (*Hesperotestudo* sp.) indicates that the Anza-Borrego region had a mild climate and frost-free winters at least until 1 million years ago.

Truth be told, Ricardo was a little troublemaker, and Celso had to get after him frequently. Estela observed that Ricardo "was a problematic child because he could not be controlled. He was very much his own person who wanted his freedom and independence to do things his own way."

Soon after Ricardo started school he began running away, either after classes or just after he got home, and no one could find him. He would stay out past dark. It was a worry for the family. Sometimes he would be playing in the streets, sometimes he went down to the river or irrigation canals to swim, and other times he took his slingshot and went hunting. The family had to do something drastic.

When he came home late one night, they locked him in the small, dark *bodega* where the family stored grain. They gave Ricardo food and water but told him they would not let him out until he promised to stay home after school.

Ricardo decided he would not make such a promise. He was determined to wait it out, believing his mother would finally feel sorry for him and release him. And it almost worked.

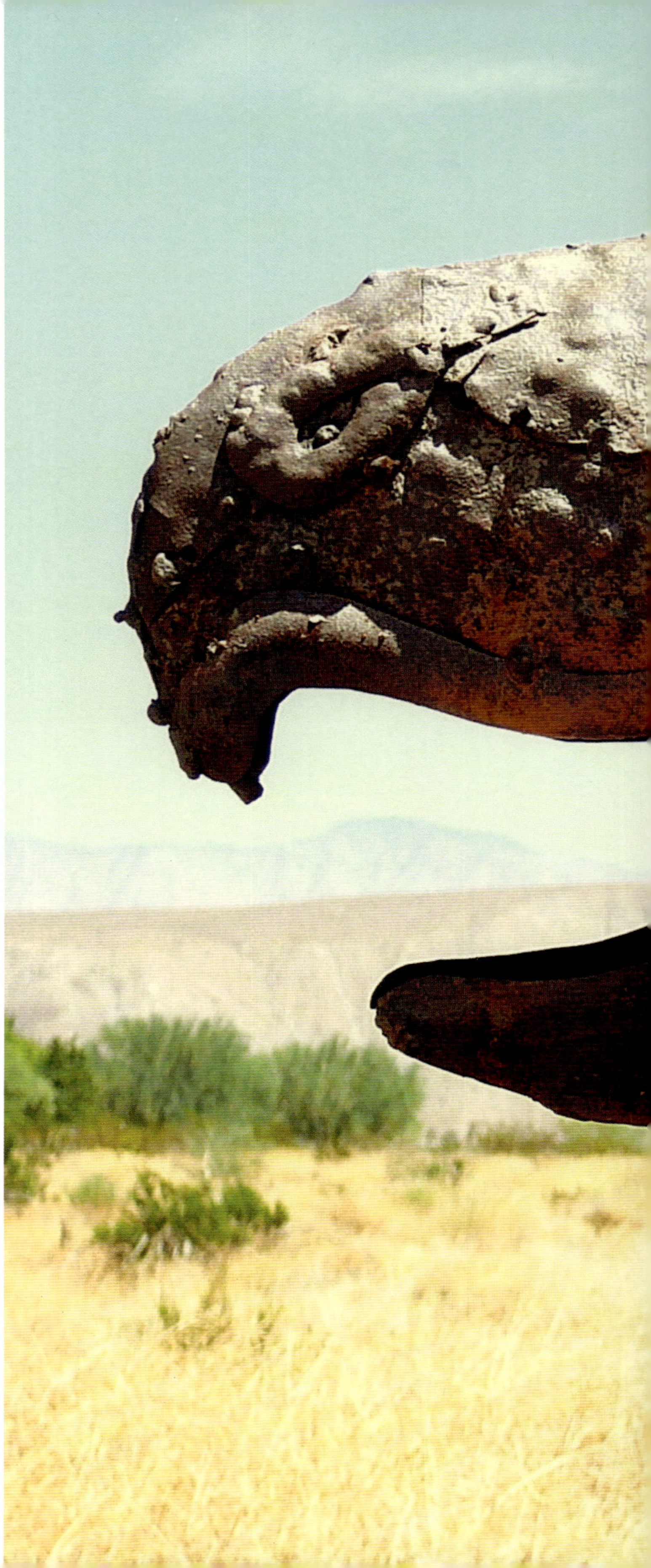

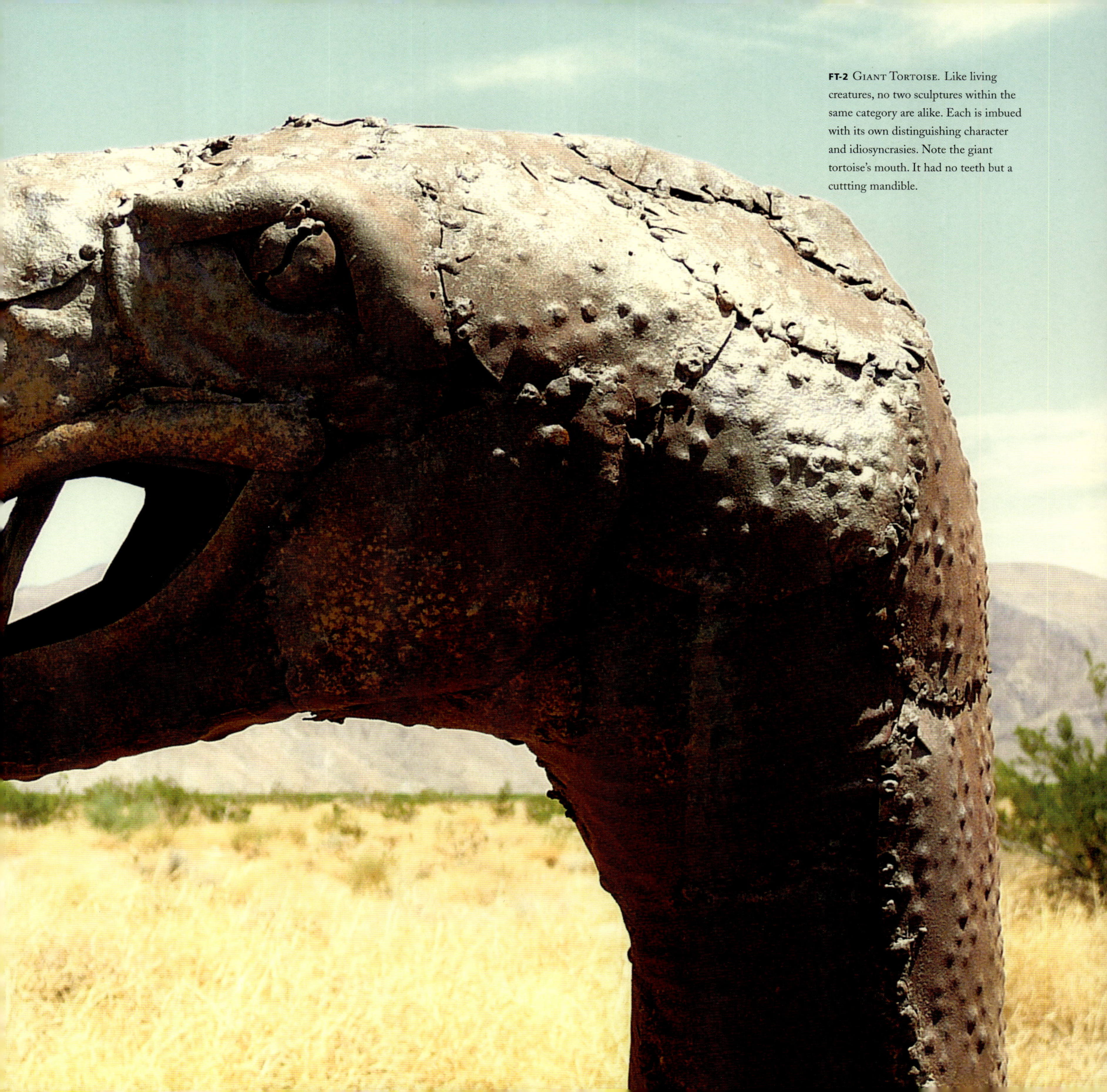

FT-2 Giant Tortoise. Like living creatures, no two sculptures within the same category are alike. Each is imbued with its own distinguishing character and idiosyncrasies. Note the giant tortoise's mouth. It had no teeth but a cuttting mandible.

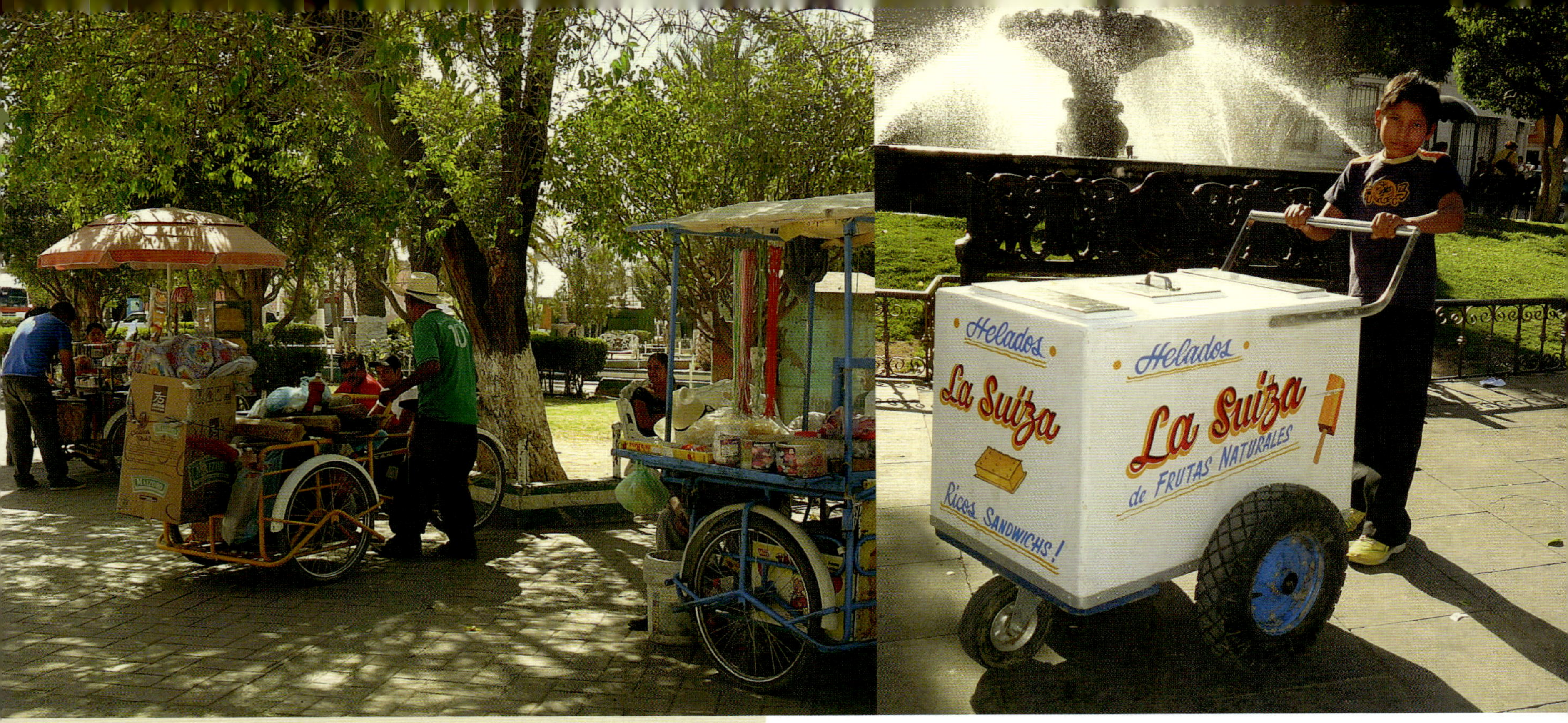

SCENES FROM VILLA UNIÓN

The central plaza is the vibrant heart of Villa Unión. There you will find vendors, a gazebo, and a large church that serves the community. It was here that the young entrepreneuring Ricardo sold his ice creams after school and on weekends when residents gathered and visited. *From left*: Vendors in the plaza; a young *paletero*, or ice cream vendor; inside the church; Ricardo at the elementary school during a recent visit to Durango.

Estela did weaken and told Ernestina perhaps they should let him out. Ernestina, as the oldest girl, always helped to keep control of the children because Estela had all she could do to manage the house and eight children. Ernestina told her mother, "No! He stays until he promises!"

Two days later Ricardo was tired of sitting in the dark and came up with a plan. He proposed becoming a *paletero*, an ice-cream vendor pushing a cart on the street. That way they would know where he was, and he would be doing something constructive. Ernestina and his mother agreed to this plan and let Ricardo out of the *bodega*. It was a fortuitous decision that funneled Ricardo's energy in a positive way.

Immediately he began earning money—his own money. From that day forward, he never had to ask the family for any money, nor did he have to account for how he spent it. He was making his own decisions at a very early age.

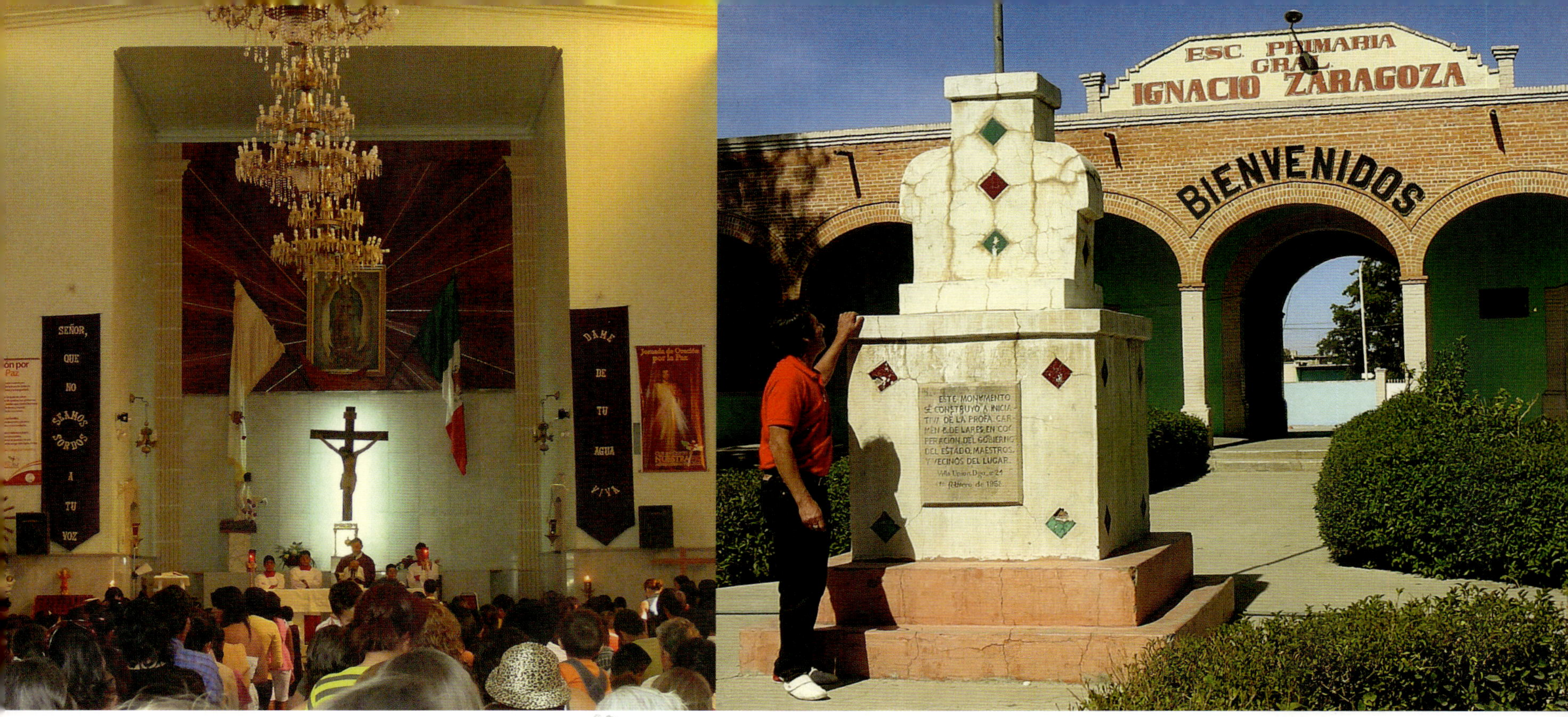

The family was also happy with his new enterprise because they knew where he was—selling *paletas* on the street and staying out of mischief. At just eight years of age, Ricardo was a businessman, and he had a plan. He would work hard, save half of his earnings, and spend the other half.

Ricardo found a loose adobe brick in the corral and decided to use the space between the wall and the brick as his bank. Each day he would take half of his earnings, pull the brick out, stuff the coins and notes in, and replace the brick.

He also decided to increase his income. In a day he could only sell so much ice cream in Villa Unión. He figured that if he pushed his ice cream cart down the road one or two miles to La Villita, he would have a brand-new market and would be able to sell more ice creams on a hot day. So, he headed toward La Villita.

Halfway there he became very tired pushing his heavy cart down the rutted road. He decided to lie down and take a nap. When he awoke, all of the ice creams had melted, and he was angry. He pushed the cart back to Villa Unión to the ice cream factory, shoved the cart into the yard, and as he ran away, he yelled over his shoulder, "I'm not coming back!"

That may have been the end of his career as a *paletero,* but it was not the end of his business career. He had tasted independence, freedom, and financial reward. He was not about to let it go.

He took some of his savings and invested in a shoe shine kit. He was now back in business, as a *volero* this time. All was well, except for Ricardo's bank. Perhaps there were too many bills and coins behind that brick. The loose adobe was in the pig corral, and one day it fell down along with some of the money. The pigs immediately scrambled after

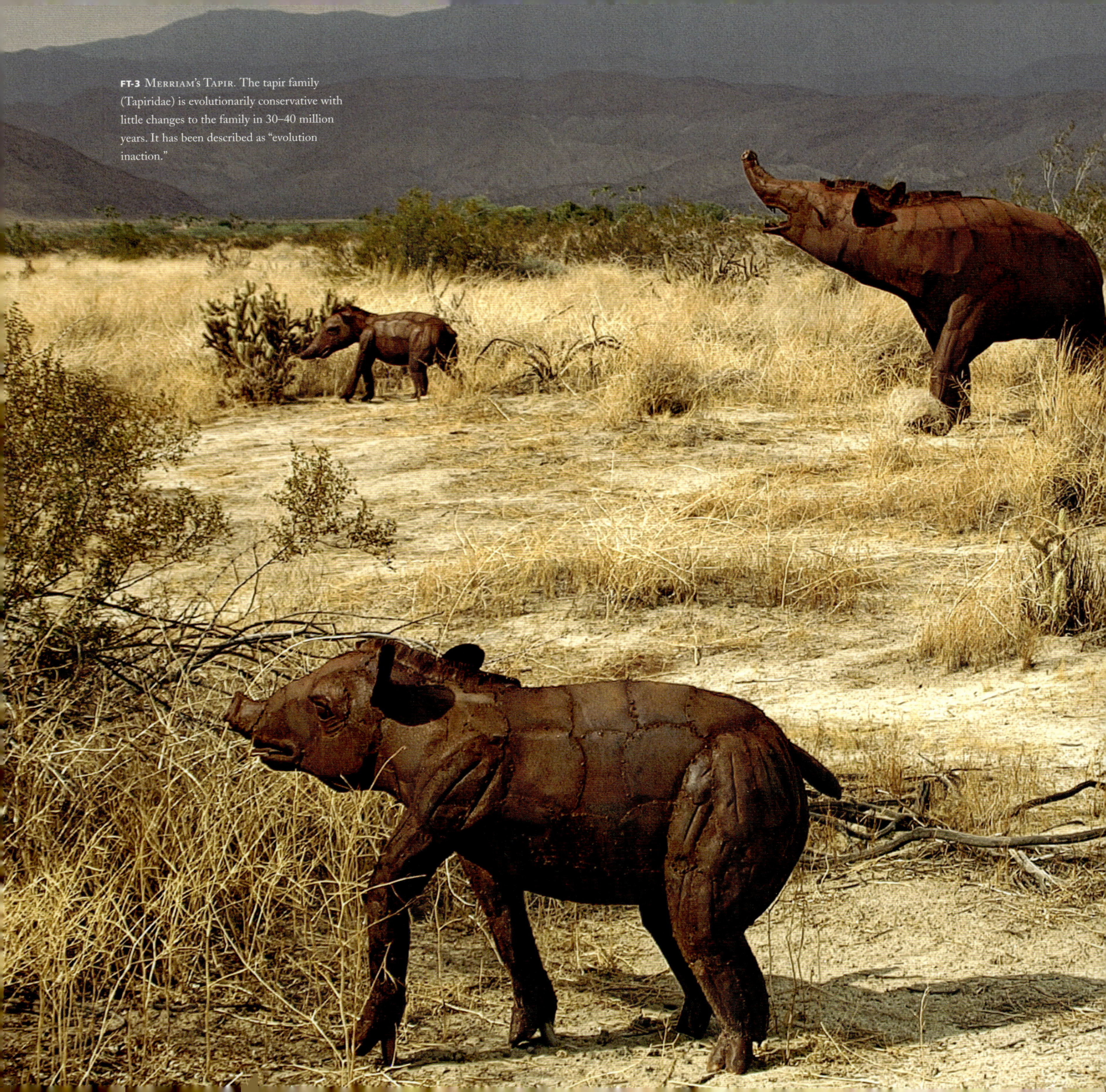

FT-3 Merriam's Tapir. The tapir family (Tapiridae) is evolutionarily conservative with little changes to the family in 30–40 million years. It has been described as "evolution inaction."

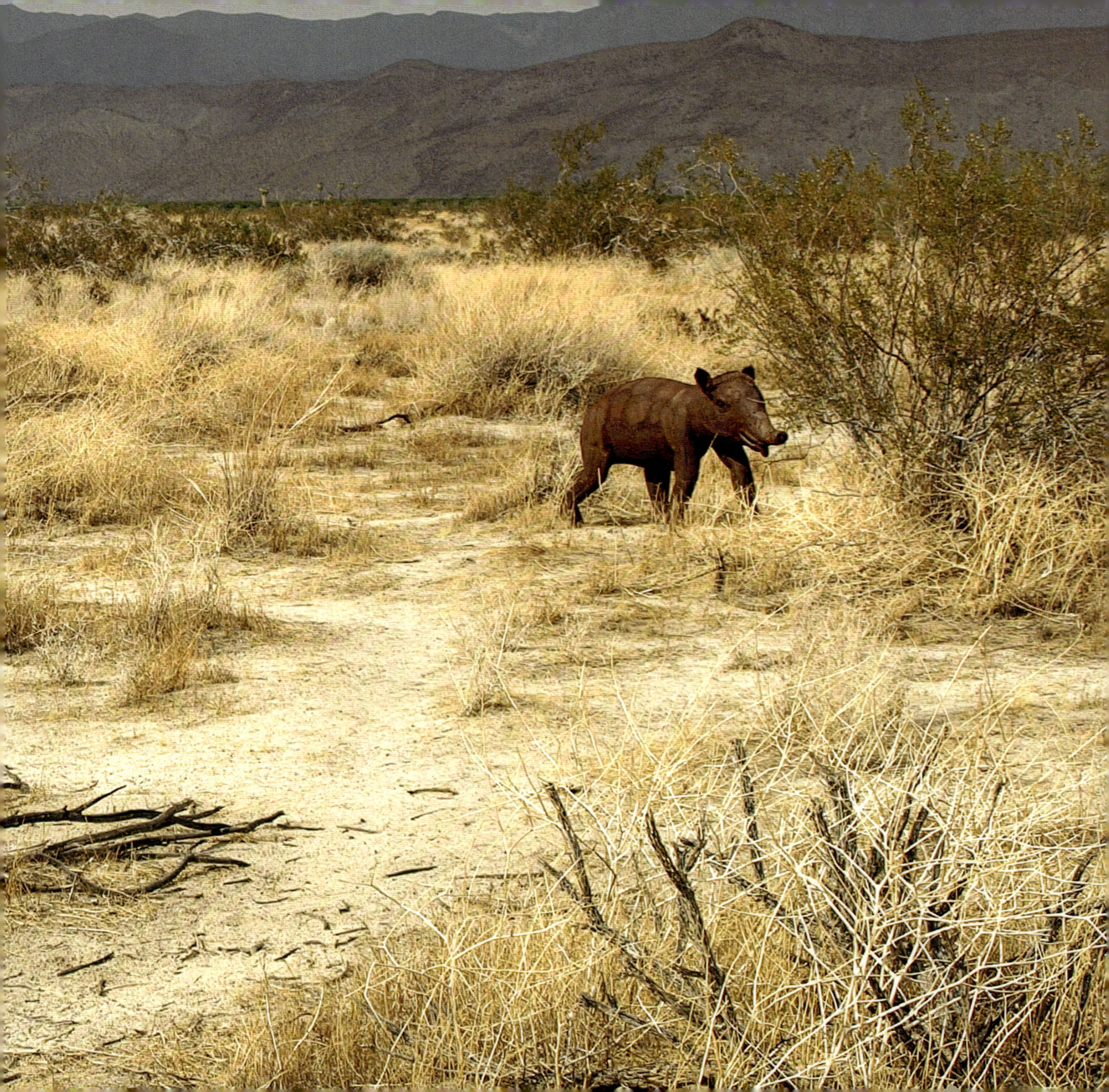

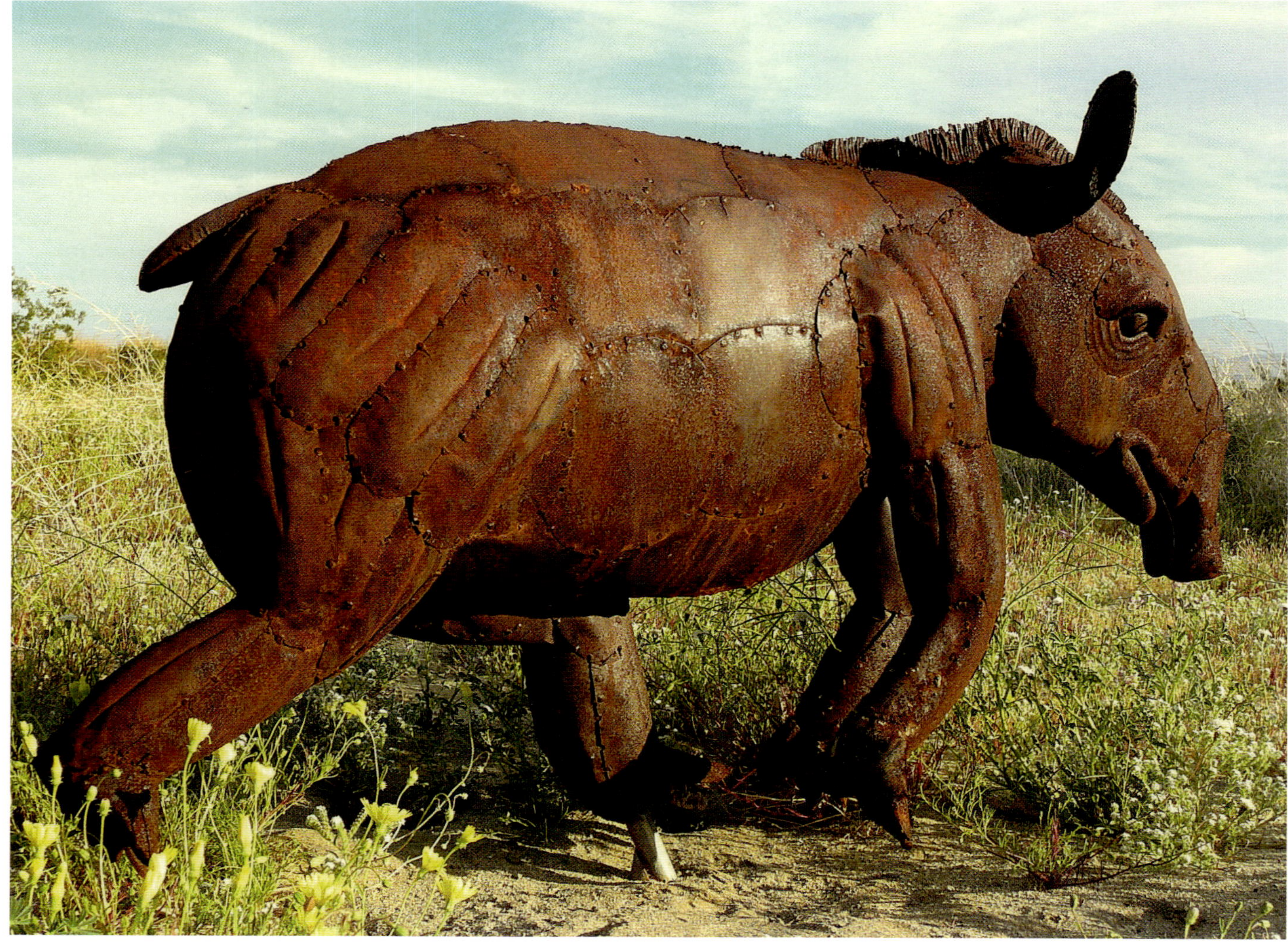

FT-3 Merriam's Tapir. The most complete specimen of Merriam's tapir (*Tapirus merriami*) comes from the Anza-Borrego area and dates from 2 million years ago. There is very little difference between the Pleistocene tapirs of Anza-Borrego and the living tapirs in Central and South America.

the scattered bills and quickly gobbled them up. They chewed the coins beyond recognition so that their value was no longer apparent. When Ricardo discovered what had happened, he was furious. He vowed from then on he would spend all of his earnings before they could disappear.

Ricardo kept up his shoe shine business for almost two years and then switched to selling pumpkin s eds that his mother roasted for him and put into little bags. He sold the bags on the street, in the park, and at the movie theater.

Ricardo was the only child in the family that had a relentless need to make his own money at such a young age. That he was hawking food and shining shoes on the street embarrassed some of his family, and they thought it demeaning. They were worried that other people would think that

Celso could not provide for his family. The criticism and rumors did not dissuade Ricardo, however. He was already making his own decisions, focused on his goals, and not distracted by others' opinions.

In the meantime, Celso was focused on his own goal for a new family enterprise. He decided that the family could make more money if they sold pigs commercially for markets in Mazatlán, Guadalajara, and Monterrey. He built a ten-room, six-bedroom adobe house on the ranch and moved the family from Villa Unión to La Villita.

Ricardo was in the fourth grade when he had to transfer to the school in La Villita for his last two years of primary education. The move also meant that everyone had to work on the new family business. Ricardo's days of entrepreneurship were temporarily put on hold as he settled into a daily routine of ranch chores before and after school.

FT-3 Merriam's Tapir (Detail). Tapirs are odd-toed browsing and grazing ungulates (hooved mammals) that are related to horses and rhinoceroses even though at first glance there appears to be a resemblance to an elephant's proboscis because of the extended snout.

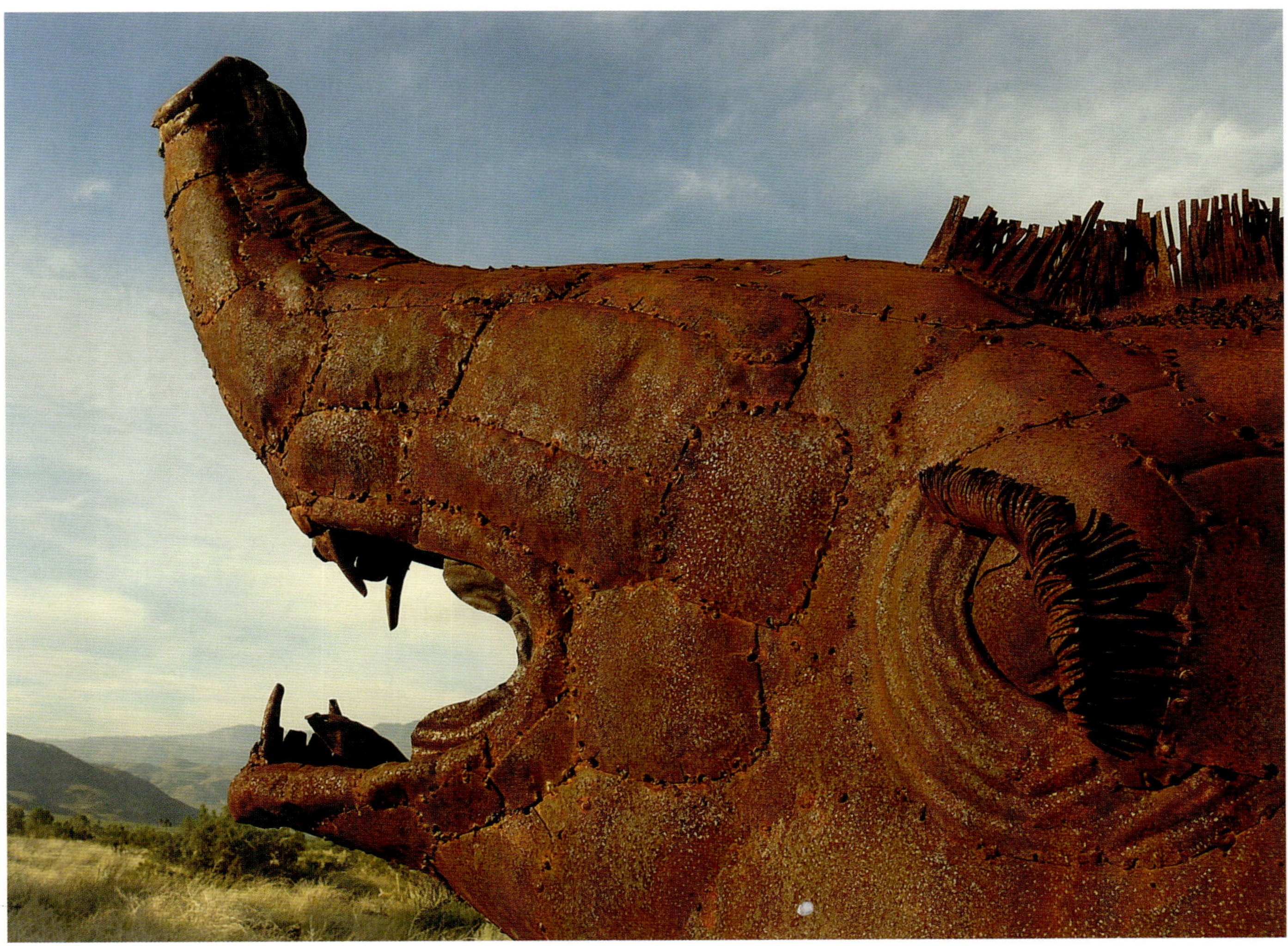

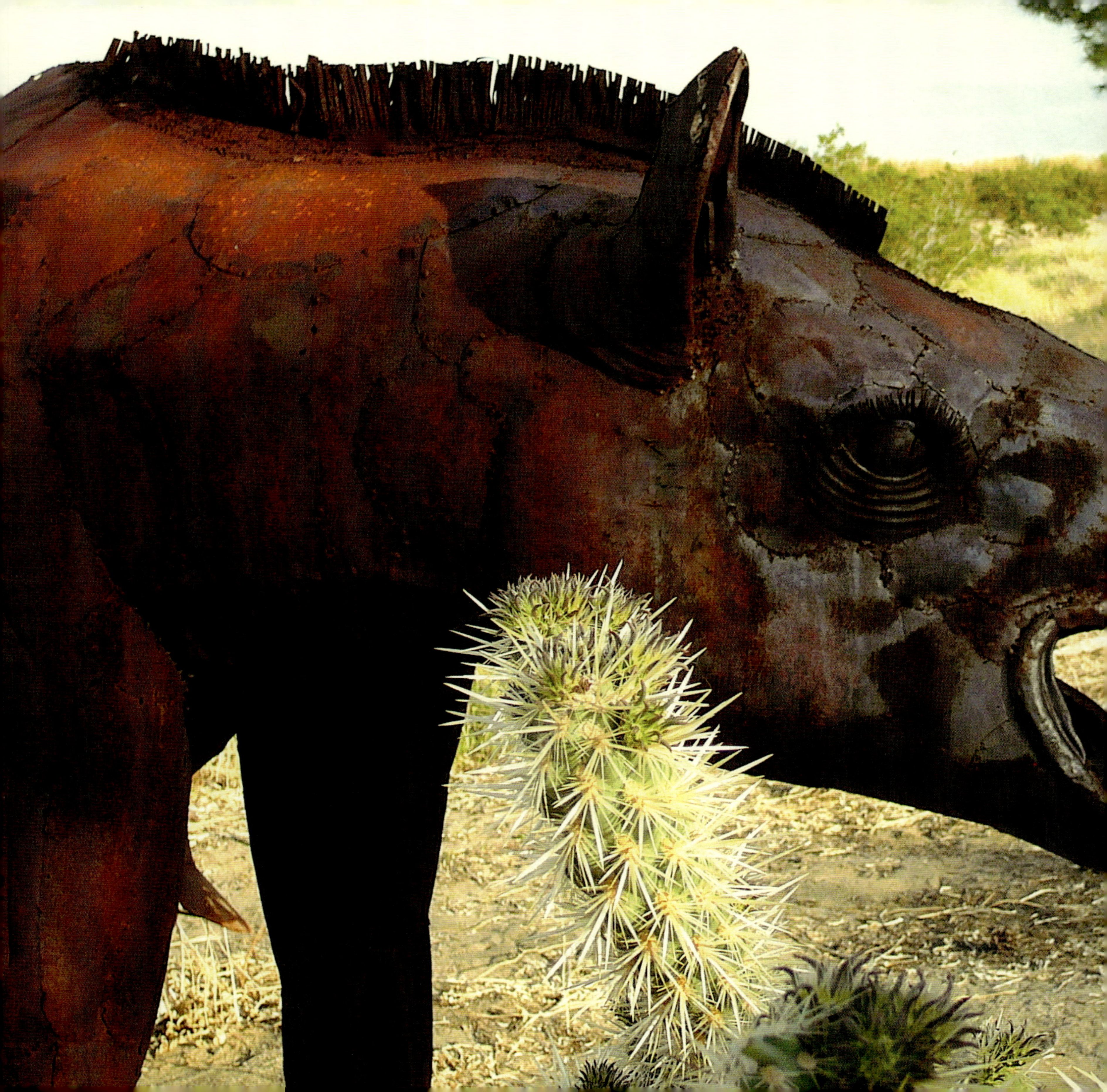

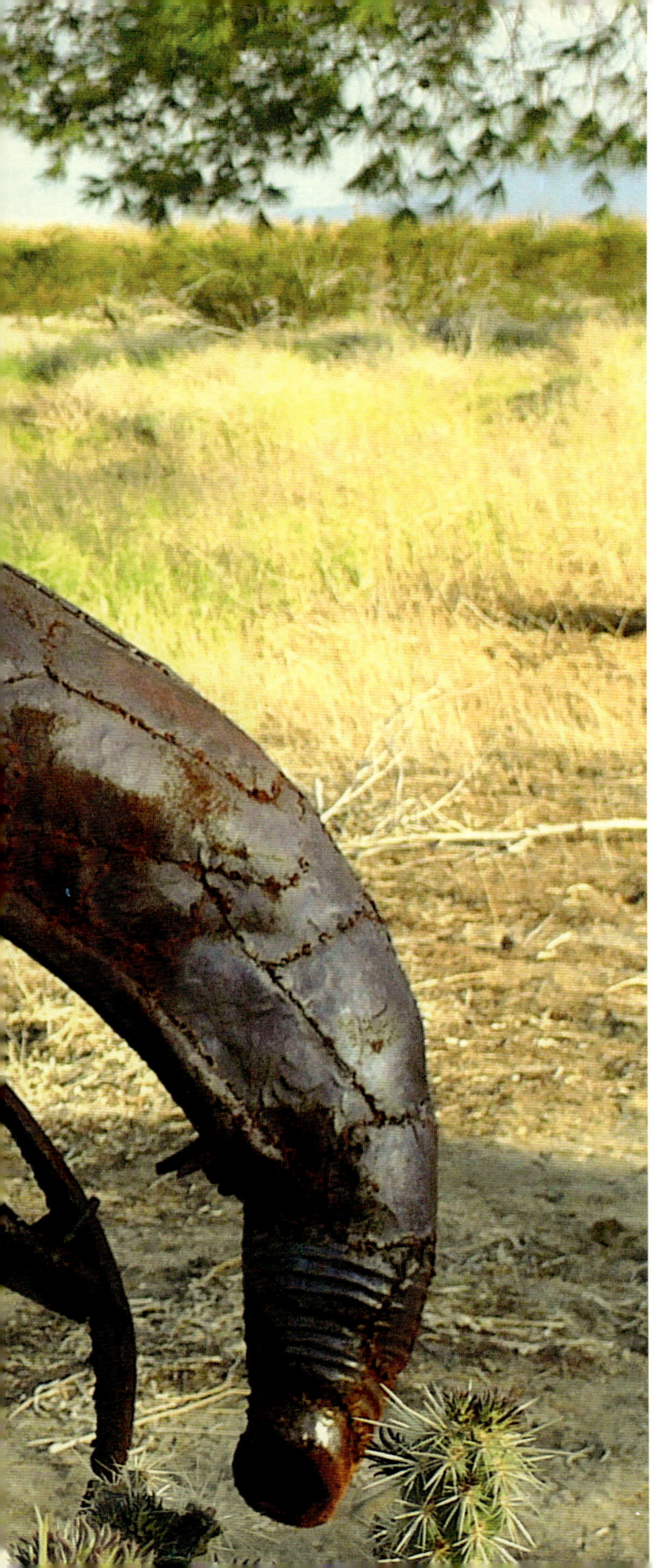

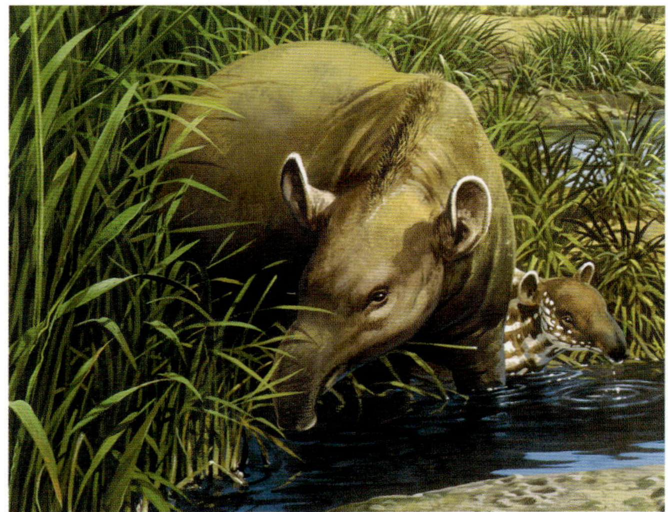

FT-3 Merriam's Tapir. The painting by John Francis (*above*) depicts a Merriam's tapir and her foal feeding along ancient Lake Borrego. Ricardo's sculpture (*left*) is accurate to the details.

Celso soon had over a thousand pigs, with trucks coming every couple of months to pick them up for market. There were crops to tend, cows to milk, eggs to collect, and many animals to feed and clean. Celso hired farmhands to help when needed.

This was a close-knit family that worked hard and strived to better themselves. Compared to others in the community, they were well off. All the children did chores before and after school and spent their evenings doing homework. If there was time left, they played with friends.

Celso was strict with the children. He expected all of them to do well in school and in society, to work hard, and to do everything he asked them to do. He did not spare the rod, and Ricardo and his older brother, Rafael, were usually the ones to get into trouble. It was Ricardo who was disciplined most often, because he did what he wanted to do and he was unwilling to do things the way anyone told him to do them.

Estela provided the softer side and was quick to protect the children if Celso was angry. Ricardo learned to run to his mother if he didn't want to get punished; she would take

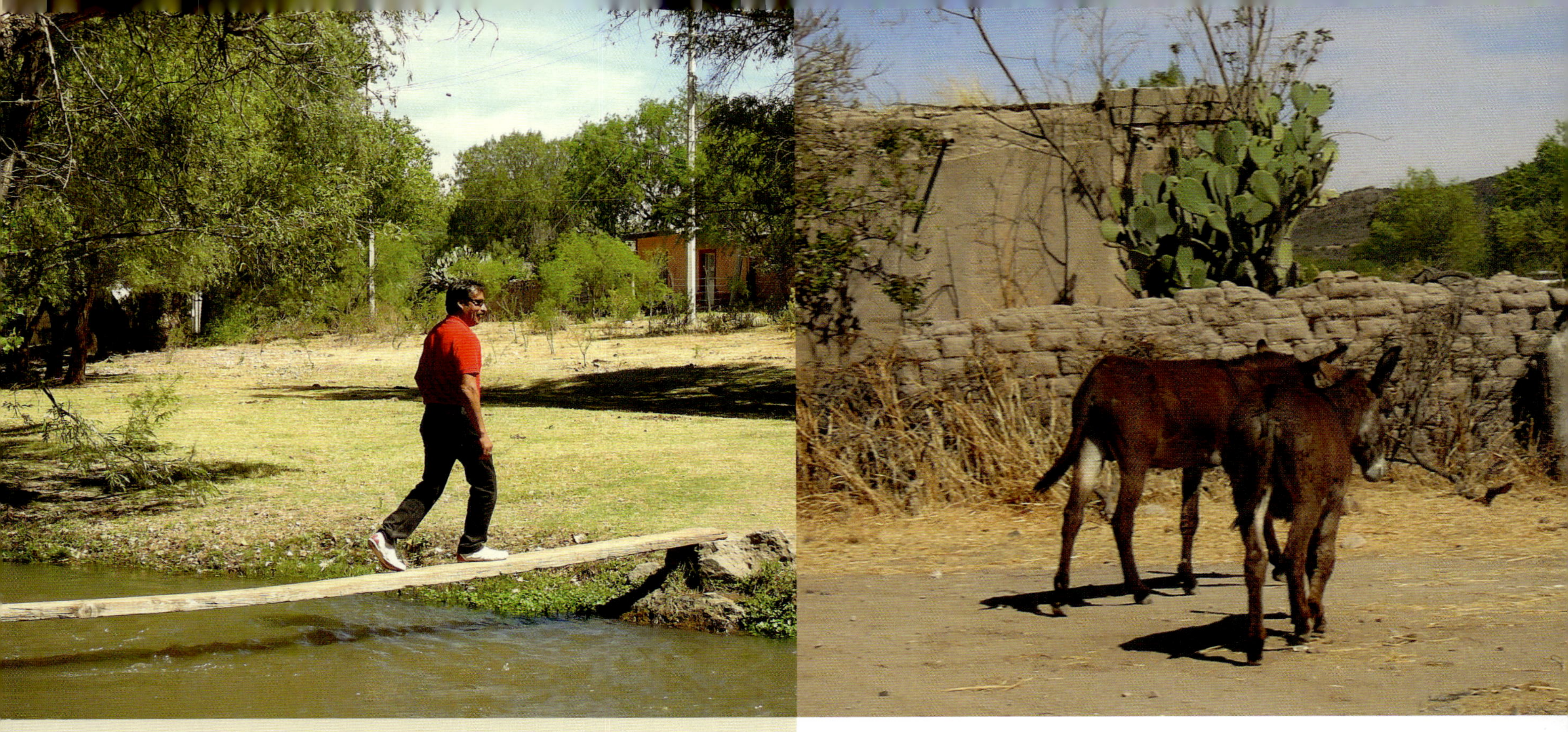

SCENES FROM LA VILLITA

From left: The Poanas River separated the ranch from the small community where the church was located. When the river rose, residents who lived on the other side of the river could not cross the plank bridge into town. That was not a problem for Ricardo's family because they had everything they needed on the ranch. It was just an inconvenience. The ranch had livestock and cultivated fields. Ricardo had an expansive view of the ranch from his window. When they could cross the river, they attended church on Sunday.

care of everything. She was understanding and gave lots of hugs and loved to tell family stories to her children. She also encouraged them to have hopes and dreams for their future. Deeply religious, Estela emphasized that one needed to have faith in God. Her strong faith was passed to her children.

Celso and Estela's hopes for their children's education and future were eventually realized. Four of their children became teachers, including Ricardo; one is an accountant, and another is an engineer, a lawyer, and a businessman. The youngest works in the family business in Durango, and the other is deceased. It was not an easy journey for them to raise eight bright and ambitious children. Most were willing to do as they were told by their parents, but Rafael and Ricardo had their own definition of independence and freedom. Rafael chose not to study beyond high school, and he decided to move to the United States for more opportunities. Ricardo

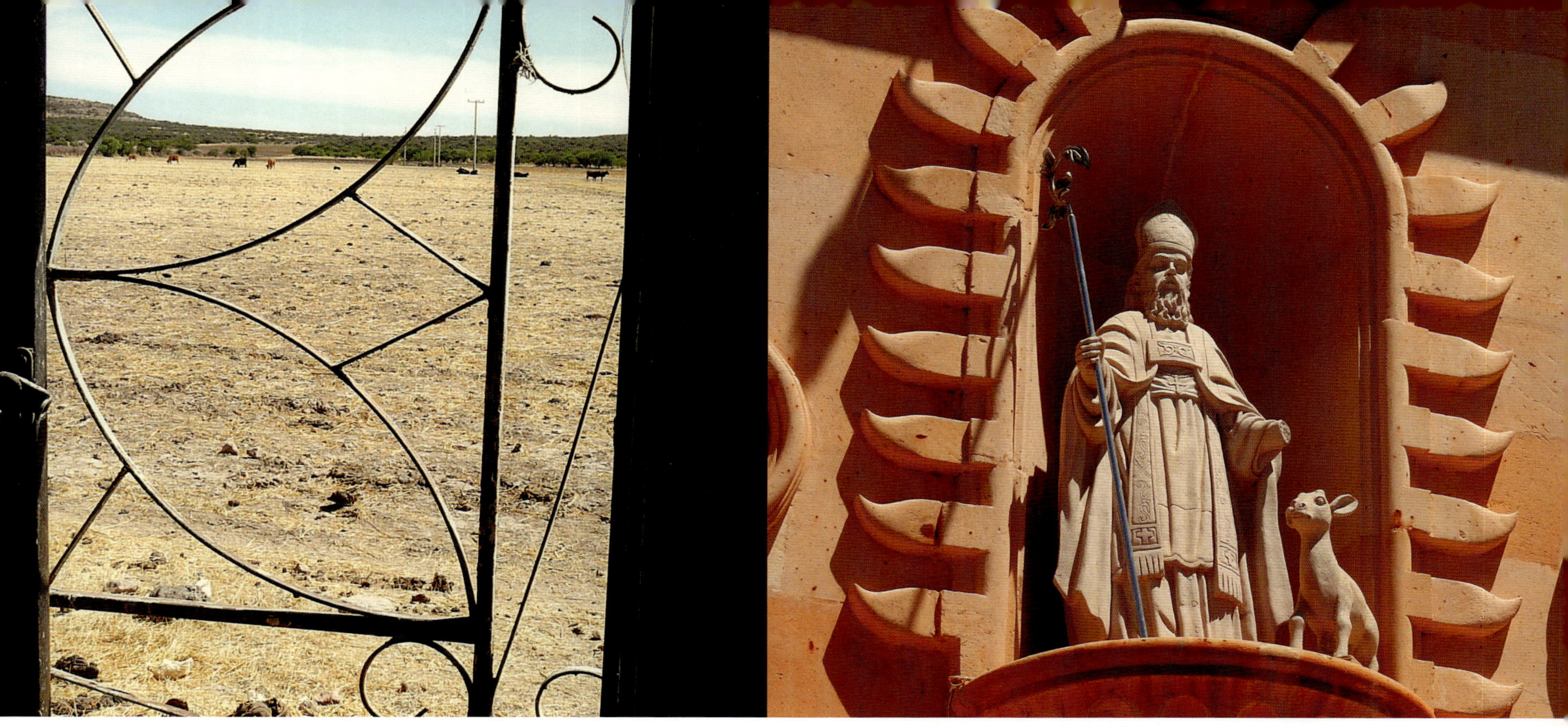

did continue his education, but his headstrong behavior was always worrisome to his parents, and Ricardo was always aware of this. It also later helped him make his decision to move to the United States.

Ricardo always knew he was well loved, and he was a happy child during the early years growing up on the ranch. His parents encouraged all their children to be self-reliant. For his ninth birthday, Ricardo was given a colt to raise. He had been riding since he was about four or five years old. He was completely responsible for the care of the orange-red or *colorado* horse. It grew into a strong and beautiful animal, which he never named. He simply whistled for it when he wanted to ride. He also took care of his pet German shepherd, and he was very attached to it. When he was ten, he was given his own rifle. There were always guns on the ranch, and all the boys learned to shoot at an early age.

Ricardo was up each morning before the sun was even a blush on the eastern horizon, riding his horse two or three miles into the surrounding hills to round up the cows and bring them into the corral. By the time the sun came up, they were already milking the cows. Then the cows were led back into the hills. Ricardo would take his .22 rifle with him and shoot one or two rabbits, bringing them home for his mother to cook. Before breakfast he also had to collect eggs and help feed the pigs and clean their pens. After breakfast it was time for school. Then after school, he had to do his homework and do the evening chores, which included cutting alfalfa and hay for the cows, feeding and cleaning the pigpens, and riding the fence line. If there were breaks in the fence, he had to repair them.

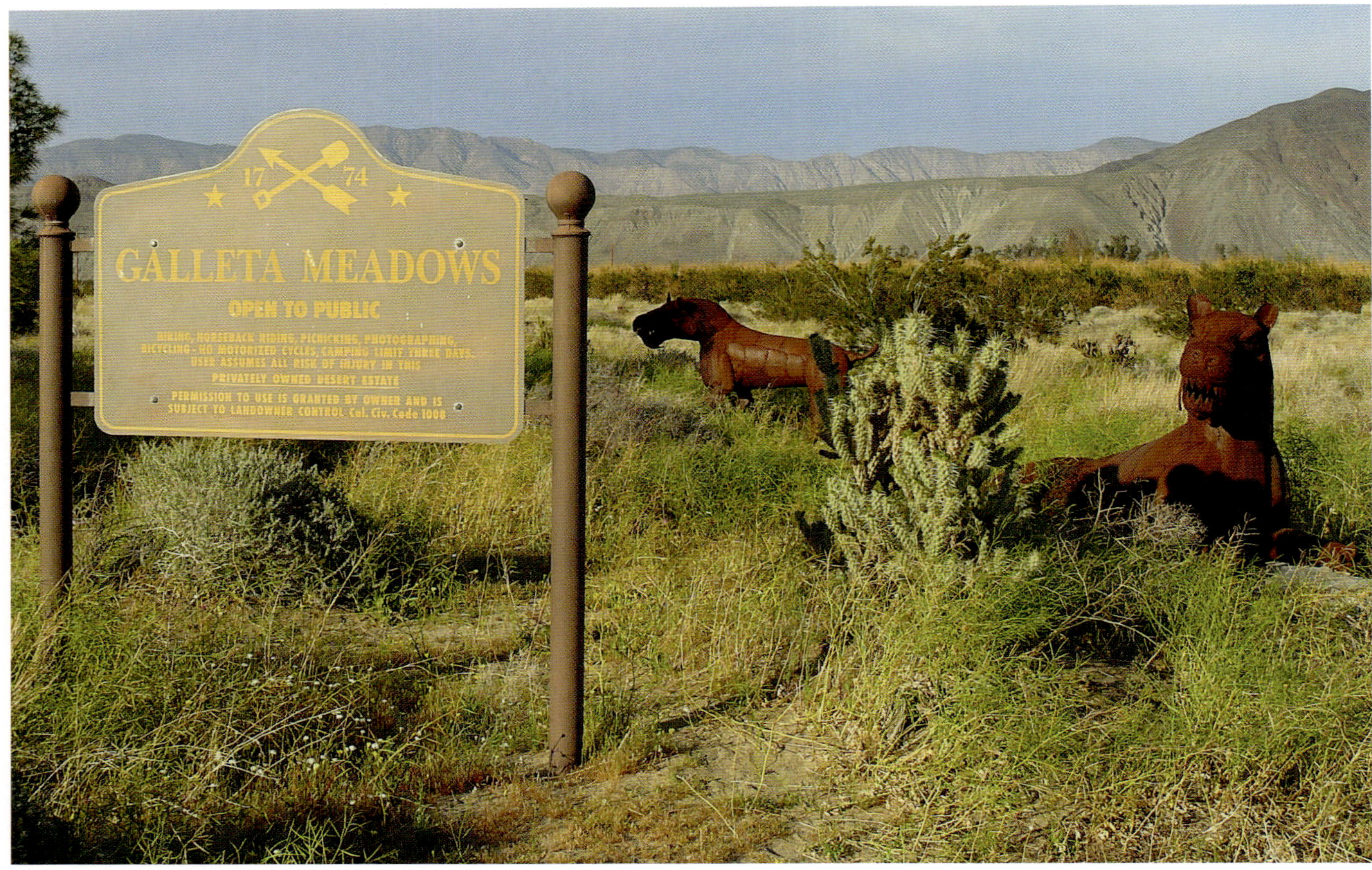

FT-4 Sabertooth Cat. Anza-Borrego offers the only fossil record for the gracile sabertooth cat (*Smilodon gracilis*) in western North America. It is a direct ancestor of the larger *Smilodon fatalis*, California's state fossil. See Chapter 3 for other sculptures of *Smilodon gracilis*.

When not working, Ricardo would take his horse and two-wheel cart into town and give his friends rides. This made him popular, especially with the girls, who loved to ride in the *carreta*. With his muscular build, mischievous hazel eyes, deep dimples, and straight white teeth that flashed into a ready smile, he always had lots of girlfriends.

His family's ranch added to Ricardo's popularity. It made him the "rich" boy in town who could sneak a pig to roast for a party. There were so many pigs that his father never knew when one went missing. He could also get a bag of beans or a pig to sell in town to get money to buy tickets for a dance or to help pay for a party. As he got older, he loved to party and go to dances.

Despite all the work on the ranch, there was still plenty of time to visit with family and friends. Sunday, after the animals were fed and the cows were milked, was a day to spend visiting. The whole family dressed up and walked ten minutes across the river to the plaza at La Villita where the church was located. After church everyone would congregate in the plaza, where they ate tacos and ice cream.

They walked wherever they needed to go. Sometimes they went to the one theater in Villa Unión that showed the

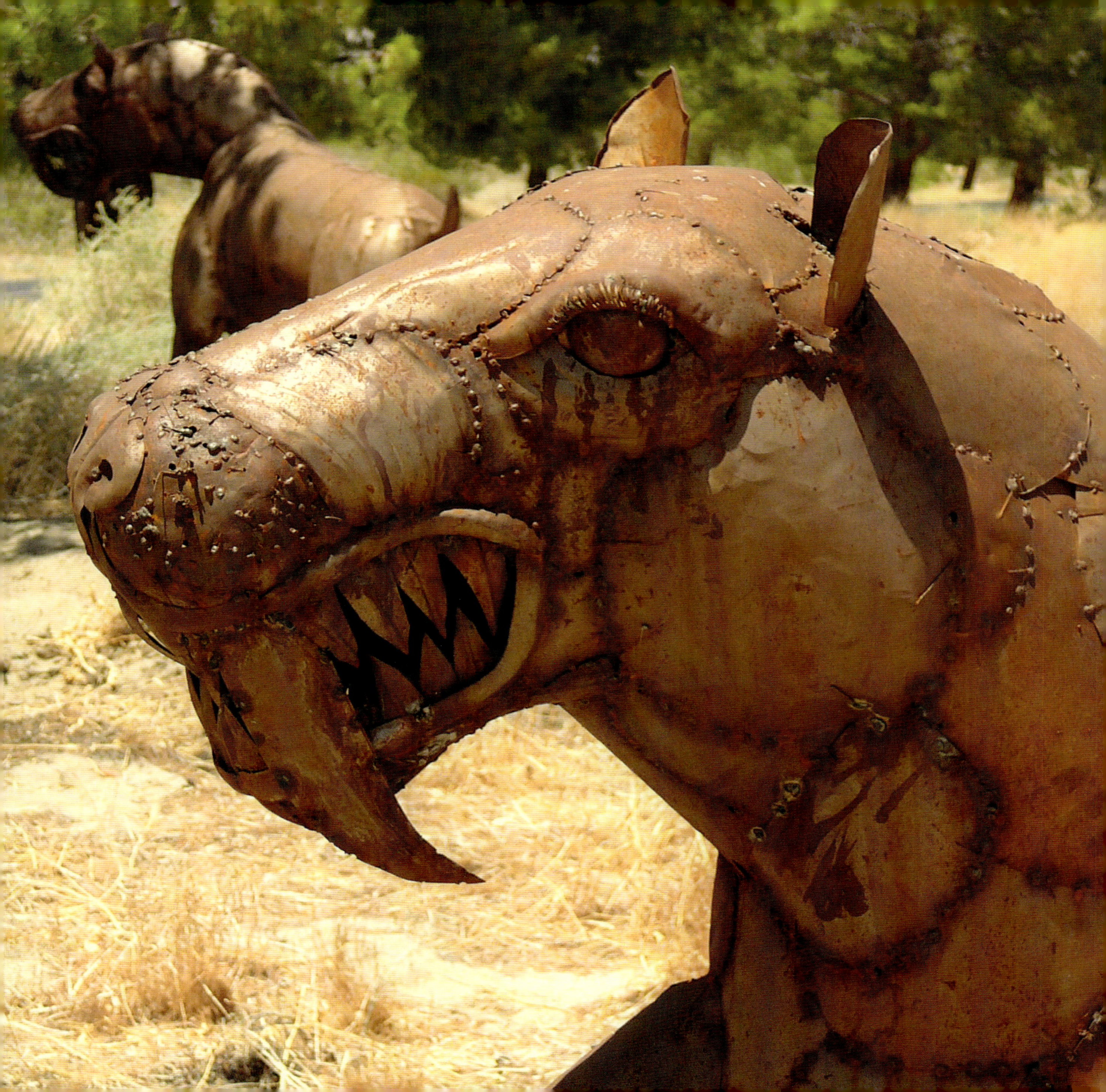

same movie for a month and charged five cents for admission. Favorite actors included Pedro Infante and Jorge Negrete, all part of the *Época de Oro,* the Golden Age of Mexican cinema. "They were all good actors and good movies—not the violence that you find in films today," Ricardo remembered.

If they did not go to a movie, friends would come over to watch television in the living room—one of only three or four televisions that existed in the whole town—or they'd listen to Mexican music on the radio.

Ricardo liked school, especially sports, and he was good at volleyball, football, baseball, and soccer. Oddly enough, he was never interested in art. In fact, if there was an art project at school, he would ask his friends to do it for him.

Ricardo feels that "life in La Villita was good." He said that it was a great place to live, although some may have thought it a little rundown with scattered, abandoned adobe homes within the village. He recalls that they had a saying about La Villita: *La Villita es fea pero engridora*—It is ugly, but it draws you back.

One time Ricardo and his friend Valentín Leal Salazár almost struck it rich. The two friends were out looking for mischief. It was Easter week—*Semana Santa*—when bread was traditionally baked. They were wandering around the ruins of an old, abandoned two-story adobe near the

FT-5 GIANT TORTOISE. California State Park Ranger Nancy Wittig and a passerby make the acquaintance of a newly installed giant land tortoise across from the entrance to Indian Head Ranch.

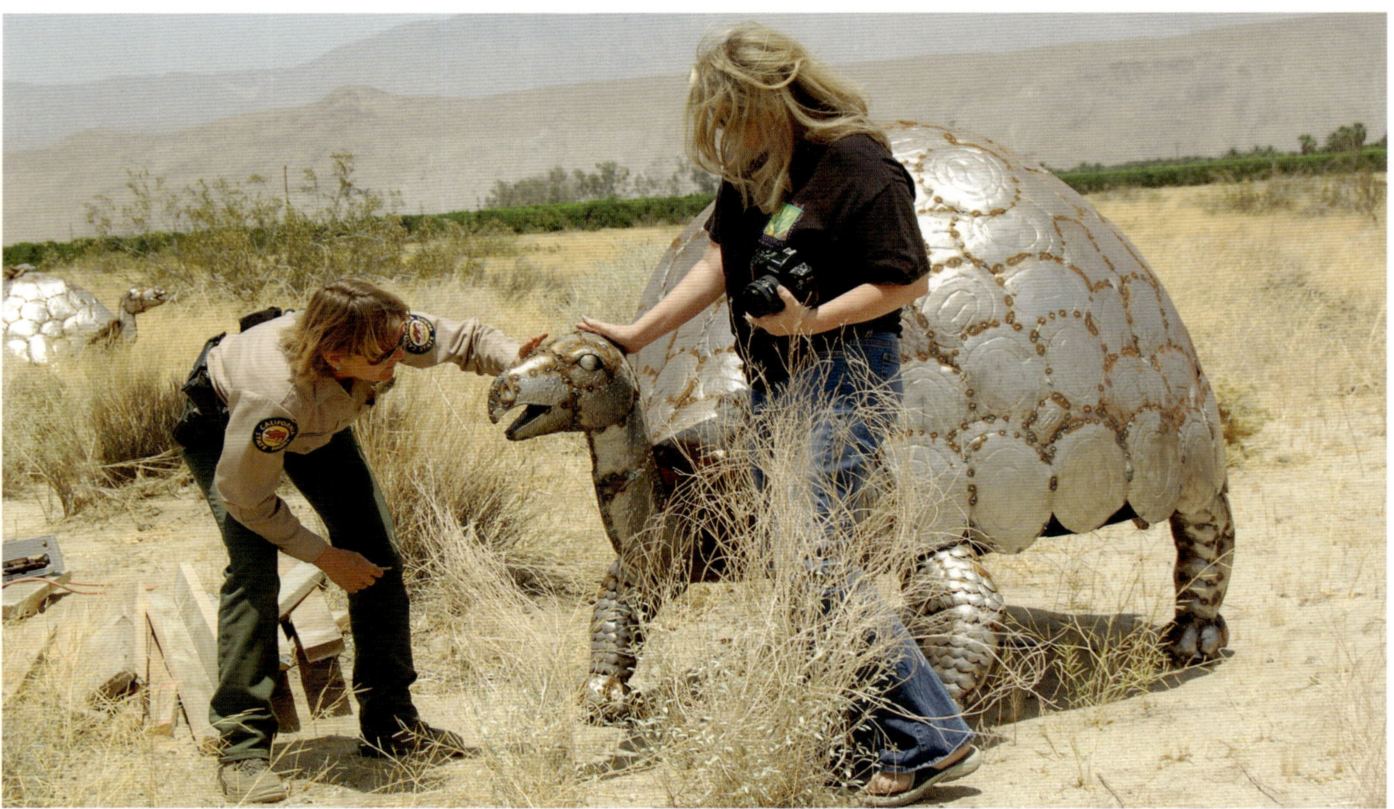

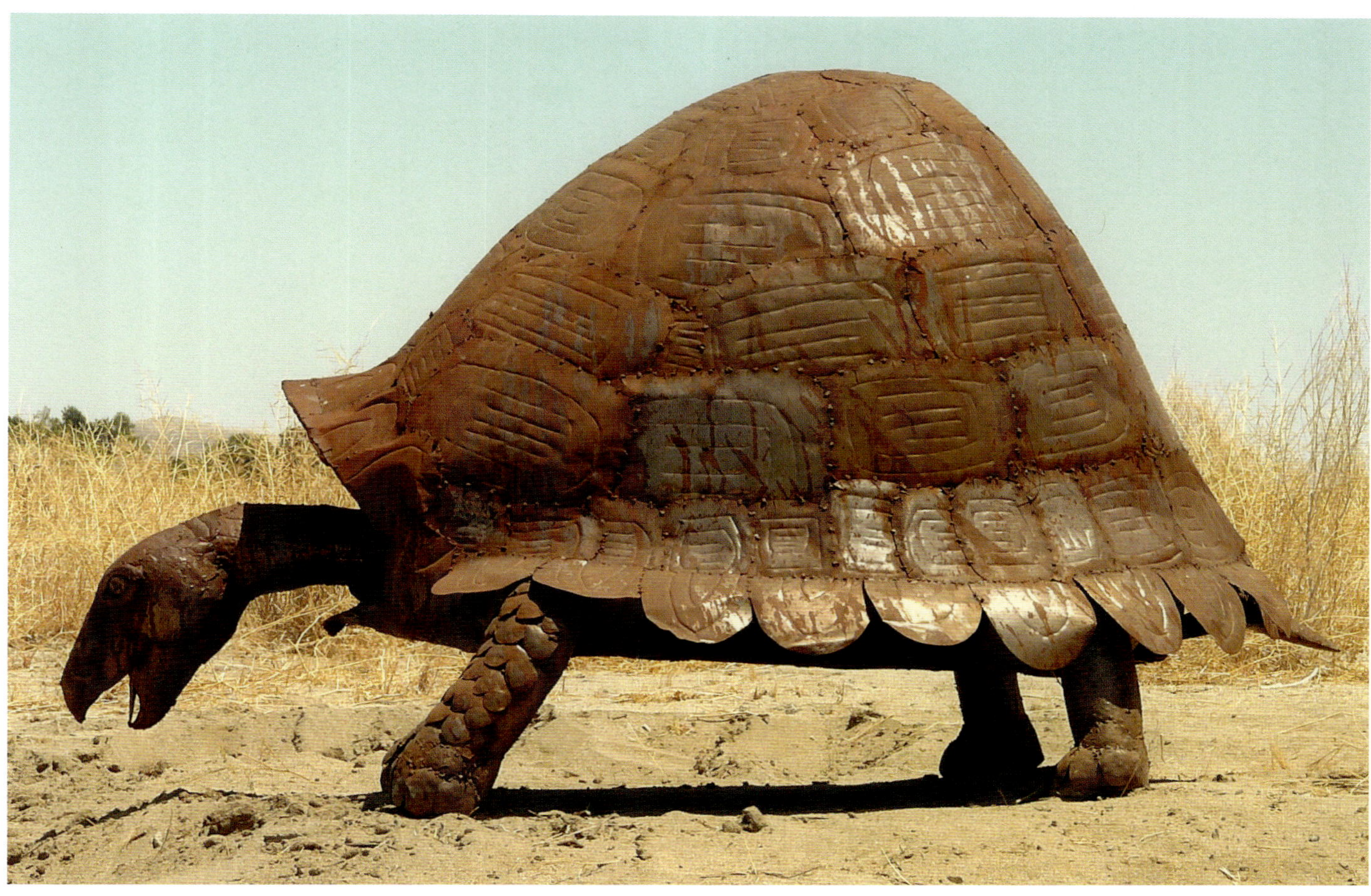

FT-5 Giant Tortoise. The giant land tortoise was a vegetarian grazer. During the Pleistocene, the tortoise would regularly visit muddy pools to keep cool. The largest land tortoise species measured almost four feet long, three feet wide, and two feet tall.

church, looking for something that they might be able to take from the rubble and use. Standing on top of the first-story wall, they noticed an old woman walking with a young girl who was carrying a basket of bread. Suddenly, they realized that they were hungry. They were well hidden in the building when they decided to frighten the woman and girl.

"Woooo. Woooo." When the girl heard the ghostly sound, she dropped her basket of bread and ran away, and the old woman followed her, hobbling as fast as she could. The boys jumped down from the wall, grabbed the bread, and ran away.

Sometime later the boys discovered a large hole in the wall where an alcove had once been. The boys had been on the wall above this alcove when it was intact. Evidently someone had decided to investigate the house after the old woman and girl had been frightened, had discovered something there, and had removed it.

At that time, because there were no banks, people hid their gold in their homes or buried it in their backyards. To this day, Ricardo still wonders what hidden treasure they may have uncovered had they just looked around the house, as they had intended, instead of playing pranks.

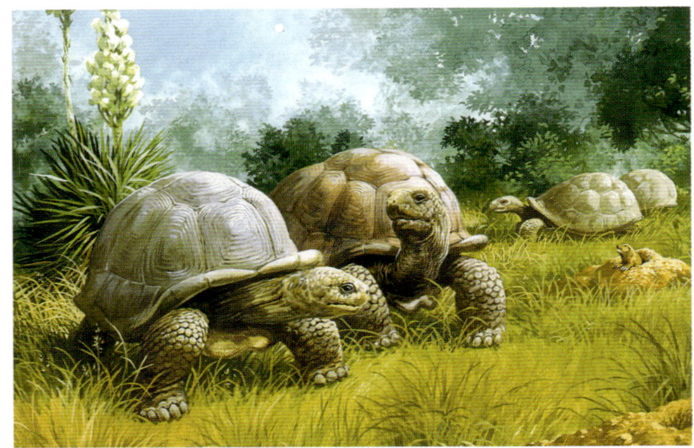

FT-5 Giant Tortoise. Today the only living giant tortoises are found on isolated tropical islands like the Galapagos. *Above:* Artist John Francis depicts the tortoise as it may have appeared in the Anza-Borrego area.

In 1974 Ricardo graduated from primary school and began Escuela Secundaria Tecnica Federal in Villa Unión, since there was no secondary school in La Villita. Secondary school turned out to be Ricardo's coming of age. He brought with him the best of what he had learned during his formative years along with his own sense of confidence, privilege, and right. He developed some good friendships and continued to push the limits of what would be considered right and wrong.

Soon after Ricardo started secondary school, his older brother, Rafael, left home and moved to the United States. Rafael did not like the confrontations with his father and thought it best to leave the house. Although Ricardo was much younger than Rafael, he was also having similar thoughts about leaving home.

Restless, Ricardo talked to his mother about quitting school, and she adamantly told him, "No!" She even offered to do his homework for him if he stayed in school, even though she had little schooling herself. Once again, she told him how education would take him somewhere and make him somebody, so he decided to stick it out, though it wasn't always easy. Ricardo's rashness and wild side still tended to get him in trouble.

FT-5 Giant Tortoise. The tortoise ate grasses, fallen fruits, and leaves, in large chunks.

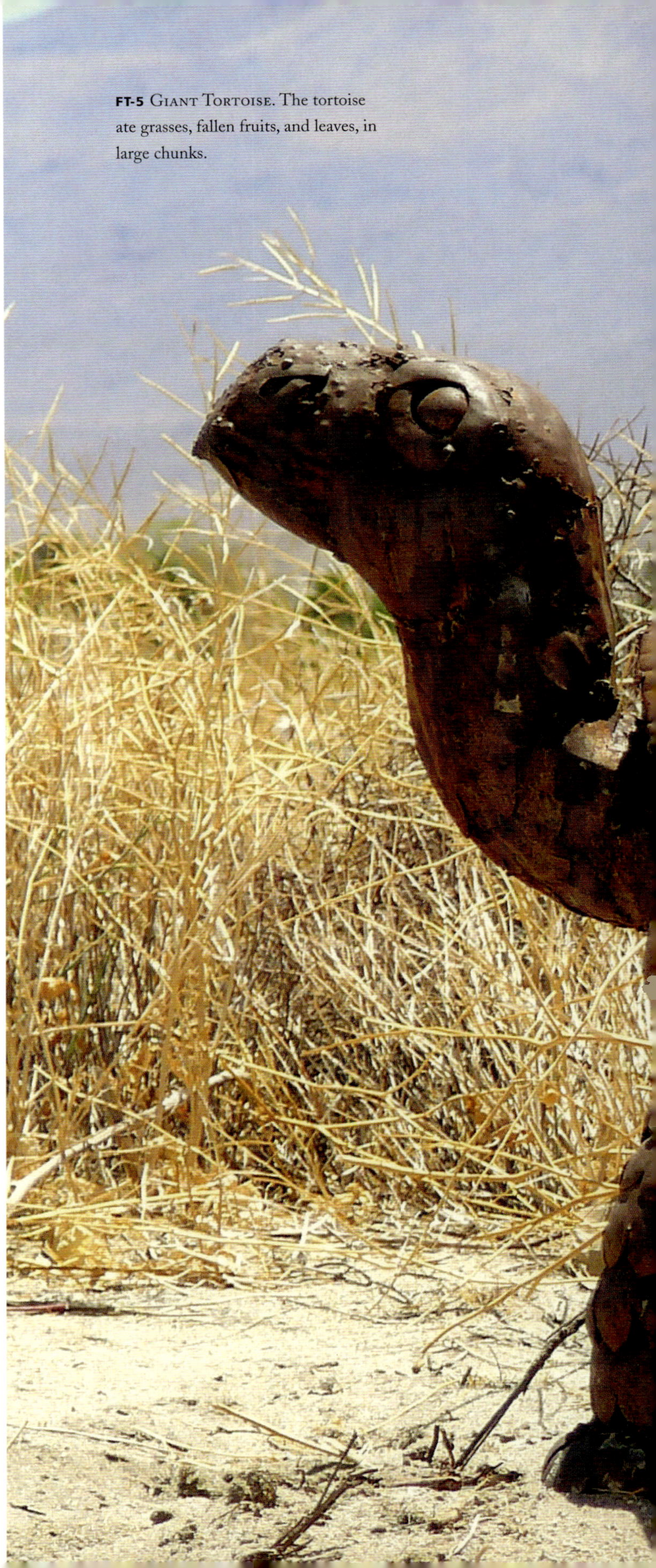

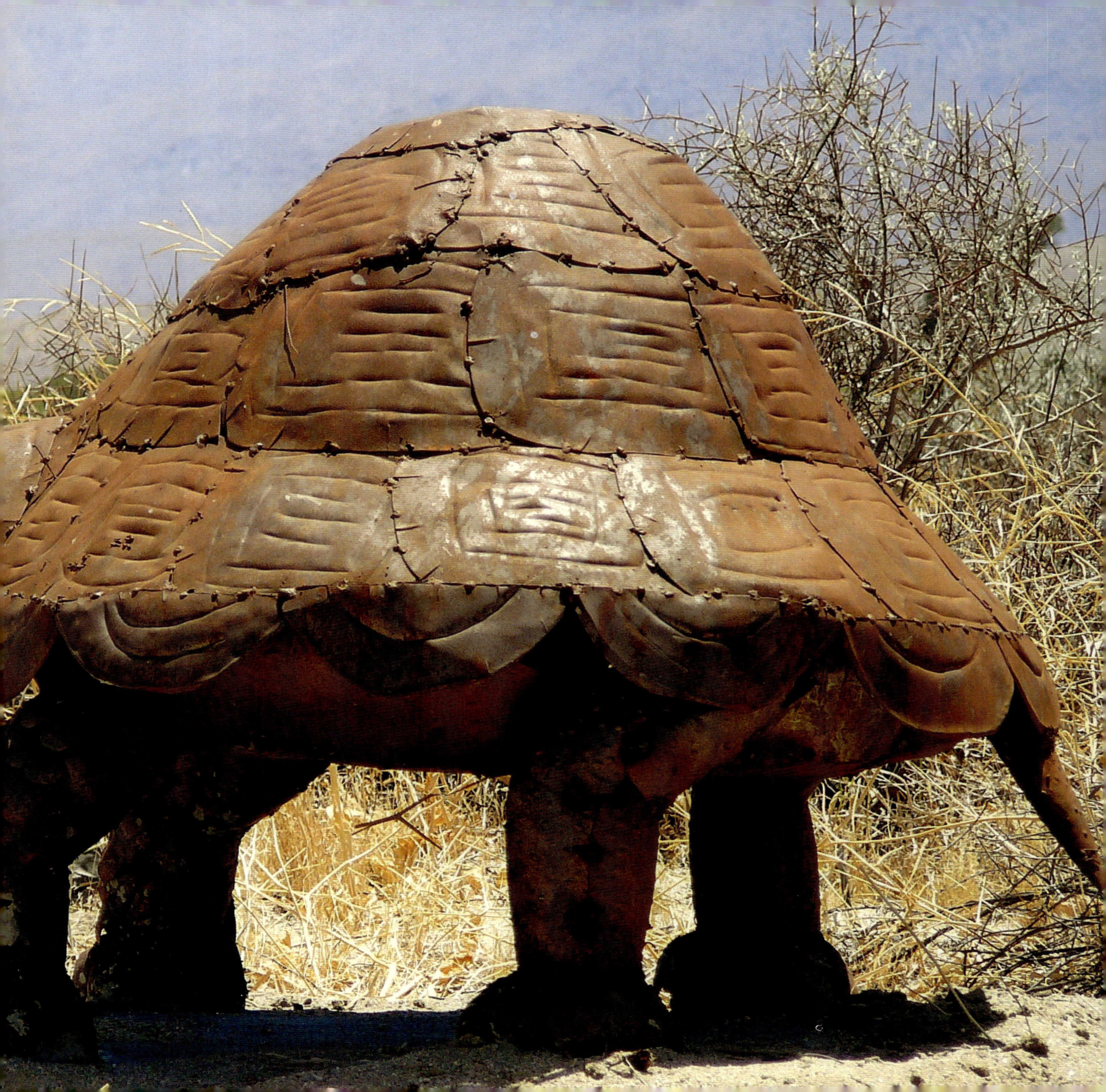

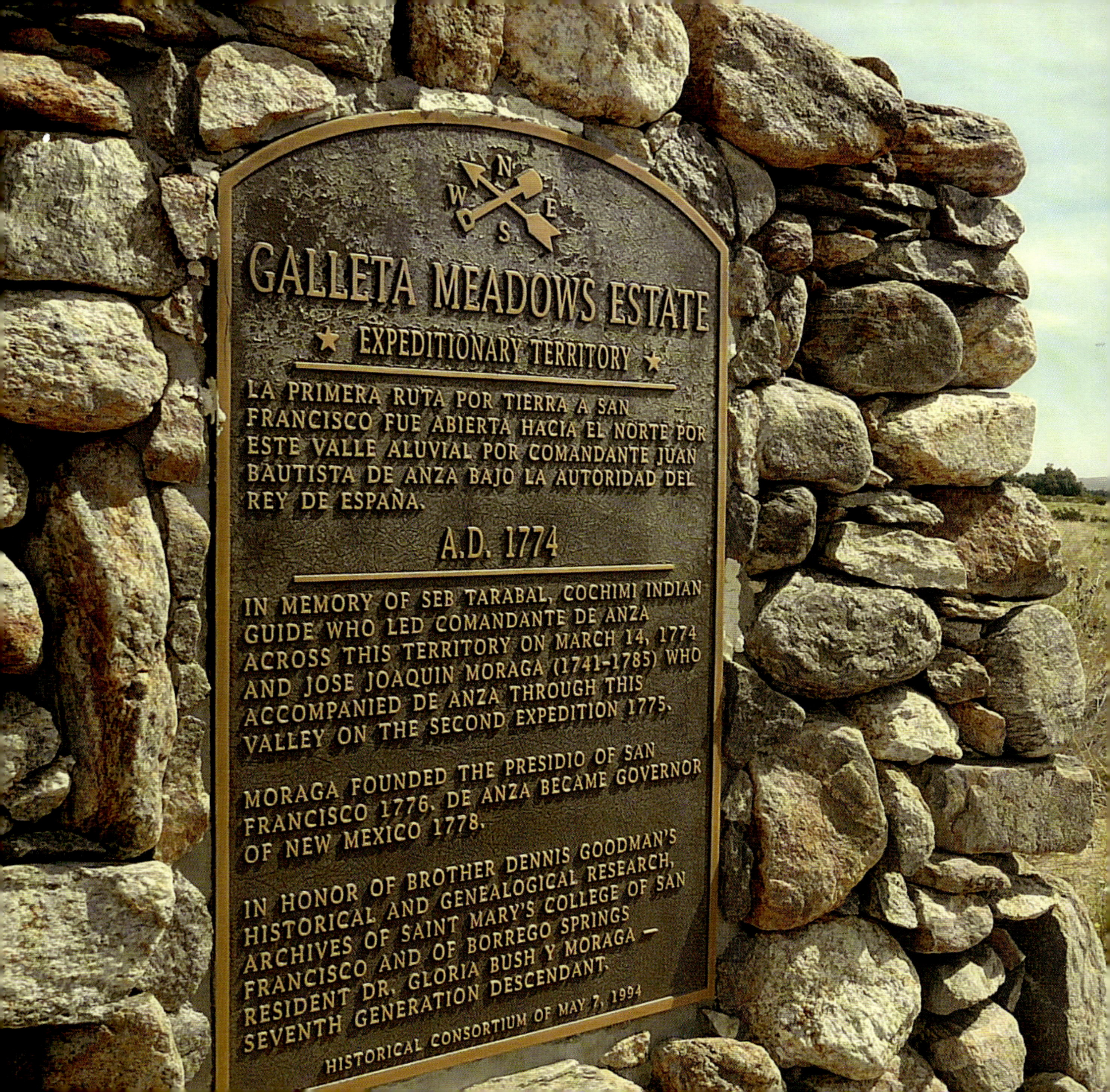
N
W
E
S
GALLETA MEADOWS ESTATE
EXPEDITIONARY TERRITORY
LA PRIMERA RUTA POR TIERRA A SAN FRANCISCO FUE ABIERTA HACIA EL NORTE POR ESTE VALLE ALUVIAL POR COMANDANTE JUAN BAUTISTA DE ANZA BAJO LA AUTORIDAD DEL REY DE ESPAÑA.
A.D. 1774
IN MEMORY OF SEB TARABAL, COCHIMI INDIAN GUIDE WHO LED COMANDANTE DE ANZA ACROSS THIS TERRITORY ON MARCH 14, 1774 AND JOSE JOAQUIN MORAGA (1741-1785) WHO ACCOMPANIED DE ANZA THROUGH THIS VALLEY ON THE SECOND EXPEDITION 1775.
MORAGA FOUNDED THE PRESIDIO OF SAN FRANCISCO 1776. DE ANZA BECAME GOVERNOR OF NEW MEXICO 1778.
IN HONOR OF BROTHER DENNIS GOODMAN'S HISTORICAL AND GENEALOGICAL RESEARCH, ARCHIVES OF SAINT MARY'S COLLEGE OF SAN FRANCISCO AND OF BORREGO SPRINGS RESIDENT DR. GLORIA BUSH Y MORAGA — SEVENTH GENERATION DESCENDANT.
HISTORICAL CONSORTIUM OF MAY 7, 1994

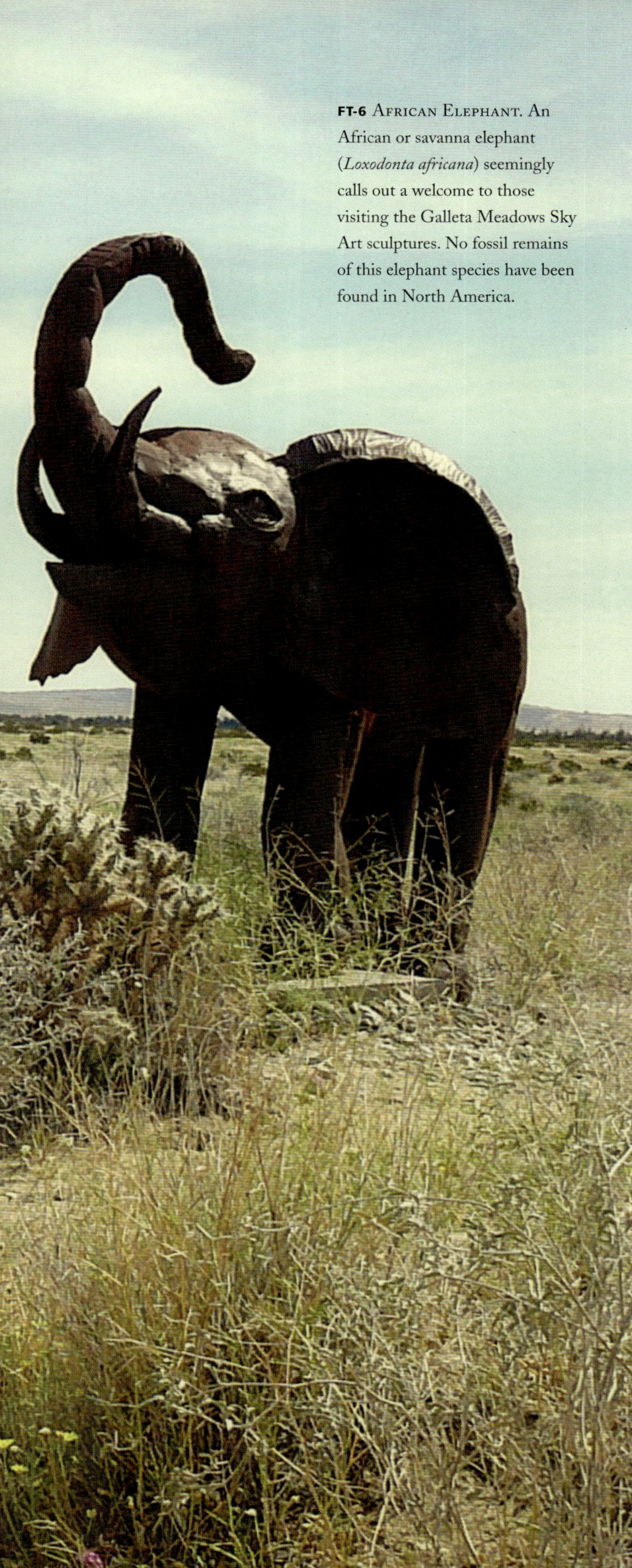

FT-6 African Elephant. An African or savanna elephant (*Loxodonta africana*) seemingly calls out a welcome to those visiting the Galleta Meadows Sky Art sculptures. No fossil remains of this elephant species have been found in North America.

CHAPTER 2

DURANGO

When Ricardo was about fifteen years old, he got into a fight with another teenager. It was a clean fight, but the police came and took only Ricardo to jail. One of his friends ran to Ricardo's father and told him what had happened.

Celso said, "Good, let the boys work out their differences in jail." But when he was told that only his son was in jail, he immediately went to the police department and offered to get the other boy so he could be put in jail, too. The police said they were not going to do that, and that Ricardo had to stay overnight.

"If you are not going to jail the other boy, then let my son go!" Celso demanded. When they refused, Celso pulled out his gun and told the policemen to open the cell door and let Ricardo out. They did. It was a little town, and everyone knew Celso had influence and money, so they let the matter drop.

That wasn't Ricardo's only trip to the jail. It happened another time when he and several of his friends were playing strip basketball at night. The guys took turns throwing basketballs from the free-throw line. Whoever missed had to take off an article of clothing. The first one to get totally naked had to run one block around the town. It was at night and not many people were around. The guy who lost had to make the run.

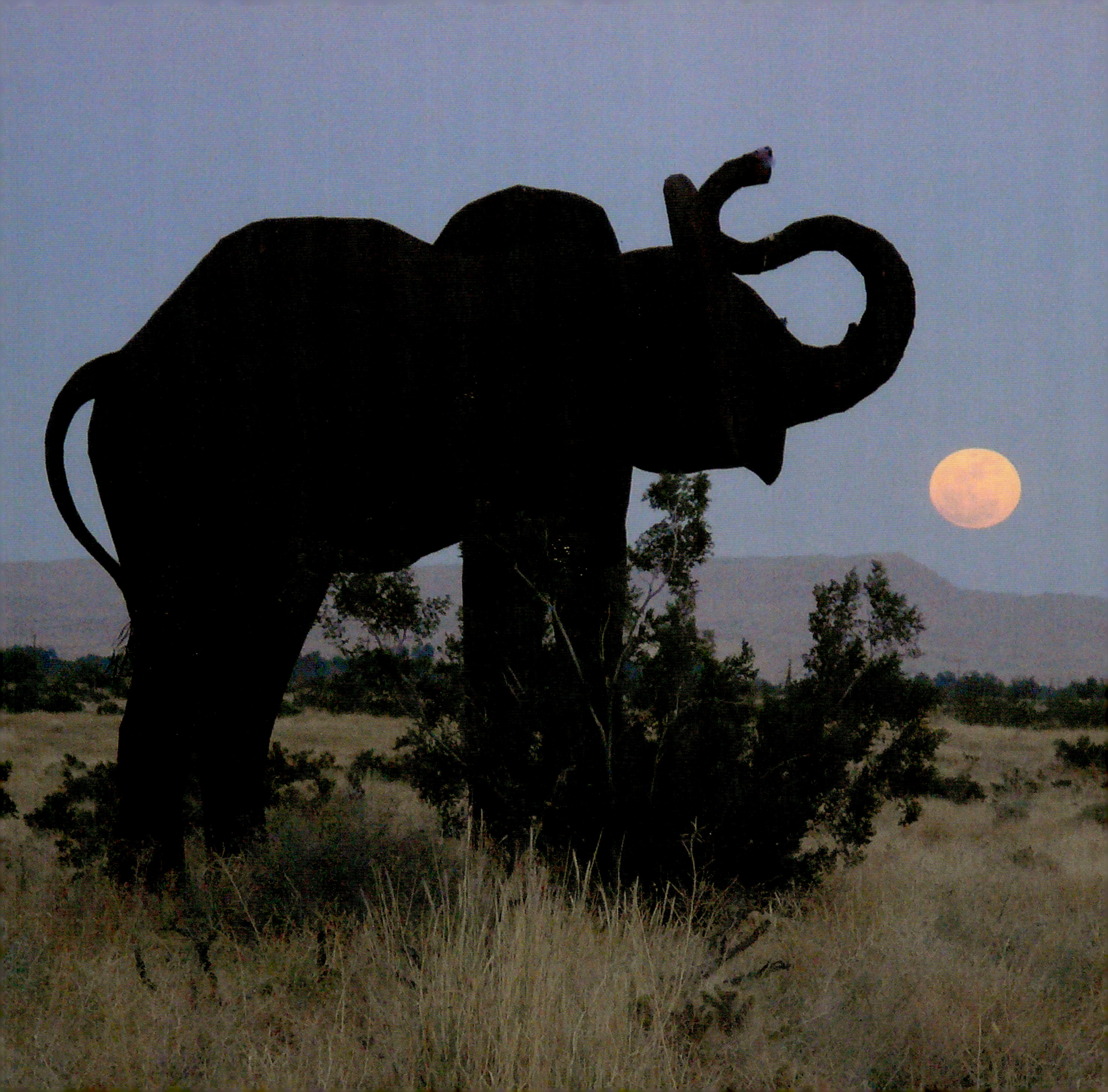

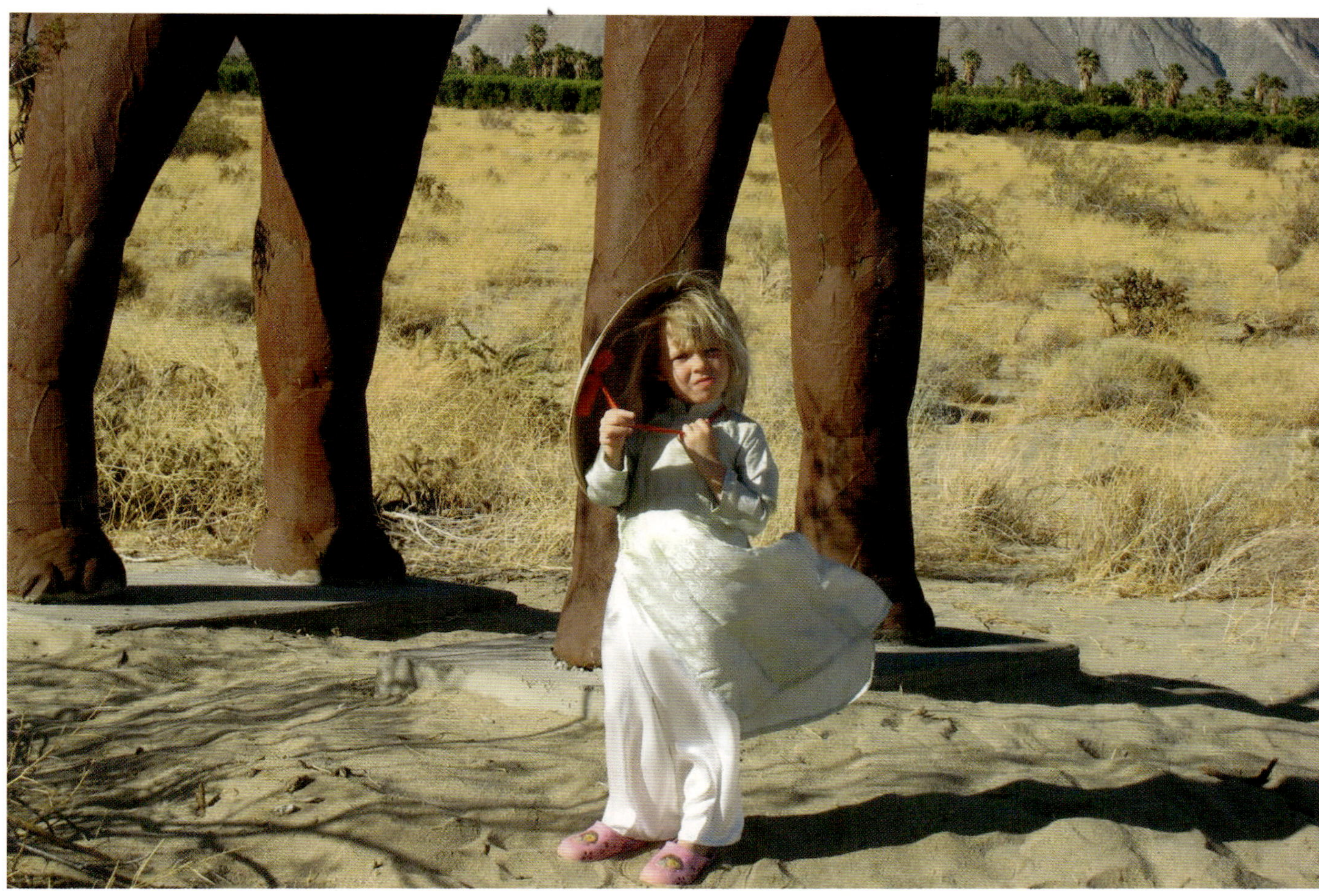

FT-6 African Elephant. The African elephant is the largest living land mammal in the world, weighing about 10,000 pounds. The little girl above is dwarfed by this behemoth. The elephant to the left observes the moon rise over Fonts Point.

Unfortunately, nearby there were two women sitting under a tree talking. When the young man ran by them, one of the ladies screamed, "Look, a naked man!" The young man yelled back something obscene to her. It turned out that one of the women just happened to be his mother, and she was so angry that she called the police and had all the boys arrested.

As punishment, they had to help repair the town's streets—filling in potholes by hauling in sand and rocks. There were about fifteen of them who had to work on the streets. Even though it was hard work, they had a good time; but, most of all, it was embarrassing because they had insulted a mother.

None of these incidents involved alcohol. In fact, Ricardo did not have his first drink until he was fifteen or sixteen years old. He remembers it very vividly.

He had ridden his horse to a *coleadura*, a Mexican sporting event in which a *coleador,* or trained horseman, catches a bull by its tail and throws him to the ground. A couple of men who were at the *coleadura* offered Ricardo

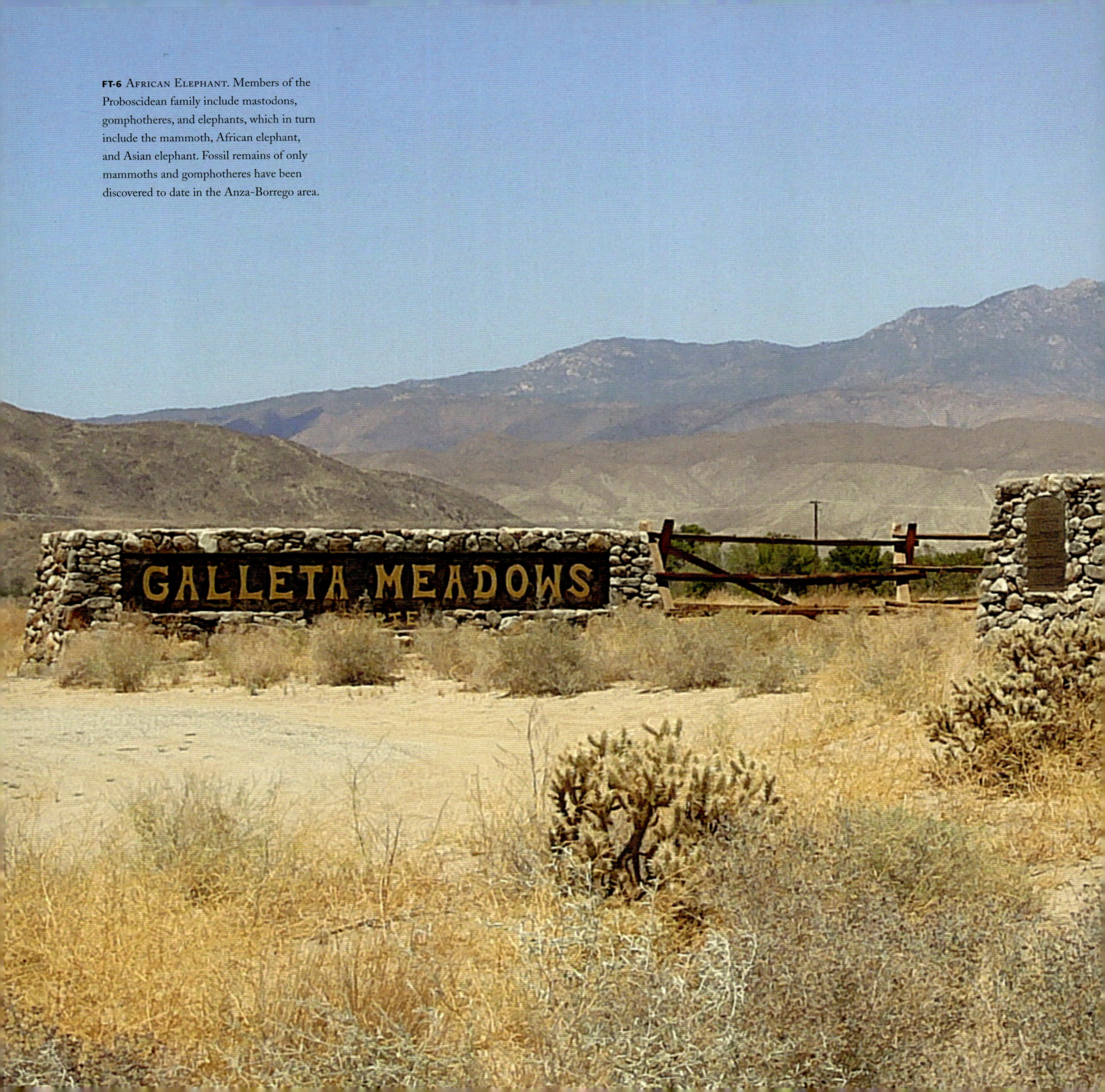

FT-6 African Elephant. Members of the Proboscidean family include mastodons, gomphotheres, and elephants, which in turn include the mammoth, African elephant, and Asian elephant. Fossil remains of only mammoths and gomphotheres have been discovered to date in the Anza-Borrego area.

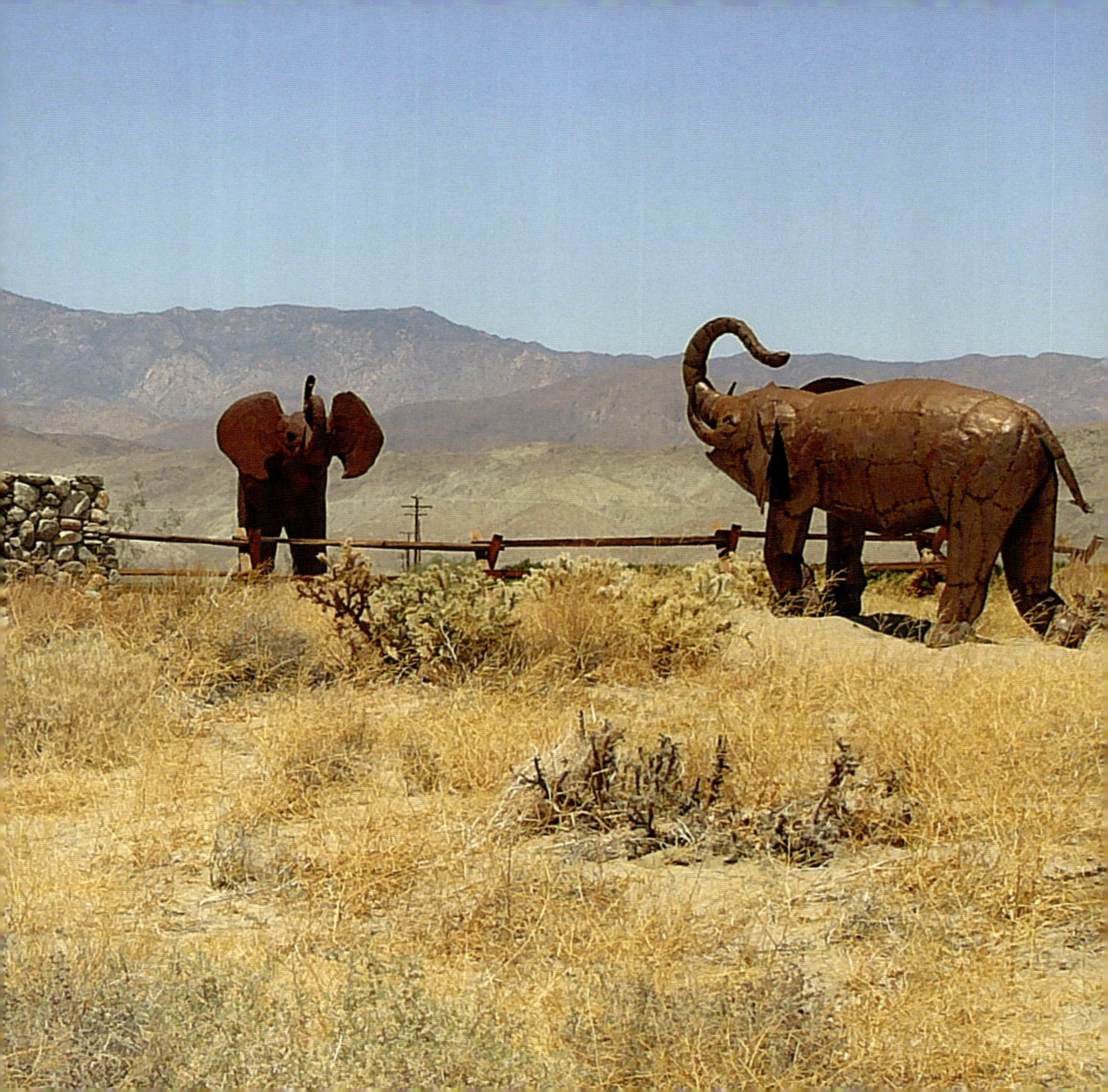

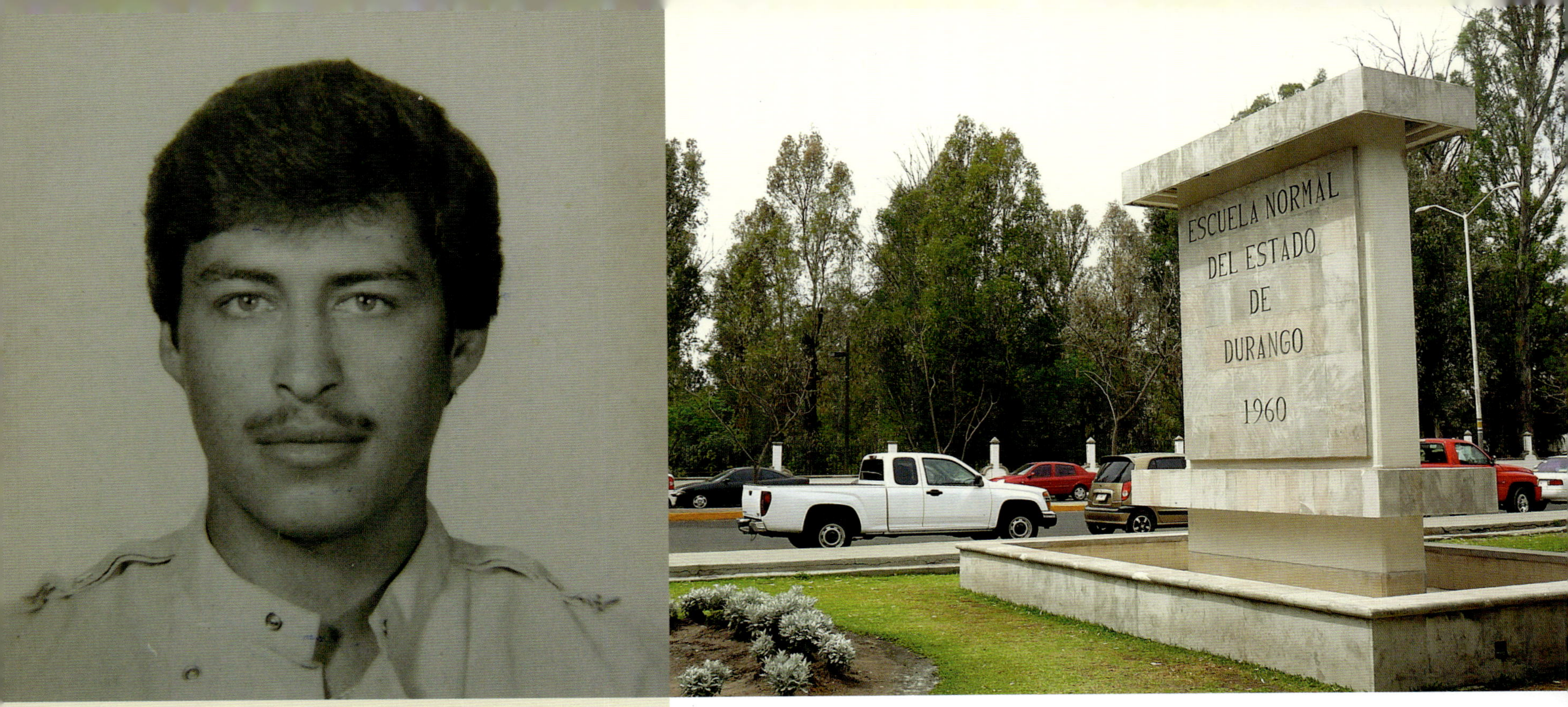

COLLEGE DAYS

Ricardo enrolled in a four-year program at a teachers' college in Durango, Mexico, graduating with honors in 1983. Like most typical students, his days were filled with college activities, studies, and weekend parties and adventures that often included his best friend, Valentín Leal Salazár (*far right with Ricardo*). Ricardo was a primary school teacher in Mexico for two years before coming to the United States.

drinks because they liked his sisters. He stayed and kept on drinking. By the time he was ready to leave, it was late and he did not want to ride his horse ten miles home in the dark. One of the men offered him a ride in his pickup. Ricardo got in and let his horse go, figuring it would find its way home. The horse was his, but the saddle belonged to his father.

When he staggered in, his sister Ernestina saw that he was falling-down drunk and ran to tell their father.

Celso was raging mad and grabbed Ricardo, dragging him out to the grain room, where he whipped him with a rope. Ricardo was so drunk that he really didn't feel anything. The next morning when he woke up, he wondered why he hurt so badly. Then he noticed lash marks where he had been beaten. He also found out that morning that his horse made it home minus his father's saddle. Someone had taken it but not the horse, because the horse had an identifying brand.

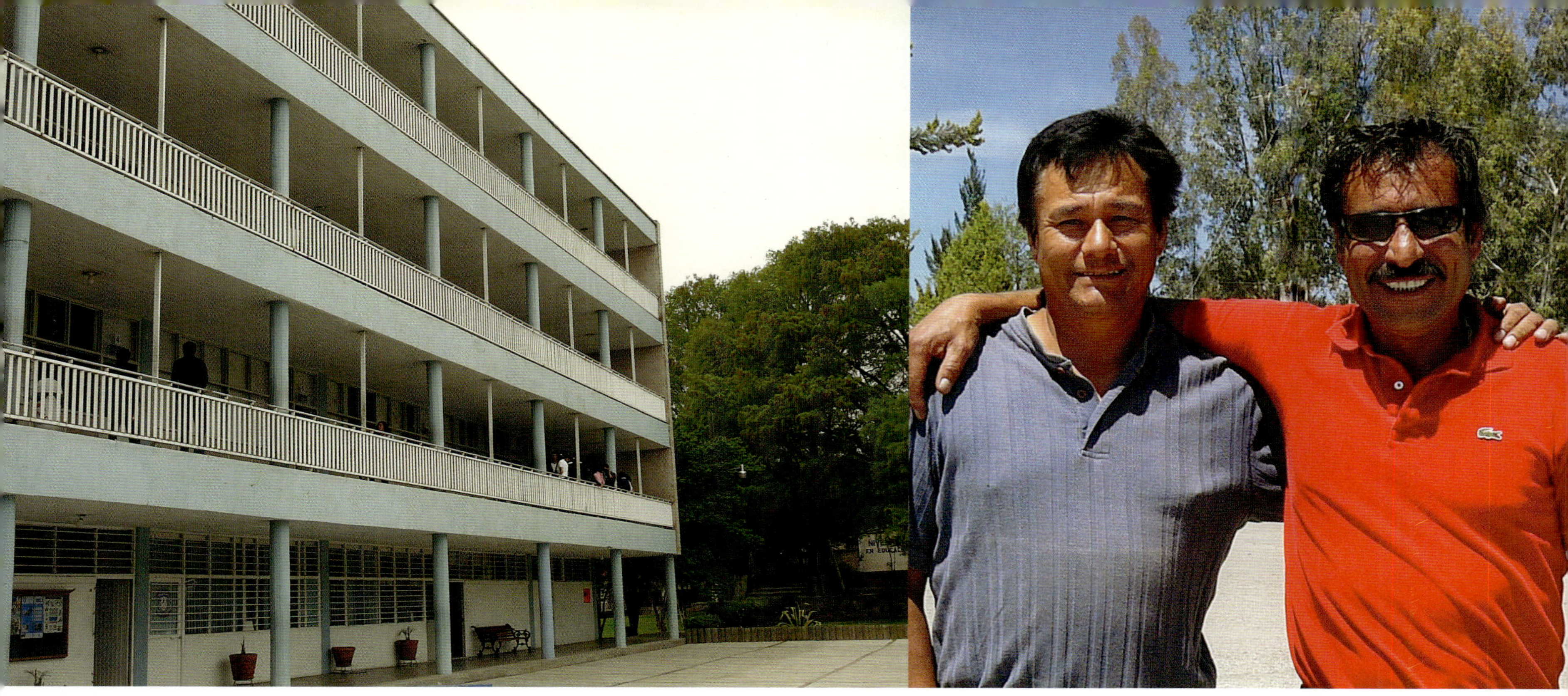

In spite of incidents like these, Ricardo appeared to be a model student, partly because he was smart enough to befriend the brightest students. Because he was well liked, his friends often did his homework for him. He was a quick learner when he had to be, but usually he didn't bother to study. He would look for the easy way out—he copied tests, charmed the teachers, and took advantage of all of his relationships. He thought school was a place to have a good time and to outwit the system any way he could.

After he graduated from secondary school, Ricardo decided to attend Instituto Tecnológico Agropecuario, an agricultural school in Durango, instead of getting higher academic education. He thought he'd have an easier and better time. The head of the school was from Ricardo's hometown and knew him. He told the teachers to give Ricardo "nice" grades. Ricardo was not required to attend classes, and he usually didn't. He ended up quitting the agricultural school because he felt he was wasting his time.

Instead, he decided to work on his father's ranch, and it proved to be a real eye opener. It was not like helping out when he was younger. He had full responsibilities thrown at him, and it wasn't one bit fun.

After a few months working as a ranch hand, Ricardo told his father he wanted to go back to school and study to become a teacher. It would take four years of training, but he would also have the freedom to party and be with his friends again. An added benefit of going to the teachers' college was that most of the students were women—beautiful women.

Ricardo enrolled at Escuela Normal del Estado de Durango, the area's best teaching school. While he was at school he worked various jobs at a number of places, including an auto body shop, a shoe store, and later a liquor store.

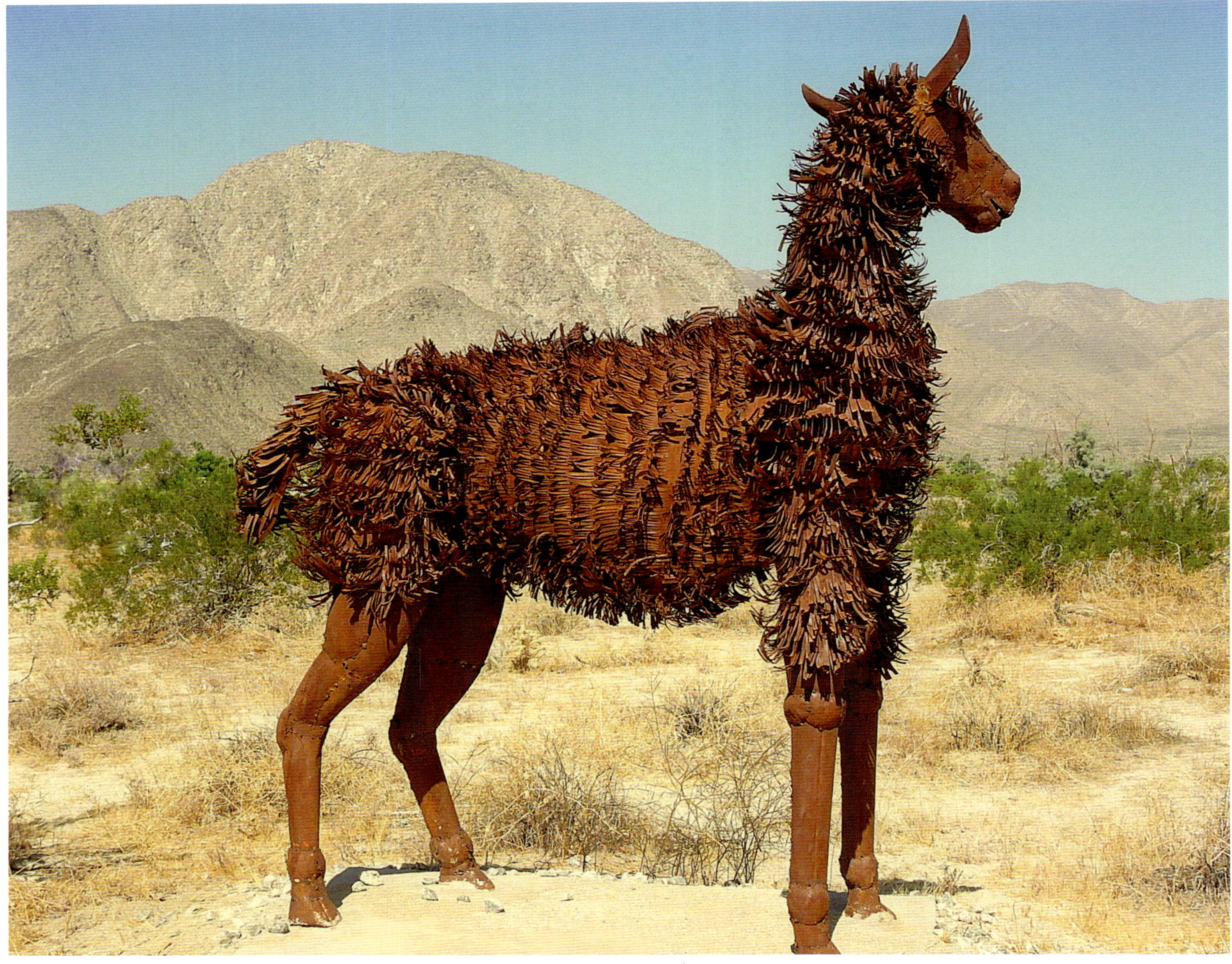

FT-7 Llama. Camels evolved in North America about 44 million years ago and went extinct about 11,000 years ago. They survive as modern llamas in South America and camels in Asia and Africa. A *Hemiauchenia* species created by Ricardo depicts the ancestor of the modern llama.

Ricardo got along well with all the teachers at the school, except for the Spanish teacher. He refused to follow the strict dress code that required blue pants and a clean, white shirt. He also had to wear shoes and not boots. The other teachers gave him some slack and he often got away without wearing the required clothing, but not in his Spanish class. To keep from having constant confrontations with the Spanish teacher, ever-resourceful Ricardo talked his classmates into swapping clothes with him when he had to attend his language class.

As in secondary school, Ricardo took shortcuts with studying to have time for partying. His friends did his homework for him, and when it was time for testing, they would all plot ways to get copies of the exam beforehand.

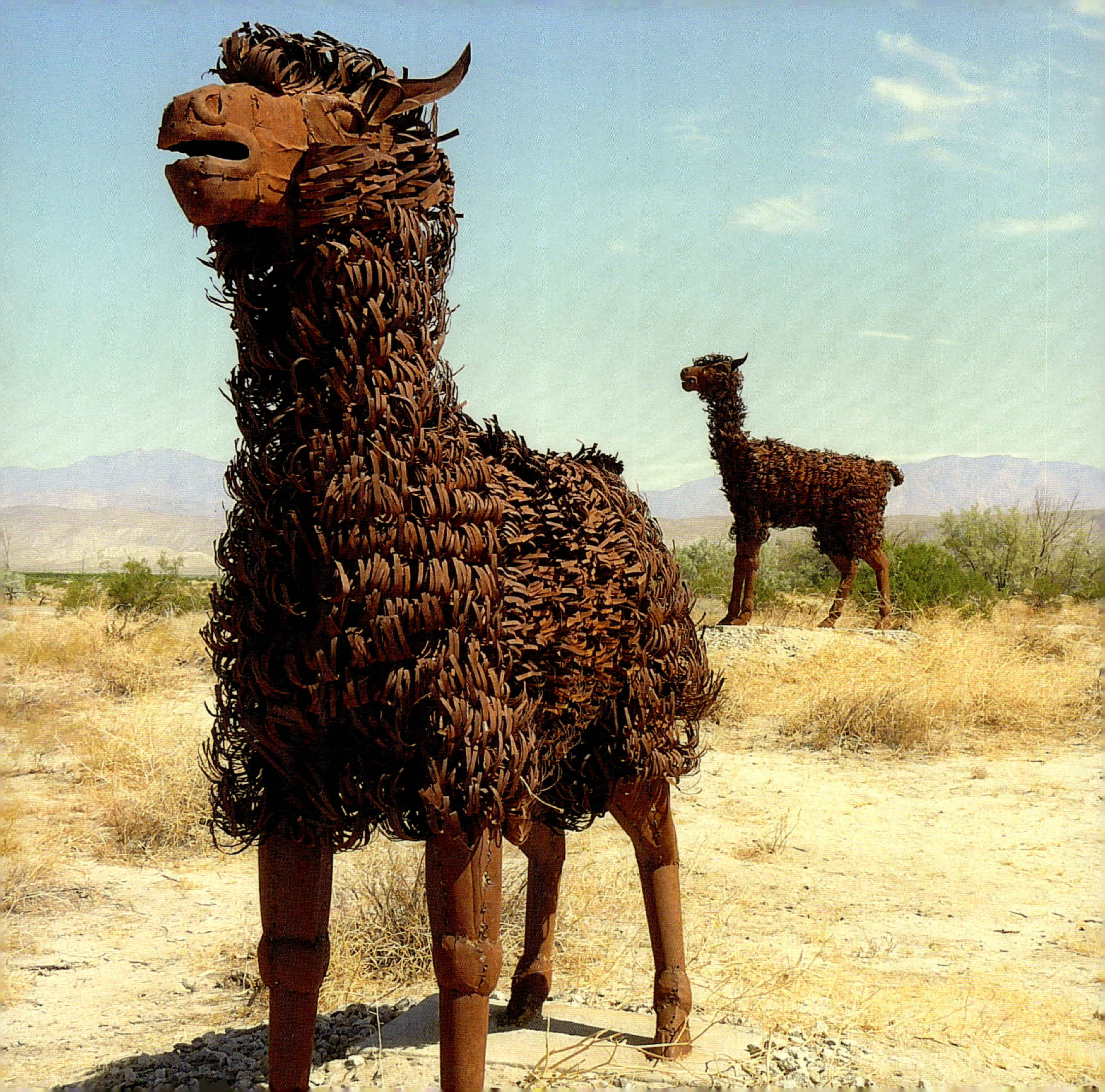

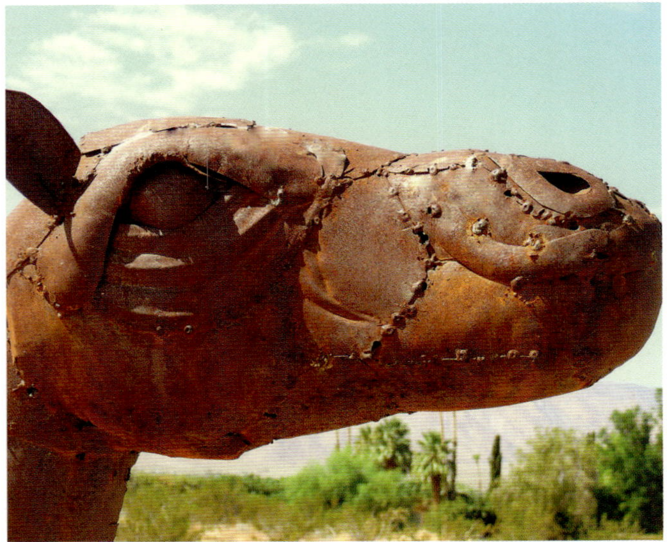

FT-7 Camelops. Despite its look and nomenclature, the *Camelops*, as rendered here, has a closer relationship to the llama than it does to the modern-day camel. *Camelops* and llamas are in the same subdivision of the family Camilidae. Modern camels are in another subdivision.

In the most daring scheme, Ricardo stepped out on a second-story ledge of the school building. When his classmates ran to the faculty room to tell the teachers that they were afraid Ricardo was going to jump, they all rushed to the breezeway and saw Ricardo standing on the ledge. The teachers coaxed him to carefully work his way back and get down. Meanwhile, his friends ran into the empty faculty room and stole a copy of the final exam. Needless to say, Ricardo and his plotting classmates passed with flying colors.

Ricardo admits that he was "a little crazy" when he was in school. His parents were always worried about him. Although his grades were good, he was basically a total rascal. He didn't want to cause them any more pain, so he always tried to make sure that his parents did not know about all the foolish and idiotic things he did.

Despite his many pranks, Ricardo managed to graduate college in June 1983 with *mención honorífica,* honorable mention.

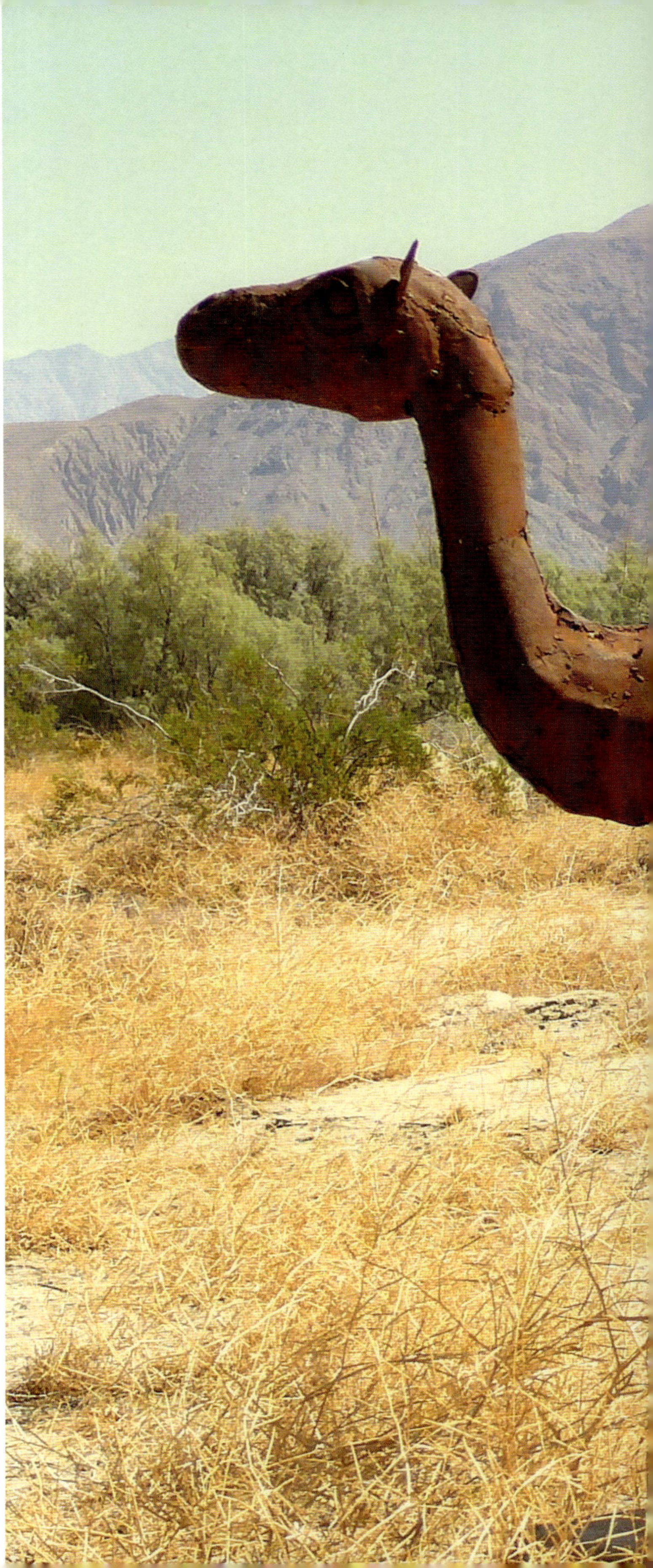

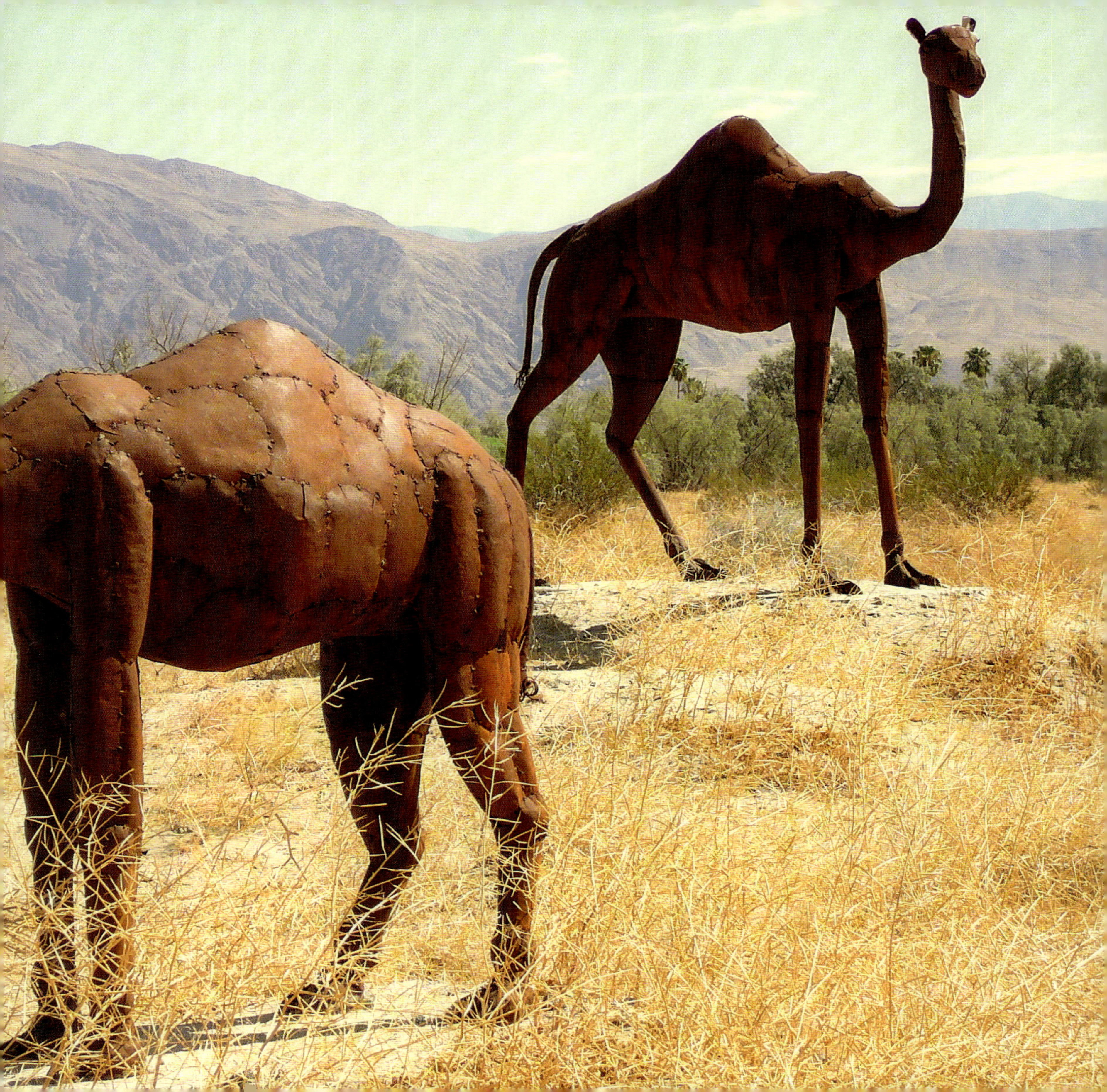

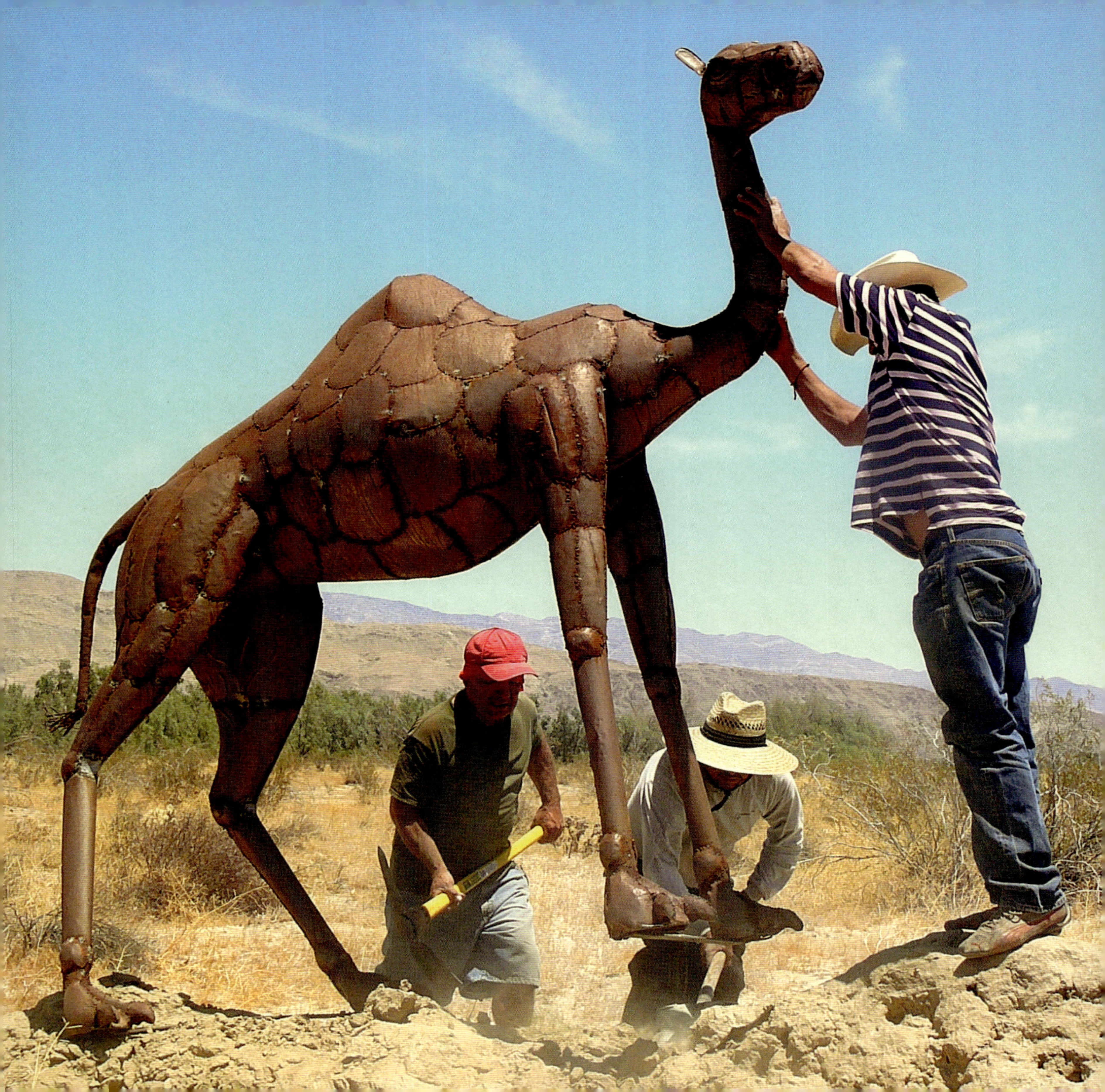

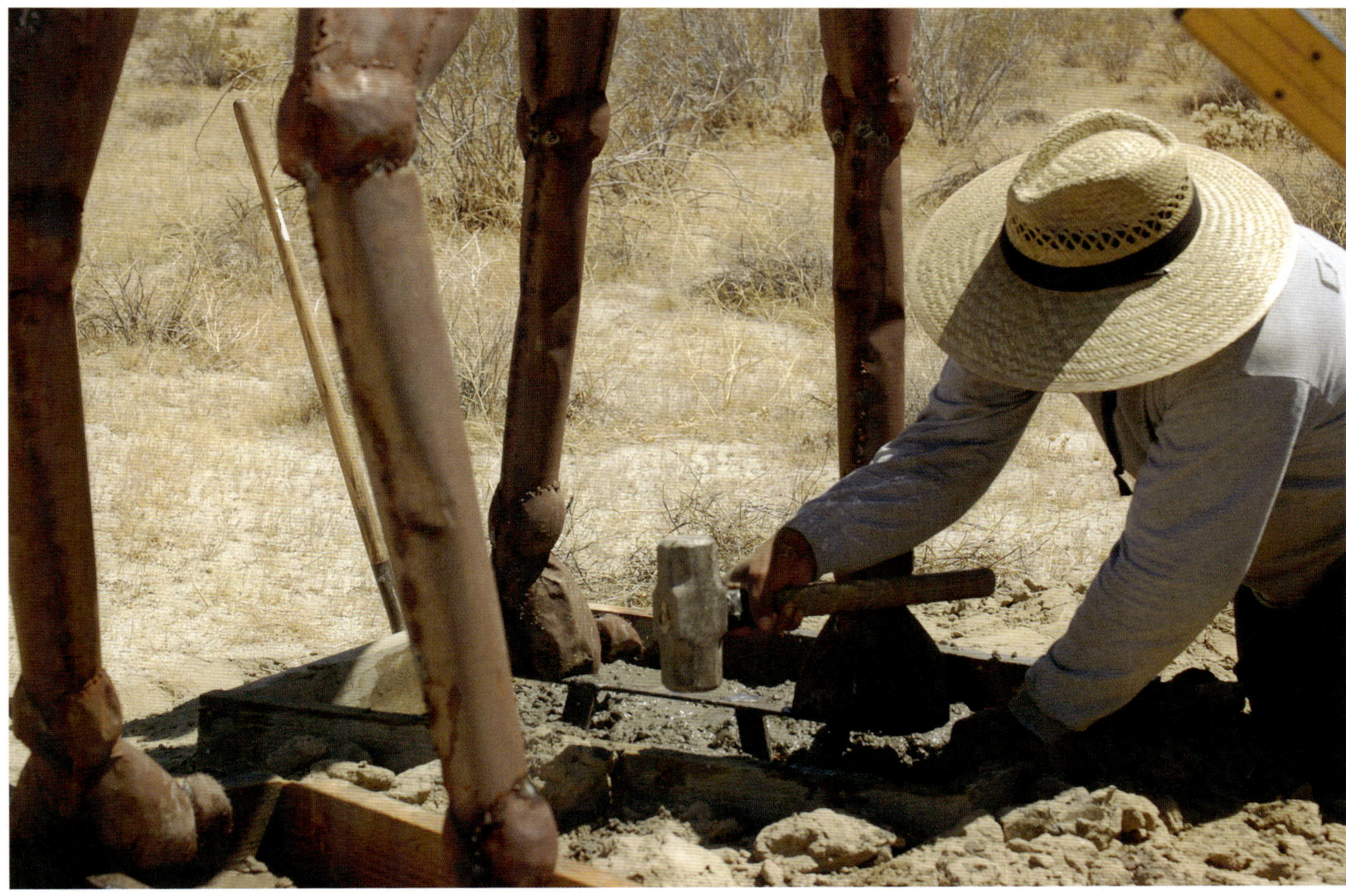

FT-7 Camelops. Ricardo and his crew install a *Camelops* in Borrego Valley. The feet are welded to a metal bar, which is in turn welded to rebar that is set in cement.

In Mexico, a teacher's first job is a yearlong placement in a remote area where a teacher normally would not want to work. In this way the government is able to provide teachers for inaccessible areas. The compensating factor is that there is no place to spend the salary and a teacher may end the year with considerable savings.

Ricardo's assignment was to go to Las Norias in El Municipio del Mezquital to work at Escuela Primaria Foránea Bidocente, otherwise known by the Indians as "Cinteoel."

Getting to Las Norias was an arduous and complicated journey. Ricardo had to travel west to Mazatlán in Sinaloa, south to the state of Nayarit to Acaponeta, then north to Huajicori, where a guide met him. Together they crossed the Huajicori River by canoe and then traveled east until they reentered Durango. They followed a mountainous trail for two days and finally arrived at Las Norias, where Ricardo would teach fourth and fifth grades for the 1983–1984 school year.

The village consisted of a few local mestizos who owned and farmed the surrounding lands and a small population of indigenous Indians representing four separate groups: Huicholes, Tepehuán, and Cora, who all speak Uto-Aztecan languages, and Mexicaneros, who speak a Nahuatl

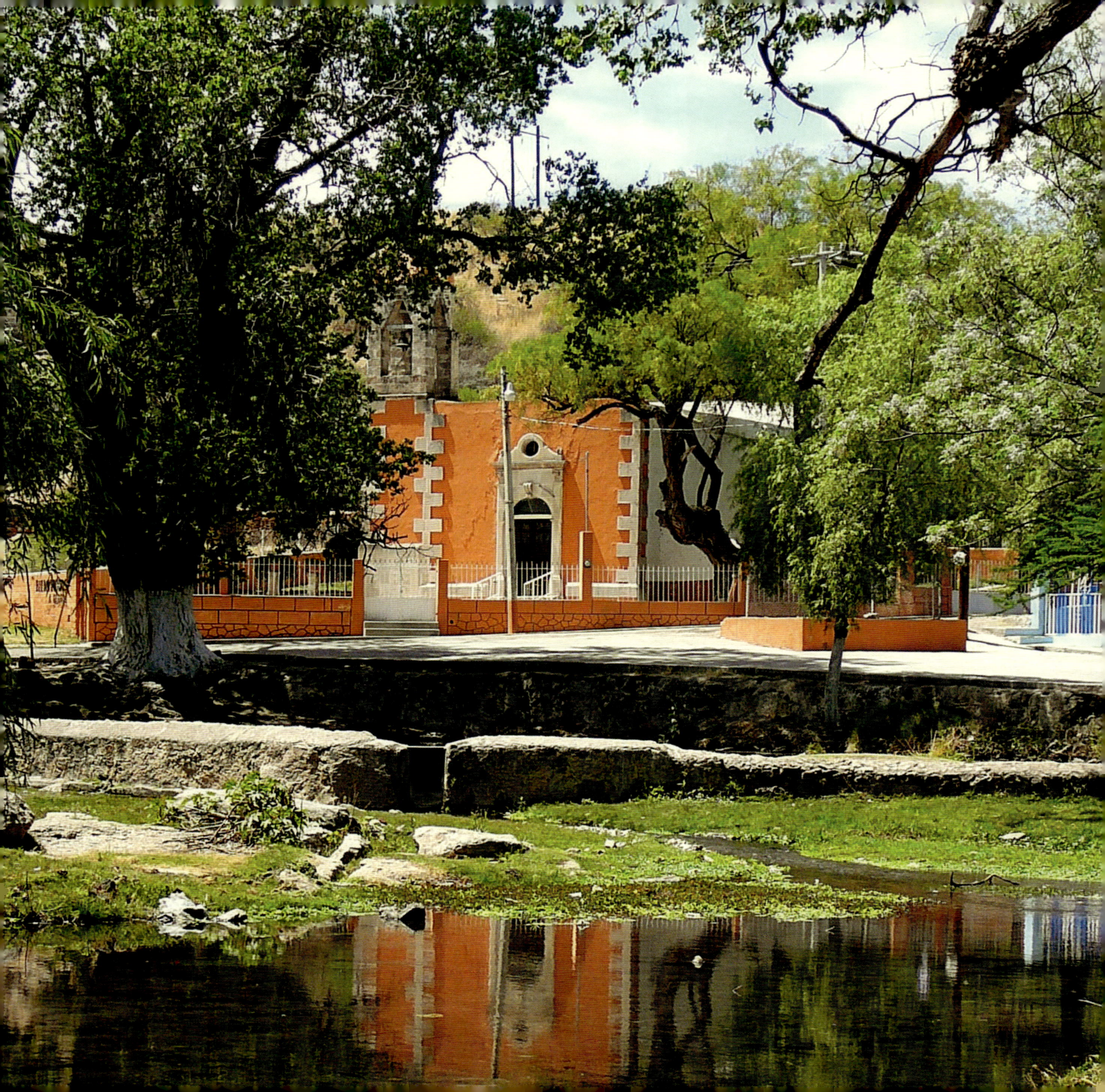

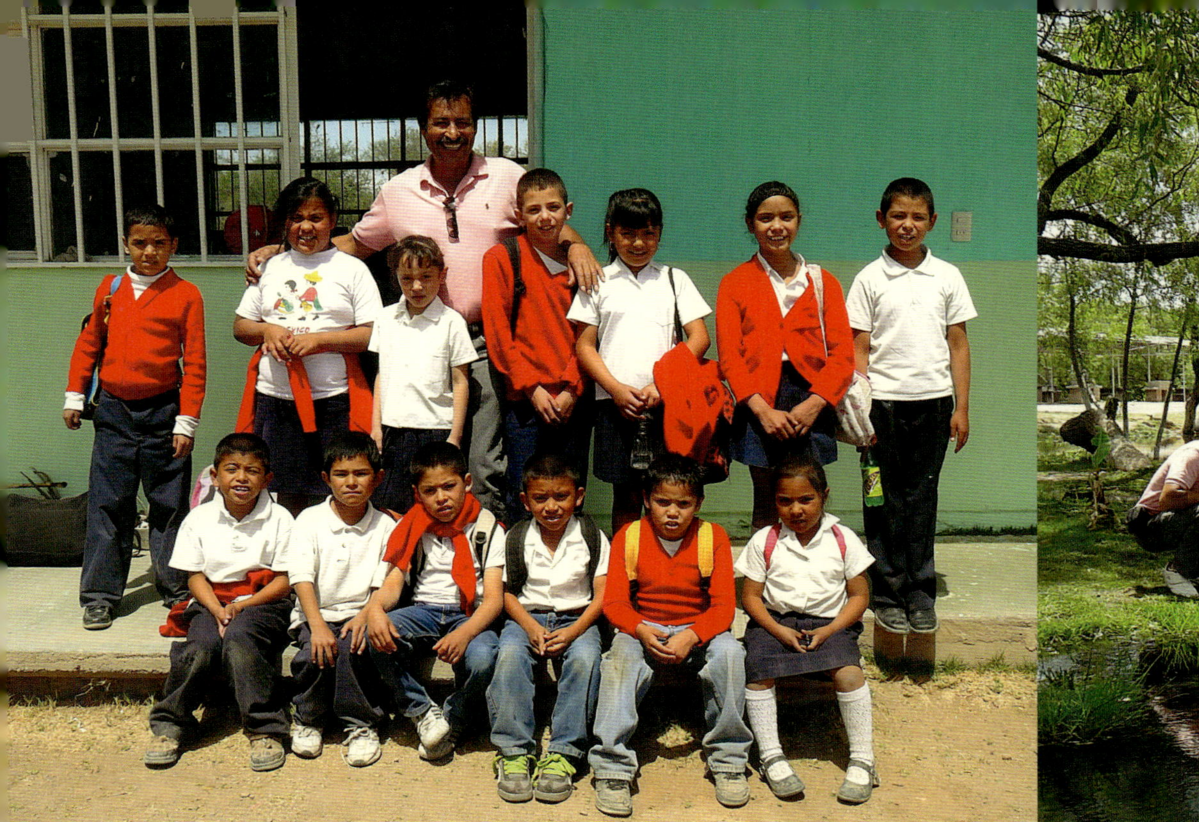

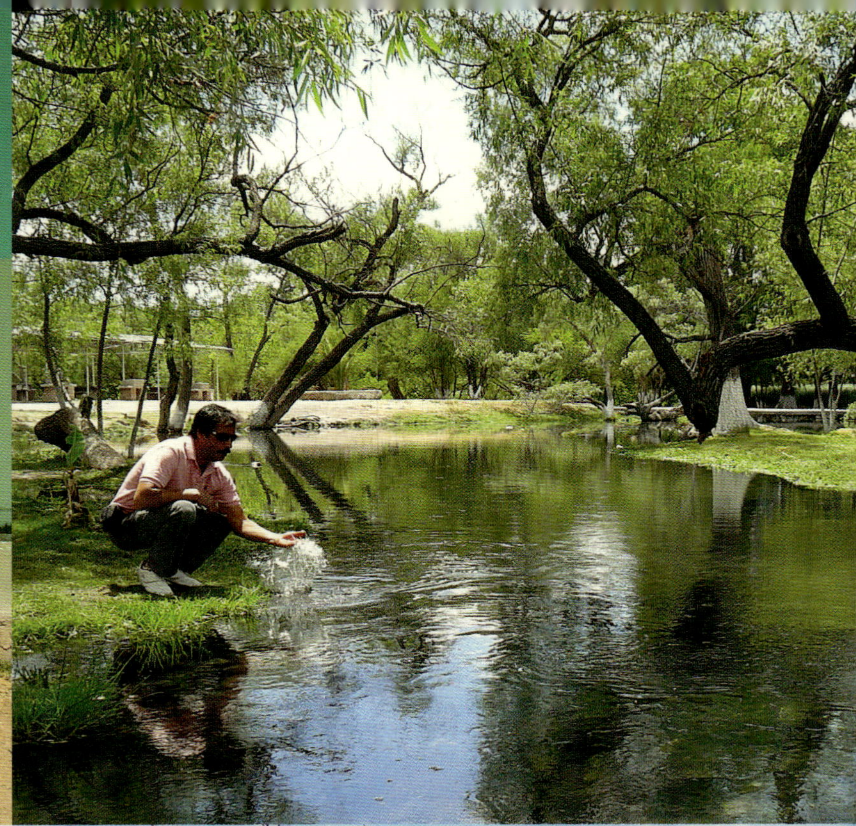

RETURN TO LOS BERROS AND SAN ISIDRO

Ricardo lived in the small community of Los Berros, known for its crystal-clear artesian lakes and streams, when he taught school at nearby San Isidro. *Clockwise from the left:* the community church is reflected in one of the lakes; Ricardo stands with students from the school where he once taught; the lakes at Los Berros teemed with fish; the rooming house where he lived was next door to the church.

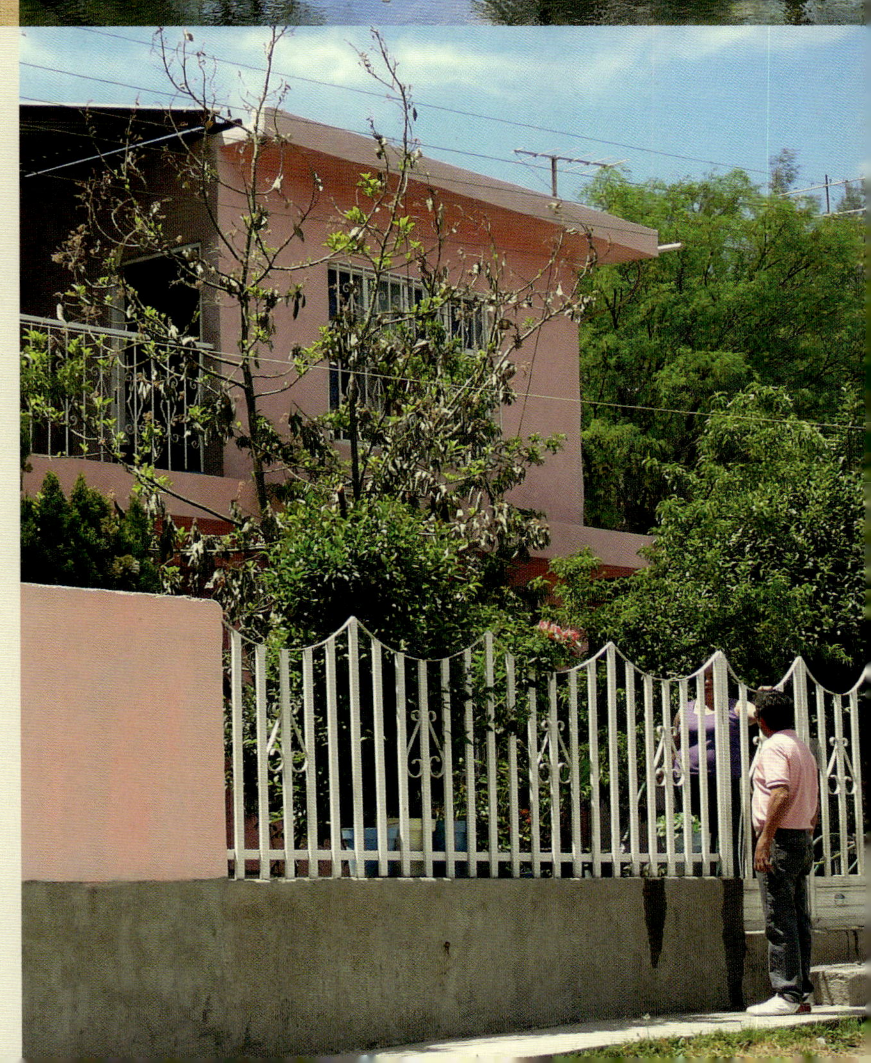

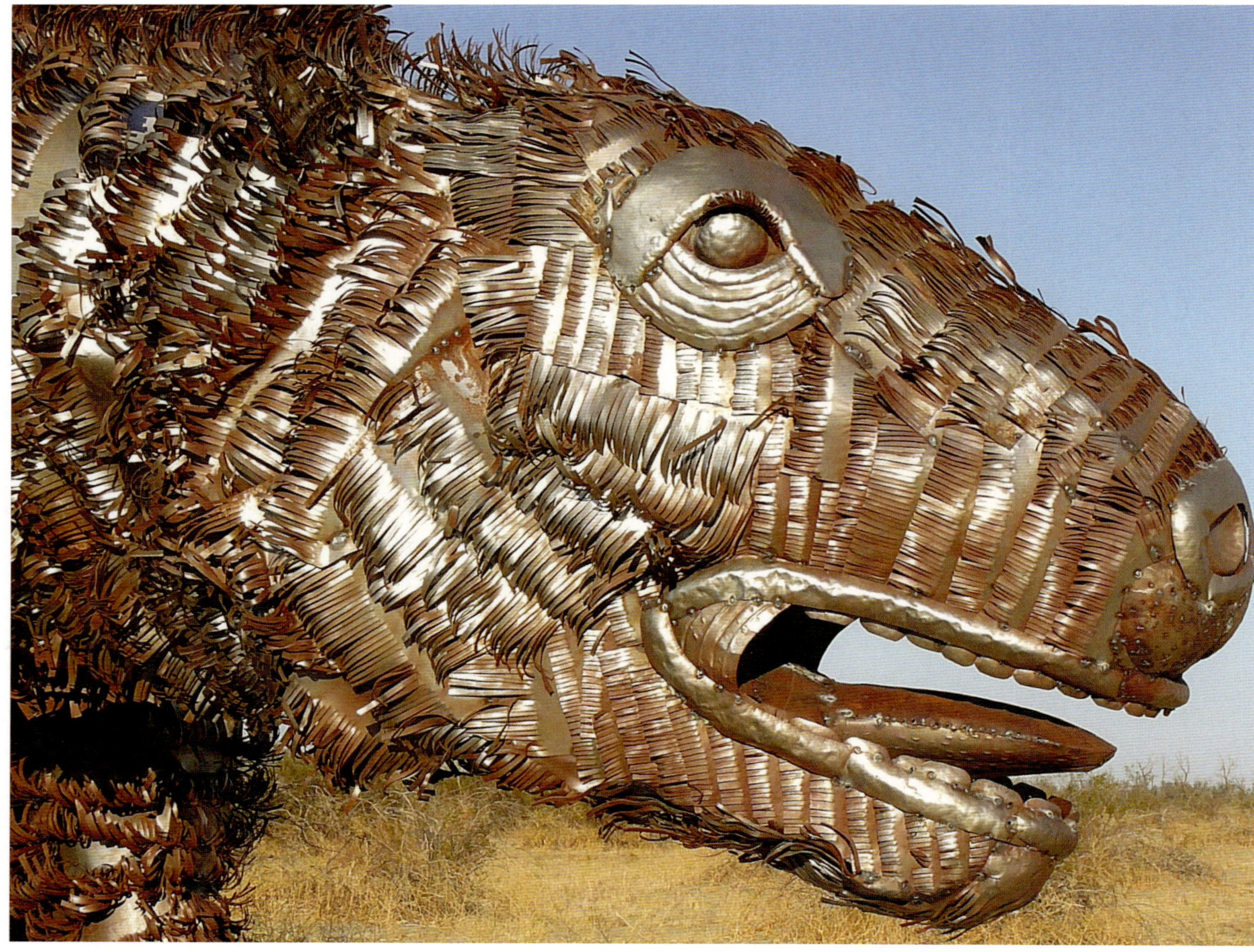

FT-8 Harlan's Ground Sloth and Baby. Ground sloths evolved in South America. The giant Harlan's ground sloth (*Paramylodon harlani*) first appeared in Anza-Borrego 2.3 million years ago. In the photograph to the right, a baby sloth rides on his mother's back as do the modern sloths of Costa Rica.

language. There were sixteen students in the school, and the two teachers taught all subjects. The students lived in such a remote area they had never seen a car or a bicycle. They saw planes in the sky and had an idea of what they were. The village provided a one-room house for the teachers, who worked there from September to July.

Ricardo was in for a rude awakening to the reality of living in an isolated area. When he arrived at the village after a two-day off-and-on rainy walk, he was exhausted, hungry, and ready for a meal.

The village provided a common area where meals were served for the teachers. He sat at the table and watched a woman rolling out the *masa* to make tortillas. Swarms of flies were everywhere. The woman had to stop every so often and

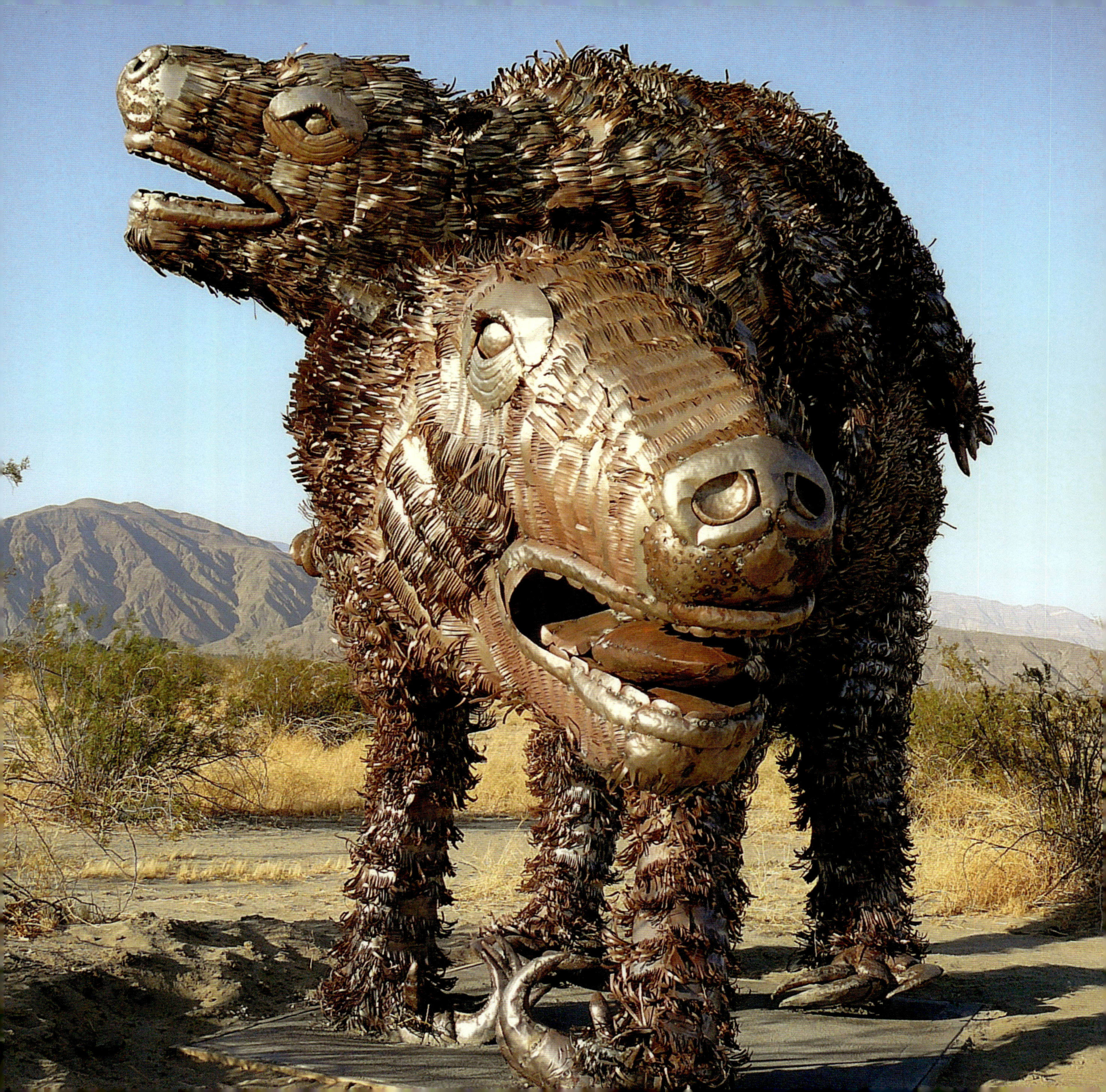

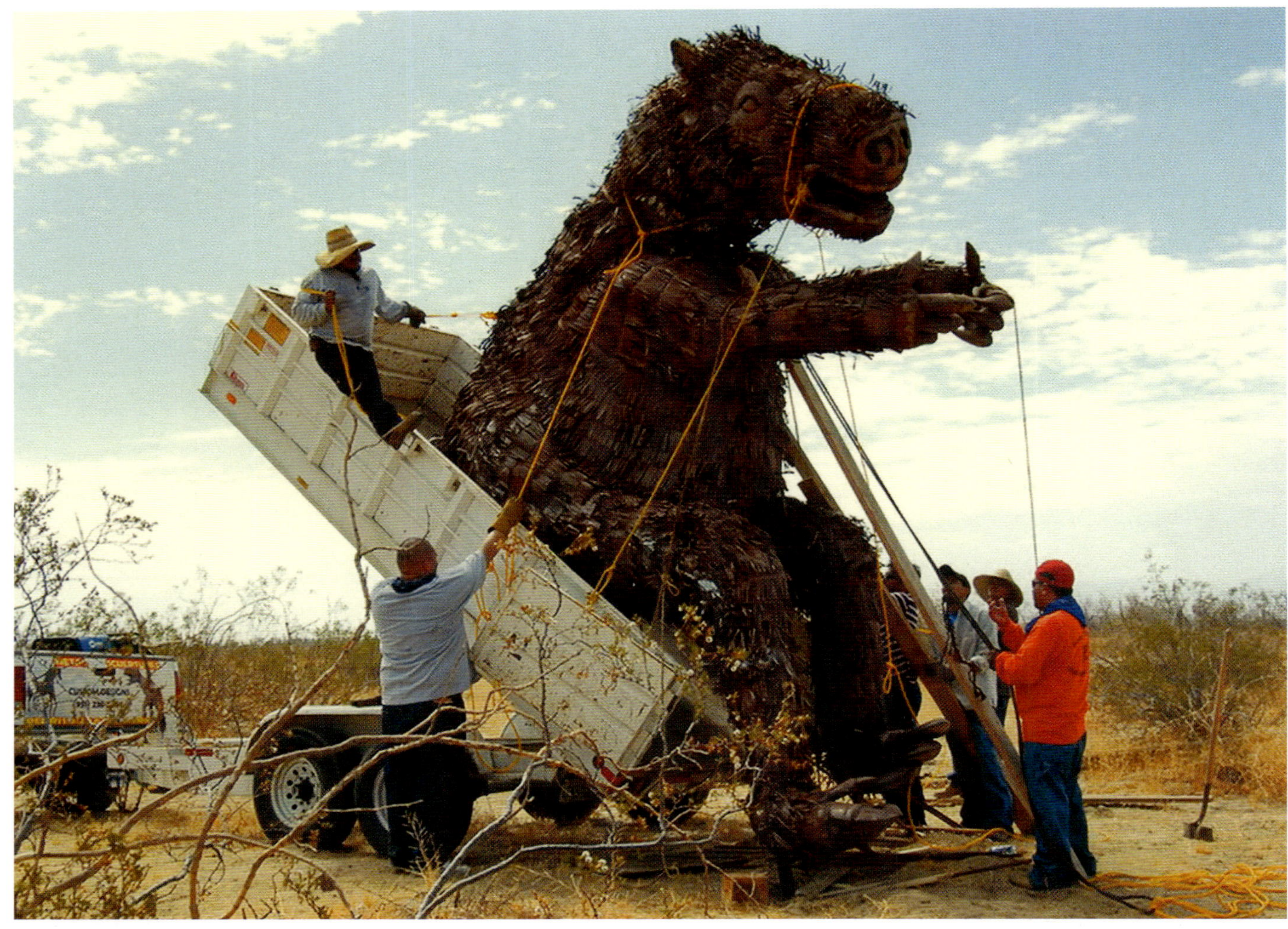

FT-8 Harlan's Ground Sloth. Installing the 1,800-pound, seventeen-foot-tall Harlan's ground sloth was very challenging to the crew without the use of a forklift or crane. It was a good thing it was not the real animal, which weighed 2,400 pounds!

clap her hands to kill flies. Then she would quickly wipe her hands on her apron and proceed to slap out the flour for tortillas. Parts of the dead flies stuck to her hands and were now in the tortilla dough. Ricardo's hunger turned to disgust.

When the nice *señora* asked Ricardo if he was hungry, he said he was too tired to eat and needed to go to bed. Also, he had a rash from walking in the rain and there was nothing to put on it. He was feeling miserable.

The next morning he was absolutely starving. He decided it would be better to die of eating fly parts than to starve to death, so he accepted a hot tortilla with his breakfast and just plucked off fly wings and legs before he ate it. "There were flies everywhere," Ricardo recalled with revulsion. "It was so nasty. But it was the way they lived, and I had to adapt."

As it turned out, he survived just fine. He learned to get along in this primitive way of life. Las Norias had cows, so there was milk and cheese available, and he could hunt for other food.

"In those days teachers were respected, so their baggage was not checked by law enforcement," Ricardo explained. He was able to bring guns and quite a lot of ammunition with him to the village. He started hunting so that he would have enough food. There were deer, wild pigs, rabbits, and doves. Whenever he killed a deer he shared it with the other families. He also sold some of his guns and ammunition to make extra money.

Ricardo had a girlfriend, a preschool teacher in another village a couple of hours away in Nayarit. He had met her

FT-8 Harlan's Ground Sloth. The *Borrego Sun* reported that an SUV came to the rescue when ropes attached to the sculpture were pulled by the vehicle to get the sculpture upright and out of the trailer.

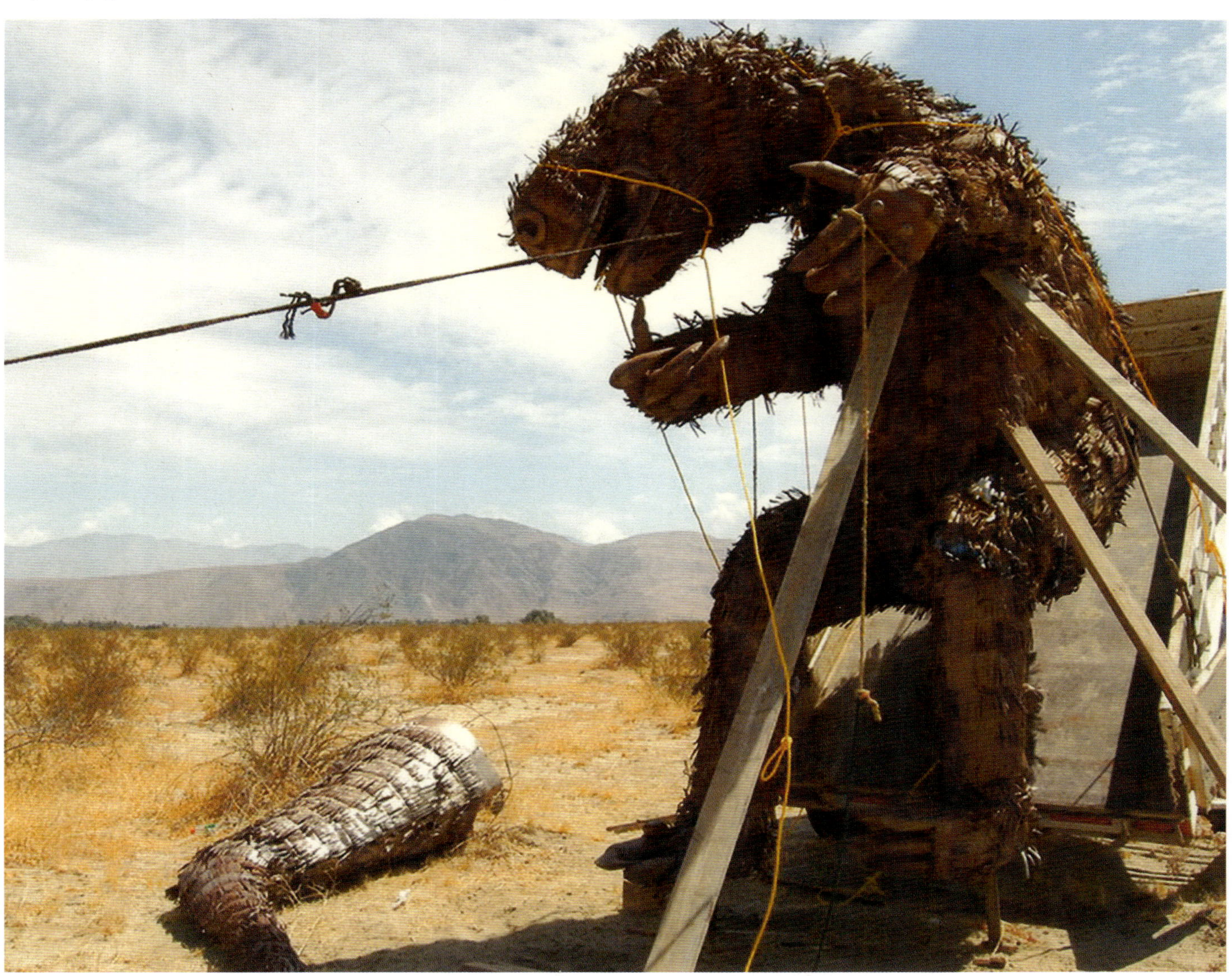

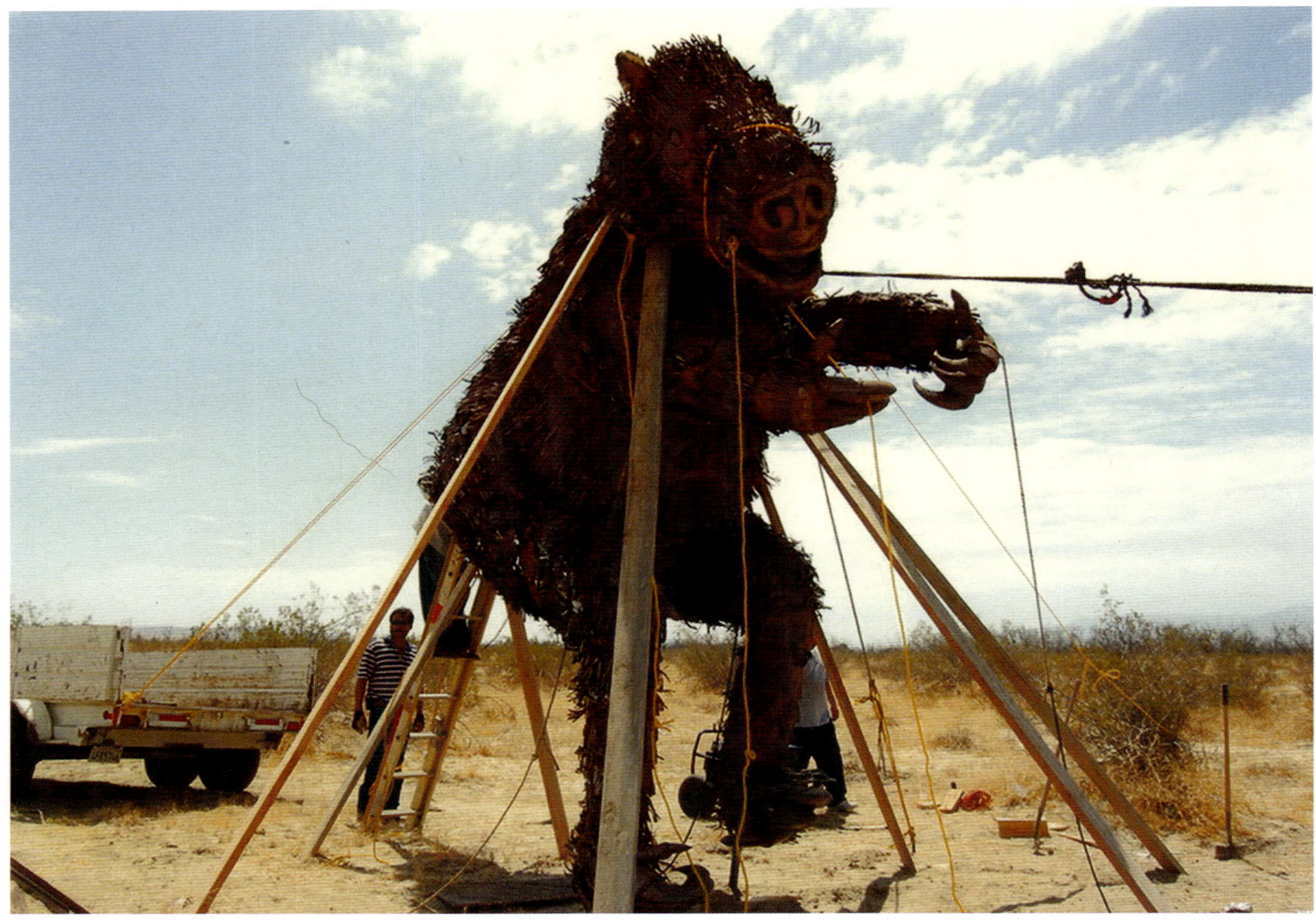

FT-8 Harlan's Ground Sloth. Supported taut ropes held steady by vehicles, the crew quickly braced the sculpture with two-by-fours. Later the crew welded the tail to the sculpture to provide stability.

when he had taken a trip to Nayarit with his fellow teacher from Las Norias. To visit her, he had to run for two hours, cross the state line, and then later run back. It was actually an hour faster to run there than it would have been to ride a horse or mule because of the steep hills. Visiting her kept him in great shape.

Teaching in Las Norias was an eye opener in many ways. The lack of any law enforcement in that isolated community meant that it was easy for the local families to grow cash crops of marijuana and heroin poppies. Because Ricardo hunted a lot, he knew where many of the cultivated fields were. Some of the plots were small, and some were very large. The crops needed to be watered and pipes had to be installed to run the water from one area to another. The going rate to help install the pipes was the equivalent of one month's teaching salary. To make extra money, Ricardo helped to install the pipes.

Ricardo took a vacation every couple of months and would go into the nearest town, where he would see locals

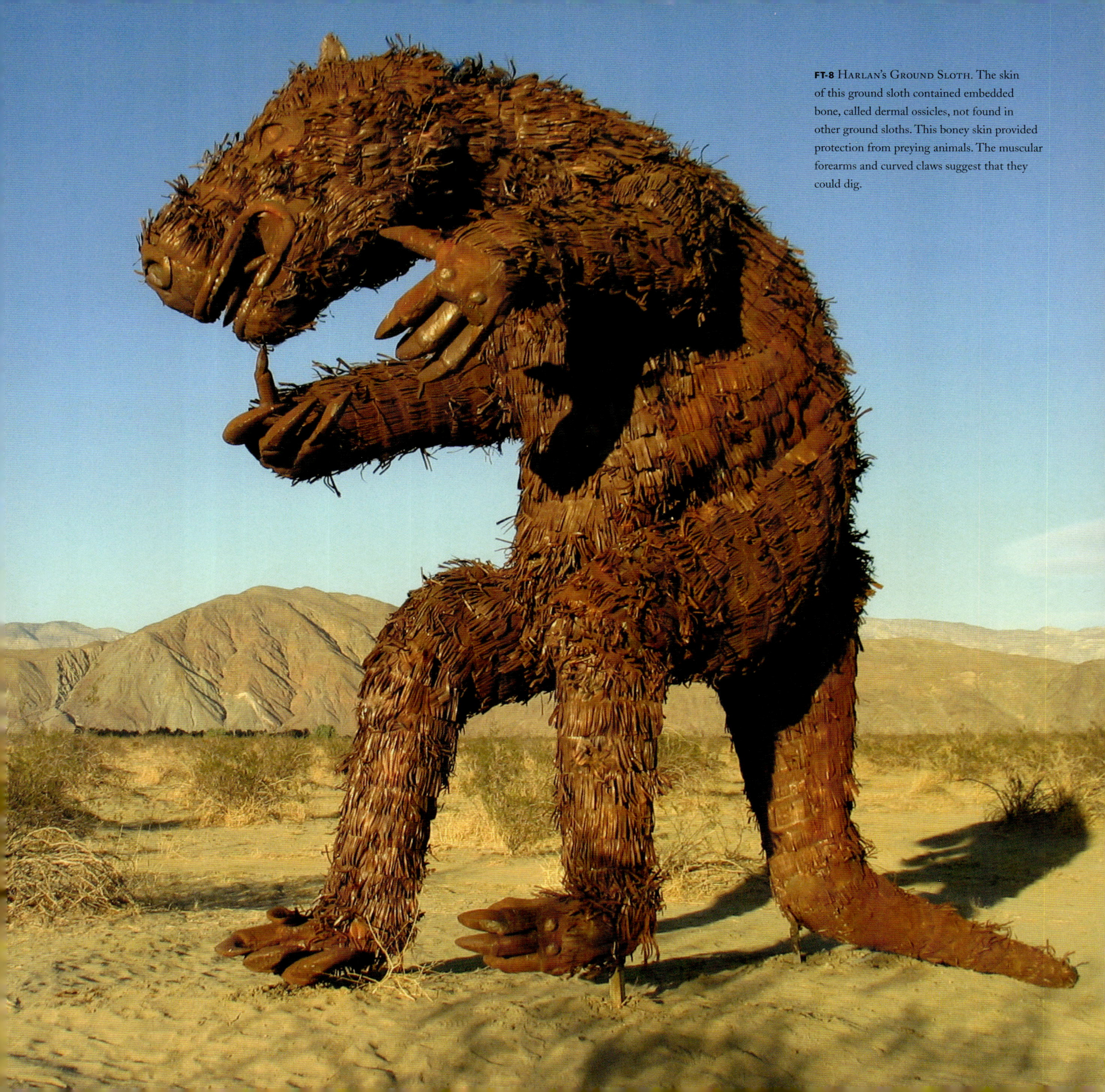

FT-8 Harlan's Ground Sloth. The skin of this ground sloth contained embedded bone, called dermal ossicles, not found in other ground sloths. This boney skin provided protection from preying animals. The muscular forearms and curved claws suggest that they could dig.

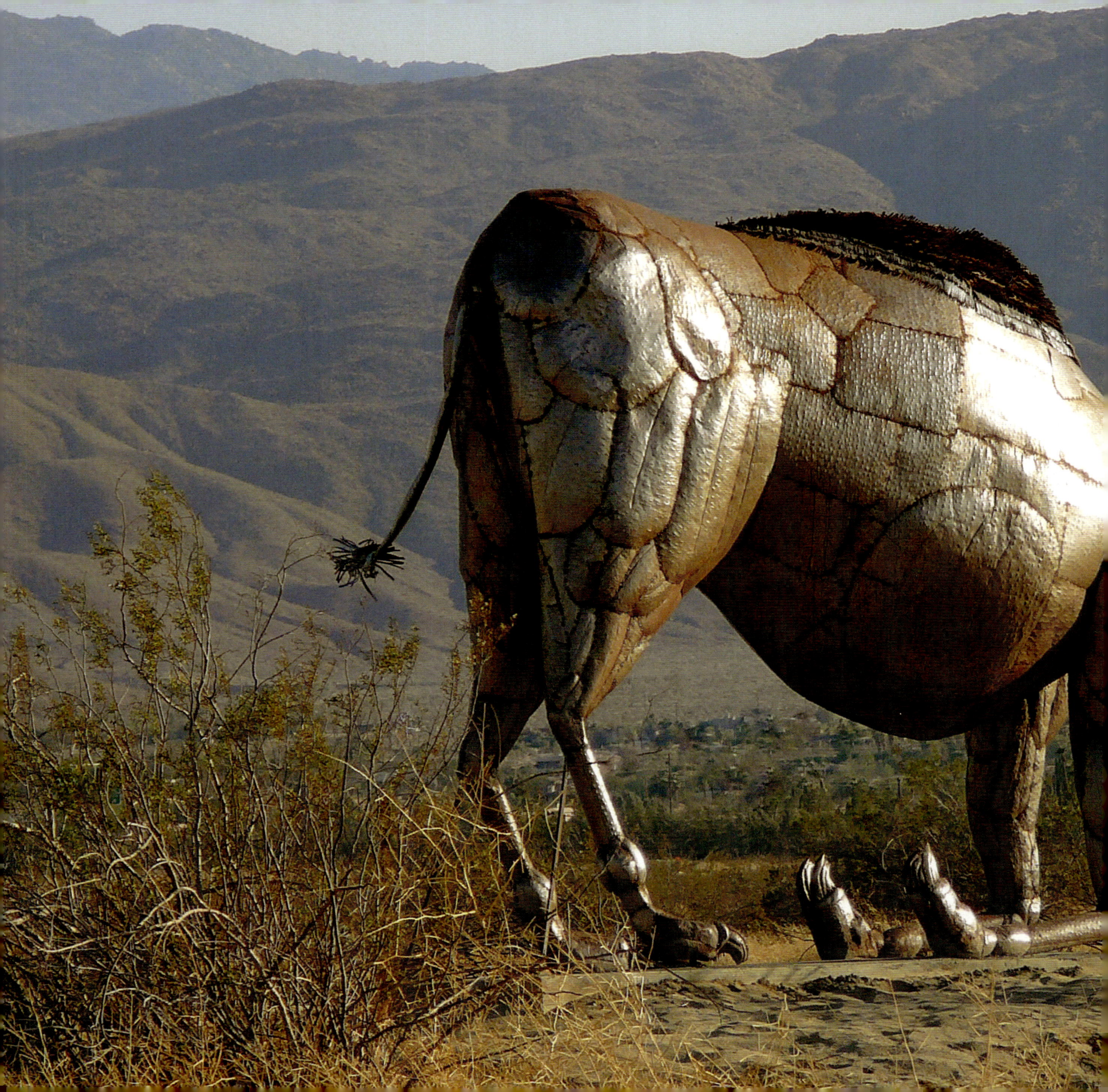

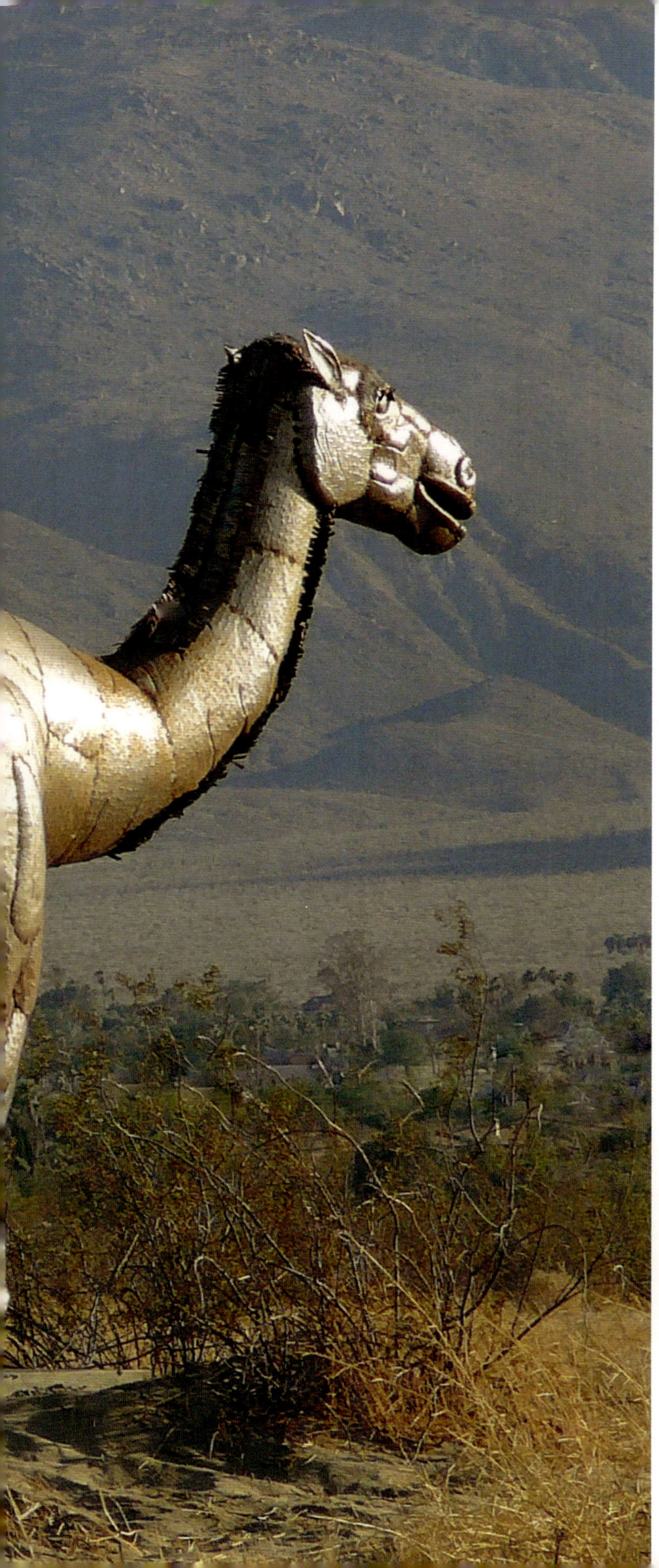

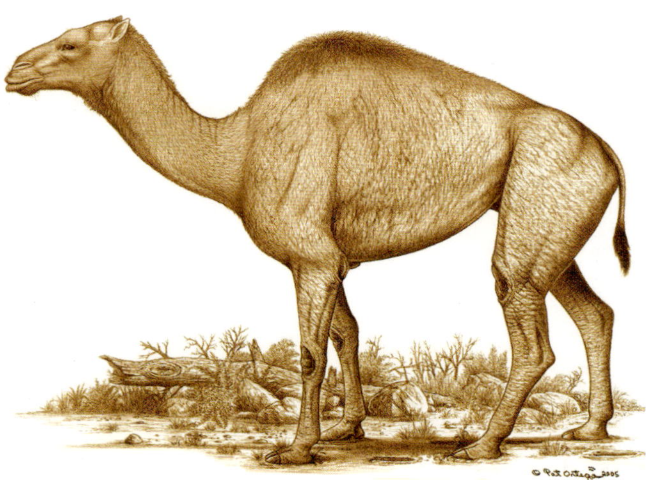

FT-8 Camelops. To lie down, a camel bends its front legs and drops to its knees. Then it folds its hind legs and sinks to the ground. Ricardo captures this action of the *Camelops* as depicted by scientific illustrator Pat Ortega.

from Las Norias with lots of money. They would have thousands of dollars, and sometimes they would go into a local bar and reserve it for the night for a party.

The locals liked Ricardo and wanted him to stay there after he finished the school year. They told him if he stayed, he could marry one of their daughters and they would build him a house. To entice him further, they would give him one hundred head of cattle. Ricardo thanked them for the offer but said he would be leaving when the school year was over.

Before he left, some of the parents of the children he taught brought bundled packages of marijuana into his classroom and told Ricardo that it was a gift. He was told to leave it there in the classroom and someone would pick it up and leave some money. The money was a good-bye gift. When he left Las Norias, he had the equivalent of two years of teacher's pay.

Ricardo's older sister Ernestina, who was also a teacher, had good connections in the administrative offices in Durango. She was able to arrange for Ricardo to get a teaching position at Escuela Primaria Rural Federal Francisco

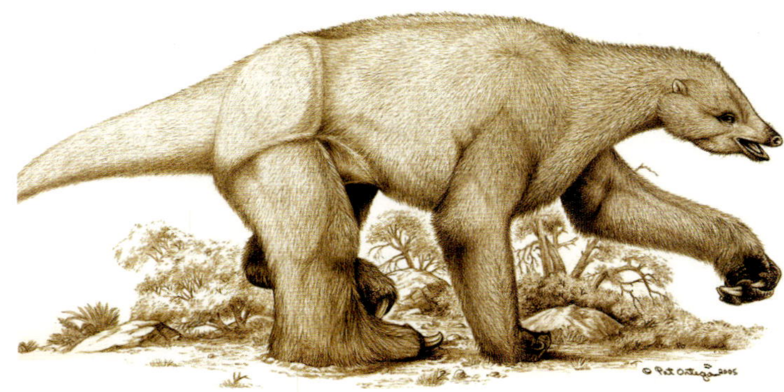

FT-9 Shasta Ground Sloth. *Nothrotheriops shastensis* was the smallest of the ground sloths and the one best adapted to a drier climate. Ricardo carefully noted details of the Shasta ground sloth sketch published in *Fossil Treasures of the Anza-Borrego Desert* and featured them in his sculpture.

Villa in the community of San Isidro, located between Villa Unión and Durango, just north of La Constancia. Ricardo was content to be closer to home, family, and friends, whom he could visit on weekends.

He found a room to rent in a nearby community called Los Berros. Across the street from the rooming house was a series of crystal-clear artesian lakes and streams teeming with fish, where he spent a lot of time. He began a routine of dropping five lines at night into the lake, and in the morning after a swim, he would pull up two or three fish that he could have for breakfast or dinner. He also used to do his laundry along the riverbank, or actually he would start to do his laundry, because one of the young ladies in the community would invariably show up and offer to wash it for him. At night he would watch television on his little combination TV–radio–tape recorder or play basketball at a nearby court.

Ricardo liked to toss the ball into the basket while jumping as high as he could. His goal was to slam his hand on the rim of the basket. Once, however, he jumped and his school ring hooked on a screw that was sticking out.

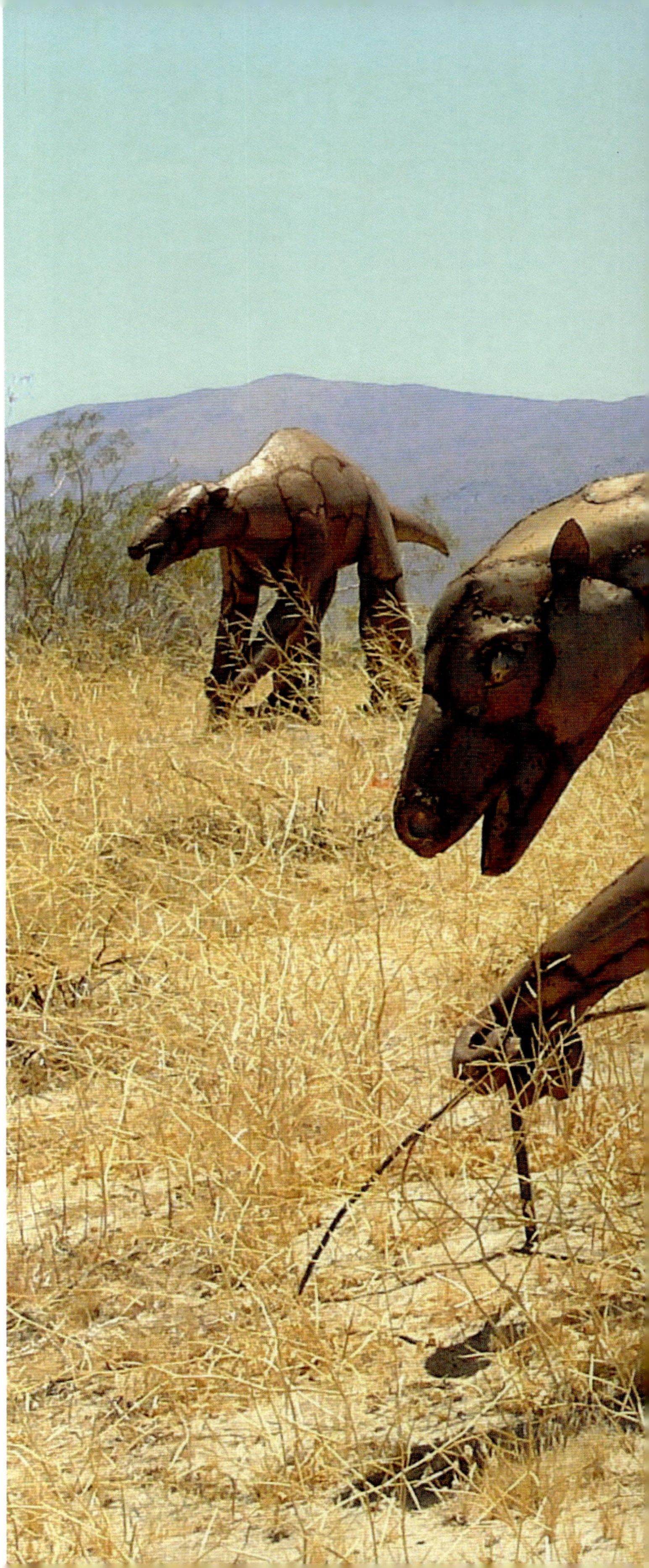

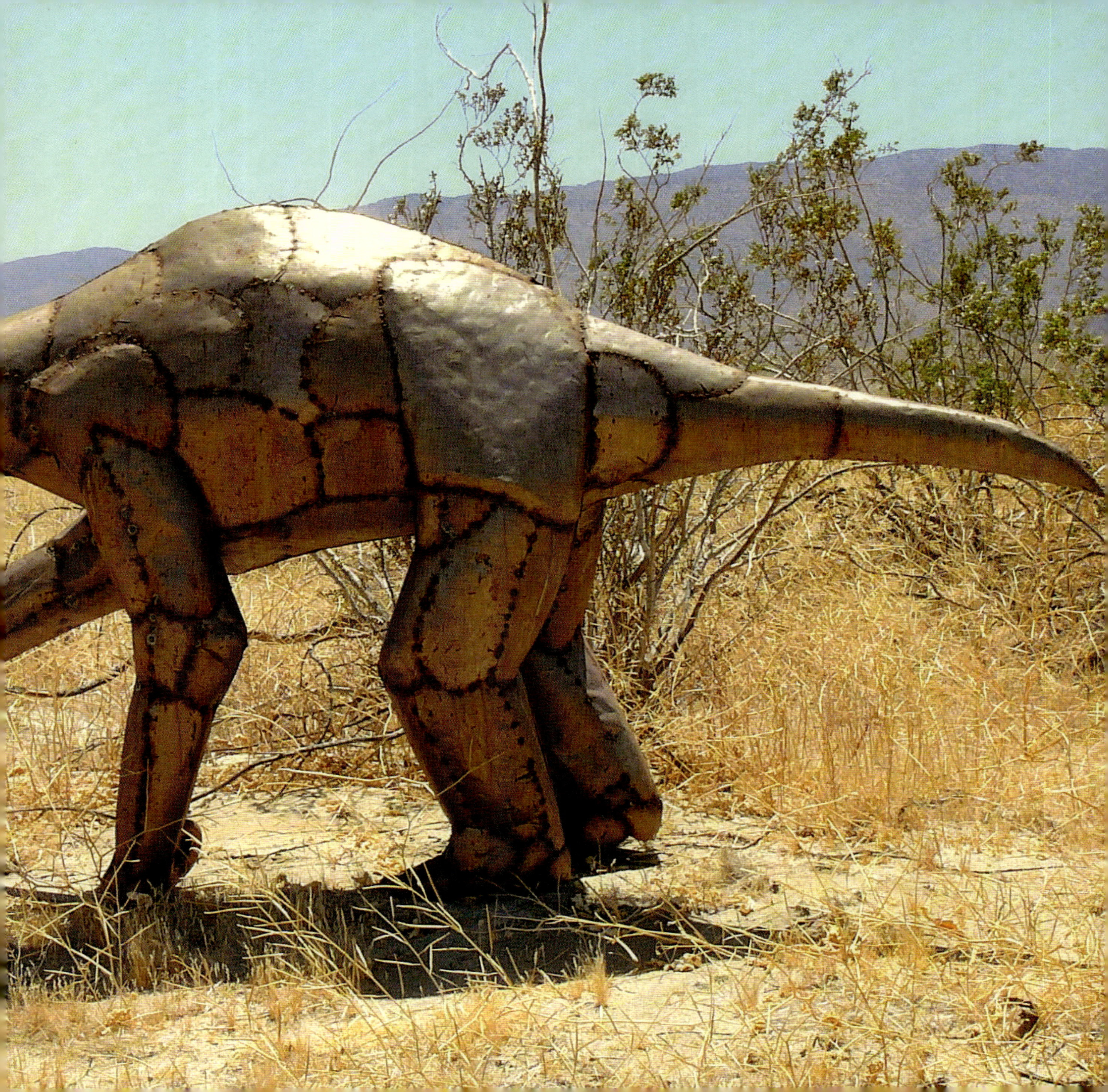

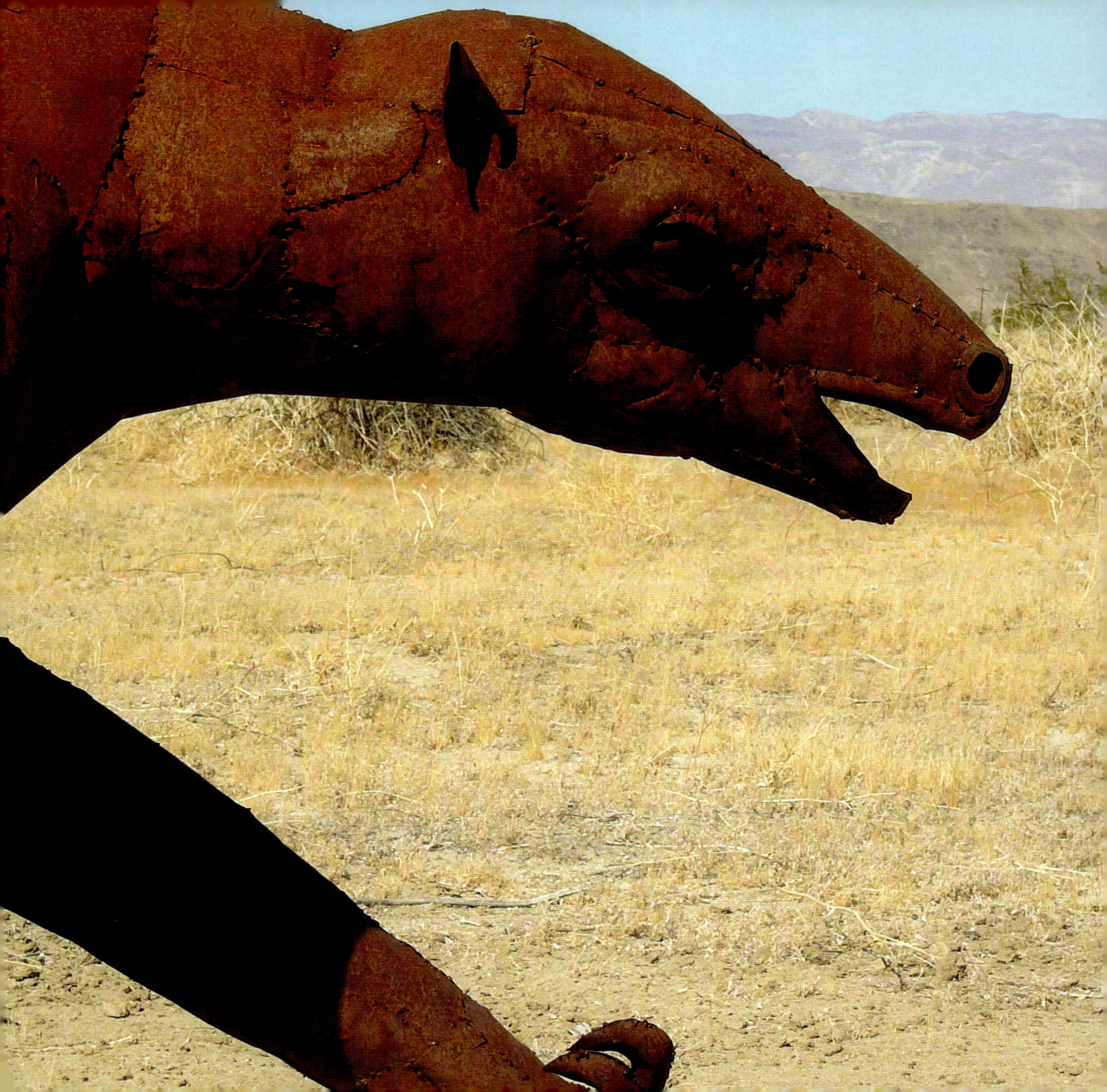

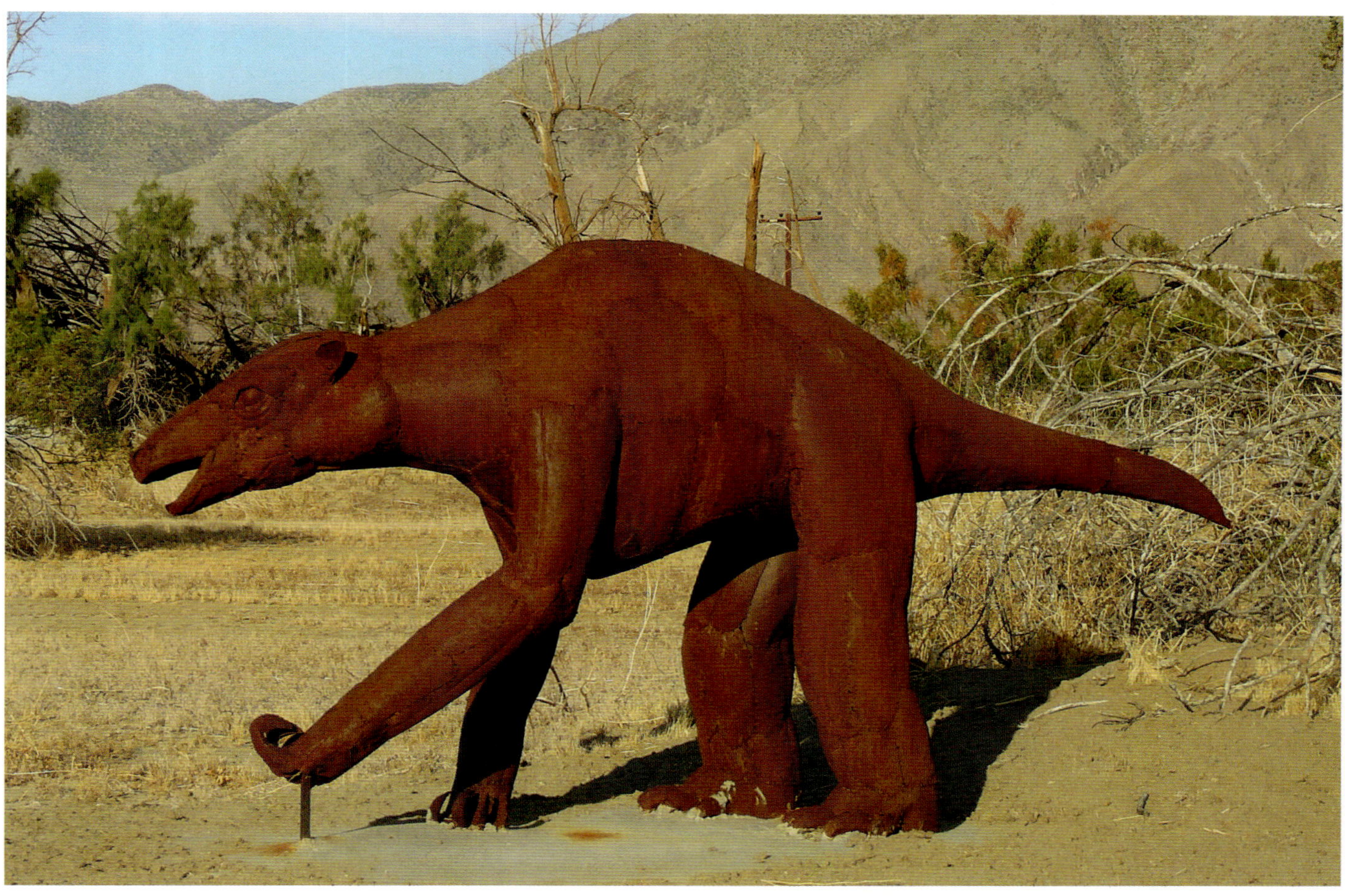

FT-9 Shasta Ground Sloth. Ground sloths are in the order Xenarthra. The only representative of this order still living today in North America is the armadillo. This sloth was probably a browser who included both desert and riparian vegetation in its diet.

Suddenly he was hanging by his ring finger. He was able to get down, but his finger was shredded to the bone.

Los Berros had a crude dispensary with limited medical equipment and a one-man staff. The ring had to be removed before the finger could be stitched back together, and there was only a small surgical clipper to do the job.

The two of them took turns clipping away at the ring for what seemed like several painful hours. By the time they were able to remove the ring, Ricardo was so angry he tossed it as hard as he could out the door. To this day he has a scar and a slight disfiguration on that ring finger. The incident, however, did not dissuade him from continuing to shoot baskets for exercise.

The small community where he taught was less than a mile away from Los Berros. He would take a quick walk across fields and hop over a few fences to get to San Isidro, where the two-room schoolhouse was located. He taught two grade levels in the same classroom and had twenty students.

Ricardo loves children and he really enjoyed teaching; he felt it came naturally to him. He was strict and would

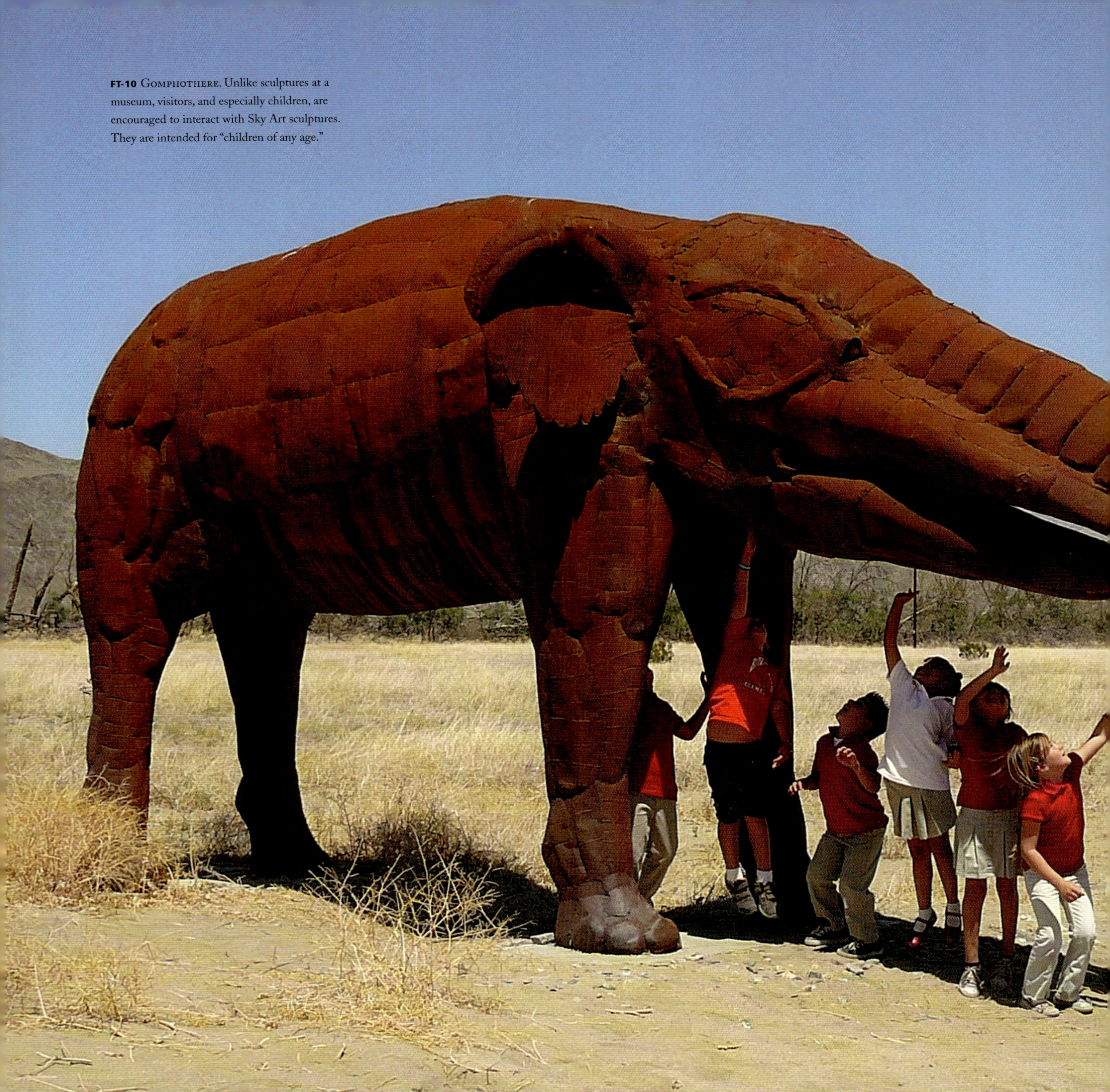

FT-10 Gomphothere. Unlike sculptures at a museum, visitors, and especially children, are encouraged to interact with Sky Art sculptures. They are intended for "children of any age."

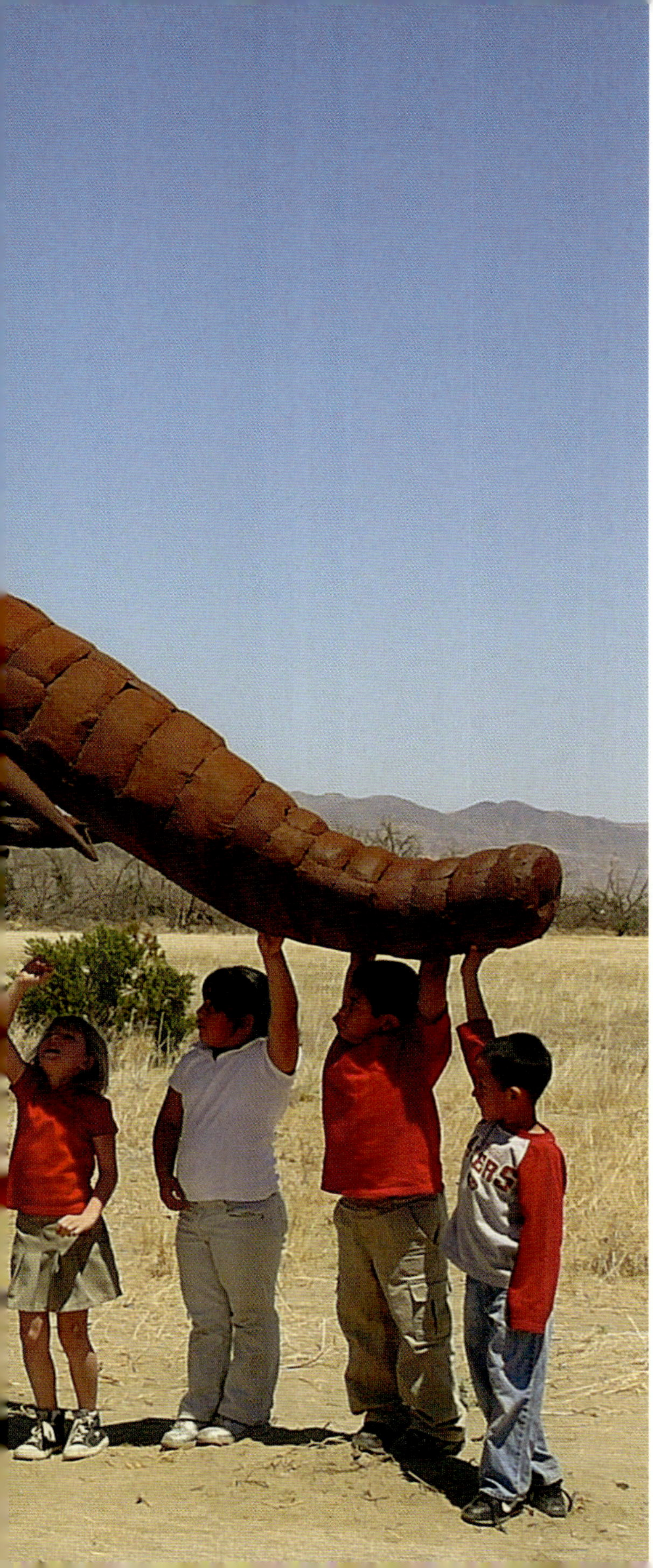

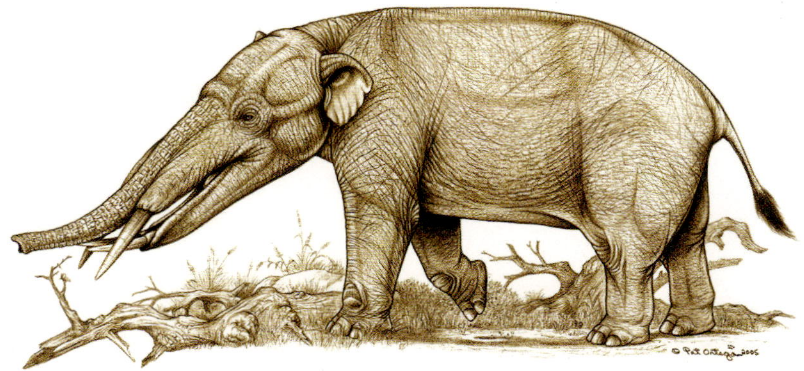

FT-10 Gomphothere. Sky Art began with this sketch of a *Gomphotherium* and an idea to bring them back to Anza-Borrego as three-dimensional representations of fossils buried for millions of years. What has vanished has been recreated.

punish any child who did not pay total attention to him with a quick pinch or tug on his ear or hair. Just as in his college days, he never felt the need to take work home, but he assigned homework for the children and checked it the next day in the classroom. He followed the chapter outlines in the book and made sure that all of the children in the class understood the lessons before he moved on to the next chapter.

If two or three children did not completely understand the lesson, he would review all the material until they got it right before moving on so that the class would stay together. Ricardo did not like to repeat his lessons from one day to the next, which is why he demanded complete attention from the students.

Ricardo's sense of competition extended to teaching also. He made sure that his students were always receiving the highest grades when there were district tests. By playing with the students at recess he developed strong, loyal relationships that made teaching much easier.

If a student came to school angry or sad, he went out of his way to find out why. He stayed in close contact with the parents to see how he could help. In such a small community where there was little to distract the students, there were seldom any problems and parents were very supportive. Occasionally, Ricardo had a troublemaker in his class, but

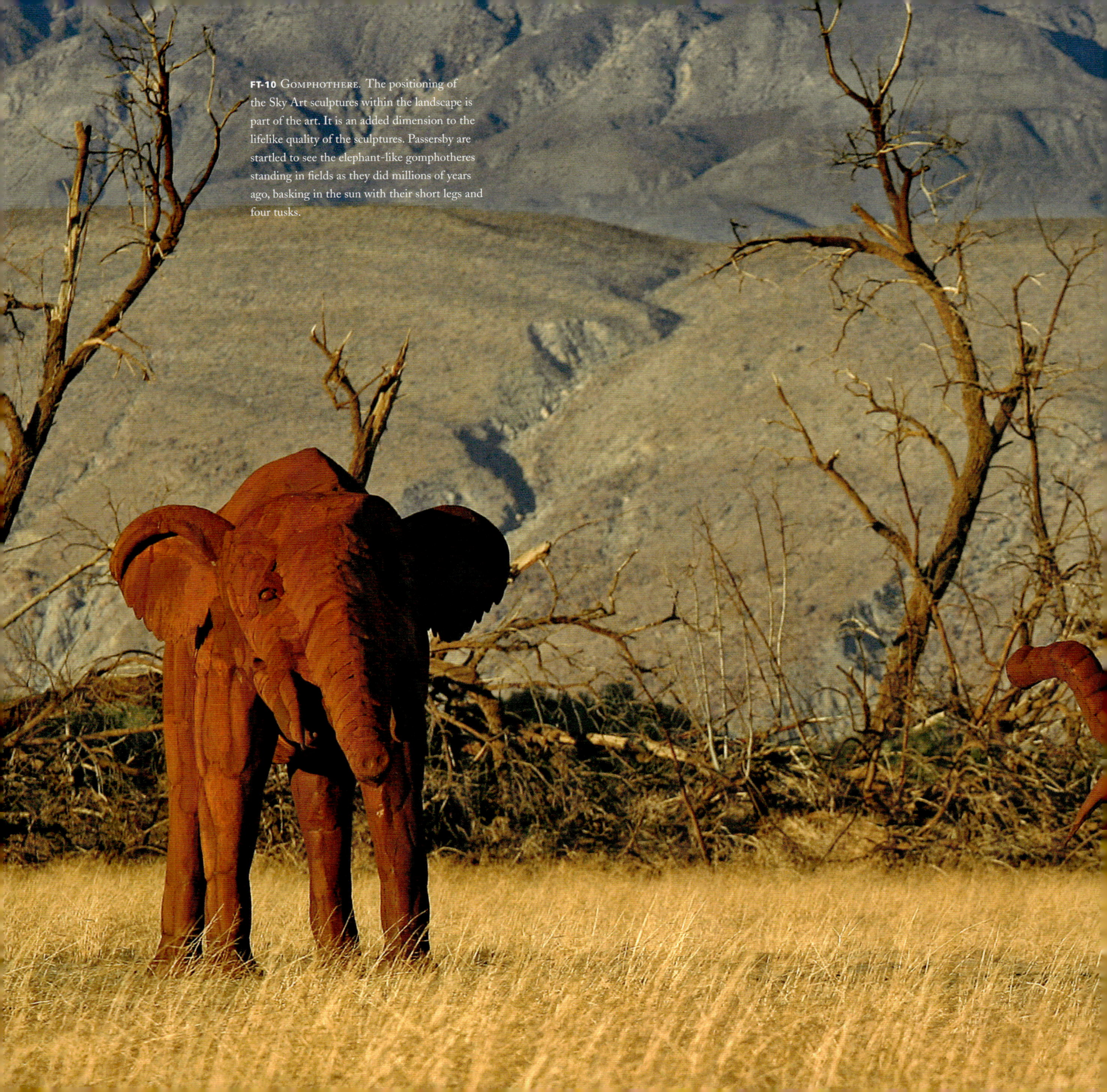

FT-10 Gomphothere. The positioning of the Sky Art sculptures within the landscape is part of the art. It is an added dimension to the lifelike quality of the sculptures. Passersby are startled to see the elephant-like gomphotheres standing in fields as they did millions of years ago, basking in the sun with their short legs and four tusks.

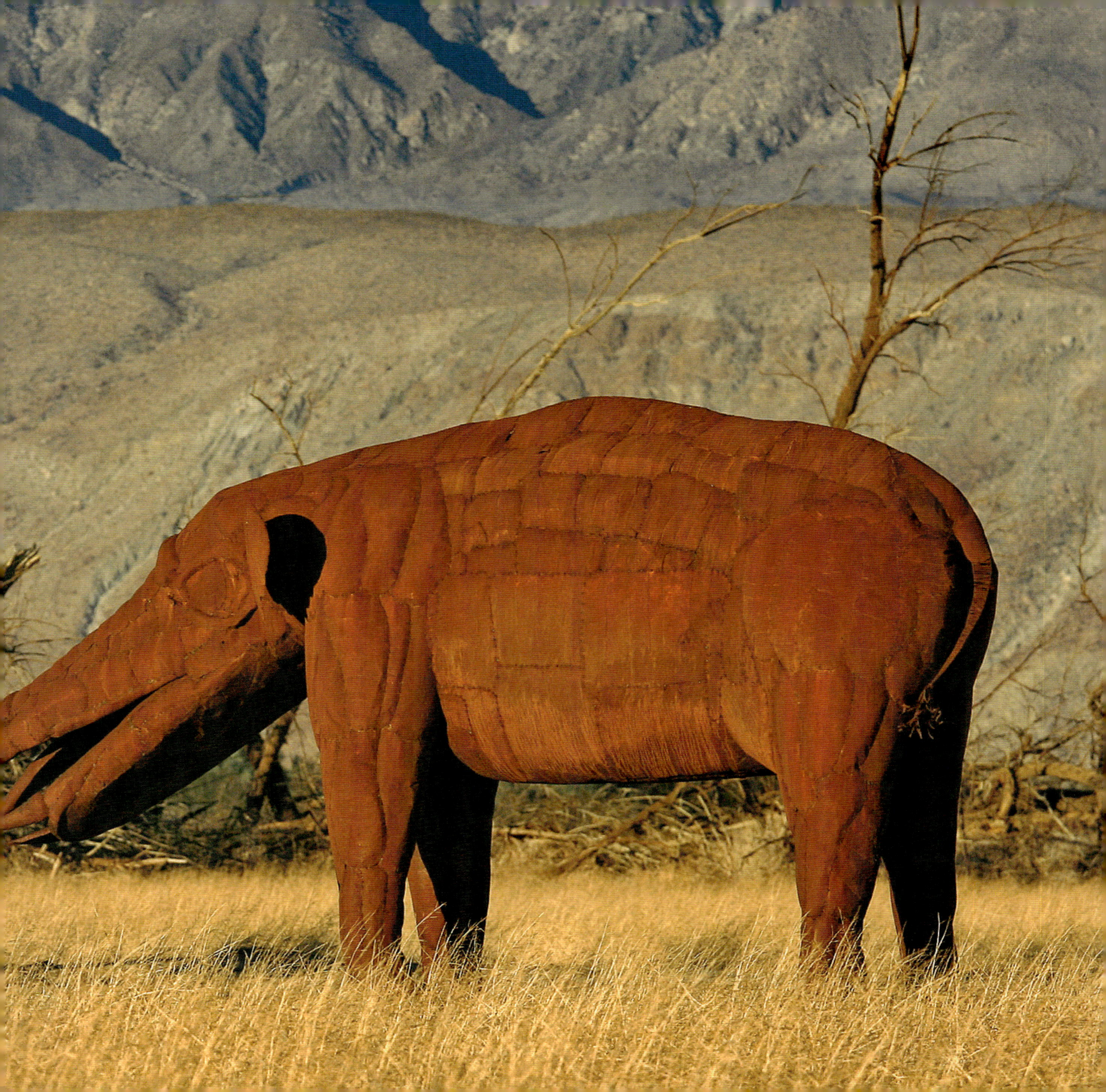

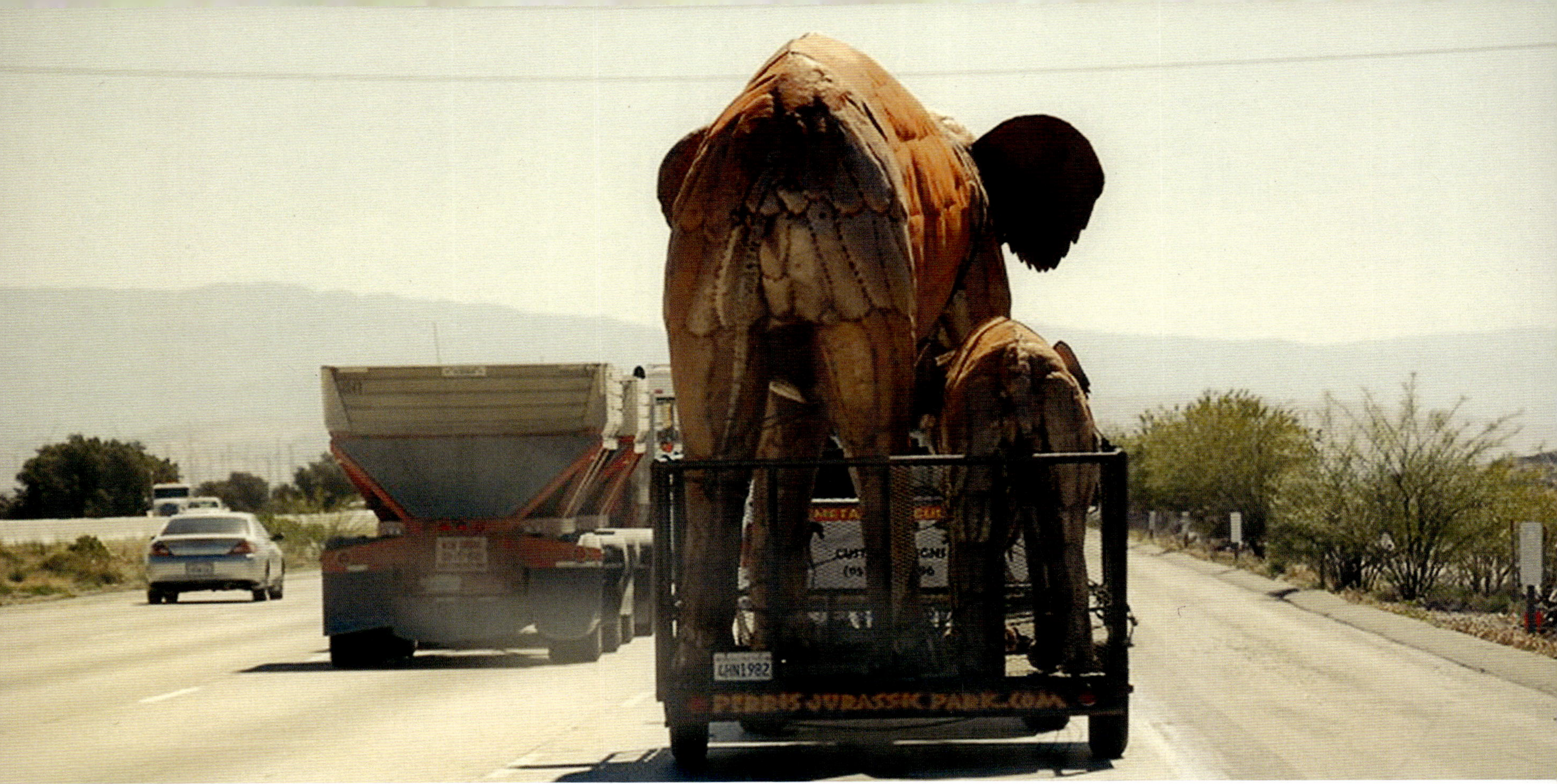

FT-10 Gomphothere. *Above:* Like a pied piper, Ricardo led a captivated entourage down the highway from Perris to Borrego Springs where he installed the first Sky Art sculptures in April 2008. *Right:* Children are particularly attracted to them and mistakenly often refer to them as "dinosaurs."

mostly the students were "sweet and noble" and they worked hard to please him. In turn, Ricardo put his heart and soul into teaching and tried to be a good model for the children.

Despite a good year of teaching with enjoyable weekends for visiting his friends and family, Ricardo made the decision to move north to the United States. His paycheck did not even cover all his weekend expenses, and he realized with his spending habits, his financial future as a teacher did not look very bright. He was still worrying his mother, because weekends found him partying heavily, staying out late, and getting into fights. Ricardo has a saying that kept coming into his mind: *¡Ojos que no ven, corazón que no siente!* If you can't see it, your heart can't feel it. If he were not around, his family would not see what he was doing and would not be hurt by his actions. Moreover, he had always been curious about the United States and was always up for an adventure.

When the opportunity arose for Ricardo to travel with his siblings to the United States in the summer of 1985, it seemed like perfect timing. He had finished the school year and was on summer break. His sisters were planning to go to California to visit an aunt in Montebello and their brother Rafael in the Fullerton area, and he was invited to join them. He did not disclose his future plans to his family.

Ricardo had no problem getting his tourist visa because he was educated, had a job, and had money in the bank—after his sister loaned him some money. In July 1985 at age twenty-three, Ricardo entered the United States, and his life took a new turn.

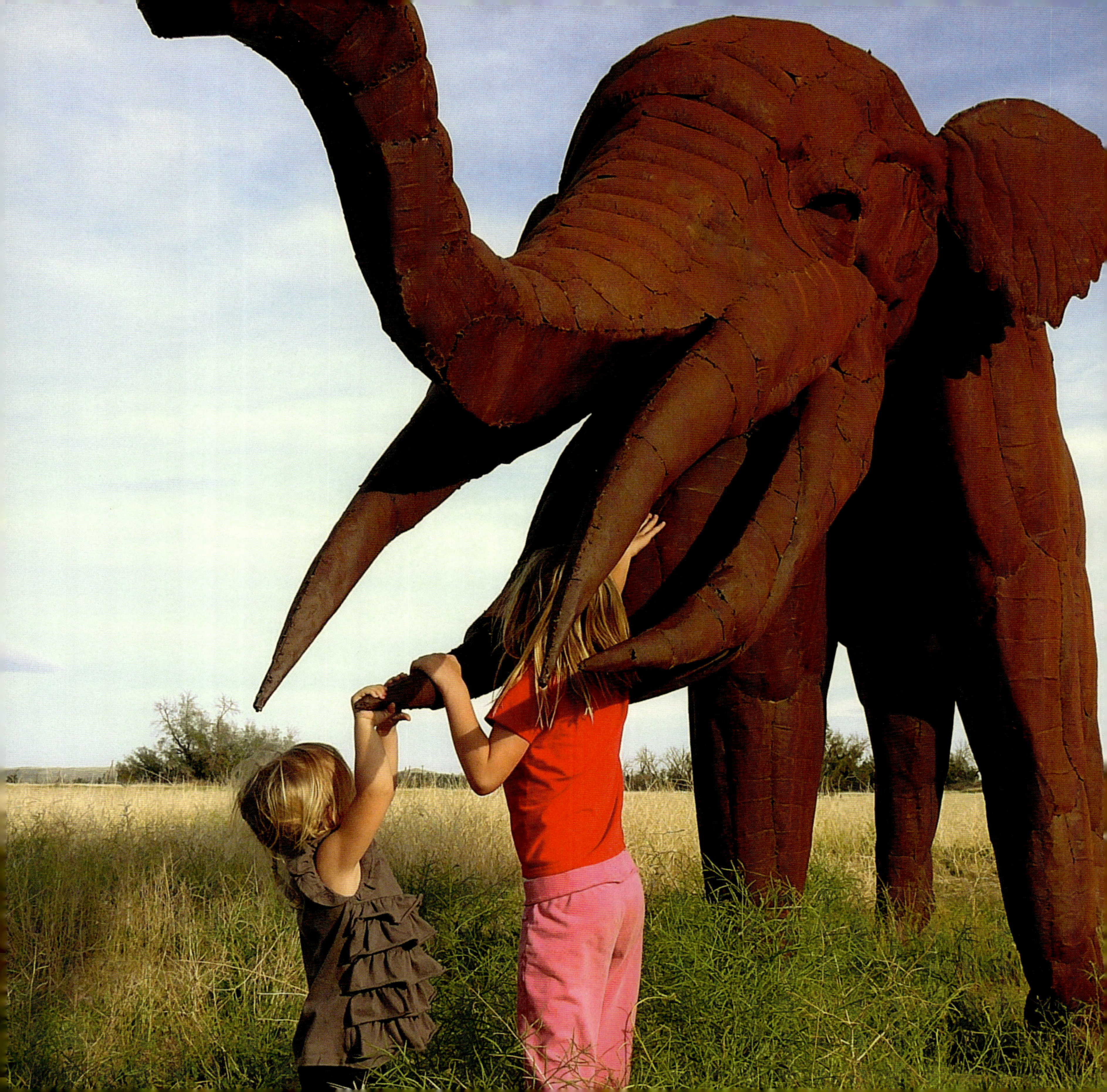

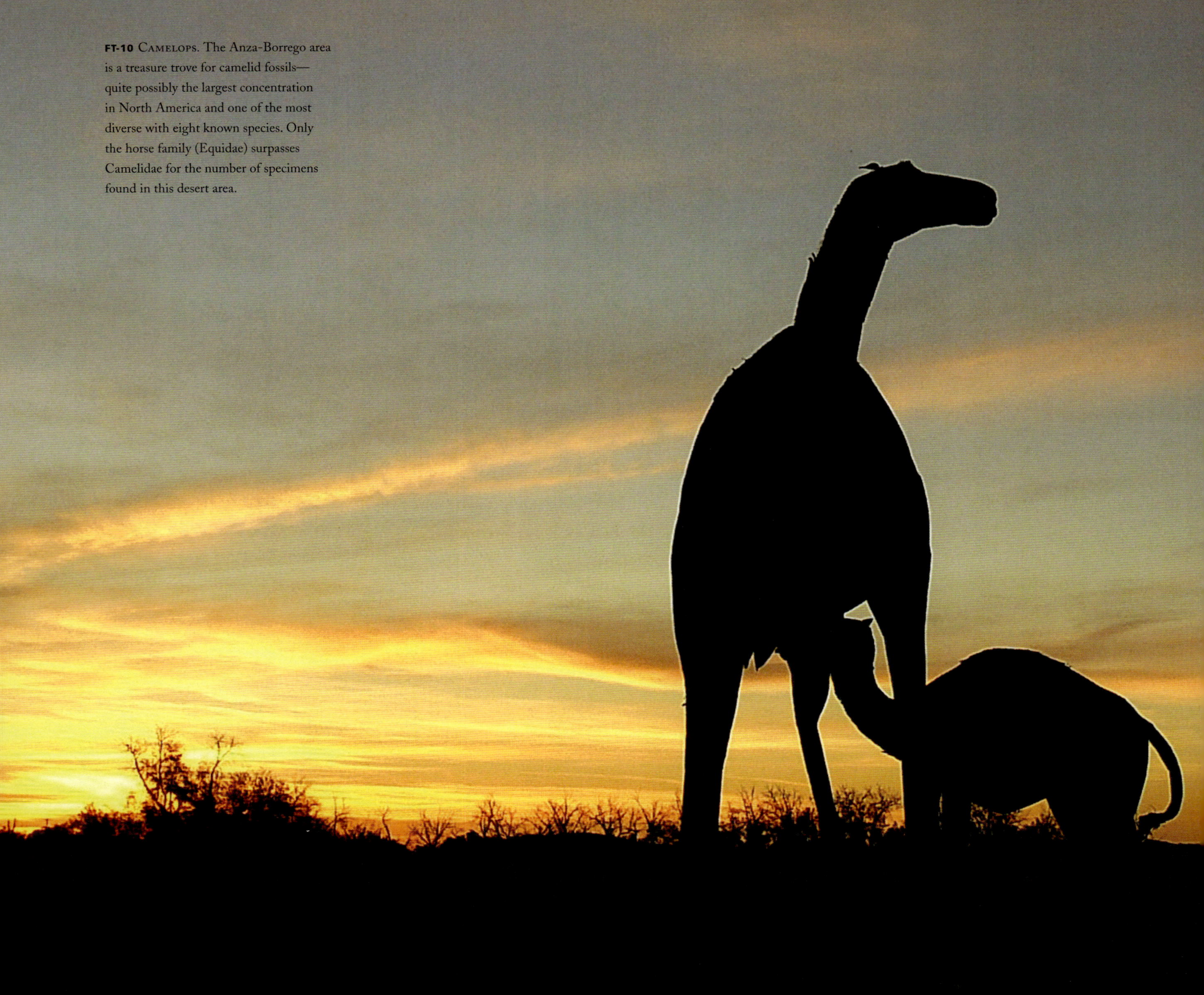

FT-10 Camelops. The Anza-Borrego area is a treasure trove for camelid fossils—quite possibly the largest concentration in North America and one of the most diverse with eight known species. Only the horse family (Equidae) surpasses Camelidae for the number of specimens found in this desert area.

CHAPTER 3

FROM BUSBOY TO BOSS

Ricardo and his sisters entered the United States at El Paso, Texas, with tourist visas and went on to California. After visiting with their aunt and brother, they made plans to return to Durango. That is when Ricardo announced that he wanted to stay, and Rafael said, "Okay."

Rafael was four years older than Ricardo and had lived in the United States for ten years. He worked as a bartender at El Torito Restaurant in Riverside and was able to get Ricardo a job there.

Ricardo did not know a word of English when he arrived in California, despite the fact that he had taken English classes in secondary school. He never thought that he would ever need English, so instead of paying attention in class, he had slipped a magazine into his textbook and had his friends help him on his tests. Now he paid the price for neglecting his studies.

The first thing Rafael told Ricardo was, "Here in the United States we speak English." To help him, Rafael blocked out all Spanish language channels on his television set and took away the radio so Ricardo could not listen to the Spanish stations.

Rafael also told Ricardo that in America the family name or surname is different than in Mexico. In Mexico the middle name is actually the surname and the last name is the

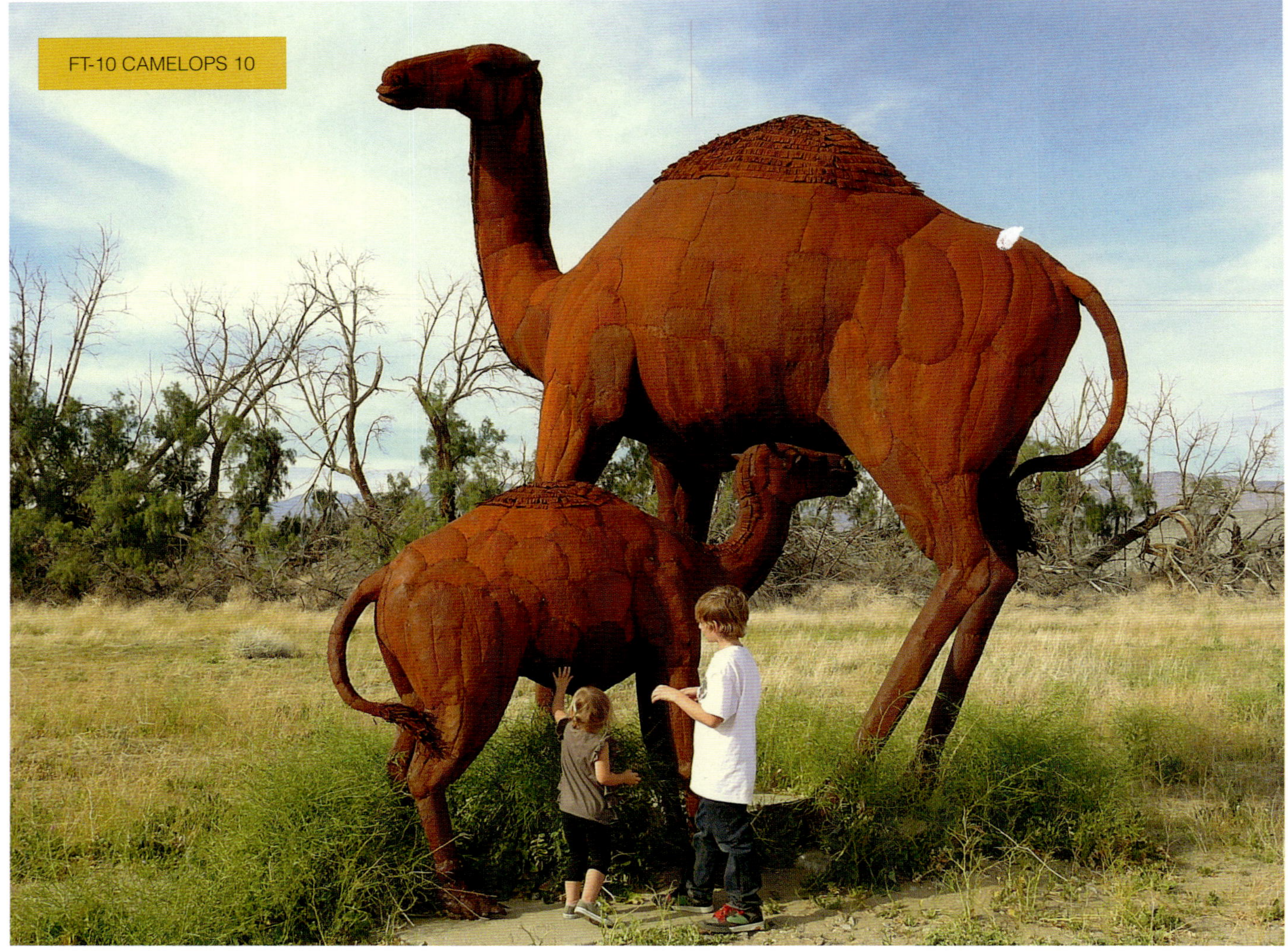

FT-10 Camelops. *Above:* Children "get it." They are delighted and amazed. No questions about whether or not the sculptures belong here or are portrayed accurately. *Right:* Astronomer Dennis Mammana captures the inverted Big Dipper in the upper right of this photo, with its two "pointer stars" at the far end pointing to Polaris (the north star) via an imaginary line drawn down and to the left to the bright star just above and left of the head of the mother *Camelops*. The constellation Draco (the dragon) winds down and to the right between the dippers. Photos like this are possible because Borrego Springs is an International Dark Sky Community.

mother's maiden name. Therefore, from now on, it would be assumed that his surname is Breceda instead of Arroyo, and he would simply be known as Ricardo Breceda and not Ricardo Arroyo Breceda.

With Rafael's prompting, Ricardo learned English rapidly, and because of his friendliness and enthusiasm, he was promoted from a busboy to a waiter at El Torito in less than four months. As a waiter, his vocabulary was limited to words that appeared on the menu. He also used a Spanish–English dictionary to help him with other words he needed to know.

His first date in the United States was with a dictionary in hand. He noticed the pretty bookkeeper Julietta at El Torito, and he offered to help her carry some books and

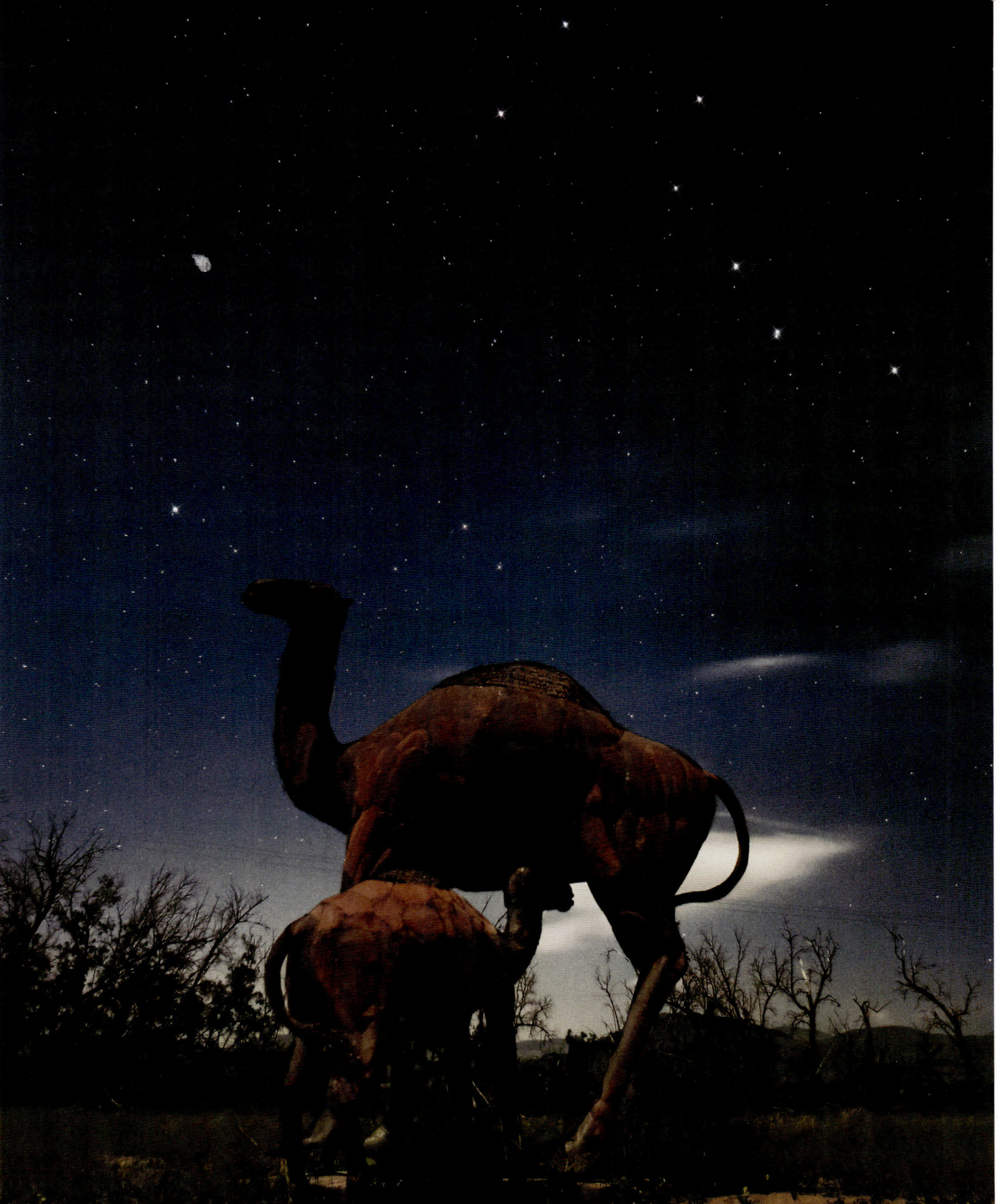

her purse out to her car. She told him, "You are very nice." Ricardo stared at her, wondering "What is '*nice*'?" Out came the dictionary, and he looked up *nice*. He flashed a winning smile, and soon he was dating her.

On his off hours Ricardo was learning to tend the bar. When he finished serving in the restaurant, he went to the bar to help Rafael until the end of Rafael's shift. He would help clean glasses and watch as drinks were being mixed to see how it was done.

After a year and a half, with more experience and a working knowledge of English, he met Victoria Valencia, who was planning to open her own restaurant. She was looking for someone to manage the place and to do the bartending. Her new restaurant would be located in Riverside

FT-11 Sabertooth Cat. Every new sculpture becomes "the best" for Ricardo in portraying movement and detail. Compare these to the first sabertooth cats made just months before, in Chapter 1. In the sabertooth assemblage, the cats fight, stalk, chase, and attack extinct horses.

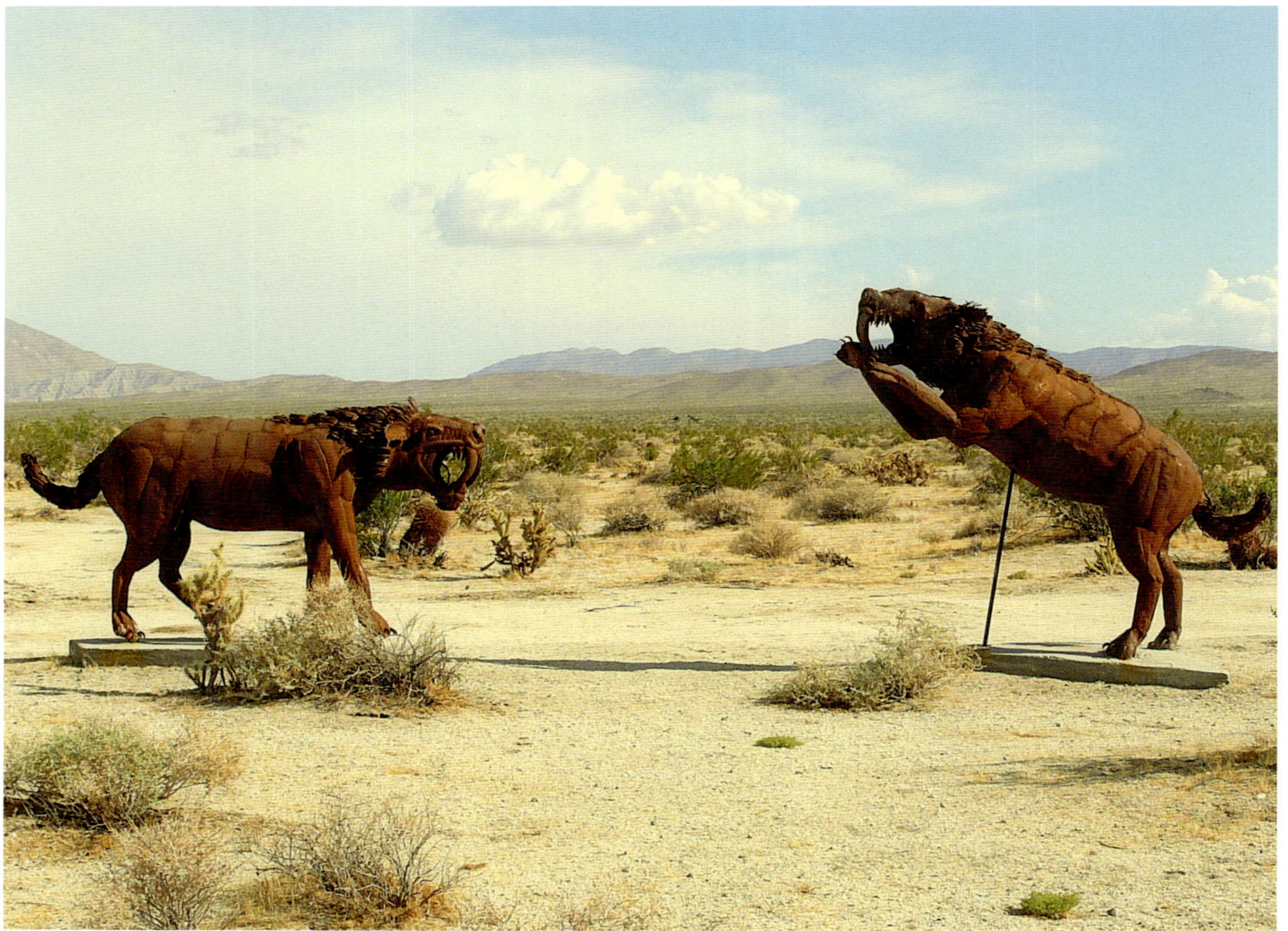

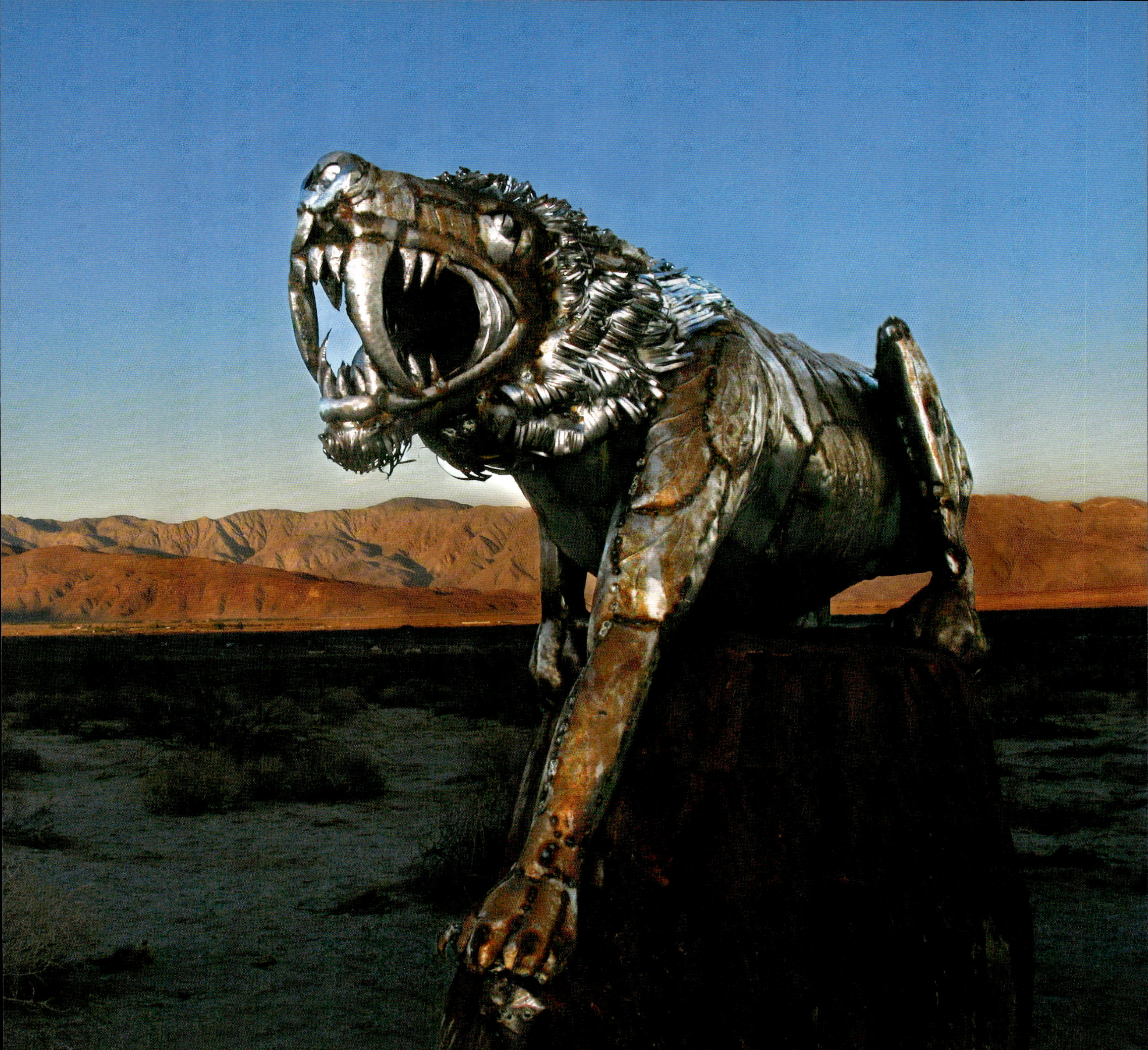

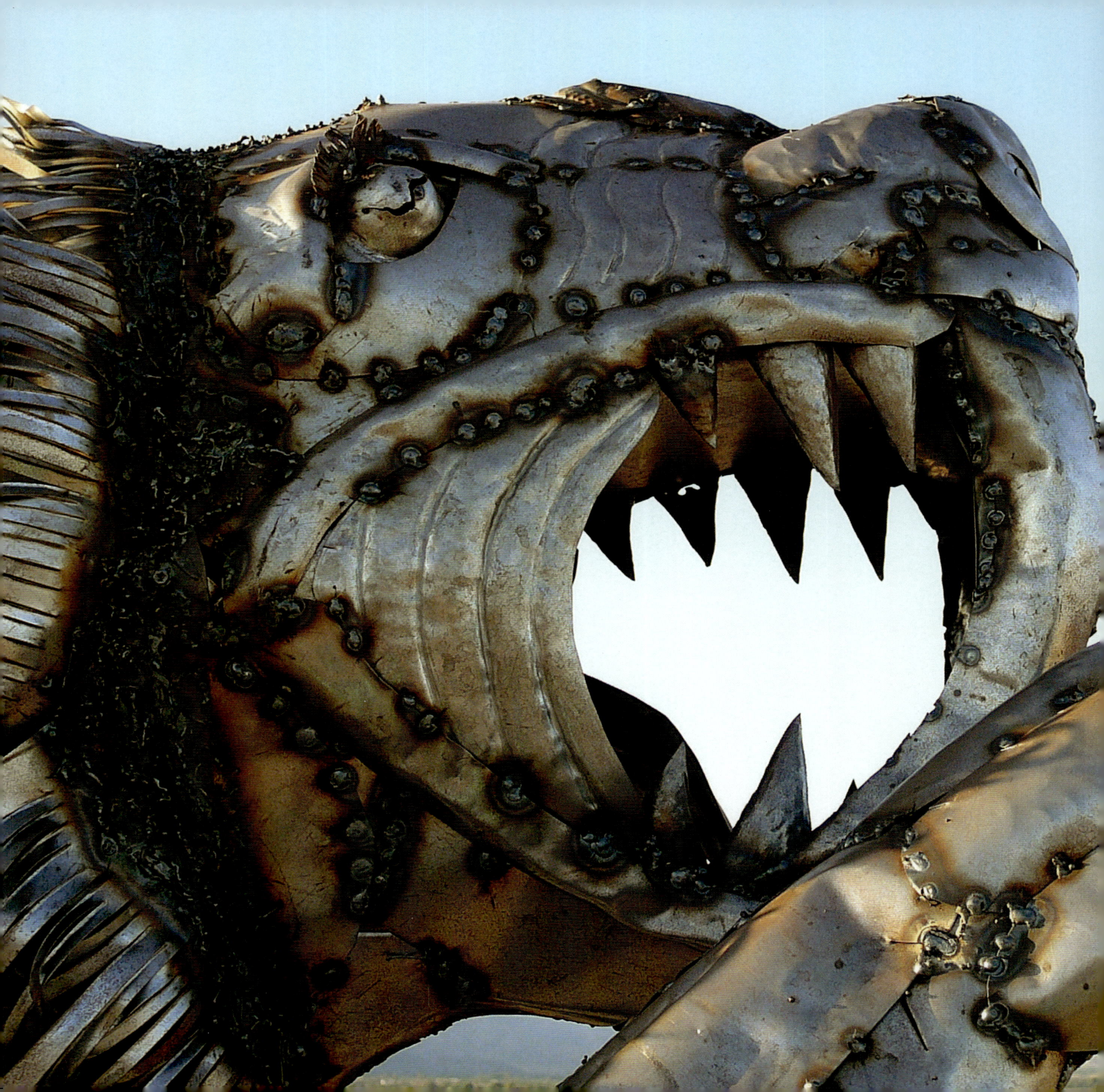

FT-11 Sabertooth Cat. The individual details found on the sculptures are best noted before the metal rusts to its lifelike dark patina. See Chapter 6 on how the sculptures are made. Note how the metal is cut and scored by hammering wires that leave impressions on the sheet metal. All is then welded together. Weld slag adds more detail.

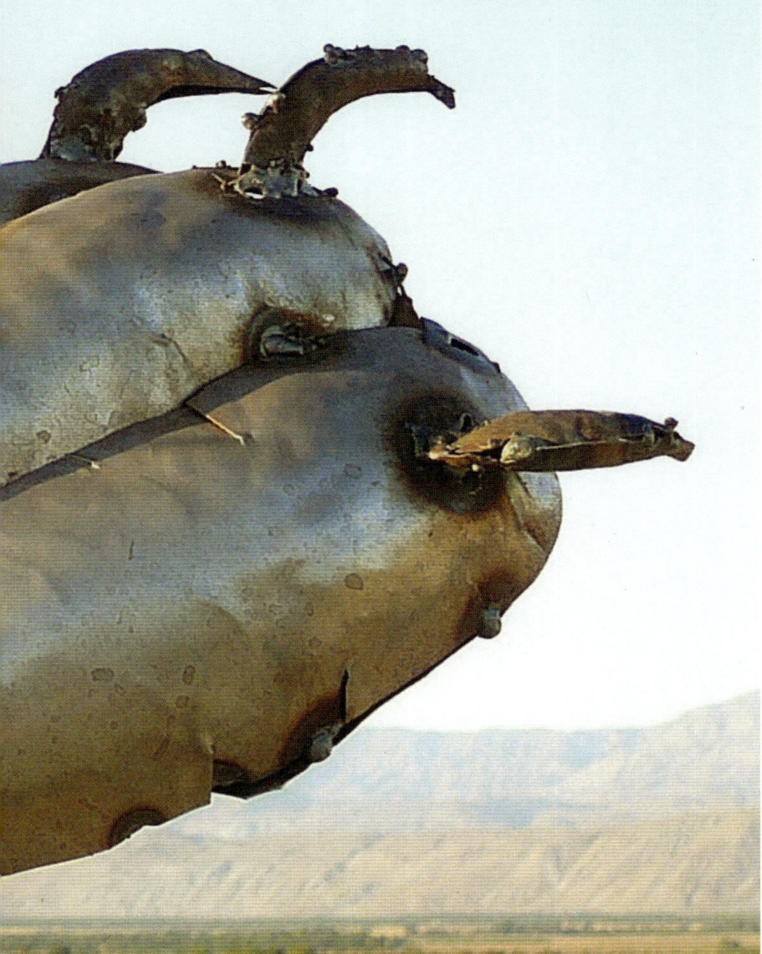

on Van Buren near Highway 91 and would be called Casa Valencia. Victoria had been watching Ricardo work, and she liked him. She offered him the job, and Ricardo accepted.

He earned good tips at Casa Valencia while he learned how to mix drinks by asking customers what they wanted and how much to pour. The more he poured, the more generous the tips. He was just getting used to his new job when tragedy struck.

Rafael was killed on May 6, 1987, in an automobile accident on the way to work at El Torito. It was a head-on collision, and he was killed instantly. Devastated, Ricardo had to call his parents in Durango to let them know that Rafael had died. At the hospital, Ricardo removed Rafael's ring from his finger and placed it on his own ring finger. He has never taken it off.

Arrangements were made for Ricardo to accompany Rafael's body to Durango for burial. After the funeral service, Ricardo returned to his job in the United States.

He still had a tourist visa. When he returned to California, he knew he needed a regular immigration card to work legally. Help came via a customer at Casa Valencia who owned a ranch and befriended him. She helped him fill out the forms for the immigration service and sponsored him. Soon they were dating.

Ricardo managed Casa Valencia for almost a year and a half. He supervised a staff of about fifteen workers that included waiters, cocktail waitresses, and kitchen crew. He opened and closed the restaurant, counted the money at the end of the night, and also worked as the bartender. He had a good working relationship with the owner, but her new jealous boyfriend named Carlos, who also became a partner in the business, thought Ricardo and Victoria were too friendly. Before anything could come to a head, Ricardo accepted an offer for an opportunity to grow in a different direction.

While he was bartending at Casa Valencia, he developed a loyal clientele. Among the regulars were construction workers who would come in at the end of the day. One of those was

FT-11 Sabertooth Cat and Extinct Horse. The sabertooth cat (*Smilodon gracilis*) used stealth and ambush rather than speed to capture its prey. It could open its mouth 120 degrees, as compared to a lion, which can open its mouth 65 degrees.

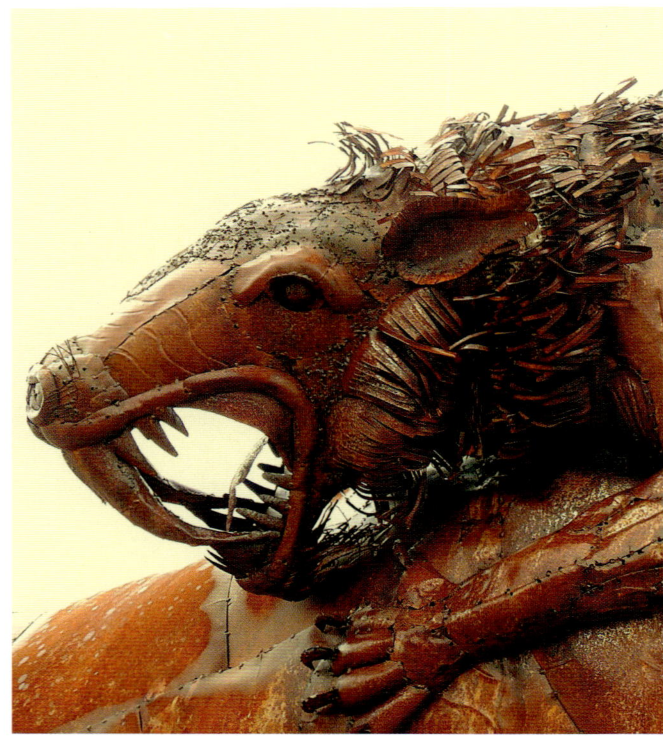

FT-11 Sabertooth Cat. The sculptures are meant to rust to develop the rich hide-like color. Rusting occurs through the natural oxidation process.

Joe Baker, the owner of B & B Construction Company, who would sometimes come in with a few of his employees. Joe's company was very large, with crews that worked all over the Southland constructing commercial buildings, apartments, and housing developments.

Ricardo became friends with Aubrey Earheart, the son of one of the foremen that Joe employed. One day Aubrey's father, Warren Earheart, offered Ricardo a job on his crew, but Ricardo told him he wasn't interested because he made good money bartending.

Joe agreed that the starting pay of $5 per hour was low, but added that he thought Ricardo was smart and he would have the opportunity to work himself up in the company. Warren also told Ricardo that as he became more experienced, his pay would increase weekly.

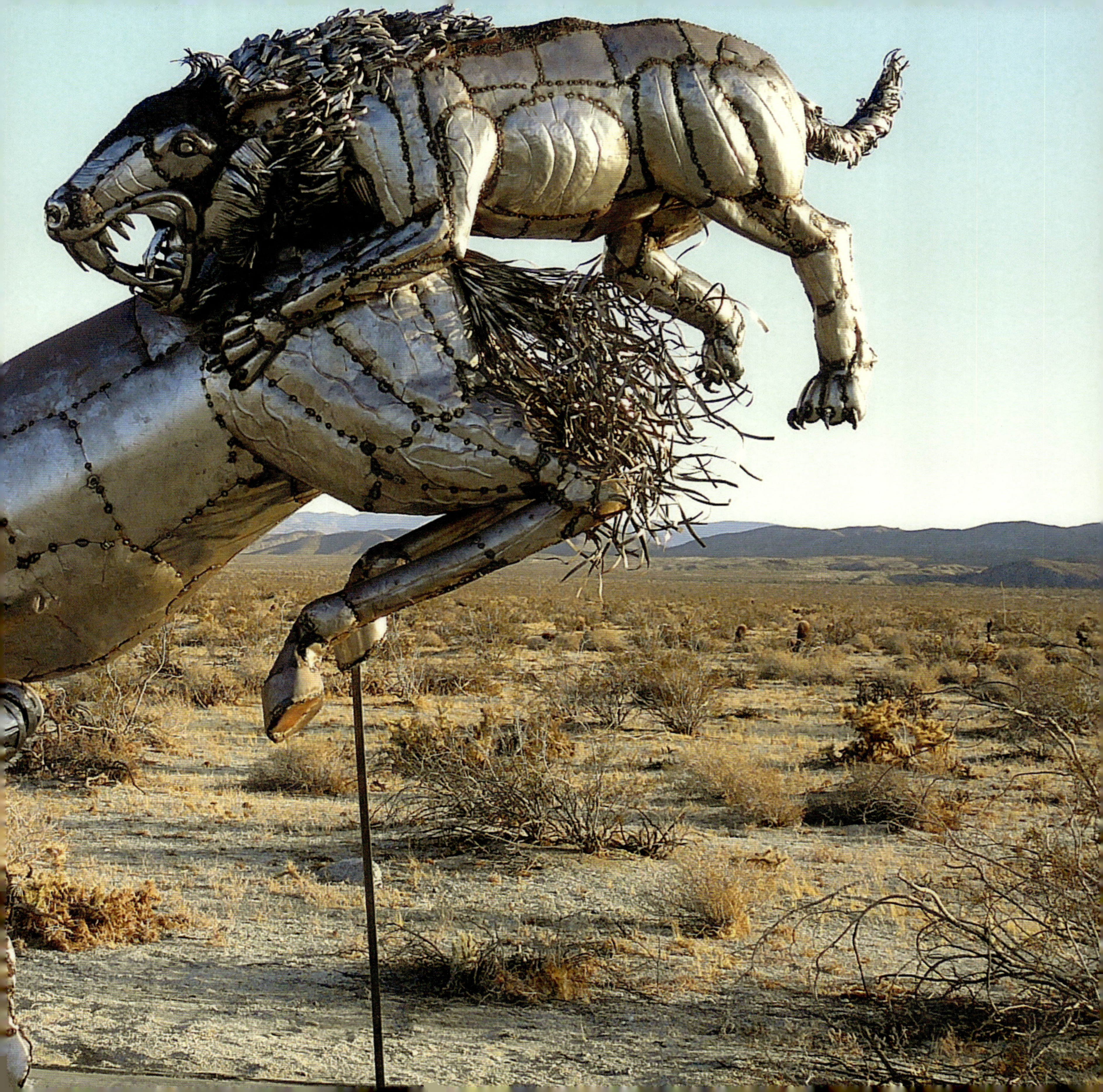

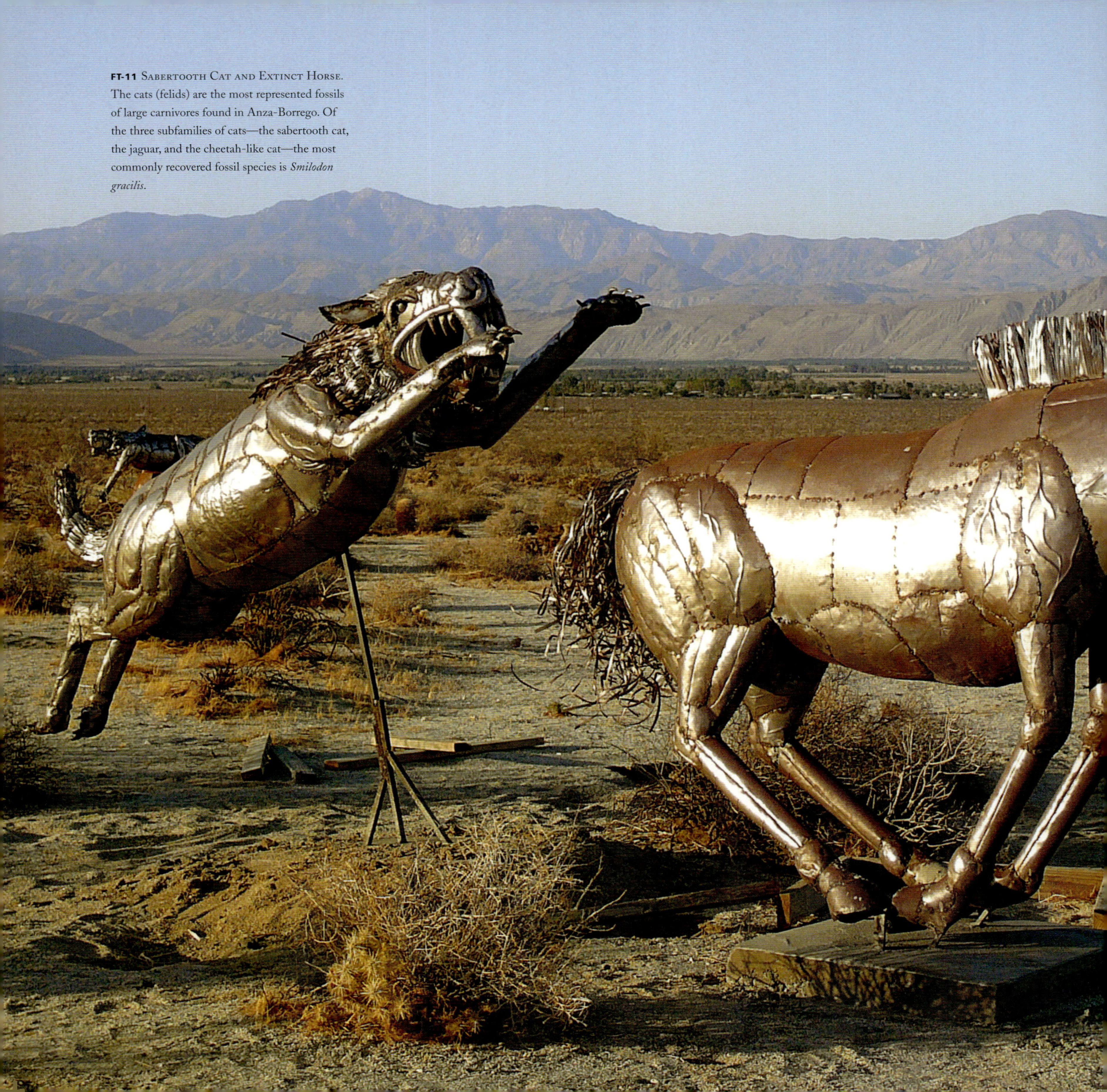

FT-11 Sabertooth Cat and Extinct Horse. The cats (felids) are the most represented fossils of large carnivores found in Anza-Borrego. Of the three subfamilies of cats—the sabertooth cat, the jaguar, and the cheetah-like cat—the most commonly recovered fossil species is *Smilodon gracilis*.

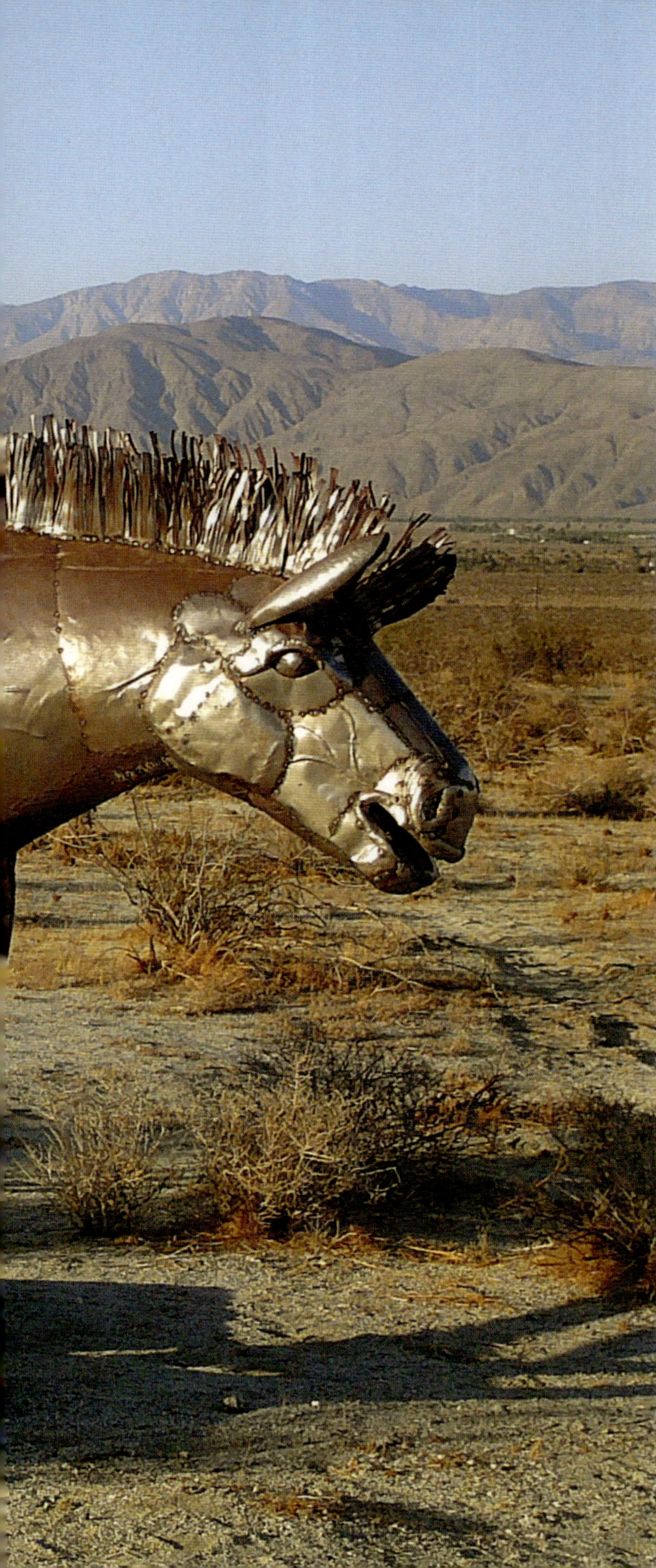

Although the offer did not interest Ricardo at first, as tension increased between Carlos and him, Warren's offer began to look like a perfect solution, so he took the job.

When Carlos came into the bar, Ricardo poured himself a drink, jumped over the bar, and with a big smile on his face told Carlos, "From now on, you can serve me!"

Warren was a good foreman and a good teacher, and Ricardo was a fast learner. Ricardo began his job at the lowest level by "holding the end of the tape." He was assigned to work with the man who had the blueprints. They would spread the blueprints on the floor and then mark where the framers needed to put in the windows and walls. After he learned to measure and mark, he then learned how to measure and cut lumber framing.

Ricardo worked on jobs all over Southern California and as far away as Las Vegas, Nevada. He was always part of Warren's crew. At the end of the workday, the crew would go to a bar or dinner and afterward play some cards or pool. Ricardo enjoyed his job, and true to Warren's word, he received a slight increase in pay every week until he was making almost $14 per hour.

He now had money in his pocket and good friends, and he lived in a nice apartment complex. When in 1989 he had the opportunity to buy a house at Kansas and Linden streets in Riverside, he became a homeowner.

One day he was cruising around his neighborhood with a friend when he noticed a pretty girl on the street. He asked his friend to drive around the block because he wanted to talk to her. She was still there when they came around again. Ricardo got out of the car and introduced himself.

To his surprise, Maria Corral was also from Durango. She grew up in a town about sixty miles northwest of the capital. She was seven years younger than Ricardo, and they shared the same birth date. Maria worked at Toro, an irrigation company in Riverside. Soon they were dating.

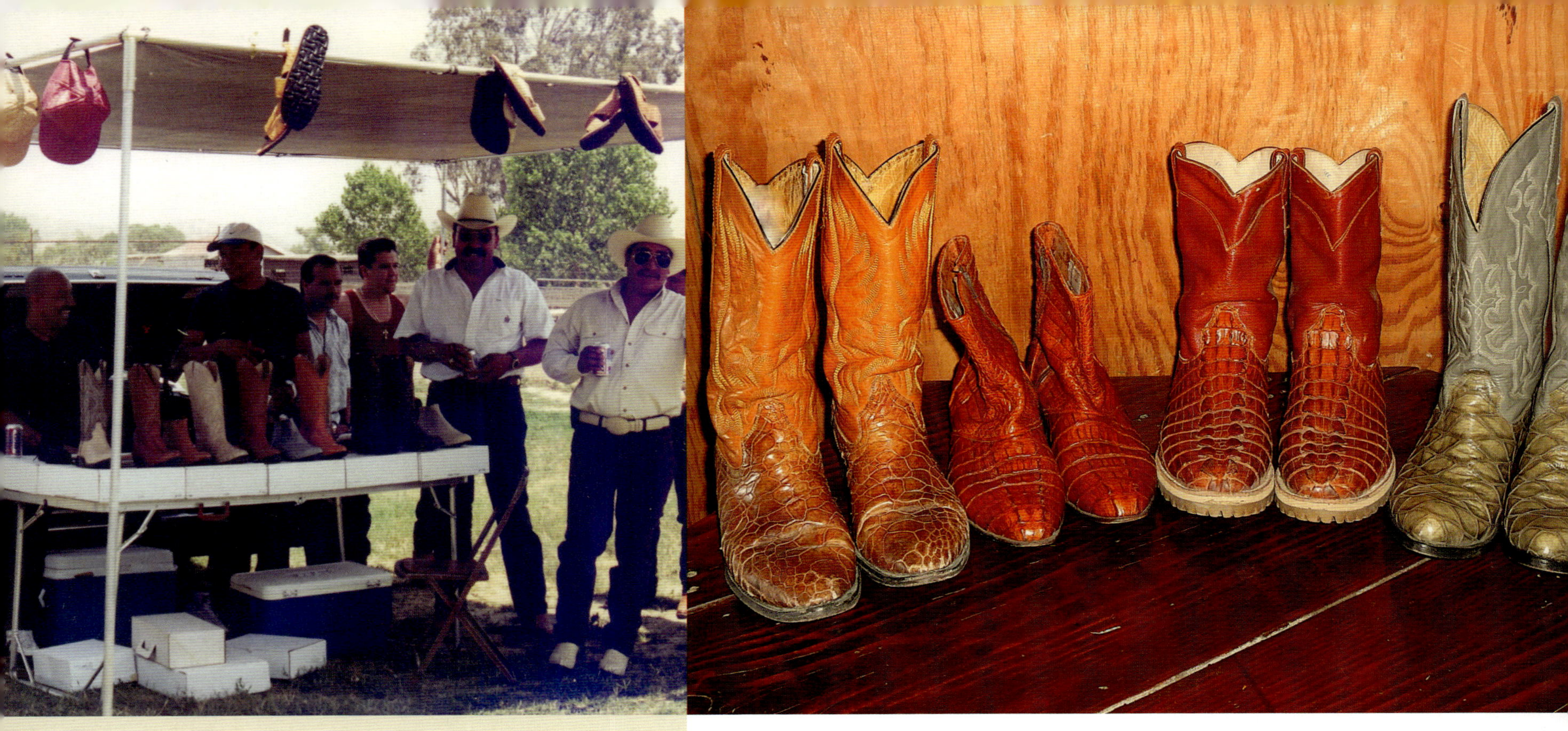

A DAY AT THE RACES

Ricardo's and Lianna's favorite race track was Rancho Los Alamos in Hesperia. *From left to right:* Ricardo had a boot sales stand that Lianna manned while he sold raffle tickets in the viewing stand; exotic skins from ostriches, alligators, eels, stingrays, and anteaters were used in making the boots that Ricardo sold; racing jockeys at the track wear casual attire; horses race in pairs, Mexican-style.

That same year Ricardo's house was broken into. Besides stealing some valuable jewelry, they vandalized the house and slashed his waterbed, causing water damage. He decided to sell his house, and he moved into an apartment with Maria.

By 1991 Ricardo was earning top pay as a member of the construction crew. As a carpenter he excelled at framing, roofing, and cutting, and he specialized in making precise cuts. He could cut the wood they needed without any waste. He had done well in math in school, and he put it to good use. Because he was such a fast and accurate carpenter, he was saving the company an impressive amount of money.

When he next asked for his weekly increase, he was told that he was receiving as much as they could pay him. He then asked for some piecework on the side so that he could add to his income. This lasted until there was no additional work available.

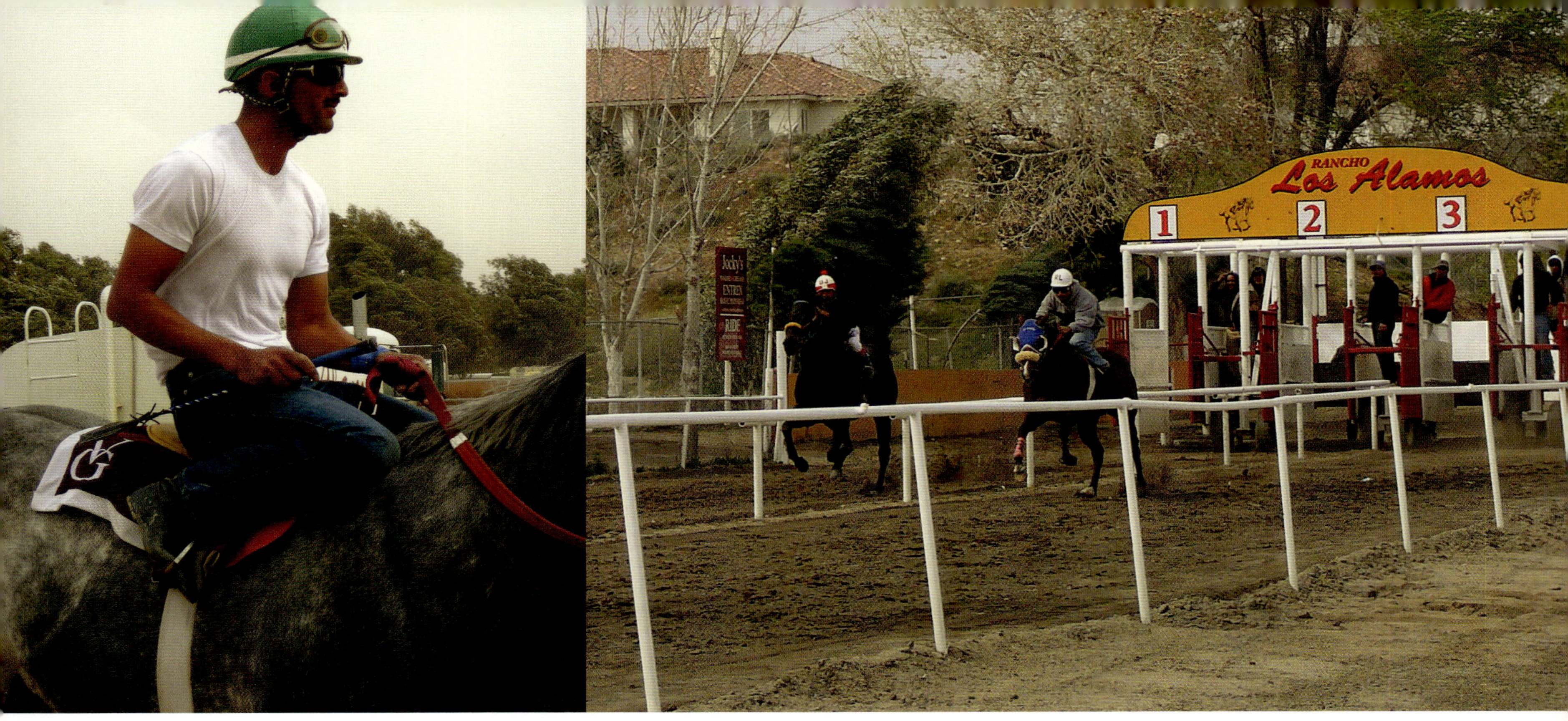

Ricardo told Warren that if he could not get some extra work or a pay increase, that he would have to quit. When no more work was forthcoming, Ricardo said to Aubrey, "Let's work somewhere else where we can earn more money." They both quit and began working for companies that could pay more. At one point, Ricardo was making $500 or more a day for his precise cutting.

Ricardo worked various jobs until 1993 when he took a job with J-Con Company. He was on the job for about six months when he had a serious accident.

Ricardo was working on framing a model for an apartment complex and needed to put soundproofing drywall in the interior between the second and third floor. The wall was high and there was no scaffolding, only an extension ladder. Ricardo mentioned to the crew that he thought it would be dangerous because he would have to hold the four-by-ten-foot panel with one hand while climbing up the ladder with the other and the ladder had no support.

One of the guys dared him by yelling, "Hey, Ricardo, you can do it!"

He thought about it and said, "It's too heavy; I don't know." The worker goaded him by shouting, "Just do it!" At that point it felt like a personal challenge, so Ricardo took a deep breath and fired back, "Okay, I'll do it!"

He hefted the drywall on his shoulder, steadying it with his hand. He used his other hand to climb up the unsupported ladder. As he neared the top of the ladder, it slid sideways and Ricardo fell about fourteen or fifteen feet from the second story and landed on his back. He immediately felt a searing pain in his back and shoulder and knew he was in big trouble. He could not get up. The workers dragged him over to the shade of the building because it was hot, and they called for help. In the first few moments after the accident, Ricardo realized he could not feel his legs or anything in the lower part of his body. He panicked because he thought he might never be able to walk again.

As he lay on the ground, he suddenly broke into uproarious laughter. The guys looked at him in utter disbelief and asked, "Are you crazy? Why are you laughing?" Ricardo gasped, "Because I can feel pain! And I can move my legs!"

When he was taken to the hospital, he was told he had shattered two discs in his lower back. Even though he was in excruciating pain, he was able to walk. The doctor recommended surgery to insert steel plates in his back to support his vertebra, but Ricardo vehemently refused. So instead, a small incision was made to suction out pieces of the damaged discs. They released him after one day.

Eventually Ricardo learned to manage his pain by exercising, maintaining his weight, and, occasionally, taking pain medication. By working out with weights, walking a lot,

FT-12 Aiolornis in Its Nest (Detail). Attention to detail is the real genius that Ricardo displays. Every element is carefully thought out and executed. Having grown up on a ranch and also having spent hours observing and hunting animals, Ricardo instinctively has a feel for the most minute anatomical details.

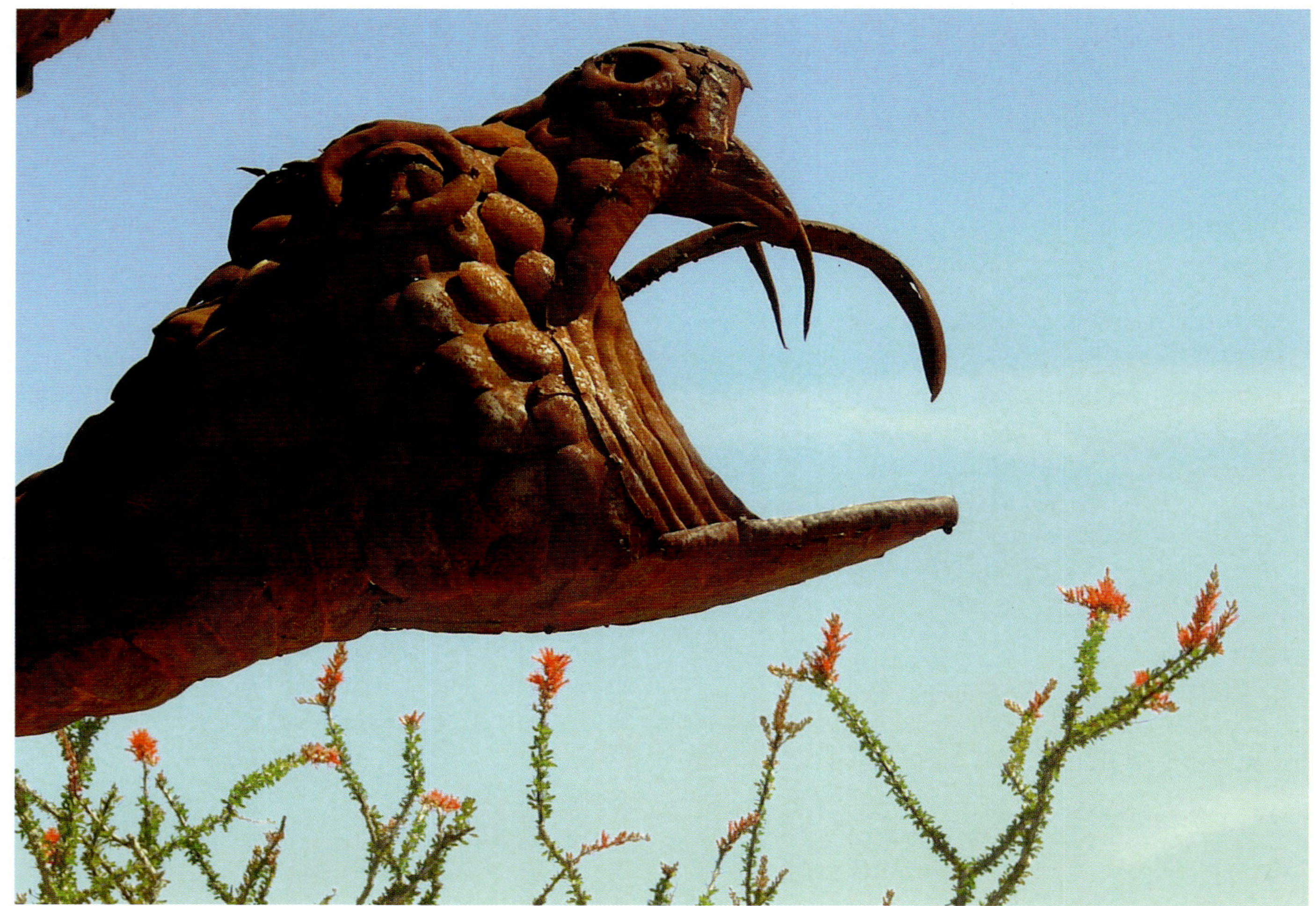

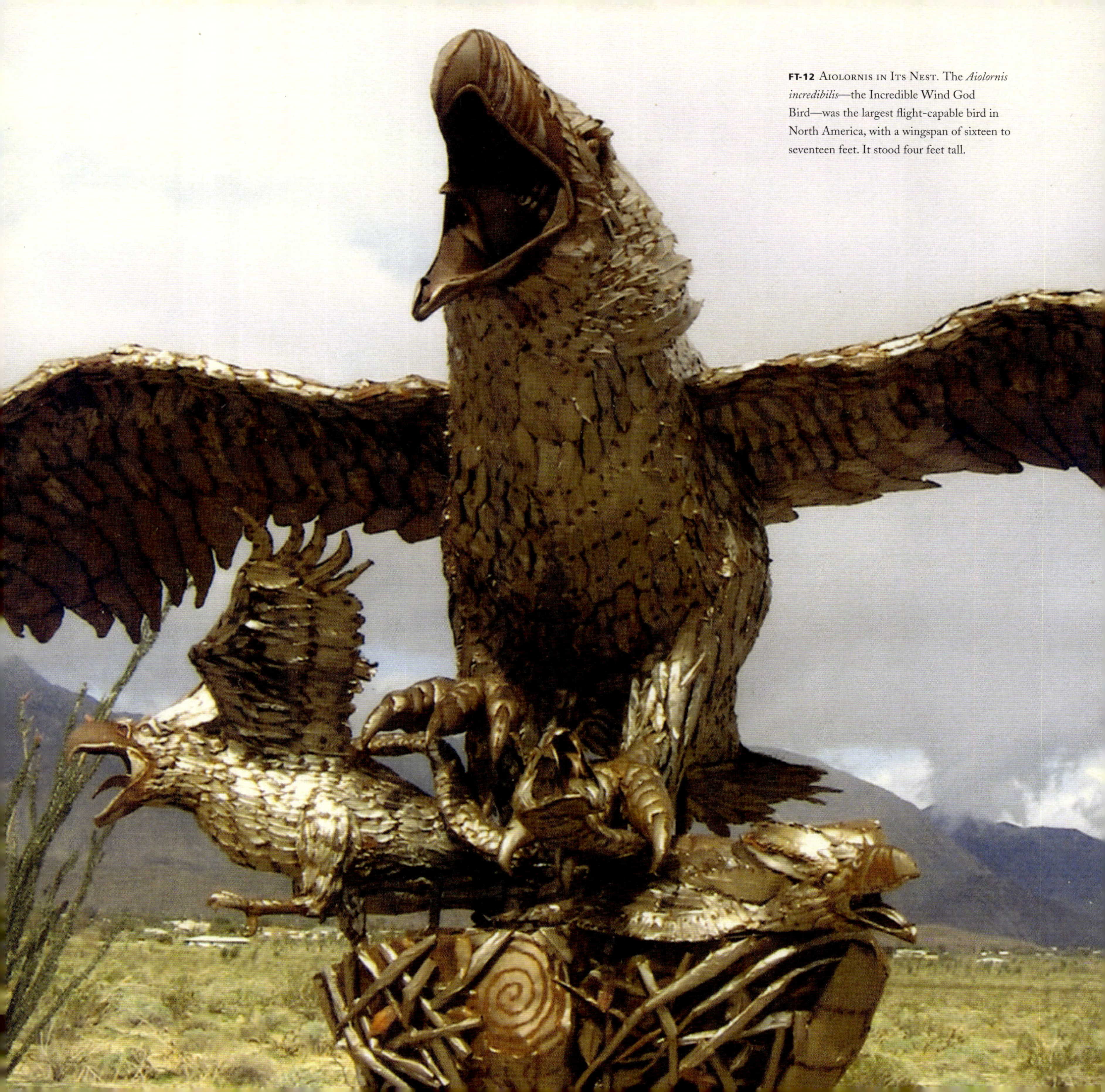

FT-12 Aiolornis in Its Nest. The *Aiolornis incredibilis*—the Incredible Wind God Bird—was the largest flight-capable bird in North America, with a wingspan of sixteen to seventeen feet. It stood four feet tall.

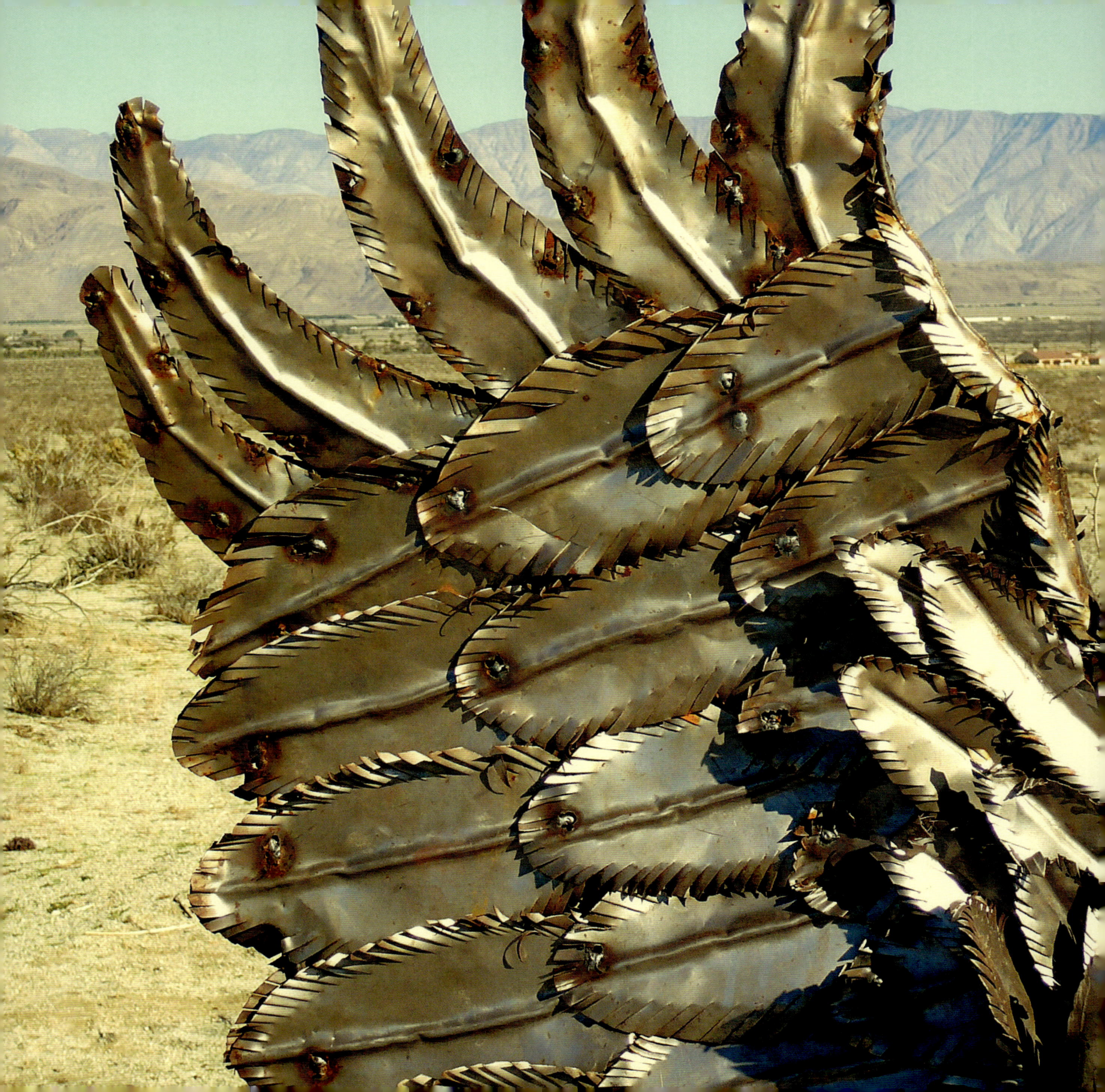

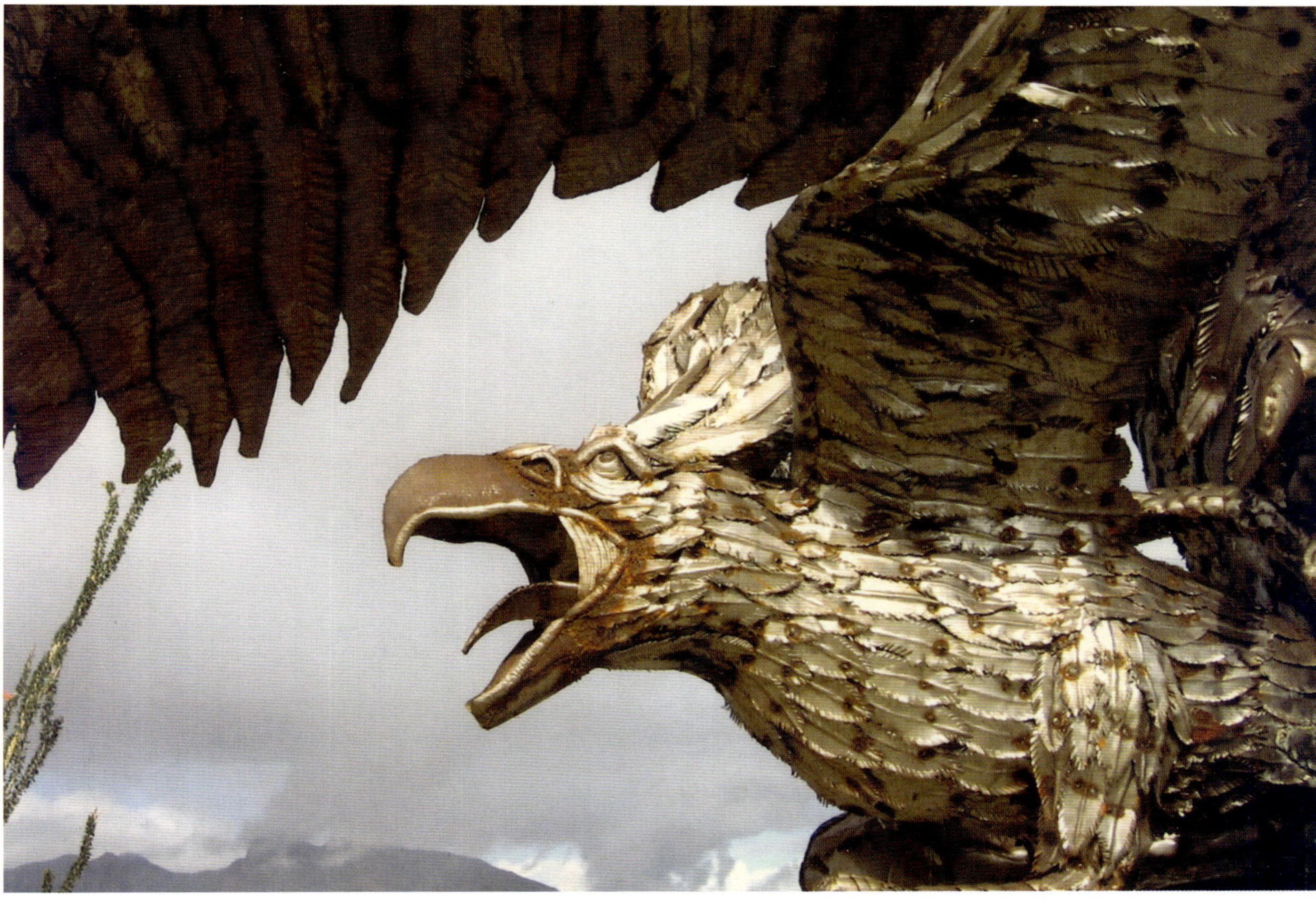

FT-12 Aiolornis in Its Nest. Each feather of the *Aiolornis* is correctly shaped according to its use whether for flight or contour. Only six specimens of this bird have been found, and three of those come from the Anza-Borrego area.

running, and shooting basketball, he succeeded in keeping his back flexible.

Ricardo tried to go back to work, but because of the injury, he was unable to continue with his job. The company had disability insurance, and he began receiving a check for $1,200 a month, which was not enough to pay his bills. And on top of that, Maria was two months pregnant.

Ricardo could do nothing but watch television all day as he waited for his monthly disability check. It was frustrating for a man who was used to working for a living and making things happen. He became short-tempered and irritable with Maria, who was working full-time at Toro and dealing with her pregnancy, and they began to fight.

In desperation, Ricardo called his brother Rodolfo in Durango and asked him for some advice as to what he could do, because he had to do something before he went totally crazy. Rodolfo suggested that Ricardo try selling Durango-made cowboy boots in the United States. Rodolfo had once

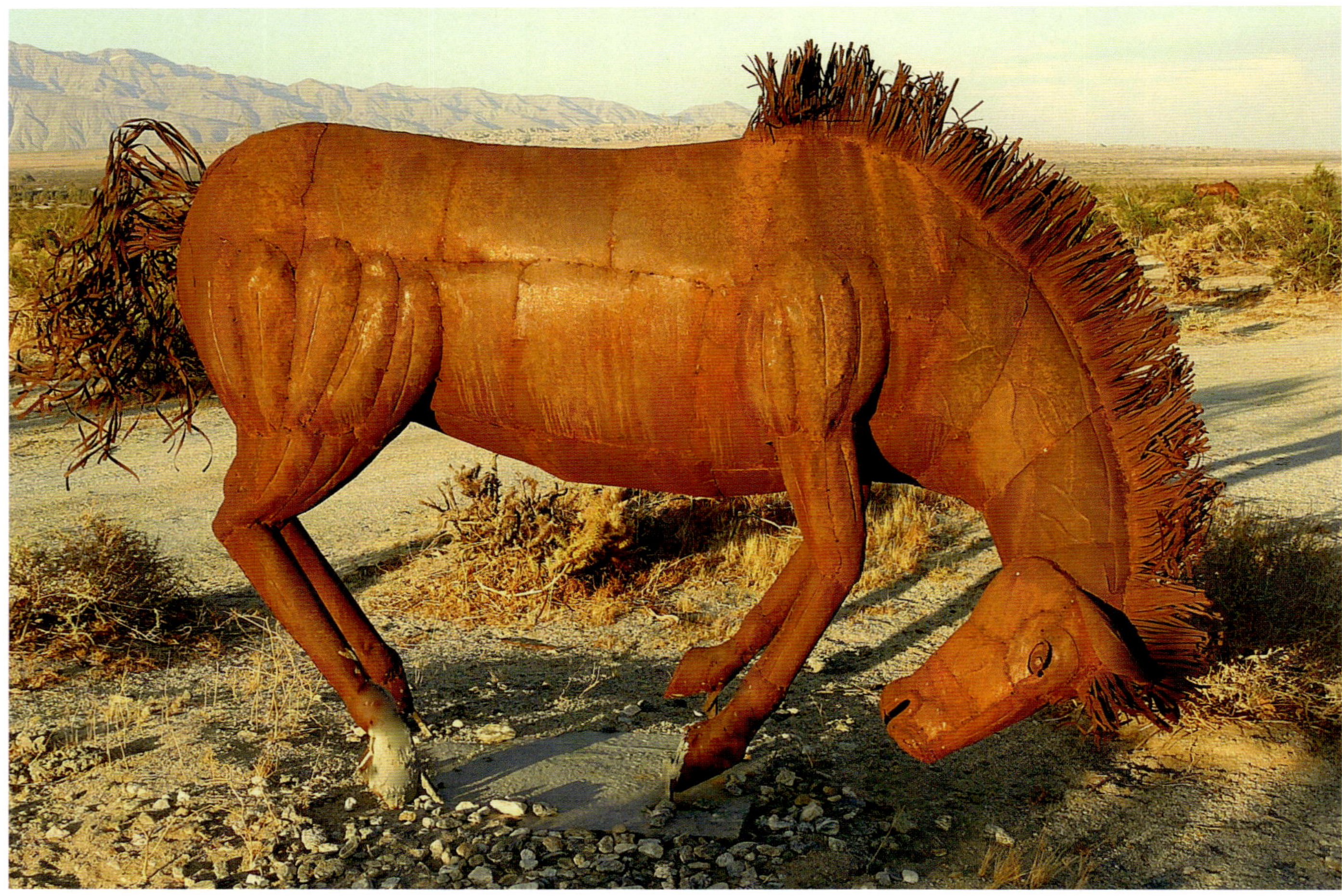

FT-13 Extinct Horse. Horses are members of the family Equidae that include true horses, zebras, and asses. Equine horses (*Equus* sp.) evolved in North America about 57 million years ago. The first fossil record for the modern domestic horse may have been recorded in Anza-Borrego. The horses to the right are just beginning to rust. Visitors today will see them with a rich reddish-chestnut coat similar to the horse above.

sold boots himself in Durango, and he knew how and where to purchase them wholesale. Ricardo decided to give it a try, and it proved to be a financial and liberating salvation.

Ricardo was a natural salesman and his philosophy was straightforward. "If you work for other people, it is for your paycheck, and you know what you are going to make each week. But if you work for yourself, you can make all the money you want if you do your best with a lot of enthusiasm. And, of course," he added, "it has to be fun." Be it boot sales or bartending or sculpting, this has always been his attitude.

Ricardo began his new business with just a few boots to see how it would go. He started selling them at local swap meets, Mexican parties, fiestas, reunions, and different ranches. "Mexicans like to party," he explained, "so there were always lots of people at the various gatherings who would want to buy boots."

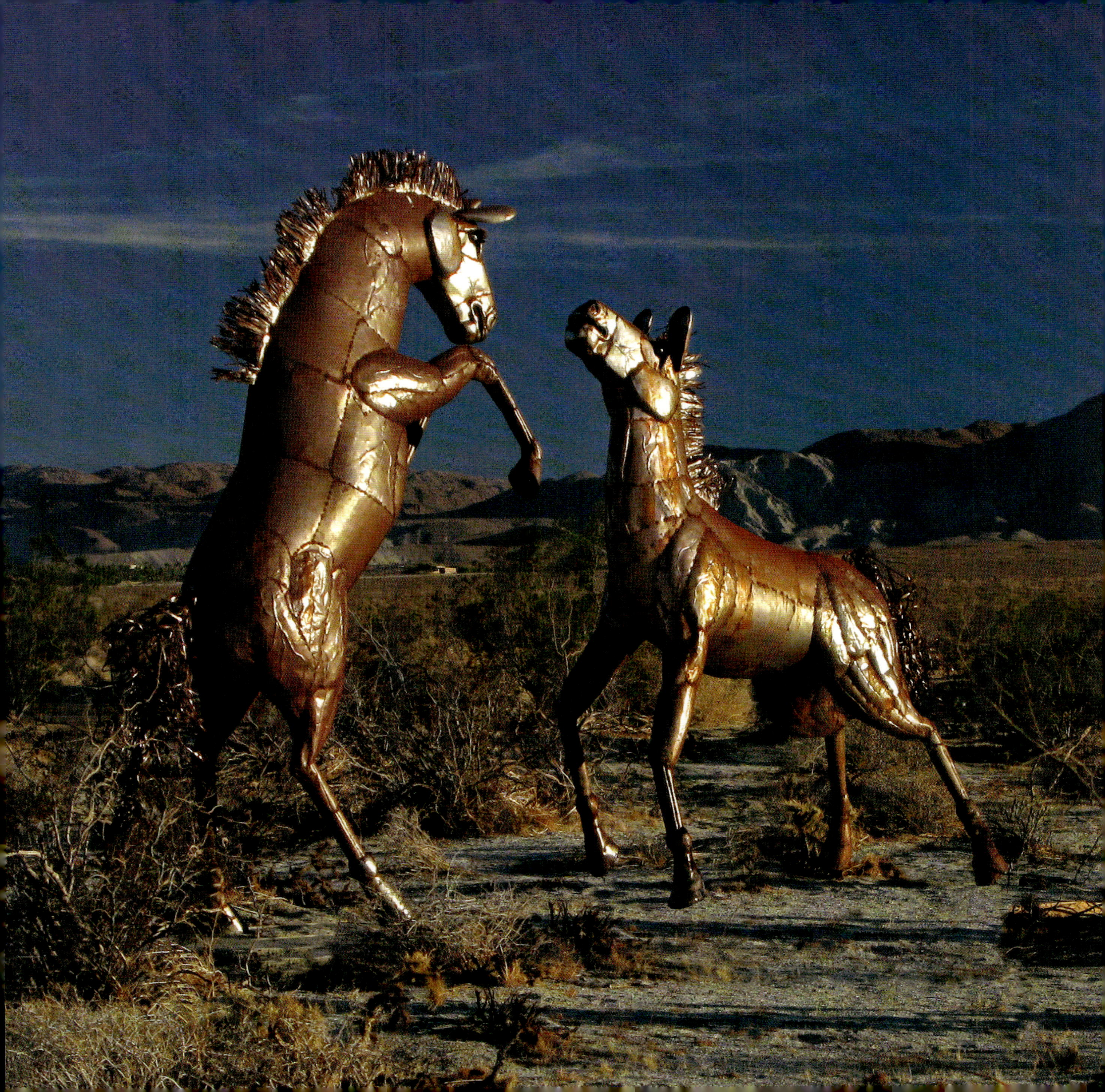

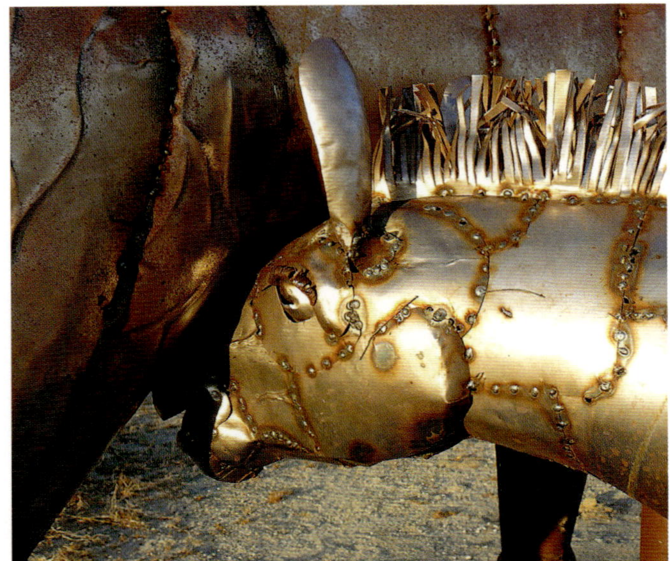

FT-13 Extinct Horse (Detail). The color of the sculptures changes with age, light, and moisture. From the silver sheen of newness, they darken as they rust.

The ranches around Chino, Riverside, and San Jacinto had lots of cattle. At the ranch parties they would serve *pajaretes*—chocolate, sugar, pure alcohol, and milk directly from a cow. A couple of cups of this hot chocolate milk made one very jovial. Ricardo would set up his stand where they sold *gorditas* and *tamales,* and began selling a lot of boots to a lot of very happy people.

As word got around that he had boots to sell at a good price, his business began to grow. It gave him a sense of purpose, pride, and accomplishment. At this same time, the birth of his daughter, Lianna Venus Arroyo, on June 13, 1994, added a great deal of joy to his life. Although it appeared that things were turning around for Ricardo, his relationship with Maria continued to deteriorate. They separated in 1995, when Lianna was almost a year old. Ricardo moved out of the apartment they were sharing and rented a house. He also found a good attorney and filed for and was granted full custody of Lianna. In addition to developing his boot sales, his main focus was now raising his daughter. On May 11, 1996, he proudly had Lianna baptized in the Catholic Church.

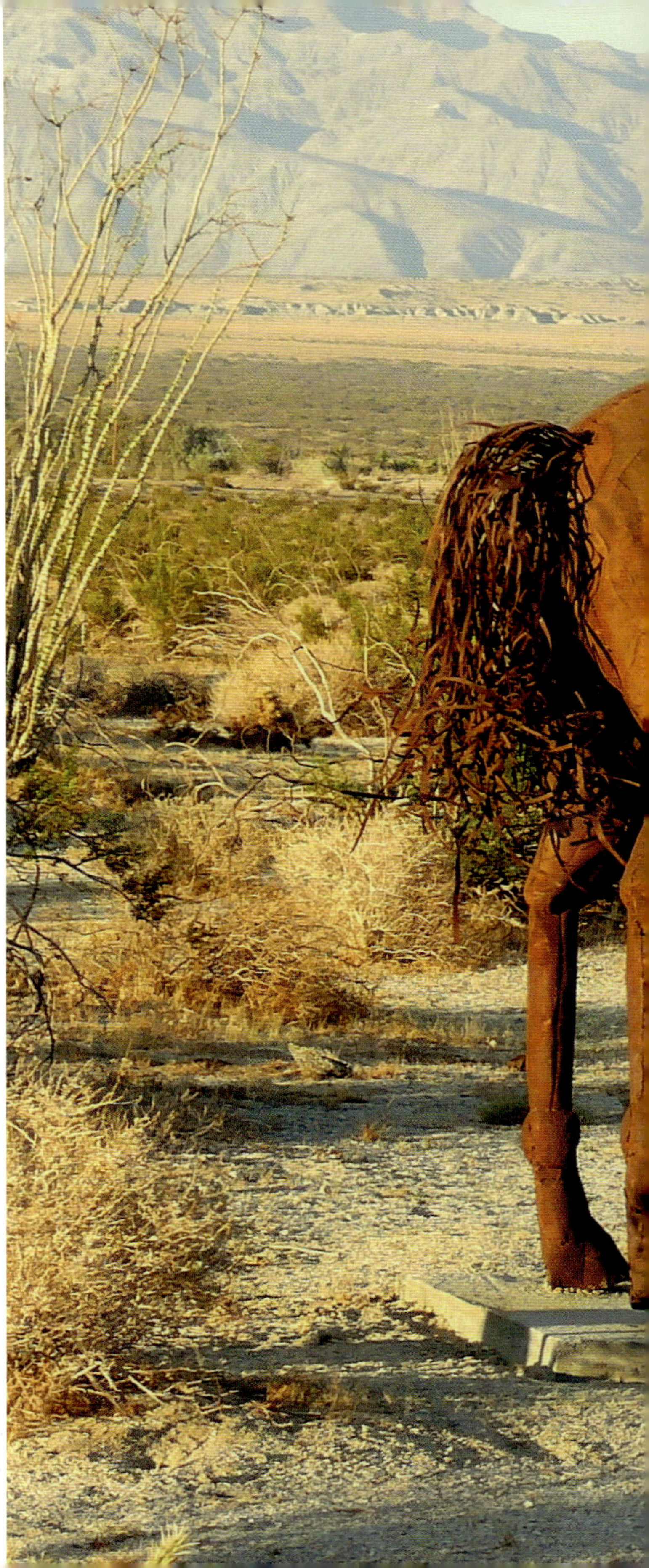

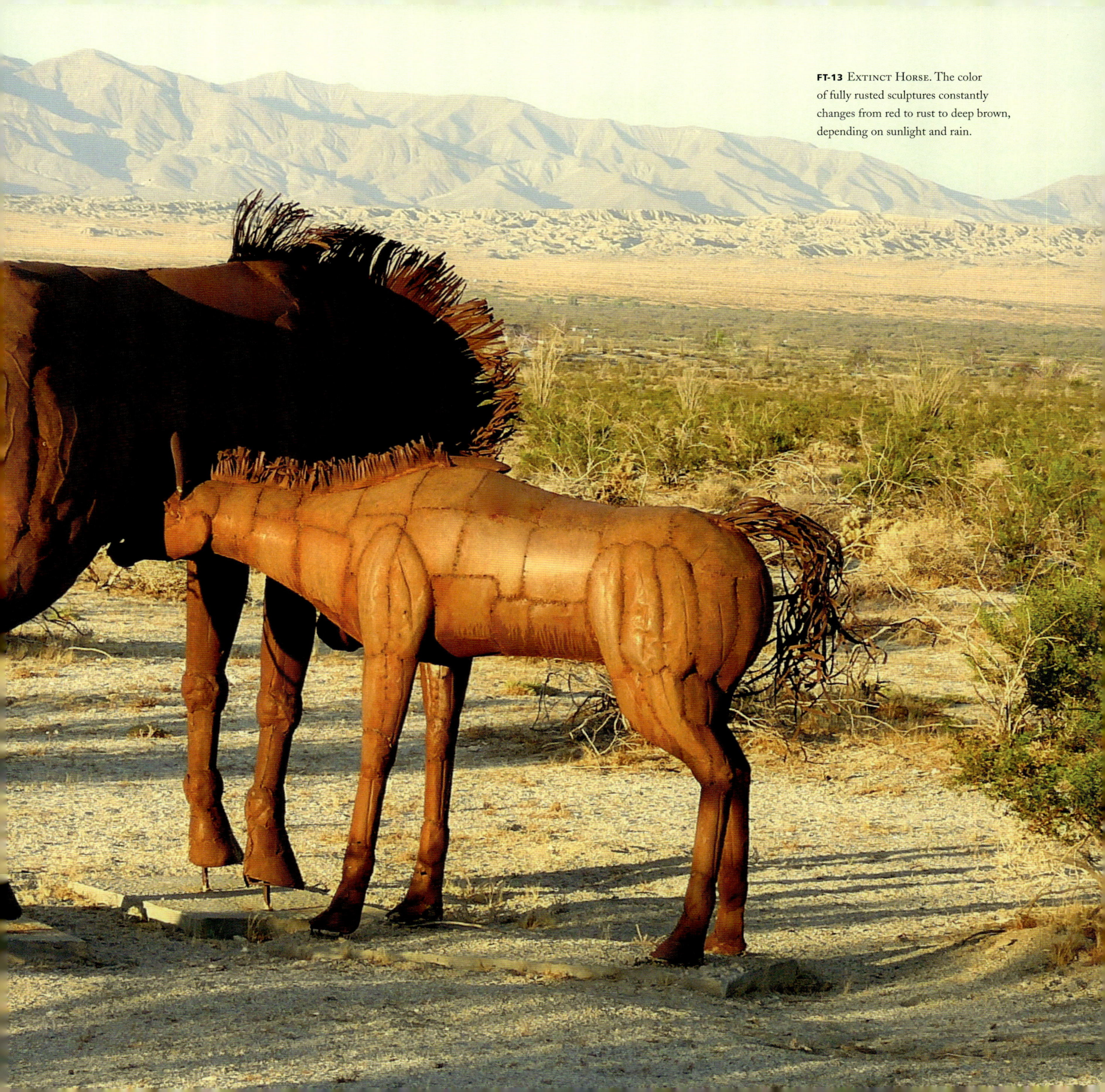

FT-13 Extinct Horse. The color of fully rusted sculptures constantly changes from red to rust to deep brown, depending on sunlight and rain.

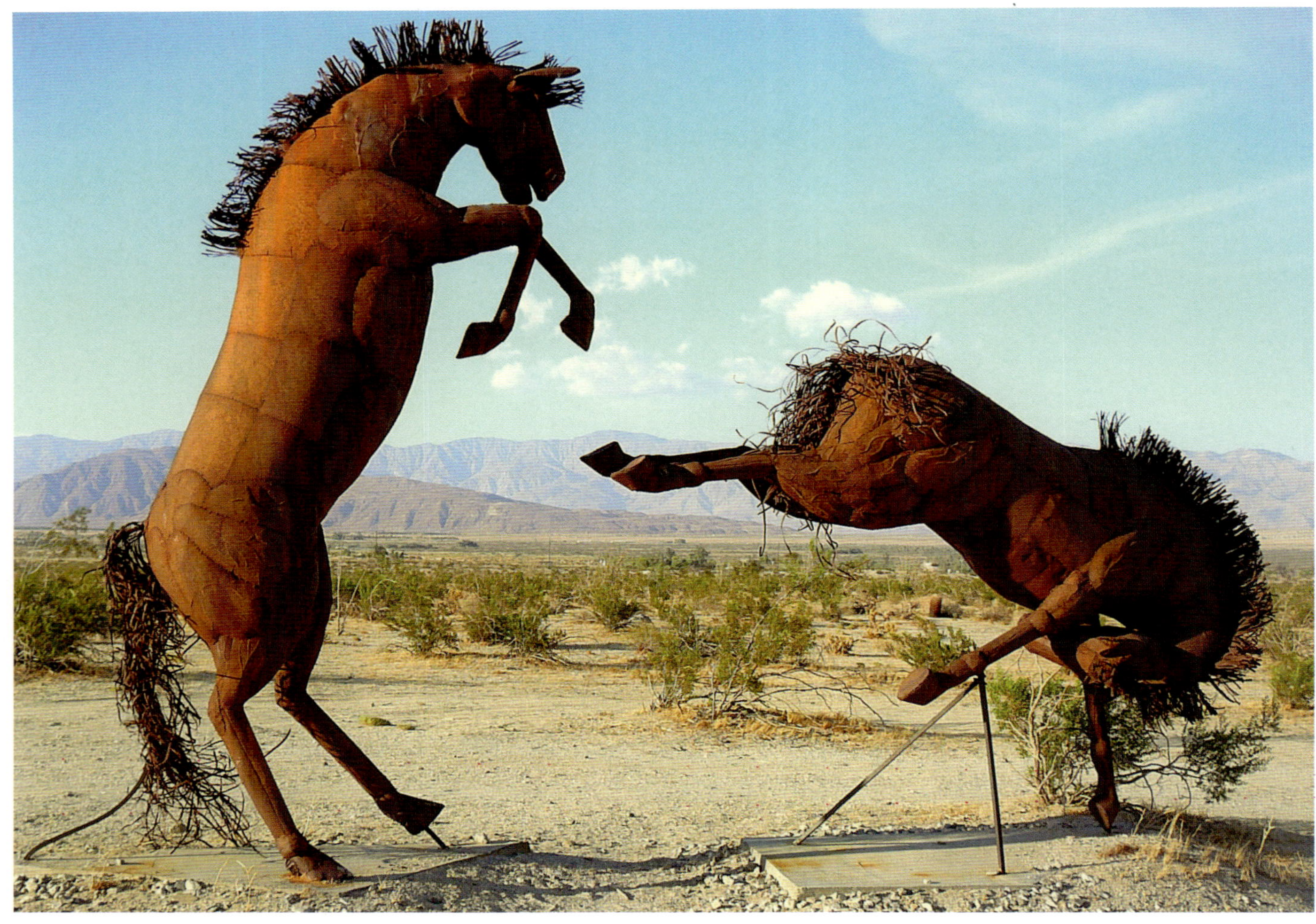

FT-13 Extinct Horse. The oldest equine fossil horses from the Anza-Borrego area are from the ancestors of *Equus.* They date to just over 4 million years ago and may possibly be the youngest occurrence of *Dinohippus* in North America.

Ricardo sold boots at ranches and weekend parties for about eight months. Then someone told him about the weekend cockfights or *peleas de gallos* held at private ranches in Arizona at Quartzsite, Cibola, and rural areas near the Colorado River. Selling at the cockfights proved to be a lot easier than the swap meets and Mexican fiestas. Cockfights remained legal in Arizona for many years after they were declared illegal in California. Arizona did not begin to crack down on cockfights until the late 1990s.

The cockfights ran all weekend, Friday through Sunday. Having Lianna with him opened many doors for Ricardo. The ranchers would provide a place for Ricardo and Lianna to stay so they could work the entire weekend.

The cockfights ran twenty-four hours a day with up to $1 million in bets placed. Ricardo sold boots to the big winners, and he usually also won when he made a bet. He had spent so much time watching the fights that he learned who had the best roosters, and he bet on those.

The weekends were a lot of fun. They weren't just about the cockfights themselves. These events were opportunities for everyone to get together, have a good time in one another's company, and relax. It brought together traditional Mexican sporting events and the camaraderie of fellow countrymen with the same cultural values.

In addition, Lianna always had friends to play with since families brought their children, and sometimes ranchers and *braceros* that came from Bakersfield or Coachella would give them fruits and vegetables to take home. They particularly liked attending the cockfights in the Blythe area because they were able to take breaks and play at the Colorado River.

As boot sales increased, Ricardo began making more trips with Lianna to El Paso, where they would stay with Ricardo's aunt. He would take day trips across the border to pick up the boots that Rodolfo had sent from Durango to their sister Estela's house in Cuidad Juárez while Lianna visited with her grandaunt. Some days Ricardo would make

FT-13 Extinct Horse. The nine Sky Art sculptures of the extinct horse on the north side of S-3 are in various poses as they may have appeared during the Pleistocene in Anza-Borrego.

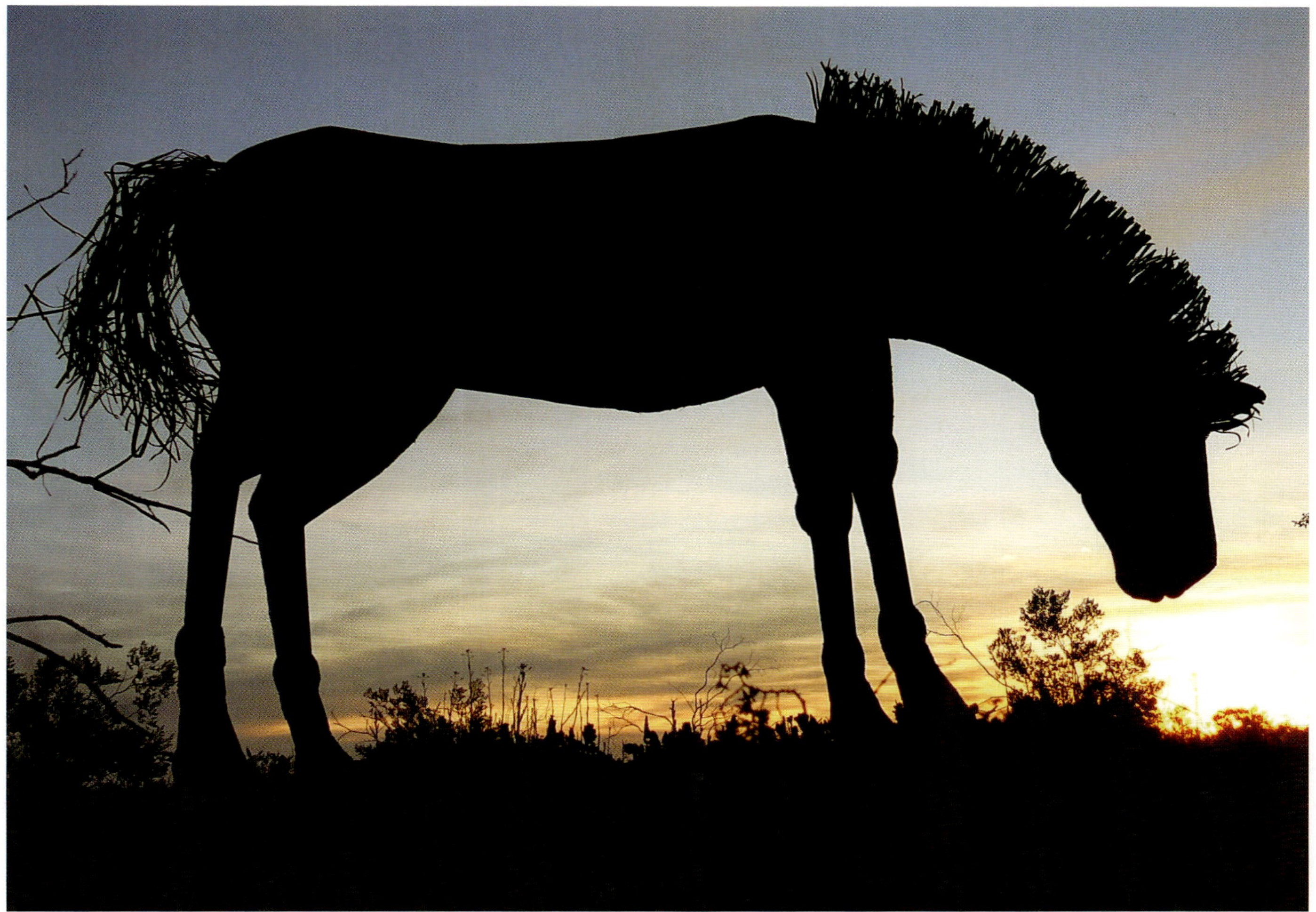

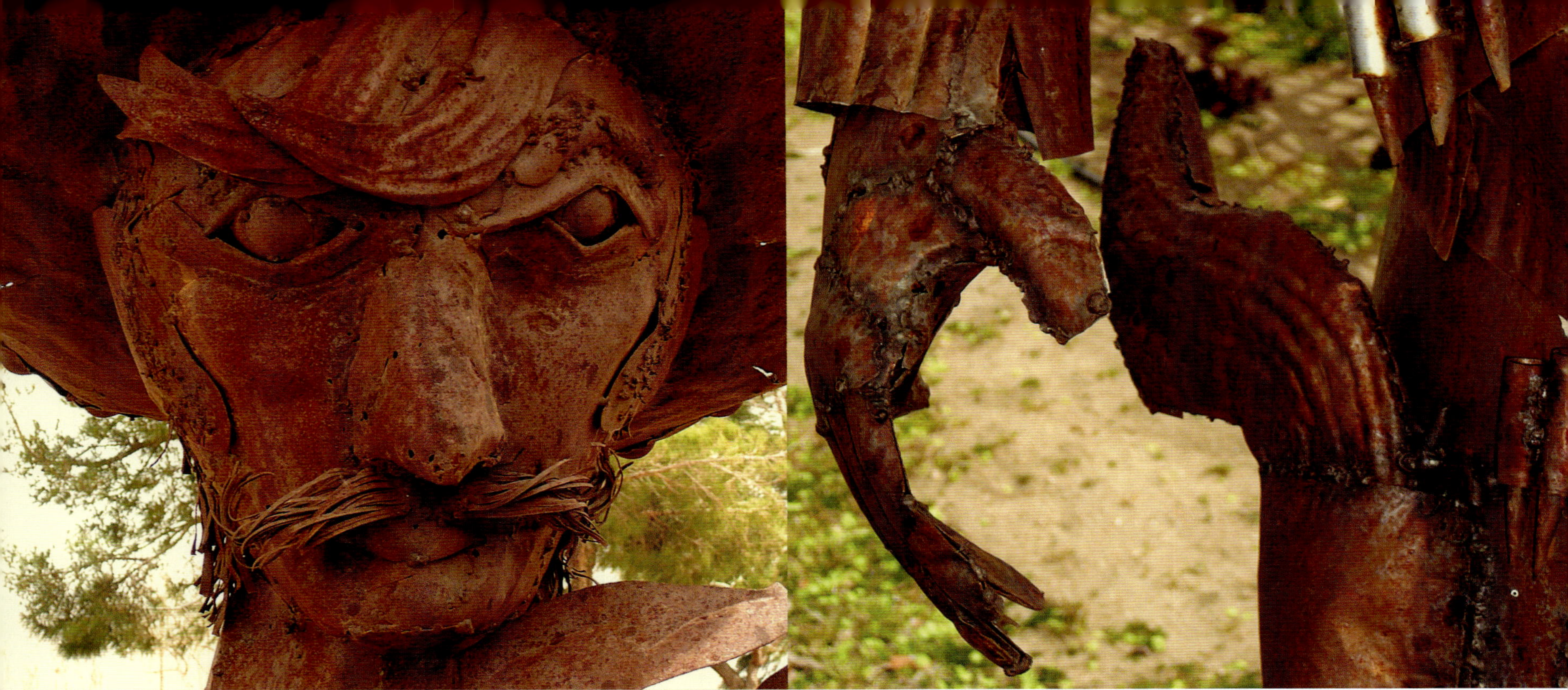

SCULPTURES AT RANCHO LOS ALAMOS

The owner of Rancho Los Alamos is Ricardo's countryman from Durango, Mexico. Several of Ricardo's sculptures are found at the racetrack including Pancho Villa–like *pistoleros* and several horses. The sculptures found here are among Ricardo's earliest works.

three or four trips, each time crossing the border with twenty pairs of boots, always the same color. He did this because it was legal to bring twenty pairs of boots into the United States without paying customs, if the boots were used for a musical band. He was careful to cross in a different line each time so that he would not have the same border guard twice.

Once a border guard asked Ricardo, "So what are you going to do with all of those boots?" Ricardo quickly responded, "They're for my mariachi band." The guard responded with, "No kidding?" Then he looked Ricardo directly in the eye and asked, "So what do you play?" Ricardo flashed one of his winsome smiles and said, "A guitar!" The guard waved him through the crossing. He was always grateful that he was never asked to play because he doesn't know how.

After he had collected a couple hundred pairs of boots, he and Lianna would drive back to California.

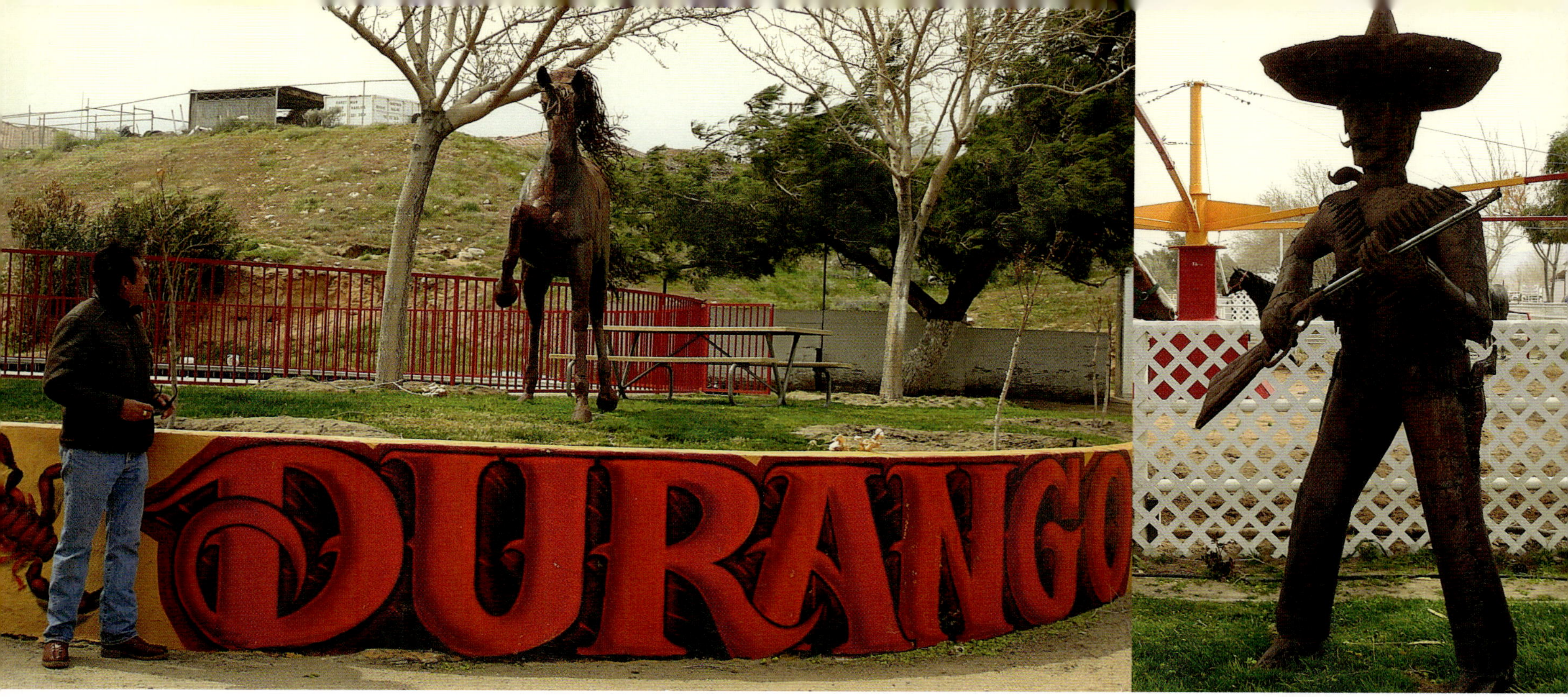

Always the entrepreneur, Ricardo got the idea to sell raffle tickets at events, Mexican style. This is how it worked: To make it more interesting and tempting for the customers, he would have twenty-six tickets in each raffle. Each ticket was marked from 0 to 25 and placed in a bag. Those who wanted the chance to win a pair of boots would draw a ticket from the bag. If a number 5 was selected, for example, then the person who selected the ticket would give Ricardo $5 and keep his half of the ticket. Whoever selected 0 would not have to pay anything, and if someone selected 25, he had to give Ricardo $25. When all tickets were sold, a winning ticket was selected, and the winner could pick any pair of boots that he wanted.

Ricardo would make $325 on each raffle and would have up to five raffles a day. After he paid for his boots, he cleared about $1,000 per day in raffle sales.

Ricardo, the businessman, seemed to attract opportunity. At one of the cockfights, a man wearing ostrich skin boots came up to Ricardo and told him he could make more money if he sold fancy boots like the pair he was wearing. He generously told Ricardo to get in touch with the supplier, a boot maker in Bakersfield, California, named José Luís.

Ricardo contacted José Luís, struck a deal, and began selling fancy boots made from the skin of eels, alligators, ostriches, stingrays, and anteaters. Some sold for as much as $800 a pair. When José Luís introduced him to a friend who made jackets from the skins of exotic animals, Ricardo expanded his wares to include wallets and jackets. His sales soared and, equally important, he no longer had to worry about getting boots across the border.

It was while working at the weekend cockfights that Ricardo learned about the private racetracks or *carriles* owned

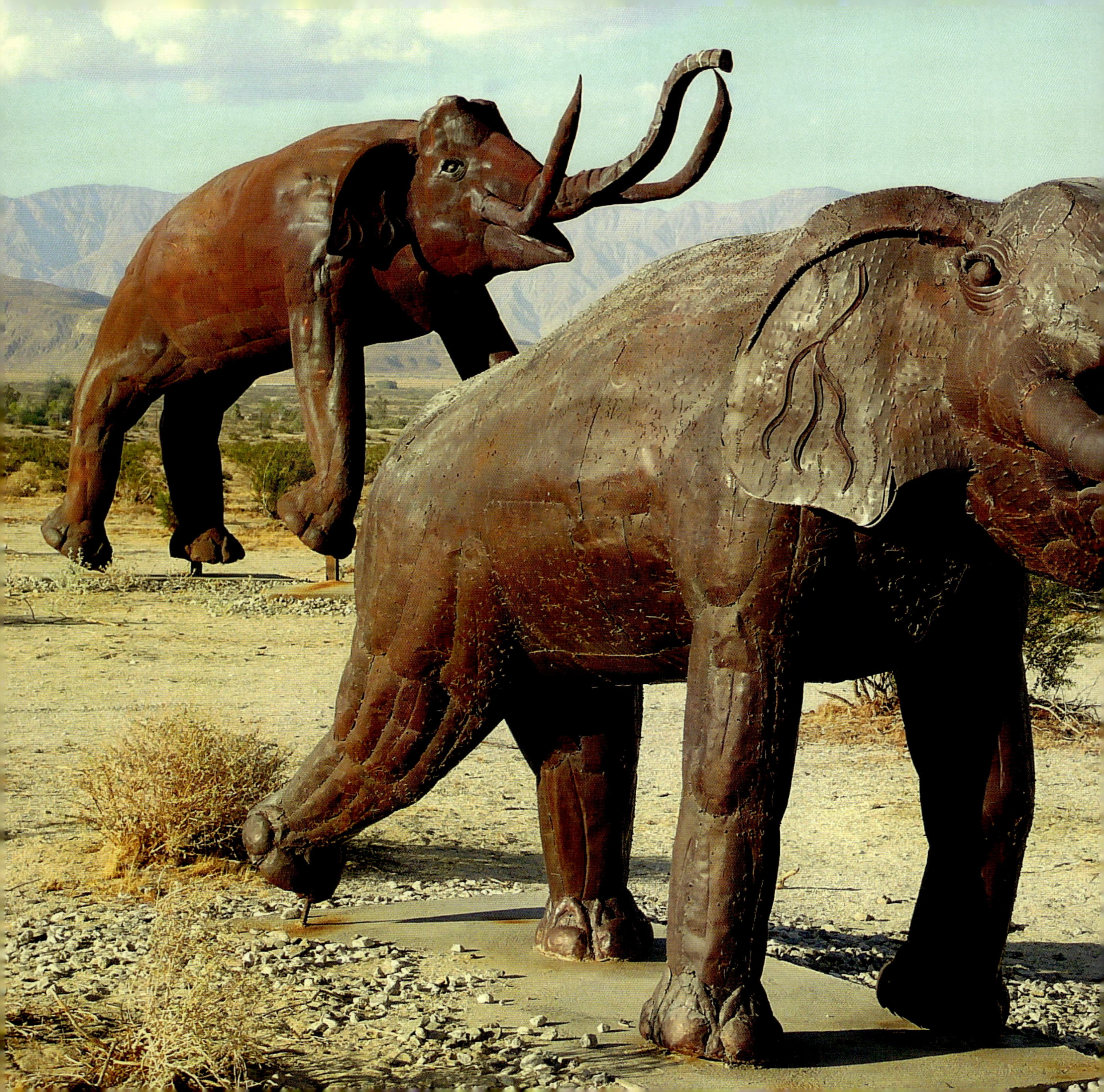

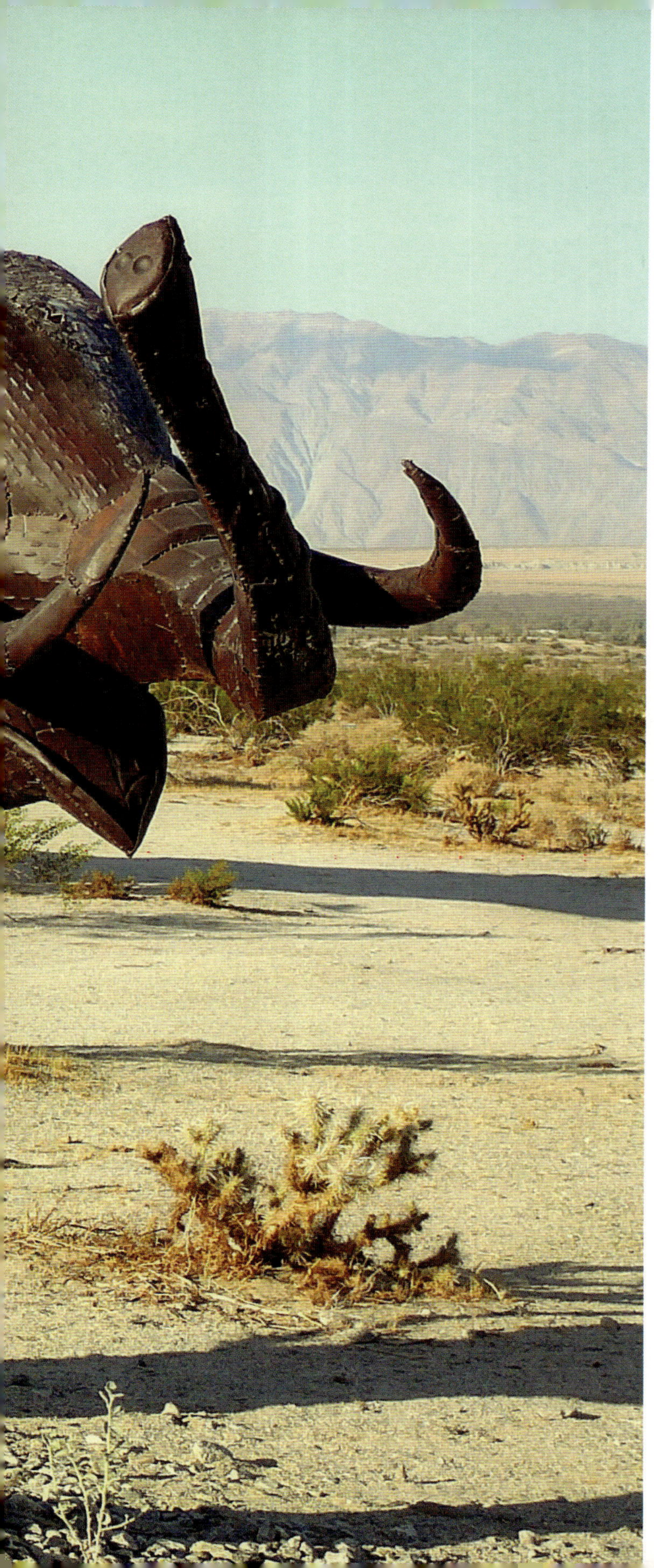

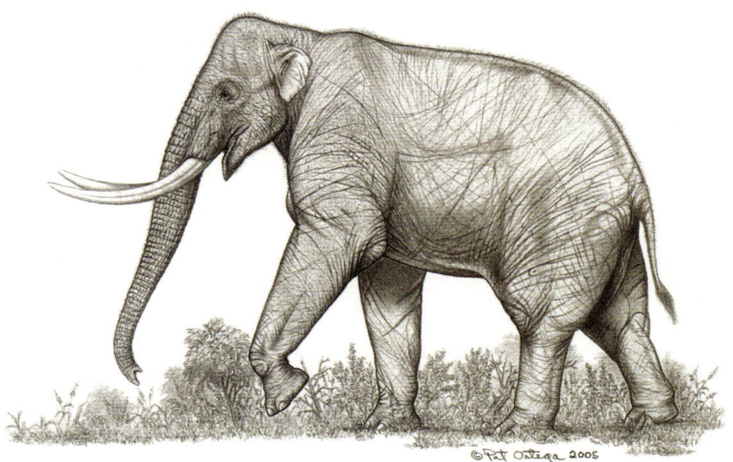

FT-14 Mammoth. The Columbian mammoth (*Mammuthus columbi*), as depicted by Pat Ortega (*above*), was the largest North American elephant. Fossil remains in the Anza-Borrego area date from 1.1 million years ago.

by Mexican ranchers. He was invited to attend one race and met the track owner, who gave him permission to sell his boots there. As he met other track owners, he always asked for permission to sell boots and was always given the go-ahead. He was never charged to set up his stand, so to thank the various owners, he always gifted them with a pair of boots.

There was an entire network of private racetracks in Riverside, San Bernardino, Imperial, and Kern counties in California as well as in Arizona, Nevada, and New Mexico. The races were held one day each weekend and, because families attended, Ricardo was able to take Lianna with him. Sometimes they worked a race on Saturday at one ranch and then drove to another ranch on Sunday.

Ricardo and Lianna's favorite track was Rancho Los Alamos' *Carril de Campeones* in Hesperia, California. It had a training center and therefore was a legal track open to the public with a paid admission fee. It was owned by Felisnando Monarrez, a *paisano* of Ricardo's from Durango, who fondly recalled the weekends when Ricardo sold tickets. "He was so fast running up and down the stands, constantly moving. He really worked hard selling those raffle tickets. Everyone bought his tickets. And he really enjoyed himself."

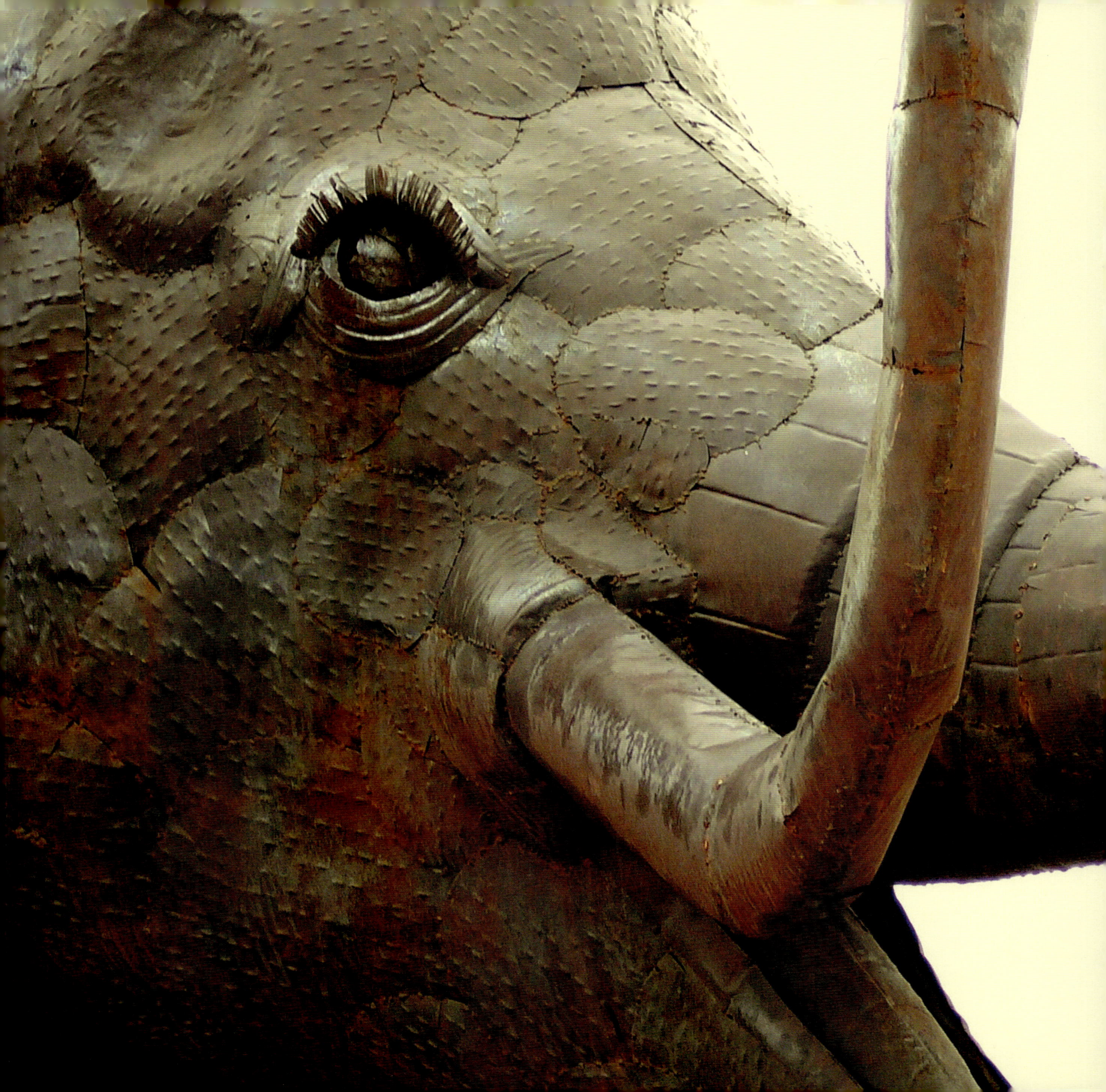

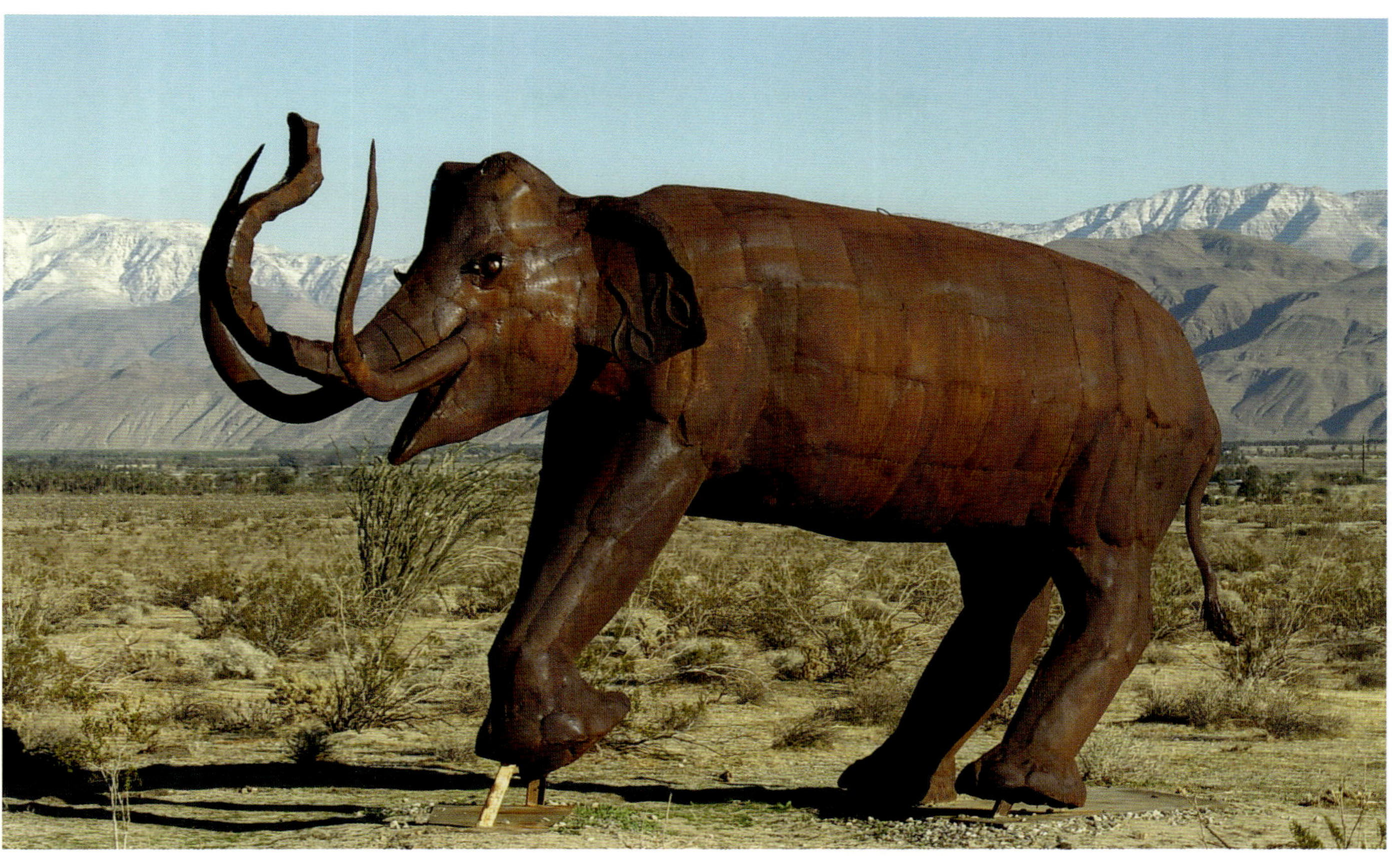

FT-14 Mammoth. *Left*: The skin texture of the head is made by hammering impressions onto small sheet metal cutouts before they are welded onto the frame. Ricardo has perfected the technique of making lifelike eyes with long eyelashes. *Above*: The backdrop of snow on the Santa Rosas transports viewers to an ice age when mammoths roamed this land.

The weekend events were also an opportunity to learn about people. One weekend, Ricardo was selling raffle tickets in the stands, while seven-year-old Lianna was watching over the boots. A man handed Lianna his ticket and told her that he had won the raffle. She believed him and let him select a pair of boots. When Ricardo returned, Lianna learned that she had been tricked. She was furious and insisted that they comb the area looking for the *cabrón*. They never found him. But it was a lesson about life for Lianna.

Overall, Ricardo had good experiences while selling boots at the various events. He developed some close friendships and earned the respect of both ranch owners and customers.

The house that Ricardo and Lianna lived in was across the street from a shopping center. He put a sign out on the front lawn and soon was selling boots out of his home. The combined income from sales at the cockfights and racetracks and from his home allowed Ricardo and Lianna to make regular trips to Mexico to visit the family.

Ricardo and his daughter came home one afternoon and immediately saw that something was wrong. There were empty boxes everywhere. Someone had broken in and stolen all of Ricardo's boots. He was livid and decided he needed to find another place to live as soon as possible—a place that would be safe for Lianna and his business.

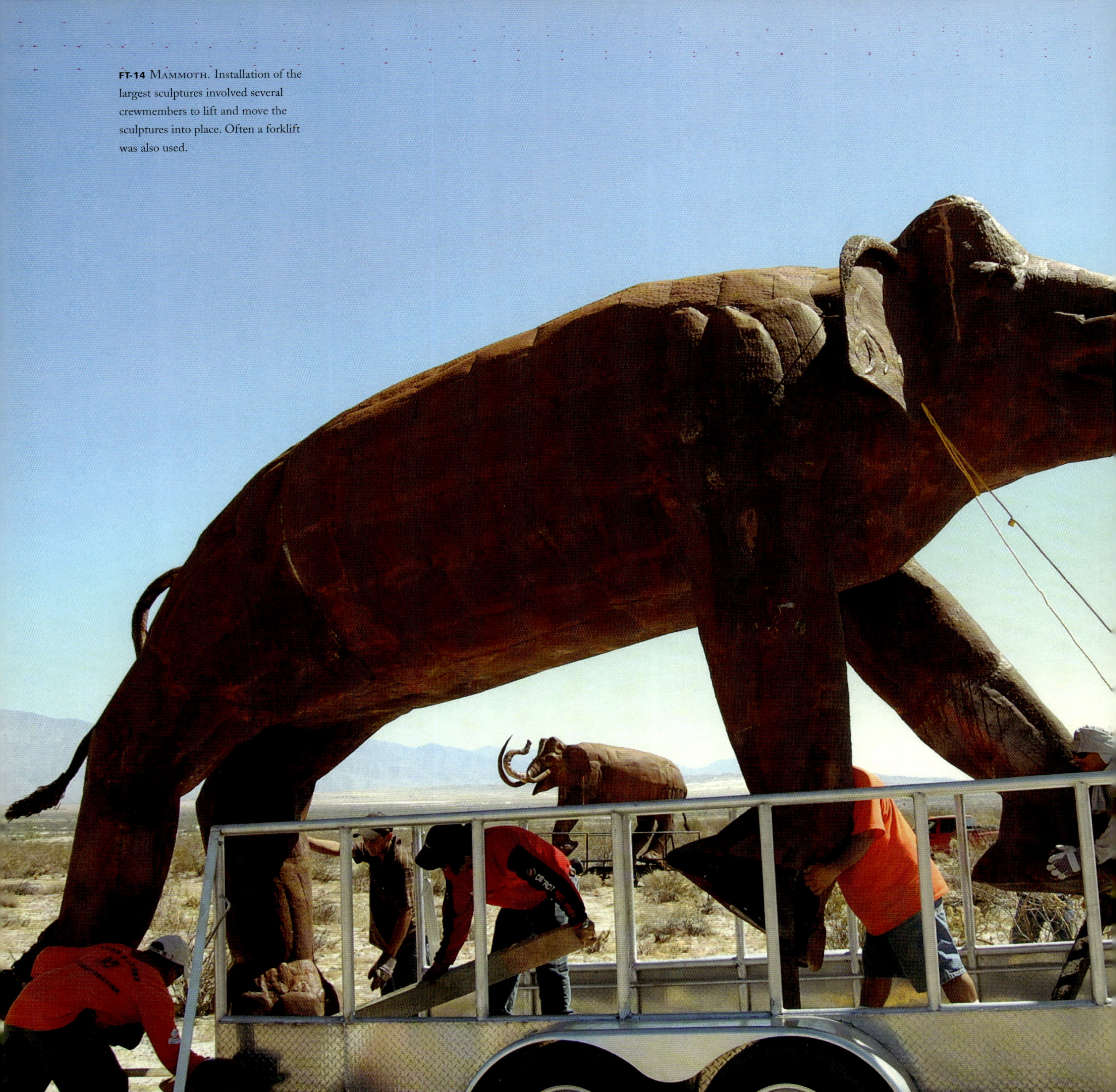

FT-14 Mammoth. Installation of the largest sculptures involved several crewmembers to lift and move the sculptures into place. Often a forklift was also used.

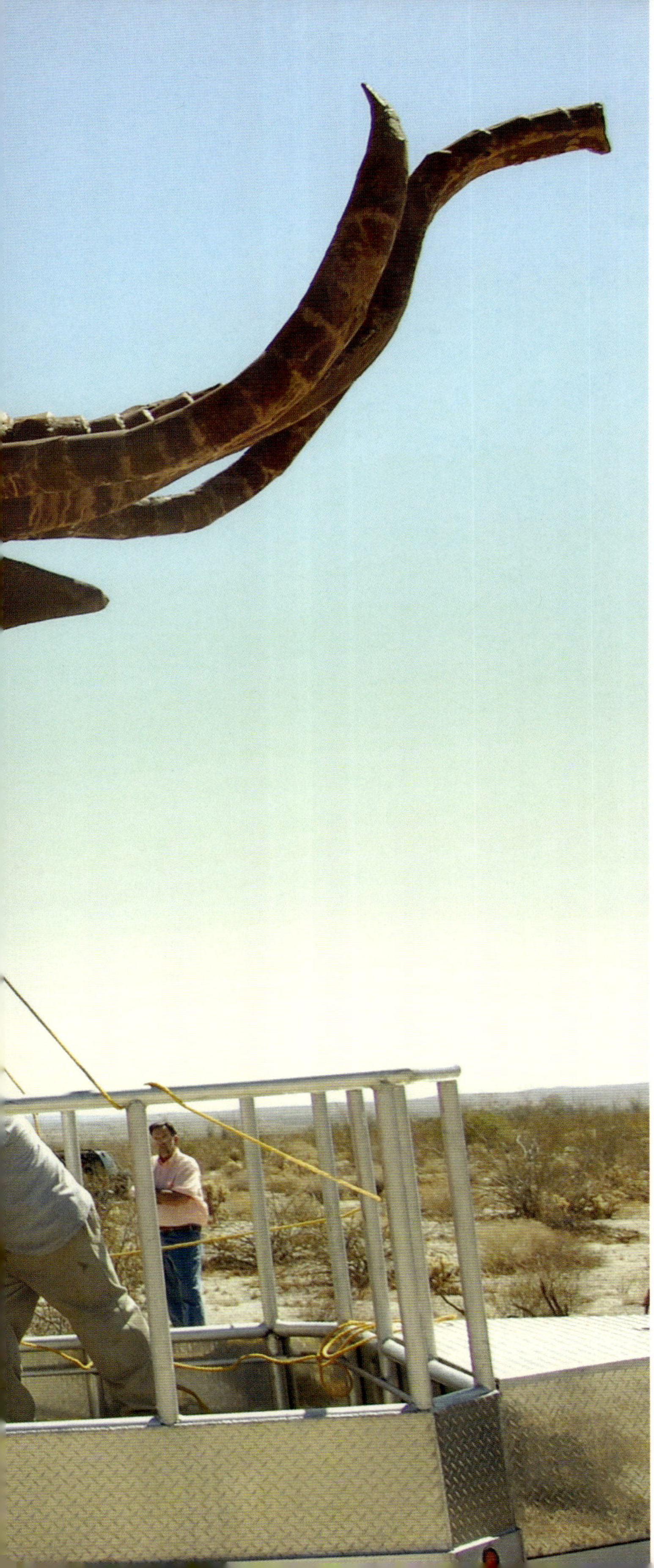

At about this same time, Ricardo got a speeding ticket and had to go to traffic school. The instructor, Joe Olaiz, asked Ricardo what he did for a living. Ricardo told him he sold cowboy boots. During their conversation he mentioned that he had just been robbed and that he was looking for a new place to live.

It so happened that Joe had commercial property along Interstate 215 that he wanted to rent. The property had an old dilapidated trailer that was uninhabitable, but the location could be perfect for a large sign advertising Ricardo's boot sales. Since the property had been vacant for a long time, Joe offered it to Ricardo at a very low price. Intrigued, Ricardo went to look at the property. It was located on the outskirts of Perris, California, in a very rural area surrounded by open fields and trees. He liked what he saw, so he and Joe struck a deal.

Ricardo called friends from his construction days, and soon they were all working to make the trailer livable, adding a new roof, walls, floors, carpeting, plumbing fixtures, electrical lines, and paint. After a couple of weeks, Ricardo and Lianna had a new home.

They added a large sign by the freeway advertising cowboy boots and leather goods, and it began to draw customers. So many people came over to his house that Joe and some of the surrounding neighbors thought that perhaps Ricardo was dealing drugs. But he was just selling boots or throwing a party for his many friends.

Sometimes people came by who really wanted to buy Ricardo's boots but did not have the money to pay for them. They would ask, "Ricardo, would you trade for your boots?" And Ricardo would always answer, "Sure. What do you have to trade?" He traded for tools, a bicycle, jobs, anything that was useful. He still trades today for his sculptures. One day a man came in asking Ricardo if he would trade a pair of his boots for a welding machine. Ricardo said, "Yeah, sure. I'll take it." He traded the boots for the machine and put it aside, never thinking he would ever use it.

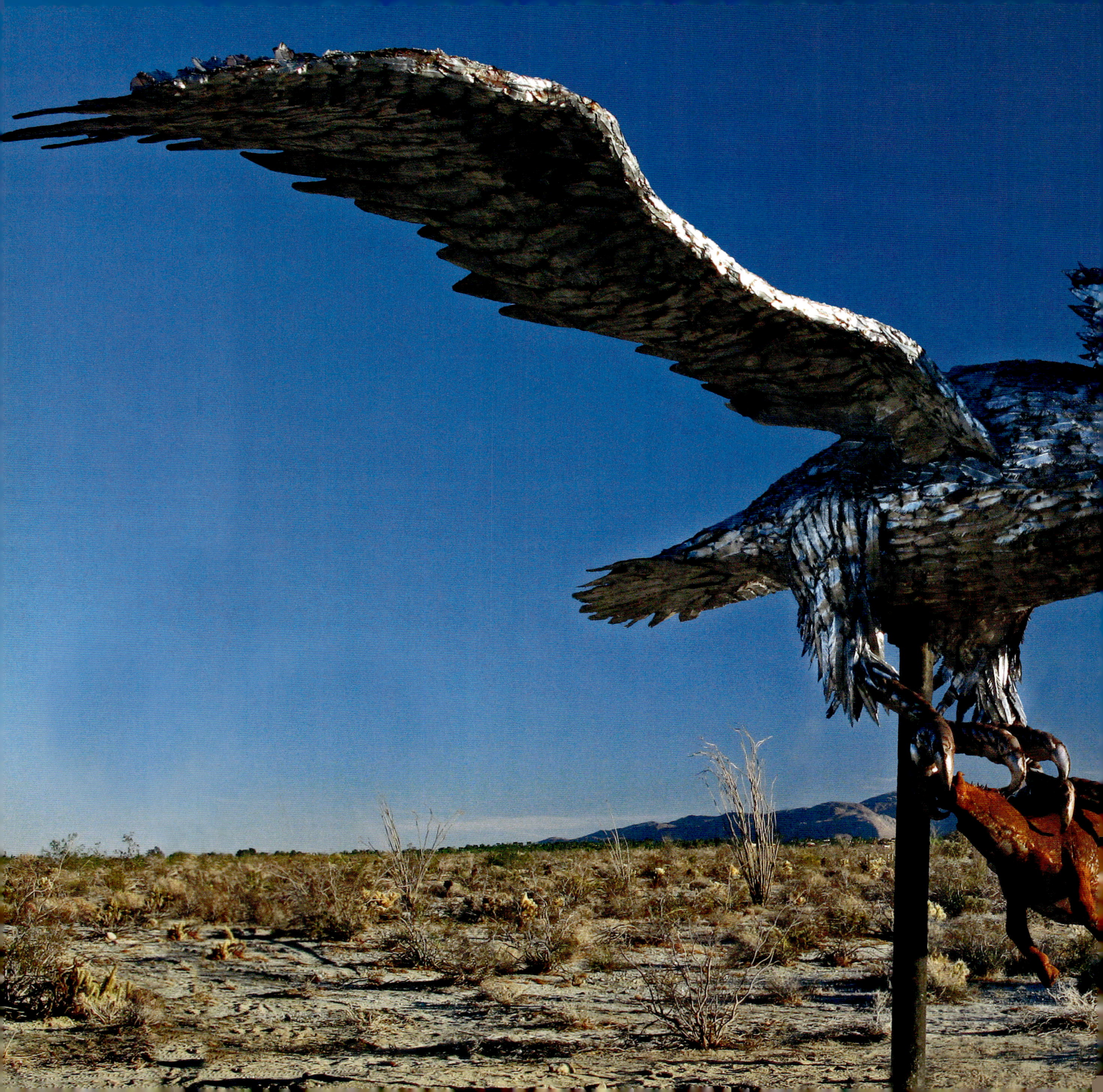

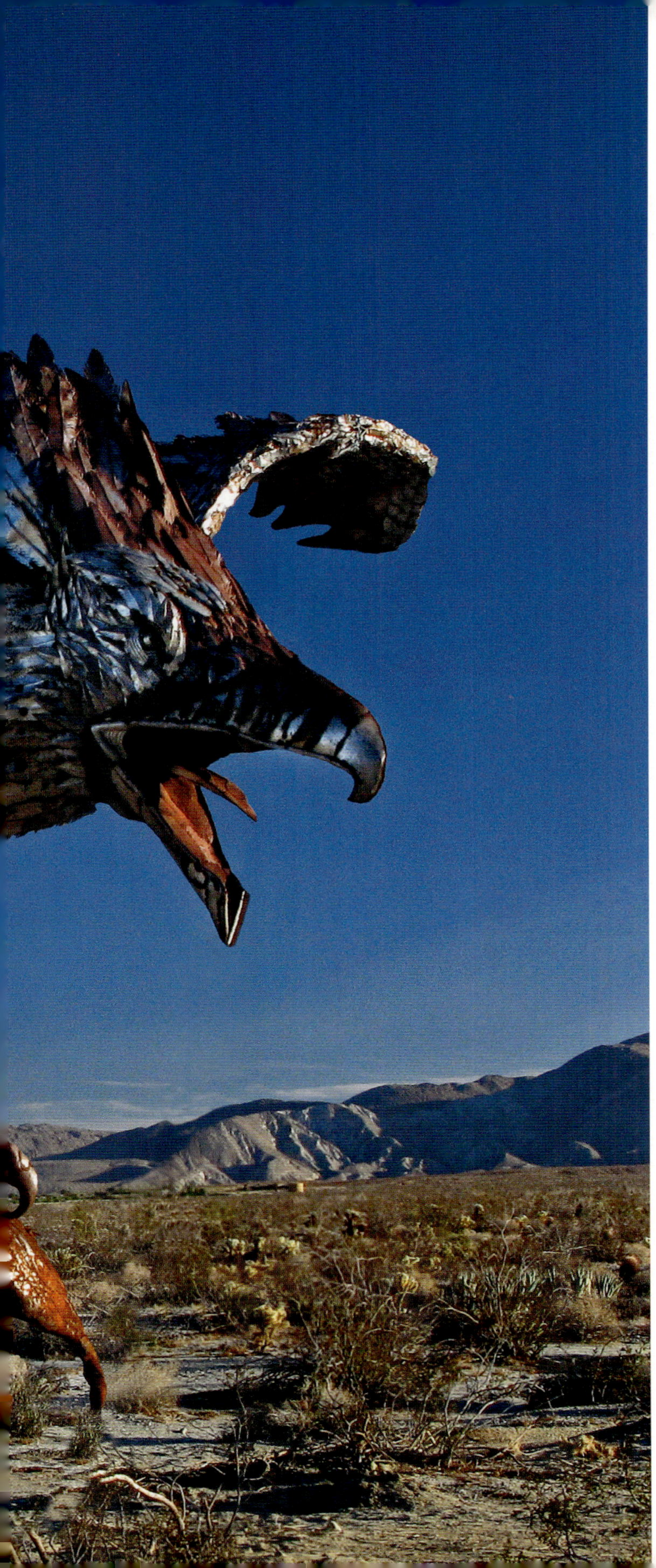

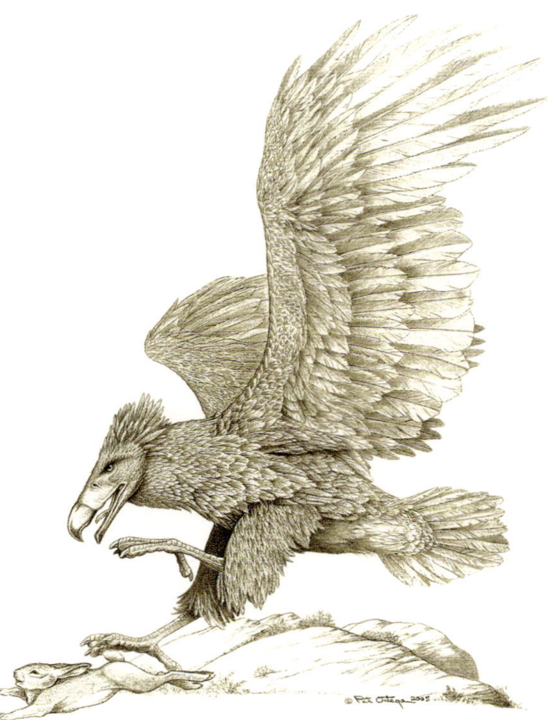

FT-15 Aiolornis with Prey. The *Aiolornis* sculpture has a wingspan of thirty feet, which is double the size of the actual bird that existed. The photograph to the left shows the *Aiolornis* as it would look without wing supports.

Several months later he took a look at the welding machine and began to wonder what he could do with it. He tried making a few crude things from some scrap and sheet metal he had purchased—a donkey, a car, a little dog, a small dinosaur.

The first piece took weeks to make. He cut the metal pieces for the sculpture with a pair of metal cutters, used a hammer to pound some shape into the pieces, and then welded them together. All of the first sculptures were about two or three feet high and were very awkward and boxy.

Sometimes the pieces made him angry because they did not come out right, and he would break them and stomp on them, yelling, "This is a piece of crap!" He got so frustrated because he knew he could make them better. When he calmed down he'd try again, because he felt that if he kept trying, he could eventually create something worthwhile. Those that he didn't break, he gave away to friends.

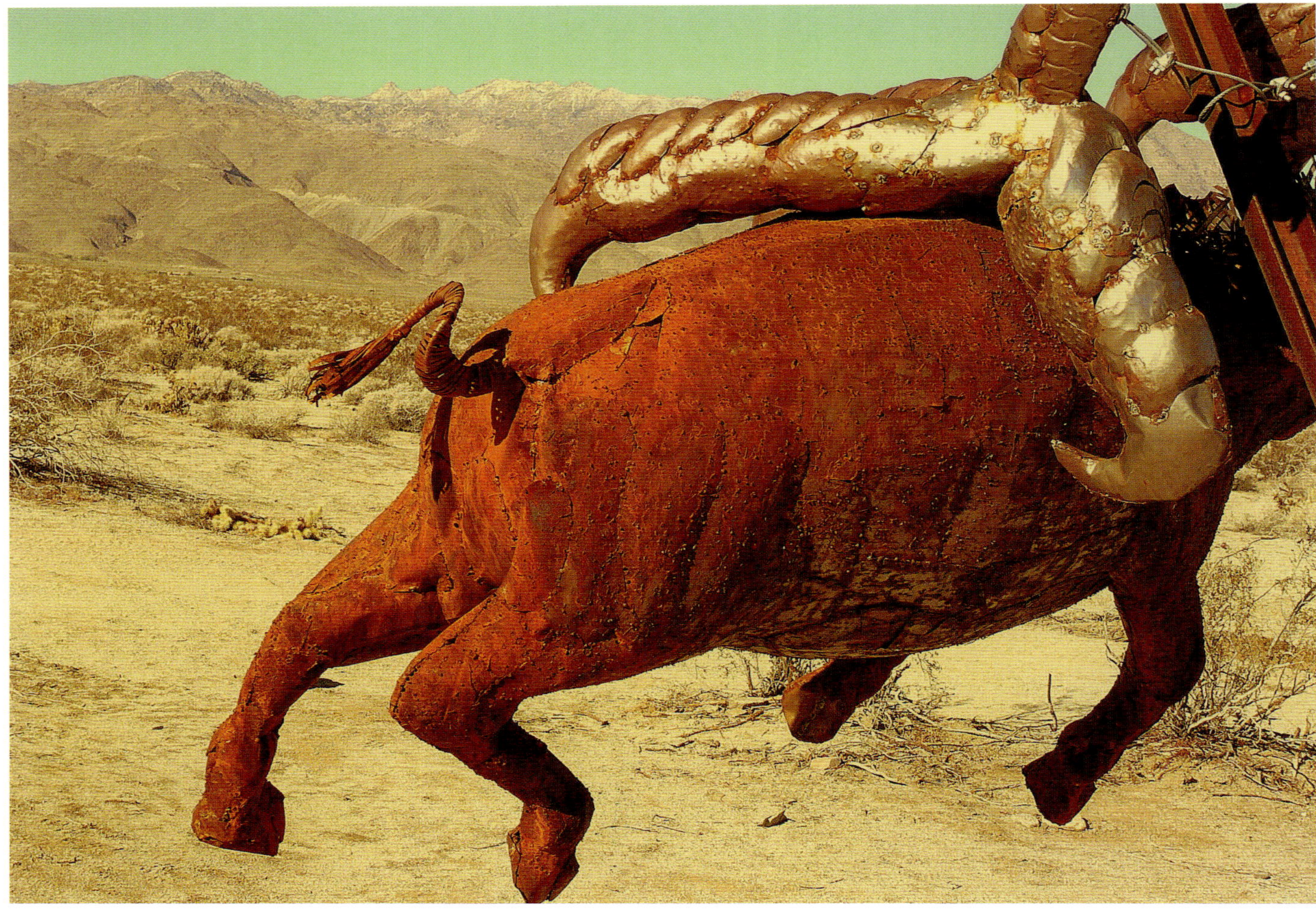

FT-15 AIOLORNIS WITH PREY (DETAIL). *Above:* The *Aiolornis* holds a peccary (*Platygonus* sp.) in its talons. *Right:* Compare the detail in this sculpture with the illustration on page 97. Because the sculpture is so large, supports were added to stabilize it.

At this point in his life Ricardo was a successful businessman with steady sales of exotic boots and leather goods. His business, Venus Boots, had been in operation since 1995 and was running smoothly. He now had the leisure to pursue his new hobby, metalwork. He had a beautiful young daughter who was the delight of his life. He was very proud of her, especially when she brought home good grades or did well in sporting events after school. They had close connections to the family in Durango, where they visited each Christmas and during summer vacation when school was out. Family members also visited Ricardo regularly in the United States.

Ricardo and his daughter enjoyed doing things together—they camped, hiked, ran through the hills, sold boots on the weekends, visited with friends, and went to the movies or watched them at home. Among their favorite movies to rent were *Jurassic Park* and *The Lost World: Jurassic Park*. They were both looking forward to the 2001 summer blockbuster release of *Jurassic Park 3.*

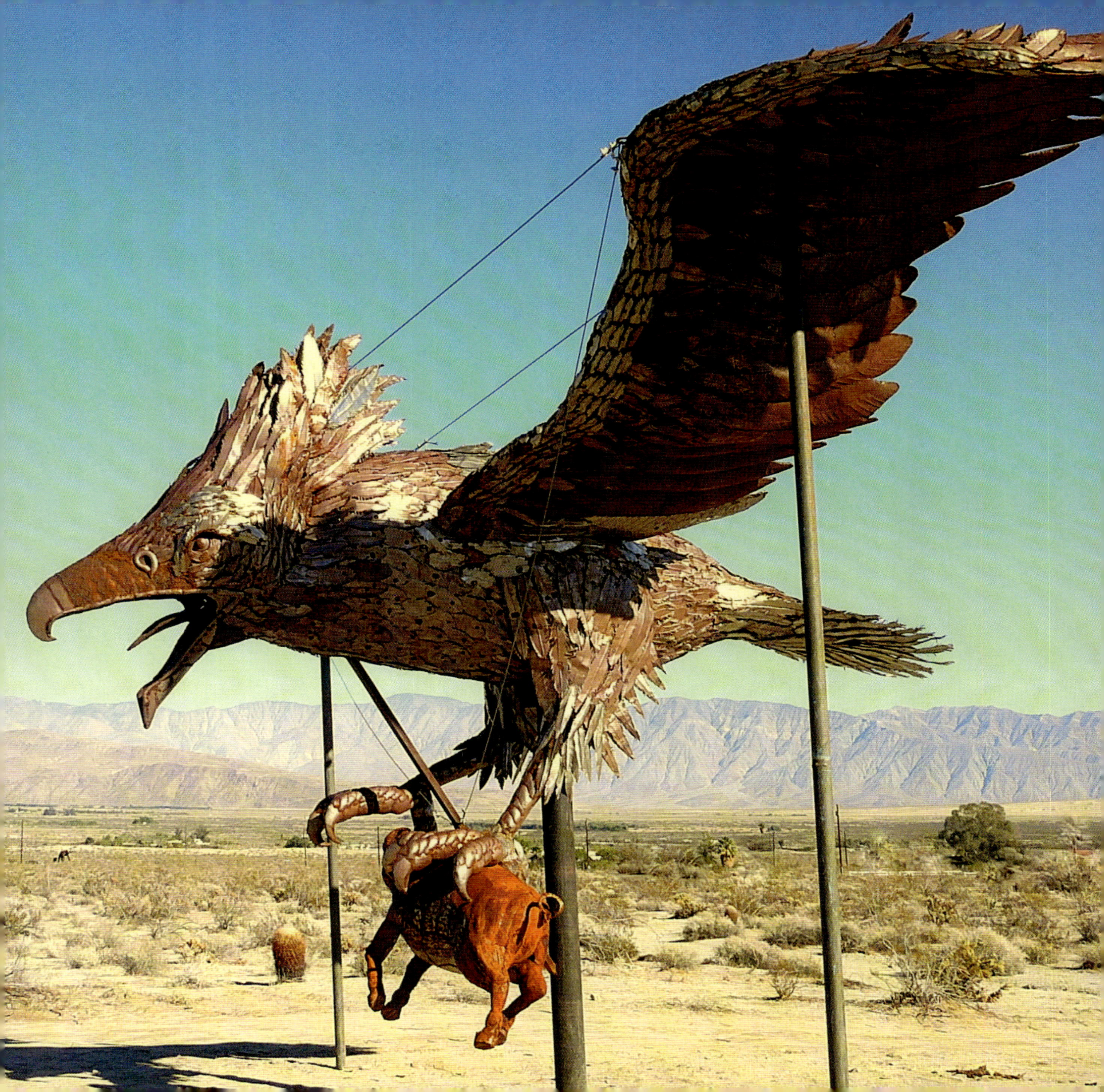

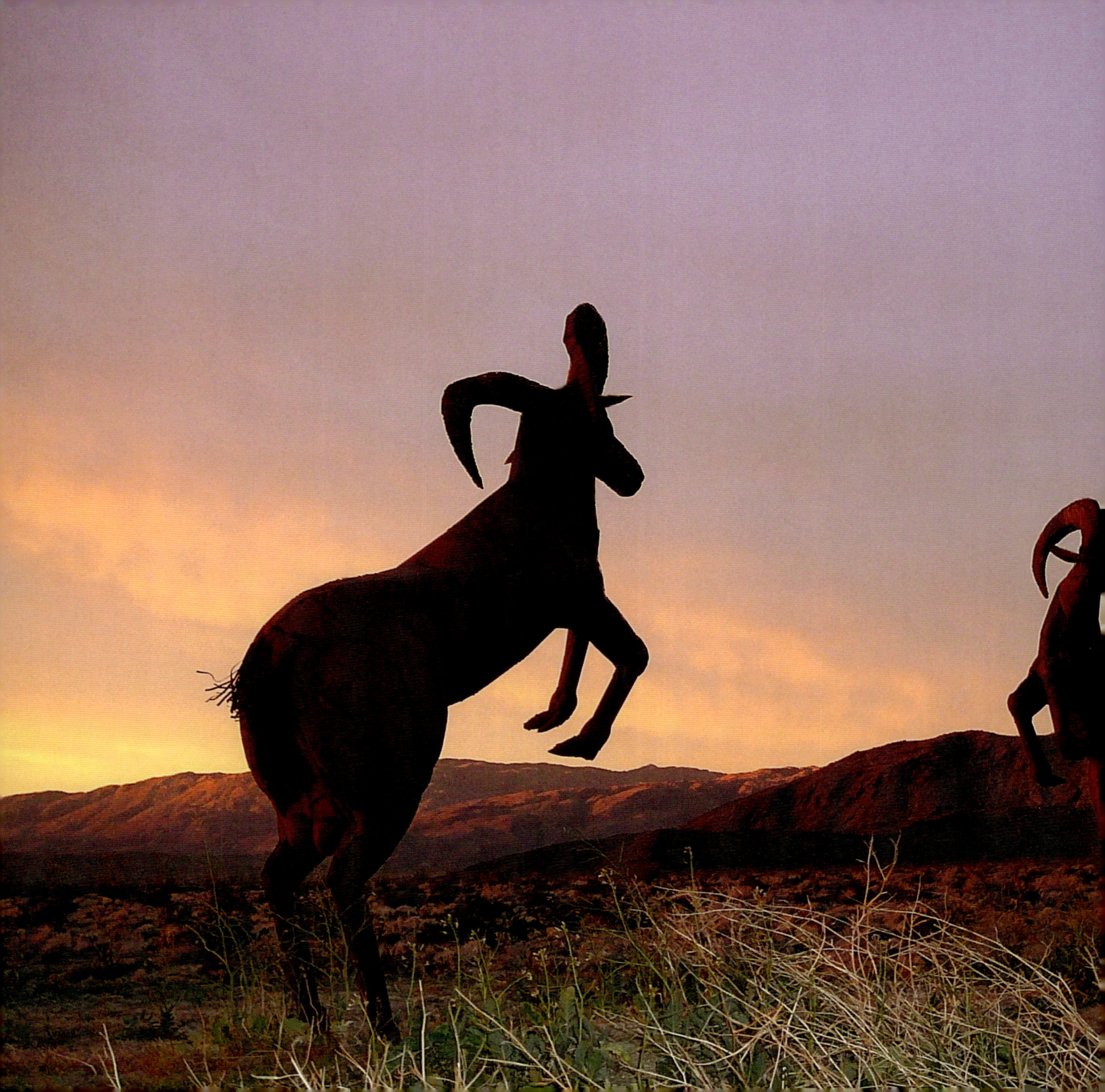

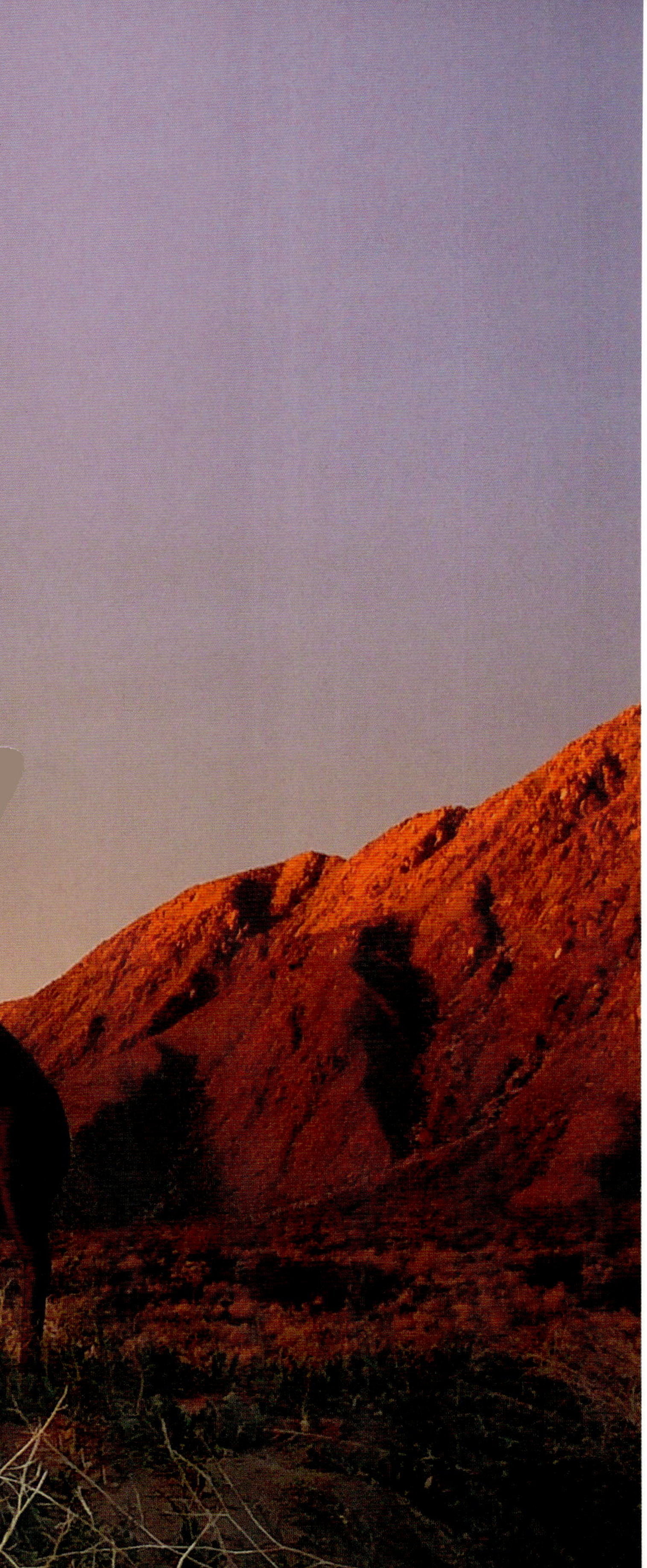

CHAPTER 4

THE ACCIDENTAL ARTIST

Ricardo has always wanted to make a difference, to be better, to be someone, to be noticed. He wants people to have fun—to enjoy themselves, and especially to enjoy something that he has done or created. He is also very self-aware and conscious of the role that chance has played and continues to play in his life.

The accident at the construction site forced Ricardo to explore other sources of income. His brother Rodolfo's connections to the Durango shoe factory opened another opportunity, as did the chance connection to the boot maker in Bakersfield. The birth of his daughter, Lianna, gave him a new focus and purpose in life. The chance encounter with the landlord of the Perris freeway frontage road at traffic school was critical for the growth of the future business. His boot business was a weekend enterprise that provided the capital to develop a new business, and most importantly, it gave him the time to learn and develop new skills. The timing of the *Jurassic Park* films coincided with his daughter's interest in dinosaurs, stimulated by her classroom studies. And so, the stage was set for something magical to happen when Ricardo traded a pair of boots for the welding machine, and Lianna asked him to make her a life-size dinosaur.

HN-1 Peninsular Bighorn Sheep. Anza-Borrego Desert State Park is a refuge for the Peninsular bighorn sheep (*Ovis Canadensis cremnobates*). The special relationship to the park is seen in its name—*borrego* is Spanish for lamb or sheep.

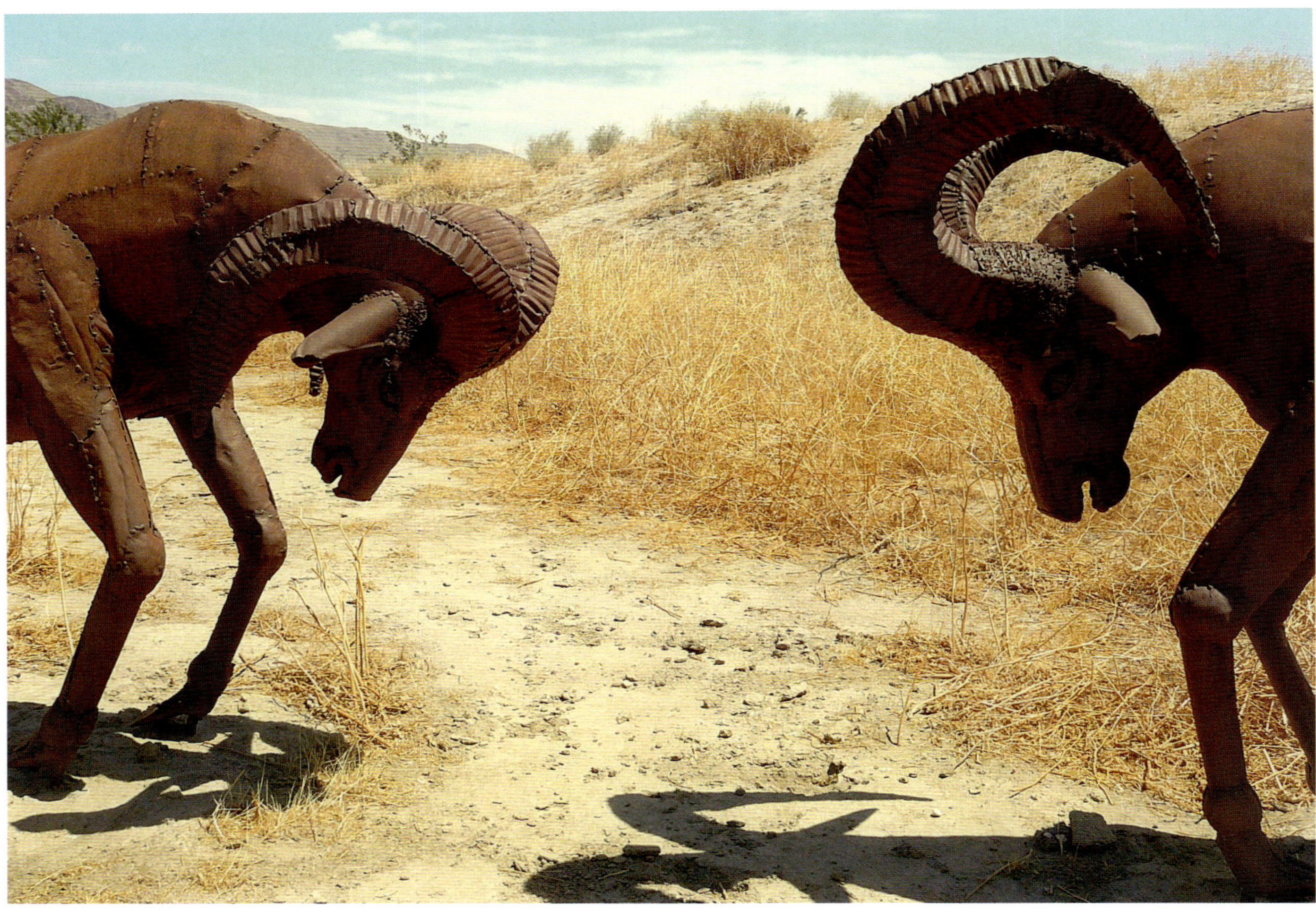

HN-1 Peninsular Bighorn Sheep. Bighorn rams will challenge each other for dominance and the right to mate with ewes in fall by head butting. They will charge each other at speeds of up to twenty miles per hour. The horns can weigh up to thirty pounds.

Lianna recalled that she always liked action movies and that *Jurassic Park* "caught her eyes." She had been studying dinosaurs and why they became extinct in school. After she and her father went to see *Jurassic Park 3,* she became obsessed with dinosaurs. "When Dad asked me what I wanted for Christmas, I think he expected me to say a doll. Instead, I told my dad what I really wanted was a life-size *T. rex* dinosaur. I really didn't think he could do that, but he always tried to do things I wanted." She added, "It was the first time I ever asked him to make something for me."

Ricardo decided that if his daughter wanted a full-size dinosaur, he was somehow going to make her one. The problem was how to start making one with the new welding machine that he had just begun to learn how to use.

While he was figuring out how to construct a dinosaur for Lianna, Ricardo saw a pickup truck at his landlord's house by the freeway. In the back of the pickup was a very crude, flat-looking eight-foot-tall dinosaur made out of sheet metal and recycled materials. One man was in the truck and another was talking to Joe, his landlord.

Ricardo went up to the truck and asked the man what they were doing with the sculpture. He was told that they were asking his landlord if he wanted to buy it and put it by the freeway to resell. Ricardo asked the man, who introduced himself as Porfirio, how much he was asking for the sculpture. Porfirio told him $700. Ricardo then asked him how long it had taken to build, and Porfirio said about two weeks.

Ricardo stared in disbelief and asked them how they made any money doing this because the $700 divided between two men less the cost of materials and gas driving around trying to sell the sculpture left very little. Porfirio said they made enough to eat. Ricardo told him that what they were doing was not a business because they were not making any money.

When Porfirio's partner, Rodolfo, came back to the pickup with no sale, Ricardo made them a proposition. If they would work for Ricardo and help him build the dinosaur for his daughter, he would pay for the tools and metal, provide room and board, and help them sell their dinosaur.

HN-1 Peninsular Bighorn Sheep. Ewes give birth to lambs in spring. Within a day lambs can climb as well as their mothers. The lifespan of bighorn sheep is about ten years.

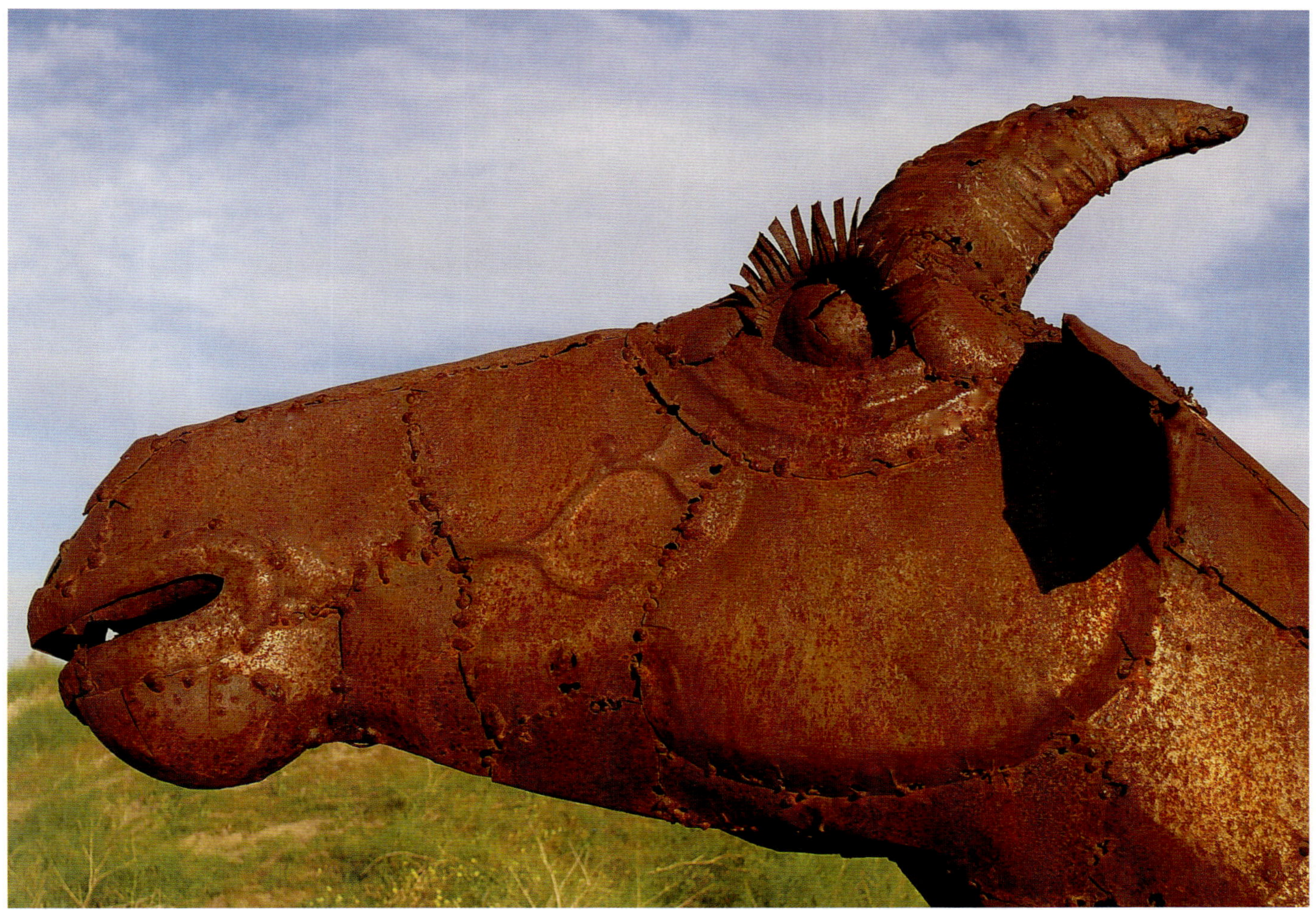

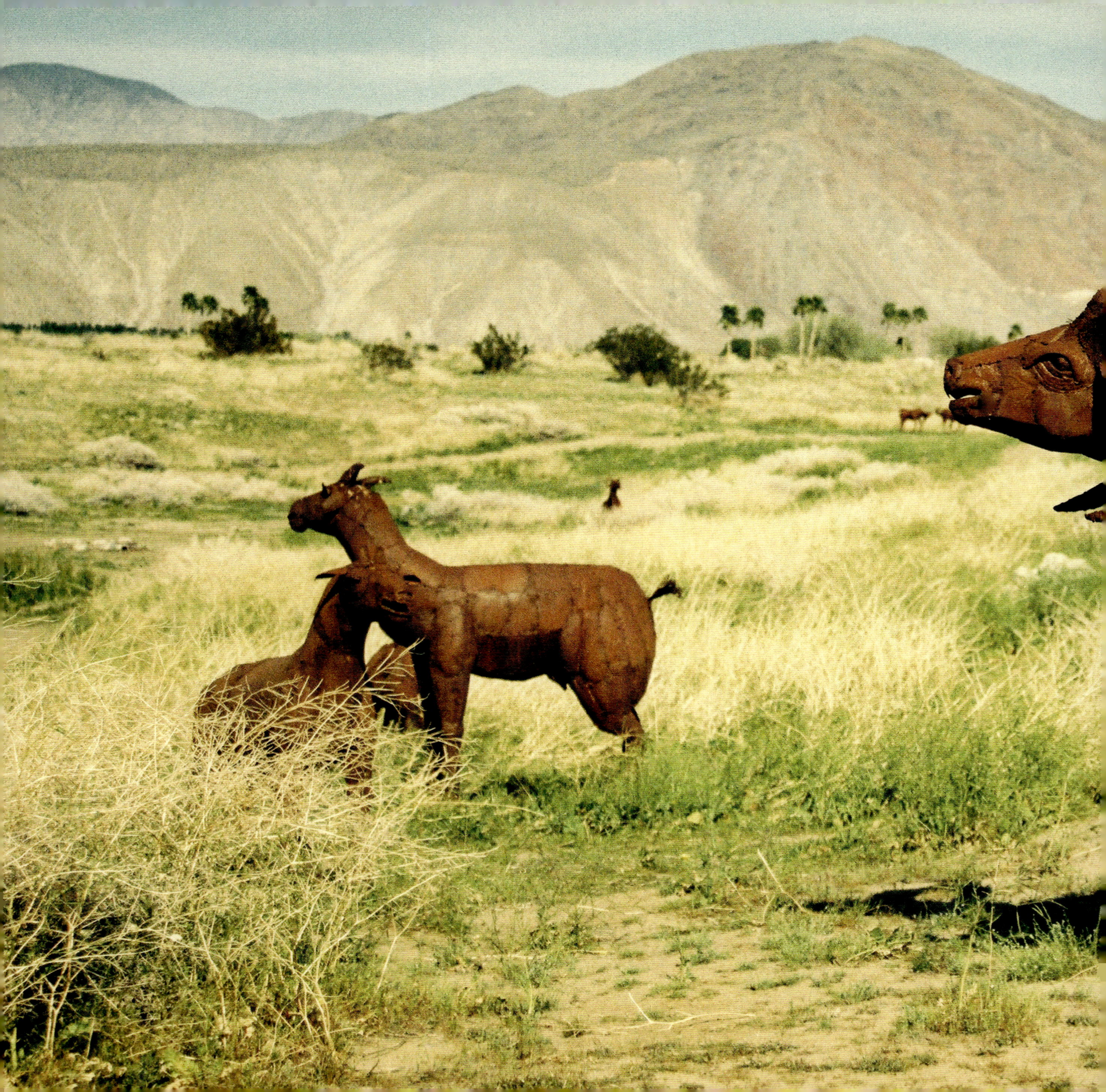

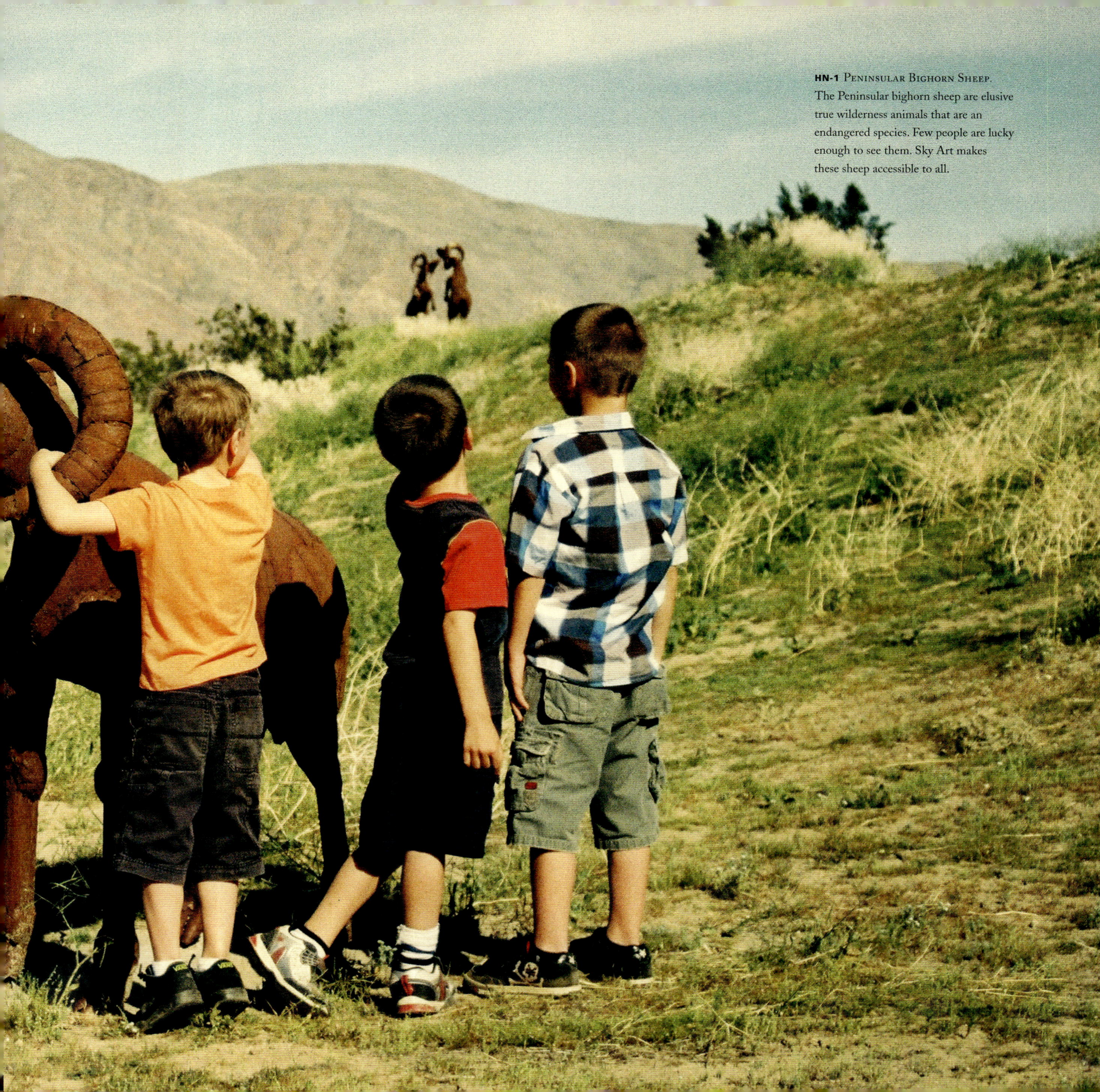

HN-1 Peninsular Bighorn Sheep. The Peninsular bighorn sheep are elusive true wilderness animals that are an endangered species. Few people are lucky enough to see them. Sky Art makes these sheep accessible to all.

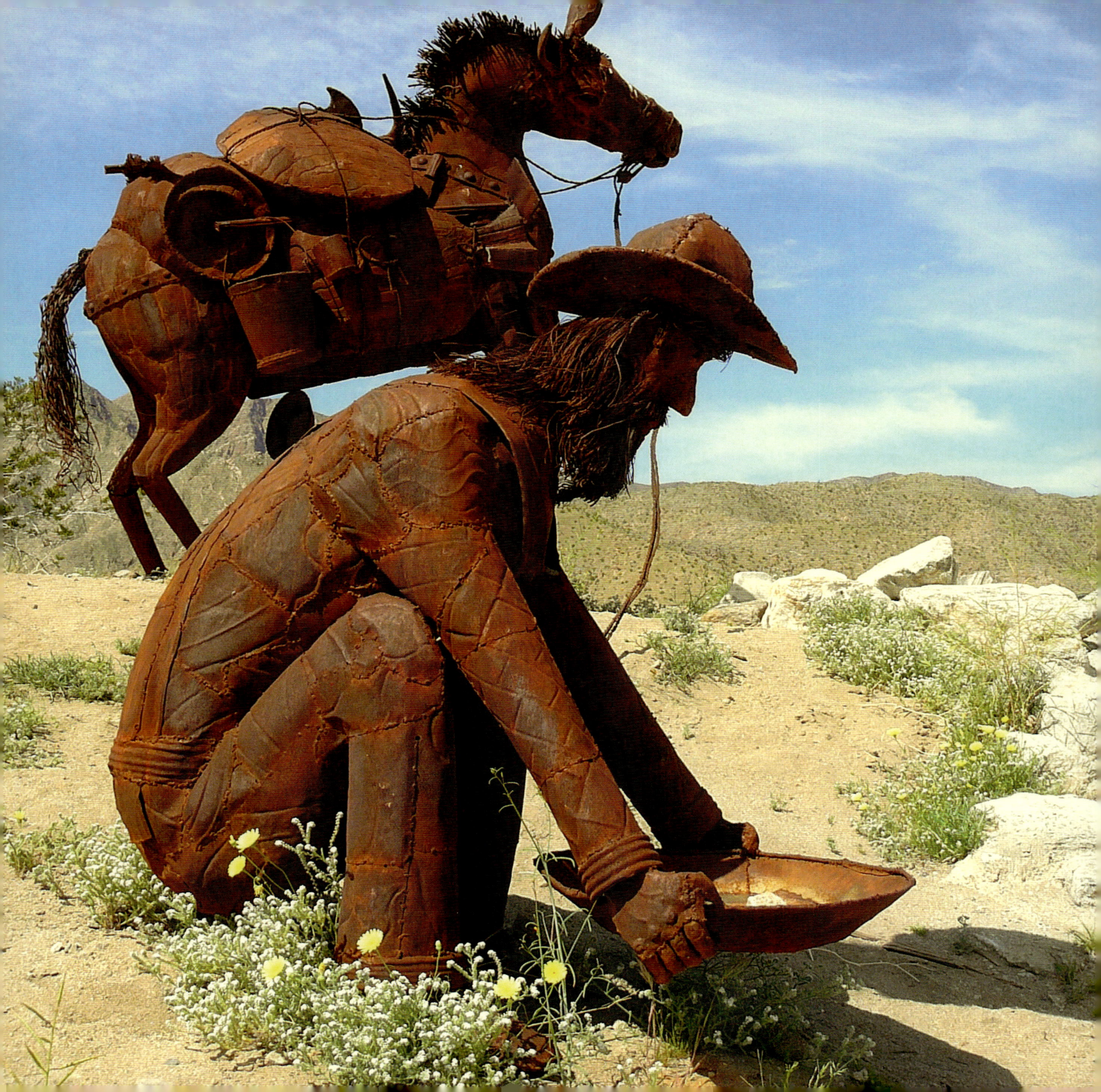

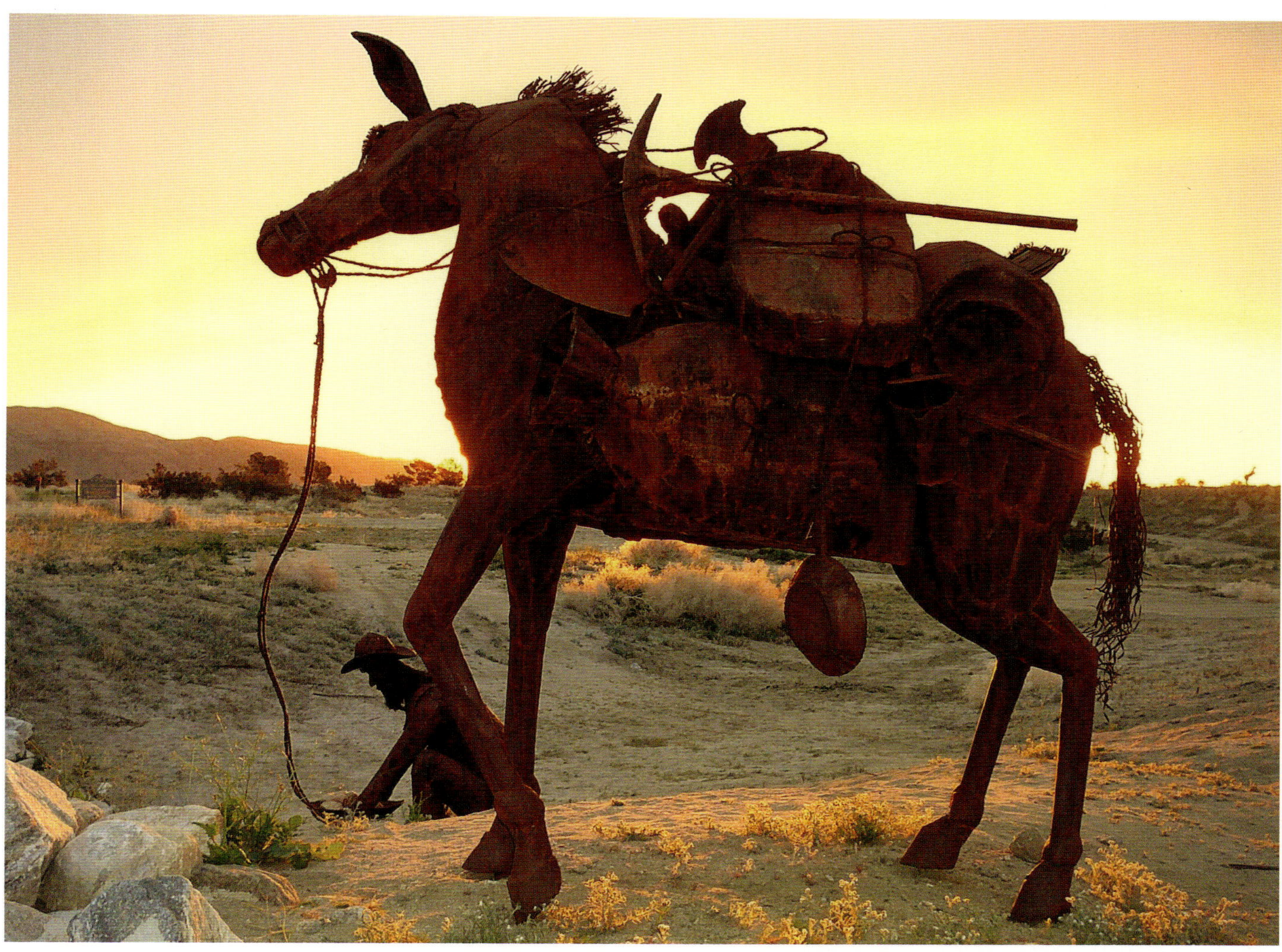

HN-2 Gold Miner and His Mule. The siren call of gold brought many miners to California who crossed the desert en route to the gold fields. After gold was discovered in nearby Julian, miners extended their search into desert areas, bringing their mules or donkeys loaded with equipment.

Up until then, Porfirio had been designing and building the pieces, and Rodolfo had assisted Porfirio by cutting metal and shaping it. Rodolfo also handled the money and customers because Porfirio only spoke Spanish.

Rodolfo was not happy with Ricardo's offer because he was used to handling the money and keeping the larger portion for himself. Ricardo remained firm, and he and Porfirio struck a deal. Reluctantly, Rodolfo agreed, too. They began their new venture about two weeks later—almost six months after Ricardo and Lianna had seen *Jurassic Park 3.* Lianna was about to get her Christmas present.

The first thing they had to do was build a shop behind Ricardo's trailer. They poured the cement for the shop floor, built an awning to provide shade, and purchased a trailer so that Porfirio and Rodolfo would have a place to stay. They put the trailer next to the shop.

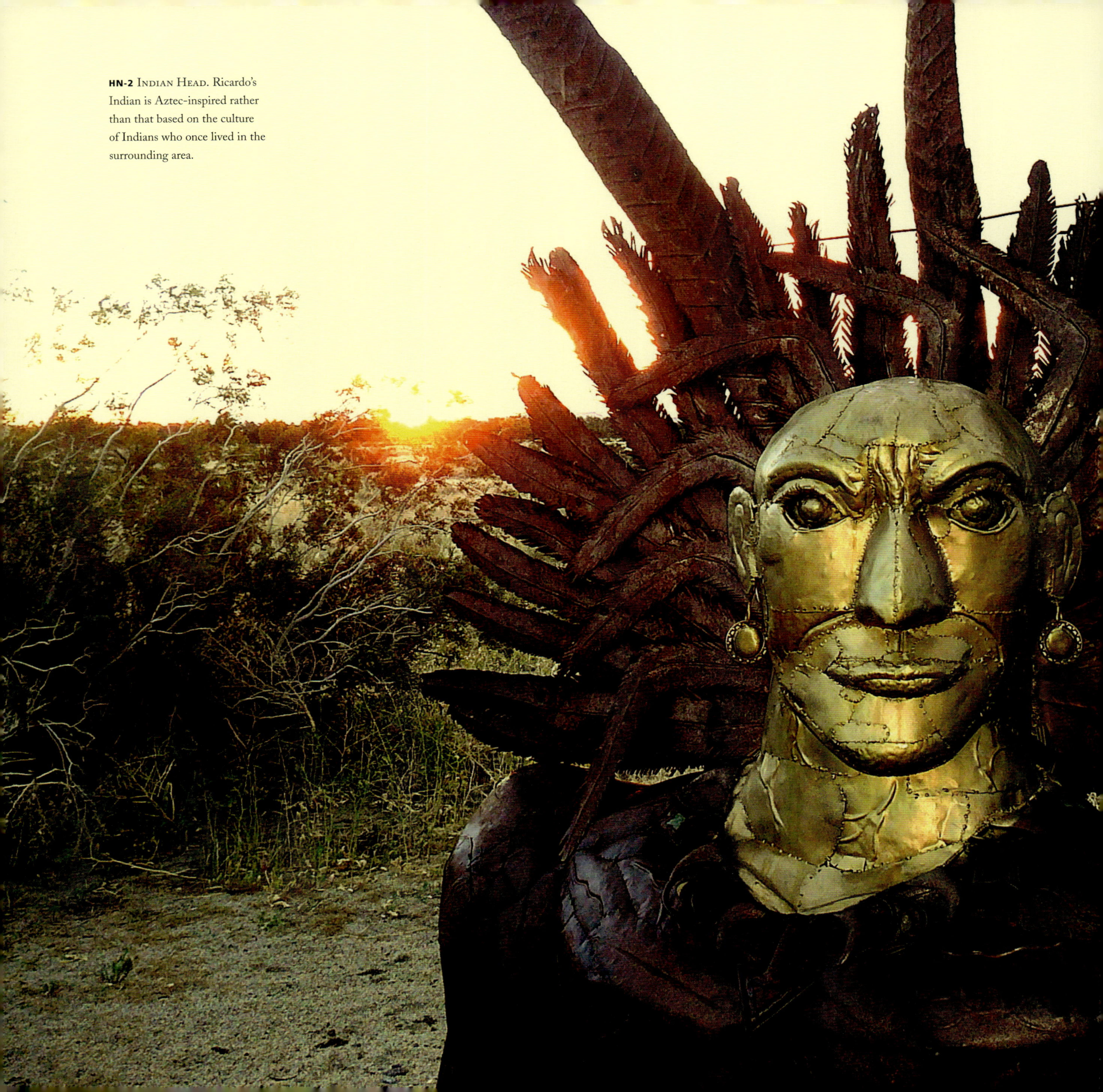

HN-2 Indian Head. Ricardo's Indian is Aztec-inspired rather than that based on the culture of Indians who once lived in the surrounding area.

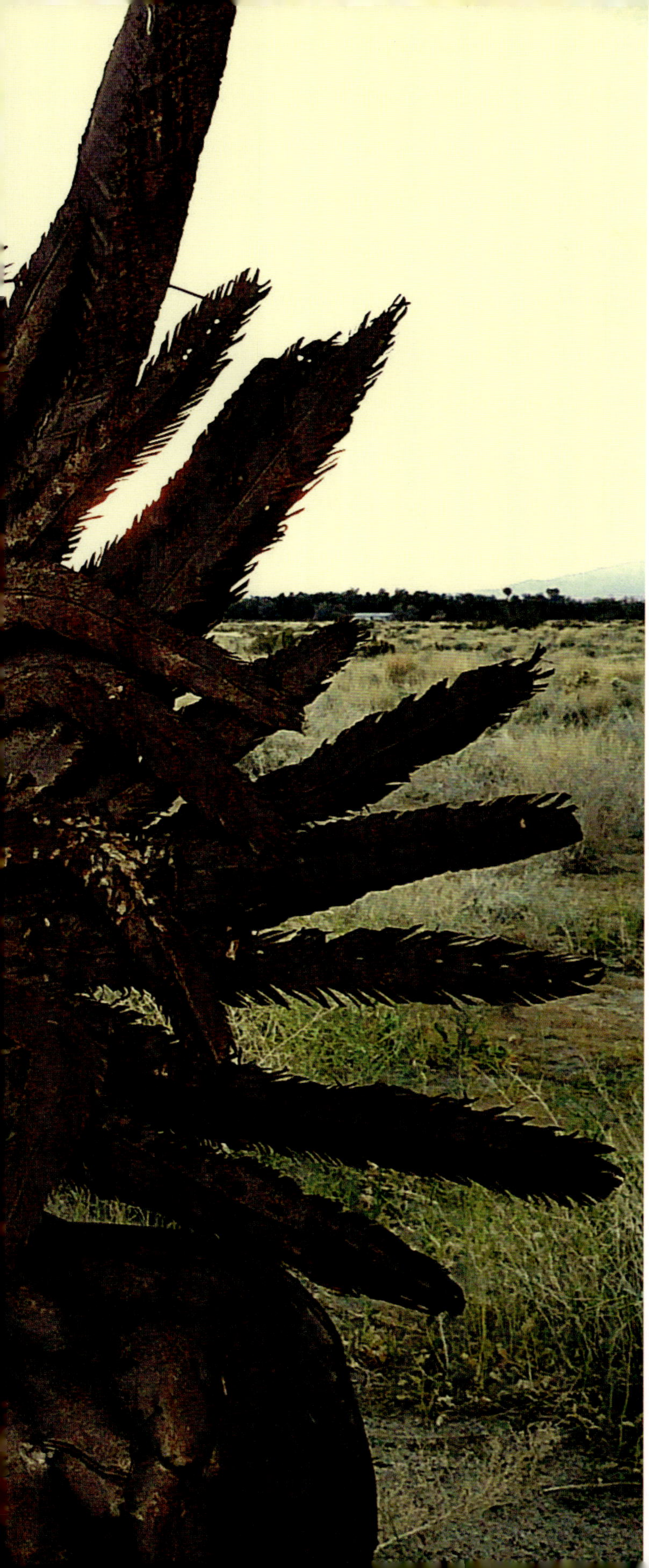

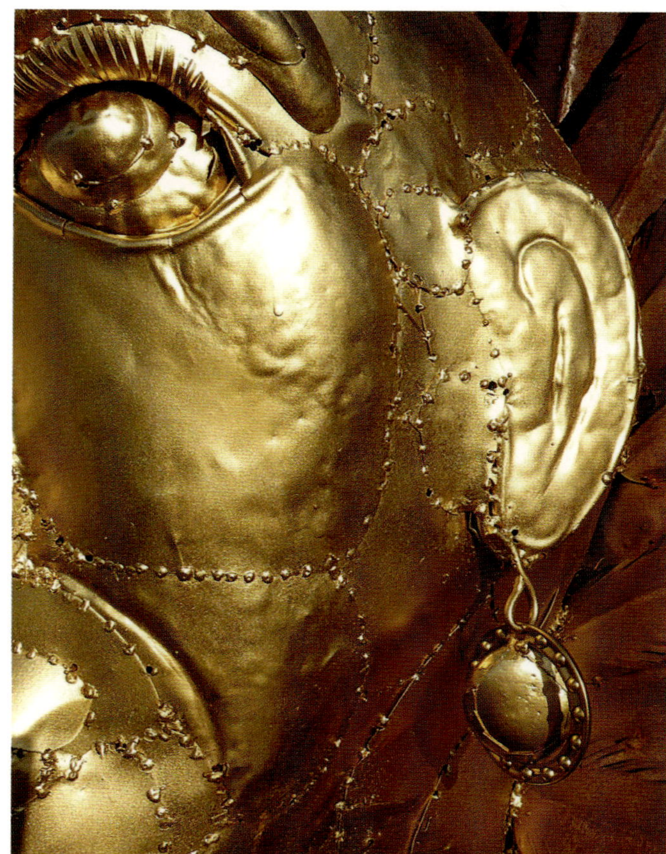

HN-2 Indian Head. Note the detail that includes the earrings and eyelashes. *Overleaf left:* **HN-2** Indian Head. A facsimile of a carved medallion holds the feathers in place. *Overleaf right:* **HN-3** Spanish Padre. Father Font views the famous point in the distant badlands that bears his name.

Rodolfo did not last much more than two weeks. He was not used to working the hours that Ricardo and Porfirio were willing to work, and he was still unhappy about not being able to manage the money in their new enterprise.

Porfirio, on the other hand, turned out to be a gem. Edgar Omar Sandoval Sanchez, nicknamed Porfirio, was fifteen years younger than Ricardo. Born in Chihuahua, Mexico, Porfirio moved to Rosarito Beach in Baja California as a young man, where he worked in an auto body shop. It was there that he learned different kinds of welding. He also worked for a brief time helping to make rustic metal sculptures in one of

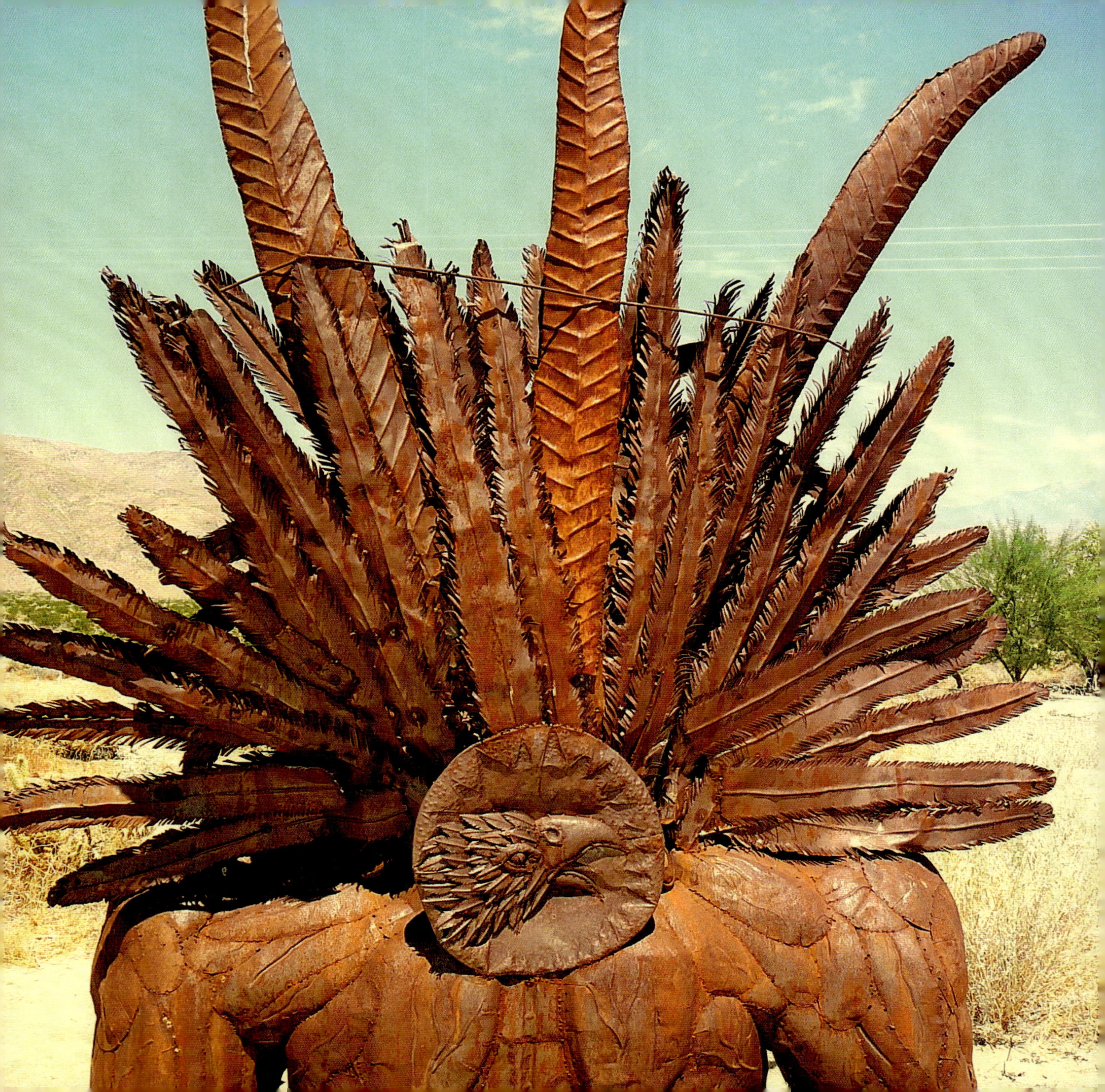

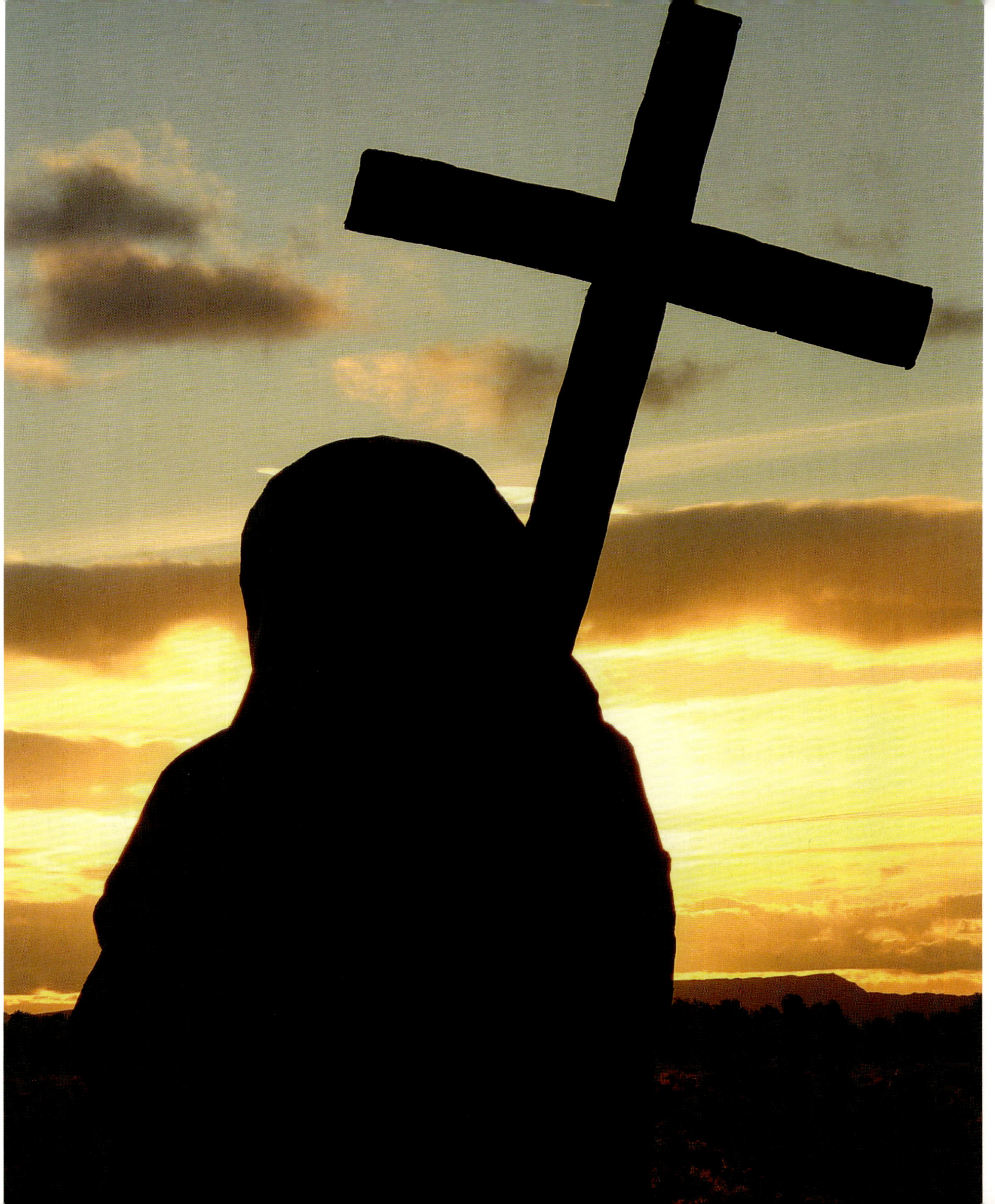

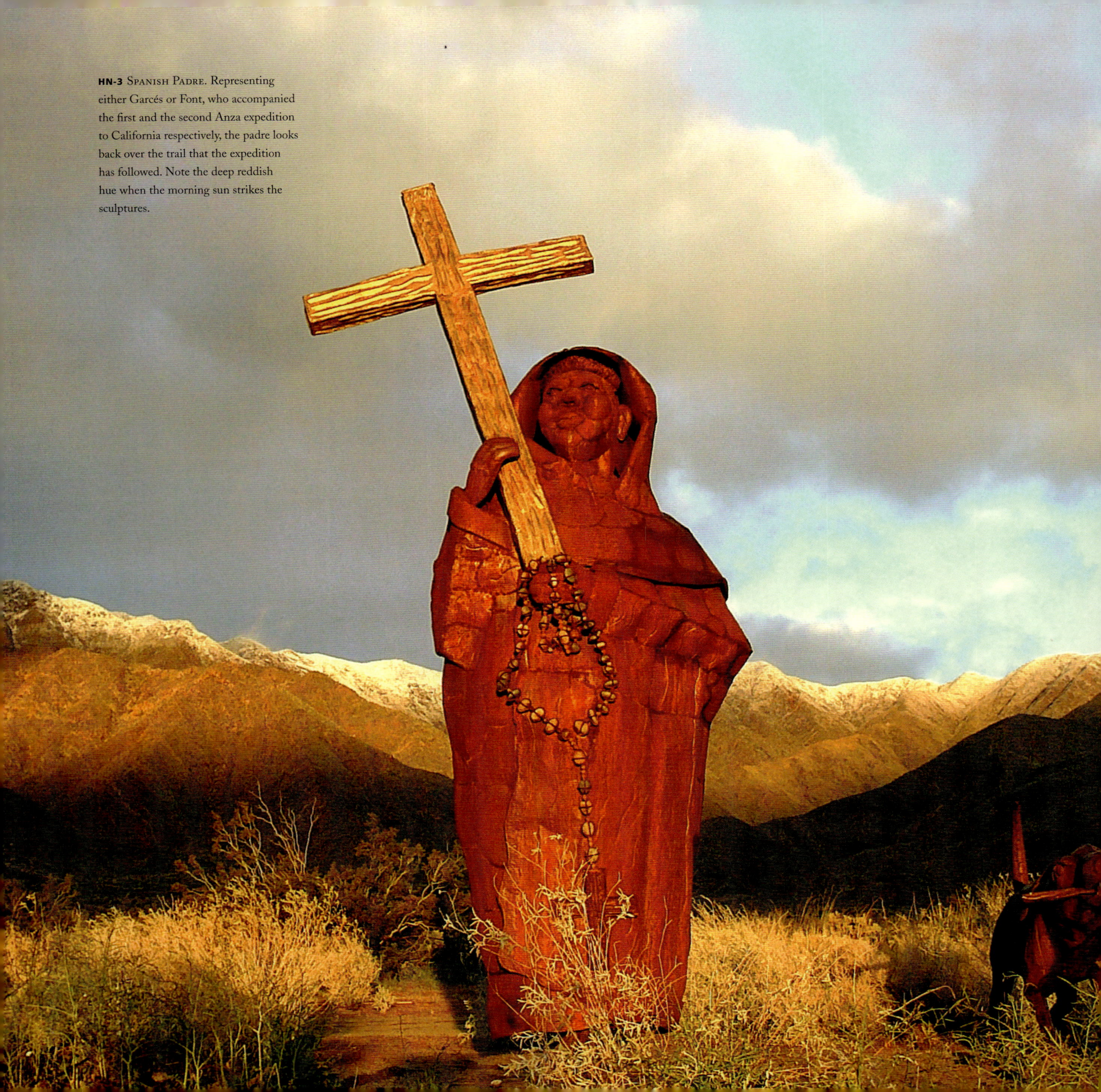

HN-3 Spanish Padre. Representing either Garcés or Font, who accompanied the first and the second Anza expedition to California respectively, the padre looks back over the trail that the expedition has followed. Note the deep reddish hue when the morning sun strikes the sculptures.

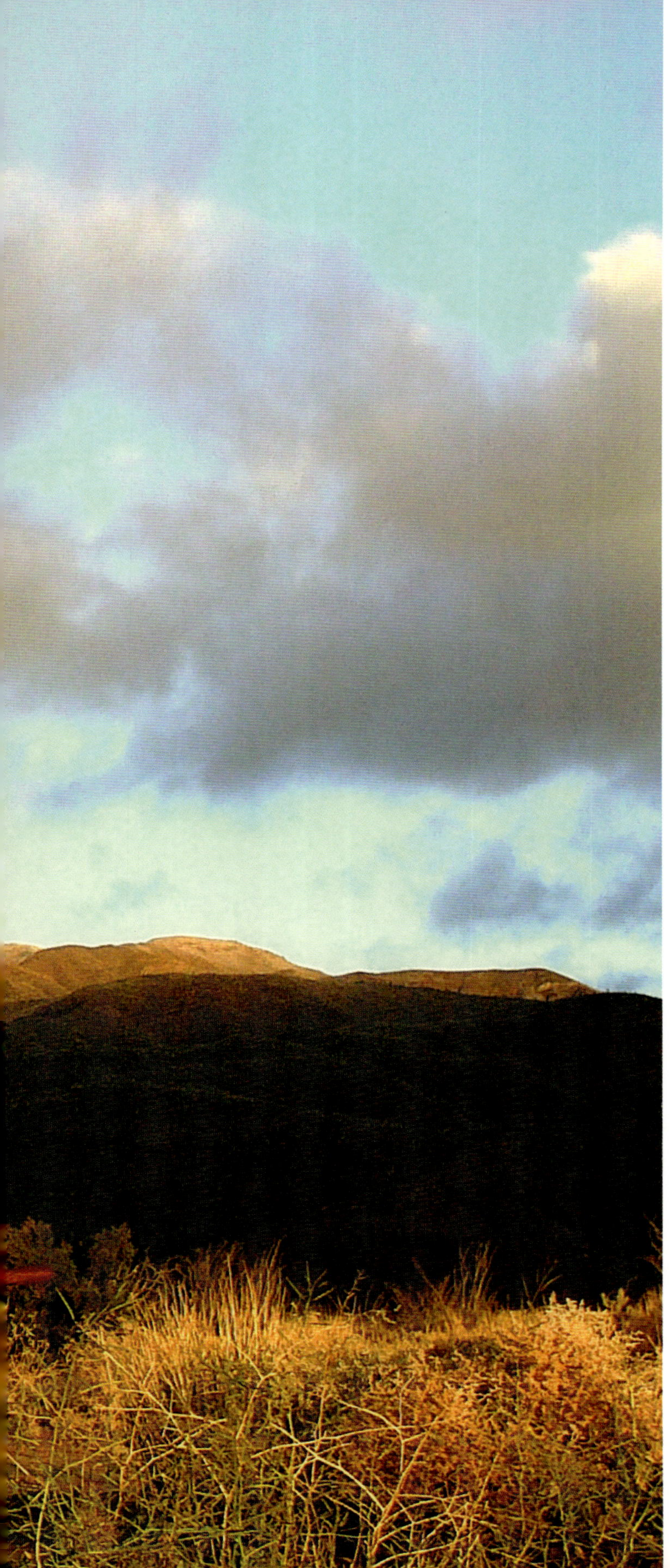

the many shops on the outskirts of town that catered to tourists. From the very beginning, Porfirio has been a diligent and faithful worker and a treasured friend.

After the shop was built, and fueled by the enthusiasm created by their new partnership, Ricardo and Porfirio began work on Lianna's *Tyrannosaurus rex.* With Porfirio able to relieve Ricardo of most of the heavy work, Ricardo had the time to design more ambitiously. When the height of the sculpture became taller than the awning over the shop, they worked on it next to the trailer. The framework was clearly visible from the road, and not long after they began constructing it, a motorist from Palm Springs stopped by to see what they were doing. He was fascinated and ended up coming by each week to watch the progress on the *T. rex.* After a few weeks, he said he wanted to buy it when it was done.

While working on the *T. rex,* they had chained it from above so it would not fall over. When it was completed and the holding chain was removed, Ricardo and Porfirio proudly stepped back to admire their first piece. Suddenly, with a mighty crash, the gigantic dinosaur fell flat on its face. Quickly, the two men gathered some rocks and loaded its tail and legs with cement and rocks so it would stand upright without additional support. Their customer never knew about this last-minute adjustment, and he liked the sculpture so much that he ordered a few more pieces.

Lianna's Christmas *Tyrannosaurus* was actually the second one built, since the man from Palm Springs bought the first one. It remains her favorite sculpture, and still stands in the Perris workshop where it was created, gazing out toward freeway traffic. These first few sculptures taught Ricardo and Porfirio about balance and reinforcement while succeeding ones taught them about the importance of adding details.

The third sculpture they made was again for the Palm Springs man, who this time wanted a *Spinosaurus.* It was followed by a *Triceratops* that joined Lianna's *T. rex* at the freeway fence. They now had two sculptures in the yard, and interest in what they were doing was growing.

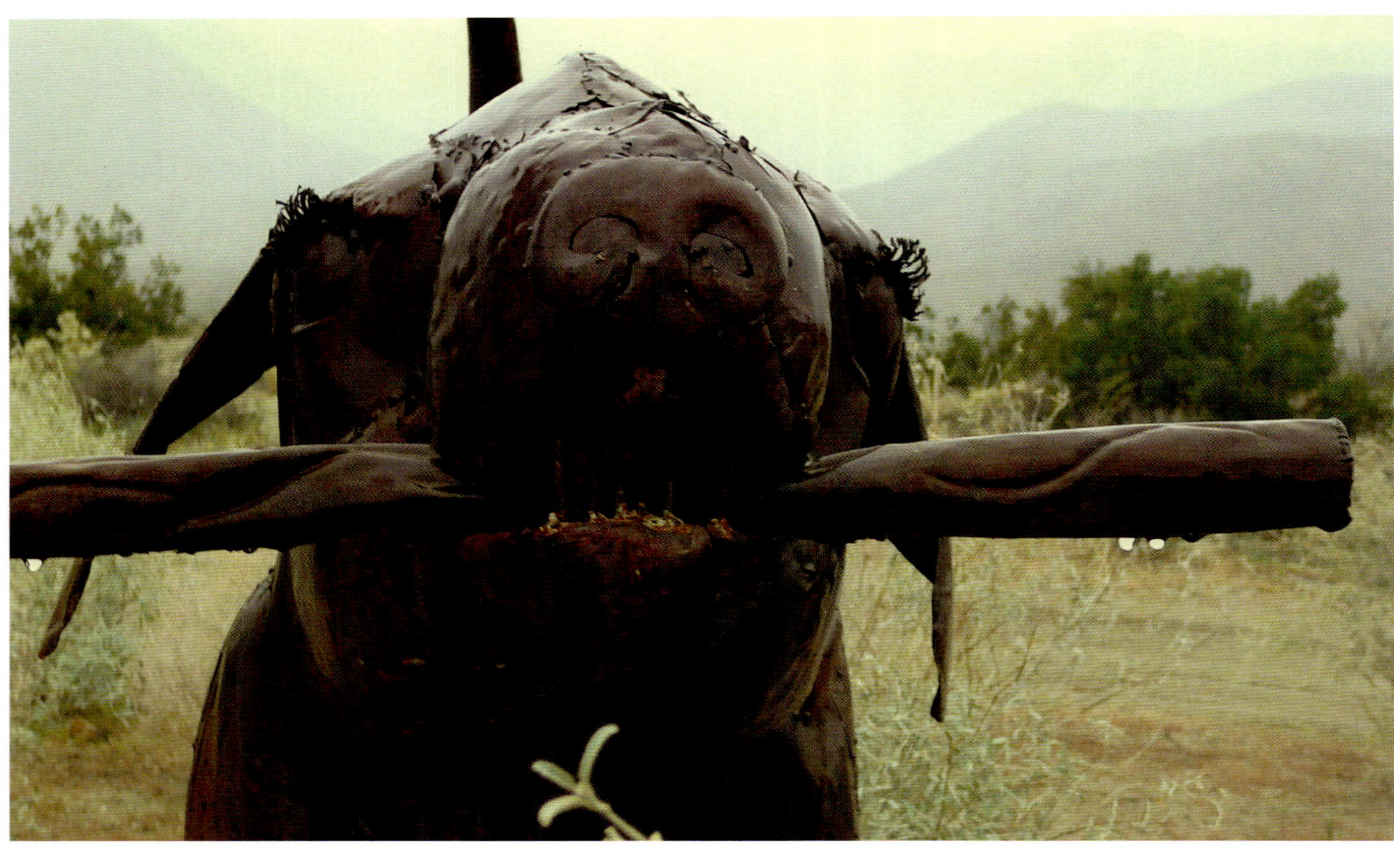

HN-3 Spanish Padre. Records do not indicate that a dog accompanied either of the expedition padres to California. Ricardo added the dog for companionship. *Above:* Raindrops fall from the dog's stick. Rain changes the color to a deep brown. *Opposite*: The padre clutches his rosary, intricately made with pebbles characteristic of the regional Peninsular Ranges.

Joe, Ricardo's landlord, came over to look at the *Triceratops*. He was so excited by what he saw that, even though he was eighty-three years old, he insisted on climbing onto it to have his picture taken with Ricardo and Porfirio. The series of pictures taken that day are the only existing photos documenting the early years for Perris Jurassic Park, as it is now called.

Each new piece they made helped Ricardo and Porfirio perfect their rudimentary techniques. But first, they had to deal with an existing customer from India.

Before Porfirio and Rodolfo's partnership with Ricardo, Rodolfo had made a deal to sell five sculptures to a man from India who had a home in the Los Angeles area. The man had agreed to pay a few hundred dollars for each piece. Rodolfo and Porfirio had completed one piece and had delivered it before they met Ricardo. Rodolfo had kept most of the money from that sale and had given Porfirio just enough to buy more materials and barely enough to buy food.

Now the man wanted the other four pieces for the price originally agreed upon. Ricardo informed him that he was now managing the business and would fulfill the obligation and honor the deal that Porfirio had made, but it would be on their schedule and not his. Ricardo told him that it might be a year or two before they could make delivery because they first

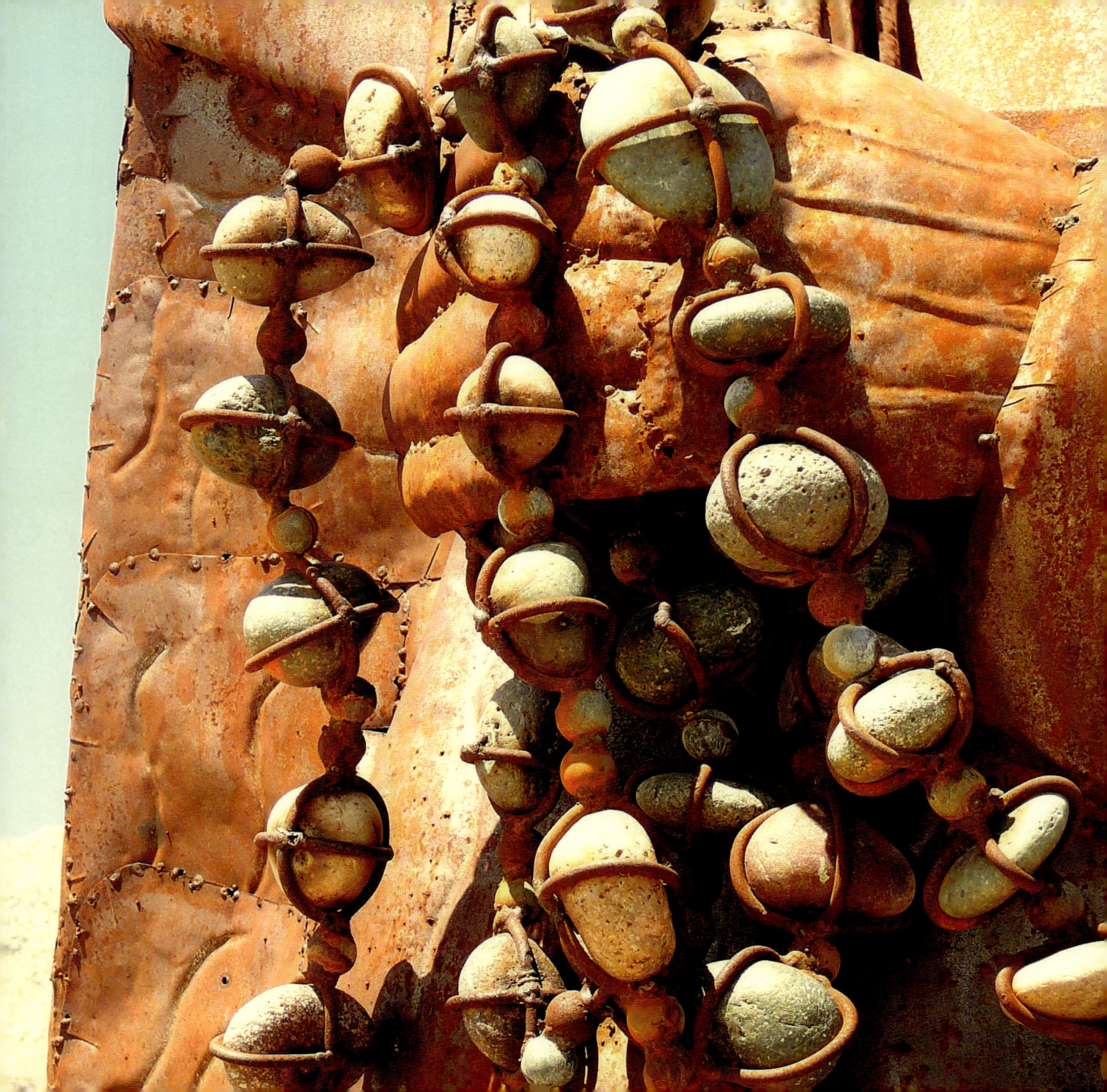

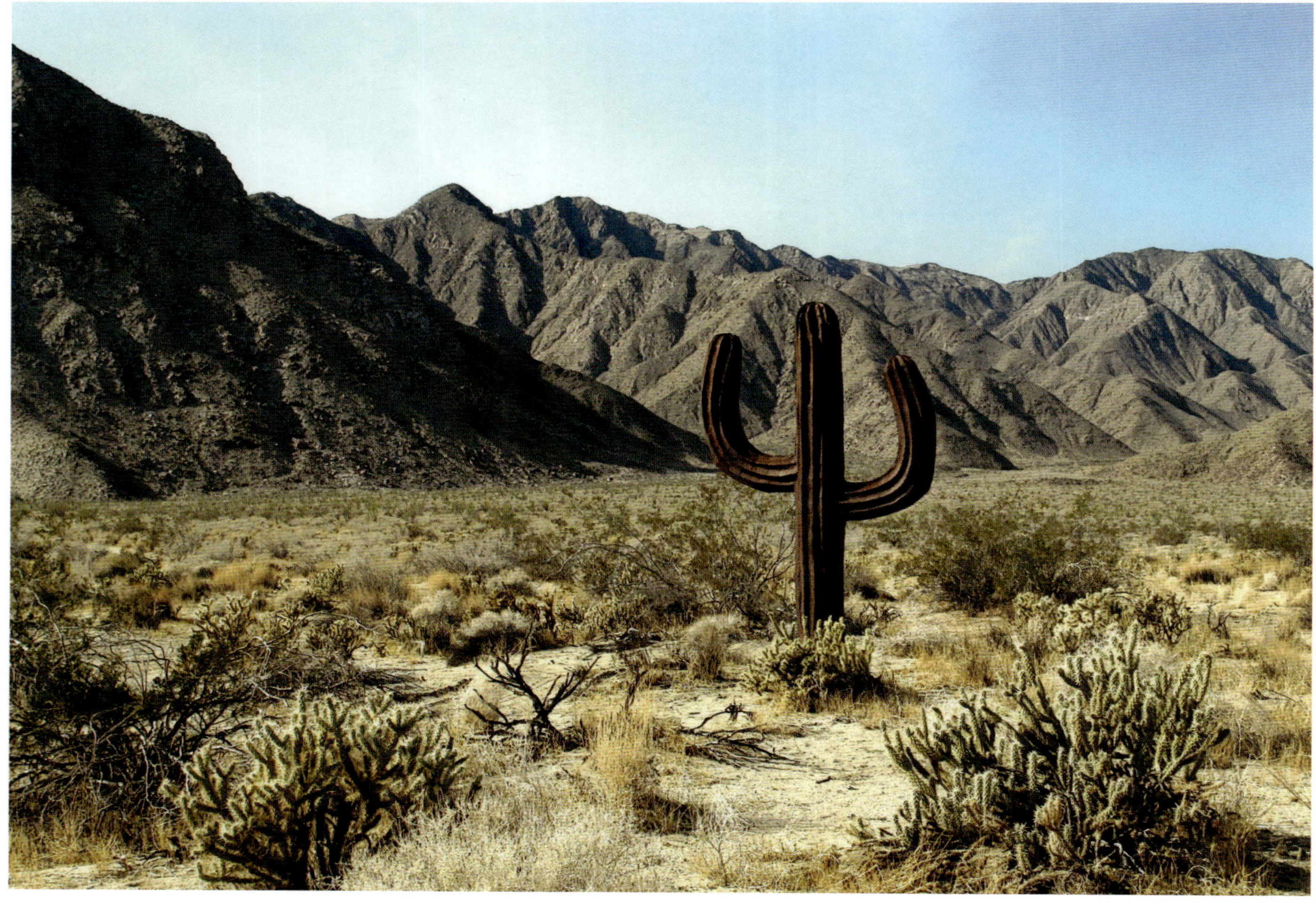

HN-3 Saguaro Cactus. A tall saguaro cactus stands west of the padre and is reminiscent of the Sonoran Desert to the east through which the Anza expedition traveled. Saguaros do not grow naturally in the Anza-Borrego region.

had to find a customer who would be willing to pay a fair price for their labor. Ricardo added that if the customer paid the new price, he could have the pieces in three to four months.

Annoyed, the man from India said, "Just forget it!" and walked away. As long as Ricardo was managing the business, no one would any longer take advantage of Porfirio or anyone else who was just trying to make a fair living.

Ricardo and Porfirio began working in earnest—fifteen hours a day, Monday through Friday. Ricardo would stop welding anytime a boot customer showed up at his door. And he and Lianna continued to do boot sales on the weekends.

Lianna recalls that when she came home from school, Porfirio and her father would be busy working, cutting, shaping, and welding the metal pieces together. She liked to watch them. She remembers that her father got quite a few cuts because the metal was sharp, and sometimes he would yell out and other times he would just laugh. Each time a piece was done, he was proud and happy, and they celebrated.

They went out for dinner, and Ricardo would take a few days off to relax before he jumped into the next project.

What was most memorable to Lianna, as she thought about those early years, was how all the pieces came together. "I was very happy with the gift my father gave me." She added, "I would watch in wonder as one dinosaur after another was built." When Lianna's school friends came over and walked among the completed pieces, they would turn to her, amazed, and say, "Your dad made this?" and "Wow, my dad never made anything like that for me." At times like this, she felt especially proud of her father.

That first year saw the creation of elephants, horses, giraffes, and a shark. The largest sculpture they made in 2002 was twenty-five feet tall and forty feet long.

While Ricardo was developing this new business, his mother, Estela, came to visit from Mexico. She took one look at the sculptures in the yard, sighed, and turned to her son to say, *Ay, mi hijo, ¿porque no te dedicas a otra cosa?* "Son, why don't you do something else?"

Ricardo recalls he seethed with anger and said to himself, "Just you wait and see!" He admits that those words, which he clearly recalls to this day, were a primary motivation to succeed. He adds that anger can be a good prod for success, if channeled in the right way.

Unlike his mother, Ricardo's sister Ernestina thought her brother had a natural talent right from the very beginning. She was very supportive, as were the rest of his brothers and sisters.

By 2003 Perris Jurassic Park was starting to get a lot of attention. The metal menagerie was beginning to tower over Interstate 215. When they brought out two of their largest dinosaur creations that fall, Perris Jurassic Park suddenly started receiving wide media attention with both newspaper and television coverage. Ricardo knew at this point that his future was assured. He had stumbled onto something big,

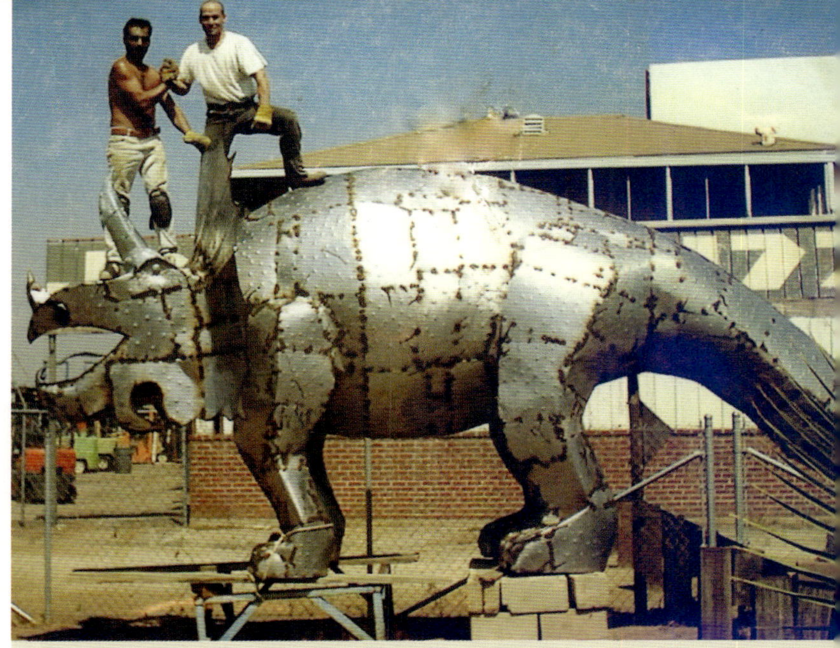

FIRST SCULPTURES

Above: Ricardo and Porfirio stand atop one of their first sculptures at Perris Jurassic Park. *Below:* The *Triceratops* has since rusted and remains part of the menagerie in the sculpture garden.

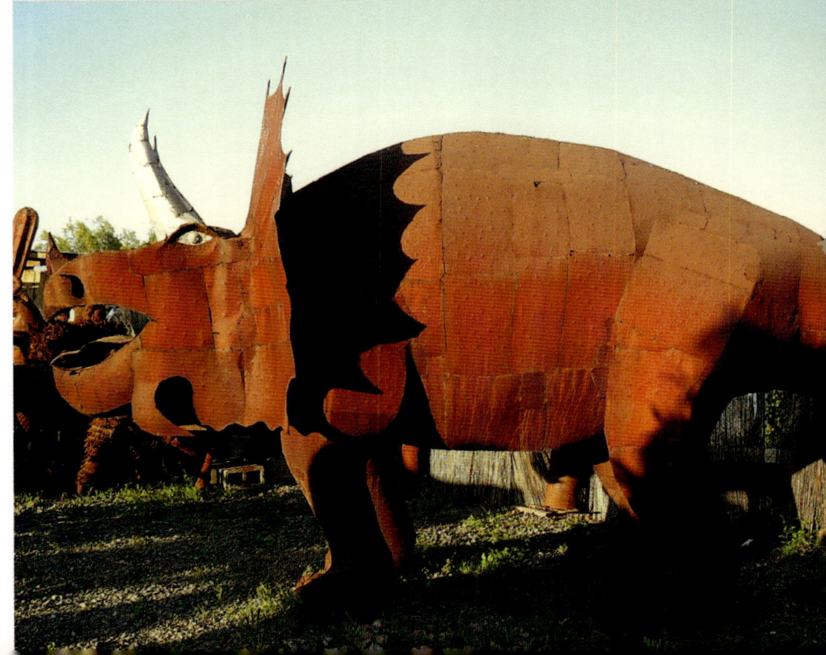

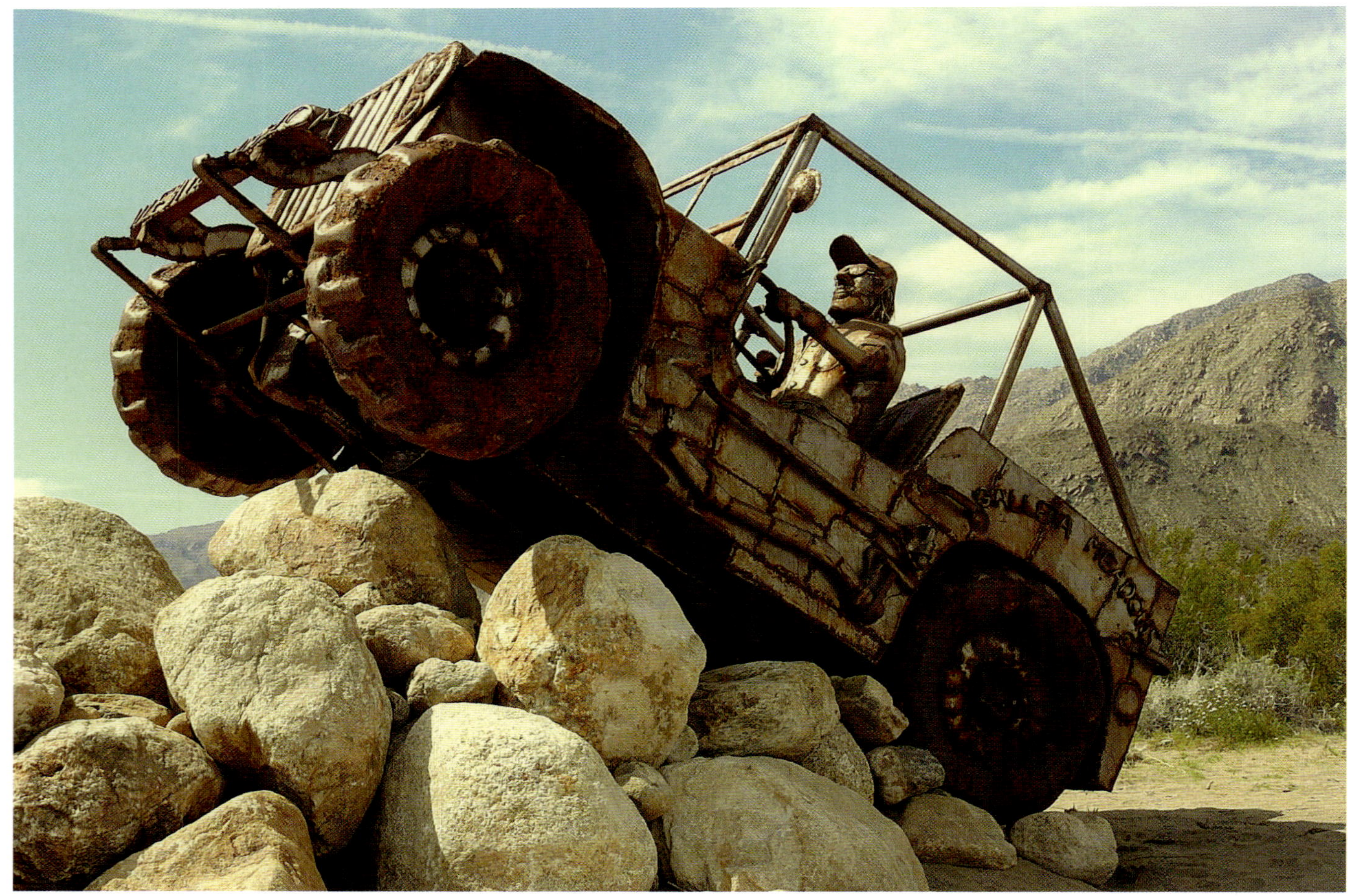

HN-4 1946 Willys Jeep. The iconic World War II military Jeep was produced in a civilian version (CJ-3A) by Willys-Overland in 1946. The Jeep forever changed desert exploration and brought challenges to park administration.

and it was fun. He could see his life's work laid out in front of him. He knew that if he could stay focused on making each sculpture better than the last one he could achieve the recognition that he wanted.

A headline in *The Press Enterprise* on November 24, 2003, read: "Dino might: Motorists are startled by a hobbyist's metal monsters along Interstate 215." The article described how traffic slowed while passing Perris Jurassic Park, and how curious motorists exited the freeway to visit the sculpture garden. In the article, Ricardo credited his daughter for the inspiration to develop his hobby and turn it into a business.

Karie Allen, the reporter for *The Press Enterprise,* wrote that "Breceda has made 20 of the metal monsters, ranging in size from 6 to 16 feet and weighing anywhere from 100 to 800 pounds."

In describing how he makes the sculptures, she wrote, "He doesn't use any blueprints. All he needs is a photograph or a scaled model. He uses small iron bars to construct a skeleton, starting with the tail, then moving into the body, and saves the head for last. He then covers the bars with small

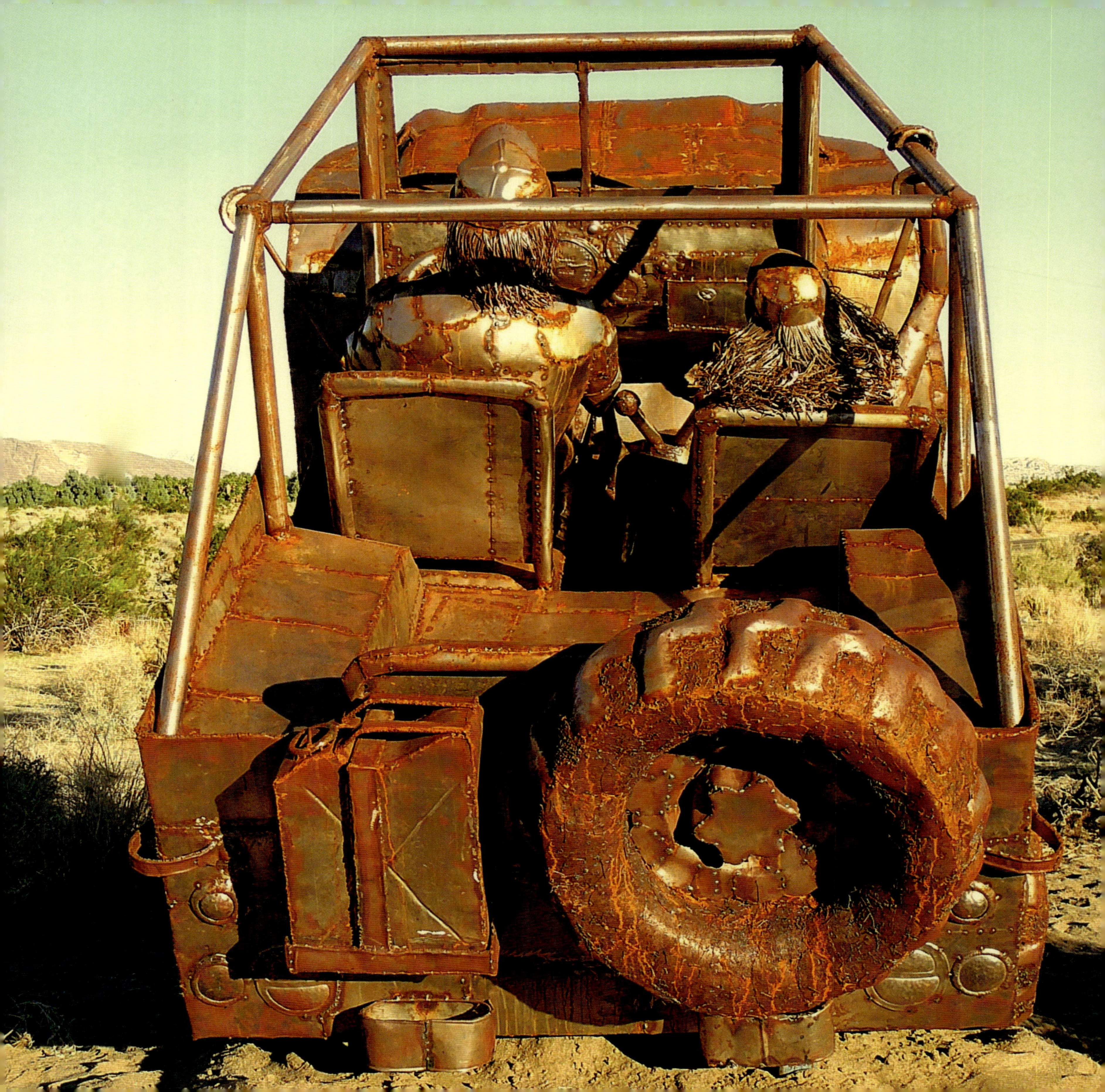

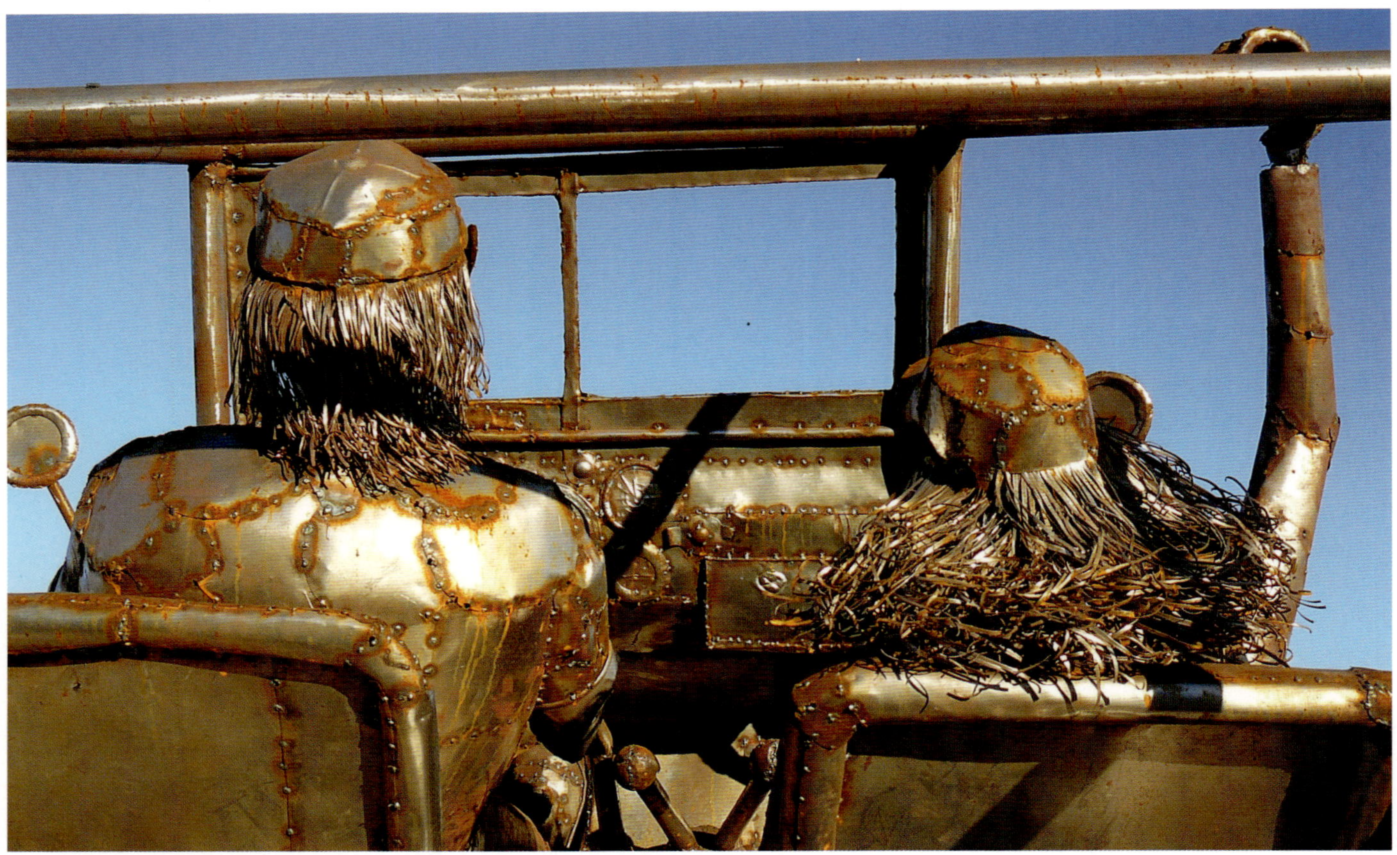

HN-4 1946 Willys Jeep. Ricardo had a neighbor with a CJ-3A. He studied every detail and replicated them in this sculpture. The undercarriage even includes details of the drive shaft. The passenger (*above*) hangs on as the Jeep rock-crawls up the incline.

sheets of 24-gauge [he actually uses 26-gauge] metal because they are best for shaping a dinosaur's body. The teeth and eyes are made with galvanized steel, so they won't rust [he now prefers using the same metal throughout the sculptures]. But for the rest of the body, it's a different story." She quoted Ricardo as stating: "The whole point is it's got to rust."

The reporter also interviewed a customer named Joey Longenecker of Sky Valley. He drove into Perris Jurassic Park, found Ricardo "very professional," and bought a *Spinosaurus* "because it was just majestic." Longenecker had had the fourteen-foot-tall and twenty-six-foot-long *Spinosaurus* placed on a six-foot hill of stone surrounded by decorative boulders and rocks in front of his masonry business. It turned out to be a good investment as it attracted new customers. He told the reporter he would be buying more.

The following month an article in the Spanish-language newspaper *La Opinión* was published. The headline read, "El Parque Jurástico de Perris." Ricardo noted the name "Perris Jurassic Park" used by the reporter. He loved it. Soon after the article appeared Ricardo replaced his boot sales sign by the freeway fence with a new sign: PERRIS JURASSIC PARK.

The Spanish-language paper also reported that the California Highway Patrol said that three major accidents had occurred in two years because of the freeway exhibit. The newspaper stated that "The animals cast a menacing shadow over the asphalt, leaping suddenly into the view of unprepared drivers. Until now, there have been no deaths, but there have been injuries of varying magnitude."

Even today, Ricardo confirms that quite regularly he hears the squeal of tires as drivers slam on their brakes, because they are distracted by the unusual and unexpected sculptures.

As a whole, Ricardo never had a problem with a drop-in customer, with one big exception. A man approached Ricardo with a plan to be his sales agent in Las Vegas. He thanked Ricardo for giving him a chance to prove himself and took about $20,000 worth of sculptures to sell. He came back to Ricardo some months later to say that sales had gone well, but he had broken up with his partner who ran off with all the money. He asked Ricardo to help him again by giving him some more sculptures. Ricardo said to him, "Look at me. Am I stupid? You owe me the money."

The man immediately took his trailer and headed for Rosarito Beach, in Baja California, to see if he could pull the same deal there. Ricardo got a call from Mexico inquiring about the man, and Ricardo explained what the man had done. He found out some time later that the man's trailer had mysteriously caught on fire in Mexico.

HN-4 1946 Willys Jeep. The Jeep's jump seat is an incredible temptation for little (and big) boys who are quick to imagine themselves bouncing along desert trails.

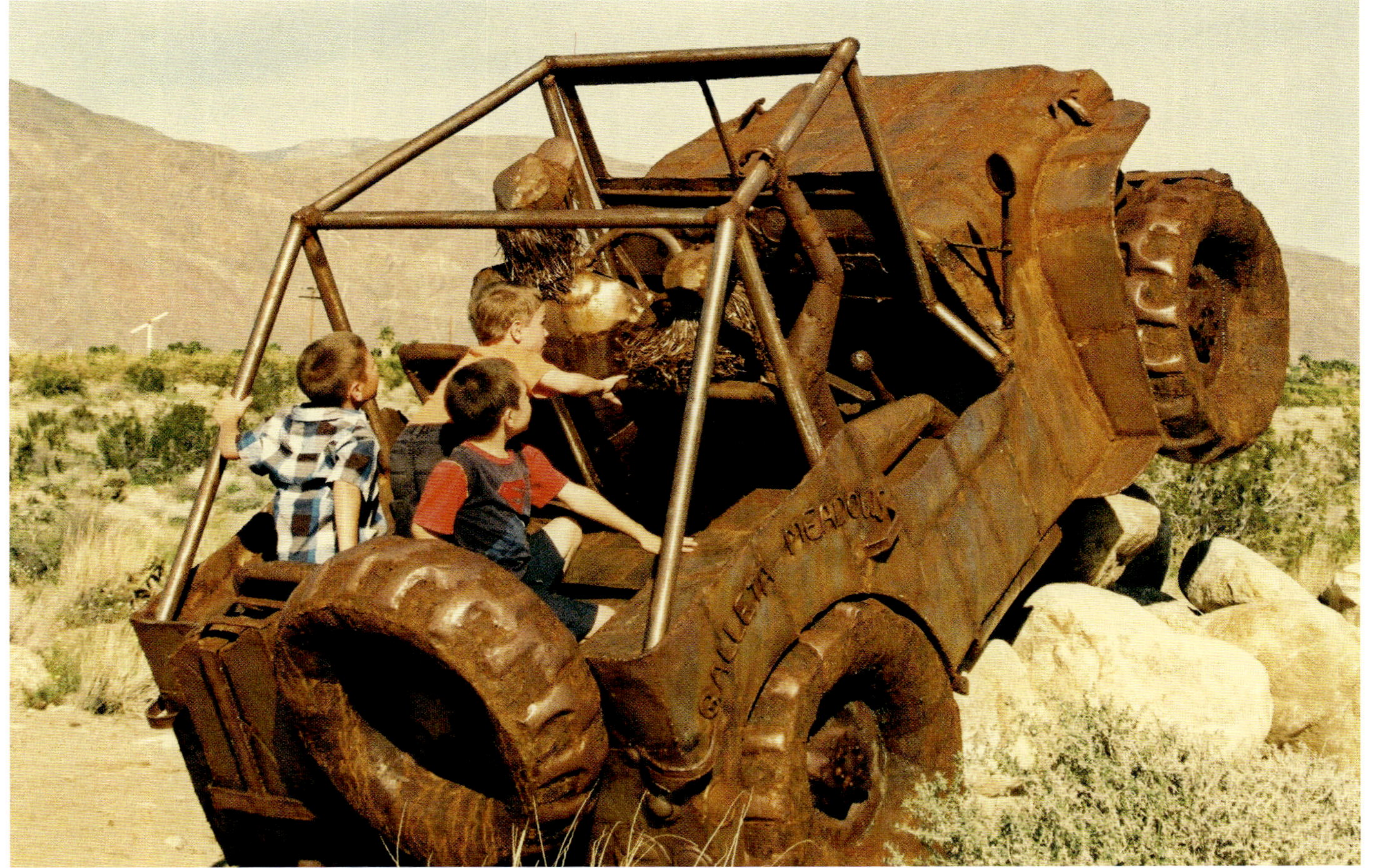

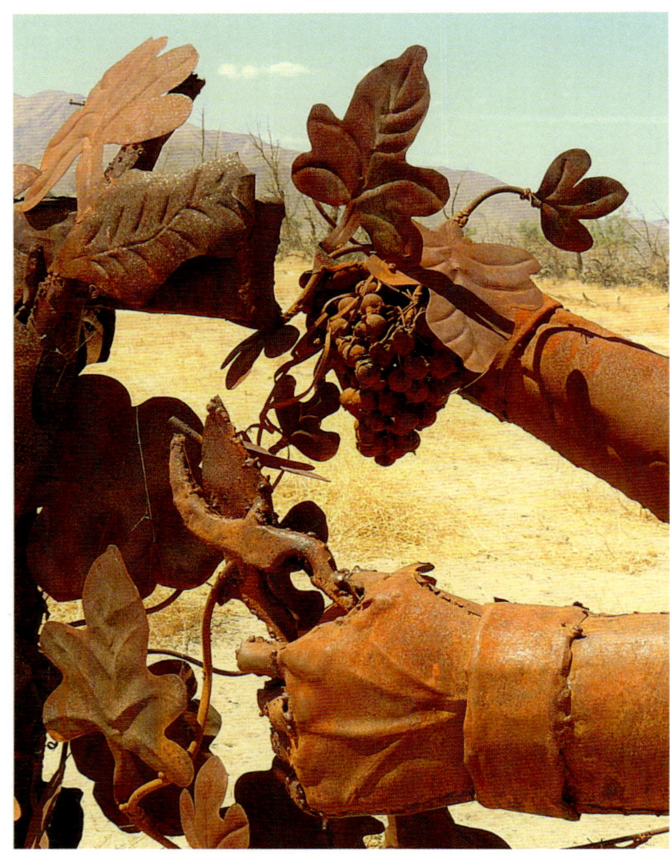

HN-5 Farm Workers (Detail). A farm worker harvests grapes for market.

From then on Ricardo dealt on a cash basis and gave credit only to those he trusted.

Shortly thereafter, Felisnando Monarrez, owner of the Rancho Los Alamos racetrack, wanted something horse-themed and dramatic at the entrance gate. To satisfy the commission, Ricardo created steel horses complimented by Pancho Villa–style Mexican revolution *pistoleros.*

Ricardo's presence is still felt at Rancho Los Alamos in more ways than one. As people walk through the gate, greeted by Ricardo's prominently displayed sculptures, many of them are wearing boots they bought from him or won at one of his raffles.

As business began to grow, Ricardo and Porfirio began experimenting; they wanted to create more intricate sculptures.

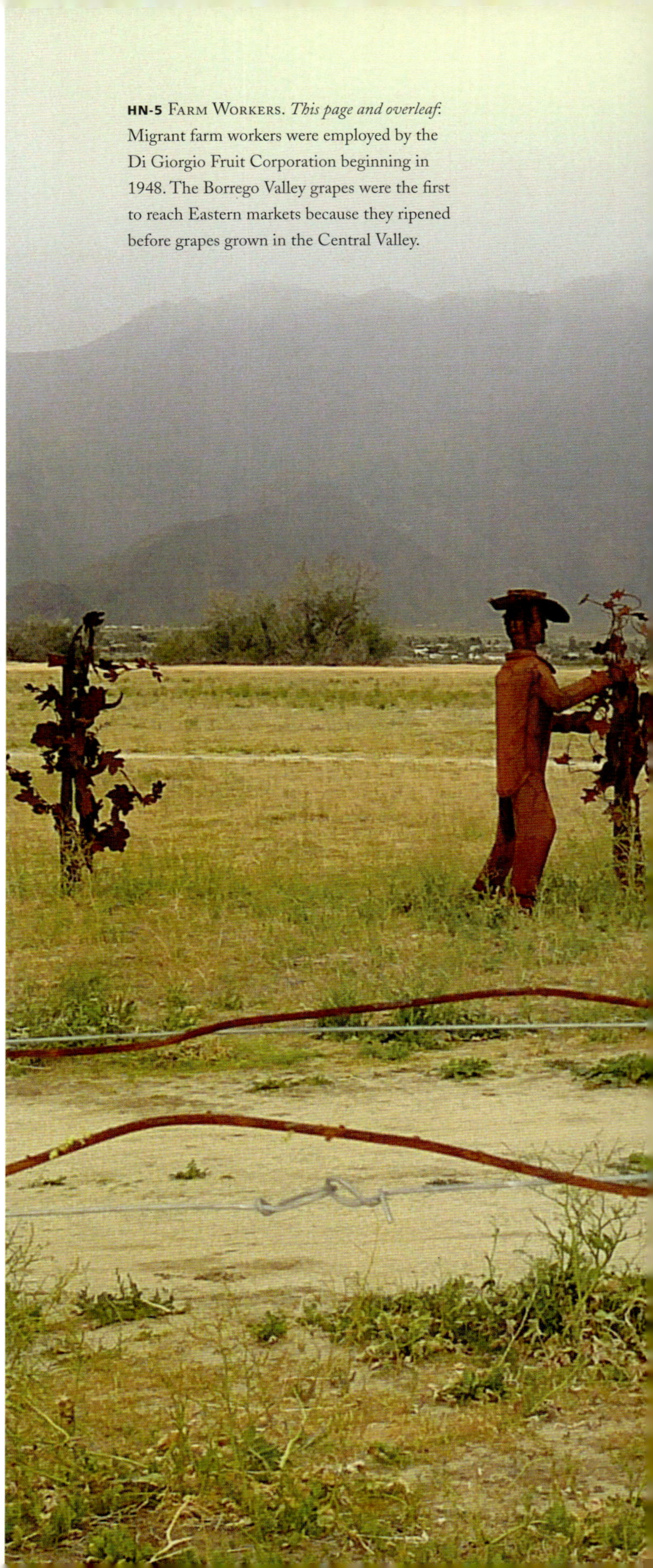

HN-5 Farm Workers. *This page and overleaf:* Migrant farm workers were employed by the Di Giorgio Fruit Corporation beginning in 1948. The Borrego Valley grapes were the first to reach Eastern markets because they ripened before grapes grown in the Central Valley.

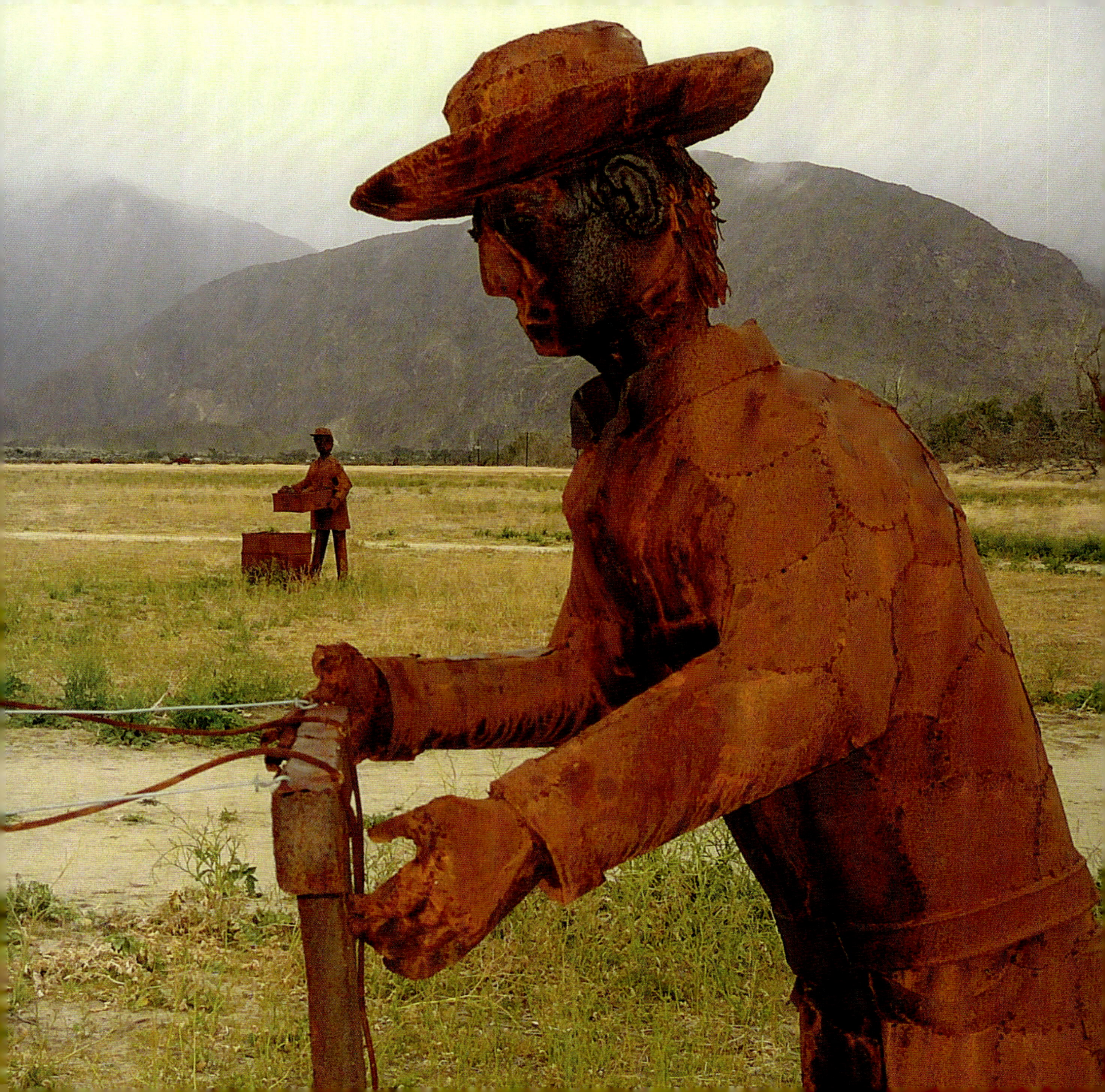

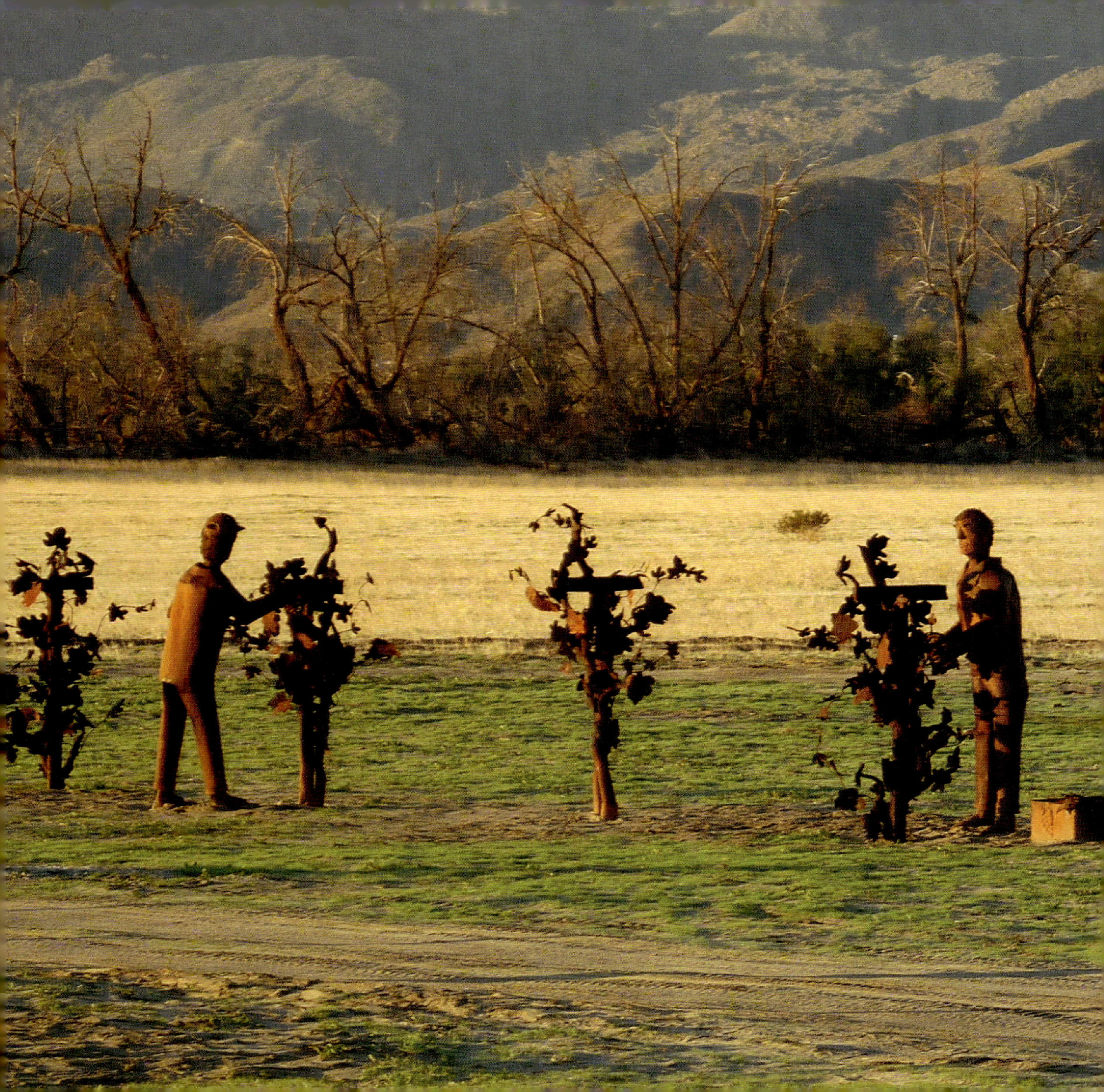

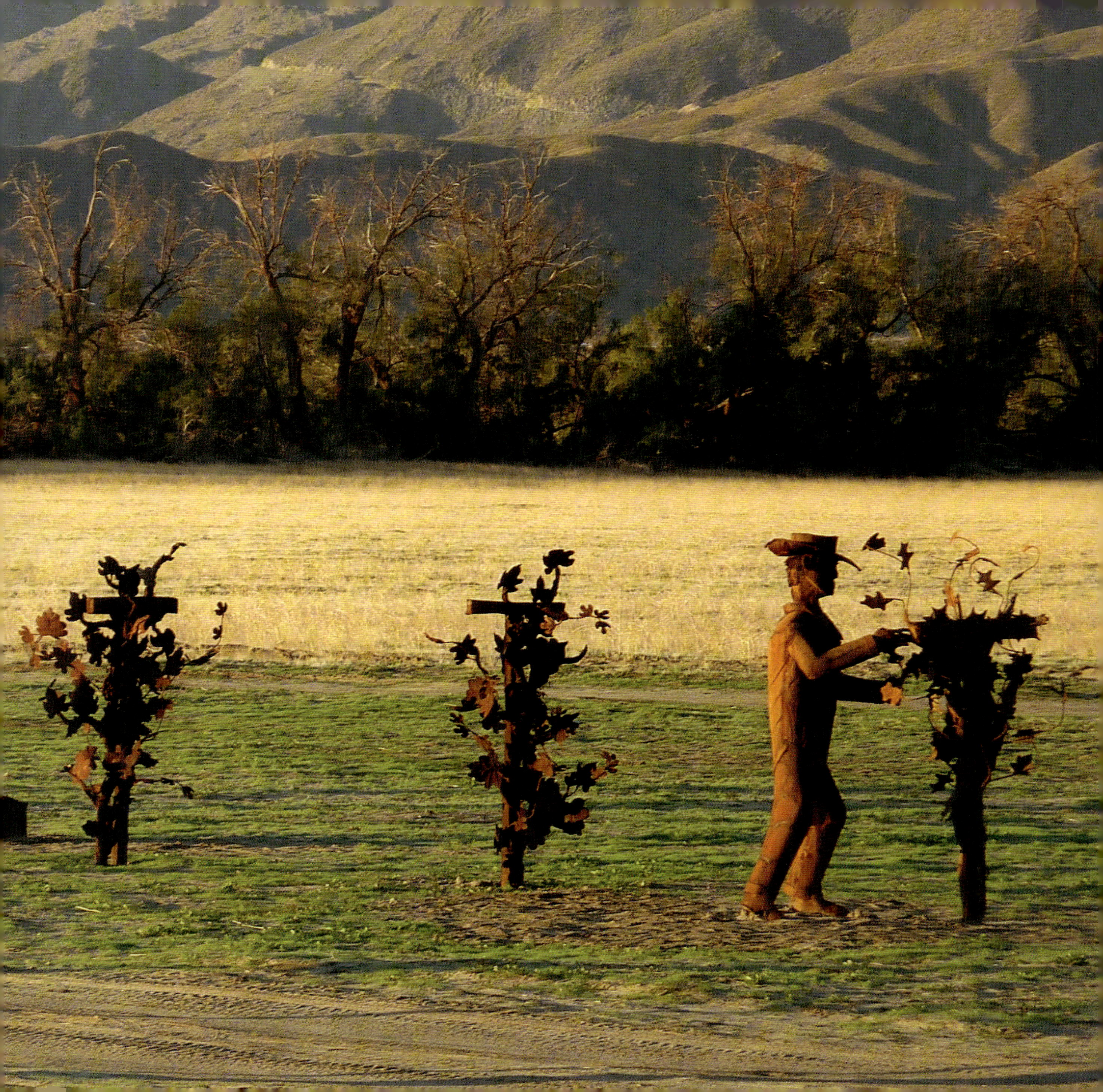

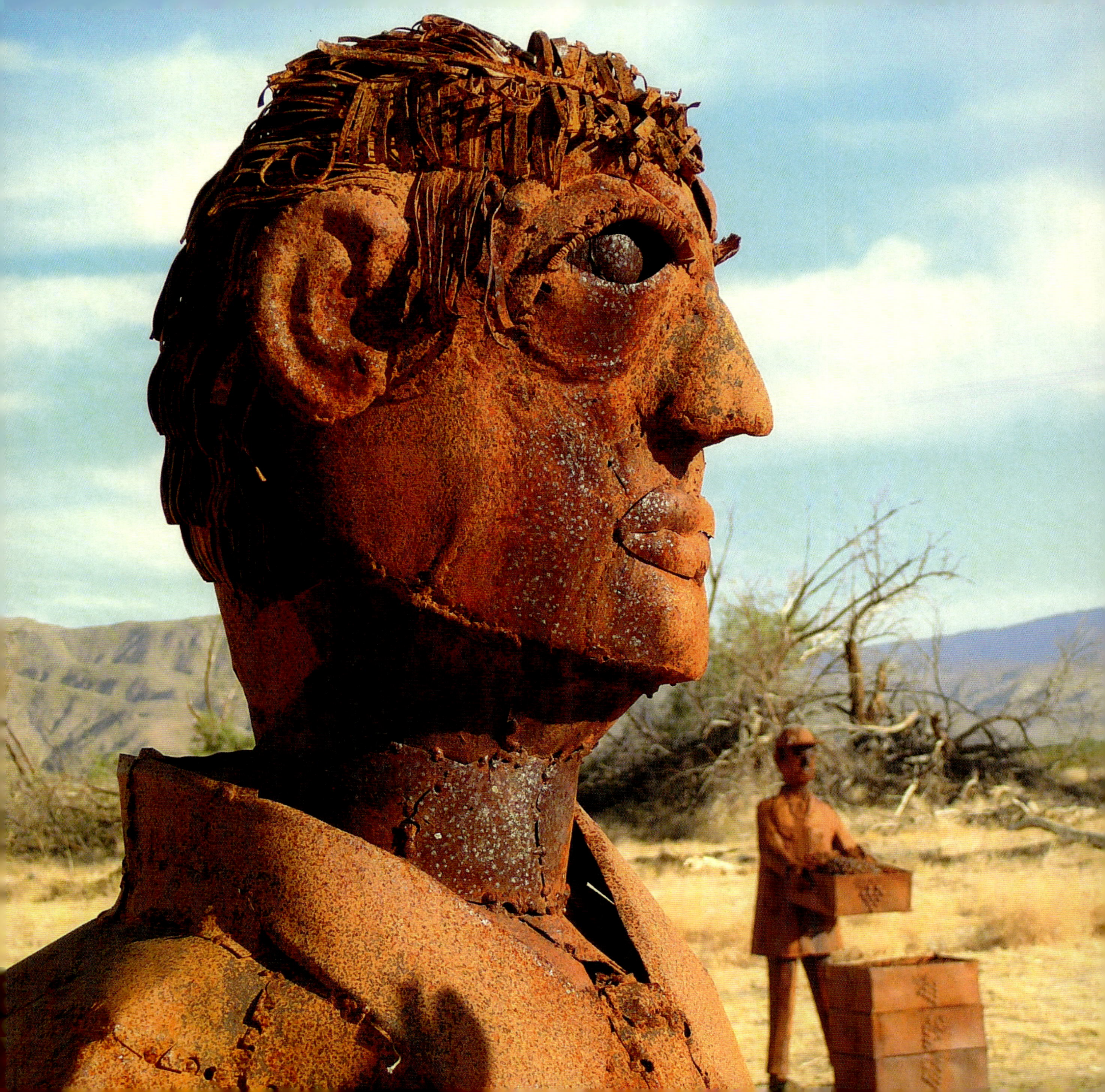

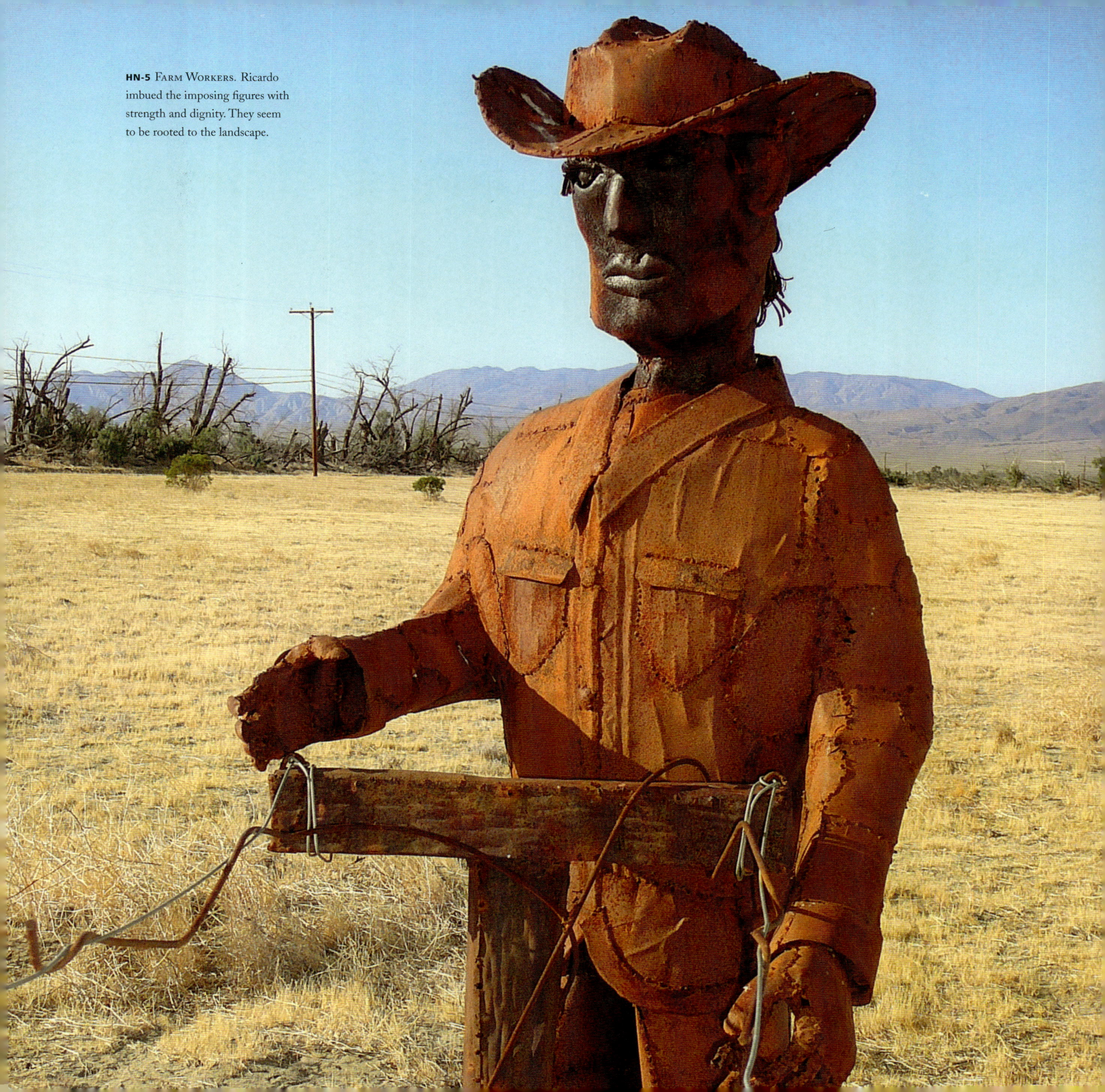

HN-5 Farm Workers. Ricardo imbued the imposing figures with strength and dignity. They seem to be rooted to the landscape.

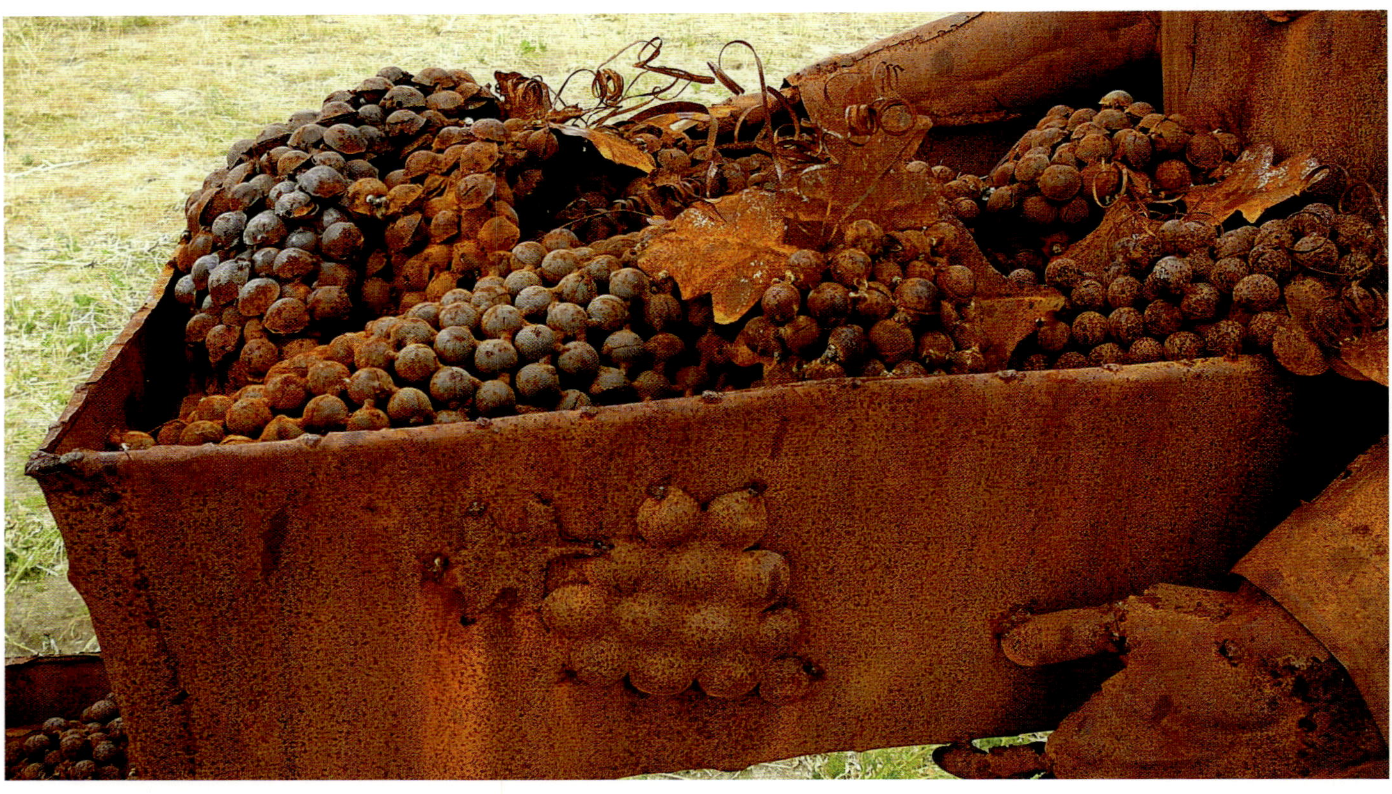

HN-5 Farm Workers (Detail). The Di Giorgio Fruit Corporation was one of the companies targeted by the United Farm Workers during the five-year grape strike from 1965 to 1970.

Listening to Porfirio talk about the artisans in Rosarita Beach piqued Ricardo's curiosity. So he took a trip across the border to see what they did and to ask questions about their technique. He figured that if he wanted his business to grow and succeed, he had to know every aspect of the process—why things are done a certain way, how to do them, who is doing them, and who the customers are. He asked shop owners endless questions and watched them work. In the process he learned every aspect of the craft.

Ricardo explained, "You can be better when you know more than the rest. That's my secret."

By 2007 Ricardo's sculptures had greatly improved. They were showing more detail and were much more lifelike. With each sculpture made, there were incremental improvements in technique and style. He now sold sculptures in several states, as well as in Canada, Mexico, and even as far away as Australia.

Weekend boot sales were still needed to cover all the expenses and to make a small profit. By now, Ricardo had a website, www.PerrisJurassicPark.com, set up for him by his nephew. If an order came in that was too big for Porfirio and him to handle, he would hire some part-time help to "cut and bang," as he described the process of cutting sheet metal and hammering it out to form the individual pieces that were later welded to a previously made frame. The "cut and bang" was the most tedious part of the job and required seemingly endless hours of work.

Occasionally even Lianna lent a hand by cutting and shaping the metal and doing some welding. Ricardo proudly states, "She is a good welder, better than some of my guys."

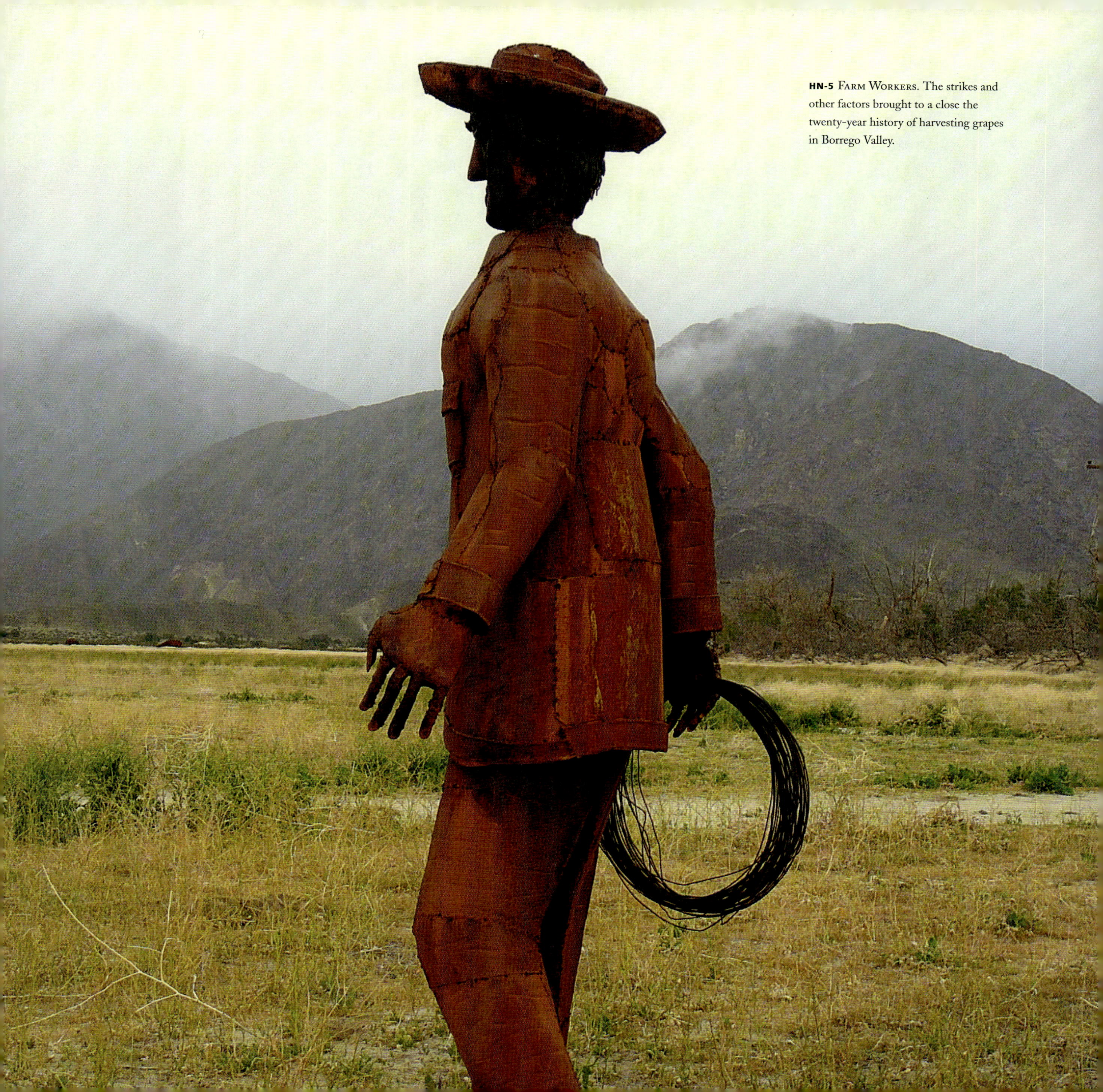

HN-5 Farm Workers. The strikes and other factors brought to a close the twenty-year history of harvesting grapes in Borrego Valley.

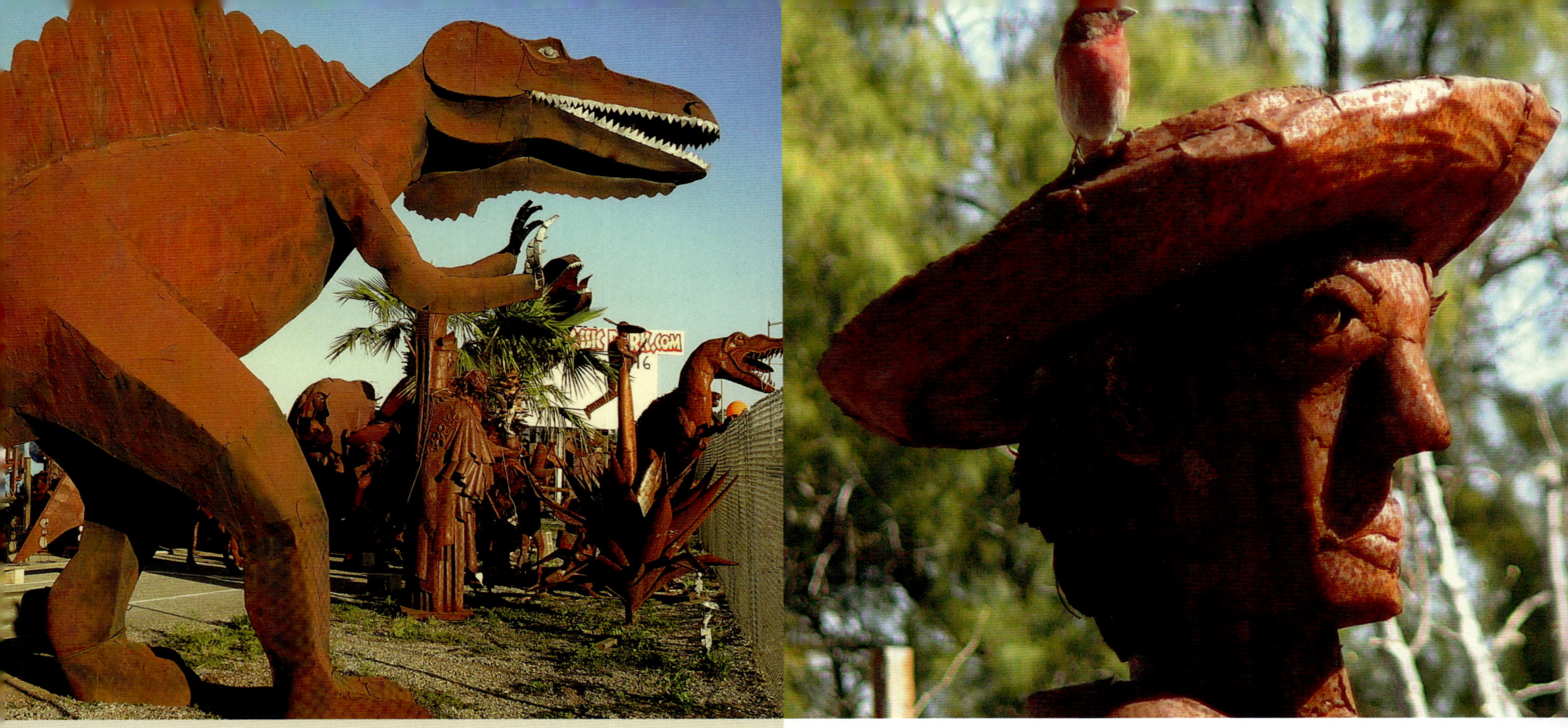

PERRIS JURASSIC PARK

Ricardo's sculpture garden in Perris, California, sits alongside Interstate 215. That is the only form of advertising that Ricardo needs to attract customers. Sculptures are positioned to peer over the fence at passing motorists. *From left to right*: Ricardo's first *Spinosaurus* is crude compared to the one found in Chapter 5; a house finch makes a perch on the head of a sculpture; a small dinosaur stands guard at the chain-link fence; Ricardo stands underneath Lianna's *T. rex*—still his daughter's favorite sculpture.

The majority of his customers continued to be attracted by the many sculptures that were clearly visible from Interstate 215. Some customers purchased completed sculptures displayed in the yard while others commissioned new creations, either showing Ricardo a picture of what they wanted or describing what they had in mind.

Dennis Avery was among the many motorists along Interstate 215. He had been peering at the sculpture garden for almost two years each time he made the trip from San Diego to Redlands and back again when he visited his sons, who attended the University of Redlands. At first, he barely glanced at the metal menagerie. Gradually it drew him in, growing in his consciousness, until one day in June 2007 his curiosity was heightened to the point that he took

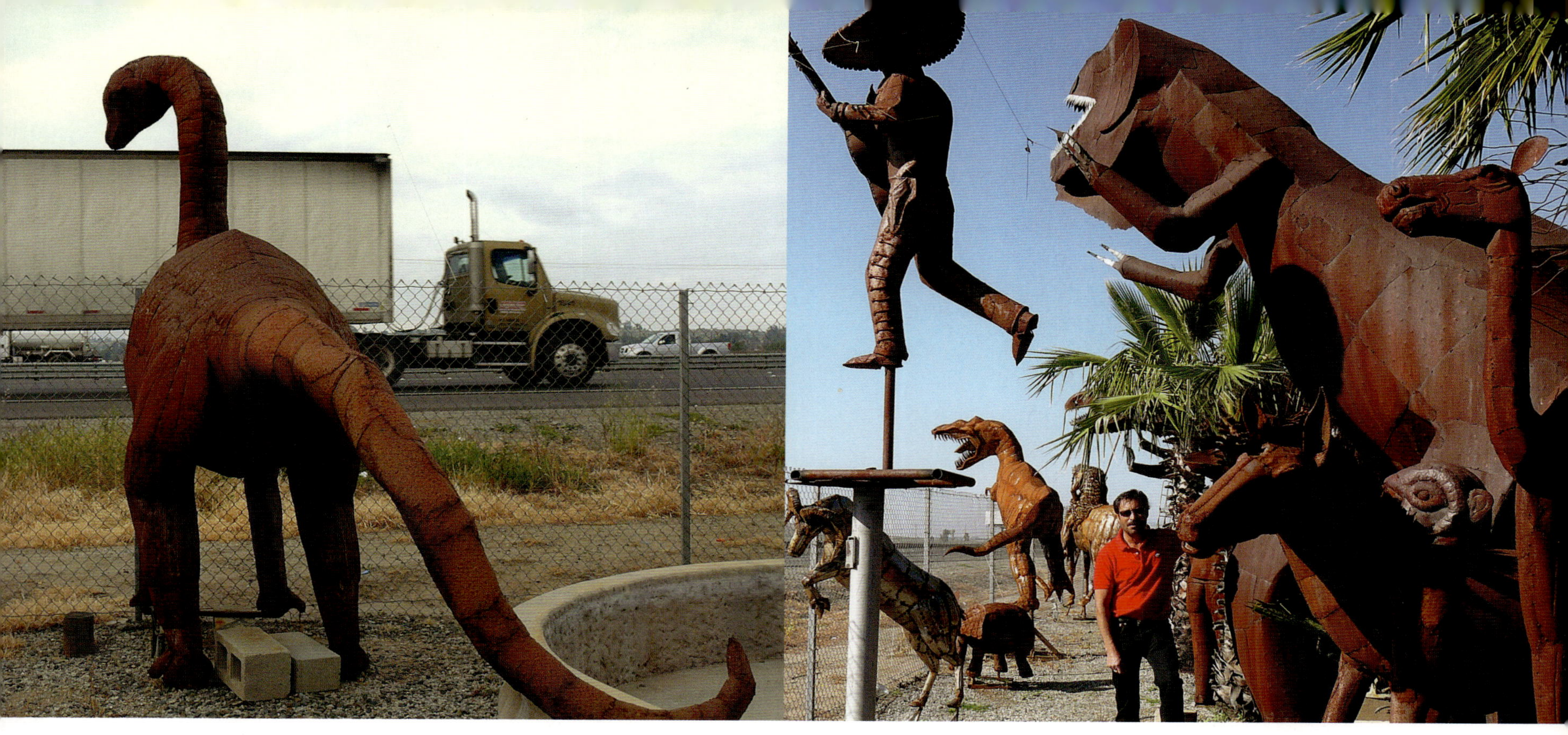

the nearest exit and worked his way back to Perris Jurassic Park like so many motorists before him had done.

Dennis drove up the frontage road, passing scattered industrial buildings, trees, and open fields until he arrived at the sculpture garden surrounded by a chain-link fence. He was met by a young man who could barely speak English, Ricardo's nephew Rodolfo, who was visiting from Mexico. Rodolfo explained that Ricardo was in Mexico and would be back in a few weeks.

Dennis walked around the grounds looking at the rust-patinaed giraffes, elephants, dolphins, alligators, horses, camels, *Velociraptors, Triceratops,* and the *Tyrannosaurus*. There was something about the primitive beauty of these sculptures, the unusual placement, and control of the metal pieces that gave them a remarkable and unique quality. Dennis picked up a price list, said good-bye to Rodolfo, and drove away.

In the next two weeks, Dennis thought off and on about those alluring works of art, and then he inquired about the purchase of several pieces from the sculpture garden. He made an offer and sent a check for half the payment, with the balance to be paid upon delivery to his home in San Diego. But that was not the end of it. Dennis began thinking of other possibilities.

In addition to a house in San Diego, Dennis had a home in Borrego Springs, a small unincorporated community completely surrounded by the starkly beautiful 660,000-acre Anza-Borrego Desert State Park, a world-renowned desert park noted for its rich Plio-Pleistocene fossils, open desert landscape, dramatic mountainous escarpment, palm tree–lined canyons, and spring wildflowers. Borrego Springs, a desert island unto itself, and in stark contrast to Palm Springs, is a quiet community where "Borrego midnight" is 9 P.M. and

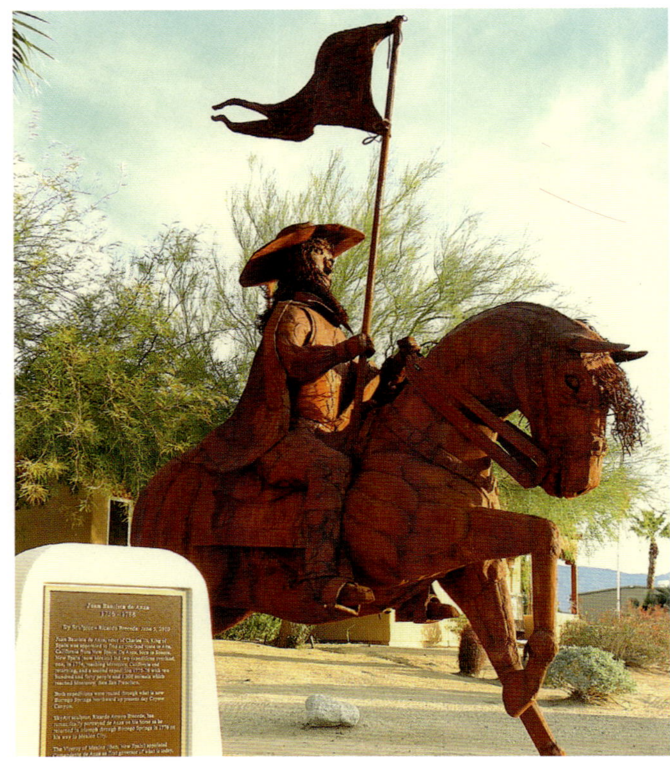

HN-6 Anza on Horseback. The Anza-Borrego area is named in part for Spanish explorer Juan Bautista de Anza, who opened the first overland trail and brought the first colonists to California in the 1770s. Ricardo's sculpture sits proudly in front of the Borrego Springs Chamber of Commerce.

the stars are celebrated. In 2009, Borrego Springs, dedicated to minimizing nighttime skyglow and photopollution, became the first official "dark-sky" community in California.

Dennis was a full-time resident of Borrego Springs from 1990 to 2001, where his children attended school and he coached Little League. In the mid-1990s in the wake of the savings-and-loan crash, Dennis purchased open lands for sale in the valley. He ended up with more than three square miles of scattered noncontiguous lands that he held in conservation.

Dennis had been holding these empty lands for more than ten years—lands that thousands and millions of years ago were the home of now-extinct Pliocene and Pleistocene animals. He could almost see giant camel-like and elephant-like creatures roaming the landscape. Dennis had a very

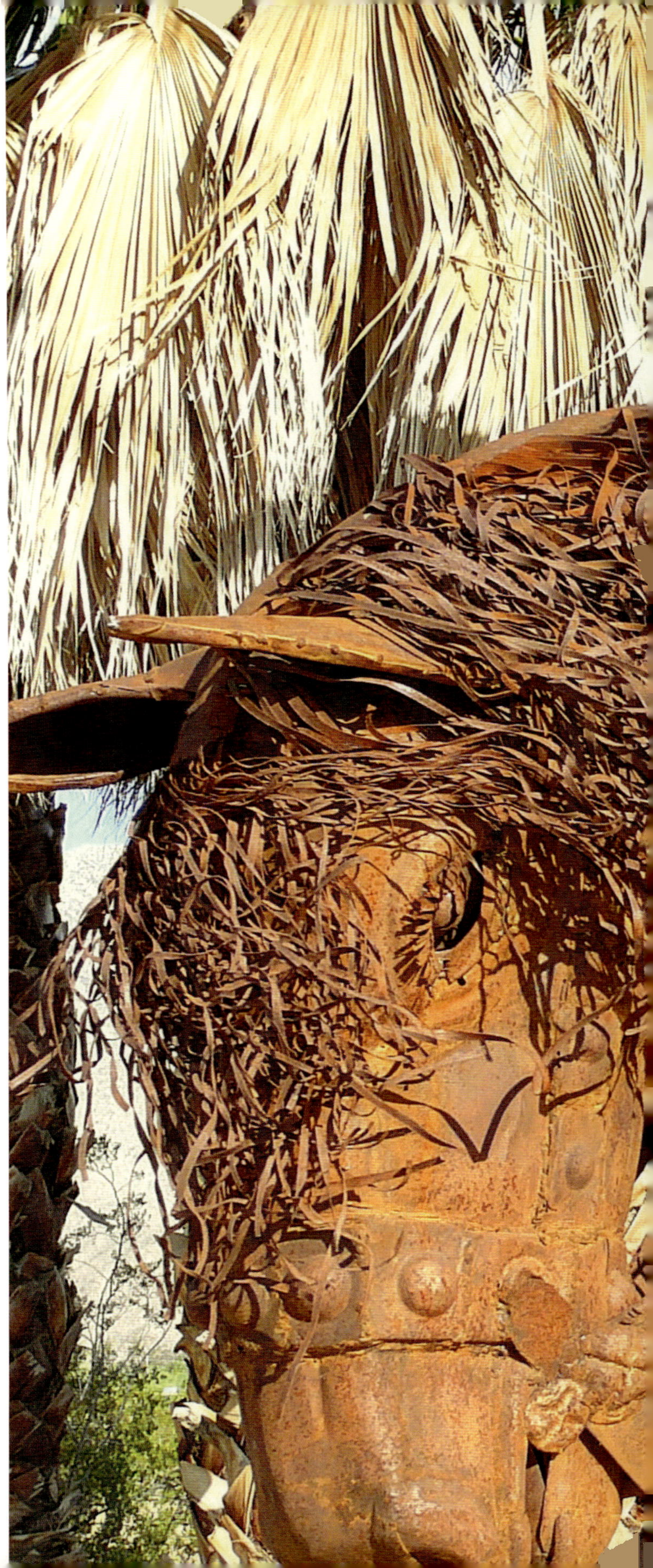

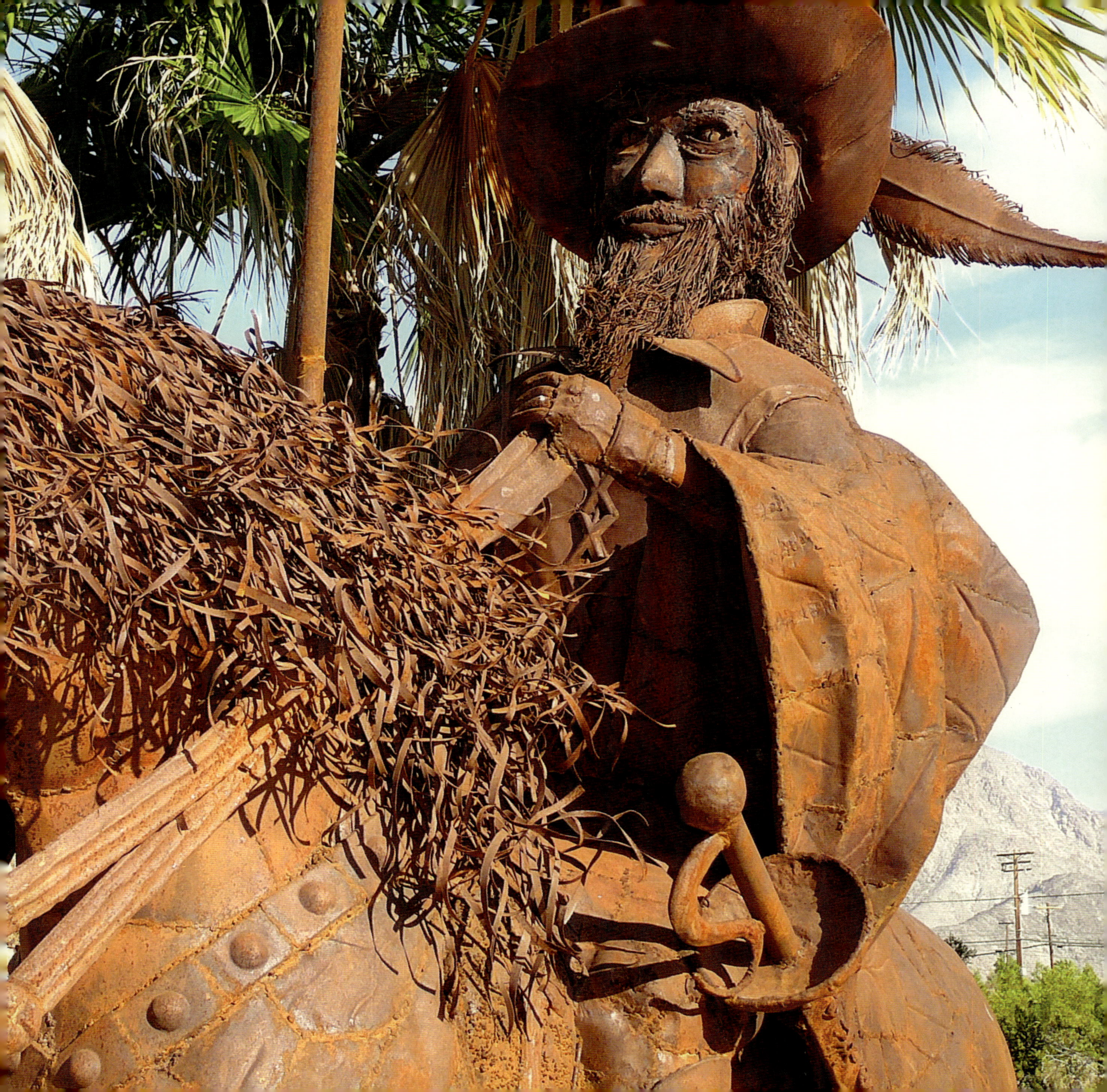

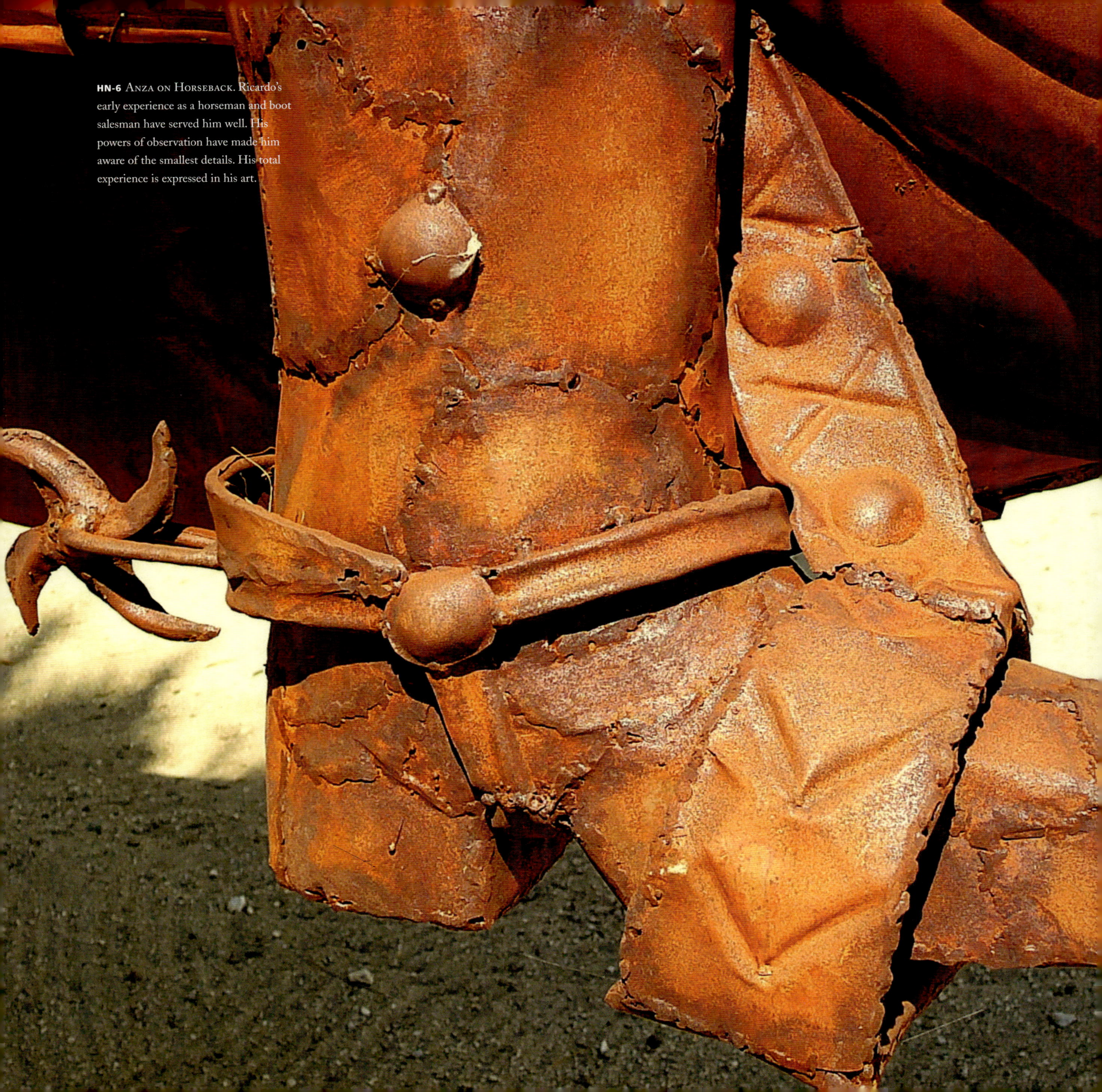

HN-6 Anza on Horseback. Ricardo's early experience as a horseman and boot salesman have served him well. His powers of observation have made him aware of the smallest details. His total experience is expressed in his art.

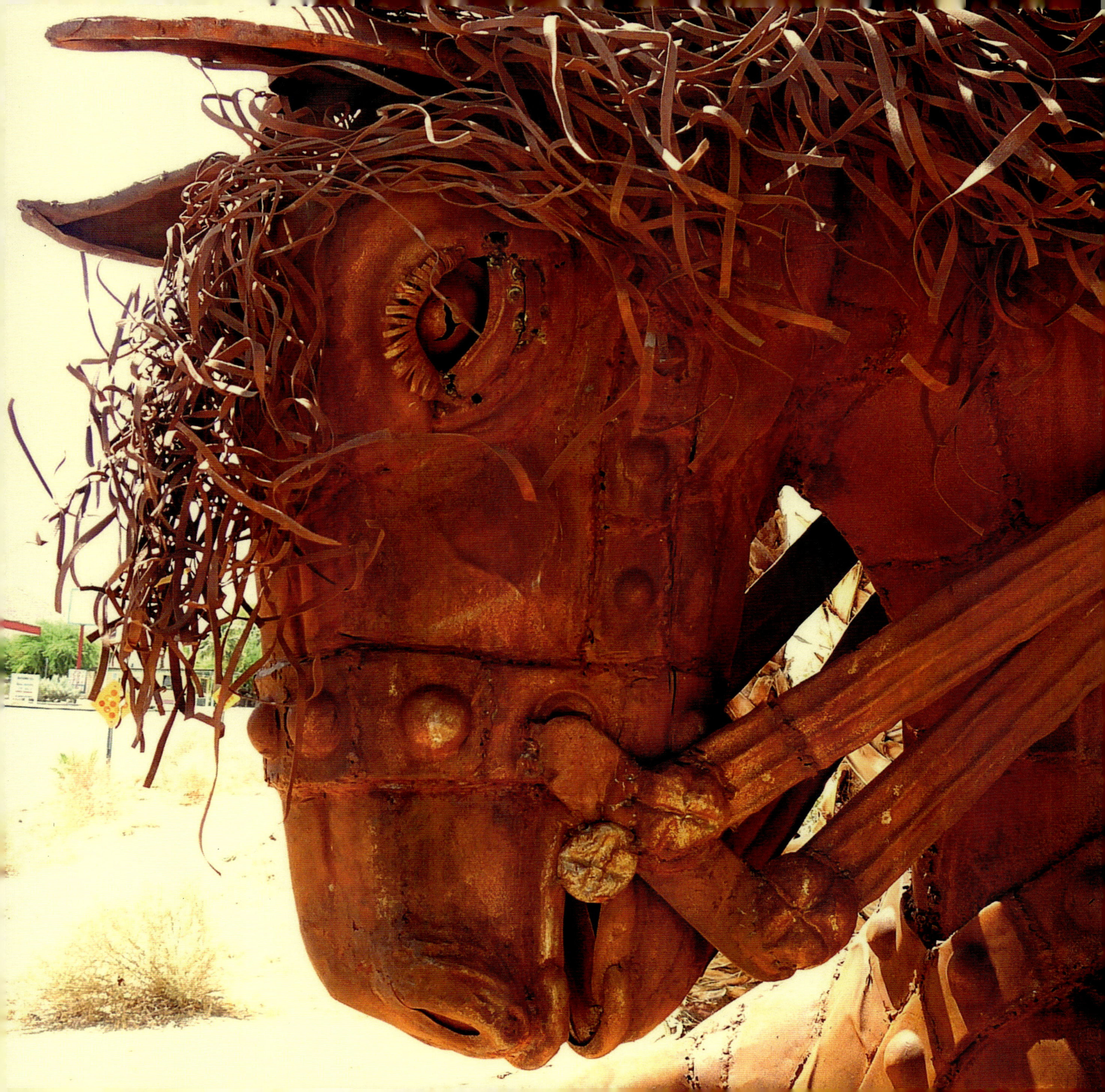

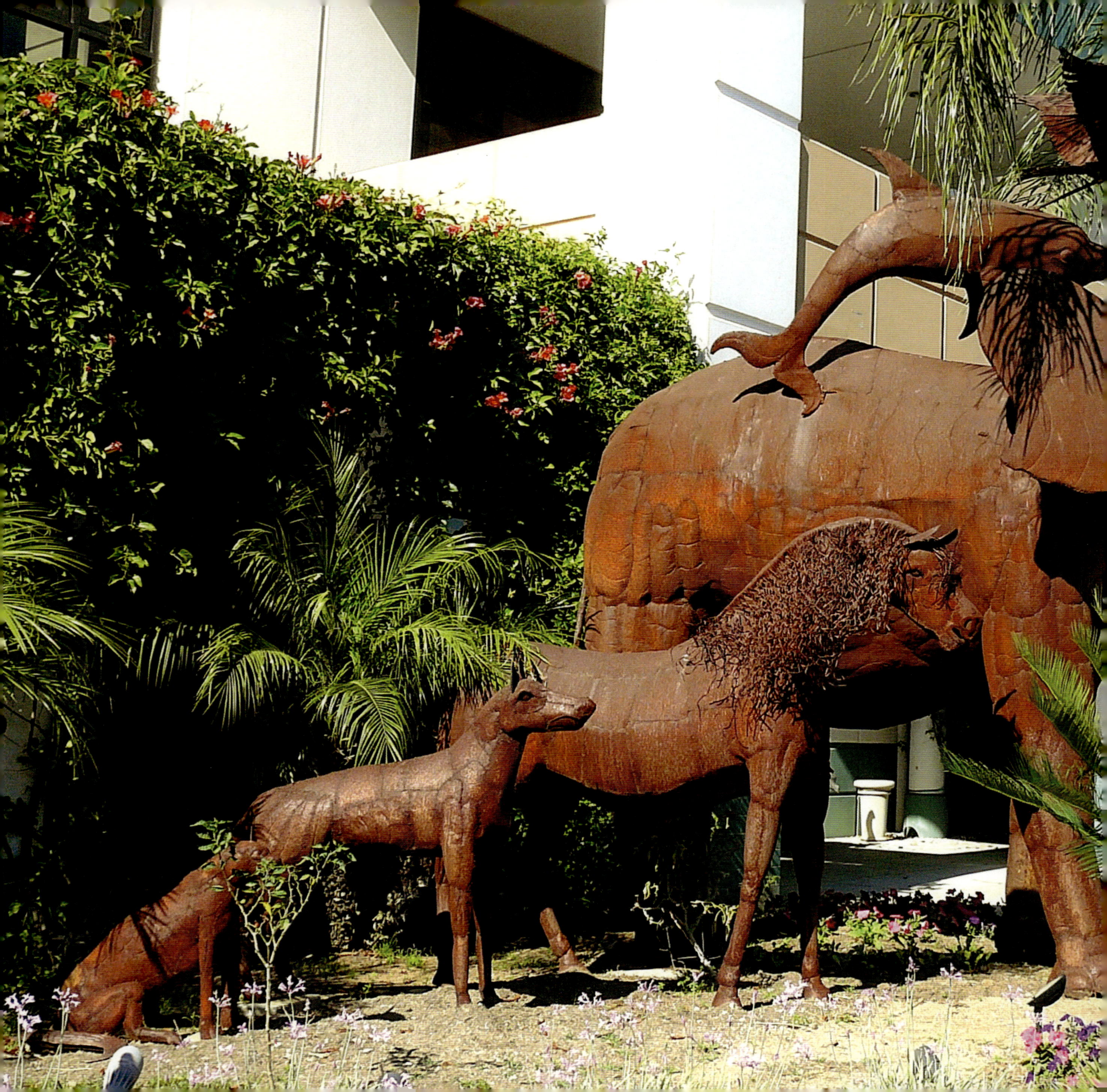

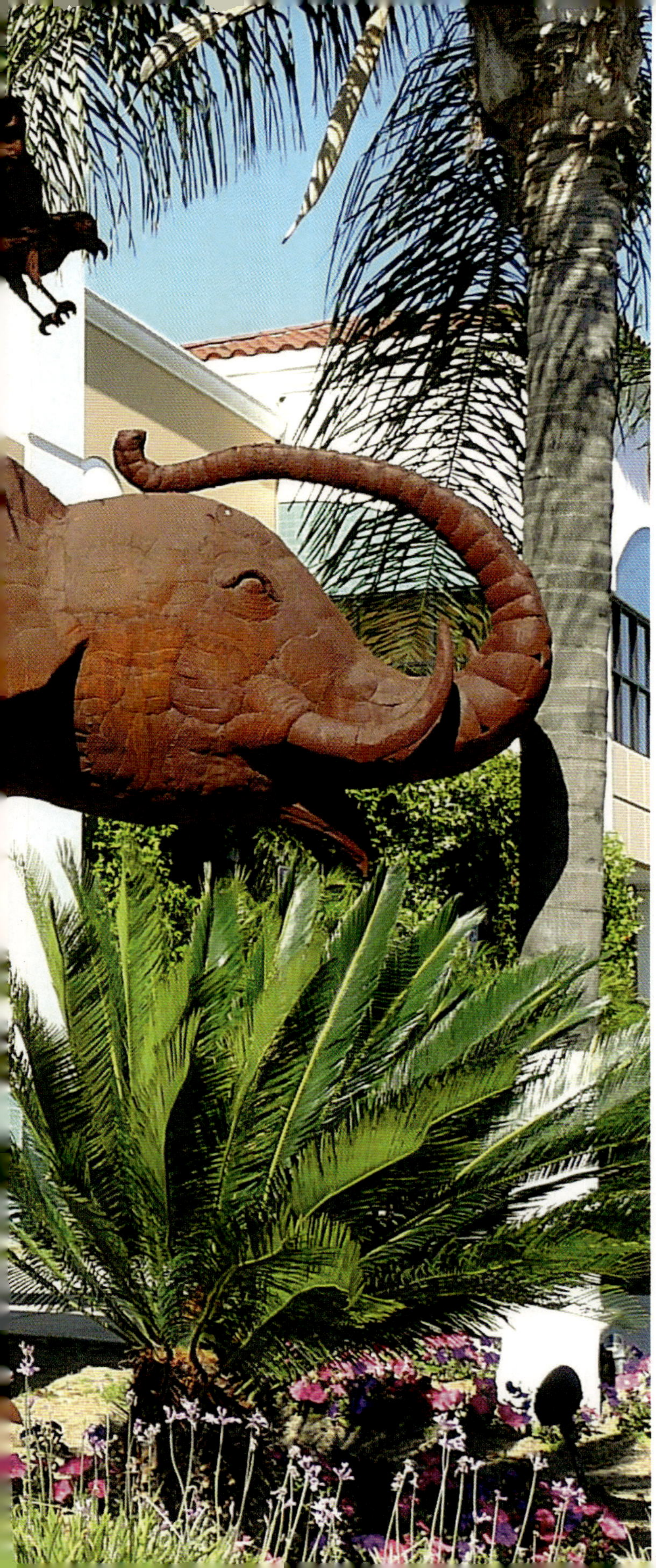

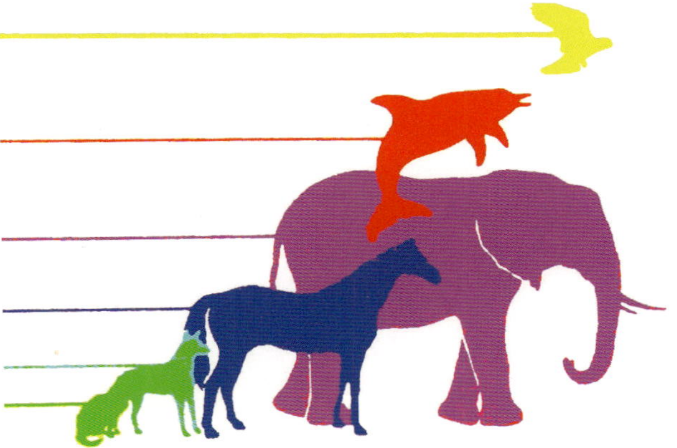

The AVID logo (*above*) comes to life in this three-dimensional depiction of an eagle above a dolphin on top of an elephant (*opposite*). Beside the elephant are a horse, a dog, and a cat, welcoming visitors to the corporate headquarters.

clear picture of these creatures, because he had been part of a 2006 major scientific publication on the paleontology of the Anza-Borrego area. His contribution had been to fund the artwork for *Fossil Treasures of the Anza-Borrego Desert,* edited by George T. Jefferson and Lowell Lindsay.

Slowly an idea began to take shape. Could this sculptor, Ricardo Breceda, build a life-size elephant-like gomphothere? Could he even create a family of gomphotheres to place on his property? It was a crazy idea, he knew, because he had no idea how residents in Borrego Springs would react to such a project. Imagine—a life-size gomphothere in its natural surroundings under the open sky. The more he thought about it, the more intrigued he became with the idea. But could an artist like Ricardo be equal to such a challenge? Especially if all he had to work with was a painting from a book?

A few weeks later, Dennis returned to Perris Jurassic Park, and this time he found Ricardo there. He showed Ricardo the drawing of an elephant-like gomphothere and asked him if he could make one. Without hesitation, Ricardo responded that all he needed was the drawing, and he could do it. Borrego Valley Sky Art was about to be born.

Ricardo sensed that there could possibly be more orders from Dennis if he did a good job on the gomphothere. He was determined to spend time creating details that would help to make it more lifelike.

In addition to the order from Dennis, Ricardo had another customer approach him that also held the possibility of future sculpture orders. In late summer 2007, Dr. Hannis L. Stoddard III, like other motorists, was drawn to the metal sculptures on the freeway and exited to find Ricardo at Perris Jurassic Park. Hannis showed Ricardo his business card and the company logo. He wanted to know if Ricardo could make a life-size logo that he could put in front of his corporate office. The logo consisted of an eagle above a dolphin on top of an elephant. Beside the elephant were a horse, a dog, and a cat.

Hannis is the founder and owner of the animal microchip identification company known as AVID (American Veterinary Identification Devices). The subcutaneous identifying chips are used in domesticated and zoo animals worldwide. The company is headquartered in Norco, California. They struck a deal, and Ricardo promised to have the sculptures ready in October 2007.

To handle these new orders, Ricardo had to hire and train new people to work in the shop, people who were used to an eight-hour workday and overtime pay. At the same time, the cost of metals, including recycled metals, was going up. In addition, Ricardo needed to devote more time to designing and working on the sculptures. He knew he was at a crossroads and needed to make new decisions.

The first decision he made was to become a full-time artist and to dedicate all of his time to designing the sculptures. He quit selling boots and closed off that source

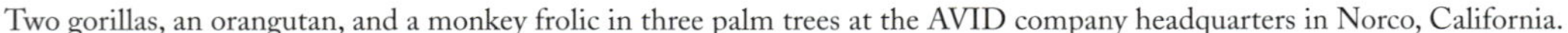

Two gorillas, an orangutan, and a monkey frolic in three palm trees at the AVID company headquarters in Norco, California.

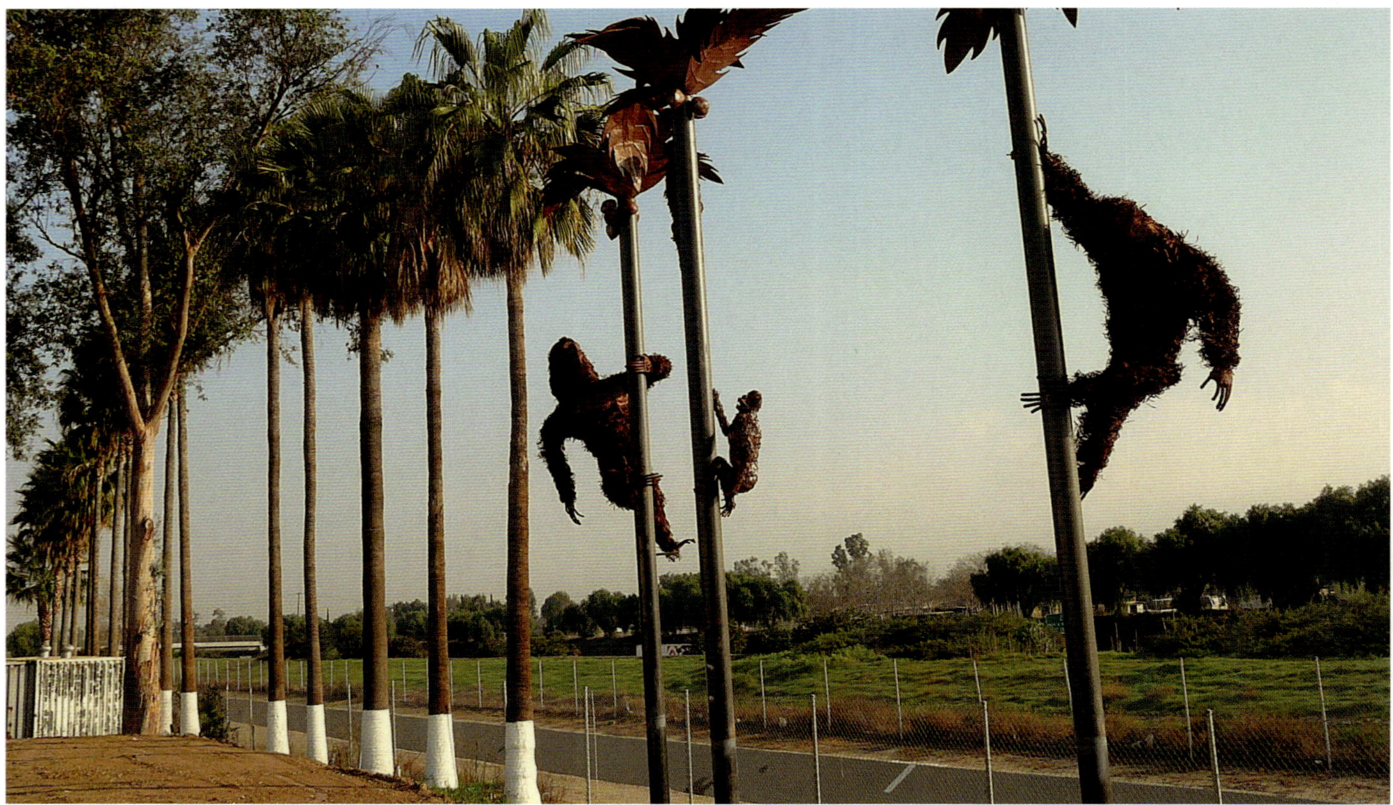

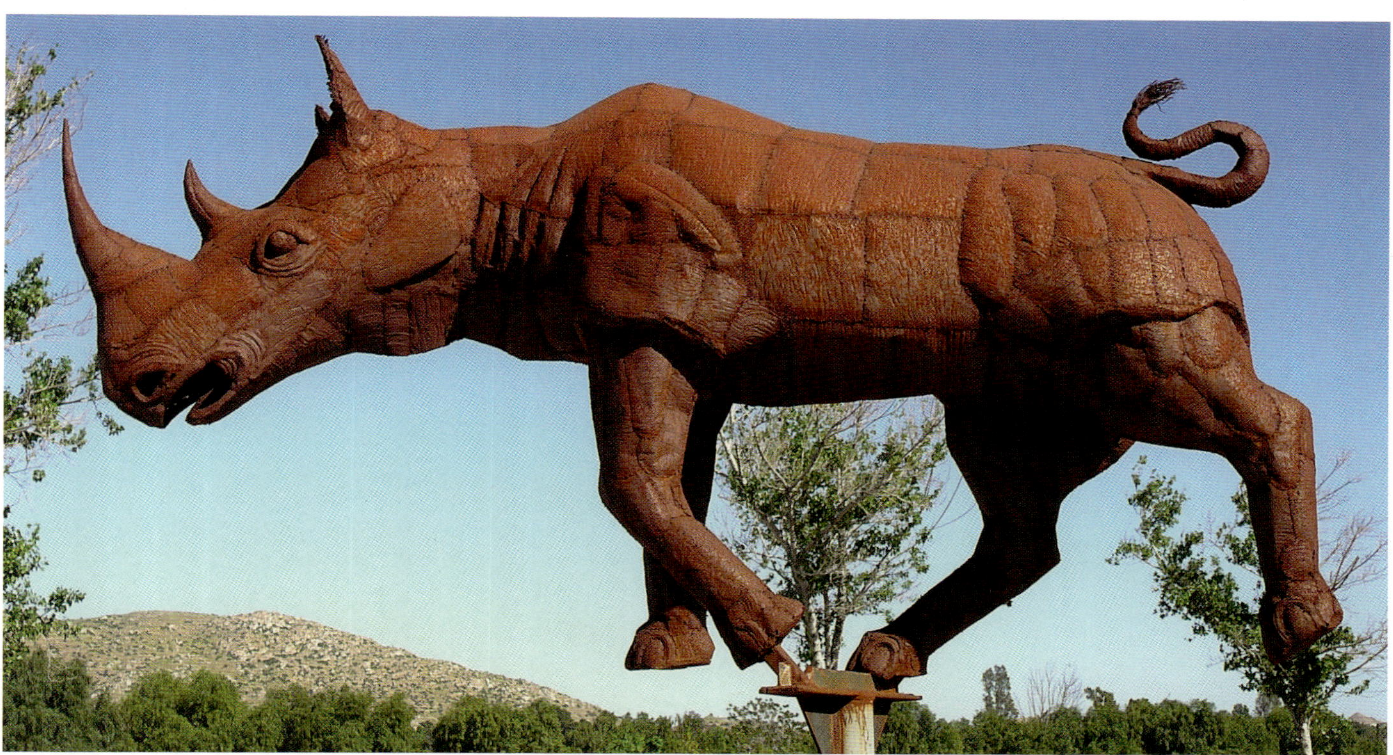

AVID is the animal microchip identification company. It has the second highest concentration of Ricardo's sculptures, including this African rhinoceros, a relative of the horse.

of income. He was now in a precarious situation. He and Porfirio had potential sales without the capital to fund the expenses and carry them over until the new orders were completed.

Porfirio had an idea how they could save money. He suggested moving their main welding shop to Rosarito Beach in Baja California, where labor and material costs were less. This would also benefit Porfirio, because his girlfriend could not cross the border and this way he could be with her and personally manage the shop in Mexico. After working out a budget, the plan made sense. They would now manage two welding shops, one in Mexico and one in Perris; Ricardo would still direct the operation and oversee the design in both shops. To help pay for the move, Ricardo began trading sculptures for needed tools for the new location.

Ricardo had correctly calculated the importance of these two customers and the potential of their future orders. Ongoing orders from Hannis and AVID have provided a permanent exhibit space for Ricardo's sculptures. And the Sky Art projects literally launched Ricardo from an artist of local interest to one deserving national attention.

The second order from AVID did not arrive until March 2010, when the company expanded its parking lot and wanted sculptures for it. The order consisted of two giraffes, one rhinoceros, and three oryx antelopes all fixed on high poles that could be seen not only from the parking area but also from Interstate 15. In October of the same year they ordered two gorillas, one monkey, and one orangutan that were all posed

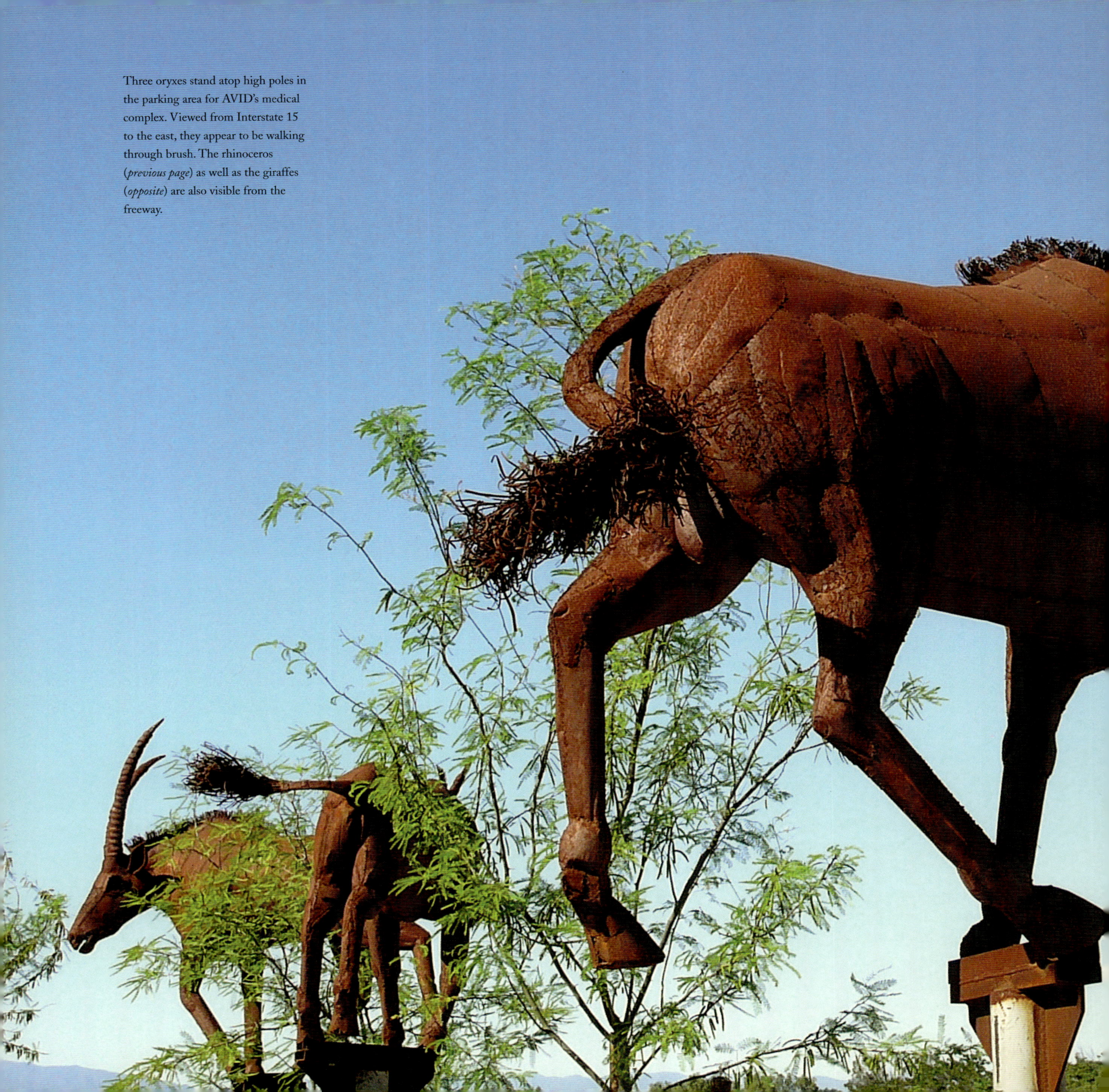

Three oryxes stand atop high poles in the parking area for AVID's medical complex. Viewed from Interstate 15 to the east, they appear to be walking through brush. The rhinoceros (*previous page*) as well as the giraffes (*opposite*) are also visible from the freeway.

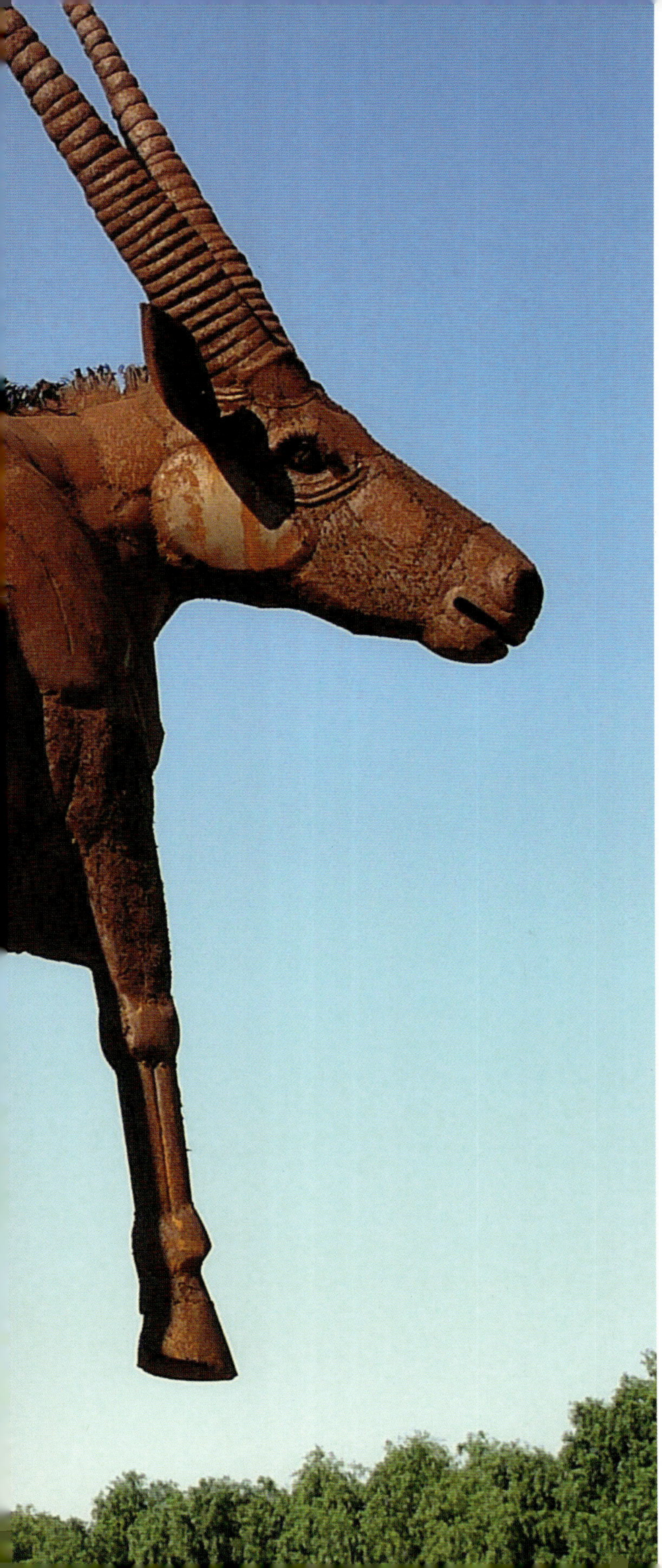

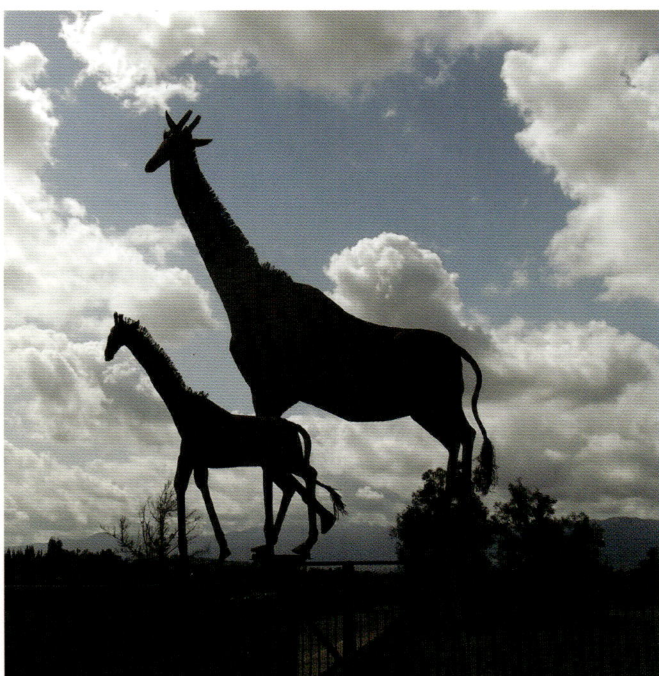

In the early morning light the AVID giraffes appear to be walking through a brushy African plain.

playfully observing or swinging from three metal palm trees, again visible from both the parking area and the highway.

In December 2010 three elephants were added. In February 2011 two zebras were placed in front of the newly constructed 25,000-square-foot animal and bird hospital. The following month, two ostriches with eggs were added. All were positioned to be visible only from the facility, not the freeway.

Gerald Gamble, Hannis's assistant, describes the doctor as "a kid at Christmas. . . . He will stop whatever he is doing when he hears that a new statue has arrived and will go down to see it. The doctor loves the lifelike appearance of the sculptures, and he thinks Ricardo is a great artist."

The parking lot has since become a tourist attraction, with visitors arriving several times a day. Small children will point to the animals and say their names. They are able to learn about the animals and see them life-size rather than in a book.

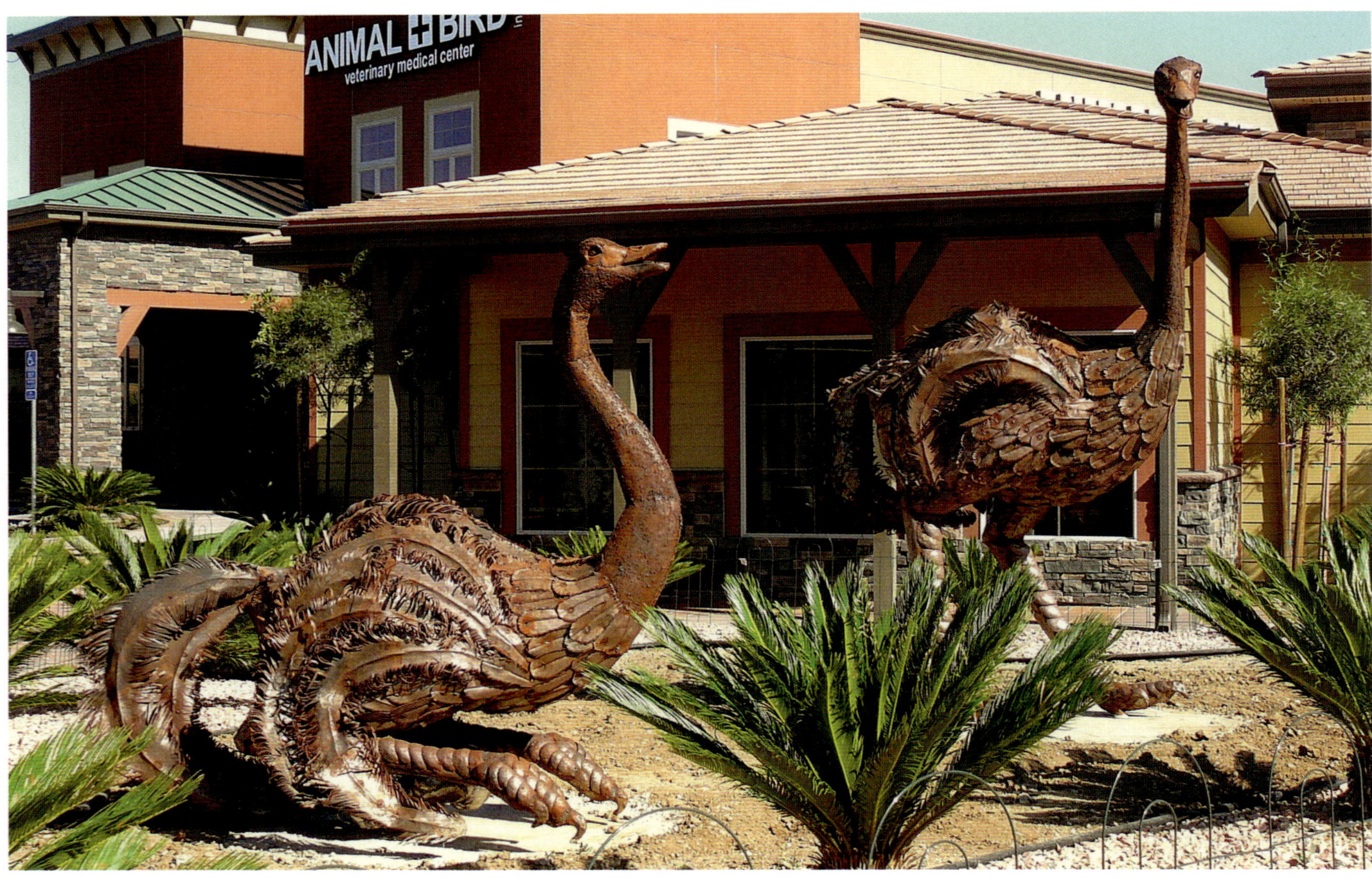

AVID has over twenty-five individual sculpture pieces displayed on their property, including this pair of ostriches.

Comments that Gerald has recorded include, "Oh my God, these are so lifelike!" and "I feel like I am driving in Africa." Probably the most common comments have to do with people talking about their lives and their relationship to animals or their trip to Africa. Gerald said, "This was what Dr. Stoddard was trying to achieve when he ordered his first statues."

From the freeway, drivers and passengers can see only vegetation with the animals seemingly walking in the brush. The poles that support them are not visible. Some interesting stories have come back to the offices as a result.

One story involved an elderly grandmother who was sitting in the back of the car. She told her children and grandchildren that she had just seen a giraffe, but they did not believe her. They were driving to San Diego. They argued for about an hour, believing she was imagining things. The family ended up driving an extra five hours on their way back to return to Norco to prove that there was no giraffe. Guess who was right?

Gerald describes the relationship between the doctor and Ricardo as very special. Hannis is very particular about things, but when it comes to the sculptures, he has total faith in Ricardo. The doctor will present an idea to Ricardo, and in turn, Ricardo will suggest how best to portray each animal for the most dramatic effect.

Gerald remarked, "For the doctor to give free rein to someone with an idea is huge. Their relationship is based on a lot of trust."

The Norco sculptures on Hamner Avenue are not yet in any guidebook. People find out about them either by word of mouth or by seeing them on the west side of I-15 between the Second and Sixth Street freeway exits. AVID has plans to add something about Ricardo and his sculptures to their website in the future. They also intend to have Ricardo create other sculptures for their metal menagerie.

Interestingly, both Hannis and Dennis had the same initial purpose in mind in using Ricardo's sculptures—introducing a subject matter through art to make it more appealing. For Hannis, it was a way to connect people with animals of the world. His purpose has not changed. For Dennis, the objective was to connect Borrego Valley residents and visitors to the rich fossil history of the area by having life-size representations of Plio-Pleistocene animals placed in areas where they once lived and roamed. Dennis's initial intent, like a living thing, continues to evolve.

Ricardo's AVID sculptures help to connect people to the animals of the world. Their lifelike mannerisms, as displayed by these elephants, are engaging.

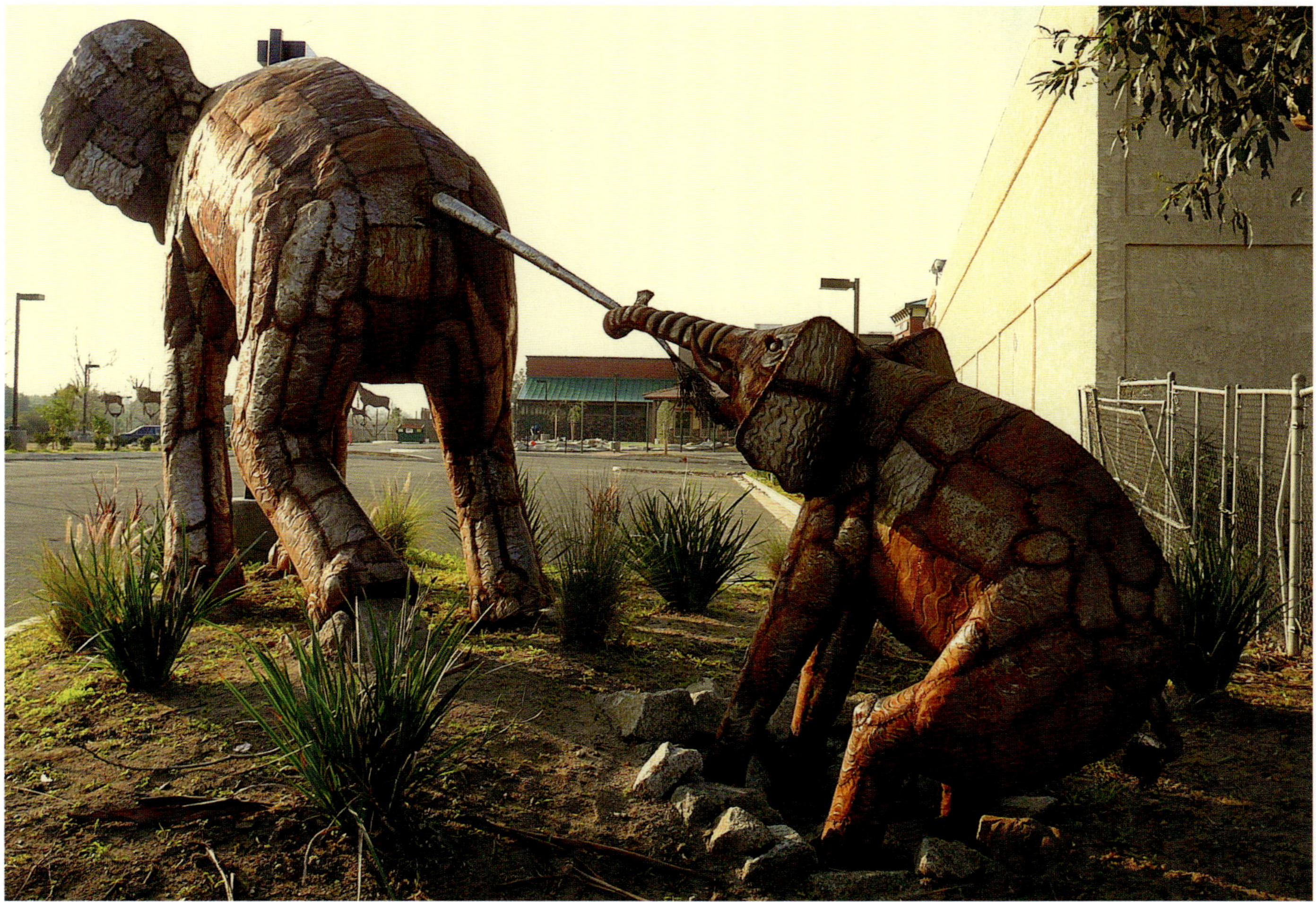

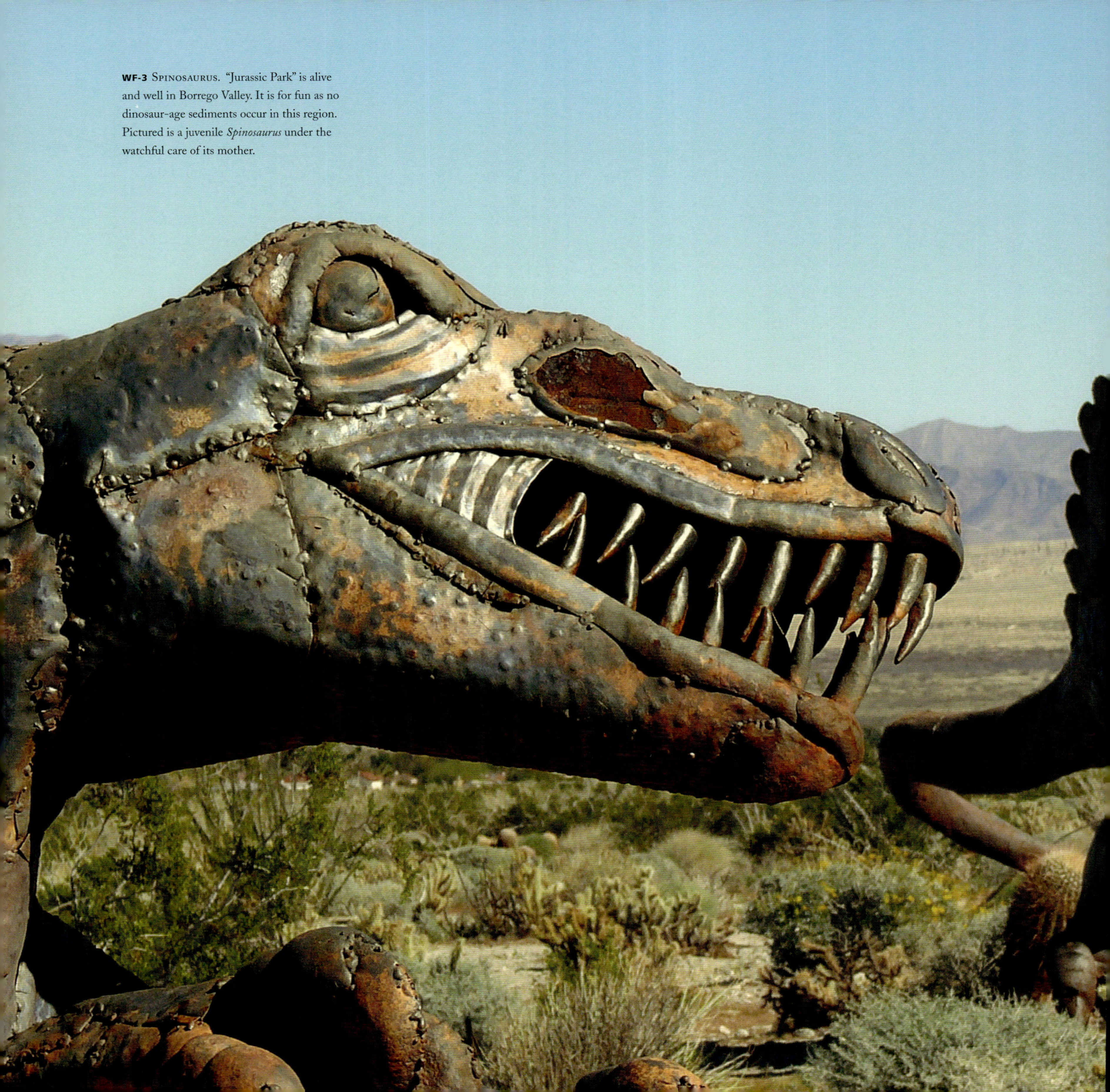

WF-3 Spinosaurus. "Jurassic Park" is alive and well in Borrego Valley. It is for fun as no dinosaur-age sediments occur in this region. Pictured is a juvenile *Spinosaurus* under the watchful care of its mother.

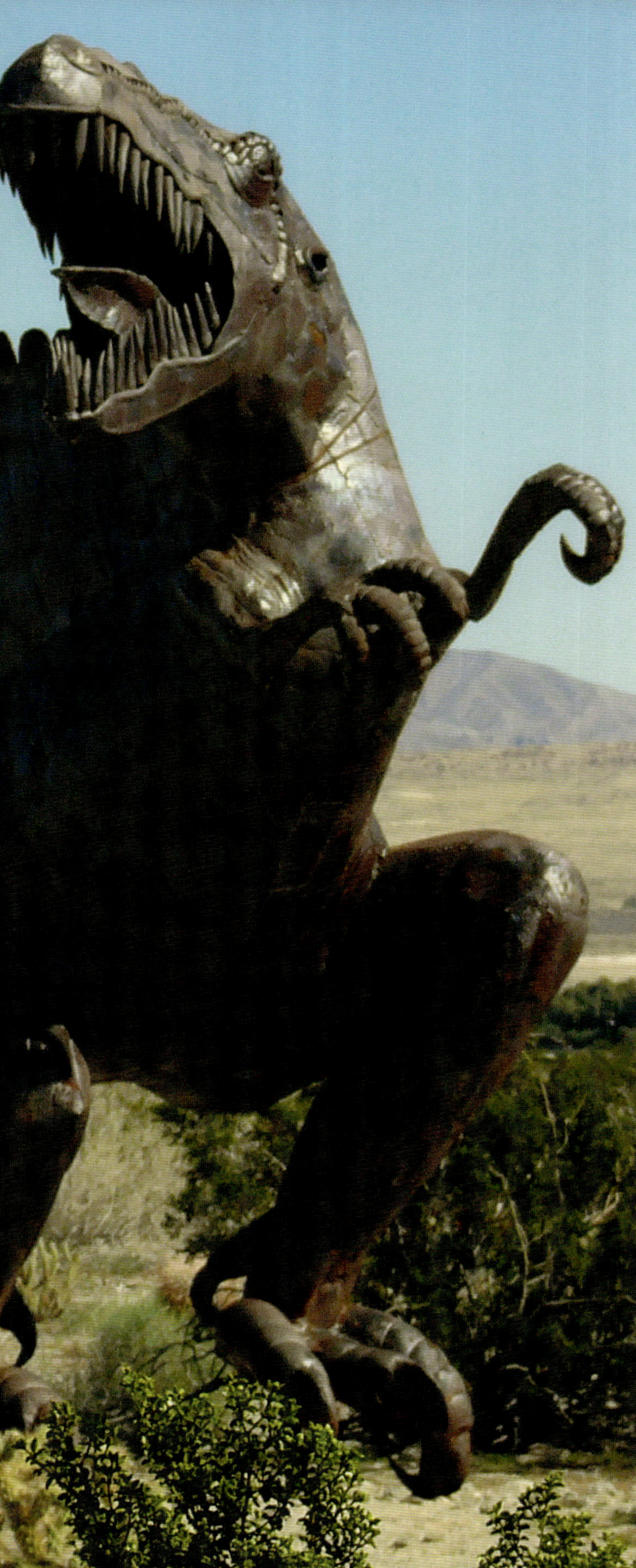

CHAPTER 5

THE SKY ART PROJECT

Like a proud father ushering the bride down the aisle, Ricardo led the procession east from Perris and then south down Highway 86 to Salton City in the early morning hours of Saturday, April 10, 2008. Secured in a trailer behind his Ford Super Duty F-350 King Ranch truck were the steel "bride" and her offspring. Following closely behind in another trailer, pulled by a beefy red pickup truck, was the twelve-foot-tall and twenty-foot-long majestic "groom."

At Salton City the procession turned west onto Highway S-22, crossing the fossil-rich Borrego Badlands as they headed to Borrego Valley and the site of the new home for the family of gomphotheres, elephant-like creatures that had once lived in the Anza-Borrego region from approximately 9 million to 1.4 million years ago.

The "wedding party" had grown since it had left Perris, picking up the curious along the way who wanted to know where these amazing half-ton creatures were going. Once in the valley, the photographer from the *Borrego Sun* was busy snapping photos as the "family" was set up in permanent pose. That afternoon, when the guests and the curious had left, the gomphotheres, displaying their unusual four tusks, seemed to be gazing over the landscape, surveying their new desert home.

Borrego residents, who are known for getting up with the sun because they go to bed soon after the sun goes down,

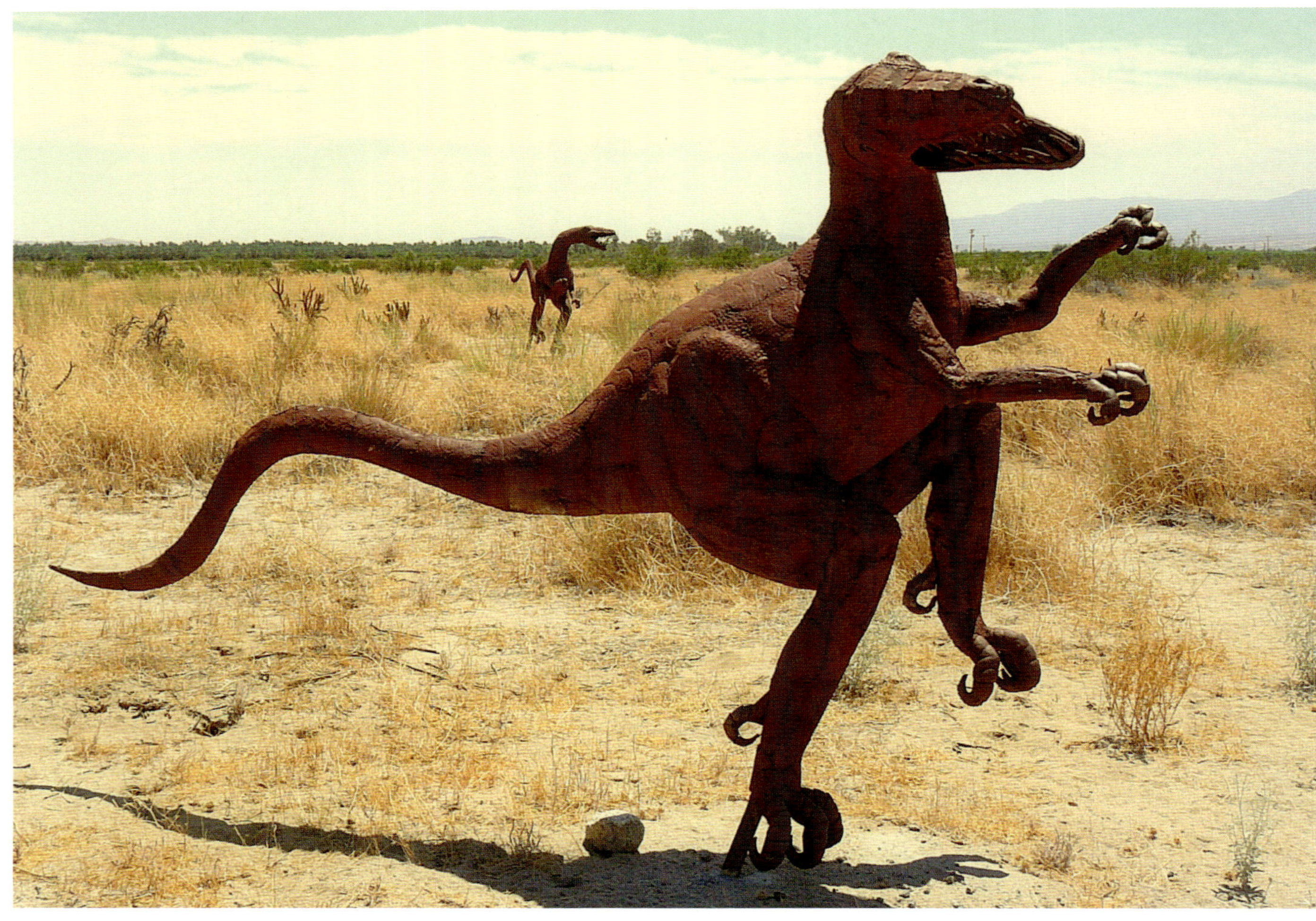

WF-1 Velociraptor. *Above and opposite*: The *Velociraptor* was made famous in the *Jurassic Park* films. However, it was portrayed dramatically larger than it actually was, which is estimated to be less than three feet tall.

were returning from their day's activities, driving along Borrego Springs Road. There, near the intersection with Big Horn Road, was a remarkable sight to behold—the Plio-Pleistocene epoch had returned to this small valley. It did not take long for this exciting news to spread throughout the town, nor did it take long for Dennis Avery to learn what the reaction might be to his bold move.

The very next day a San Diego television news crew from Channel 8 showed up at Dennis's office wanting an interview, and the *Borrego Sun* wrote a very positive piece about the installation. This was sculptor-artist Ricardo Breceda's debut in Borrego Springs, and it was largely love at first sight.

Ricardo's metal gomphotheres and the other silent behemoths that followed actually fit perfectly in this open and naked land—a primitive landscape for primitive art. The Plio-Pleistocene-inspired sculptures in particular increased the awareness and importance of the scientific aspect of the

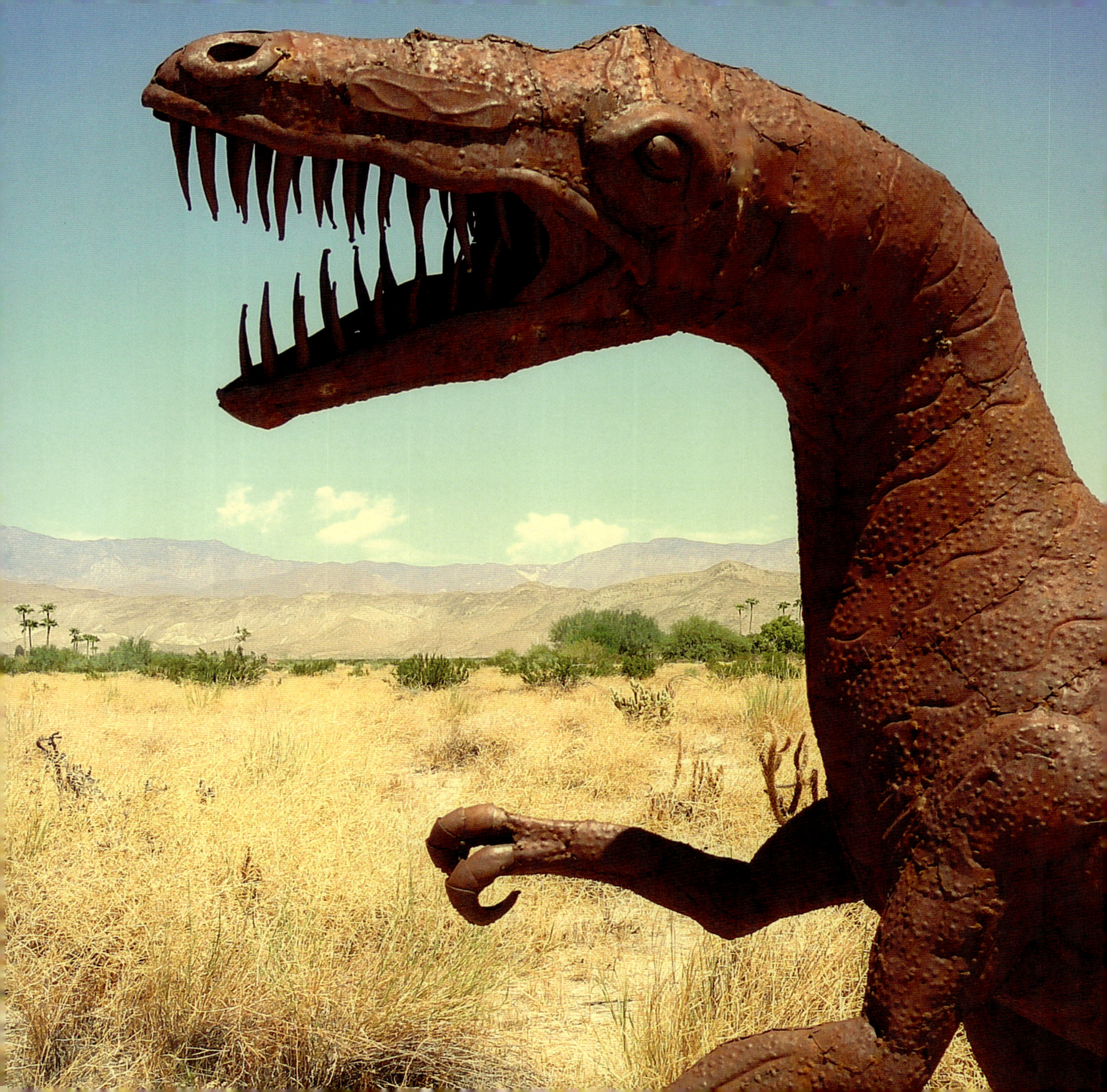

area's long past, especially in children. As an art form, all of the sculptures added to an already rich catalog of art expression visible in this community. They also helped to attract tourists, who are so essential for the area's businesses. Dennis may be the patron for Sky Art, but it has been Ricardo's own abilities as an artist that has truly earned him the respect of this community.

Borrego Springs is surrounded by the pristine and rugged Anza-Borrego Desert State Park. Many of the area residents actively support the park's mission to preserve and protect its many resources. One of the resources is the rich trove of paleontological specimens found in the park. A very active volunteer Paleontology Society works closely with the district paleontologist to collect, prepare, and curate fossil specimens. The society also has an educational component that works with school-age children to increase their awareness of and interest in science. The presence of sculptures that are scientifically inspired fits well with these programs.

From the very beginning, Dennis thought that life-size sculptures would ignite the imagination of children and possibly more interest in science and in the Plio-Pleistocene animals of the area. He viewed the sculptures as three-dimensional representations of fossils buried for millions of years. "My idea might not be completely rational," he said, "but it is certainly pretty amazing. Especially if you're eight years old!"

WF-1 Velociraptor. The forelimbs of the *Velociraptor* had digits with three strongly curved claws. It also had a large sickle-shaped foot claw.

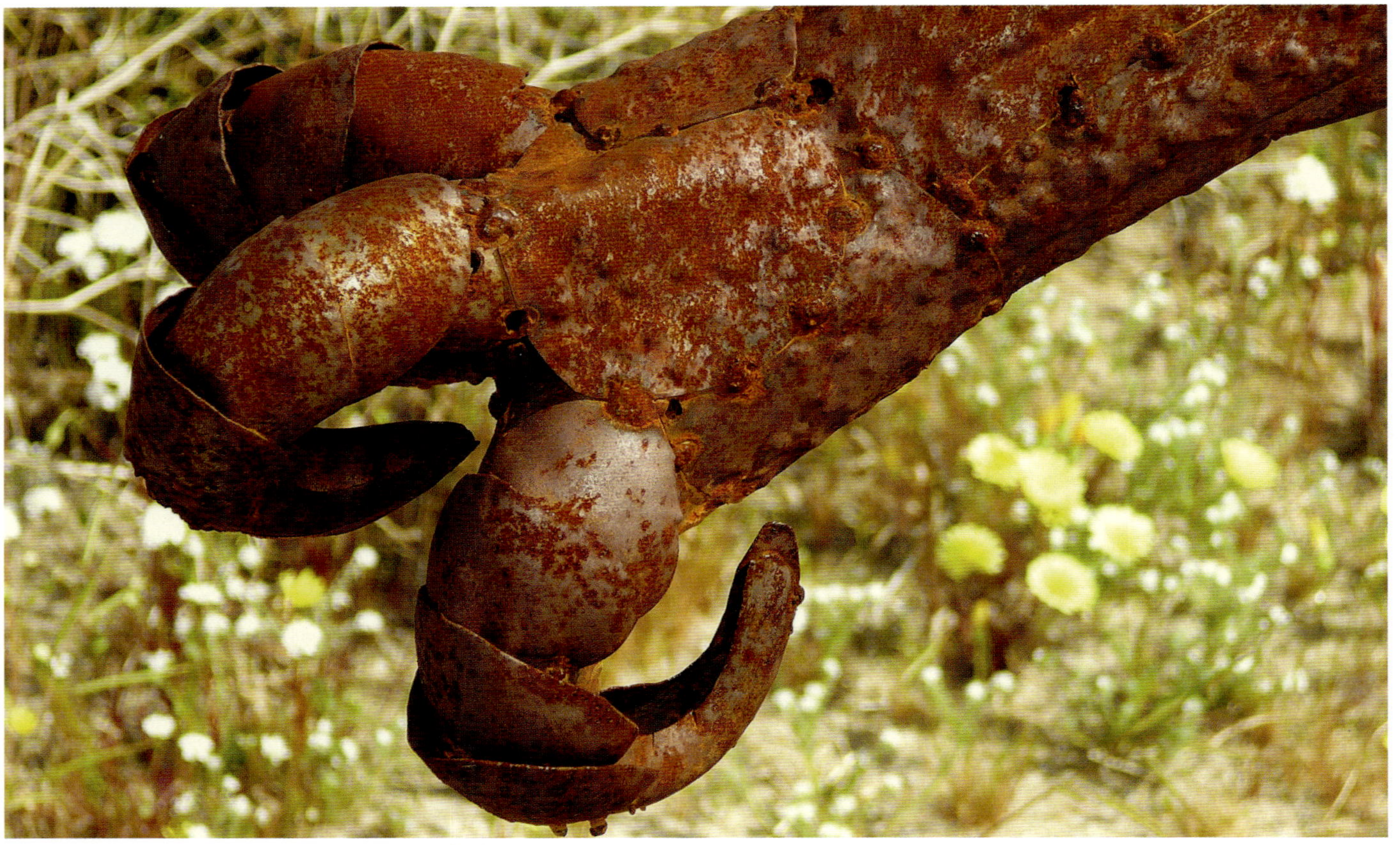

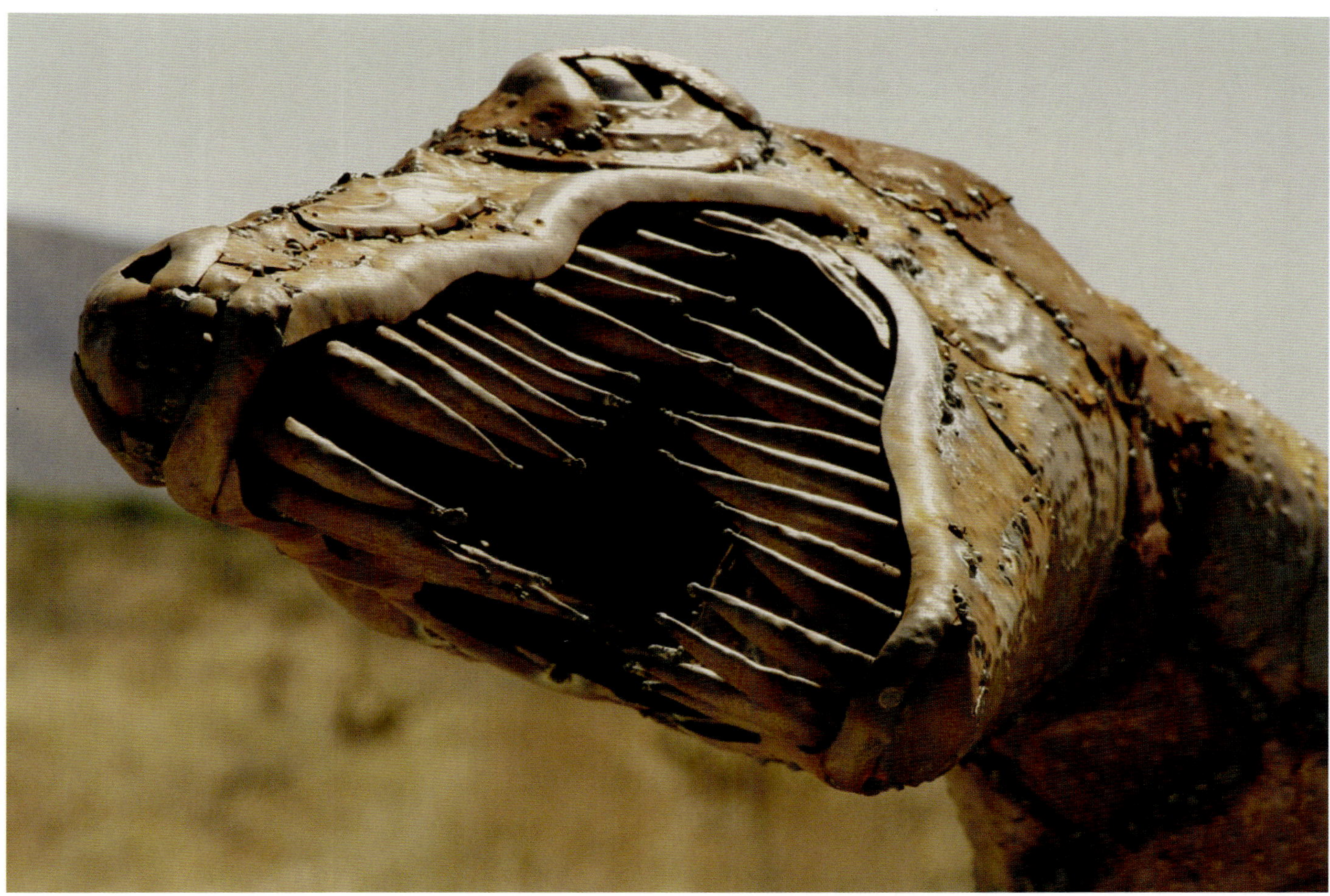

WF-1 Velociraptor. The *Velociraptor* was a bird-like theropod dinosaur with feathers that lived during the late Cretaceous period, about 85 to 80 million years ago. It was the first dinosaur to be installed in Galleta Meadows.

The model for the first sculptures was based on drawings by Pat Ortega, an award-winning scientific illustrator, and John Francis, a renowned landscape artist whose illustrations are now the background paleolandscapes at the Anza-Borrego Desert State Park Visitor Center. Their drawings are found in the 2006 publication of *Fossil Treasures of the Anza-Borrego Desert,* a landmark publication featuring the comprehensive work of twenty-three leading scientists and specialists from scientific and educational institutions across the United States. This book, which opens a window into the region's long-vanished past through its scientific interpretation and analysis of fossil finds, was the direct inspiration for the creation of the original sculptures. Certainly Dennis was absolutely delighted with the detailed work that Ricardo demonstrated with his first commissioning. He was also pleased with the immediate acceptance of the gomphotheres from a wide audience, which was encouraging because he had already ordered more sculptures from Ricardo based on other drawings found in *Fossil Treasures.*

He dubbed the sculptures "Sky Art." Sky Art refers

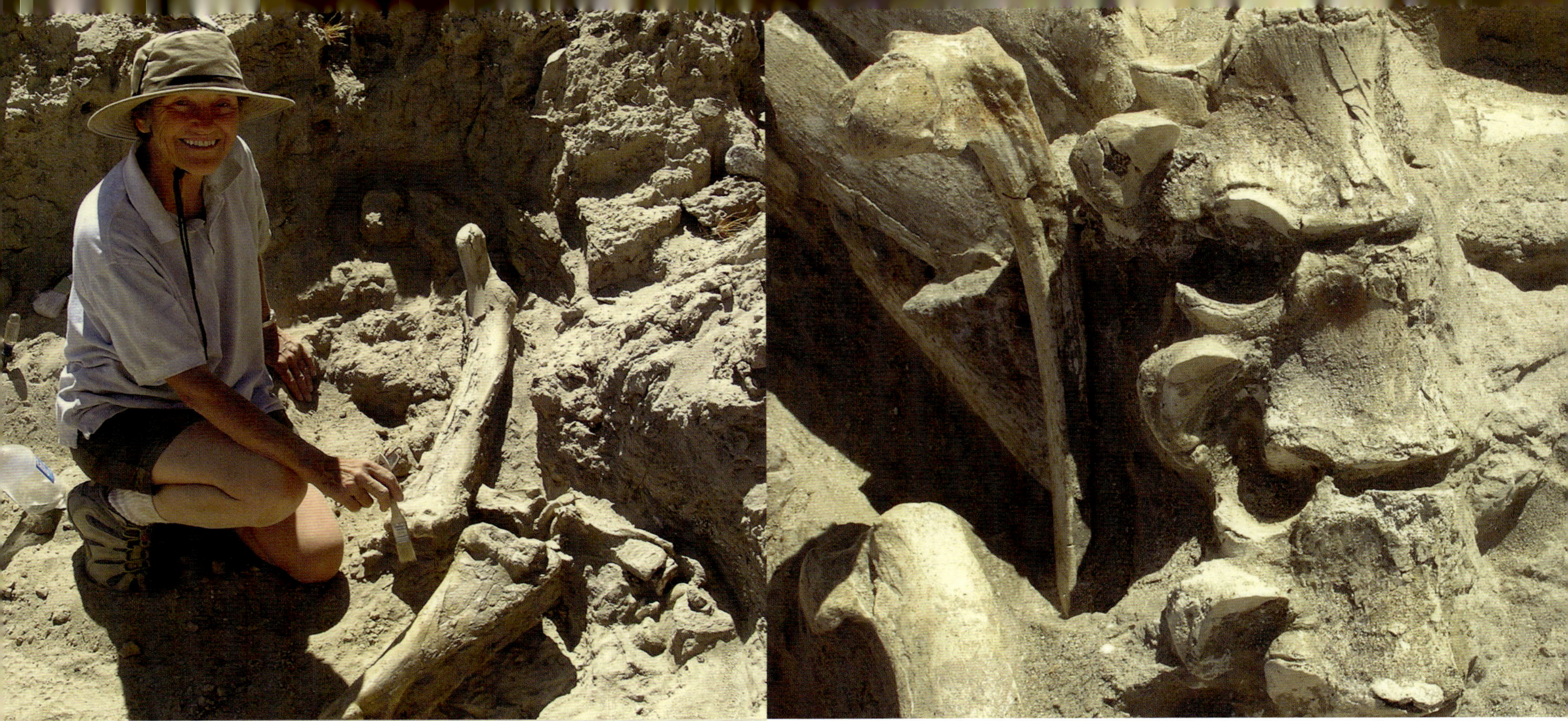

PALEONTOLOGISTS AT WORK
A very active Paleontology Society, made up of volunteers, works closely with the district paleontologist to collect, prepare, and curate fossil specimens. *From left*: Sandra Keeley carefully brushes leg bones; a close-up of fossil remains found in the field; Linda Gilbert documents her discovery of a nearly complete giant tortoise shell fossil (*Hesperotestudo* sp.) while attending the annual field camp in 2010; in celebration of her very rare find, Linda purchased one of Ricardo's giant tortoise sculptures where it now graces her yard in Borrego Springs.

to art under the sky that is integrated into the surrounding landscape. Where the work of art is placed is an integral component of its effect. It is also a relative art form that depends on and varies with the human experience. One's perspective becomes part of the art itself. Dennis muses that it is "fantasy, foible, fact . . . fun, folly, and turmoil. Finite. Eventually a pile of rust. Everyone senses that: the life, the death of it." The art of Christo and Jeanne-Claude or the buried Cadillacs all lined up on Highway 66 in Amarillo, Texas, are other examples of this perspective.

When the first article about the placement of the gomphotheres ran on the front page of the *Borrego Sun* on April 17, 2008, a paid announcement also appeared on the interior pages inviting the public onto the privately owned land to view the sculptures. The headline called the sculptures "Inspired Art of Past as Present for Children of Any Age." It was also the

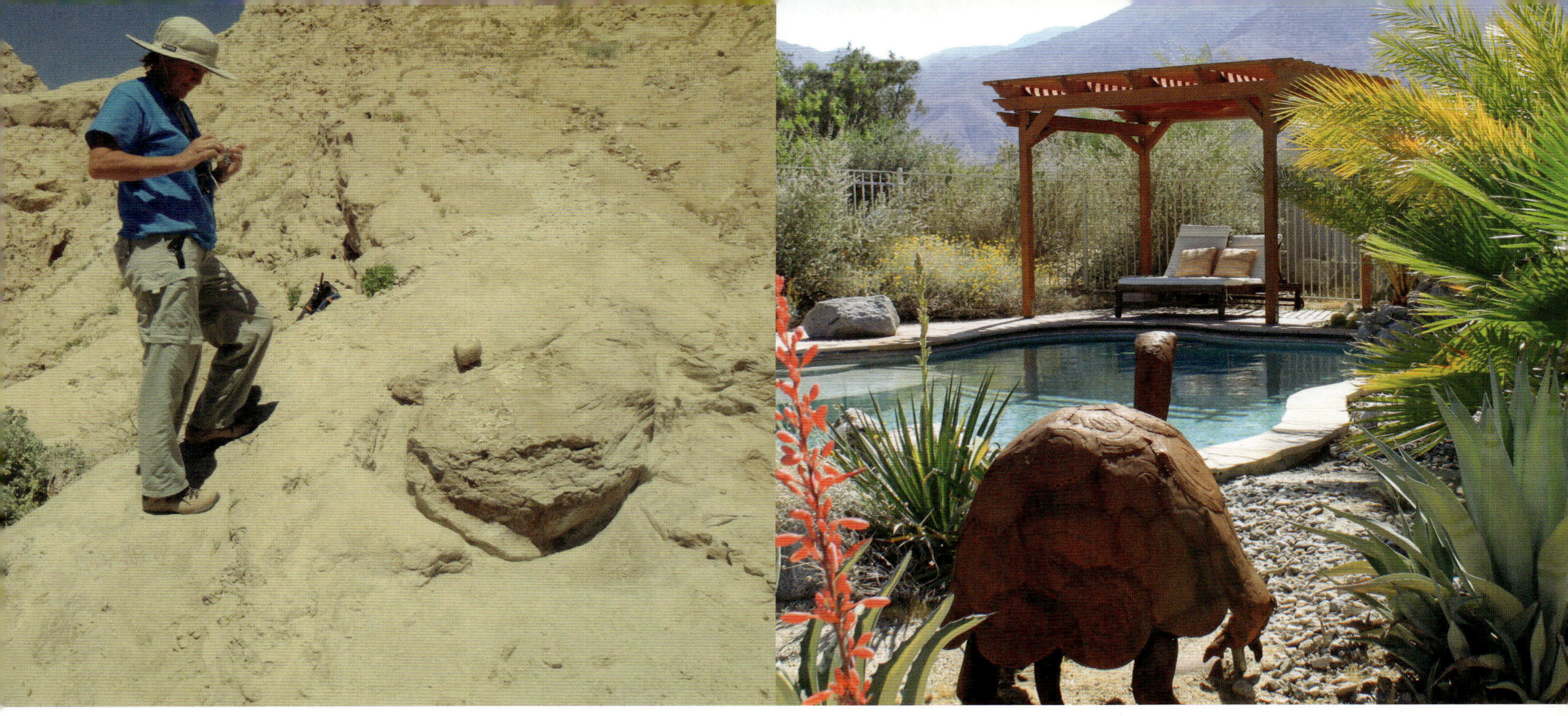

first time that the term “Sky Art” appeared, and Ricardo was formally introduced to the community. The ad (with typographical and grammatical errors corrected here but not errors of fact) also announced that more sculptures were coming, and the purpose of the sculptures was explained:

> Borrego Springs celebrates its wildflowers, bighorn sheep, open skies, and mildly populated land. Tourists, residents, and sightseers enjoy, each knowing Anza-Borrego desert is North America’s greatest preserve of vanished species. Their bones, fossils, remain; no greater diversity or scientifically proven habitat exists in North America.
>
> Hispanic Sculptor *Ricardo Breceda*’s art brings alive again, in sculptured form, Borrego’s early residents of epochs past.
>
> *Ricardo Breceda*, over extended time, re-created for today what vanished yesterday. His natural talents and creations from ready materials distinguish his expressions of vertebrates, born of fantasy and fossil fact.
>
> His art births expression of life which may enthrall or inspire appreciation and awe of the Pleistocene to Miocene Eras. *Ricardo Breceda*’s master talent of storied creations, combined with outdoor sculpture, impresses our landscape with past ever present.
>
> During 2008, his masterworks, outside roadways and in fields of Borrego Springs, are shared, bringing closer the present and past for visitors and residents.
>
> **One by one, they are appearing:**
>
> The Gracile Sabertooth (*Smilodon gracilis*),
> The Elephant (*Gomphotherium*),
> The Ground Sloth (*Paramylodon harlani*),
> The Single Hump Camel (*Camelops*),
> The Bird Giant (*Aiolornis incredibilis*),
> Turtles, Llamas, and more . . .

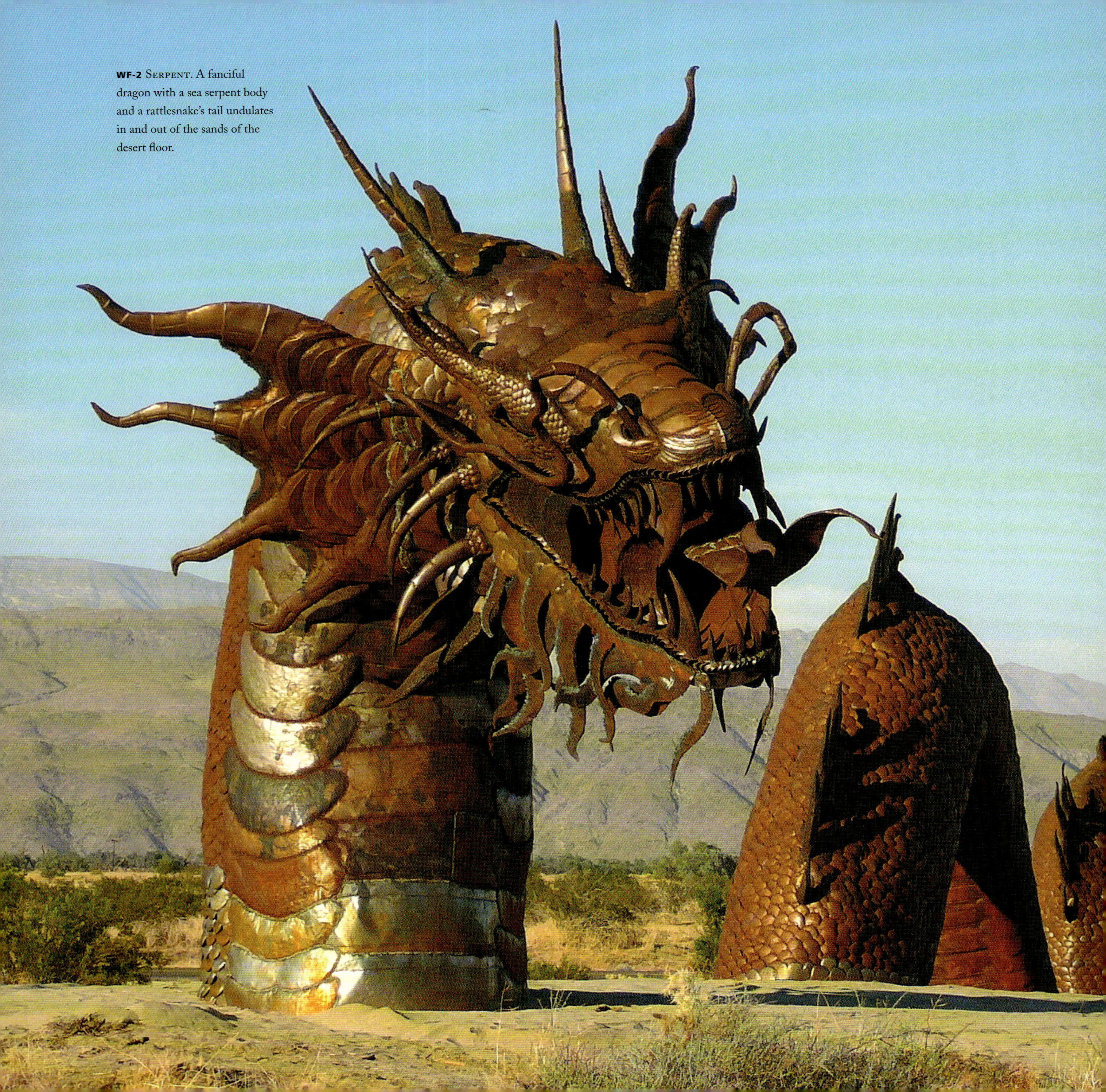

WF-2 Serpent. A fanciful dragon with a sea serpent body and a rattlesnake's tail undulates in and out of the sands of the desert floor.

Sculptor *Ricardo Breceda*'s fantasy and fact reaches beyond 100 million years to his creation of the extinct dinosaur, aired again in Breceda's sculptured forms.

Something else was also happening. Ricardo and Dennis were working well together. Early on, Dennis had recognized not only Ricardo's innate artistic ability but also his drive to make something of himself through his own efforts. This was as much an attraction to Dennis as Ricardo's growing talent. Ricardo, in turn, realized that he had an opportunity with Dennis to develop his business. He became his own taskmaster, continually looking for new ways to make his sculptures more and more lifelike and to express movement and emotion. Certainly Porfirio and his Rosarito Beach crew could see the greater emphasis on creating something out of the ordinary. Porfirio credits Dennis with furthering their artistic growth by giving them the freedom and opportunity to create new and more exciting pieces.

Ricardo and Dennis also discovered they had many things in common. They both shared a deep love for children and a real delight in making them happy. Both shared unlimited imagination and a love for life. They were also both willing to risk folly for the sake of creating something spectacular. And, more than anything, they wanted people to *enjoy* the sculptures. They both agreed the sculptures needed to find "A Place in the Heart & Sight of Children of Any Age," as stated in the April 17, 2008, *Borrego Sun.*

During this collaboration, they developed a solid trust, agreeing on a project with a nod of the head. No written contract has ever been needed. And like with Hannis Stoddard at AVID, Ricardo has been given virtual free rein to develop his ideas and to present a finished product with plenty of flourish. In addition, Dennis had an abundance of undeveloped land, and Ricardo required a huge landscape to accommodate his creations.

Making the decision to install metal sculptures on his undeveloped private property meant Dennis needed to

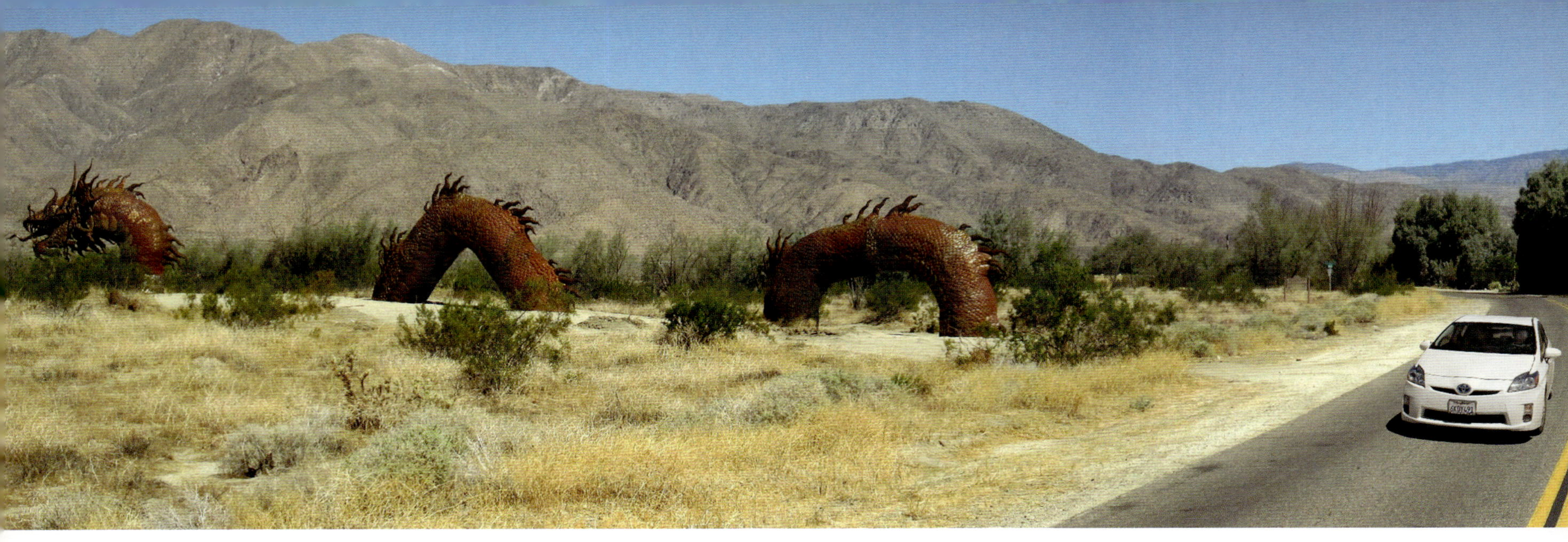

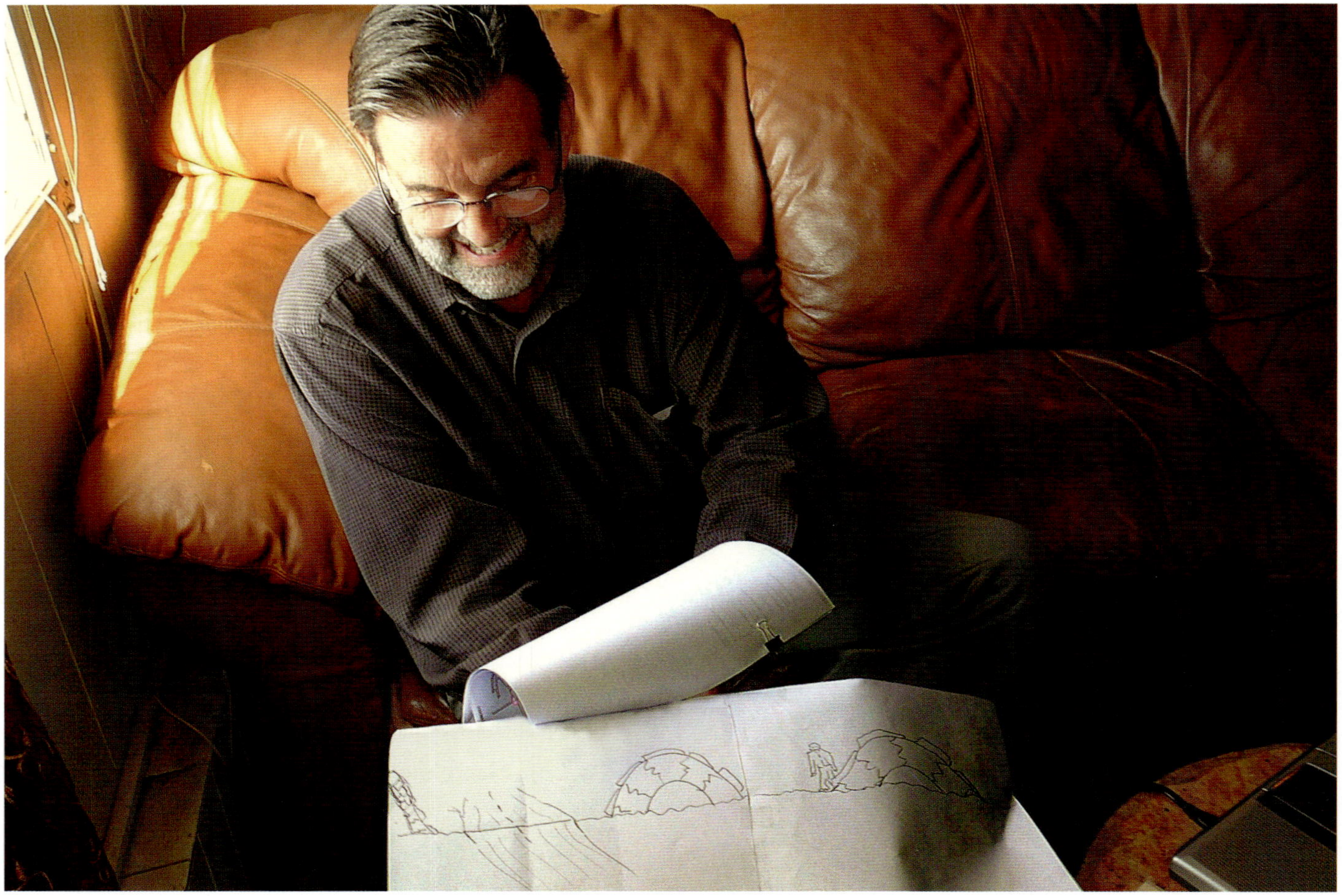

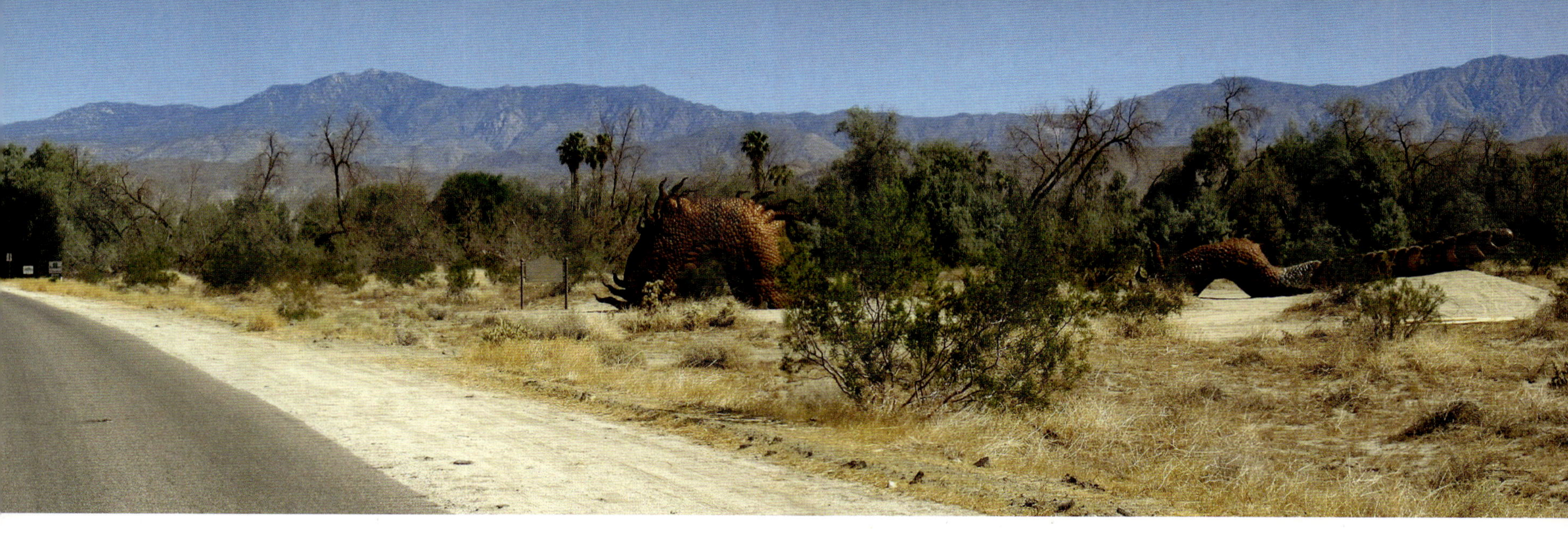

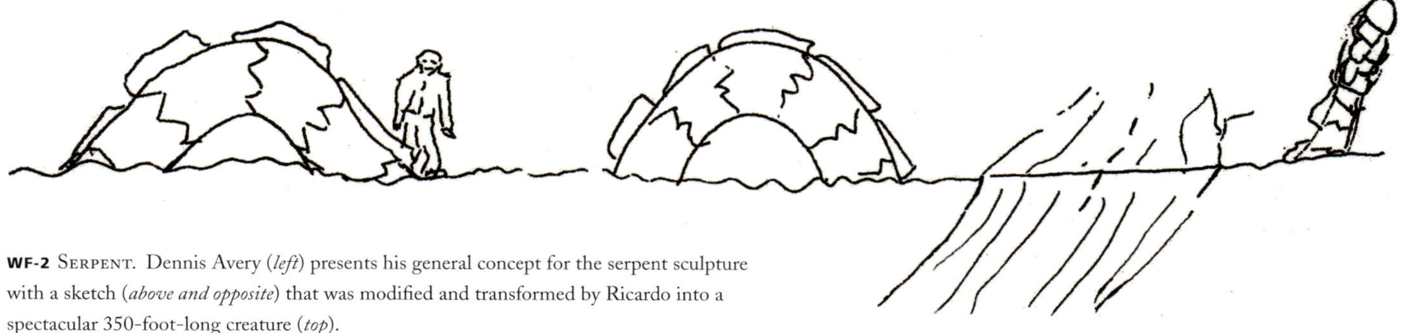

WF-2 SERPENT. Dennis Avery (*left*) presents his general concept for the serpent sculpture with a sketch (*above and opposite*) that was modified and transformed by Ricardo into a spectacular 350-foot-long creature (*top*).

clarify the use of his land for the public. Part of that decision was made when he created an LLC for his Galleta Meadows properties and transferred all then-existing art into the corporation. Any art acquired after October 2008 would be automatically included.

While Dennis welcomes the public onto his land, he also had to establish guidelines for visitors. He had signs installed on all of his properties indicating that the privately owned estate was open to the public, but was subject to landowner control, and all risks of injury would be assumed by the users. Generously, the signs also stated that the public is free to camp on the property for up to three days and that hiking, picnicking, photography, horseback riding, and bicycling are allowed. Only motorcycles are prohibited.

The sculptures are not a typical public exhibition of art. There are no interpretive signs, roadway signs, bathrooms, or drinking fountains. They are there as "pure, expressive art" that is not subject to county regulations and is, according to Dennis, a magnificent embodiment of First Amendment rights to free expression.

It was only a month after the gomphotheres arrived and the buzz had not quite settled before new sculptures appeared, again taking the community by surprise.

Sabertooth cats and giant tortoises were installed near the Indian Head Ranch gate, and two elephants were situated at the Galleta Meadows sign and the Galleta Meadows

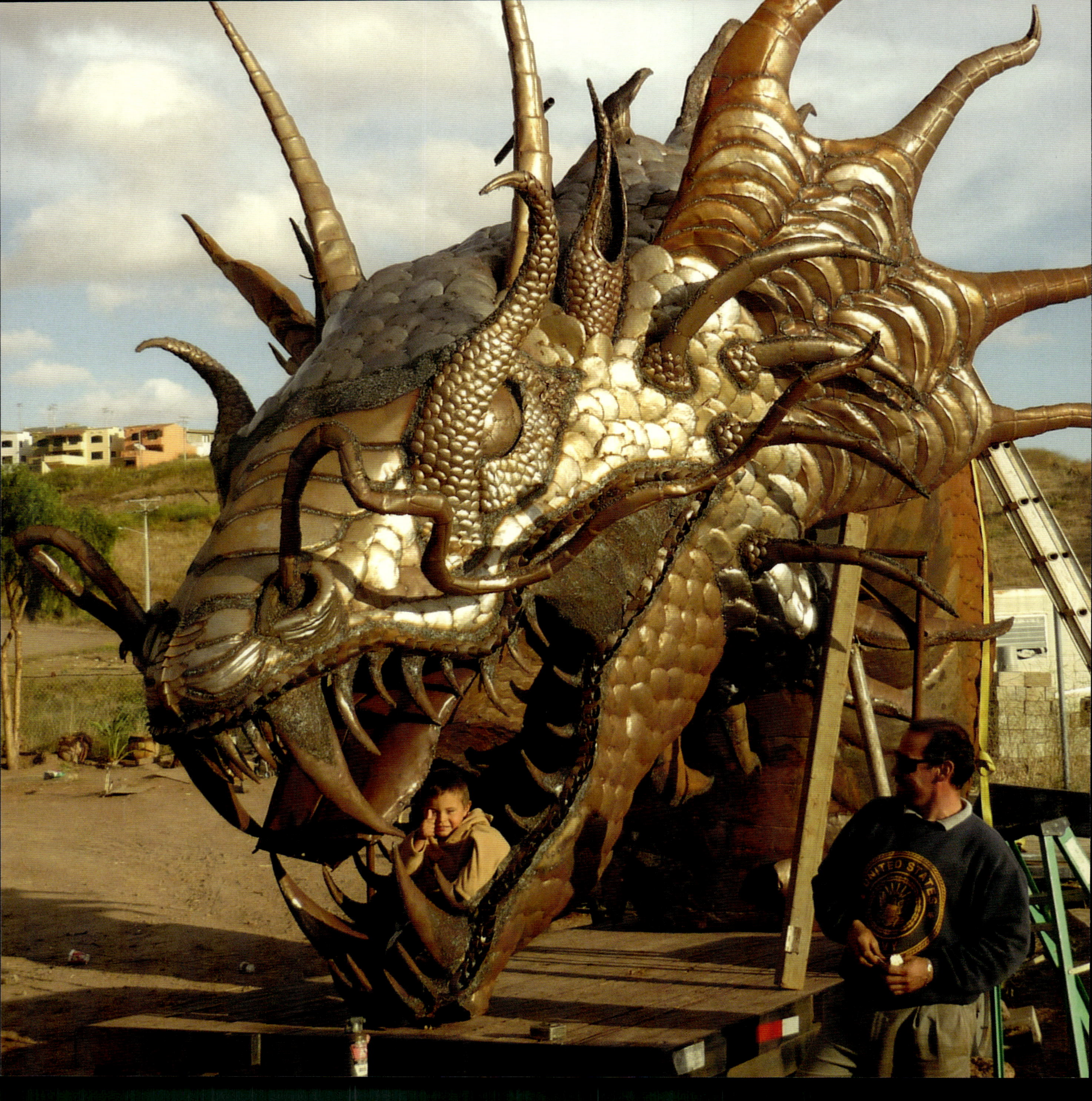
UNITED STATES

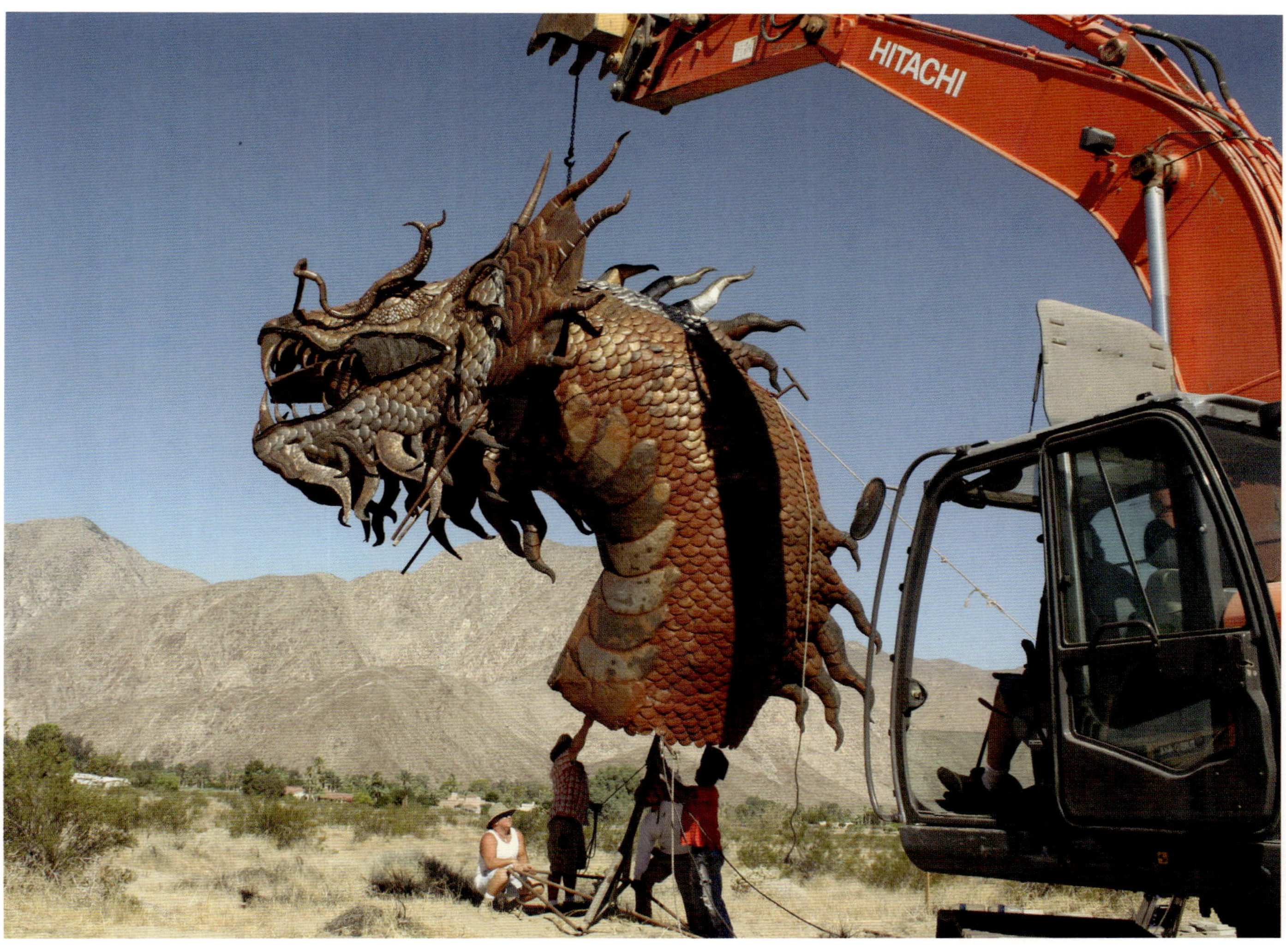

WF-2 Serpent. Porfirio (*left*), with his son Nicolás sitting in the mouth of the dragon, admiringly approves the finished head ready for transport to Borrego where it is installed (*above*) in Galleta Meadows by the crew of Okie McNatt.

Estate monument on Borrego Springs Road near Santa Rosa. All were made specifically for Galleta Meadows except for the largest elephant, which came from the Perris Jurassic Park sculpture garden. This large elephant is an example of one of Ricardo's earlier works and lacks some of the flow and relaxed natural appearance of his later pieces.

Like clockwork, each month new sculptures arrived. Those who lived out of town could get the flavor of what was happening by reading it in the *Borrego Sun,* or they could look at the new website www.galletameadows.com to see photos of the installations, comments from the public, and recent news articles. A map indicated where the new sculptures could be found. The list of sculptures began to look like a roll call on Noah's Ark: llamas, *Camelops*, Shasta ground sloths, Harlan's ground sloths, Columbian mammoths, peccaries, extinct horses, more sabertooth cats, and the incredible *Aiolornis.*

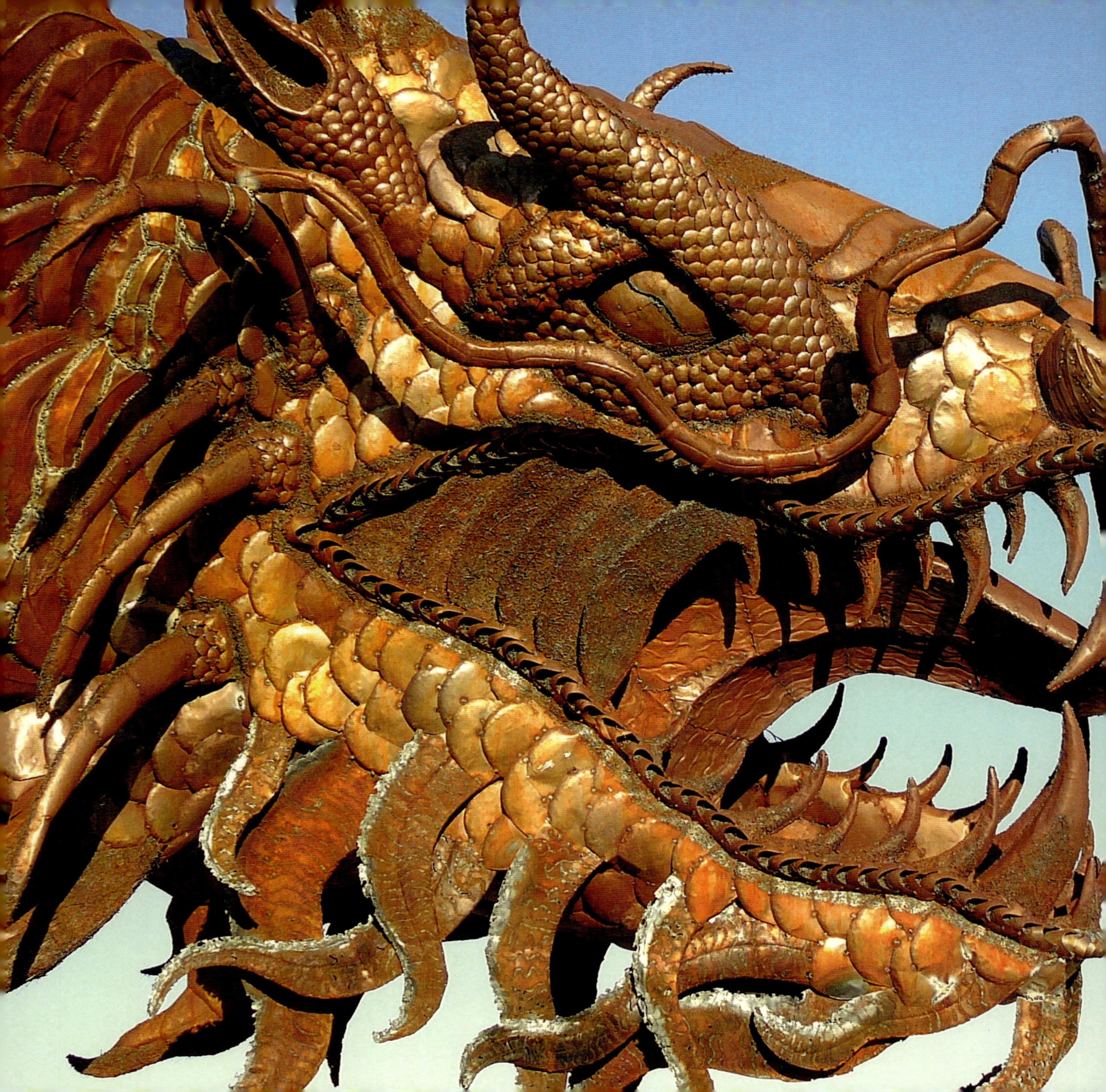

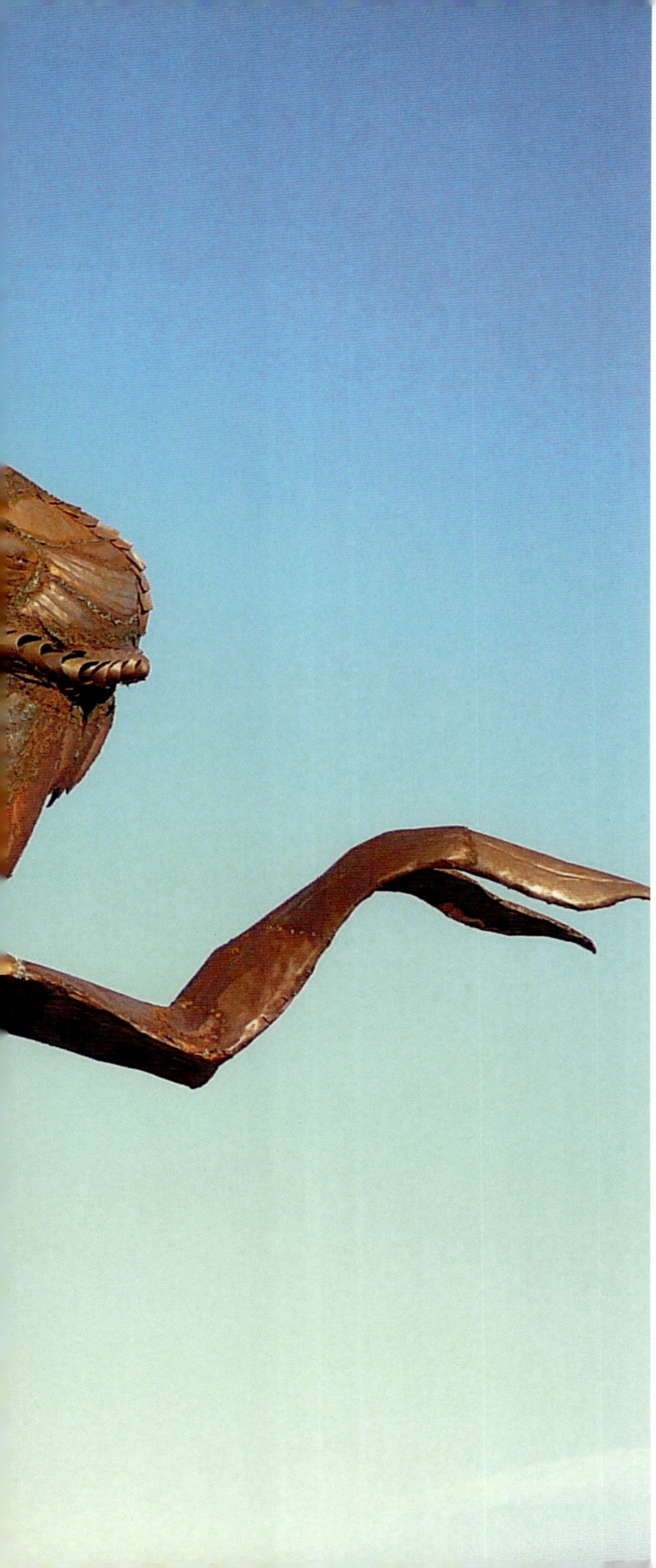

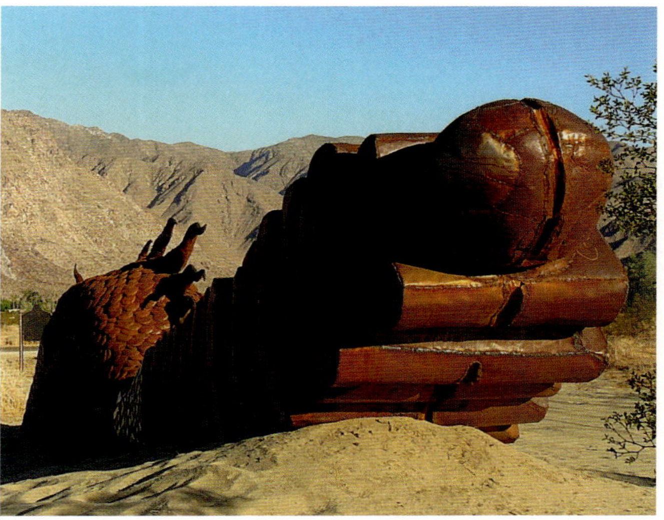

WF-2 Serpent. The detail in the dragon head (*left*) and rattlesnake tail (*above*) surpasses all of Ricardo's previous works. It is his new "best" work.

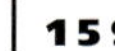

The rate at which they appeared was a reflection of the obsessive focus of the artist. His world, sunrise to well past sundown, was a world surrounded by scrap metal, welding tools, and loud hammering. This was his chance, and, like a long-distance ultra-marathoner, Ricardo was running with it nonstop, keeping his cool, plotting his strategy, seeing his destination, reaching for the brass ring.

With the rapid arrival of so many sculptures, the creatures began to look like they were interacting with one another. Sabertooth cats were stalking and attacking the extinct horses on the south side of Highway S-3, while horses were sparring with one another to the north of the road. Nearby a mother horse suckled her young, while north on Borrego Springs Road a *Camelops* also suckled her offspring.

Finding the perfect spot and position for the sculptures sometimes took a large crew. Because of their sheer size and weight, moving them around was not easy. The extreme summer heat made it even more challenging. The Harlan's ground sloth (*Paramylodon harlani*) was a particular struggle because no forklift was available to lift the 1,800-pound, seventeen-foot-high giant.

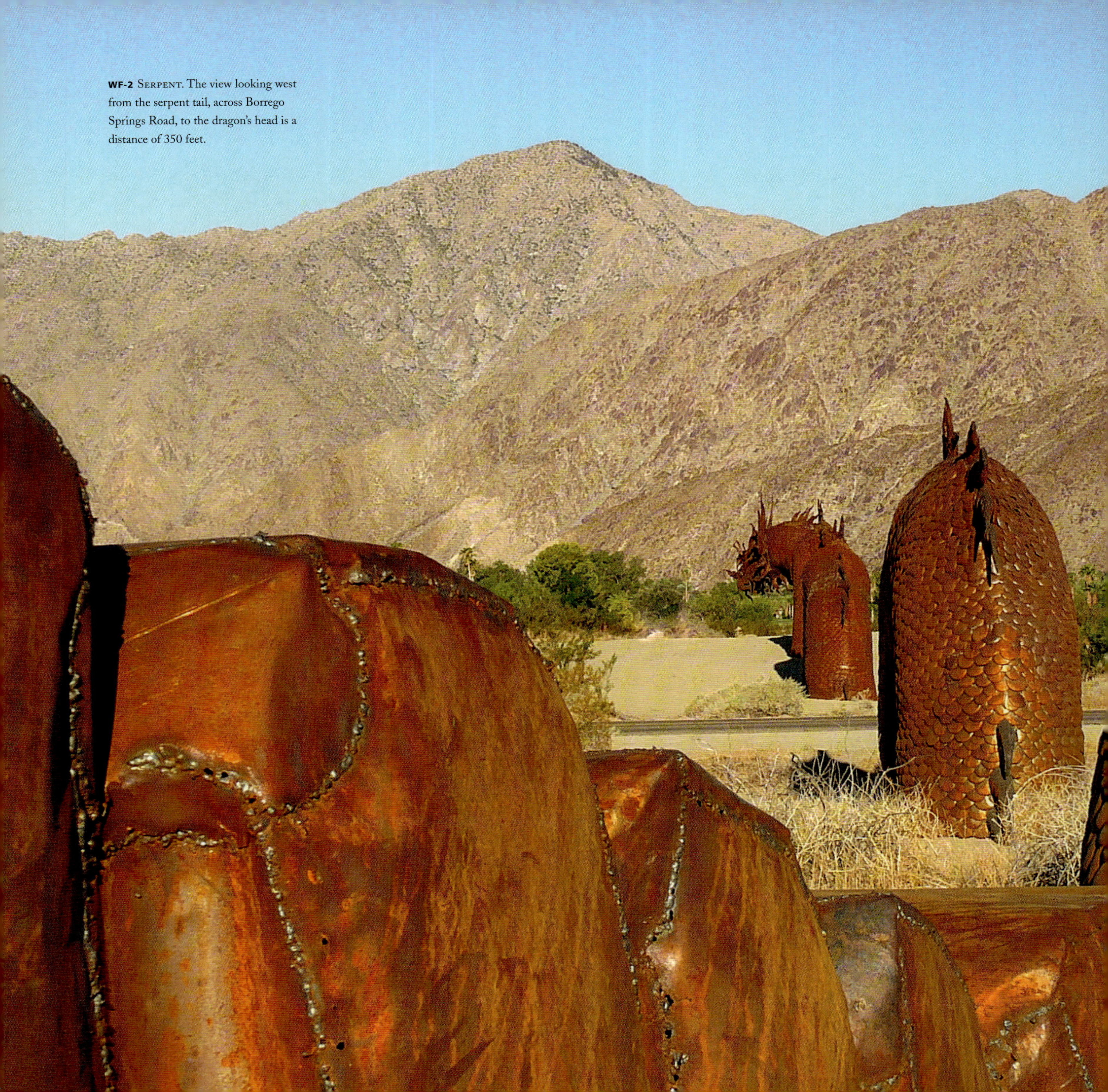

WF-2 Serpent. The view looking west from the serpent tail, across Borrego Springs Road, to the dragon's head is a distance of 350 feet.

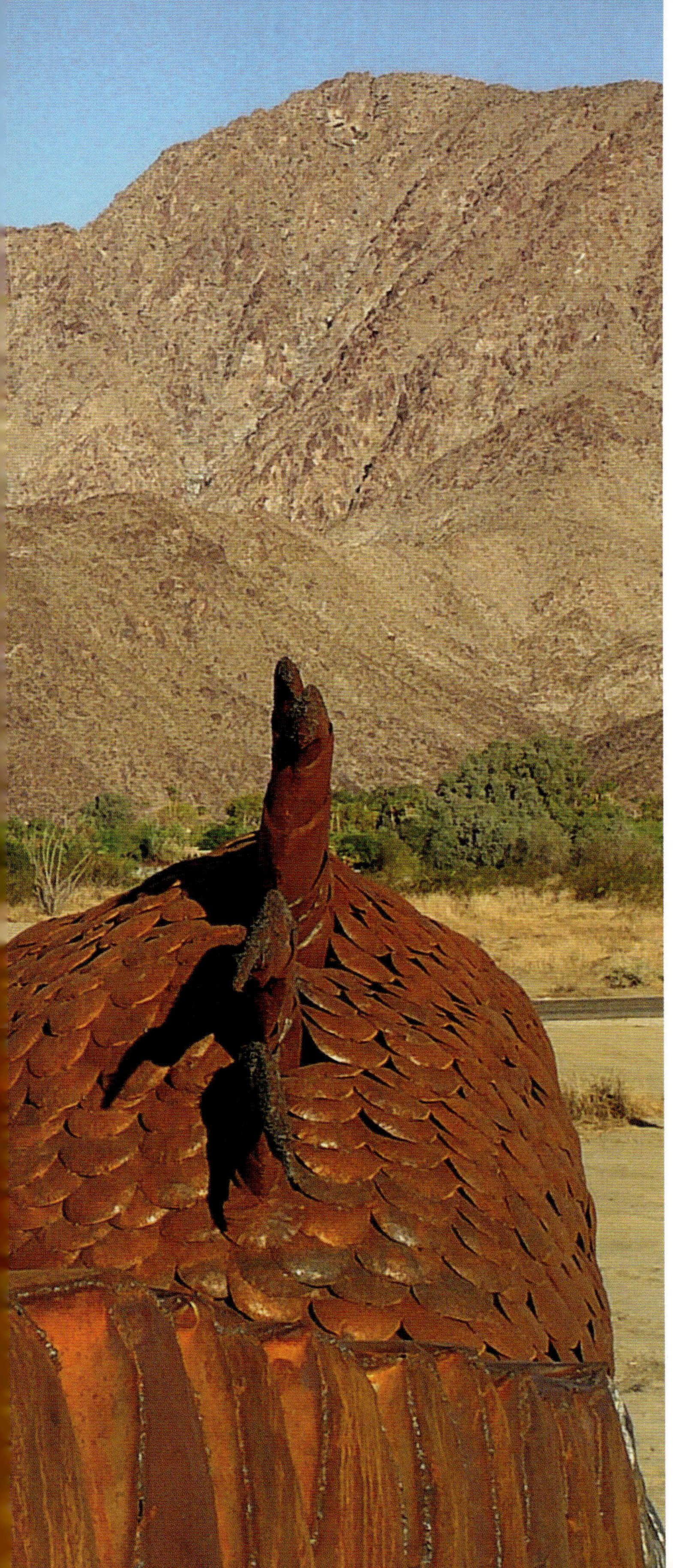

Maris Brancheau, reporting in the *Borrego Sun* on July 24, 2008, wrote, "Avery used his SUV to pull ropes attached to the sloth's body as it sat upright in the back of a lifted trailer. The sloth jangled like a giant metal puppet as Breceda guided his crew." Later the crew welded the tail to the body to help stabilize it.

Even more challenging was the installation in November of the two *Aiolornis incredibilis.* Both the construction and installation of these two giant birds had been the most demanding to date.

The *Aiolornis* located off Anzio Drive took two weeks to install and plans had to be modified because of the strong winds found in that area. First, to act as a stabilizer, a truck axle was buried in cement four feet into the ground. Then the body of the bird was reinforced with steel, and cables were attached to support each fifteen-foot-long wing. Next, it was hoisted onto an earth mover and fixed on top of the truck axle. Finally, the feathers and other structural and artistic features were added to the 1,400-pound colossus, including a prehistoric *Platygonus* or peccary upon which the *Aiolornis* was preying.

When they were finally installed, Dennis quipped, "Ricardo, 'the maestro,' has met his match with this one." Even Ricardo admitted that he had lost a lot of sleep trying to figure out how to affix the bird so it appeared to be airborne.

The other *Aiolornis,* located north of Highway S-3, was equally difficult to install in its nest, but at least the wings were easier because they were not as long. Ricardo had to dig deeper within himself to ascend to yet a new level of skill.

By November 2008, sixty individual pieces were installed at a total of thirteen sites in seven months. With the exception of the African elephants, all were based on Plio-Pleistocene vertebrates as described in *Fossil Treasures.* By now Ricardo was becoming a local celebrity, and he was invited to ride in the Borrego Days Desert Festival parade that fall.

Sky Art took a new turn beginning in December 2008. From science-based inspired sculptures there was a shift first

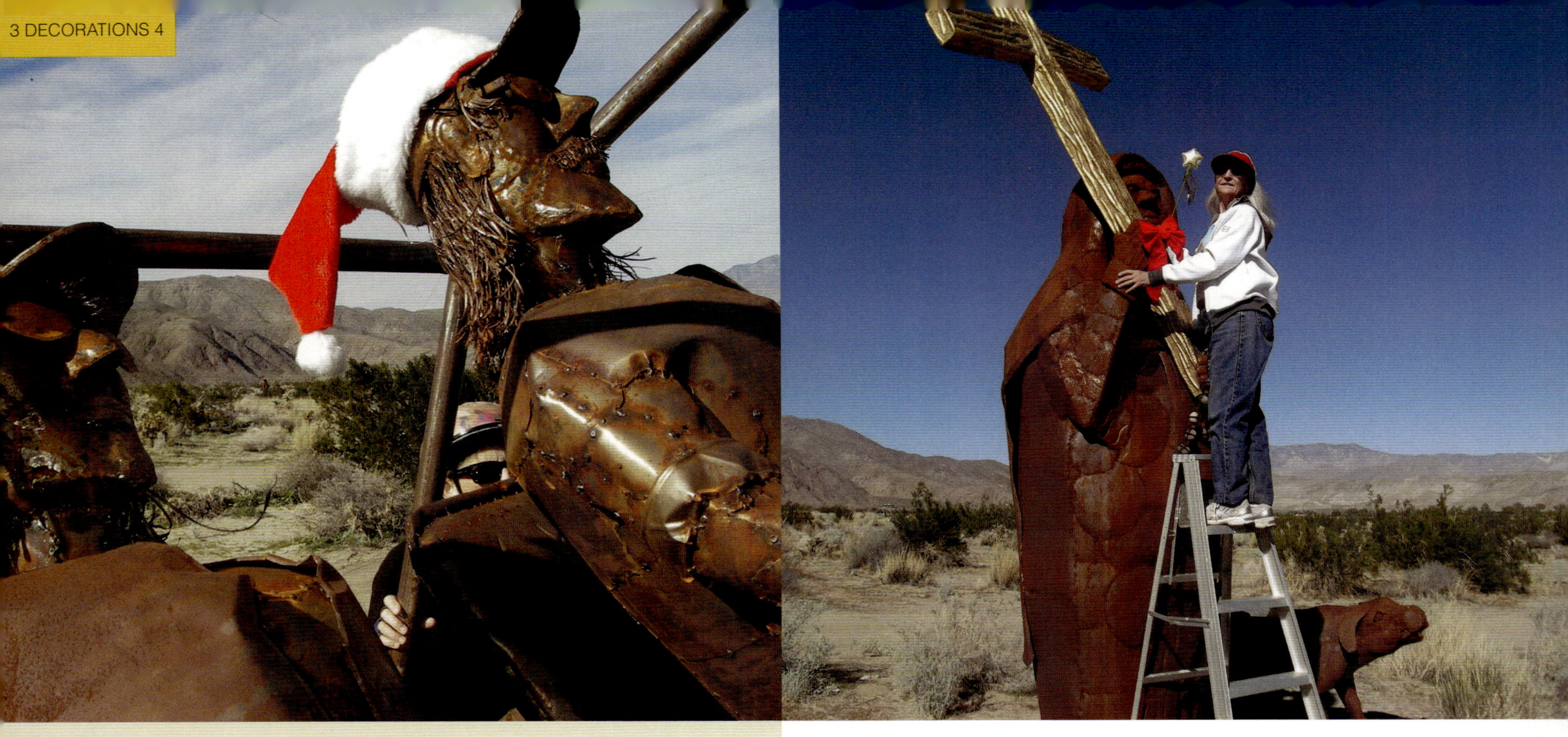

ENJOYING THE SCULPTURES

Sky Art is now very much a part of the community. *From left to right*: Residents of Borrego Springs decorate the sculptures for the holidays; resident Grace Rickard started the "new" holiday tradition; visitors find "friends" to camp with them; the Jeep sculpture becomes a float in the fall Borrego Days Desert Festival parade before being installed in Galleta Meadows. *Far right*: Dennis Avery poses as if he is holding up the Jeep while Ricardo smiles at those lining the street who are enjoying the parade. This "last" Sky Art sculpture became the last one before the next "last" one.

to interest in historical subjects, then nature, and finally whim. The November 27, 2008, edition of the *Borrego Sun* announced that new sculptures were on their way—an Indian, a padre, and some dinosaurs.

After moving to Borrego Springs in 1990, Dennis had begun reading about the early Spaniards and their expeditions. In May 1994 he had bronze plaques installed on his property commemorating the eighteenth-century Anza expeditions. It was not a stretch for Dennis to consider honoring members and players of this significant historical event, considered by some historians as the third most important event in California history after the discovery of California and the establishment of the first mission in San Diego.

Dennis gave Ricardo complete freedom to express himself artistically, which included design choices for sculptures. For the dinosaur installations, for example, Dennis

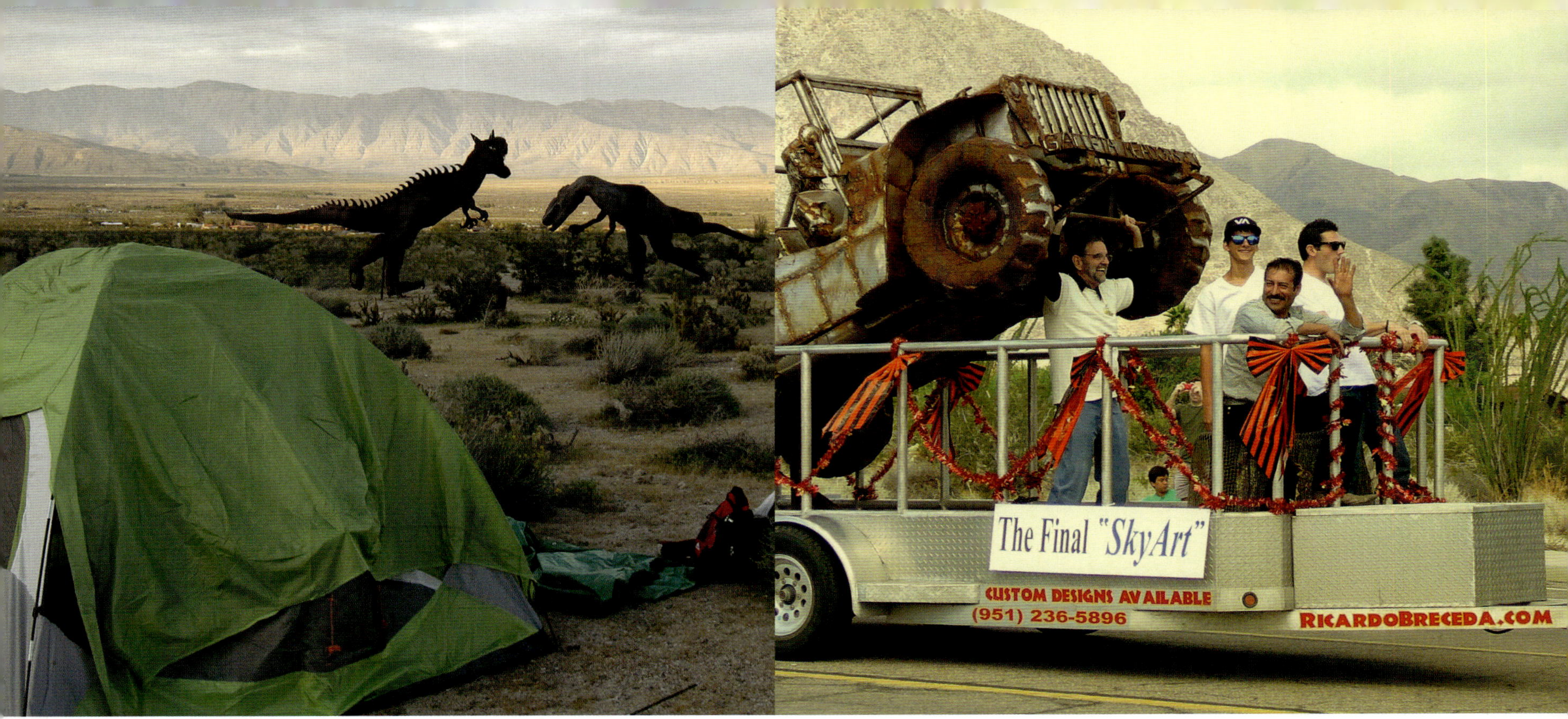

presented Ricardo a copy of *The Encyclopedia of Dinosaurs* and left it to Ricardo to choose what he wanted to make.

The same artistic license applied when Ricardo was instructed to make an Indian head. The very stunning Indian head (and upper torso) sculpture represented either Sebastián Tarabal, the Cochimí Indian guide used by Spanish explorer Juan Bautista de Anza on the first overland expedition in 1774, or Salvador Palma, the Yuman chieftain who was the critical link for crossing the Colorado River into California. The head he made is Aztec-inspired rather than one typical of either tribe of the Indian guides.

The impressive Indian head and the padre were installed in December 2008. The padre holds a cross and is accompanied by his dog. The padre represents either Fr. Francisco Garcés or Fr. Pedro Font, who were part of the first and second expeditionary forces, respectively, that opened up the first overland trail to California from New Spain. The second expedition brought colonists to California and secured the area for Spain.

That December was also the first year that sculptures were decorated by residents in Borrego Springs. It has become an annual event since then. Judy Meier, editor of the *Borrego Sun,* made note of all of the holiday decorations on the sculptures in her January 8, 2009, column. She wrote, "Hundreds—if not thousands—of valley residents and visitors saw the embellishments adorning some of the Galleta Meadows sculptures in the past few weeks."

She also noted that "Most of the iron creatures wore a cloak of newly acquired rust, compliments of our midmonth rains." The more the sculptures rusted, the darker they became, developing a rich brown patina that made the metal animals even more realistic.

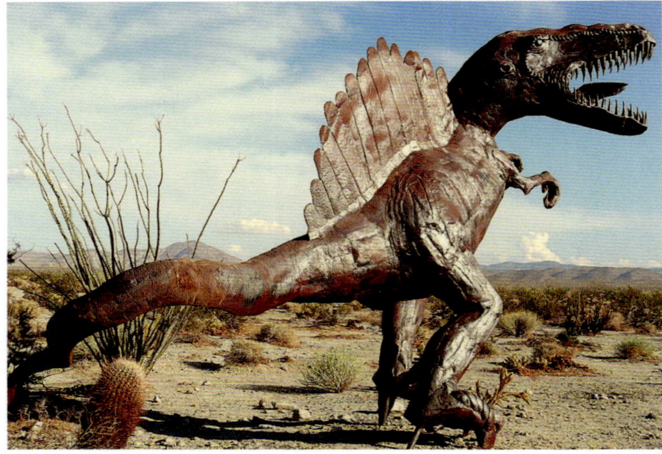

WF-3 Spinosaurus. The four-ton, forty to fifty-foot-long *Spinosaurus* had a six-foot-long sail-like structure protruding from its back vertebrae.

A variety of sculptures were installed at various locations in 2009, including twelve bighorn sheep, two giant tortoises, and two *Velociraptors* at Indian Head Ranch, a saguaro cactus near the padre, and thirteen dinosaurs south of Highway S-3 on the cactus-studded alluvial plain below Yaqui Ridge. The concentration of dinosaurs on this plain, known as Yaqui Meadows on the United States Geological Survey maps, has created Borrego's own "Jurassic Park." All of the dinosaur sculptures are herein referred to as whim because no fossils are known to exist in the park from the Jurassic period, a part of the so-called Age of Dinosaurs.

As such, the sculptures should be viewed as interpretive art because in some cases they were not portrayed accurately. Children, however, often don't know the difference. Dennis and others take delight in hearing children call the Plio-Pleistocene sculptures "dinosaurs." Technically that is incorrect because the dinosaurs lived more than 65 million years ago and the area's Plio-Pleistocene terrestrial vertebrate fossils are largely no older than 5 million years. But to children, any extinct vertebrate, such as a mammoth or gomphothere, can be a "dinosaur," according to Dennis. He finds this fact "very revealing of children" who are easily delighted and whose contact with these creatures may be the first step toward an interest in expanding their knowledge.

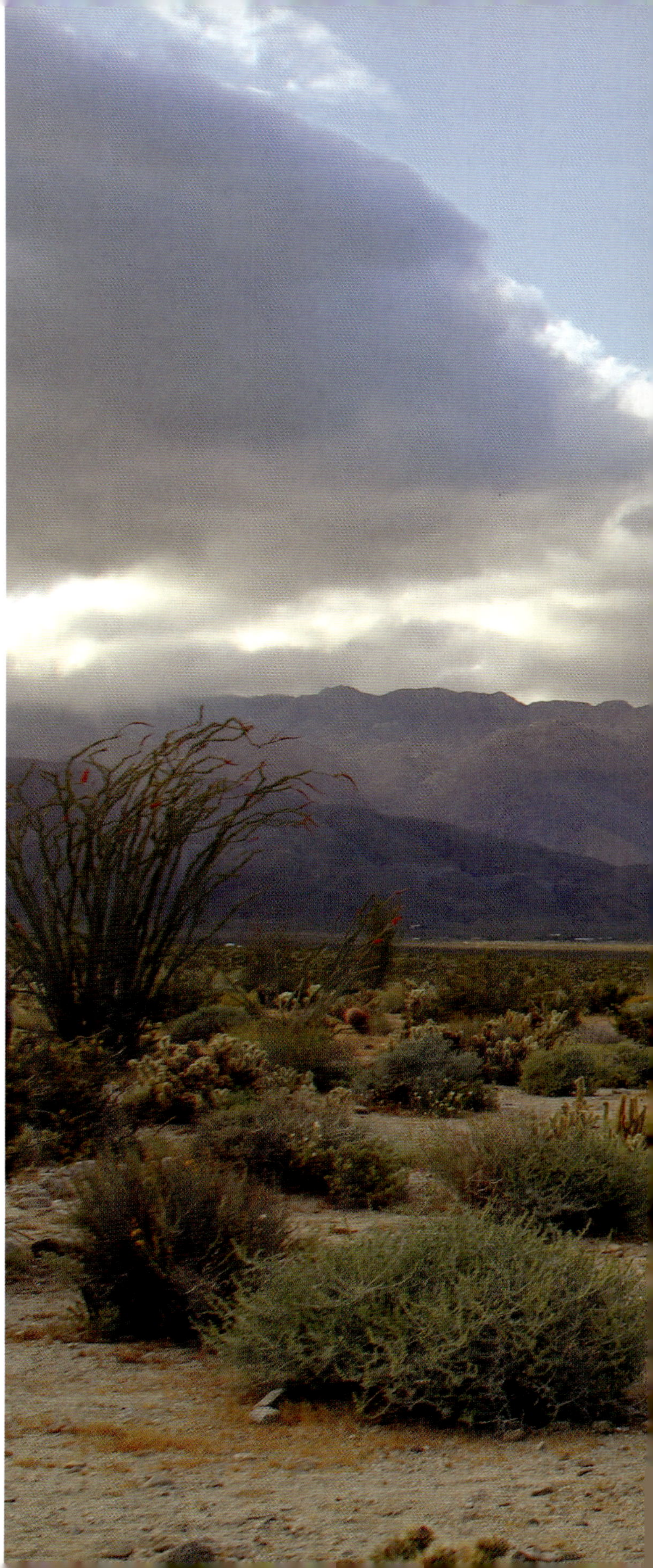

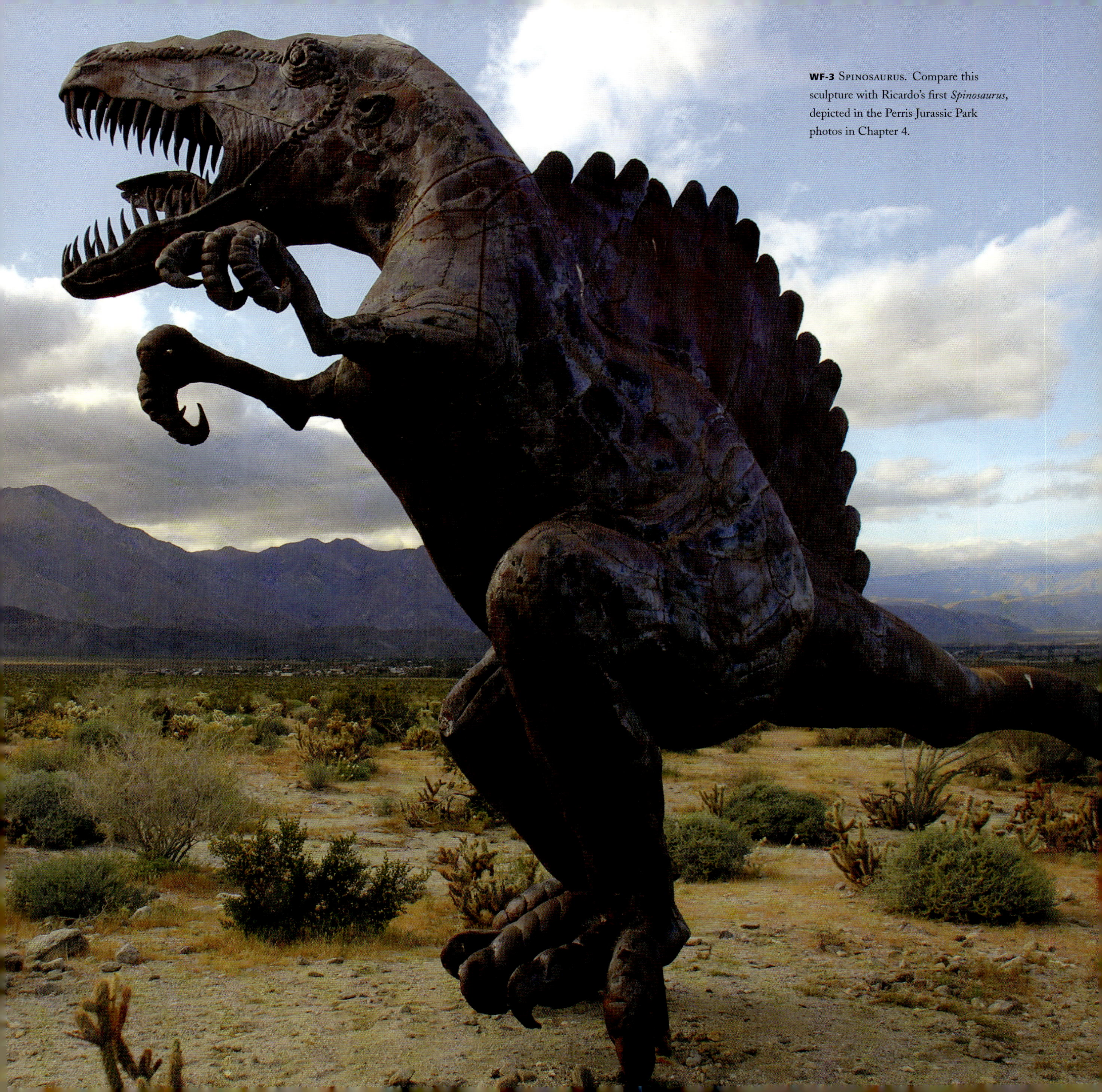

WF-3 Spinosaurus. Compare this sculpture with Ricardo's first *Spinosaurus*, depicted in the Perris Jurassic Park photos in Chapter 4.

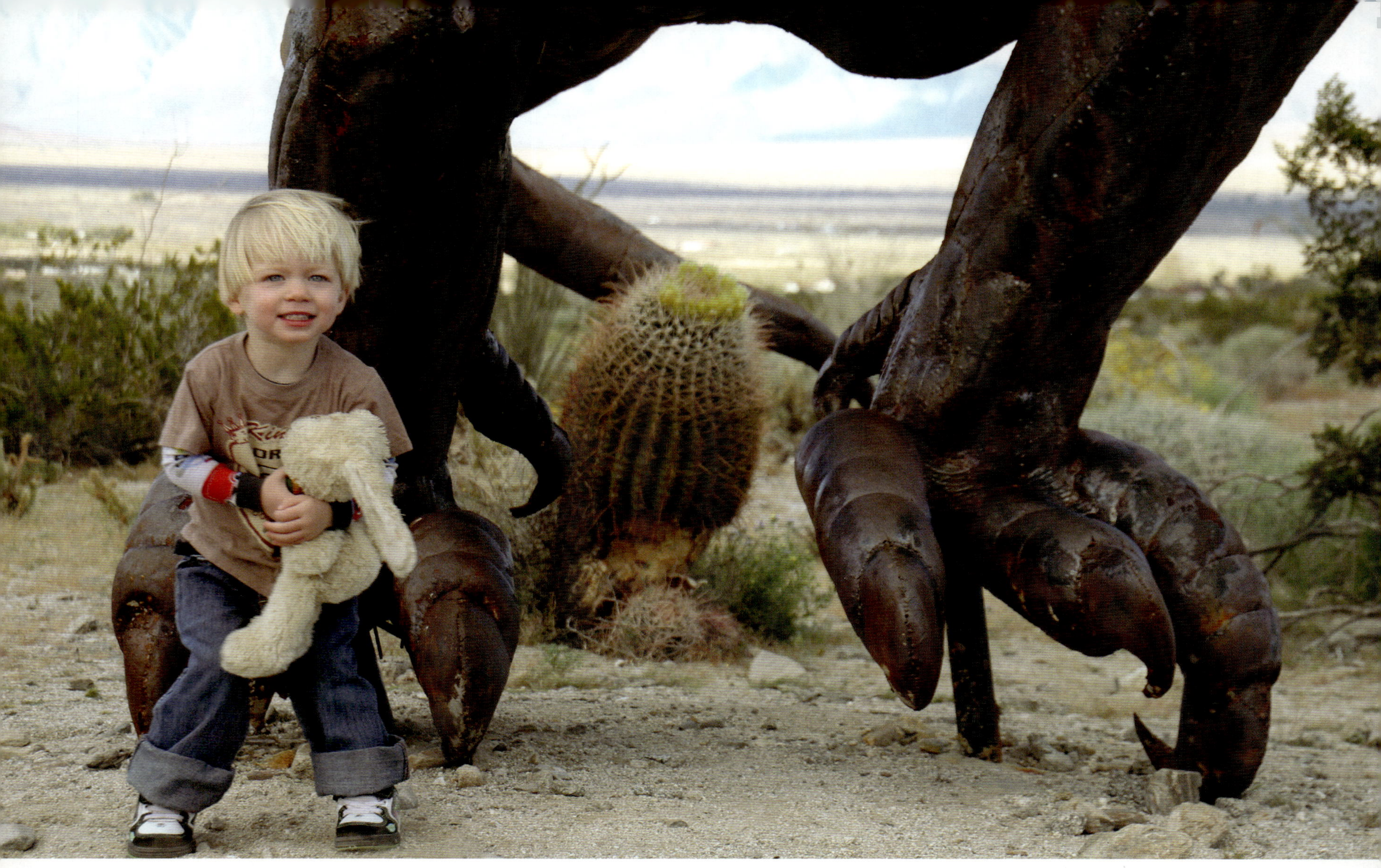

WF-3 Spinosaurus. This little visitor (*above*) is not intimidated by being dwarfed by a dinosaur that lived in Cretaceous time, about 95 million years ago.

More important to Dennis is the fact that some of the best sculptures that Ricardo has made are dinosaurs. Inspired by the *Jurassic Park* films that he watched with Lianna, Ricardo chose to make all of the dinosaurs in Borrego Valley to date carnivorous theropods—bipedal dinosaurs whose front legs were not intended for locomotion. All had powerful jaws and sharp teeth and were active in the early to middle Cretaceous Period following the older Jurassic Period of the Mesozoic Era.

Some might argue with Dennis and say that Ricardo's bighorn sheep are the most realistic of the sculptures. Certainly they were in the forefront of Dennis's mind when he first contracted Ricardo in 2007. Dennis's daughter Chasa had included her father in some of her research projects involving Peninsular bighorn sheep when she attended the University of California at Davis. Chasa participated in sheep captures in Borrego. She was able to include her father on hunts, helicopter rides, and inoculation of sheep.

Dennis was delighted with Ricardo's rendition of the bighorn sheep. He was especially impressed with the way Ricardo positioned the sculptures so that they appeared in a natural pose. Ricardo's artistic eye includes a keen sense of placement, which is very much a part of Sky Art. The twelve bighorn were set in a hilly area resembling their nearby habitat.

Ricardo also had the opportunity to do a piece for the Woolcott Memorial Auction in 2009. Dennis commissioned him to make a dragonfly suitable for a garden or home interior. The auction is an annual event that raises money in support of the Borrego Community Health Foundation. Ricardo's participation in this event provided an opportunity for him to be among the other artists whose works were being auctioned.

Although it is a small town with a permanent population of less than 3,000, and with a seasonal population of about 10,000, the arts in Borrego Springs are remarkably well supported. There are several art galleries, an Art Guild, and the Circle of Art exhibition that raises money through art sales for educational grants and scholarships. Borrego's Art Institute offers classes for children and adults and has

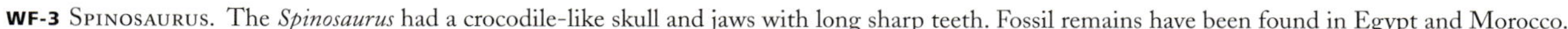

WF-3 Spinosaurus. The *Spinosaurus* had a crocodile-like skull and jaws with long sharp teeth. Fossil remains have been found in Egypt and Morocco.

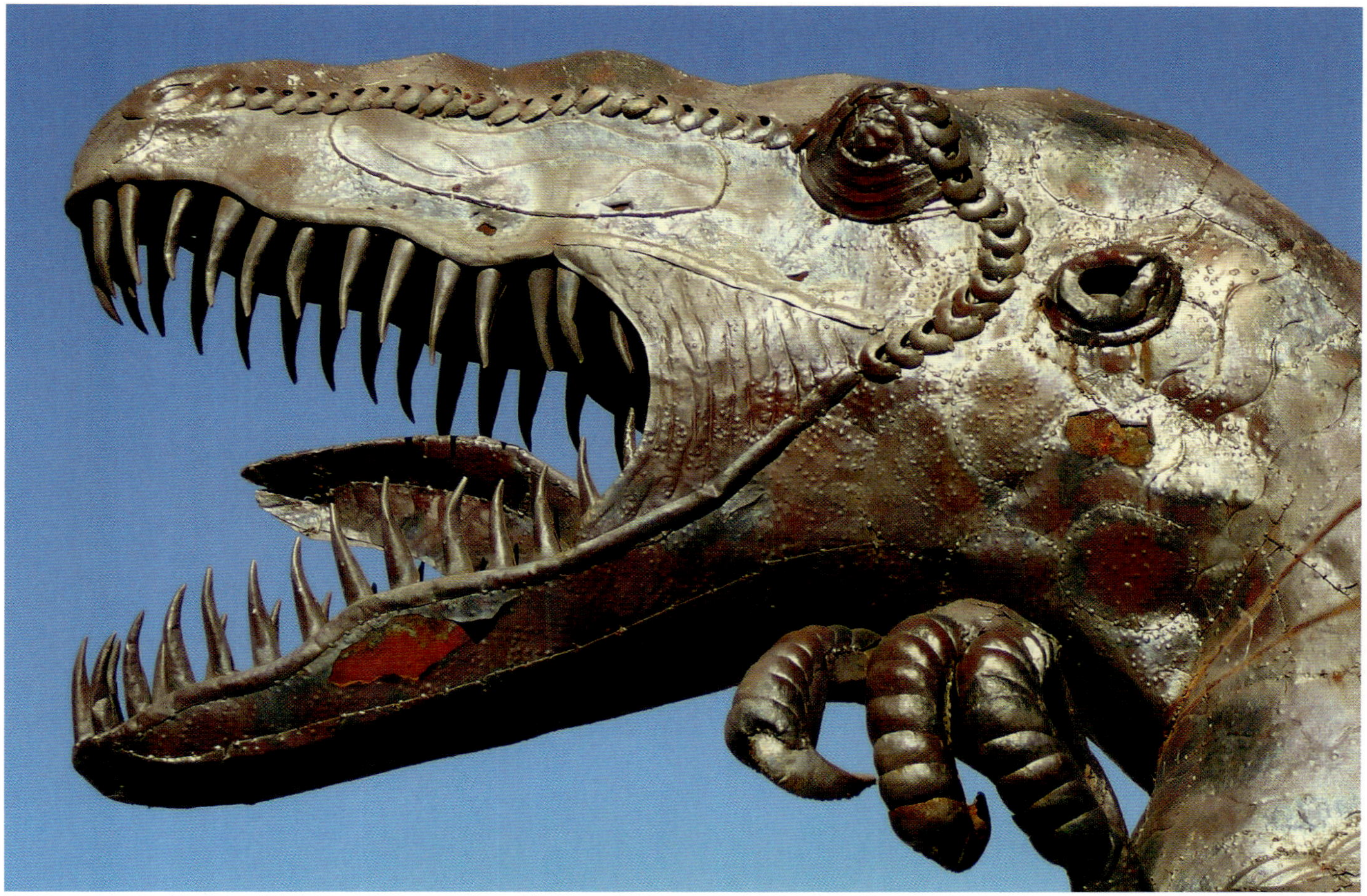

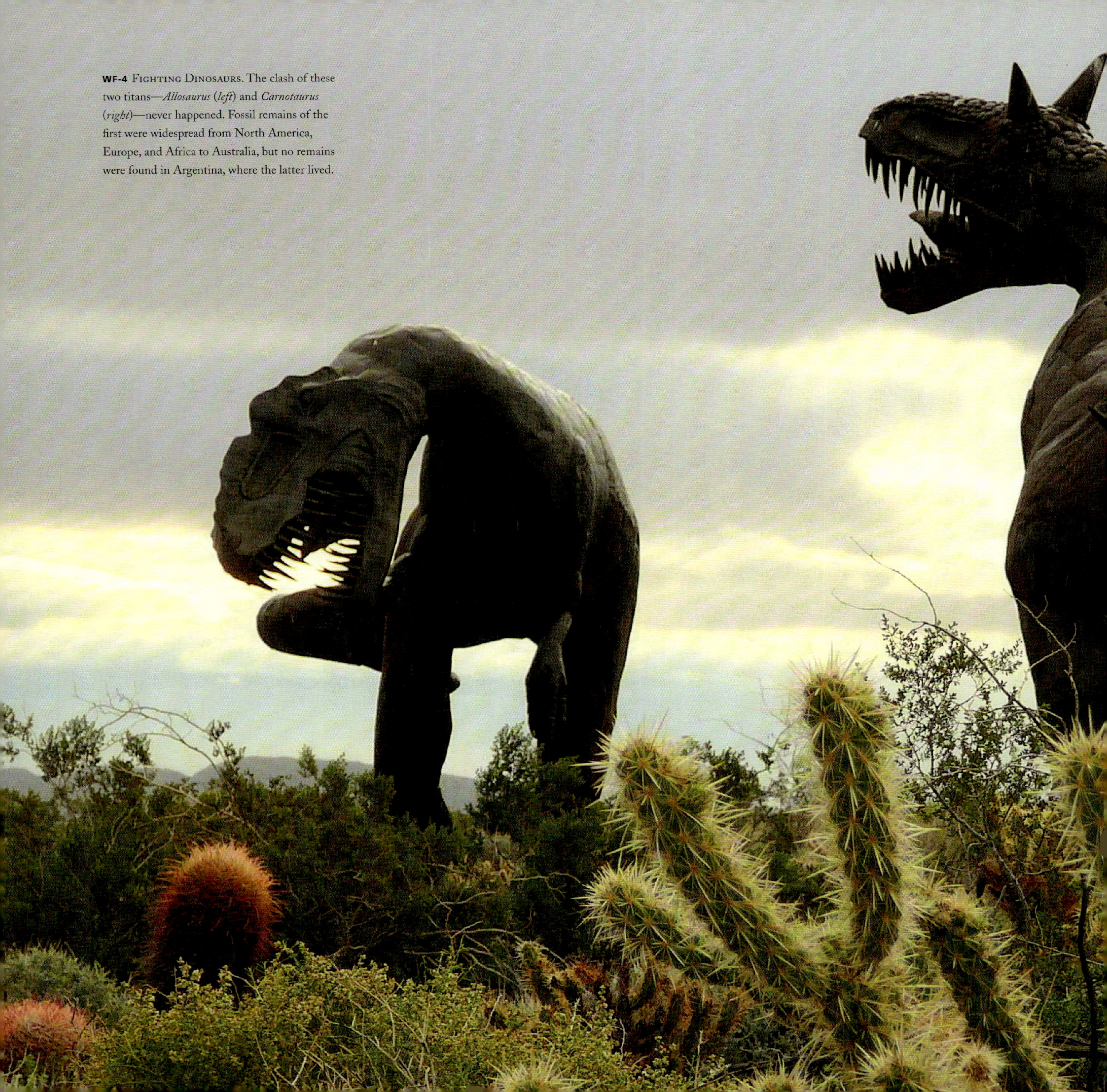

WF-4 Fighting Dinosaurs. The clash of these two titans—*Allosaurus* (*left*) and *Carnotaurus* (*right*)—never happened. Fossil remains of the first were widespread from North America, Europe, and Africa to Australia, but no remains were found in Argentina, where the latter lived.

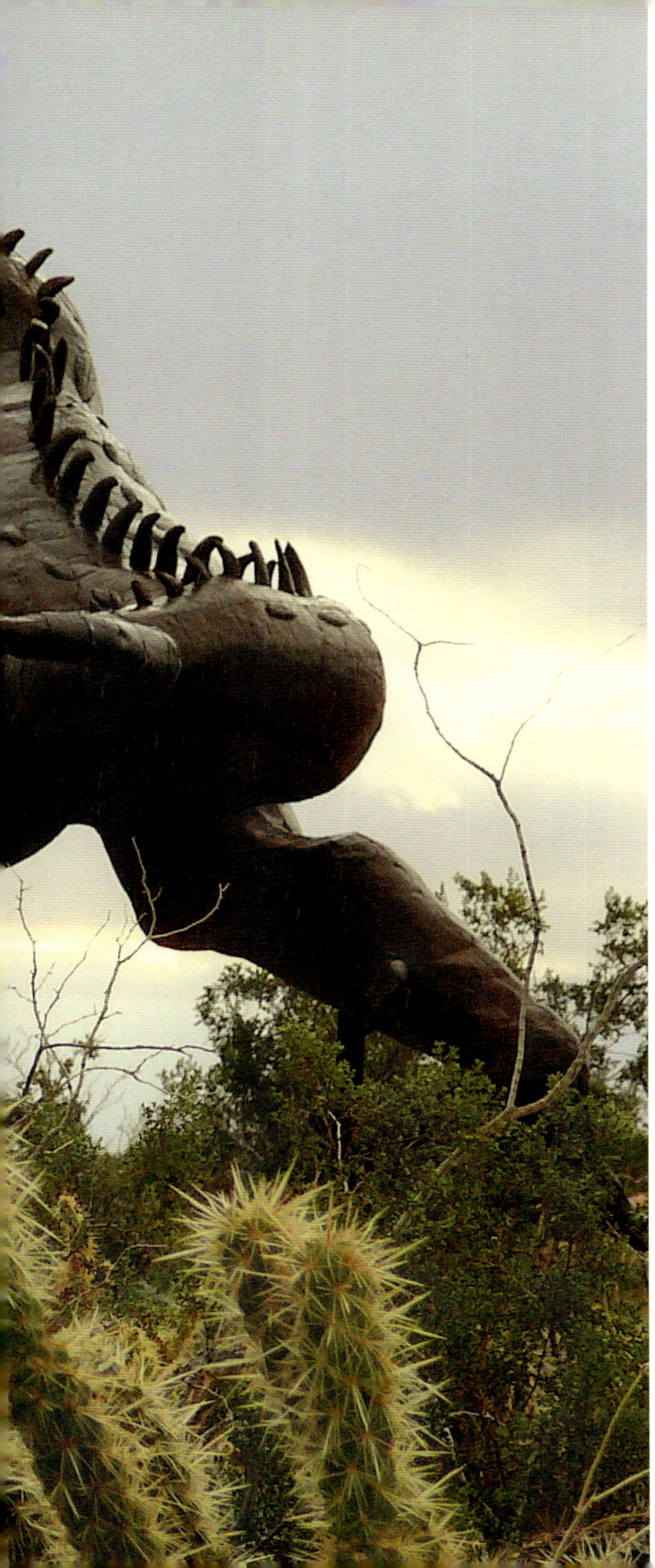

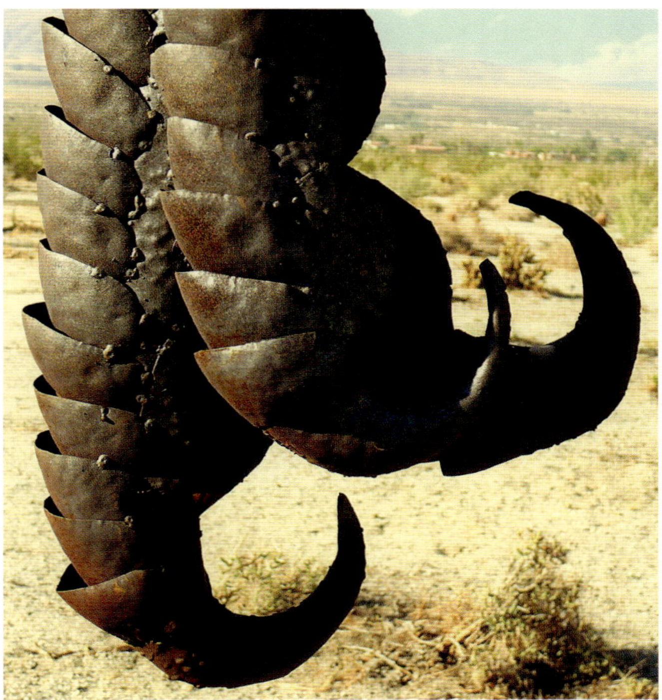

WF-4 Fighting Dinosaurs (Detail). The forearms of theropods were not meant for locomotion. The claws, such as that of the *Allosaurus* (*above*), were used to hook into the meat of their victims.

exhibition space. Include the presence of a Performing Arts Center and an Institute of Photography, and there is something of interest for everyone.

Some well-known artists call the Borrego area home, including metal sculptor John Richen, wood sculptor Craig McCloskey, potter Ginger Dunlap-Dietz, glass artist Breta Matson, and painters Carol Lindemulder, Leslie Duncan, Cheryl Criss, Nancy Bartusch, Barbara Matson, Liesel Paris, and Barbara Nickerson. Well-known area photographers include Paul Johnson and Dennis Mammana.

When asked how Ricardo is viewed by the various artists and art organizations in town, Barbara Nickerson, executive director of the Borrego Art Institute, said, "We are proud of him and his achievements. We are proud that he was chosen to give this community a real gift of his talent. We are made special by his artwork."

Ricardo also received recognition for his art in 2009 when television personality Huell Howser filmed a segment about Borrego Springs for his KCET (PBS affiliate) *California Gold* series. (The segment featuring the Borrego sculptures may be viewed at www.galletameadows.com.) Howser viewed the gomphotheres and the bighorn sheep and interviewed both Dennis and Ricardo. Dennis told Huell that Sky Art was a little project—a dream. Then Huell shot back, "There is nothing little about this!" Dennis grinned and confessed, "It sort of got away from us."

In September 2009 Ricardo created sculptures of a group of farm workers busy in the Di Giorgio grape fields of Borrego Valley, recalling that moment in history when the United Farm Workers under César Chávez went to battle against the Di Giorgio Fruit Corporation. Immediately, there was an outcry from some residents, claiming that no women worked in the field as Ricardo had depicted, and that the water boy was not authentic. Several of the pieces were removed in November and replaced with others in January 2010. This was the only time that direct criticism actually resulted in a change of sculptures. The change was made hastily, before the allegations were fully researched. As it turned out, only the women with babies needed to be removed as women had worked beside men harvesting the grapes.

By the end of 2009 more than 100 Sky Art sculptures had been completed. Ricardo had also negotiated with the

WF-4. Fighting Dinosaurs. The concrete truck on the left awaits the positioning of the *Carnotaurus* to pour cement for the installation. It takes a coordinated effort to handle sculptures that weigh hundreds of pounds. Borrego Springs Mayor, Okie McNatt, usually provided a forklift for the installation.

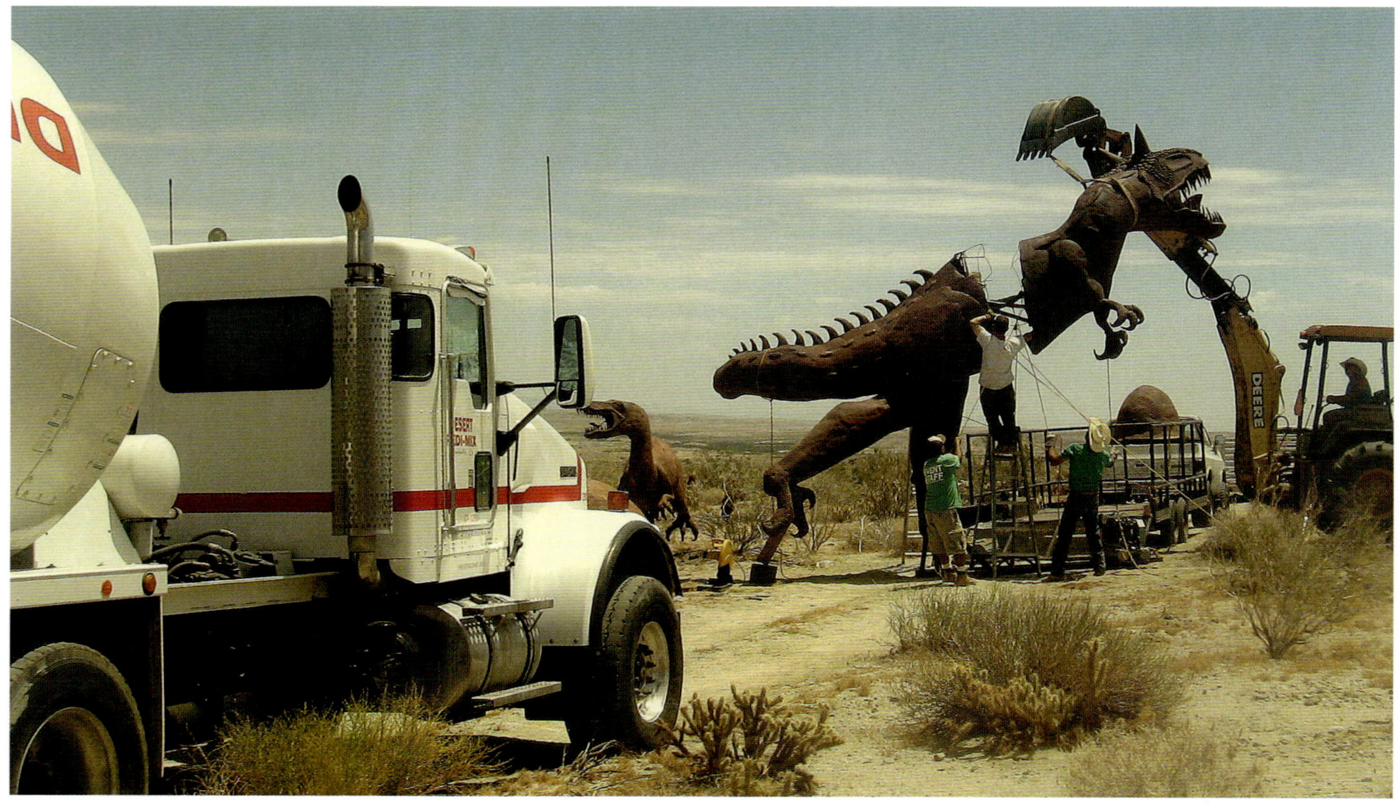

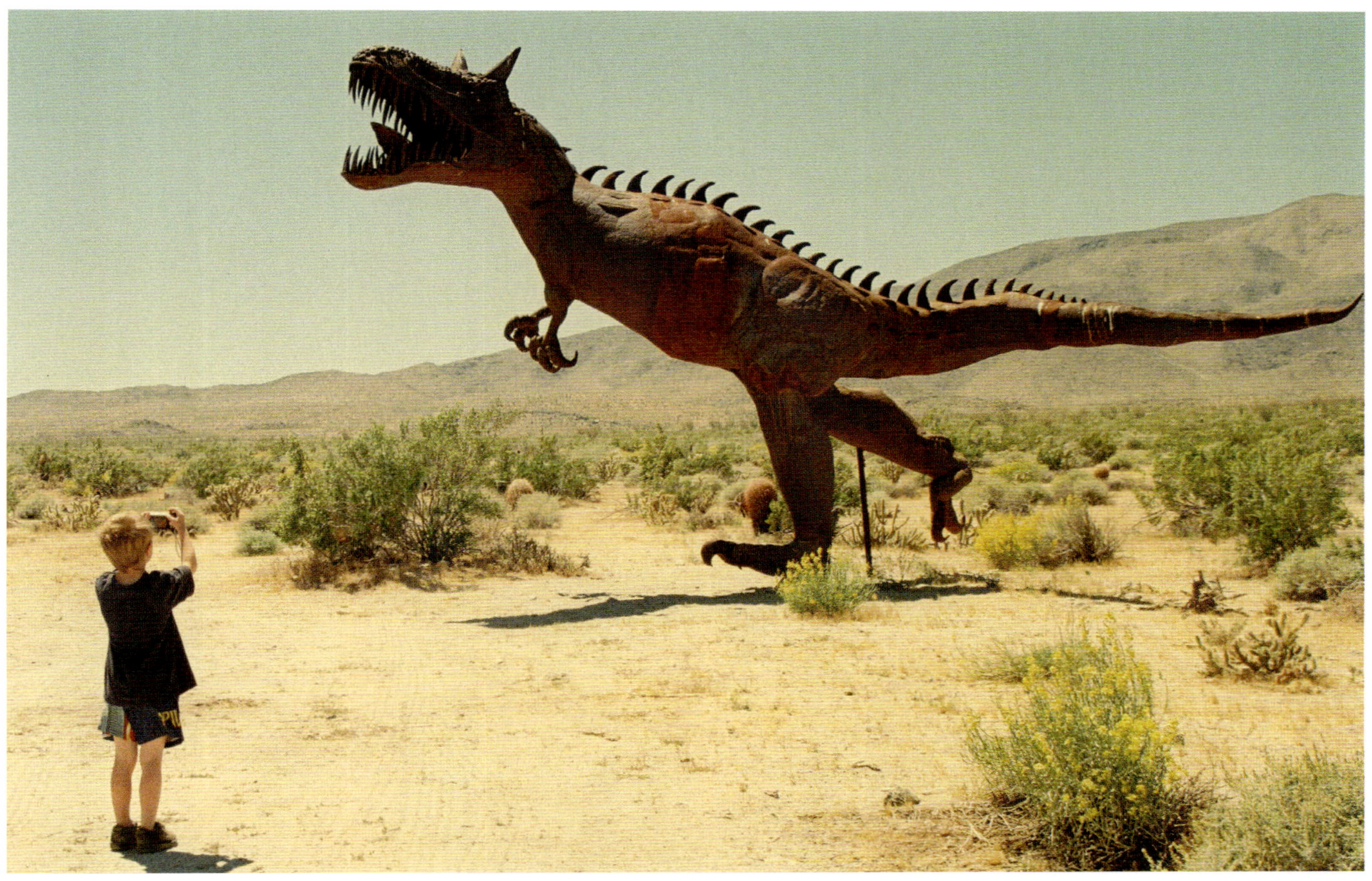

WF-4. Fighting Dinosaurs. The fascination with dinosaurs could lead children to a lifetime interest in the sciences and a possible career in paleontology. A young man snaps a photo of the dinosaur for his collection.

owner of El Borrego Restaurant to carry some of his sculptures on consignment in the restaurant's side yard. The restaurant has since become an outlet for Ricardo's art in the valley.

Sky Art projects were finally winding down in 2010. The largest projects that year included the replacements for the farm workers and a grouping of Plio-Pleistocene tapirs at Indian Head Ranch. Then there were another three assemblages that were historical in nature.

A statue of Captain Anza on his horse was placed in front of the Borrego Springs Chamber of Commerce. A bronze plaque summarizing Anza's history was also installed. The plaque clearly noted that Ricardo Breceda was the sculptor of this larger-than-life Basque explorer whose name forevermore is linked to this desert area.

A lone miner searching for gold was placed near the bighorn sheep on Indian Head Ranch. His mule, overloaded with all his possessions, is tethered nearby. The mule's posture suggests that perhaps a snake has startled it, but the bundled load of work tools, bed roll, supplies, and coffee pot remain secured.

What was touted as the very last piece of Sky Art was a commission to replicate the original civilian Jeep, the

CJ-3A. It was inspired by a group of desert explorers called the Herd of Turtles. The group had sought out Ricardo and Dennis after the 2009 Borrego Days Desert Festival parade to thank them for the Sky Arts they had enjoyed. In turn, they were invited to visit Perris Jurassic Park. In the 2010 Desert Festival, Ricardo and Dennis became part of the parade as they escorted the completed Jeep that was a "float" for the day. Later that afternoon, the Jeep was planted in a permanent location near the junction of Borrego Springs Road and Henderson Canyon Road. Hardly a detail was missing from the Jeep. Ricardo had found an old 1946 military Jeep that he had used as a model. Even the worn-appearing leather jump seat begs for a passenger to climb aboard and be photographed before the driver rock-crawls up the steep incline.

By the end of 2010, 128 pieces had been installed at twenty-six separate sites. There were thirty-two separate groupings and three themed categories: art inspired by science, art inspired by history or nature, and art inspired by pure whim—just for the joy of it. Galleta Meadows was now a full collection, and Sky Art had become a popular tourist attraction and a boon to Borrego Springs.

WF-4 Fighting Dinosaurs (Carnotaurus, left; Allosaurus, right). Movement is clearly visible in Ricardo's sculptures as seen in this charging *Carnotaurus*. Because of their size, these fighting dinosaurs are visible a mile distant.

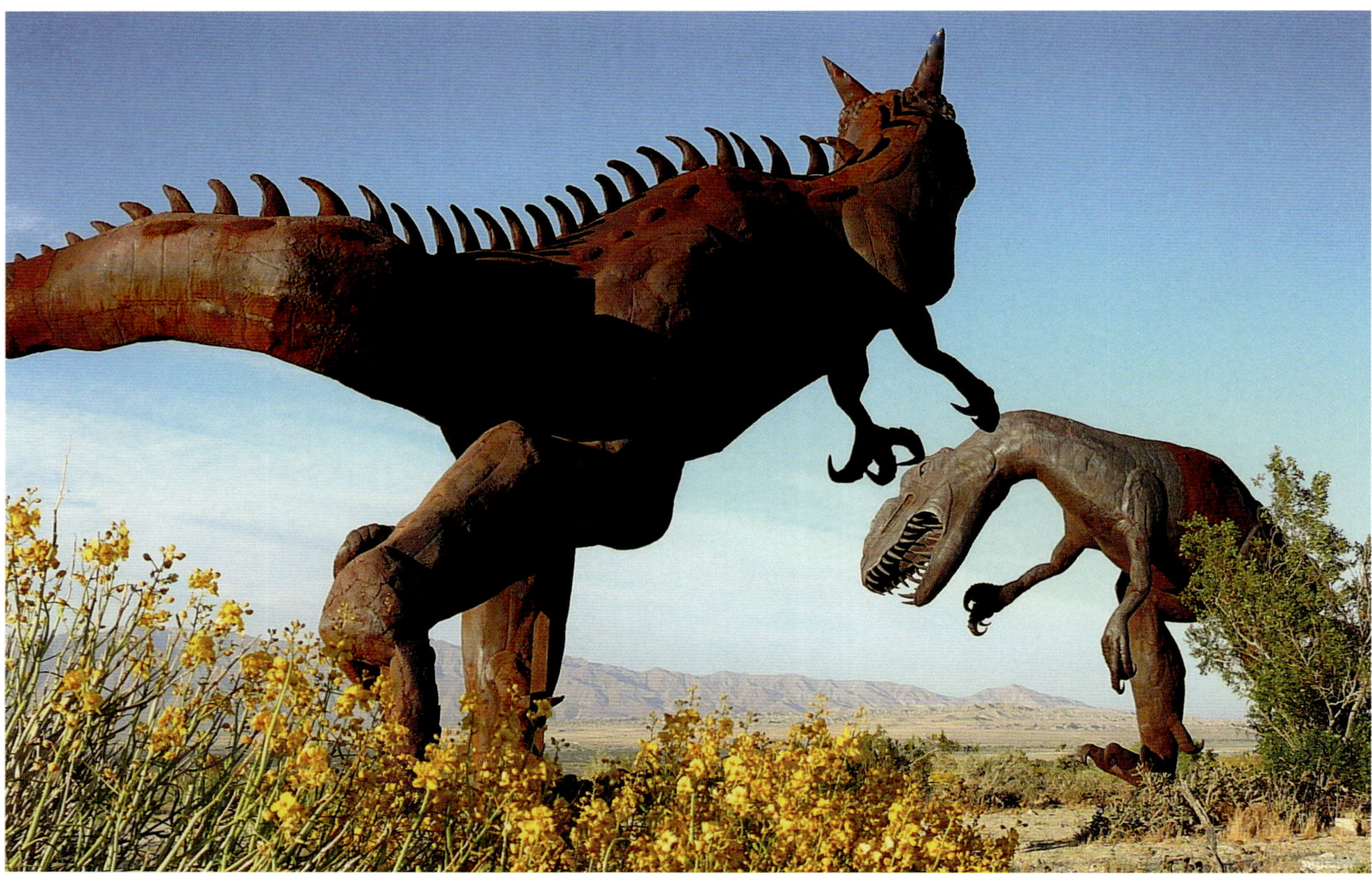

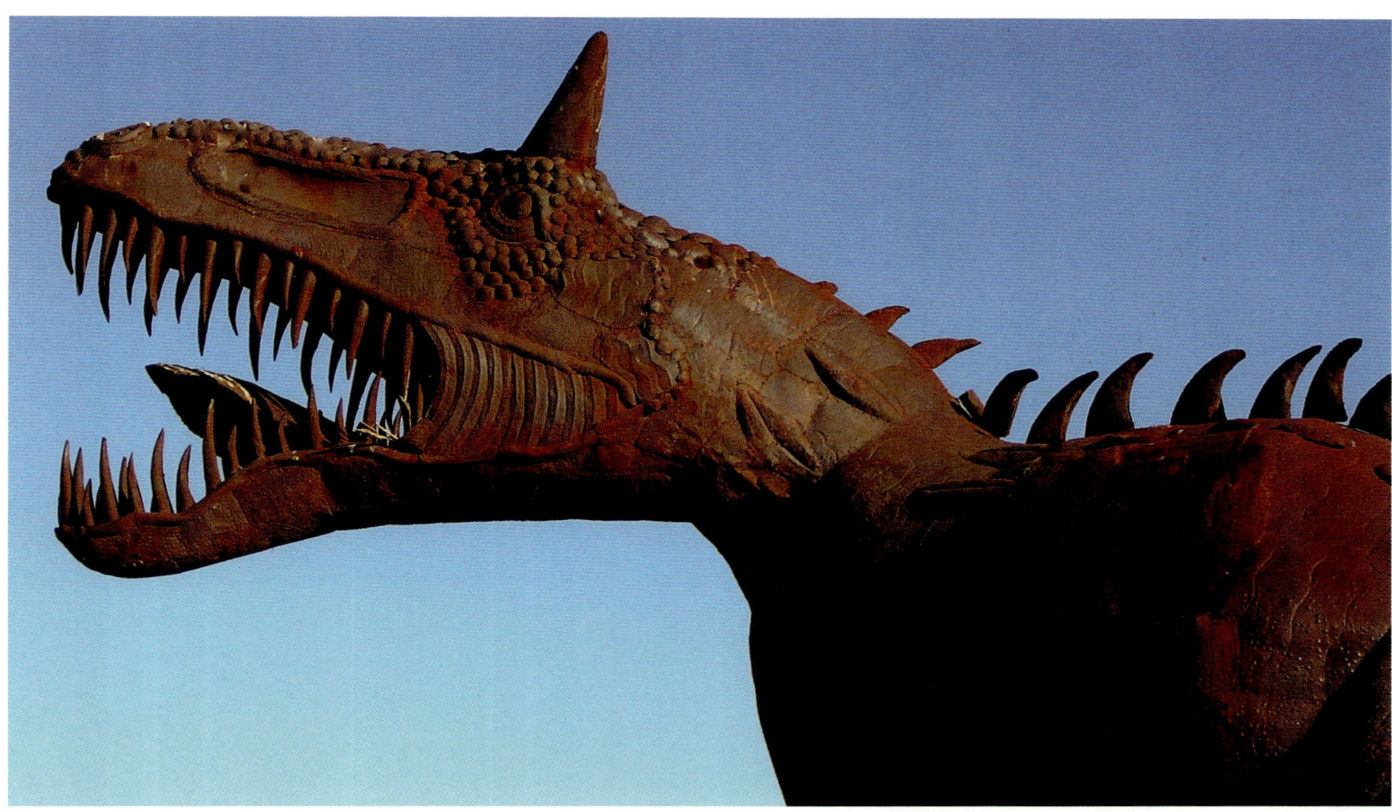

WF-4 Fighting Dinosaurs. The *Carnotaurus* or "Flesh-Eating Bull" was unusual for its two hornlike protrusions above its eyebrows. Only a single fossil specimen has been found for this dinosaur that lived some 113 to 91 million years ago in Patagonia.

While Borrego residents support local businesses, most of those businesses are very dependent on tourism. The draw has always been park visitation, especially during the wildflower season, or some self-generated events such as the Borrego Day's Desert Festival, the Circle of Art, the annual Plein Air Invitational, and other such activities. The sculptures have added a new dimension to tourism in Borrego Springs.

The Borrego Springs Chamber of Commerce President Pat Havens announced:

> The sculptures have, indeed, put Borrego Springs on the map! The first year they were accidentally discovered by visitors who came in to the Chamber of Commerce. By the second year, visitors to the Chamber were saying: *"Where are the sculptures? We came all the way out here to see the sculptures!"* By now, we are nationally famous for the sculptures and have good maps to show the location of all of them to visitors.

Pat added that the Borrego Springs Chamber of Commerce considers Ricardo as "part of the art community." From the chamber's viewpoint, he has made a very real and positive impact on this special community.

The overall reaction to Sky Art from visitors to the area has also been very positive, as noted in the guestbook found on the Galleta Meadows website. Comments are posted by visitors, and frequently they have to do with the unexpected

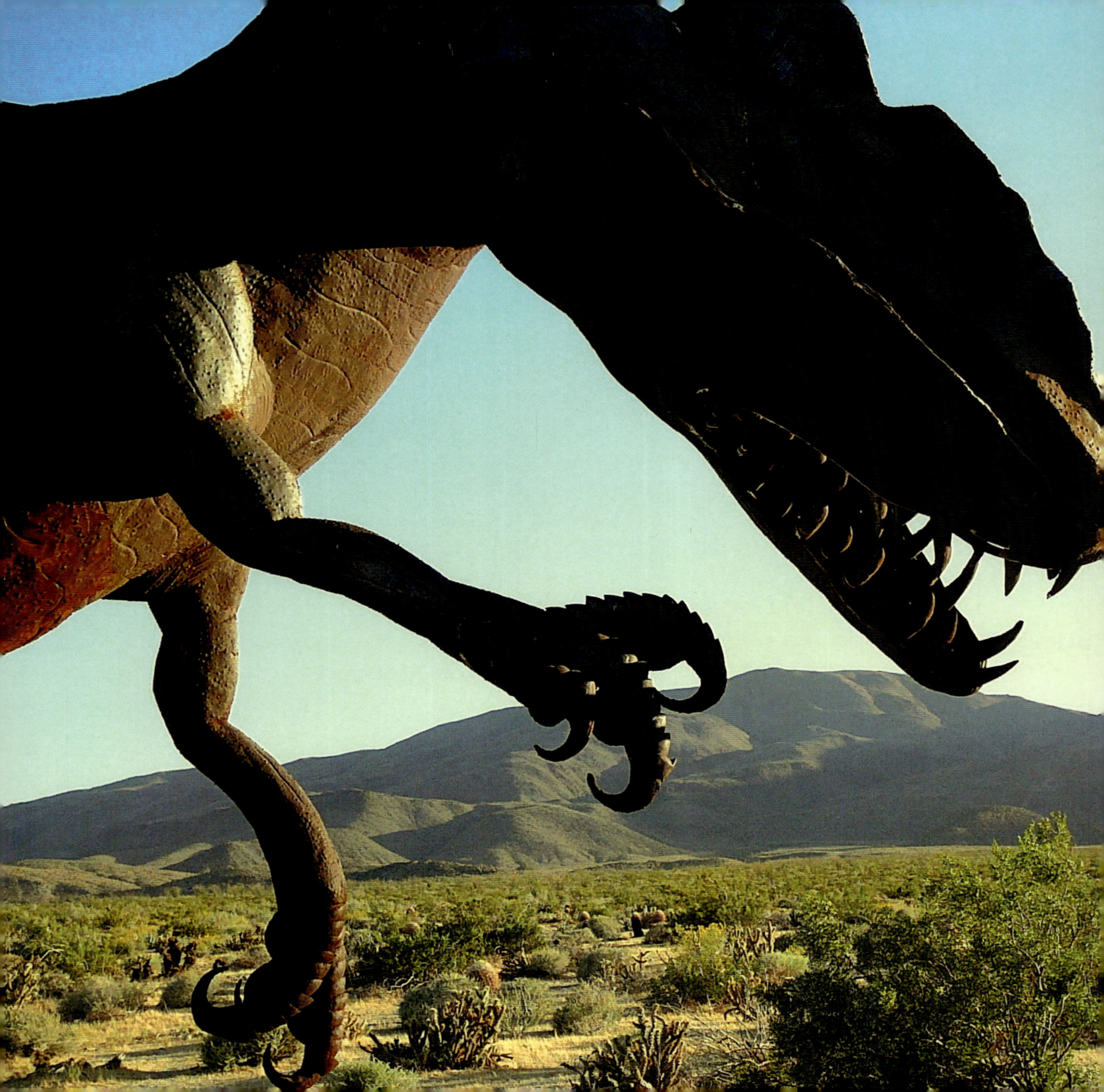

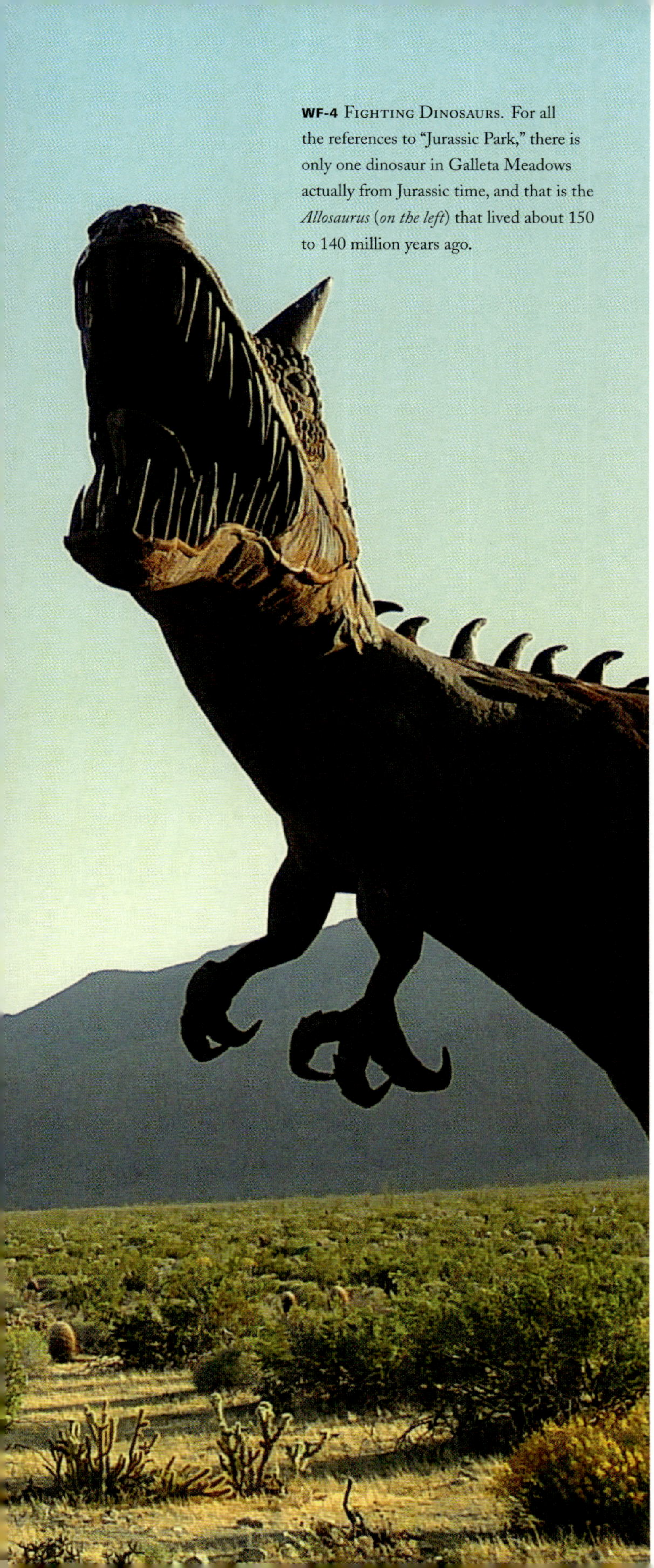

WF-4 Fighting Dinosaurs. For all the references to "Jurassic Park," there is only one dinosaur in Galleta Meadows actually from Jurassic time, and that is the *Allosaurus* (*on the left*) that lived about 150 to 140 million years ago.

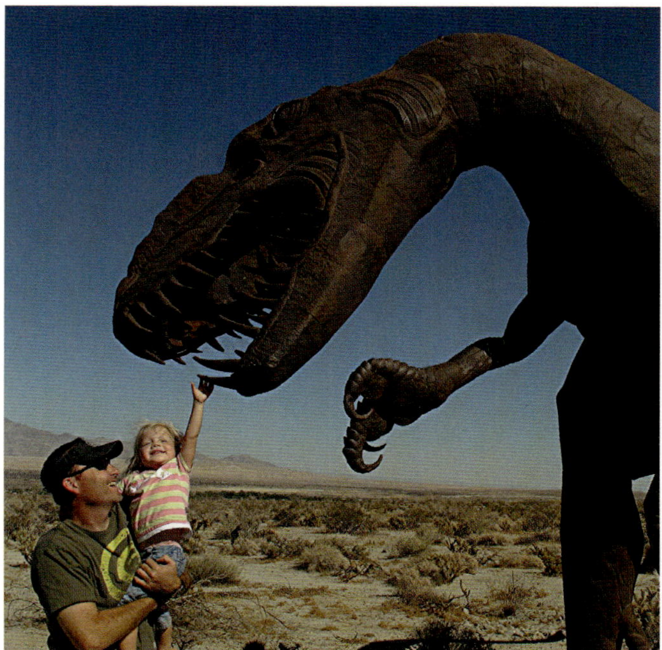

WF-4 Fighting Dinosaurs. As frightening as dinosaurs appear, children find them fascinating.

surprise and delight in finding them, such as in this posting by Cayenne in March 2010:

> I cannot begin to describe my utter delight to discover these upon making my first foray in Borrego Springs. I went to find wildflowers, but serendipitously happened upon these precious treasures. I was truly awe-struck, and I think finding them unexpectedly heightened the mystery and joy of the experience . . . a perfect fit for a town with such strong support for visual artists.

Some of the comments have to do with specific sculptures that provoke deep personal connection, such as the posting from Heather Rodriguez in February 2010:

> . . . as an artist myself . . . I have to say, this is the best display of art I could have imagined. Not just the pieces, but the location and history behind them. Of all the pieces that stand out most in my mind and will always be remembered are the farm workers. As

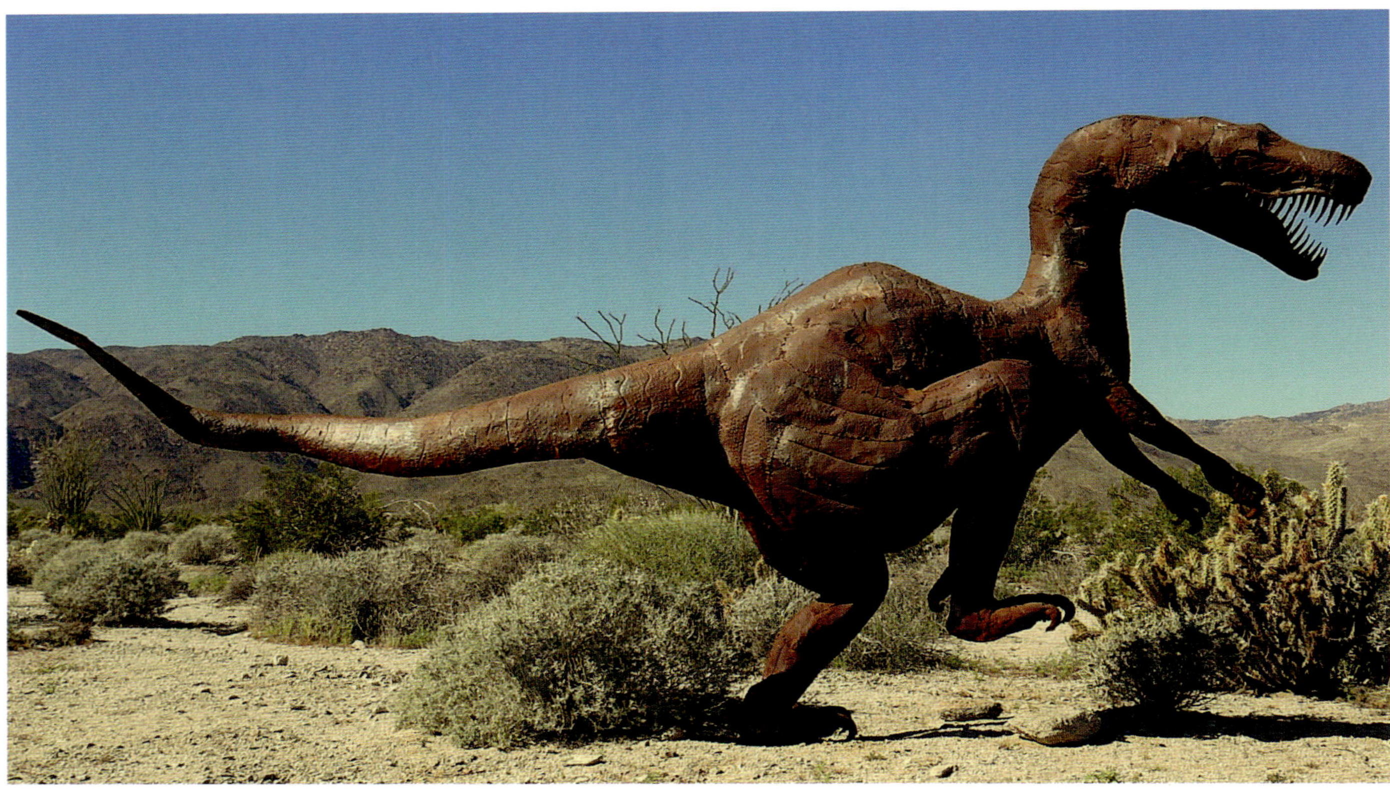

WF-5 UTAHRAPTOR. The discovery of the fossil remains of *Utahraptor* after the release of the *Jurassic Park* movie justified the size of the raptor depicted in the film. *Utahraptor* was twice the height of the three-foot-tall *Velociraptor*.

> a Mexican descendent it personally touched me that these would be out here among all of the other wonderful pieces.

Several comments have to do specifically with the many Plio-Pleistocene animals that are represented. Eric Scott, the curator of paleontology at the San Bernardino County Museum and the author of the chapter on horses in *Fossil Treasures,* said in a posting that the sculptures are "fantastic." In regard to the area's geologic and paleontological history, he wrote, ". . . it's nice to see that prehistoric wonder captured not only in the Park's visitor center, but also artistically with these sculptures."

A couple from Sedona, Arizona, even went one step further when they wrote, "Great idea, much more interesting than museum fossils; gives a fascinating feel for size and shape outdoors."

Many visitors comment on the setting. A man from Encinitas, California, said it is a "perfect blend of art and terrain. And like the desert, open and free. Unique in the USA."

Almost all of the comments express either appreciation or laudatory remarks such as "Awesome vision; amazing execution" to "Ricardo u r a genius and Mr. Avery a visionary," written in texting style. In May 2010, a couple from La Crescenta, California, even dubbed Ricardo "the Picasso of Steel," an expression that has become synonymous with the sculptor.

There have been a few negative comments, but those have pretty much been restricted to the selection or location of sculptures rather than to the art itself.

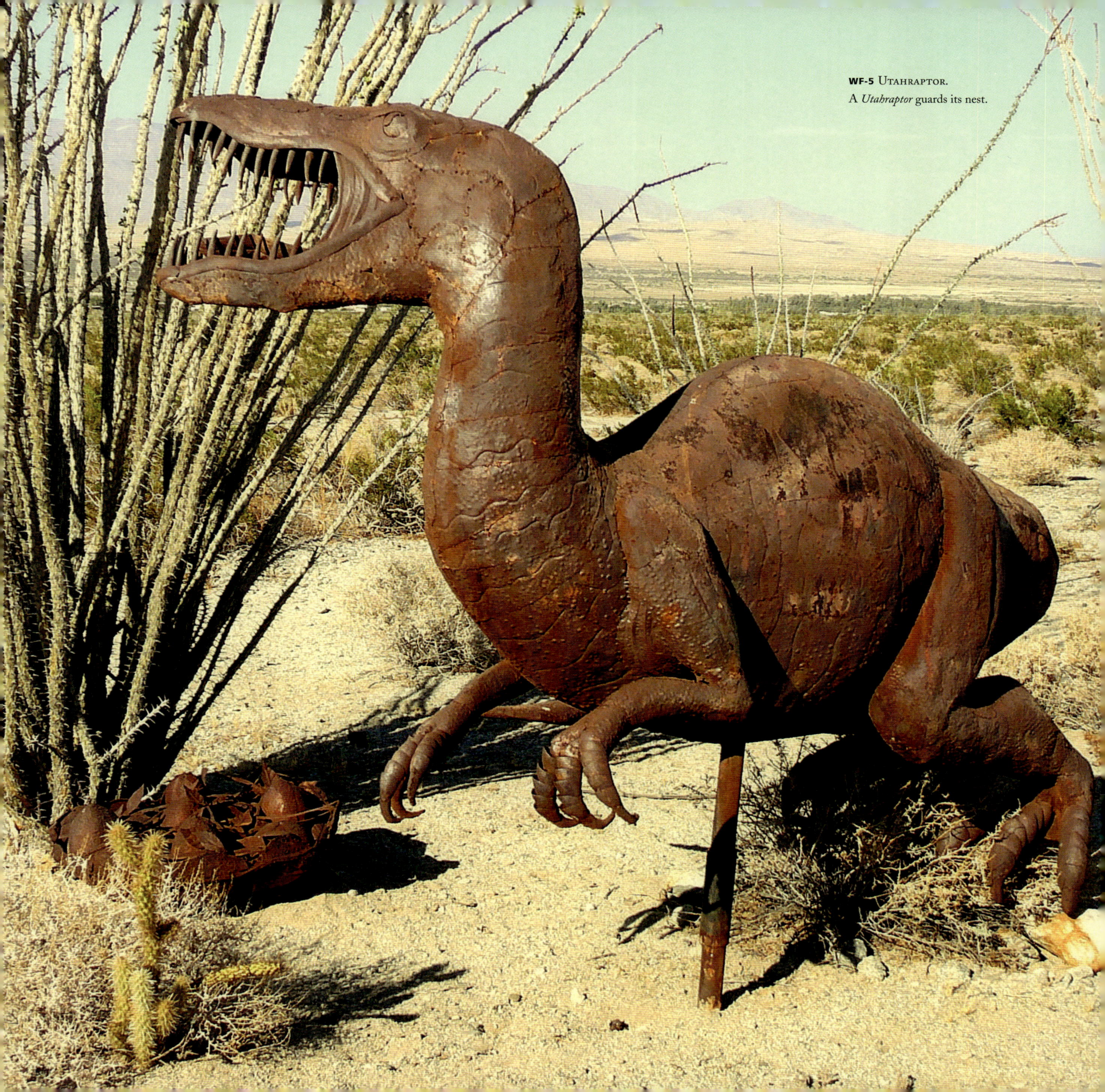

WF-5 Utahraptor.
A *Utahraptor* guards its nest.

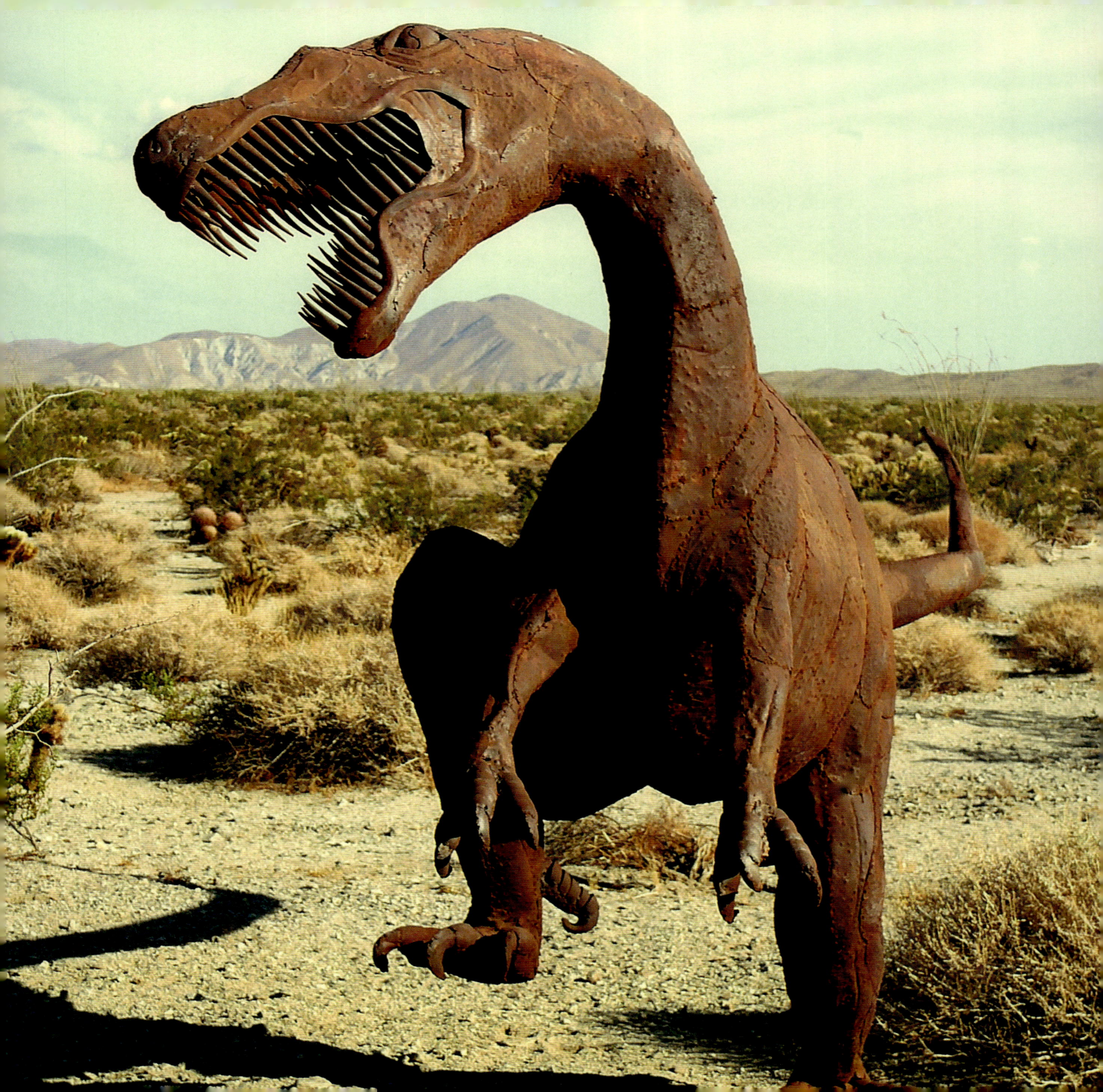

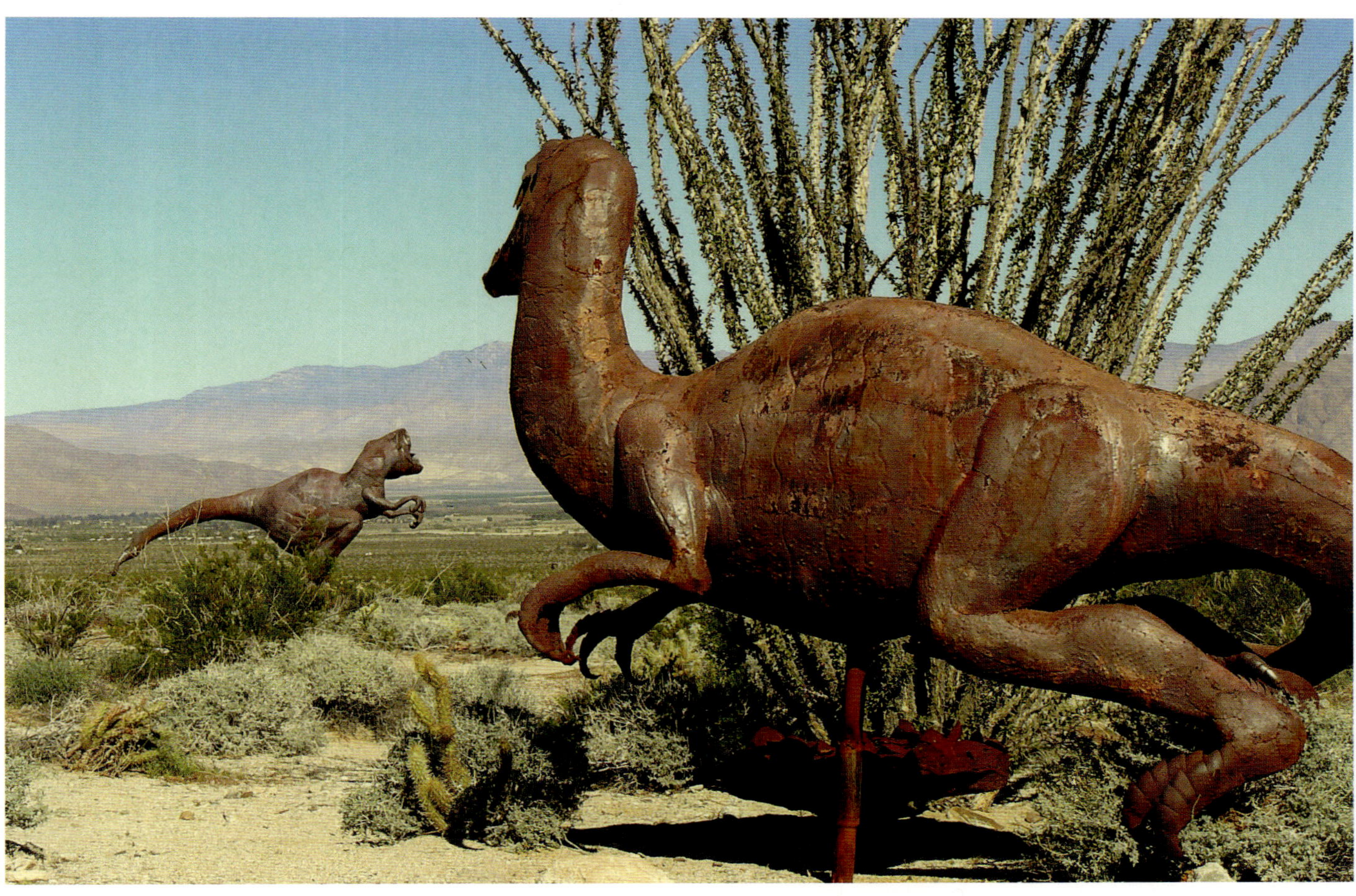

WF-5 UTAHRAPTOR. The *Utahraptor* was a light, fast, agile, and giant birdlike dinosaur with large, sharp, serrated teeth and powerful jaws. It was highly intelligent and may have hunted in packs. The Galleta Meadows raptor (*above*) cautiously views the neighboring *T. rex*.

The dinosaurs have also stirred controversy. Much of the criticism had to do with their introduction because their fossil remains have never been found in this area. Clark Shimeall's letter to the editor of the *Borrego Sun* on March 19, 2009, accurately reflected the sentiment of some: "I am much opposed to including dinosaurs in the collection, at least until fossils of these animals are locally found. The display should authentically represent the prehistoric and historical past of the Borrego basin."

Another complaint has been the saguaro cactus situated to the west of the padre. Saguaros are not found in the Anza-Borrego area. They are located in the deserts to the east of the Colorado River and south into Mexico. However, this saguaro can be seen as symbolically representing the Sonoran area from which the padre began his trek or the area he passed through before crossing the Colorado River along the Anza Trail.

There was also initial concern about the baby sloth riding on its mother's back because some thought there was no proof that sloths carried their young that way. Dennis put that to rest when he took a trip to Costa Rica and confirmed it through direct observation.

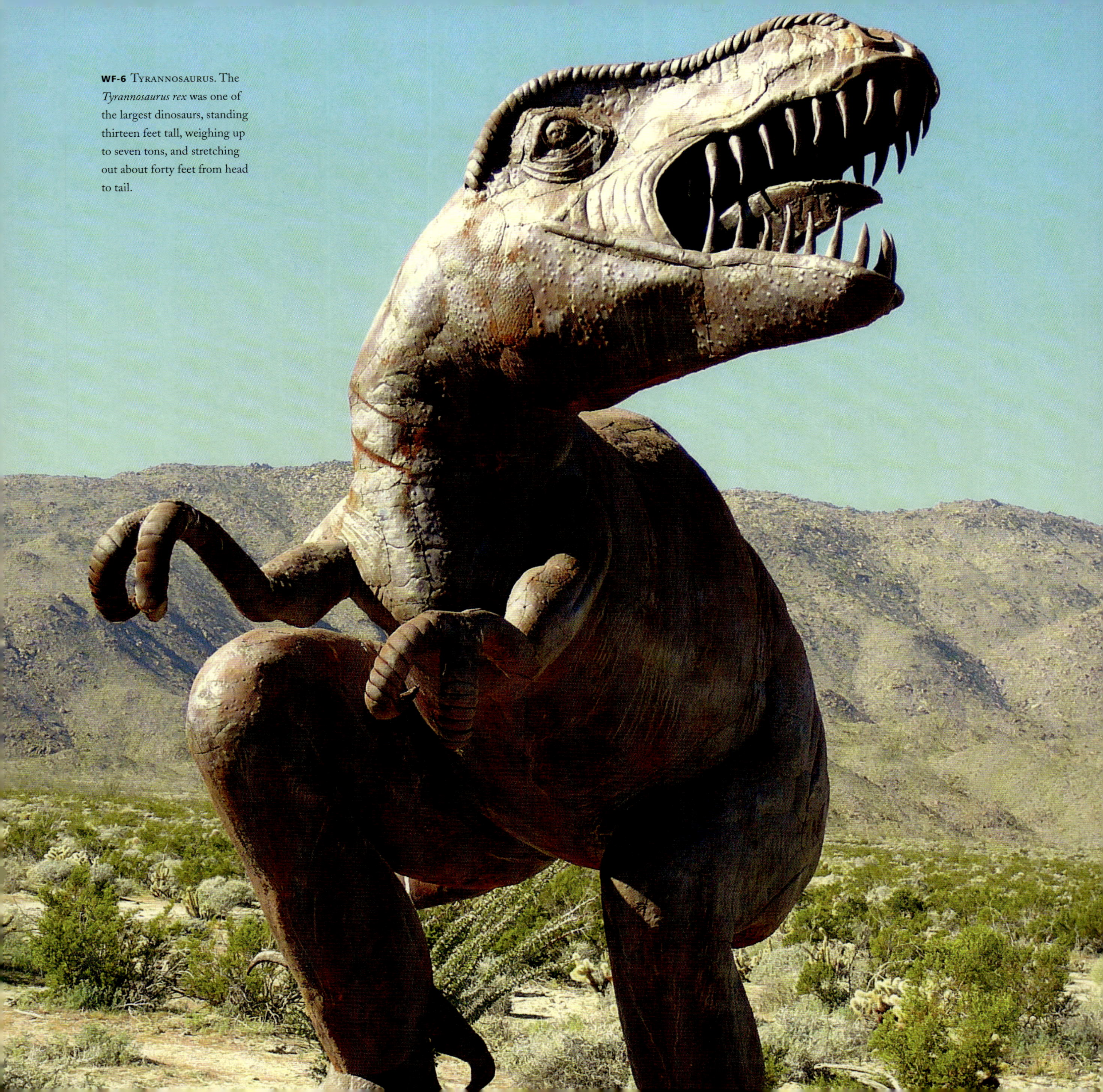

WF-6 Tyrannosaurus. The *Tyrannosaurus rex* was one of the largest dinosaurs, standing thirteen feet tall, weighing up to seven tons, and stretching out about forty feet from head to tail.

Some homeowners have grumbled about the location of sculptures, especially those who now have their open view of the desert disrupted. Others complain about added traffic. One homeowner was unhappy when he was asked to assist a visitor whose vehicle became stuck on a dirt road leading to a sculpture.

The three-day free camping policy for Galleta Meadows has caused various reactions. Those who have not abused the privilege react with sheer delight, as reflected by a couple from Vancouver Island, British Columbia, who wrote in the guestbook on the Galleta Meadows website: "As visitors we have felt blessed to be allowed to camp beside these incredible sculptures and get a feel for the land. It has given us a completely different experience and appreciation for the present and past of the areas Borrego Springs has to offer."

Others abuse the privilege, as one visitor from St. Louis, Missouri, reported in a letter to Dennis in March 2011: "The campers take over the area and make it unsightly. The vehicles tear up the desert vegetation in a large area around the sculptures. Others wanting to view the sculptures have to dodge their chairs, cars, grills, rugs, and extra vehicles." The visitor suggested changing the camping policy

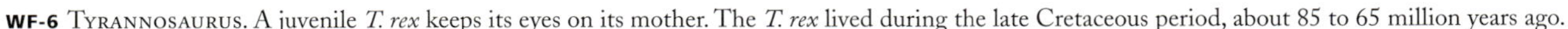

WF-6 TYRANNOSAURUS. A juvenile *T. rex* keeps its eyes on its mother. The *T. rex* lived during the late Cretaceous period, about 85 to 65 million years ago.

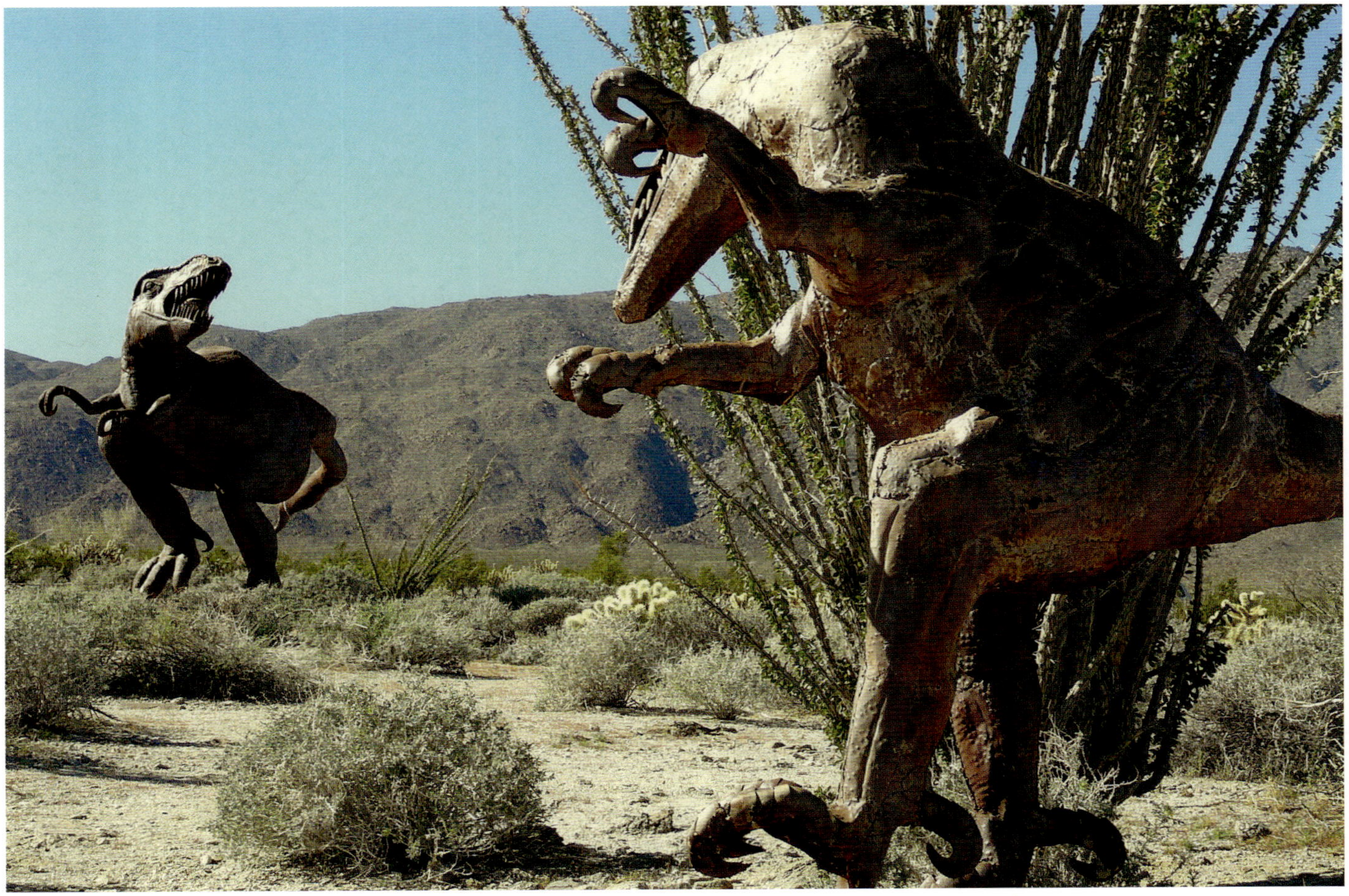

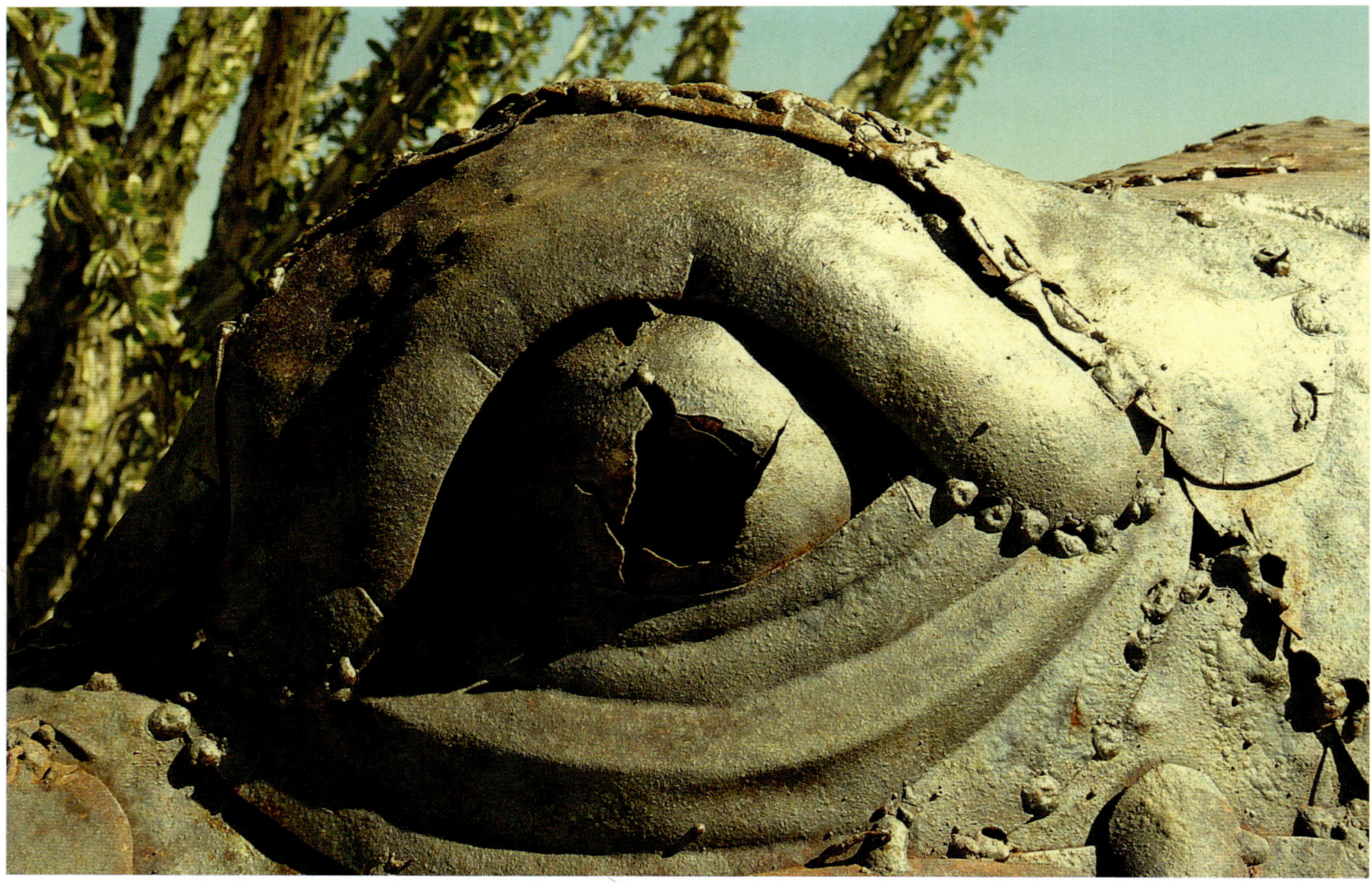

WF-6 Tyrannosaurus. The fearsome eye of the *Tyrannosaurus rex* keeps watch on its territory. Ricardo has used different styles in making eyes for his sculptures, sometimes cutting a hole for the pupil (*above*) and other times just cutting a slit—as in the *Velociraptor*.

at Galleta Meadows "to allow tent camping but not motor vehicle camping."

There were some complaints from young earth creationists who took exception to references that some of the animals lived almost seven million years ago.

None of these complaints or concerns had to do with Ricardo's art or genius in building his sculptures. The only noted criticism was the experimental use of a clear varnish on the baby mammoth. A post on the Galleta Meadows website from a Borrego Springs resident exhorted, "Please don't ruin these great works of art!" The resident was concerned because "now the details are obscured" with the glaze. Both Ricardo and Dennis later regretted adding the shiny surface. Their preference is to keep it natural.

Overall, the many comments have helped to spread Ricardo's fame and encouraged more people to visit Borrego Springs.

There was, however, one comment that Ricardo really wanted more than all the others, and he finally got it when his mother visited him during Easter week 2011.

For years Ricardo had been driven to prove himself—to prove his mother wrong when she had said to him, "Son,

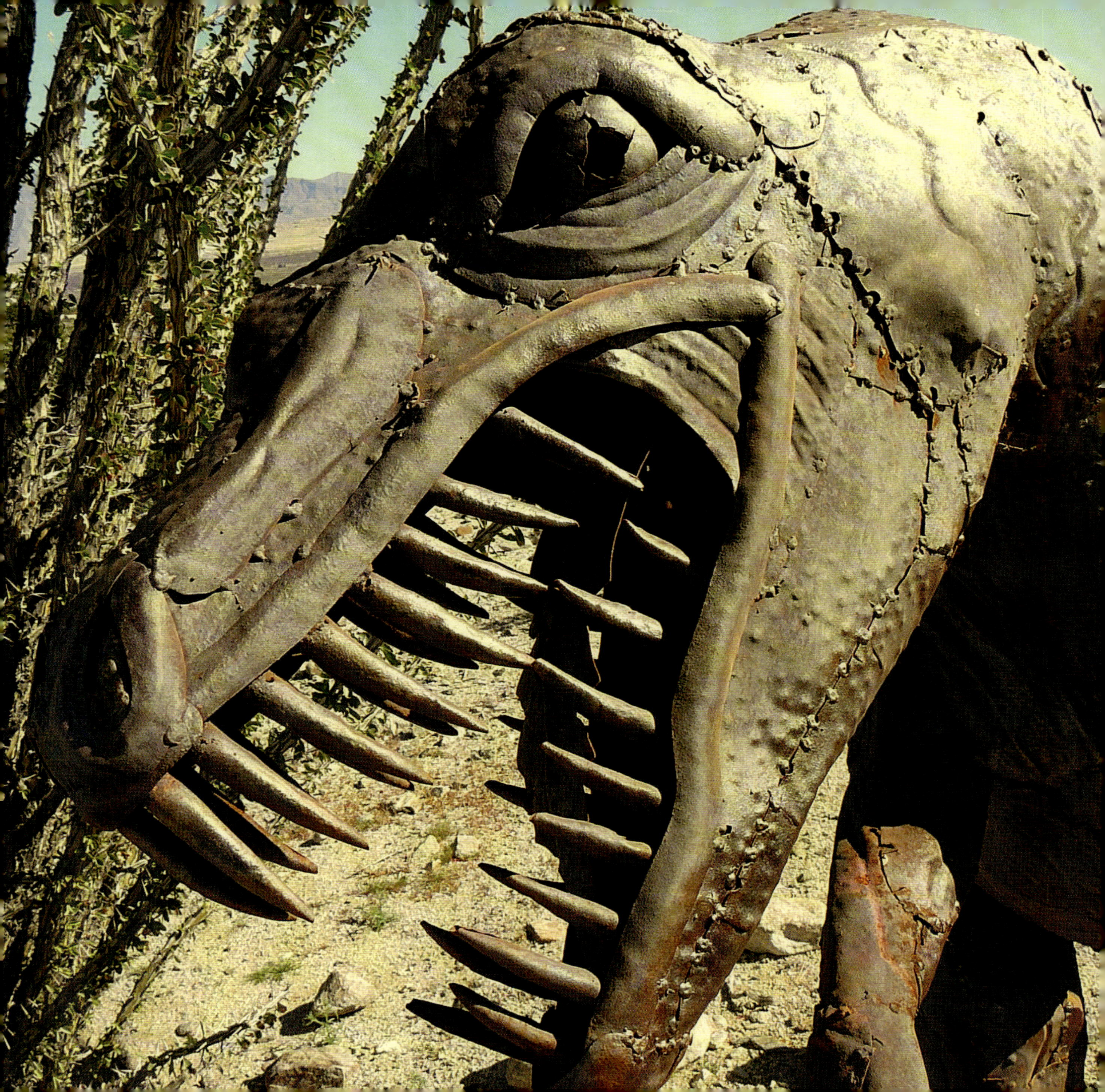

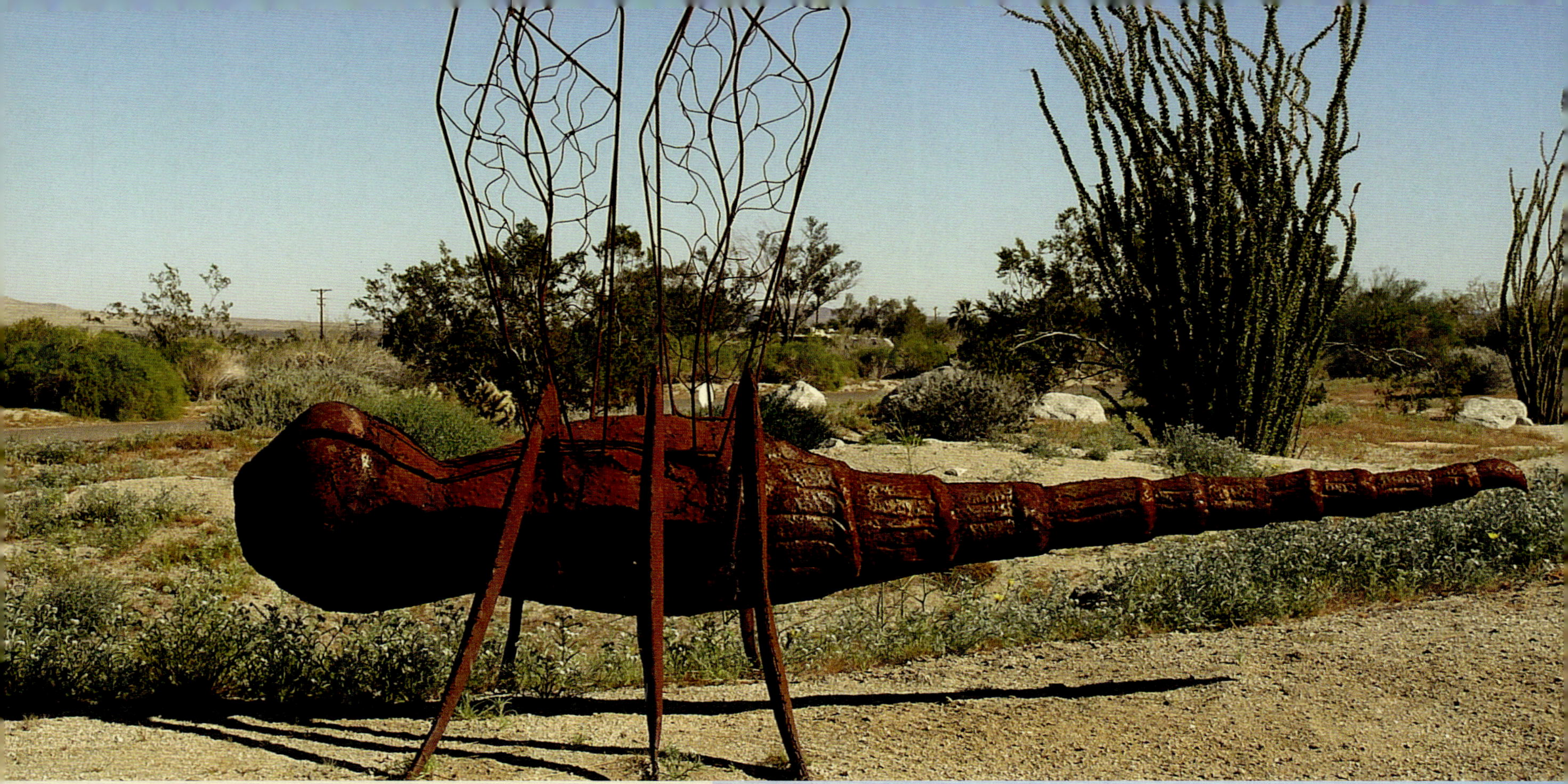

YARD ART

As Ricardo's art has become more popular, several residents of Borrego Springs have purchased their own sculptures to display in their yards, such as in the dragonfly (*above*) and the bighorn sheep (*to the right*) shown here.

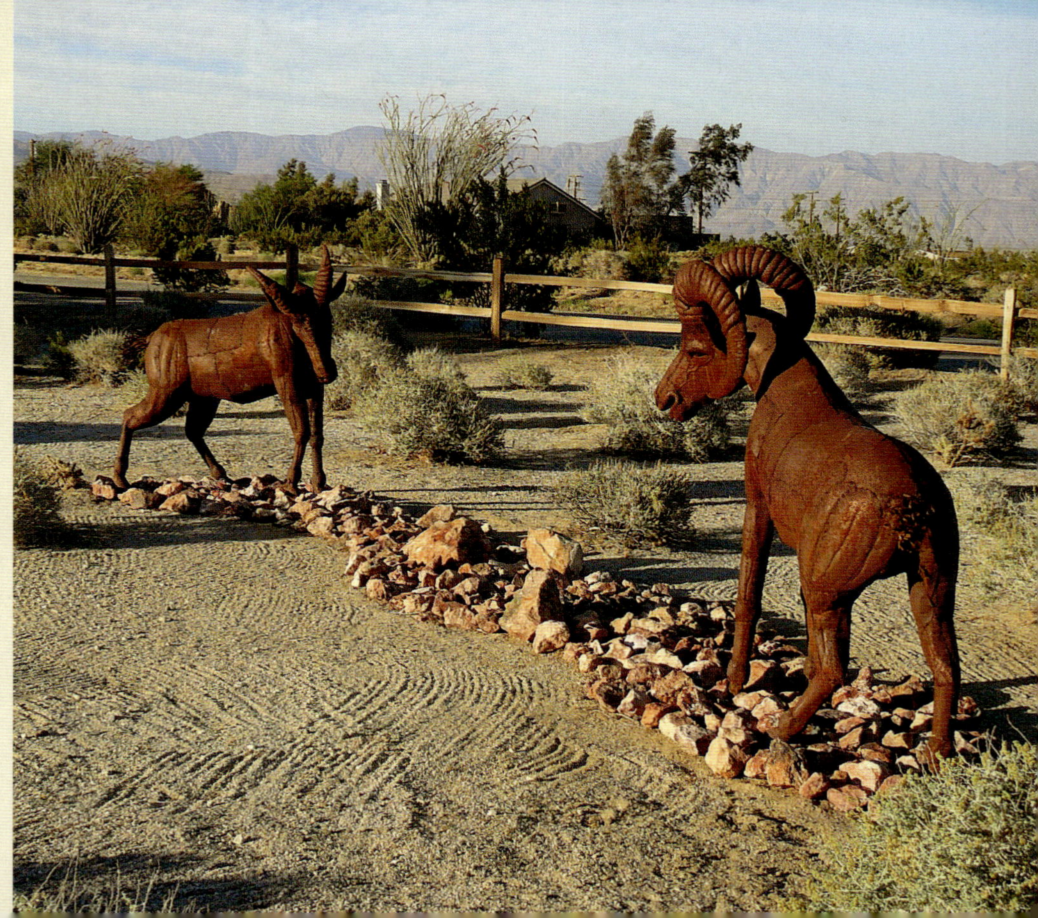

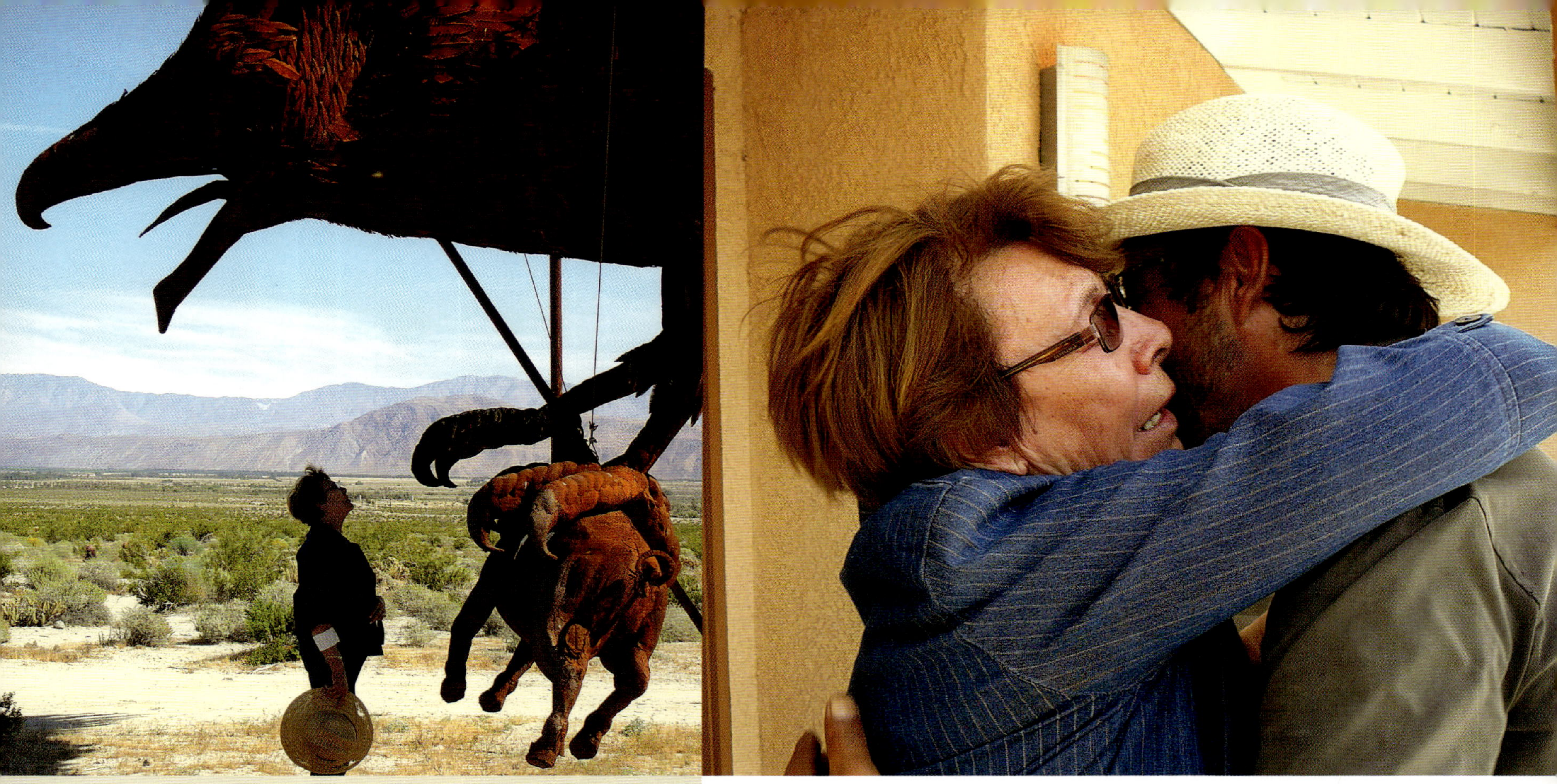

ESTELA AND RICARDO

Initially Estela did not encourage Ricardo in his new career. However, in 2011, she came to the United States and visited Galleta Meadows for the first time. She was astonished and found the sculptures incredible. After her tour she found Ricardo and embraced him, admitting she had not understood what Ricardo wanted to do and now was doing in this stage of his life.

why don't you do something else?" She had inadvertently thrown out a challenge and Ricardo had met that challenge. He had told himself, "just wait and see," and now the time had come.

His mother Estela, and sister Yolanda, along with his nephew Leonardo, came to Borrego Springs in April 2011. It was their first visit to the desert and their first time to see Sky Art.

As his mother was driven from one sculpture to the next, she kept saying, "Incredible." She gently touched some of the sculptures. Then hours later when she saw Ricardo, there were tears in her eyes as she grabbed and hugged him, admitting that she had never understood and now knew that her son was doing what he was meant to do.

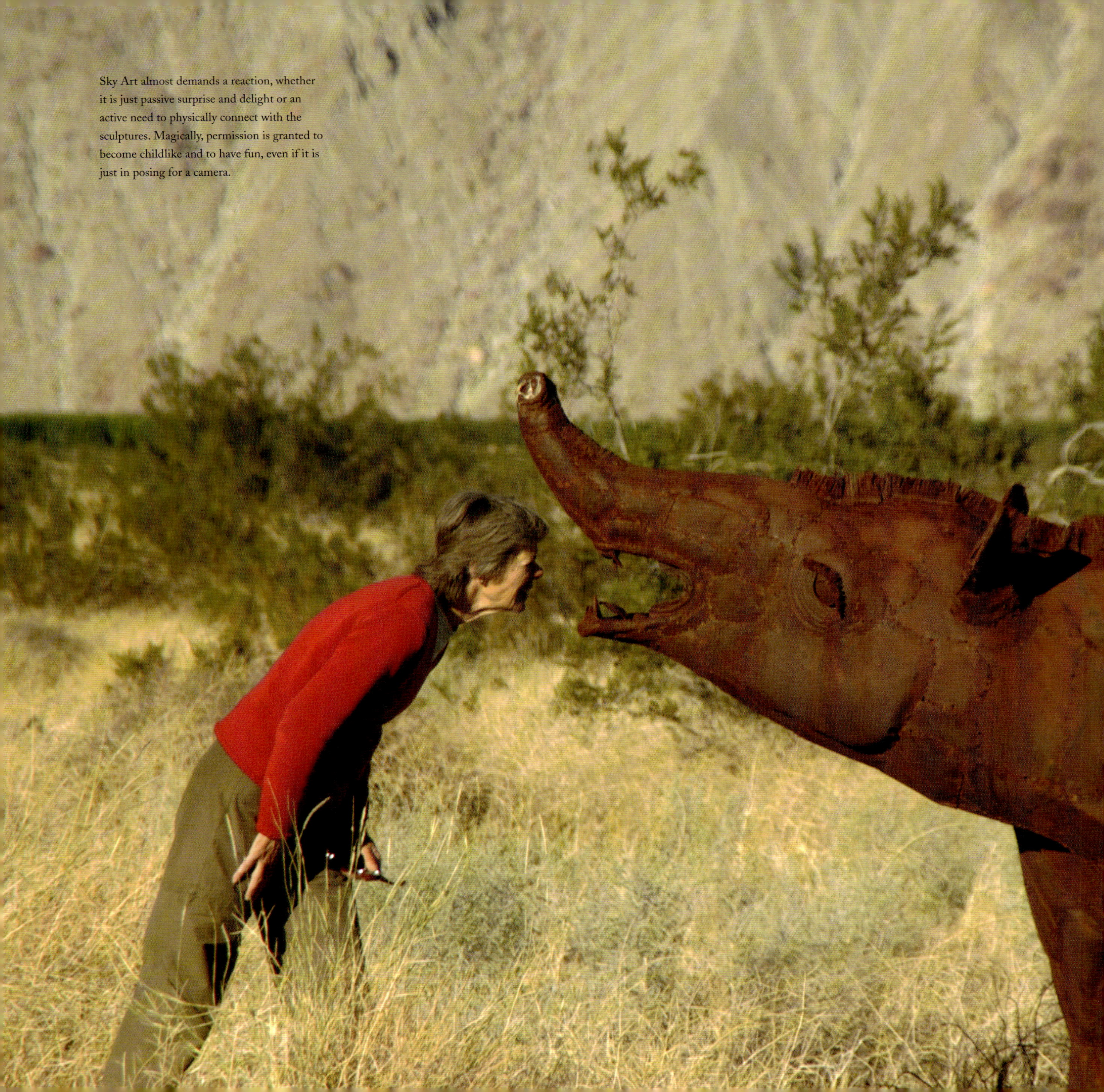

Sky Art almost demands a reaction, whether it is just passive surprise and delight or an active need to physically connect with the sculptures. Magically, permission is granted to become childlike and to have fun, even if it is just in posing for a camera.

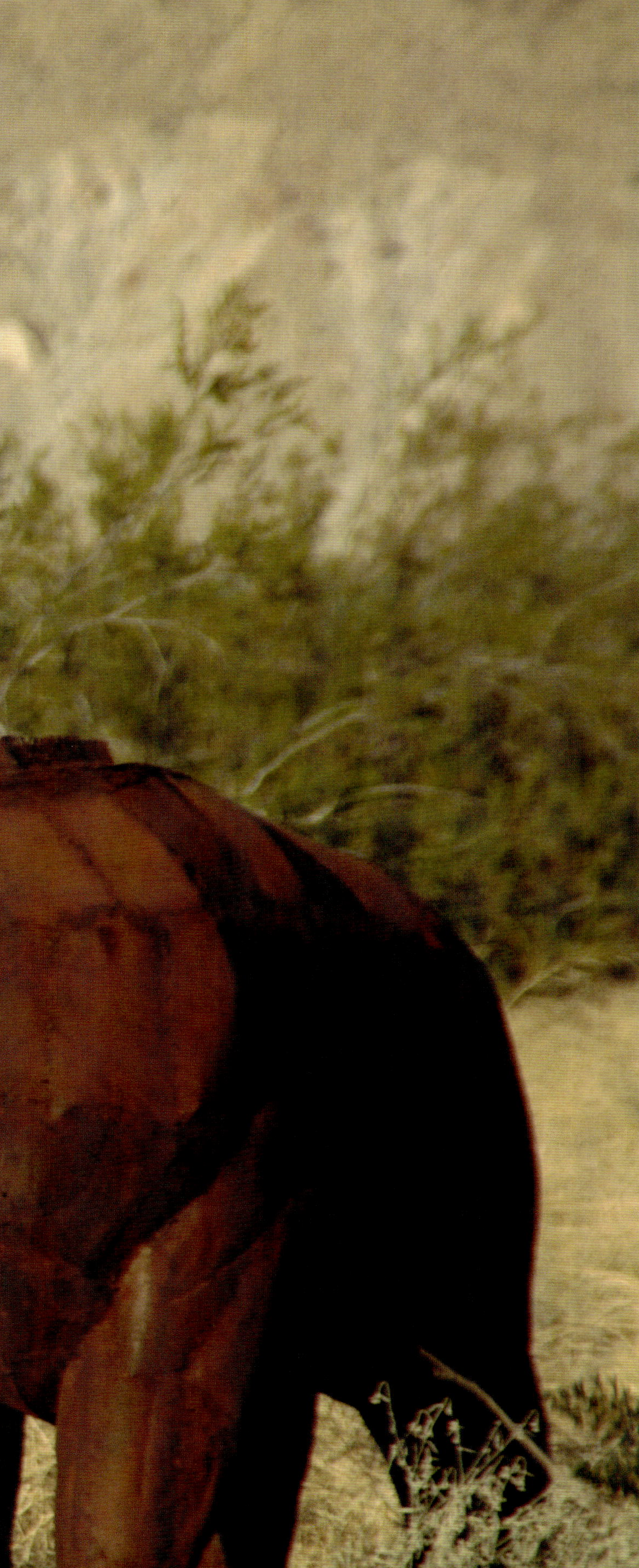

CHAPTER 6

STEPPING OUT

Ricardo often jokes that each of his sculptures carries his DNA. In a sense they do, both literally and figuratively. Cutting, hammering, and welding metal is hazardous work, often leading to injury. Scars on his hands and arms prove that. In a figurative sense, his sculptures carry his charisma and allure by inspiring a reaction of playfulness and joy, and a sense of connection. And connect he does—to individuals, groups, residents, and other artists.

One only has to look at photographs taken by families and friends, often readily available online at such sites as Flickr and Shutterfly, to see people interacting with the sculptures. Sometimes a photo is taken with the person's hand or head placed near a sculpture's gaping mouth or teeth. A sculpture's pose may be duplicated in a stance, or a person may show surprise or feign fright. Often a group shot is staged in front of a sculpture. There is something about the metal structures that draws one in, creates delight, and leaves a sense of wonder.

Group field trips to this desert area often include a tour of the sculptures. Several Imperial County schools participate in the Anza-Borrego Foundation's Fifth Grade Camp program in which students, accompanied by their teacher, spend three days and two nights at the Anza-Borrego Desert State Park school camp. Part of the program involves tours of the Stout Paleontology Lab to learn about the Plio-Pleistocene

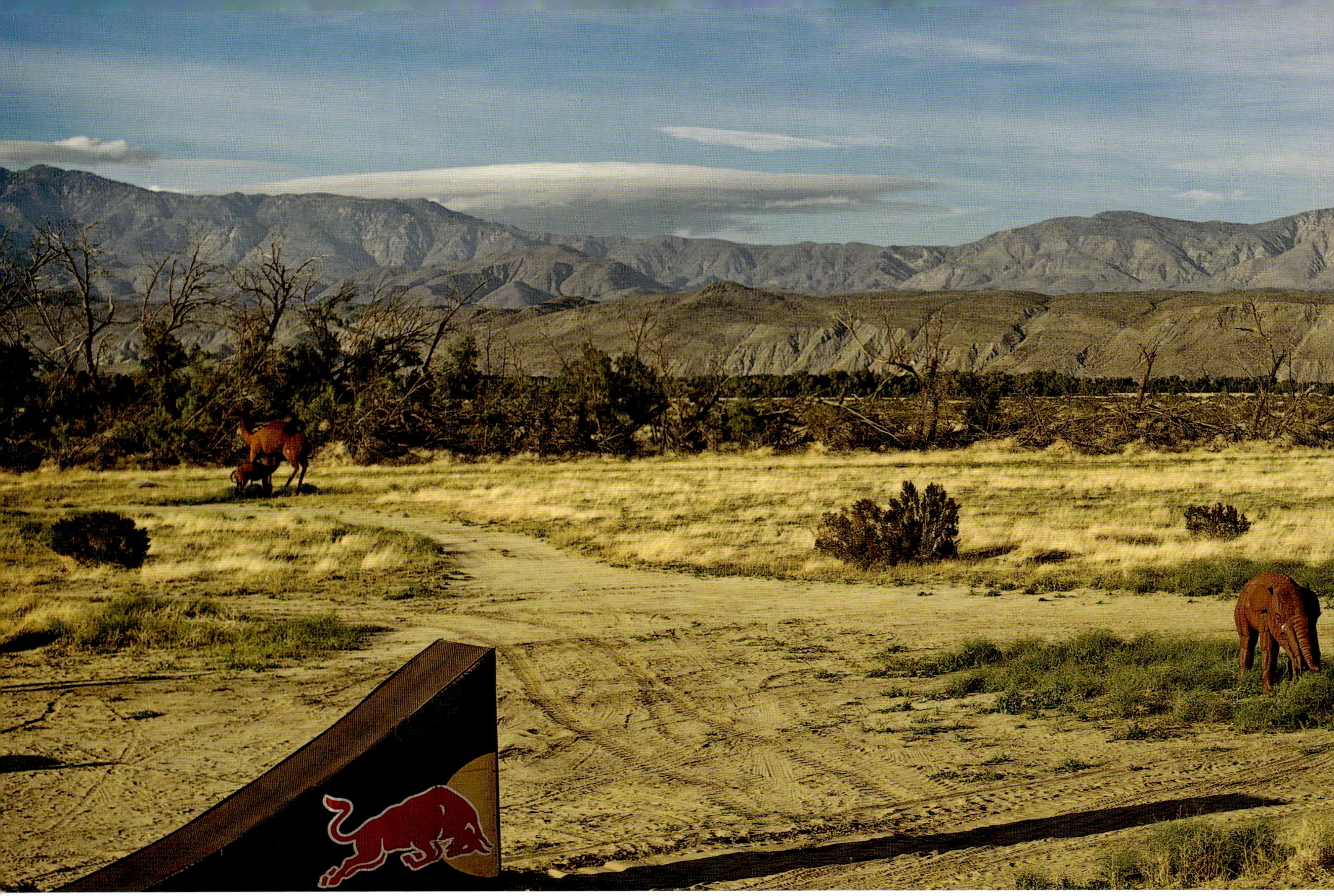

Robbie "Maddo" Maddison, the world's most famous stunt biker, performs a "scorpion" as he soars over the gomphotheres. The photo shoot was sponsored by the energy drink company Red Bull.

animals that once lived in this desert area. Often classes visit the sculptures either en route to camp or upon their return to Imperial County.

The Desert Protective Council sponsors a Salton Basin Living Laboratory program for fourth through sixth graders at five Imperial County schools, which also includes a trip to the state park and the Stout Paleontology Lab. Students spend part of their time visiting the Plio-Pleistocene sculptures with their teacher.

Adult geology field trips also take advantage of the learning opportunity that visiting the sculptures provides.

The South Coast Geological Society and the San Diego Association of Geologists publish books annually on a given study area that includes a two-day field trip. In 2010 the

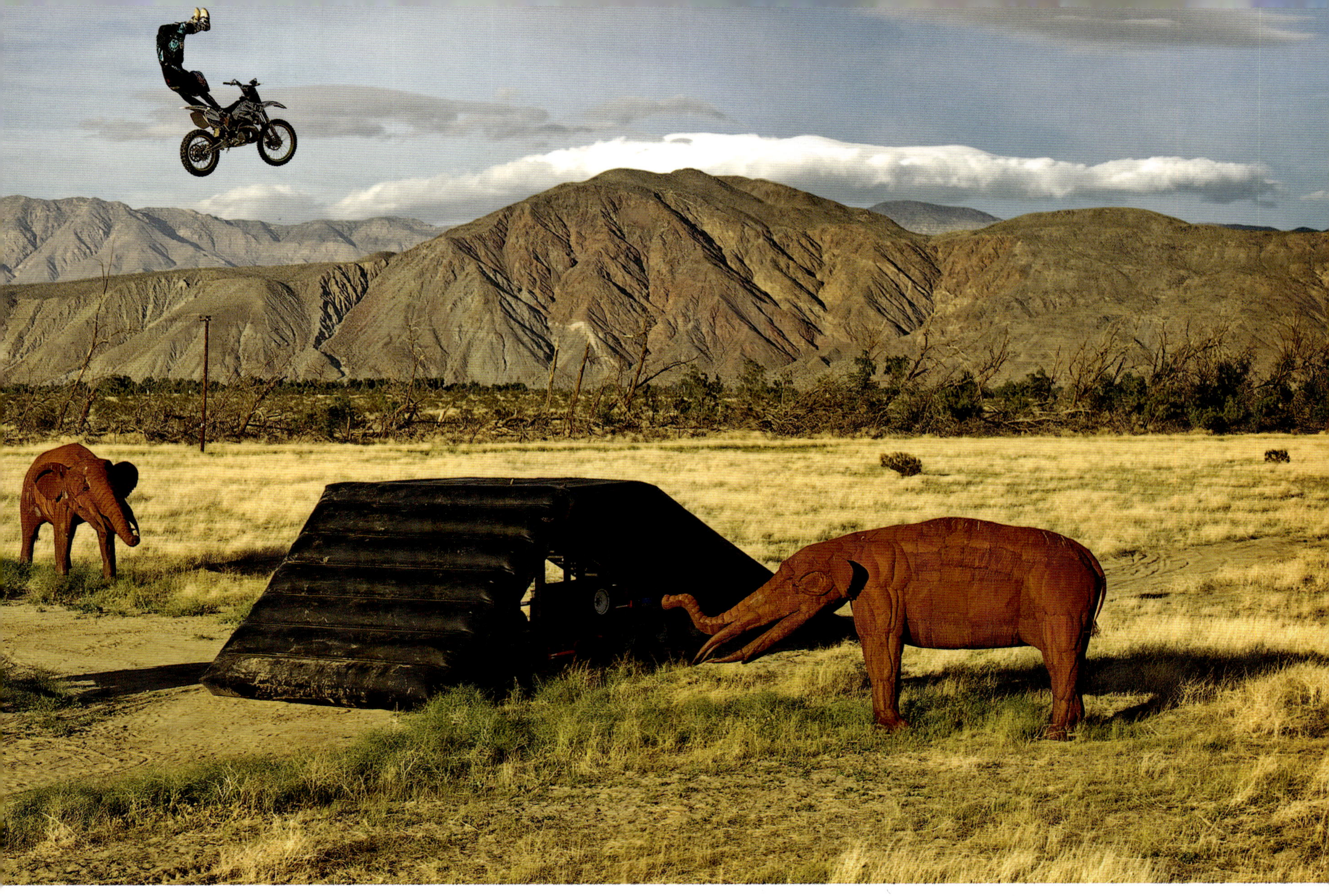

two organizations published a joint study titled *Geology and Lore of Northern Anza-Borrego Desert Region* that included fifteen scientific papers. One of those papers focused on the sculptures: "Galleta Meadows Sky Art, Inspired by Science, History, Nature, and Whim: A Catalog and Guide to Sky Art Assemblages in Borrego Springs, California." The detailed report includes maps, spreadsheets, charts, illustrations, and photographs of the sculptures.

The attraction extends to residents of Borrego Valley, who are drawn to the sculptures for a weekly afternoon "happy hour" that rotates from one sculpture assemblage to another. It is an open affair with folks bringing chairs, food, drinks, and news to share for a couple of hours. Some residents have purchased and display their own Breceda sculptures in their yards. A lone mule gazes at the mountain ridge while standing in a cactus garden. A giant tortoise

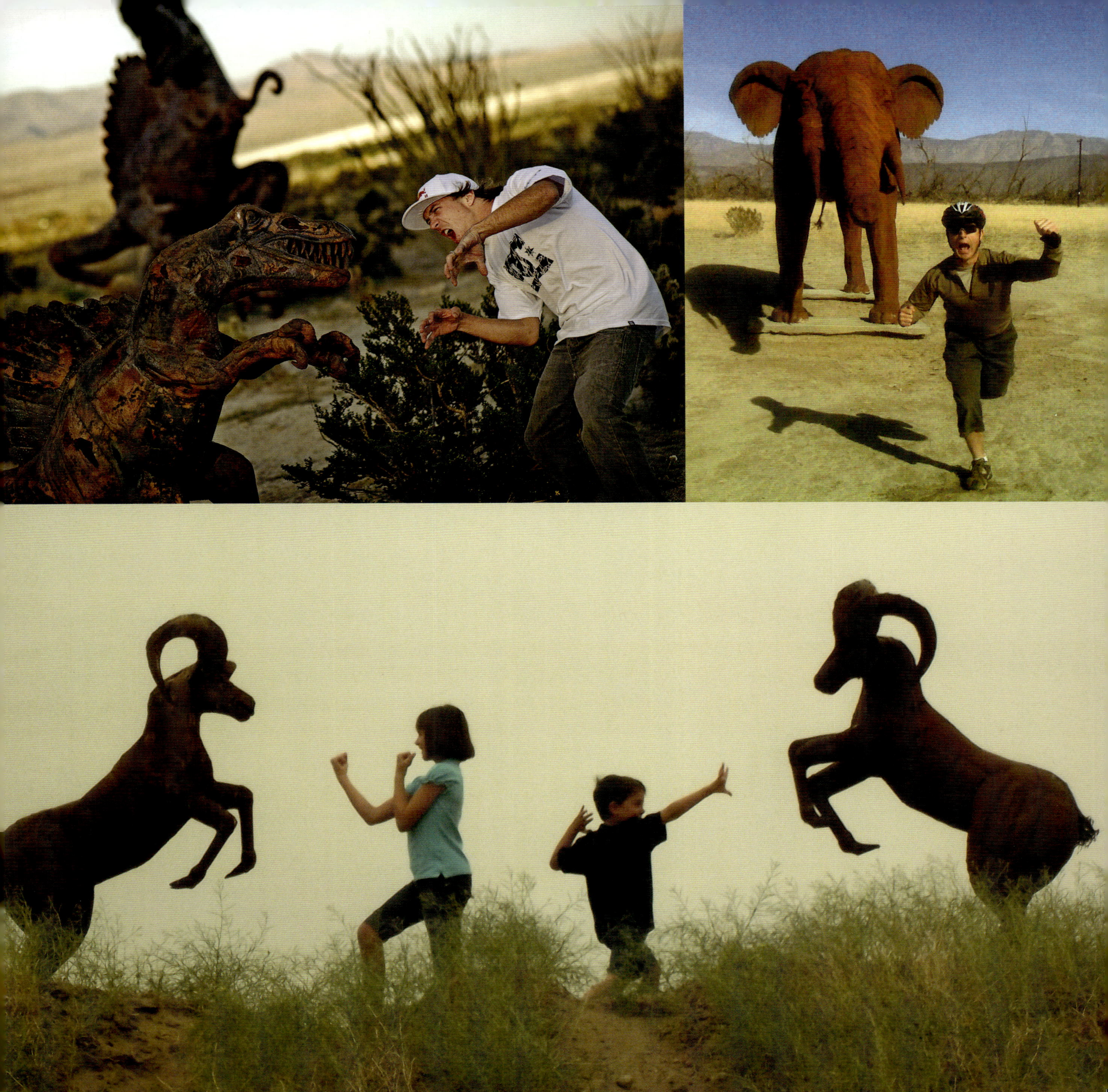

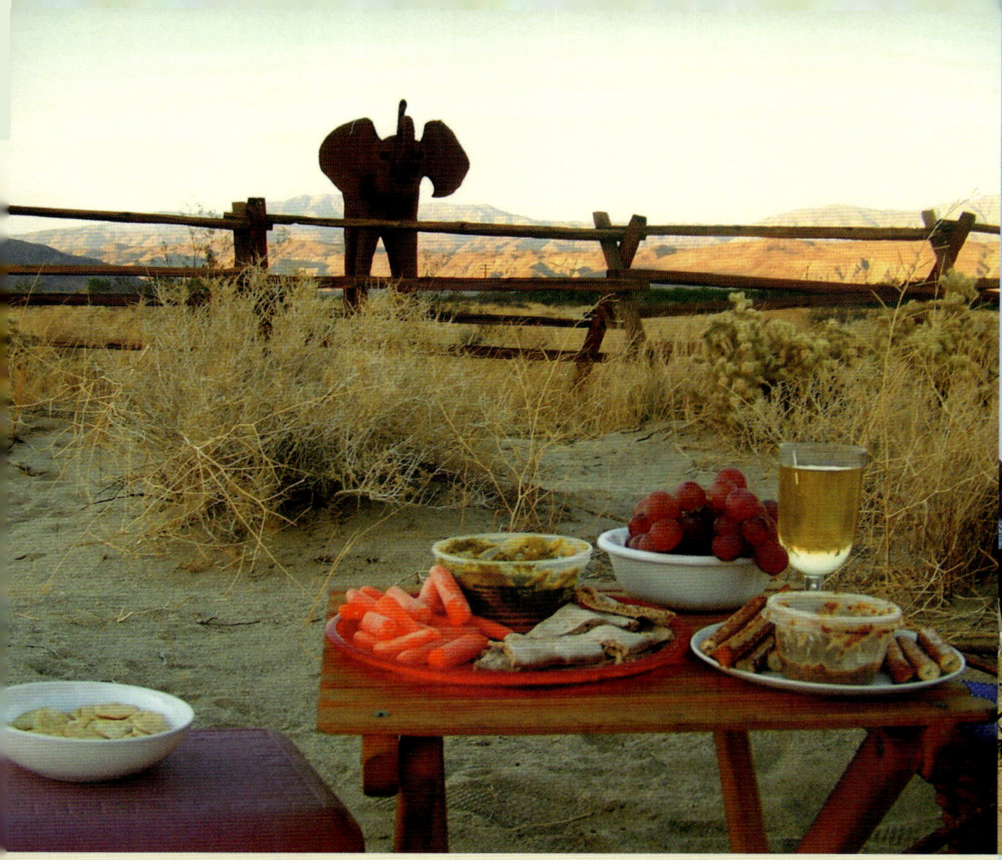

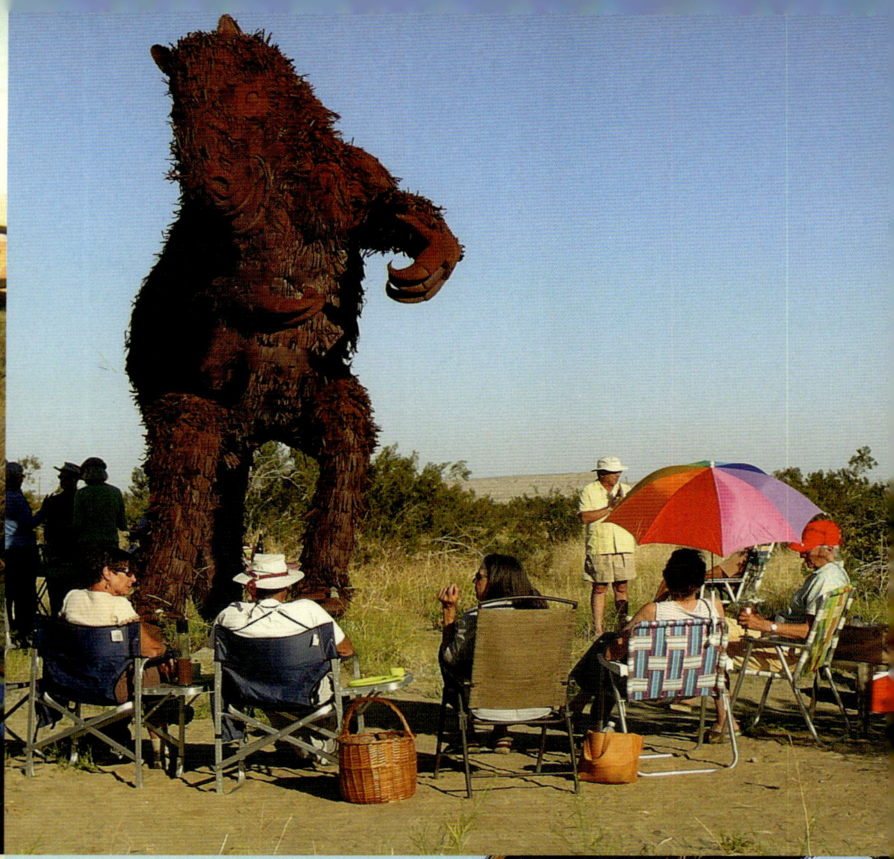

HAVING FUN

Most often Sky Art is the catalyst for play and fun. *Clockwise from bottom left*: Time to duke it out with some bighorns; stunt rider Robbie Maddison meets his match; a visitor flees from a charging gomphothere; sundown happy hour is "so" Borrego; weekly happy hour gatherings rotate through the sculptures; Ricardo enjoys comments about his sculptures at one of the get-together soirees.

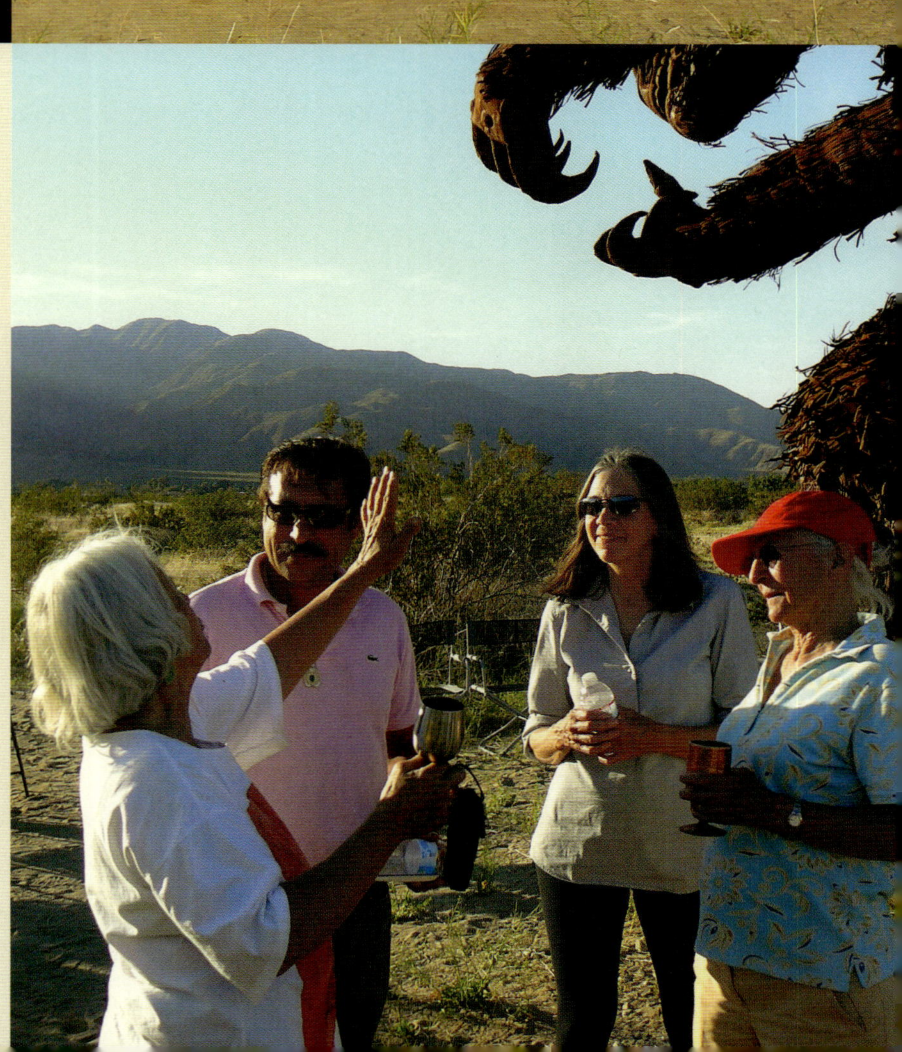

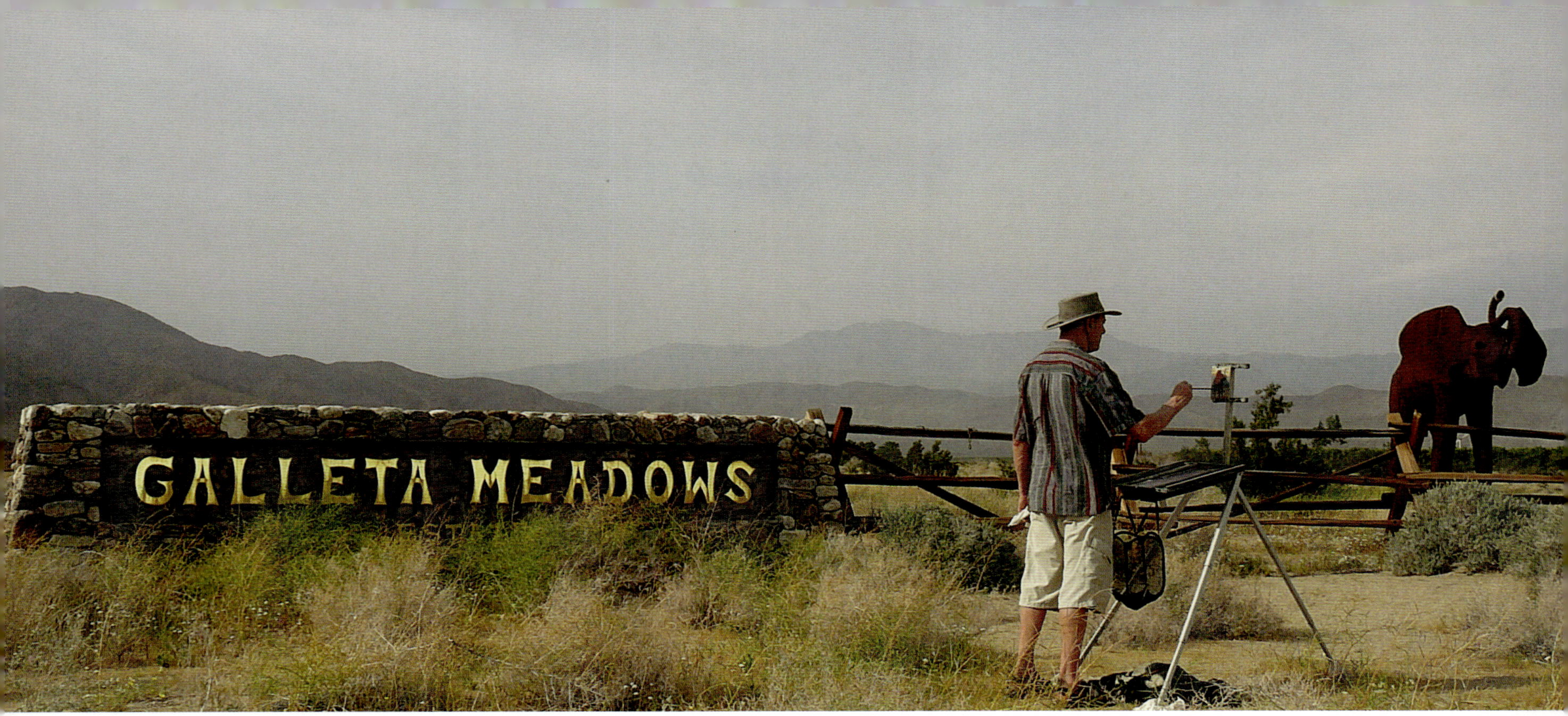

The Borrego Art Institute hosts a juried annual Borrego Springs Plein Air Invitational each spring. In 2011 artists spent one day using the Sky Art sculptures as a subject. John Eagle (*above*) chose an elephant (*below*) for his subject.

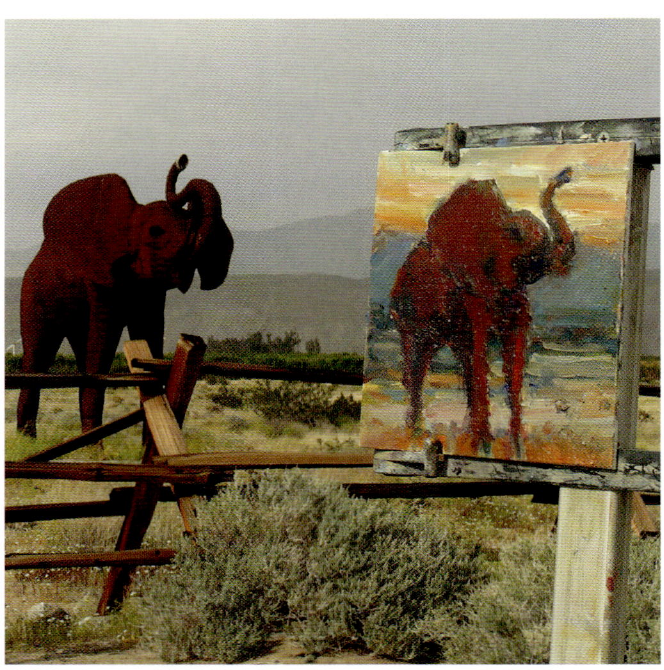

eyes the pool. Some *Velociraptors* guard a front gate. A pair of bighorn sheep strike a majestic pose in the corner of a yard while another one observes golfers on a nearby course. A giant dragonfly views passersby on the street.

Artists have also used the sculptures as inspiration for their drawings. The Fifth Annual Borrego Springs Plein Air Invitational in March 2011, hosted by the Borrego Art Institute, scheduled one of the six days of the festival to paint likenesses of the sculptures that were later displayed in the gallery in town. From hundreds of applicants, only fifteen artists were invited to participate.

"Plein air" is a French expression and, like "Sky Art," means "in the open air." It describes painting that is done outdoors. Inspired by Impressionists Claude Monet, Pierre-Auguste Renoir, Edouard Manet, and others, artists use various media such as paper, canvas, Yupo, oils, acrylics, watercolors, pastels, colored pencils, and even crayons to catch

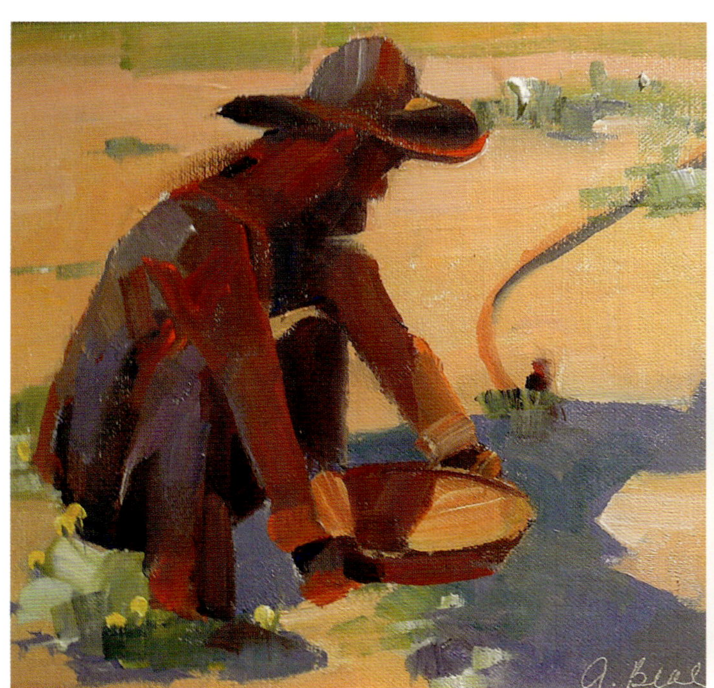

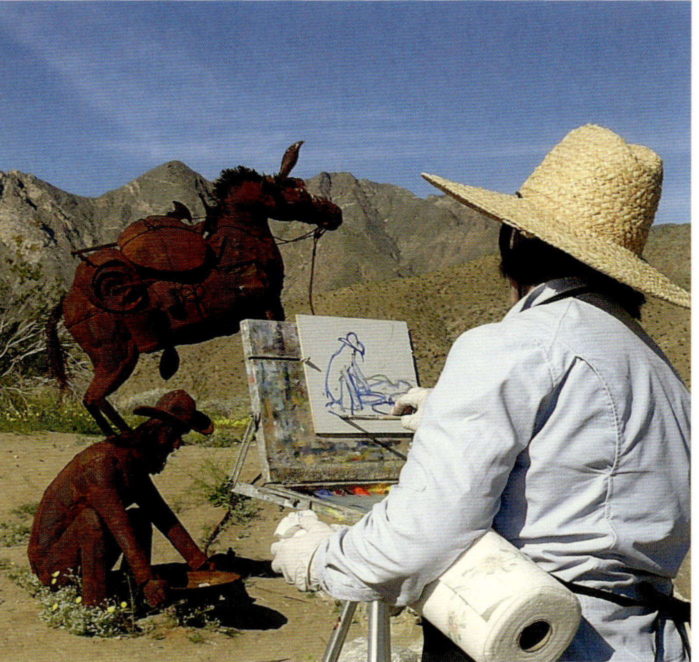

"Plein air" is a French expression and, like Sky Art, means "in the open air." It describes painting that is done outdoors. Joli Beal (*above*) selected the miner as her subject.

the always changing conditions and light on their subject. They paint quickly and without hesitation to capture the moment. Those portraying the sculptures for the 2011 invitational finished their renderings well before noon. Subjects selected included the miner, a tapir, elephants, camels, and a dinosaur.

Photographers are also inspired to use the animated sculptures as subjects with varying lighting and weather conditions, including dramatic sunrises and sunsets, early-morning and late-afternoon shadows, and rainclouds and rainbows. The sculptures are used as subjects for photography classes as well as in human interest shots.

One of the most interesting photo shoots occurred on March 6, 2011, when Robbie "Maddo" Maddison, the world's most famous stunt biker, did a "scorpion" sailing thirty feet into the air over the Plio-Pleistocene gomphotheres. Once he soared off the launching pad, Maddo threw his body out into an arch above his handlebars so that he was completely upside down as he sailed over the gomphotheres, then he swung his body back to riding position just before he hit the ground. Maddo holds the world record both for the highest jump and the longest jump on a motorbike. The photo shoot, sponsored by the energy drink company Red Bull, posted the photos from the jump over the gomphotheres on their website.

Interest in Ricardo's sculptures also extends south into Mexico and especially the Rosarito Beach area of Baja California. There has been a collateral benefit to those artisans as Ricardo has perfected his skills and ability to add incredible details to his sculptures. Adding those details and taking extra time to give a more realistic form to his artwork means that he must charge more for his labor to cover the costs involved.

Ricardo will not bargain when it comes to the cost of his art. When a customer cannot meet Ricardo's price, he

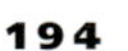

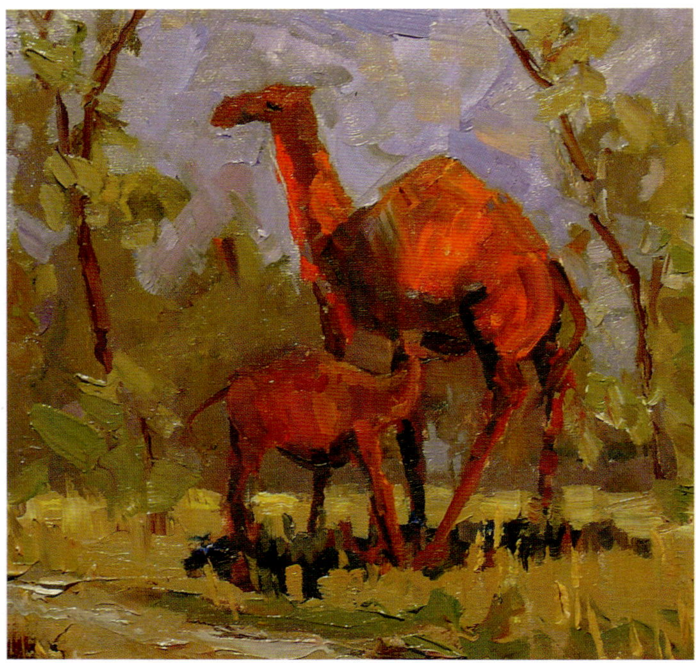

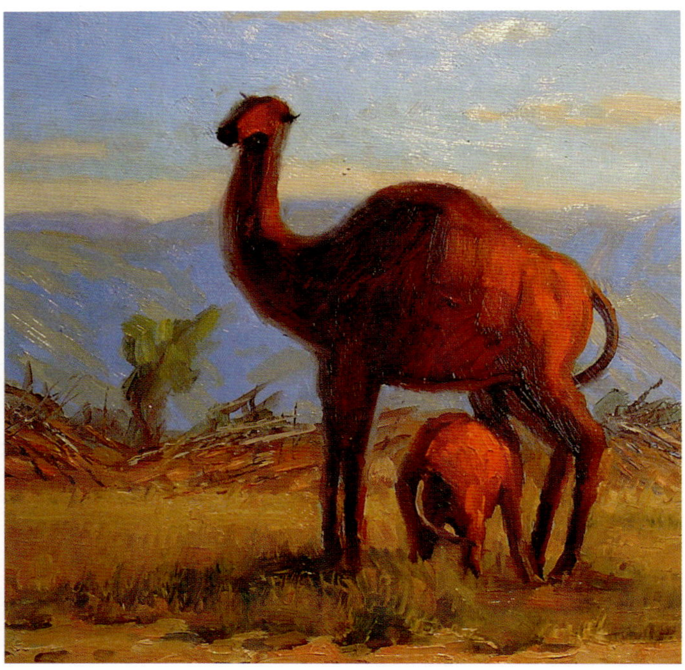

Plein air artists use various media such as paper, canvas, and Yupo, painting with oils, acrylics, watercolors, pastels, colored pencils, and even crayons to capture the ever-changing light on their subject. Artist Toni Williams (*below*) used the *Camelops* for her subject (*above, left*). Artist Steve Wang used the same subject (*above, right*).

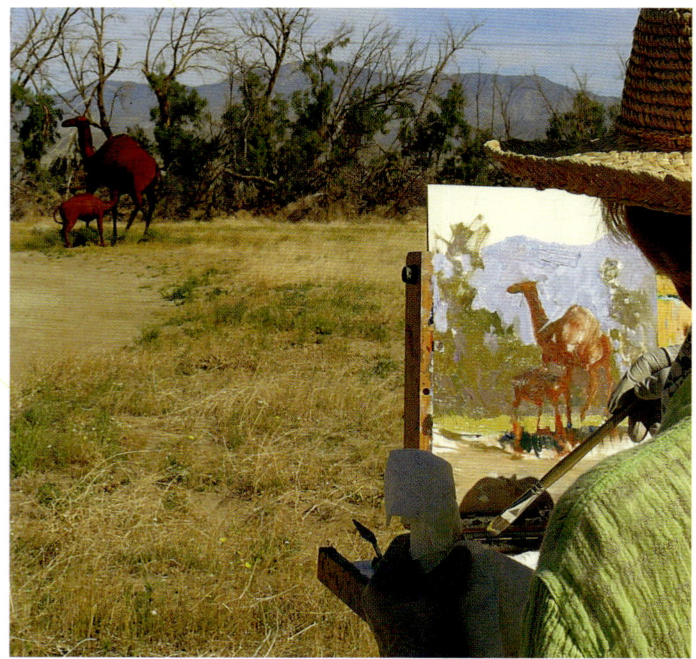

generously refers them to other rustic art welders on both sides of the border. He knows that when he does that he is helping individuals whose very livelihood, from day to day, depends on selling their sculptures. It wasn't that long ago when Porfirio, now the backbone of Ricardo's business, was doing just that.

When Ricardo began creating metal sculptures, he was not really aware of who else was making them. It wasn't until Porfirio began working for him that Ricardo became conscious of the artisans in Baja California. Ricardo still keeps in close contact with many of these artisans and shop owners, and now some of them come to visit him. As a result of this exchange of information, Ricardo says the quality of Mexican sculptures has improved and his own techniques have evolved as well.

The art of making rustic metal sculptures or *arte rústico* probably originated in Tlaquepaque, Jalisco, a municipality

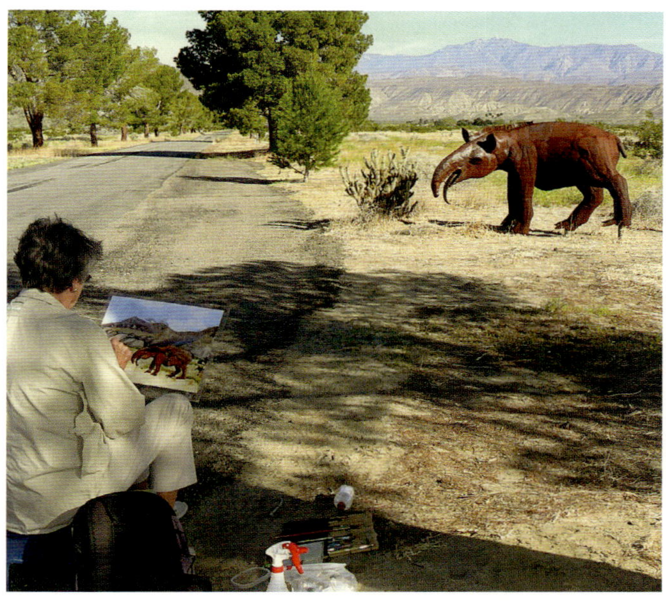

that is now part of Guadalajara. Although it has been around for many years, this folk art did not exist in Ricardo's native Durango. Without knowing about this tradition he has taken the craft of metalwork and elevated it into an art form.

Ricardo's sculptures are environmentally friendly in that they are made from scrap metals or slightly damaged 26-gauge sheet metal if he can find it. He is able to use rebar, pipes, tubes, rods, wire, and metal plates in creating the heavy frame. He will use whatever he can put his hands on for the frame, as no one ever sees inside of the sculpture. He has even used a truck axle for reinforcement and bracing. Wire is used around the reinforced center to form the basic framework.

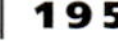

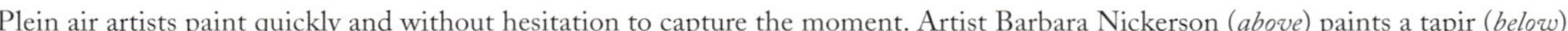

Plein air artists paint quickly and without hesitation to capture the moment. Artist Barbara Nickerson (*above*) paints a tapir (*below*).

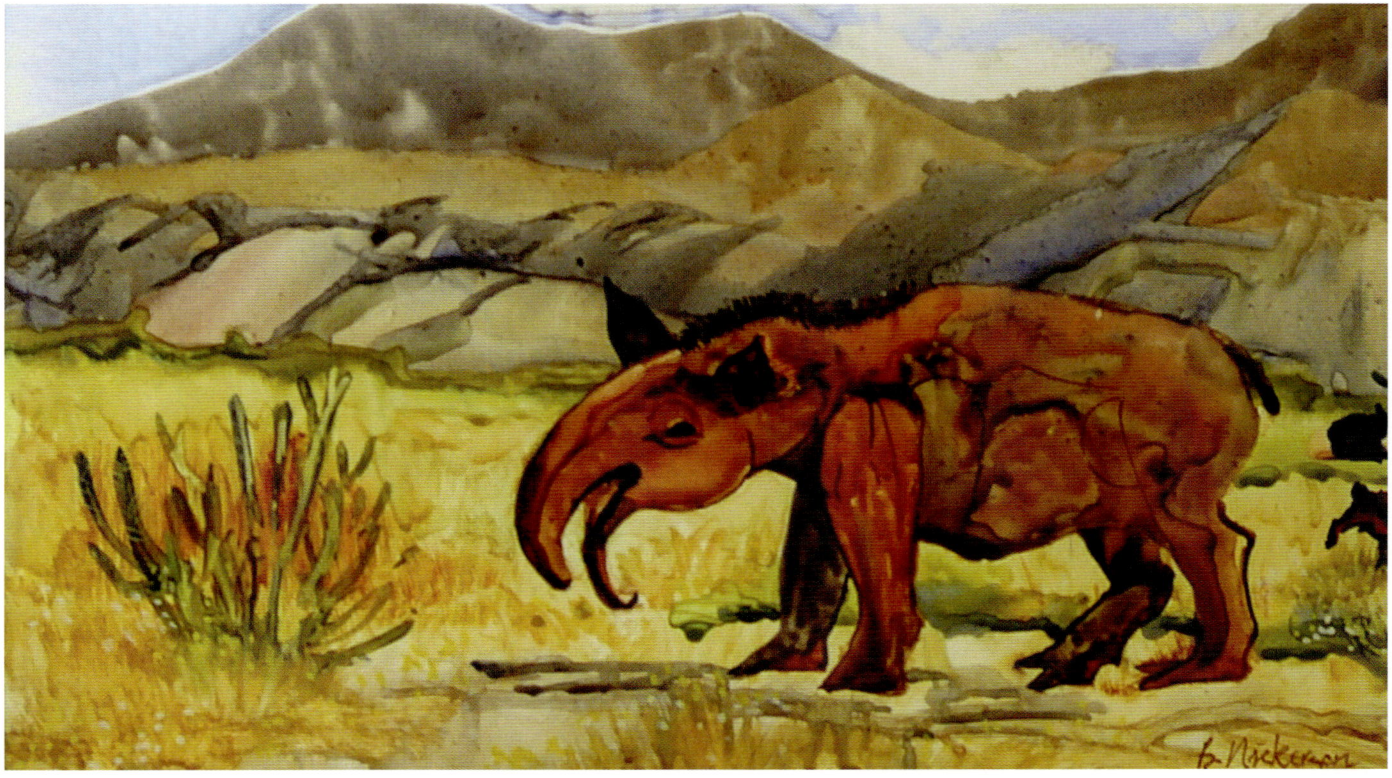

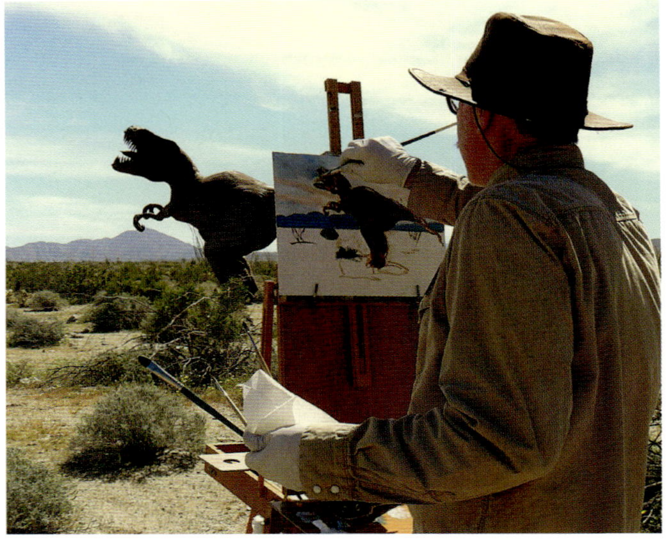

Ricardo tries to buy the metals from recycle centers or scrap metal dealers to save money. Steel works perfectly for the sculptures because the major component of this metal alloy is iron, which corrodes, creating the rich rusty hues that make the sculptures particularly attractive in a primitive way. As the sculptures rust, they take on a more lifelike look, especially from a distance when it appears that the animals have a thick dark hide.

The welding machine is his main tool besides various hammers, wires, pliers, and metal cutters. Welding joins metals by melting the parts using the concentrated heat of an electric arc and using filler, usually provided by a consumable electrode, to form a joint. Two types of welding processes are used in creating the structures.

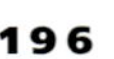

Artist Mark Slusser (*above*) chose the *Tyrannosaurus rex* (*below*) for his subject.

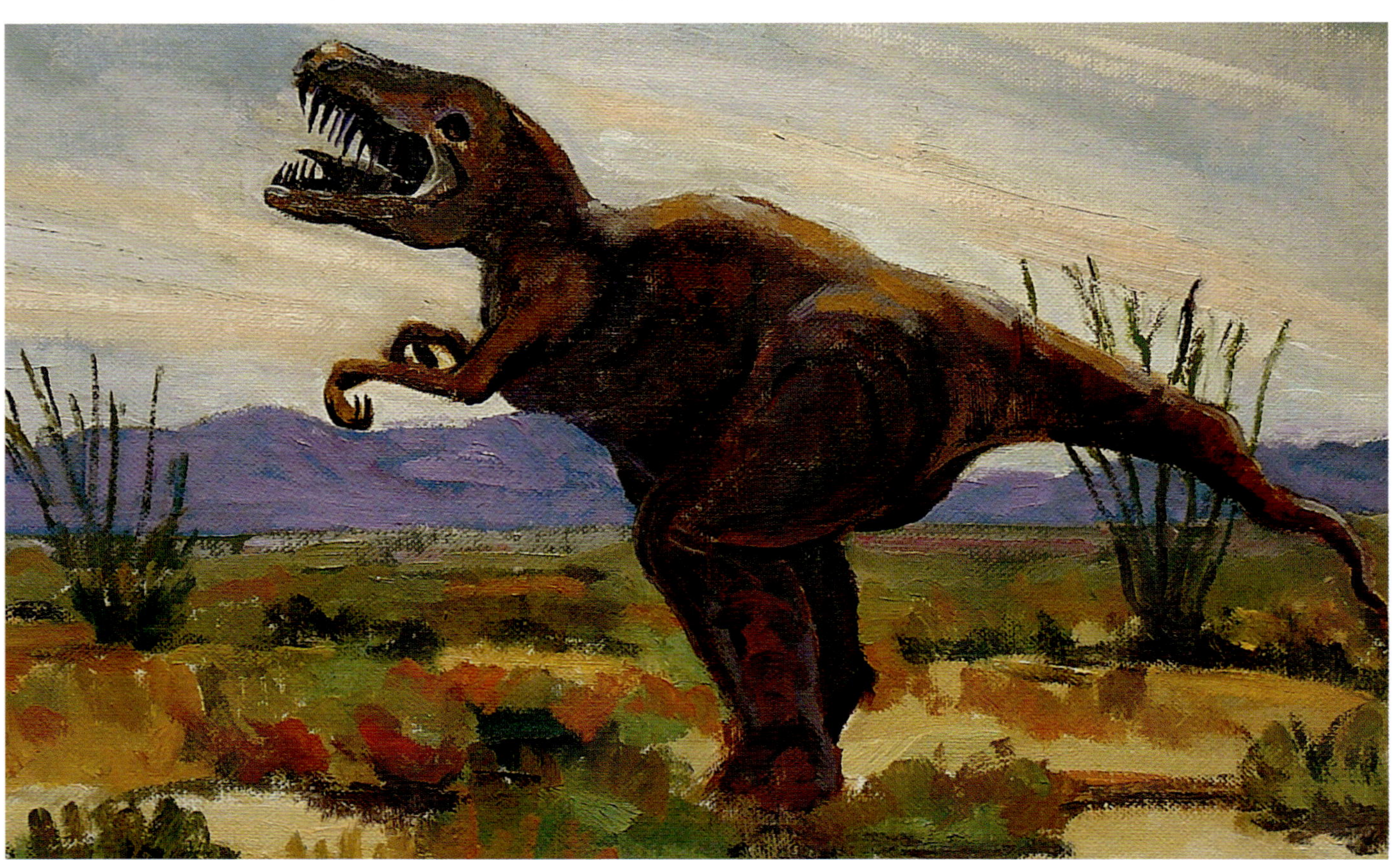

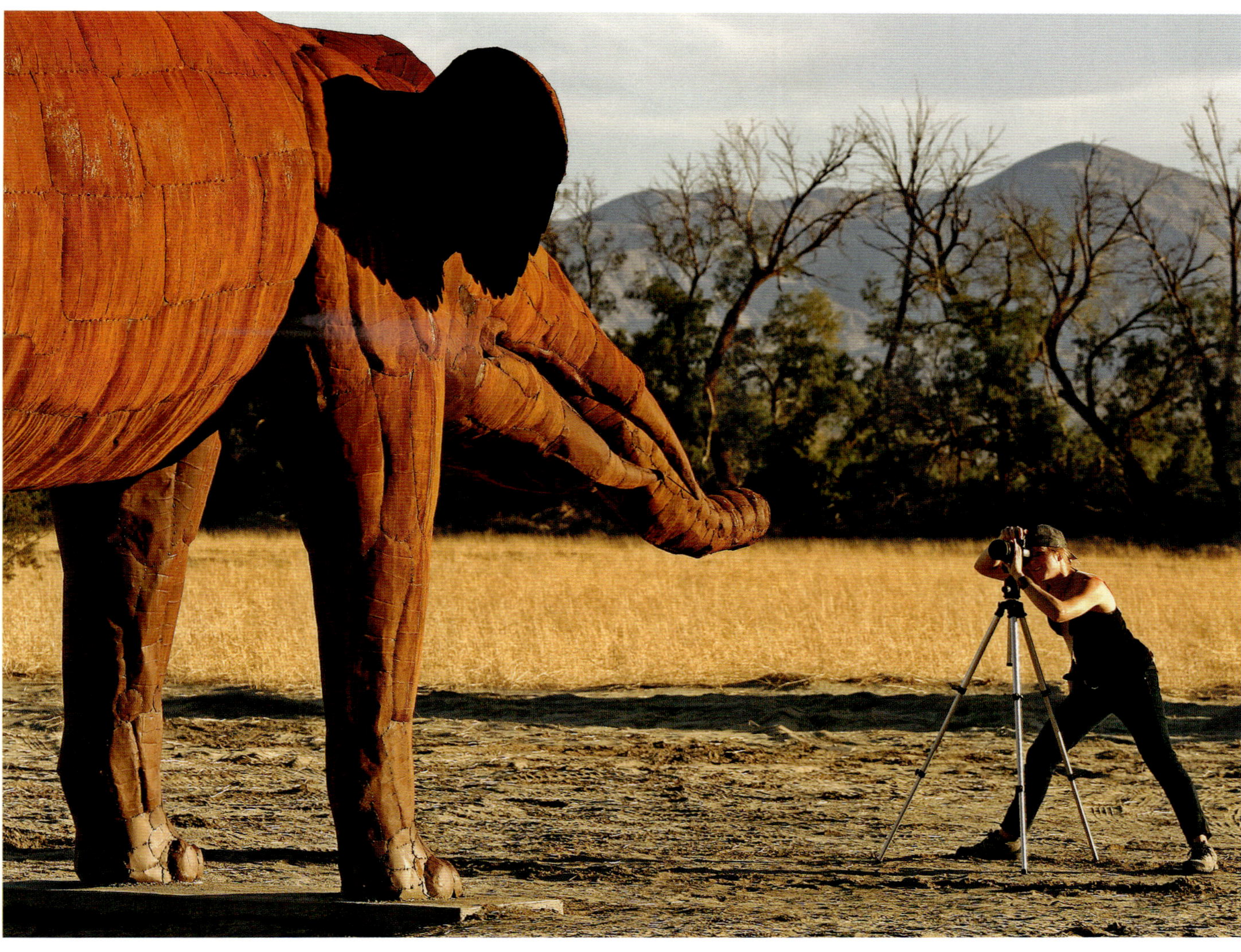

Amateur and professional photographers are drawn to Sky Art at all times of the day and night, hoping for the perfect picture.

Shielded metal arc welding or stick welding is used on the heavy frame. In this type of welding an electric current is used to strike an arc between the base material and a consumable electrode rod or stick. The covered electrode rod is made from a material that is compatible with the base material that is being welded. The heat generated from the arc melts a portion of the electrode tip, its coating, and the base metal in the immediate area. The weld forms out of the alloy of these materials as they solidify in the weld area. Welding time is slower and the consumable electrodes must be replaced frequently, but the weld is hotter and stronger and necessary for the frame.

Gas metal arc welding, more commonly called MIG (metal inert gas) welding, is used to attach the sheet metal to the frame and to add the many details. This type of welding uses a gas during the weld, typically carbon dioxide when

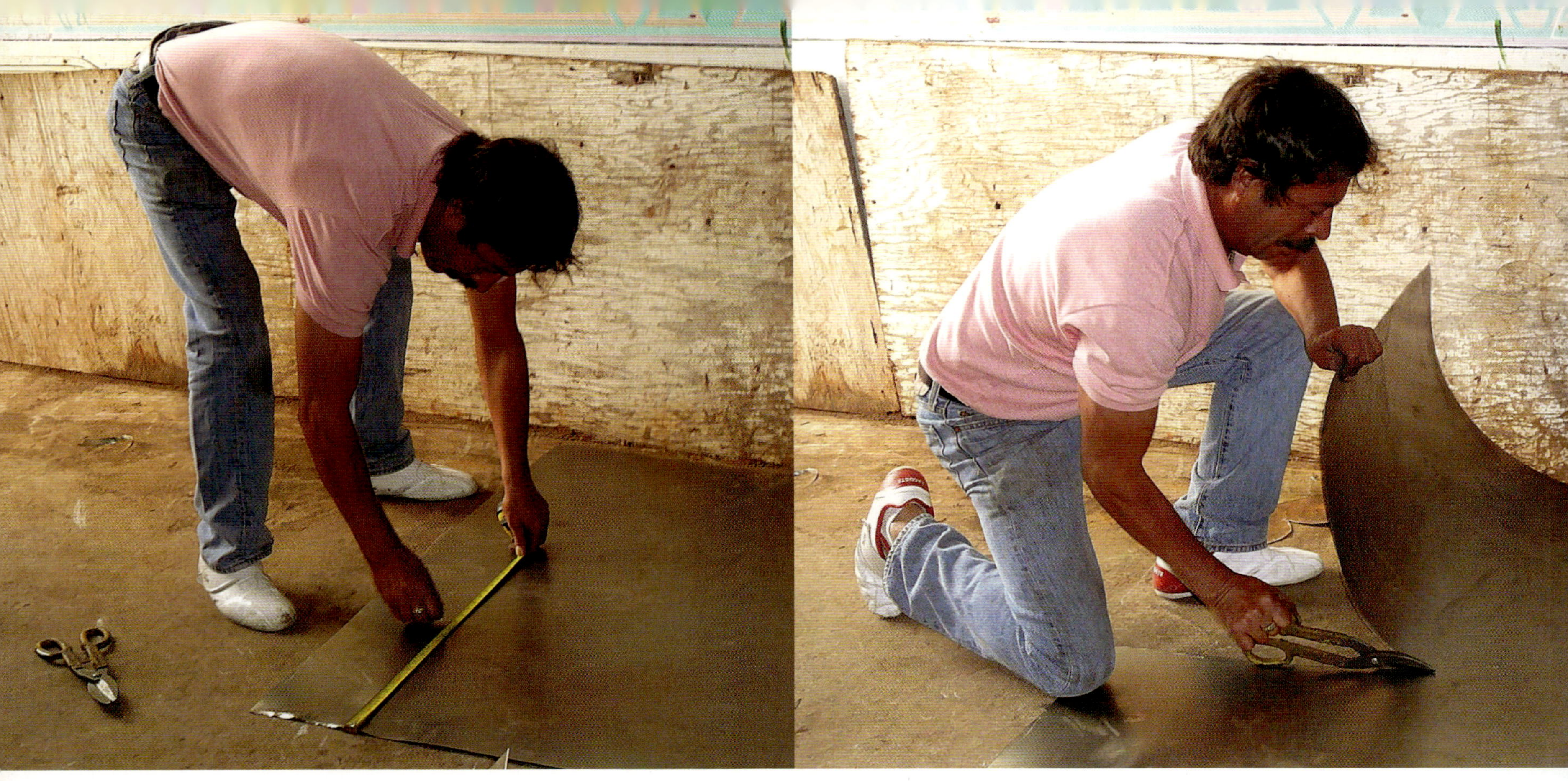

Measuring and Cutting. Once the vision of the sculpture is formed in Ricardo's mind, (*clockwise left to right*) 26-gauge sheet metal is measured and cut. Ricardo will give one of his crew a pattern to trace, and they may literally cut hundreds or thousands of the same form for a sculpture. Cut pieces are then trimmed as needed for placement.

welding steel. Wire is continuously fed from a spool, making it a semi-automatic welding process. The wire acts both as the electrode and filler metal and is fed through the gun. The shielding gas flows around the weld to prevent weld contamination. Multiple weld layers can be made at the joint. Temperatures involved are relatively low and are suitable for thin metal sheets. The residue or weld slag is a key element left on the sculptures or purposely added to create details, such as hair on the head of the baby mammoth.

Welding can be dangerous. Heavy gloves are used to protect the welder from the extreme heat, while a welding helmet is necessary to prevent eye damage from the ultraviolet light of the arc. Obviously, the sharp metal pieces have to be handled very carefully.

The most tedious part of construction is cutting the individual pieces of metal needed to create the body and details. Ricardo uses sheet metal in four-by-eight-foot sections. A pattern is drawn on the sheet and then cut out. Literally hundreds to a thousand or more pieces may be required for an individual sculpture, and each one of those must be hammered into shape before it can be welded onto the frame. Ricardo will make a sample of what he wants and give this to his crew to duplicate hundreds of times.

The hammering creates the texture. Hammering various size gauges of wire or rebar placed over the metal creates lines of large or small veins and arteries. Various hammers or mallets are used to form muscles or to stamp a design into the metal, such as in the dinosaur hides. Some of the metal

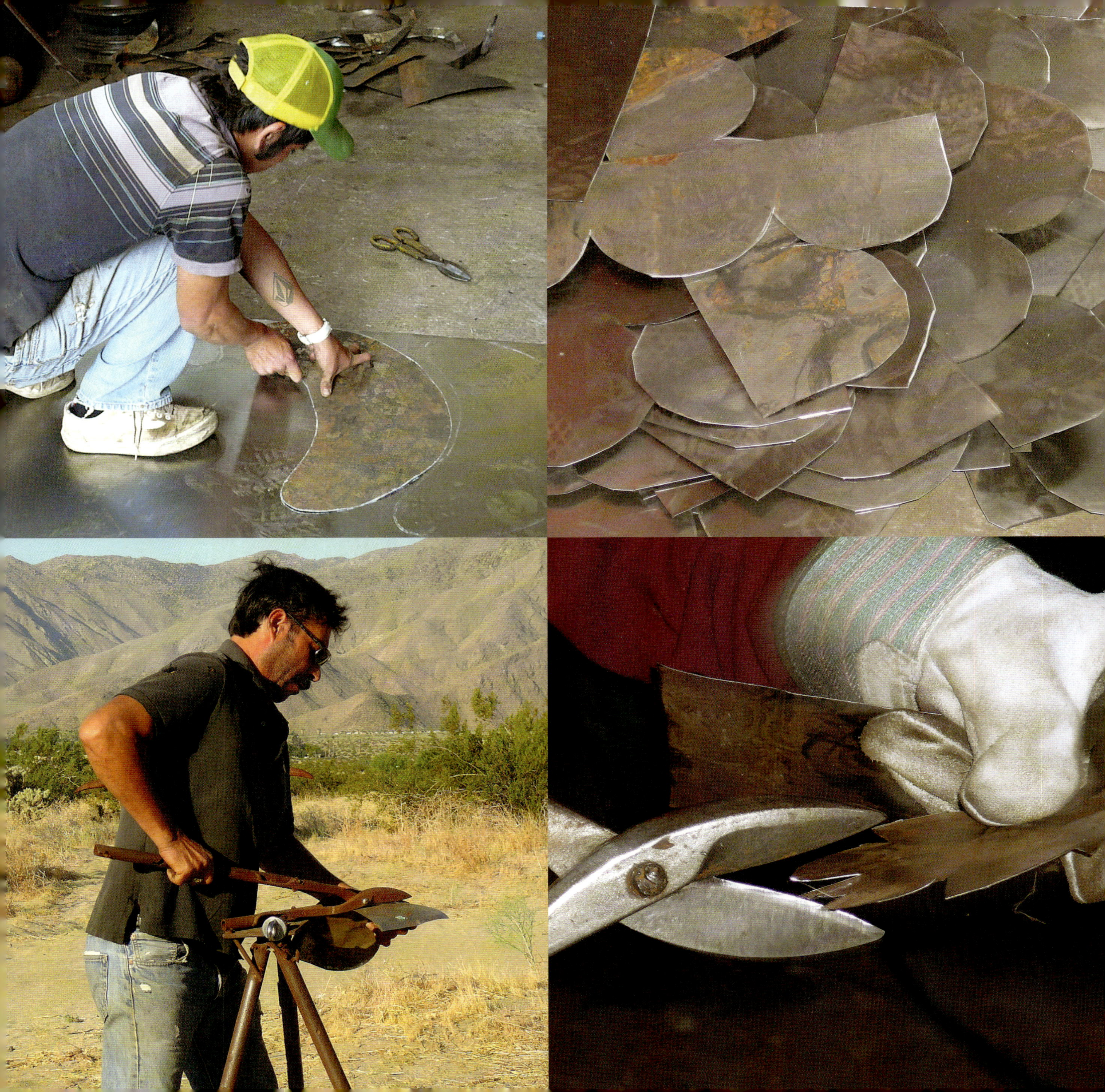

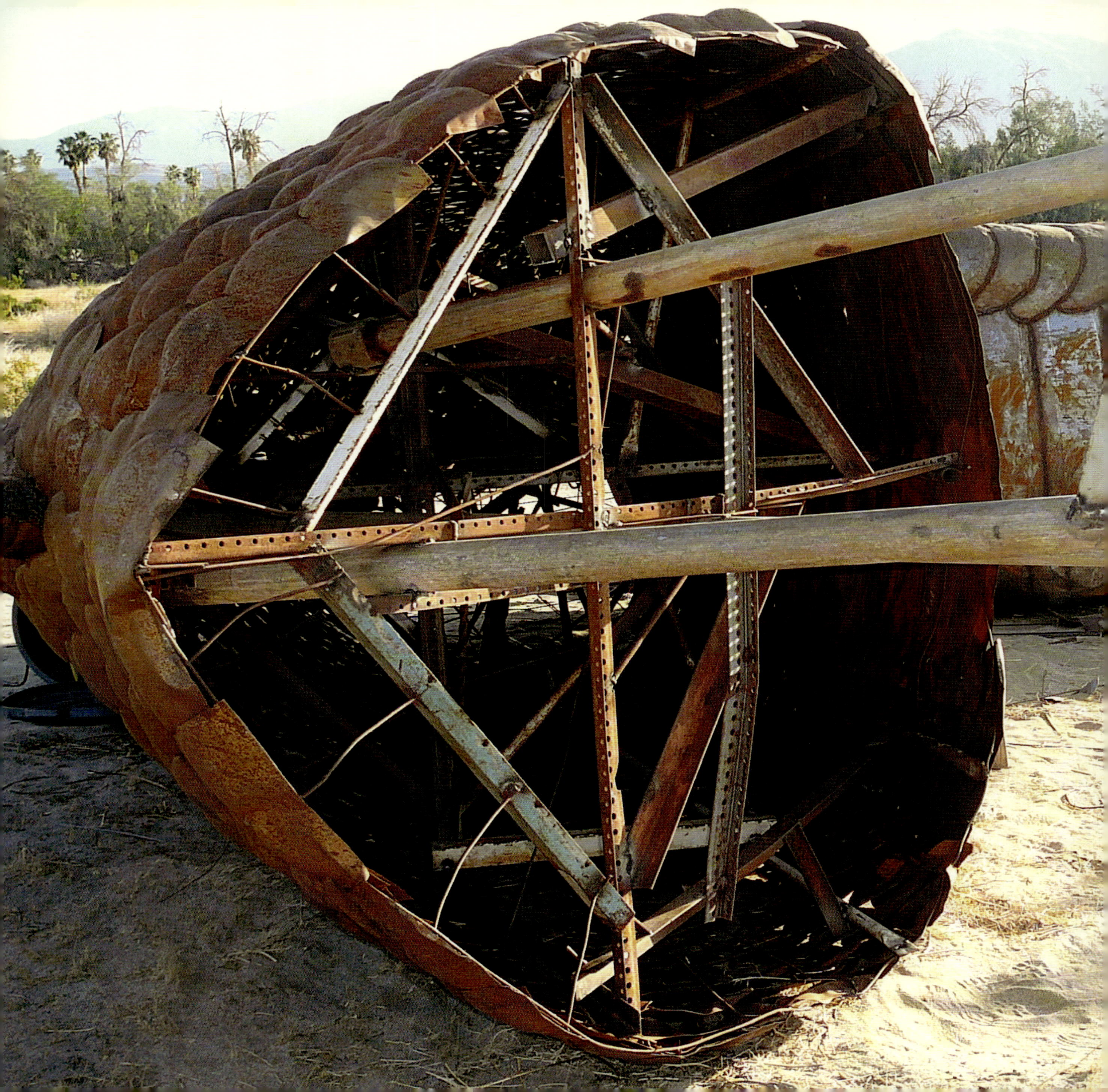

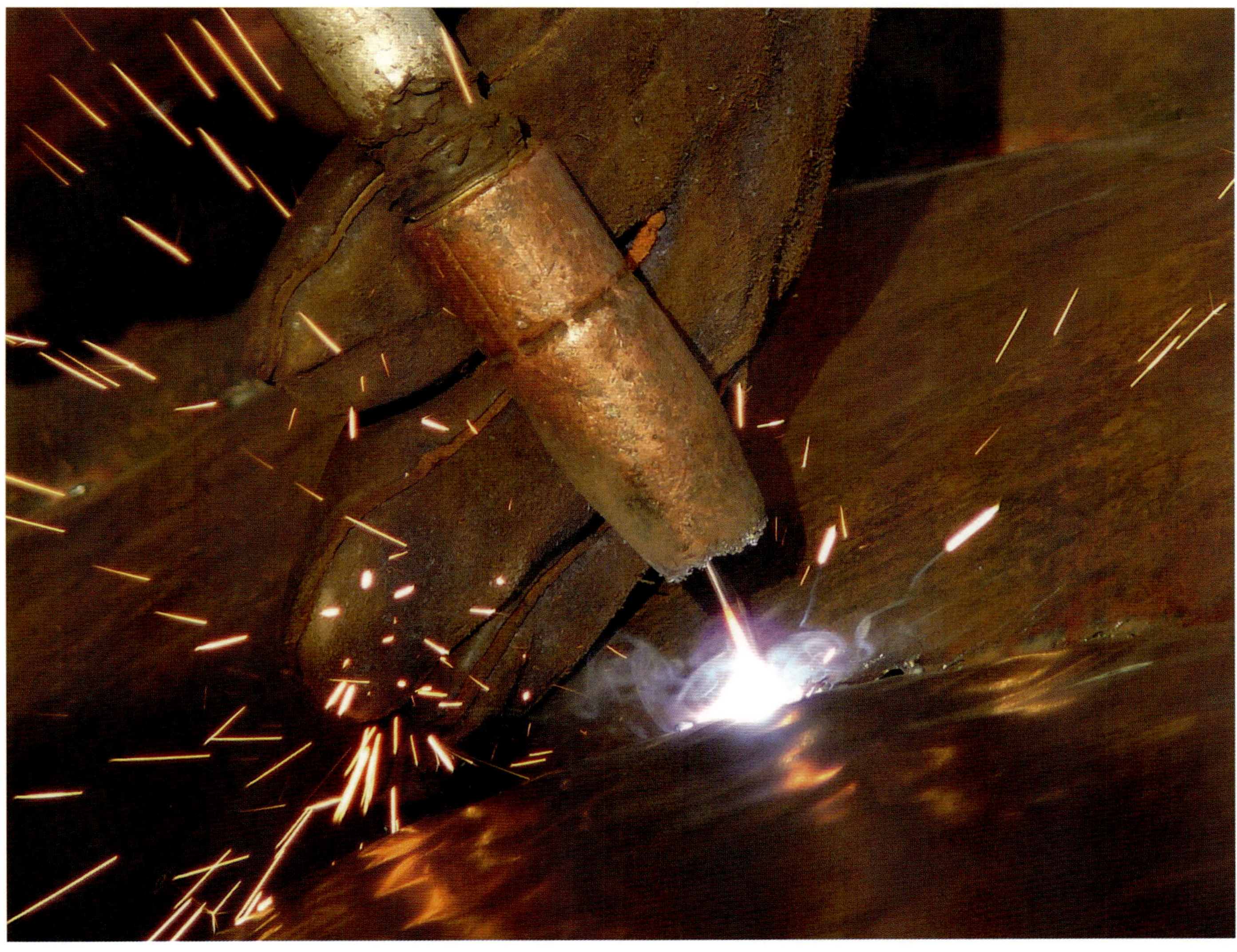

Welding. *Left:* First a frame is constructed for the sculpture, welding together whatever scrap metal is available, to give the interior the support and strength it needs. *Above:* The body will be welded around this frame, section by section.

pieces also need to be ground down to create a lifelike texture. "Since each piece is individually made, no two sculptures are ever exactly alike. Each has its own personality," according to Ricardo.

The larger structures take longer to make and weigh more because of the reinforcements they require in the frame. Large structures such as a mammoth can weigh well over 1,400 to 1,800 pounds and can take several weeks to make. By contrast, one or possibly two regular horses, which weigh about a hundred pounds, can be made in a week.

Ricardo learns by a combination of observation, experience, paying attention to customers' comments, and drawing on some innate ability that enables him to see the internal frame of each sculpture and every piece needed to support it.

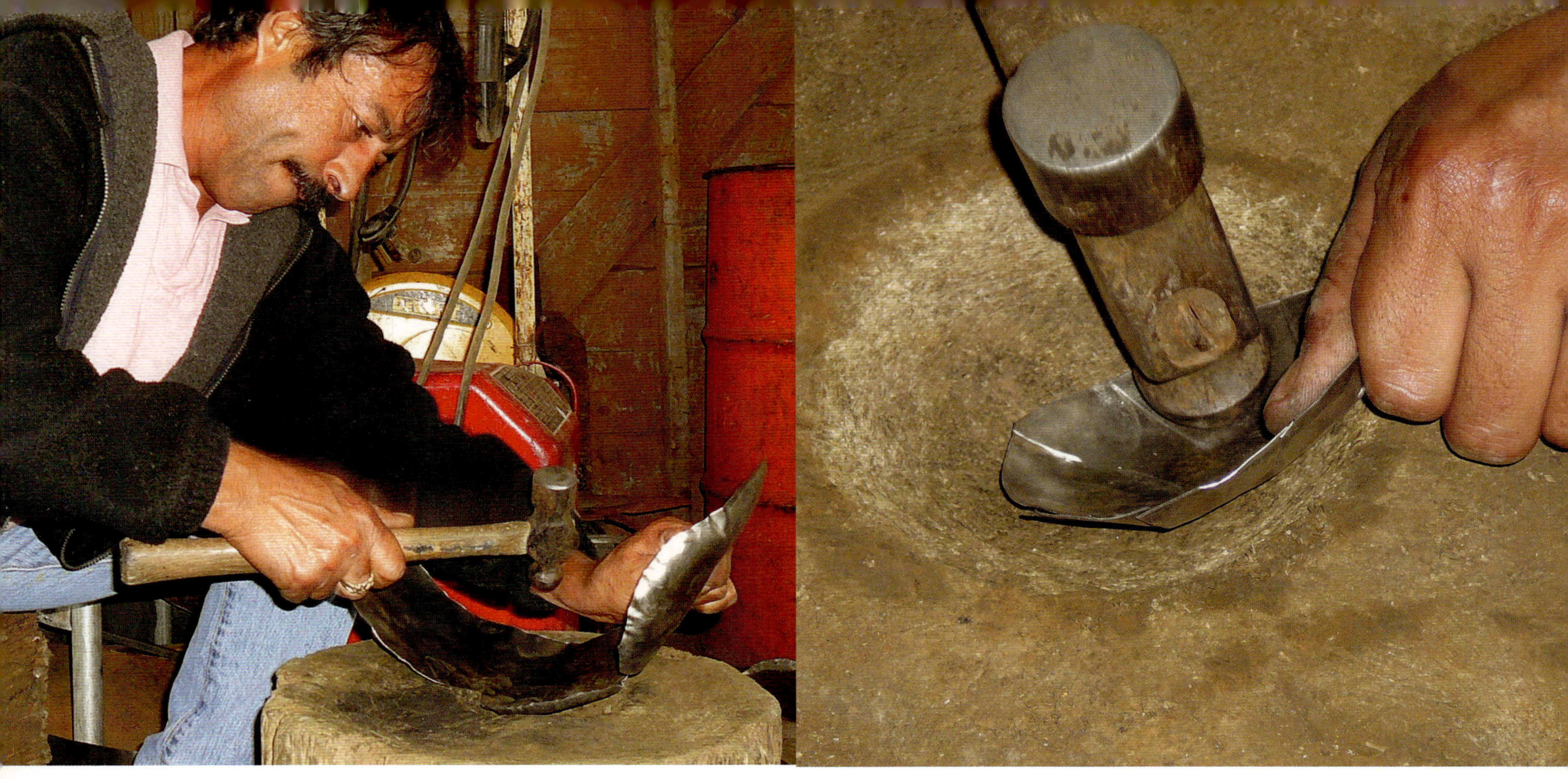

Hammering Shape and Texture. Besides cutting, the most tedious part of creating the sculptures is hammering the pieces into shape while adding texture to the cut pieces (*above, left to right*). Special textures require specialized hammers (*far right*) or wires to create patterns (*next page*).

Sometimes he makes mental corrections even before he explains to Porfirio what he has in mind.

The "map" for creating each piece is entirely in Ricardo's head. With no art training and little ability to draw, Ricardo has developed an uncanny skill for sensing proportions, animal locomotion, and anatomy. He actually sees the whole piece three-dimensionally and is able to turn the piece around, viewing it from the top, bottom, front, and back. As he has perfected this skill, he now also sees some of the details that he is able to add to each new piece. "The picture tells me the whole thing. It's only when I start working that I change details," he explains.

Porfirio admits it is not always easy to see what Ricardo has in his head, and there have been plenty of times that almost-completed pieces have been dismantled because they were not quite right. Ricardo strives for perfection above all else. Each new piece must be better than the last one. It's also important that his sculptures have a lifelike quality. It is this demand for quality that ultimately makes Porfirio happy to work with Ricardo.

For Ricardo each new sculpture is a challenge that takes his full attention and will not be considered complete until he is absolutely satisfied. He explains:

> I am kind of a perfectionist. I don't like to just let things go—not me. I don't care if it takes me three times, five times, ten times, or more, but it has to convince me that it is good. If it doesn't, then I have to start again. It has to be good, at least to my eyes. My people say that if it looks good to me, then it will look good for anybody.

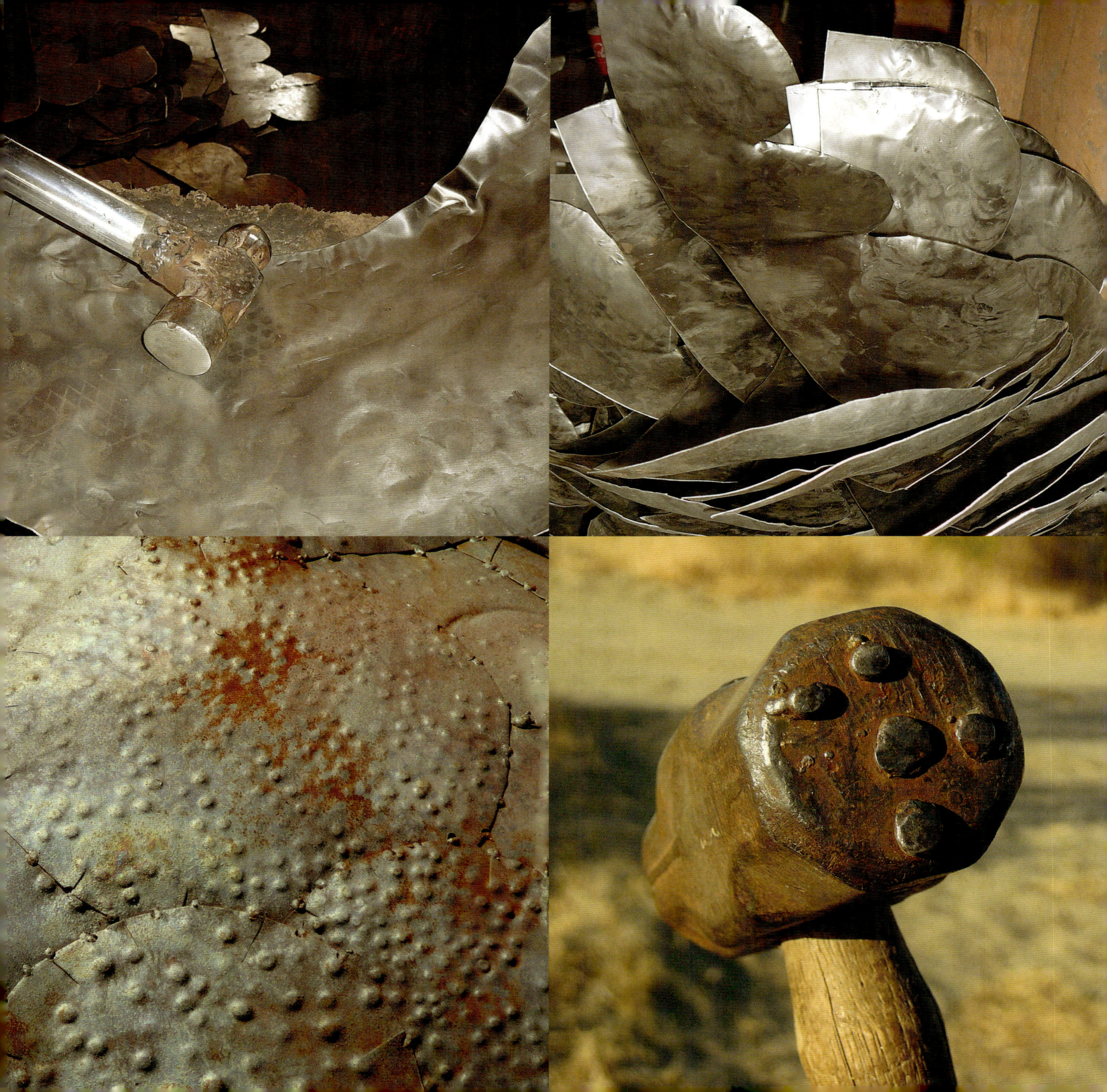

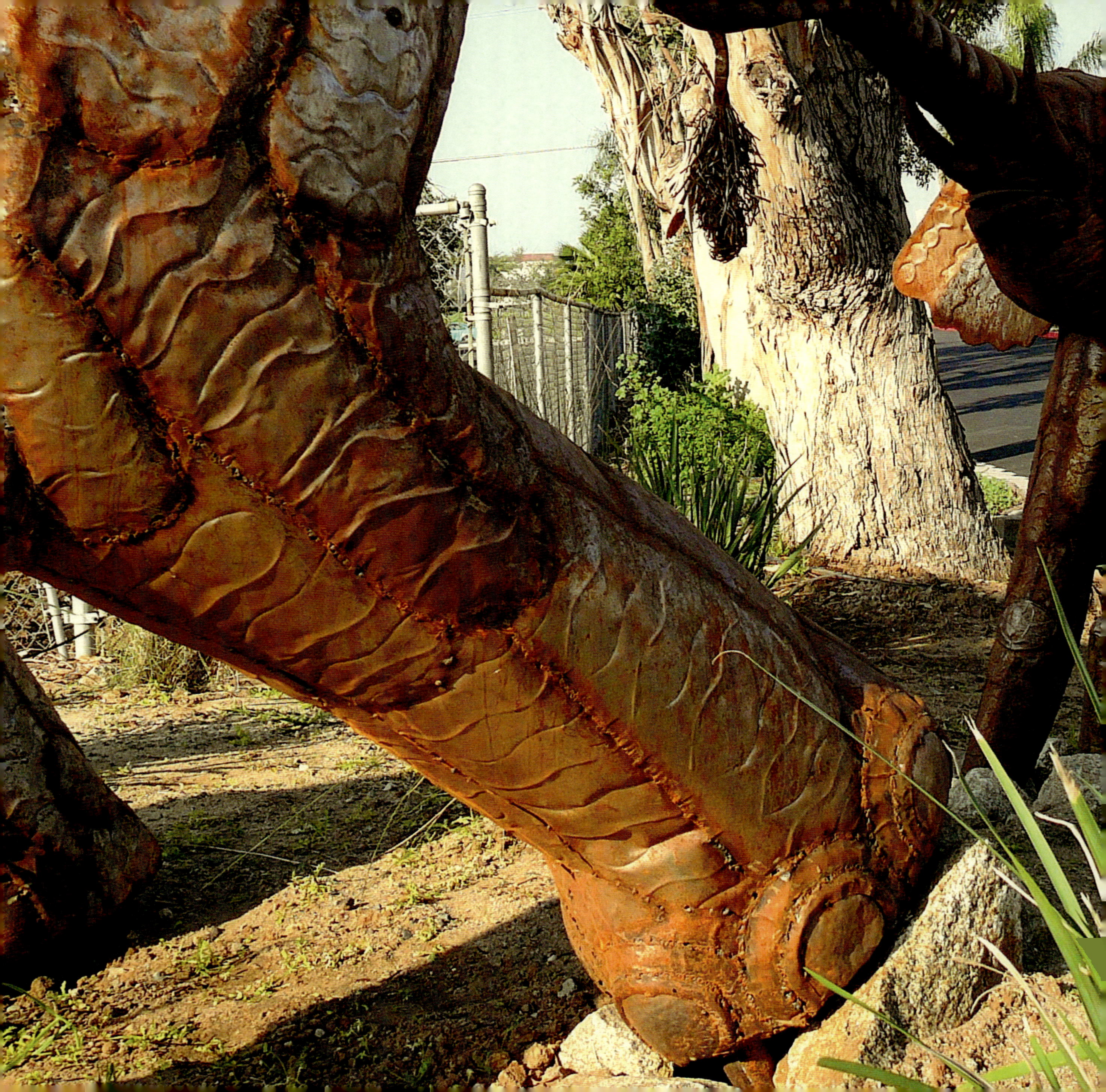

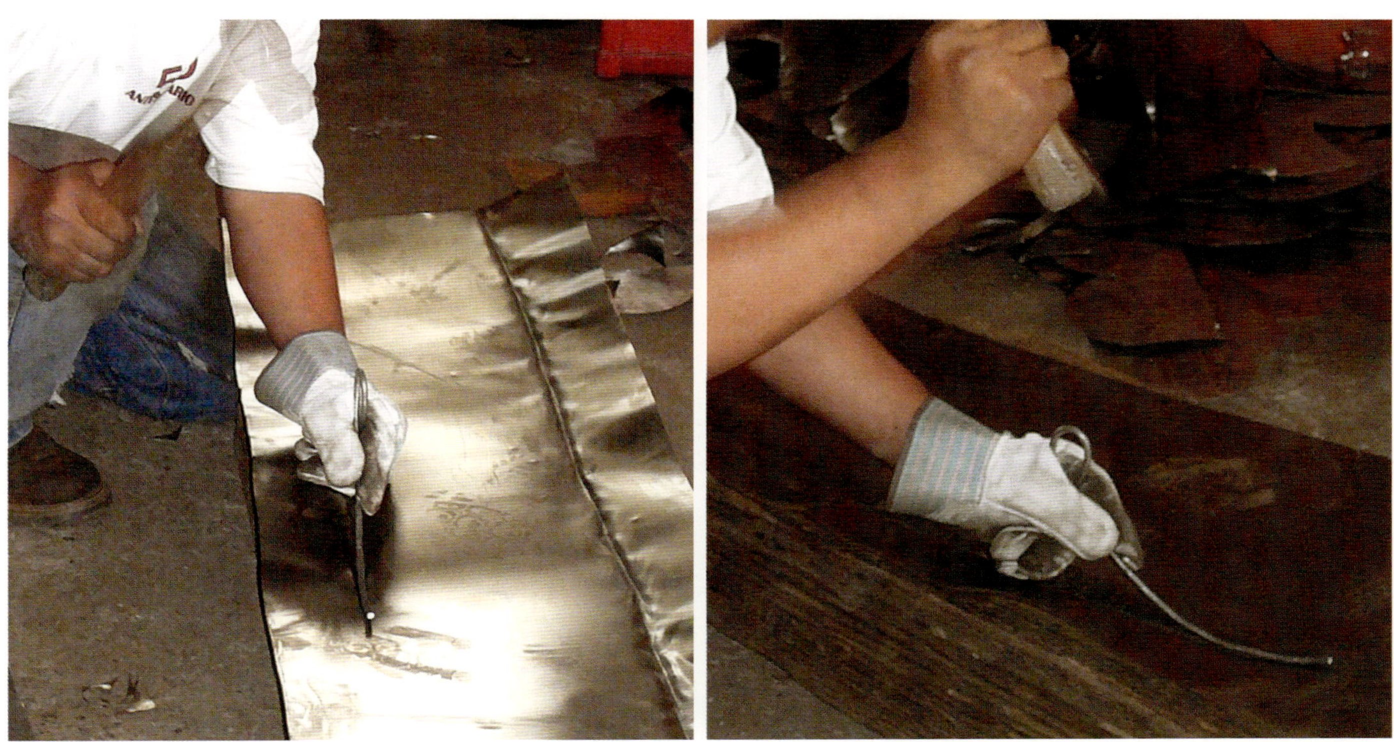

HAMMERING DETAIL. To create wrinkles and veins, a wire is hammered into the sheet metal (*above*) so that it leaves a permanent impression. The thickness of the wire will vary according to the imprint that is needed. The result is dramatic (*left*), as seen in the elephant's leg at AVID medical offices.

When the Willys Jeep was installed on November 1, 2010, it was announced that this was the last Sky Art for Galleta Meadows. And it was . . . at that point in time.

Then just two months later, Dennis attended festivities to celebrate the approaching New Year at the Chinese Language School of San Diego. Above the heads of the 250 guests hung a fifty-four-foot-long dragon to help usher in the Year of the Rabbit. That dragon caught Dennis's attention and fueled his imagination.

About a year earlier, Dennis had researched information on the Internet about Ohio's Serpent Mound, which is the world's largest serpent effigy, constructed about 1000 A.D. on the edge of an ancient impact crater. It is 1,370 feet long and in some sections almost three feet thick. The thought of the enormousness of this earthen mound fascinated Dennis. About six months later, he considered having a giant serpent as part of the Sky Art works. But not until he saw the New Year's dragon did it all come together.

Dennis has always been conscious of Chinese and Japanese dragons and serpents. He recalls that in the early 1940s his parents had a silk embroidery depicting Chinese dragons. A decade earlier his father had lived in China for a period of time when he dropped out of college. Dennis also is keenly attuned to Chinese culture through his wife, Sally Tsui Wong-Avery, who is the founder of the Chinese Service Center in San Diego and the principal of San Diego's Chinese Language School.

When Dennis gazed at that dragon on the ceiling, he knew what he wanted to do. He called Ricardo and immediately went to see him in Perris on Tuesday morning,

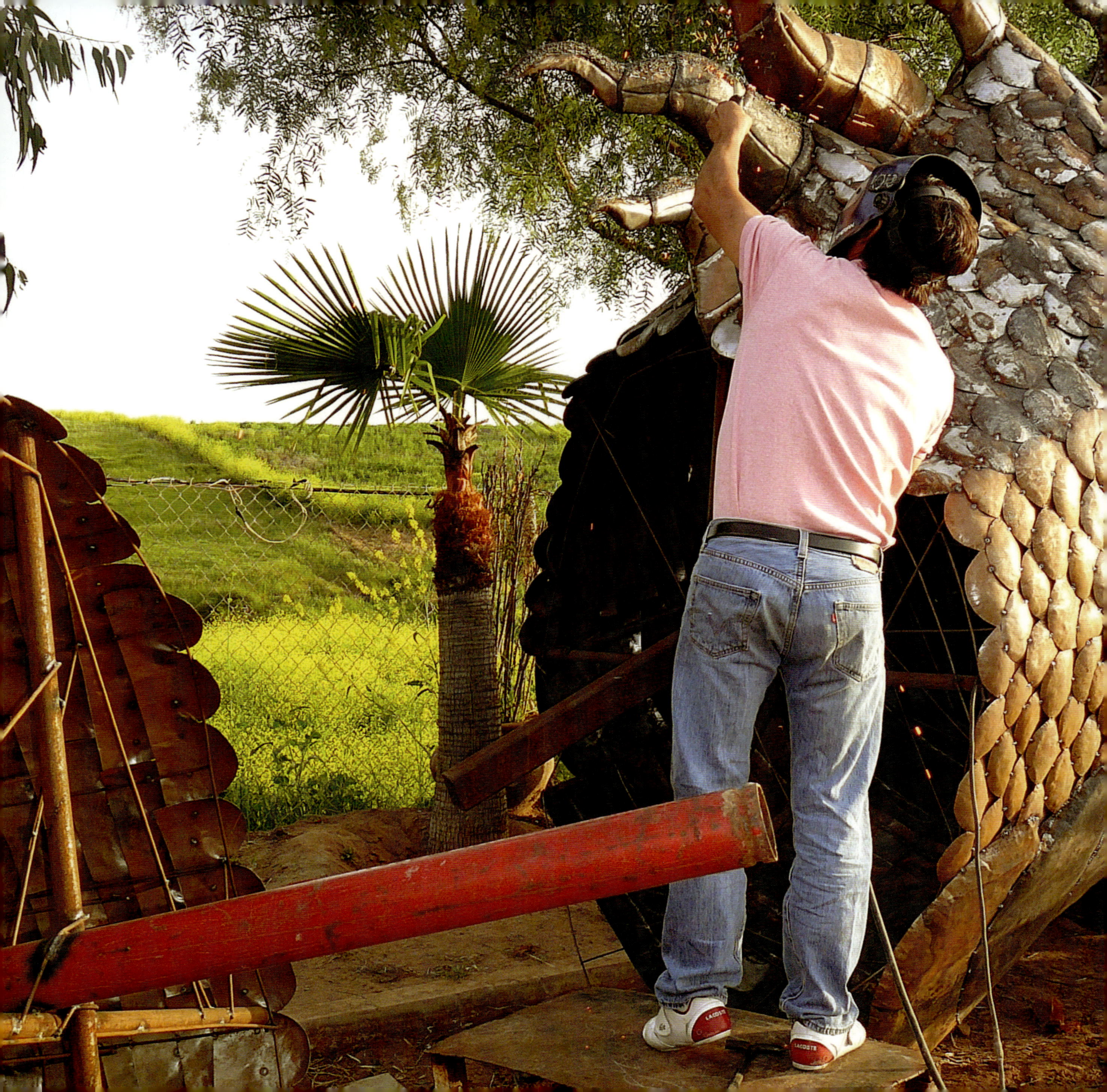
LACOSTE
LACOSTE

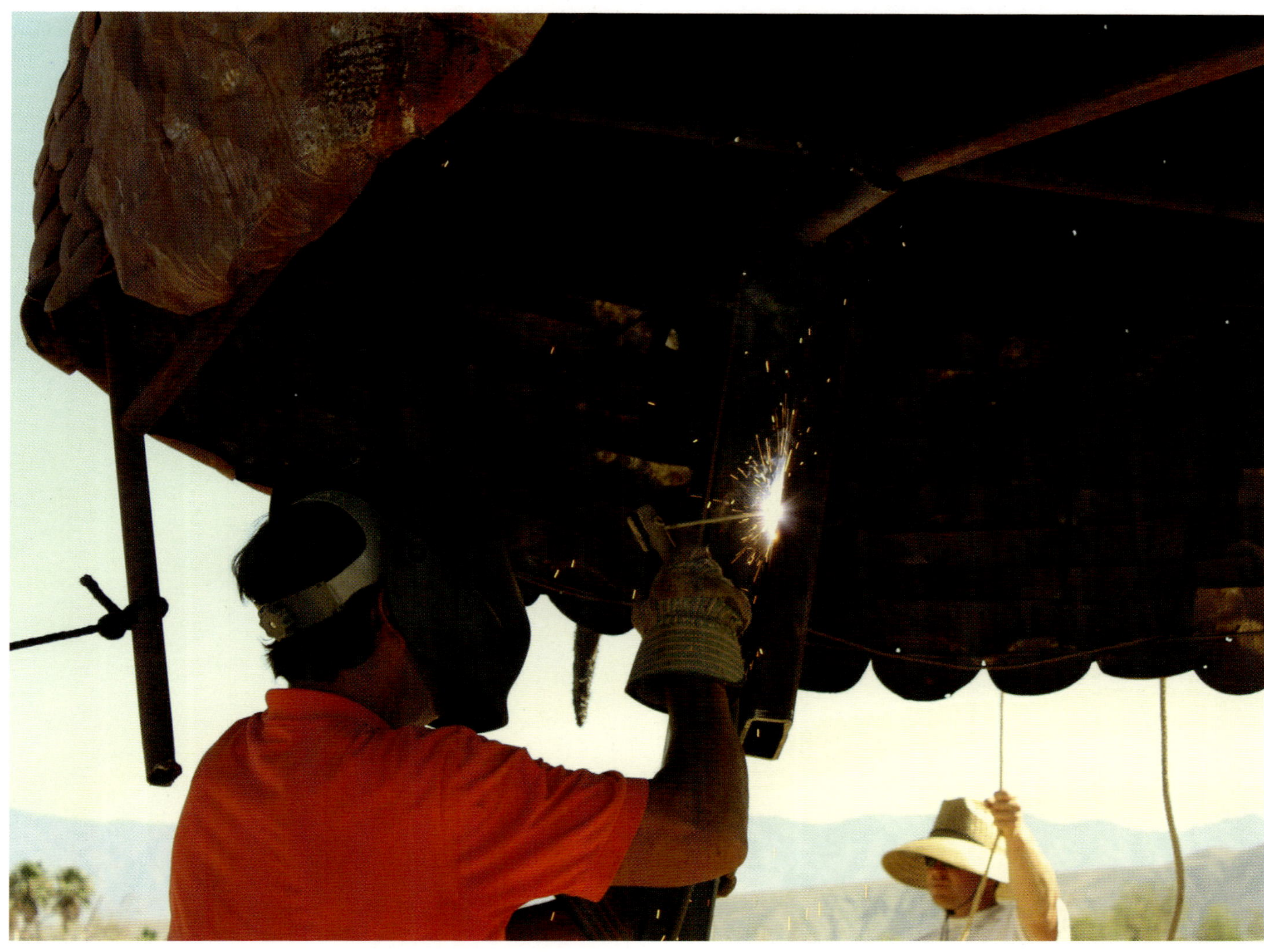

Welding Detail. Once the various parts are welded together onto the frame, the process of adding welding details begins. It is in the detail work that Ricardo distinguishes himself.

February 1, 2011, and presented his idea to him. Instantly, Ricardo "got it."

Ricardo began adding and modifying Dennis's ideas to make the proposed serpent as dramatic as possible. Dennis brought a computer printout from the Internet showing a photograph of the Ohio Serpent Mound, and he told Ricardo it was about 1,400 feet long. Ricardo suggested making the Sky Art serpent about one-tenth that size or at least 140 feet long. Dennis quipped, "That IS big." Sky Art was about to enter a new phase. From science to history and nature to whim, this grand idea was now moving to total fantasy.

The serpent would have a tail like a rattlesnake because it would live in the desert. It would have the body of a sea serpent as it dipped in and out of the shifting desert sands, and it would have a head of a dragon to stir the imagination beyond limits of what should be.

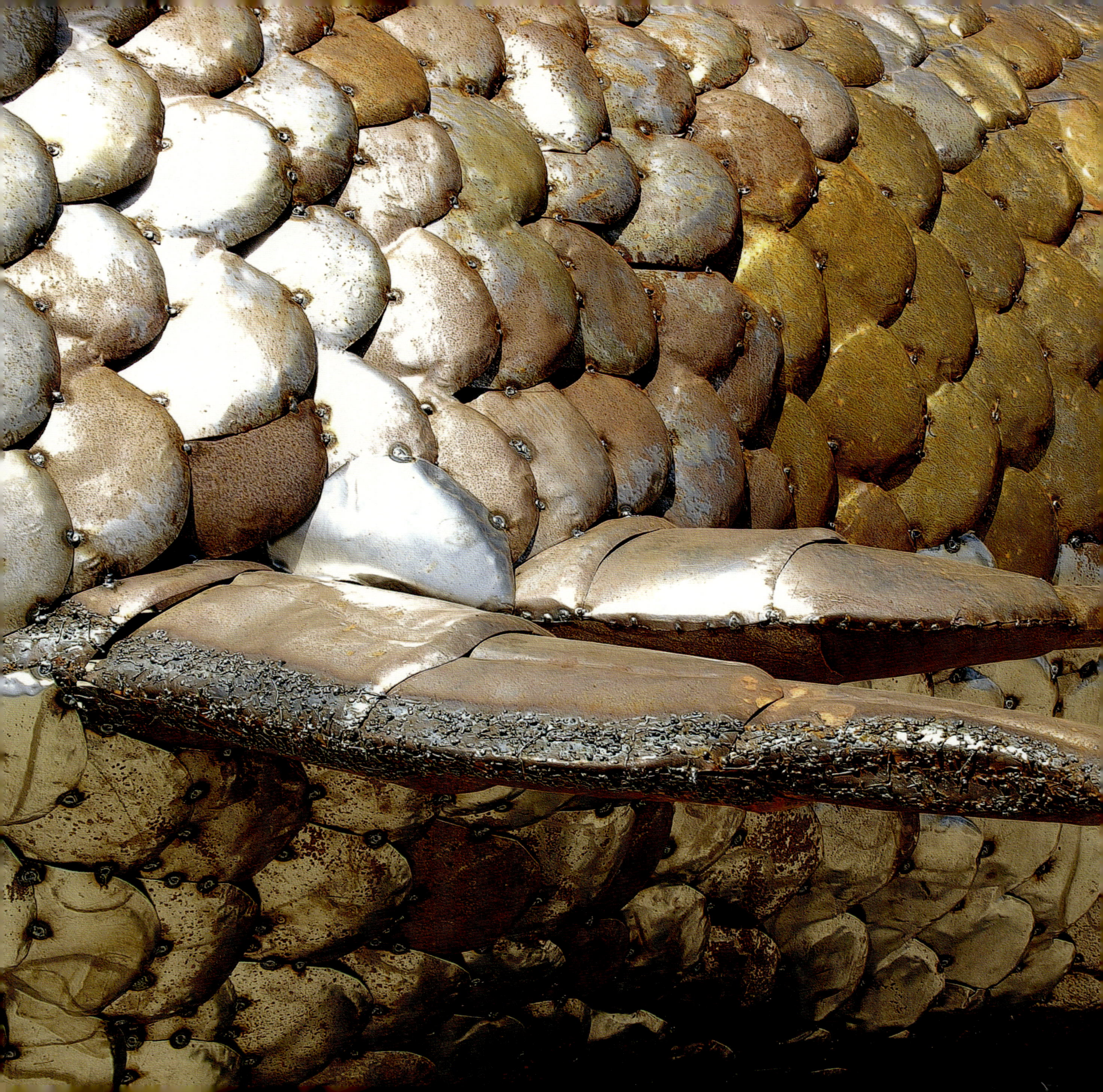

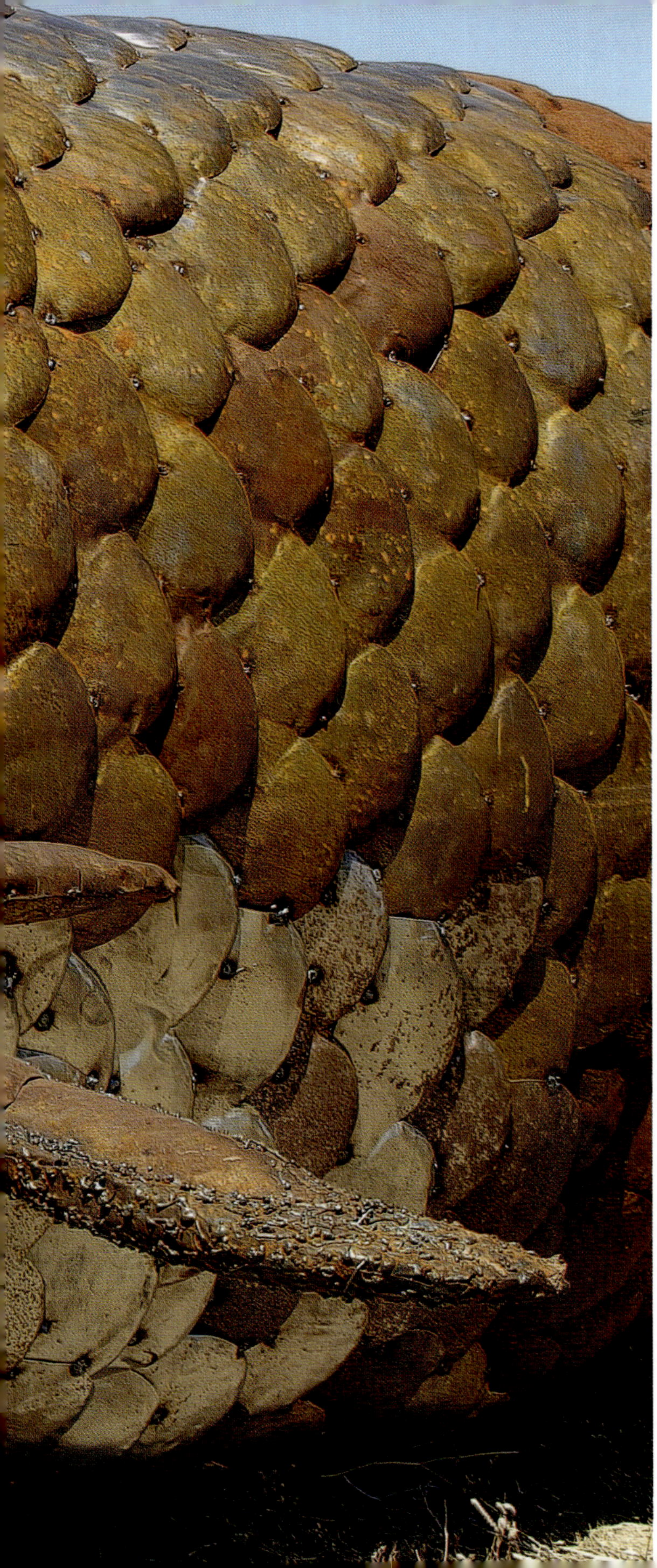

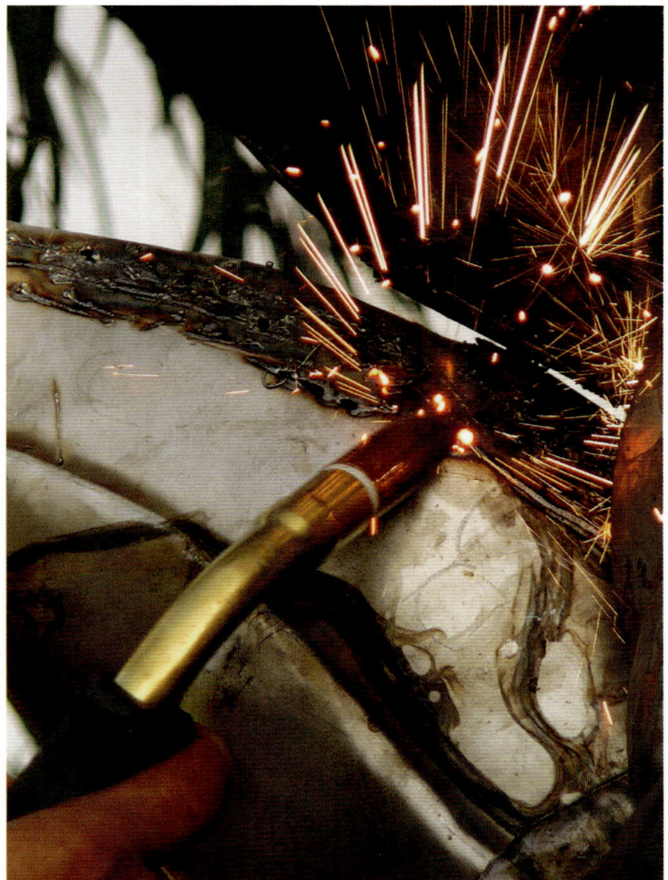

WELDING DETAIL. Weld slag, or the debris left in the welding process, is not removed but rather used to create the needed detail (*above*). Note the two fins (*left*), one with slag and one without.

Like all commissions that Ricardo had received from Dennis, once the idea was presented, it was in the maestro's hands to develop.

Dennis showed Ricardo a sketch he had made showing a serpent's tail protruding out of the ground on one side of a road with the illusion of having its body dip under a road with two undulating loops and the head on the opposite side of the road. He thought the diameter of the body could be about three feet.

Ricardo thought for a few minutes and immediately altered the original plan to make it more dramatic.

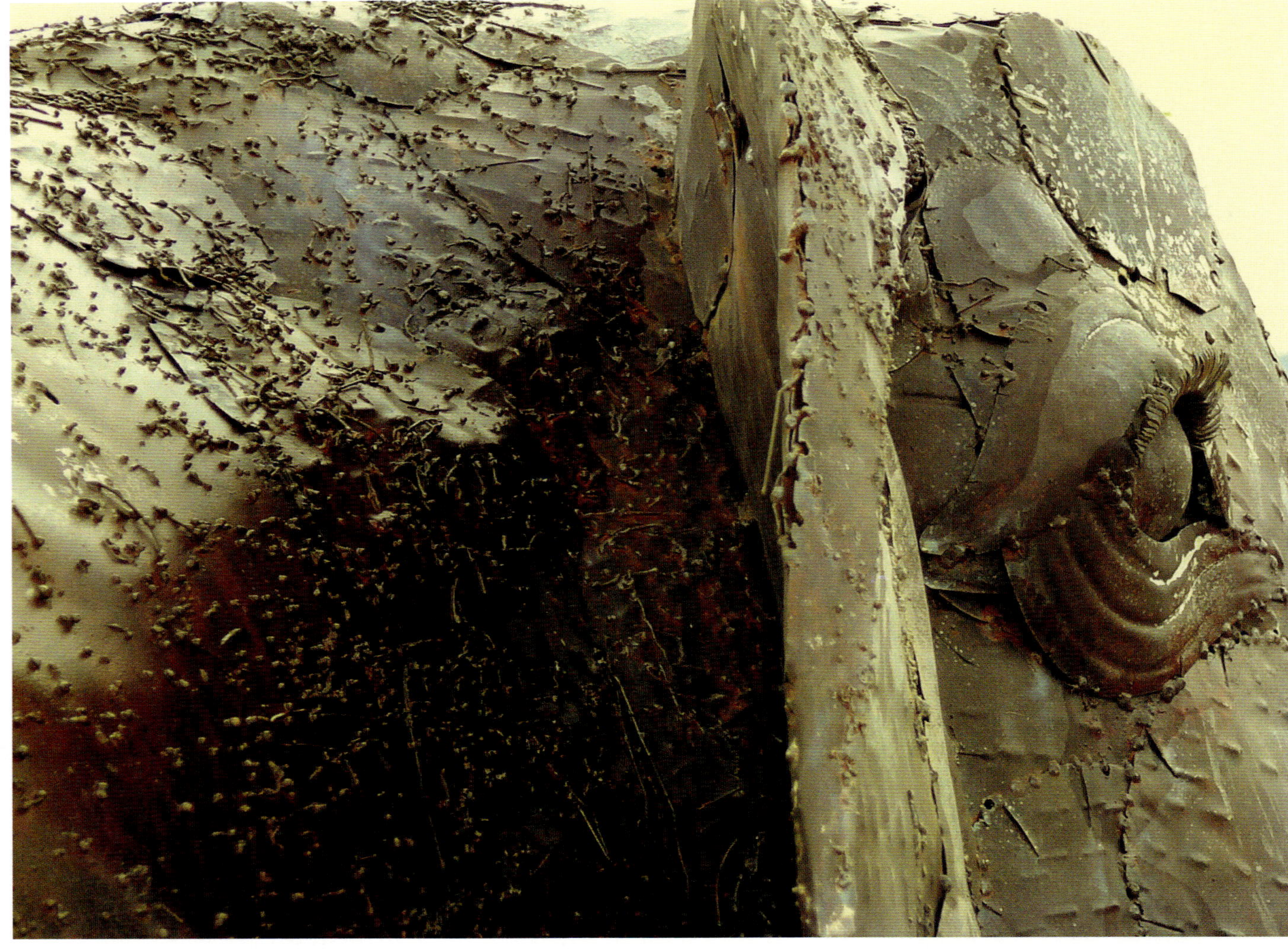

WELDING DETAIL. For Ricardo, weld slag has many possibilities. It can be used to create realistic hair on the elephant-like gomphothere and mammoth (*above*).

A loop would be added to the side of the road with the tail to keep it more balanced. The size of the serpent would be increased so that the underside of the largest loop could be at least six feet high so that people could walk under it and easily view the belly of the serpent. The diameter of the body needed to be at least six feet so that it really looked like a serpent and not like a giant worm. Each loop would have to be made in two sections of fifteen feet each, making the length of the total loop thirty feet. The total length of the serpent with all the loops and the space in between where it appeared to go under the ground would make the serpent 350 feet in length. It would take literally thousands of scales to cover the body, and it would take months to build. Installation alone would take three months on site.

The positioning of the serpent was very important. The sheer size and drama of this sculpture would easily draw attention and perhaps detract from the subtle charm of the other smaller sculptures. Care needed to be taken so as not to overpower other pieces. This magnificent creature needed to be by itself—a "final" crescendo to an overwhelming performance.

As word spread in Borrego Springs that another sculpture was coming, anticipation also grew. The curious began to appear to see what was happening.

The serpent was so large that eight trailer loads of sections had to be transported to Borrego, one at a time. Each section was largely constructed in the shop in Rosarito Beach under Ricardo's supervision. The tail was particularly burdensome to Ricardo's crew as the maestro kept rejecting it and tearing it apart to begin anew. Ricardo's perfectionism was in high gear as he announced that his latest creation needed to be "the best."

Welding Detail. A close up of weld slag shows its texture. See Chapter 3 to see how Ricardo uses weld slag for detail on the sabertooth cats and, in Chapter 5, note how weld slag is used on the head of the dragon.

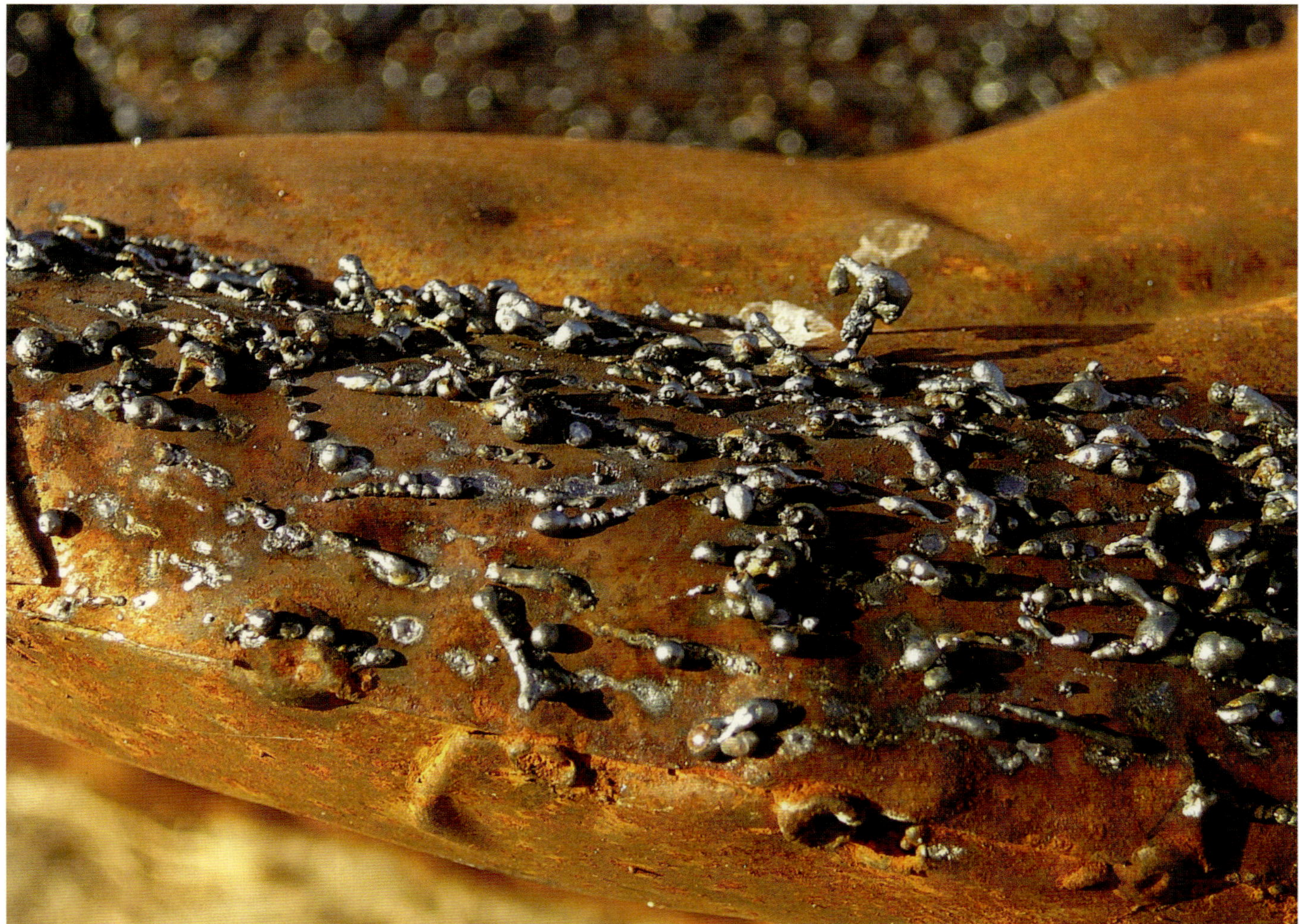

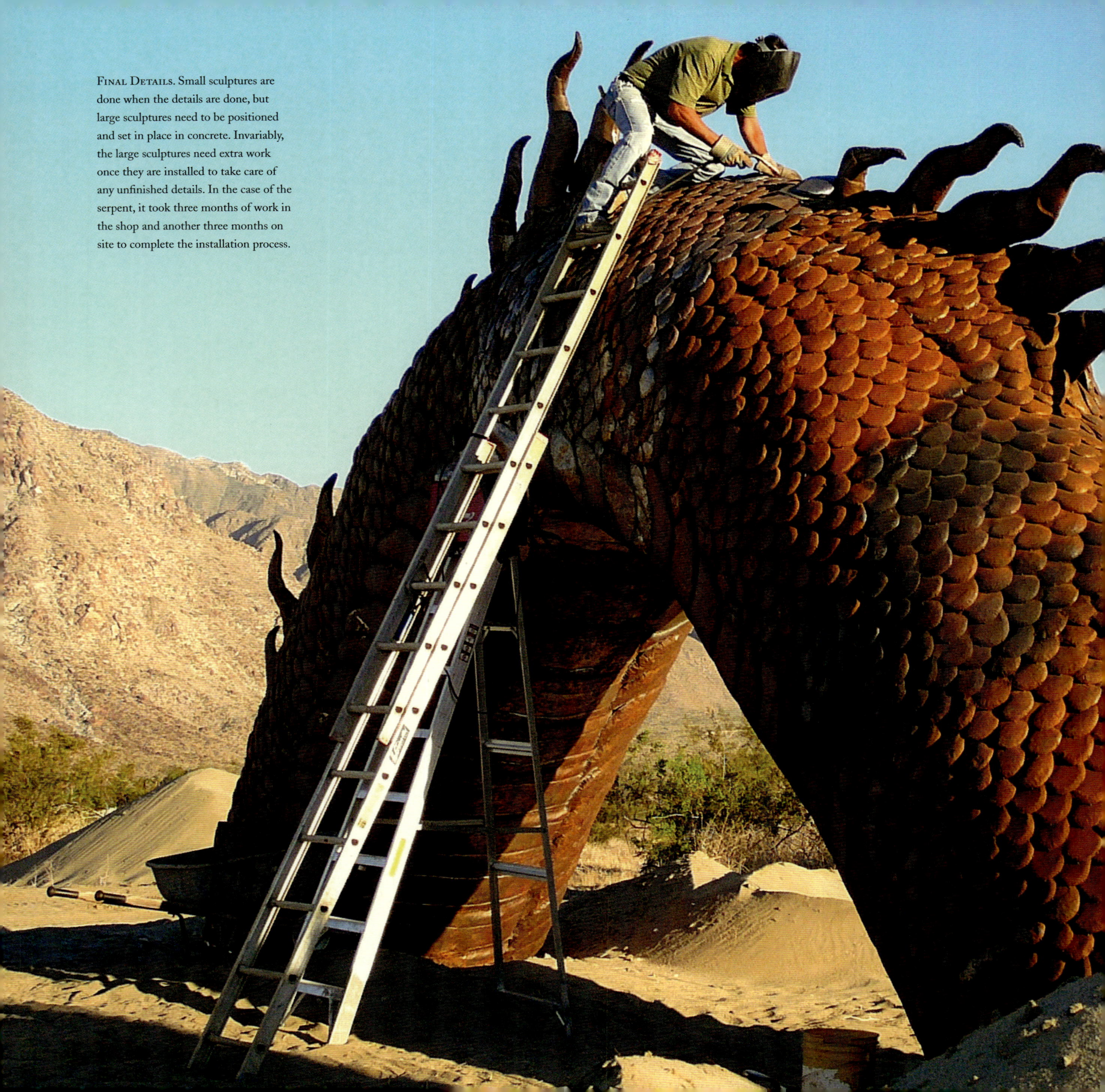

Final Details. Small sculptures are done when the details are done, but large sculptures need to be positioned and set in place in concrete. Invariably, the large sculptures need extra work once they are installed to take care of any unfinished details. In the case of the serpent, it took three months of work in the shop and another three months on site to complete the installation process.

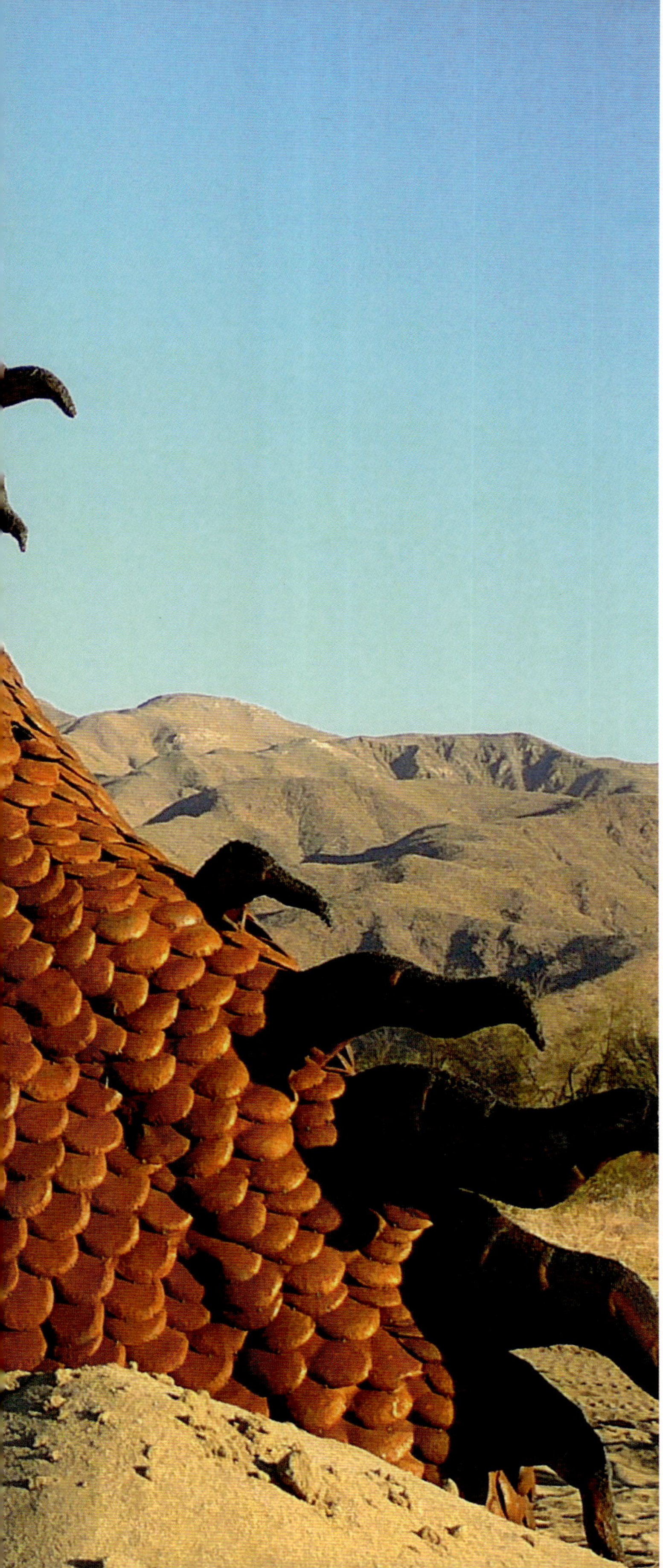

For three months, Ricardo's energy level was running on maximum from sunup to sundown as he obsessively and passionately worked daily to assemble the various sections that were spread on the ground along Borrego Springs Road. The smaller Shasta ground sloths that were in the area had to be removed and reinstalled farther down the road so as not to be completely dwarfed by this behemoth.

Ricardo was in his element with a welding helmet on his head, a MIG welding gun in one hand, and a heavy leather glove in his other hand. He would lift his face mask to assess his latest move, drop the mask, and begin welding, sparks flying in every direction. He moved from one piece to the next, always remaining intensely focused.

Visitors drove along Borrego Springs Road throughout the many weeks watching Ricardo work as the serpent slowly grew. Some drove by to only catch a glimpse of the fantastic creature as it gradually came together. The more inquisitive parked and walked over to get a closer look. They were always met with a smile and a warm greeting from Ricardo, who liked nothing more than getting praise for his art and being the center of attention. His work was joyful to him, and he wanted to share his joy, so he never minded having his photograph taken as he assembled and welded. He worked contentedly, knowing that when his serpent was completed, it would be a source of wonder and delight to all those who viewed it.

Perhaps Dennis had some satisfaction in knowing that serendipitously he was helping to usher in 2012—the Year of the Dragon.

The great serpent may be the final piece in the Sky Art collection, but, for sure, it is not the last sculpture for Ricardo. When a sculptor's imagination is boundless, deep inside its recesses lies endless inspiration for even more fantastic future creations. Ricardo is that amazing artist. He is always thinking, ready for the next challenge, and eager to continue his accidental journey.

GEOLOGIC TIME SCALE

ERA	PERIOD		EPOCH	START DATE (mya)*
Cenozoic	Quaternary		Holocene	0.01
(*Age of Mammals*)			Pleistocene	0.25
	Tertiary	Neogene	Pliocene	5
			Miocene	24
		Paleogene	Oligocene	34
			Eocene	55
			Paleocene	65
Mesozoic	Cretaceous			144
(*Age of Reptiles*)	Jurassic			208
	Triassic			245
Paleozoic				570

Source: *Fossil Treasures of the Anza-Borrego Desert* (2006); adapted by D. E. Lindsay per correspondence with G. T. Jefferson (2010)

* million years ago

A GUIDE TO GALLETA MEADOWS SKY ART

The Sky Art sculptures fall into three general categories: (1) sculptures inspired by science, (2) sculptures inspired by historical events or natural features of the Anza-Borrego desert, and (3) sculptures inspired by whim and fantasy. The designations below indicate the category and location for each sculpture. Refer to the location map on page 228. The legend for the location map lists all sculptures in each category.

FT: SKY ART INSPIRED BY SCIENCE

All of the sculptures in this category are based on fossil evidence as presented in *Fossil Treasures of the Anza-Borrego Desert.* The descriptions that follow are based on the text found in this book. The Sky Art sculptures in this category are numerically listed as they are generally found in a north-to-south order.

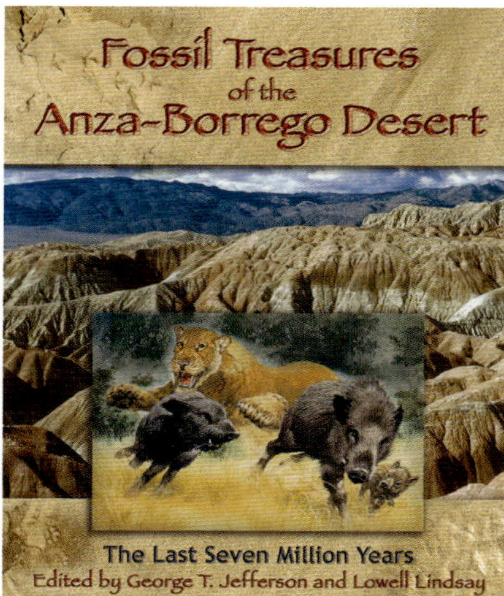

FT-1: Peccary—*Platygonus* sp.
Even-toed ungulates or hoofed animals belong to the order Artiodactyla as opposed to Perissodactyla, the odd-toed ungulates. The artiodactyls include peccaries, llamas, camels, deer, sheep, goats, cattle, giraffes, and pronghorns. The perissodactyls are browsing and grazing animals that include horses, tapirs, and rhinoceroses. Peccaries are members of the family Tayassuidae, endemic to North America from the Miocene to the present. Fossils from the extinct genus *Platygonus* have been found throughout North America. In Anza-Borrego they date from 3 million to 1.7 million years ago. Although artiodactyls are basically herbivores, the peccaries were like their living pig relatives, eating leaves, seeds, roots, fruits, worms, larvae, small vertebrates, and eggs. They were probably gregarious and hunted in packs. Their bodies were larger than modern

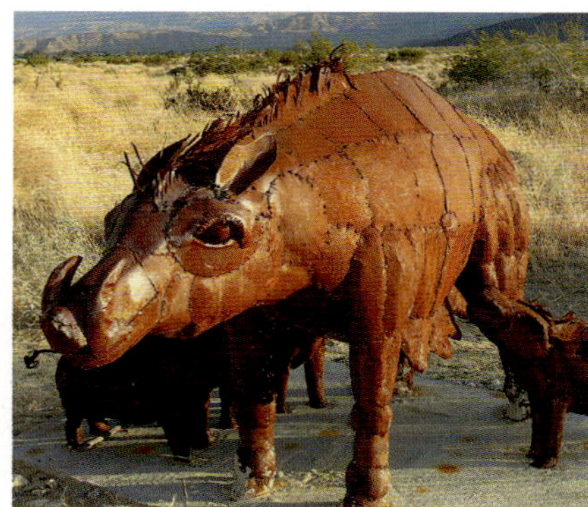

peccaries and they had long legs and carnivore-like tusks.

The Sky Art peccary metal sculptures are located on the southwest corner of Galleta Parkway and Stagecoach Way within Indian Head Ranch. Four piglets are suckling a sow as the boar observes.

FT-2: Giant Tortoise—*Hesperotestudo* sp.

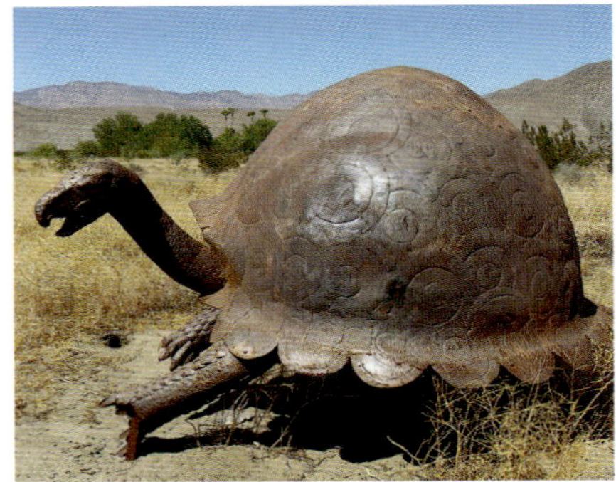

Hesperotestudo is an extinct species of the family Testudinidae, which are the tortoises or land turtles. The presence of this tropically related fossil in Anza-Borrego has significant implications regarding the early climate of this desert region during the Pliocene and early to middle Pleistocene. It would indicate warmer winters, cooler summers, and enough precipitation to create permanent bodies of water. Two species of the giant tortoises have been identified based on their size. The largest measures almost four feet long, three feet wide, and two feet tall. They first appear in the fossil record in Anza-Borrego about 3 million years ago and are found in various strata up to 1 million years ago. Since these animals did not burrow, they could only survive in a frost-free area that had pools of water where they could cool themselves. Fossils from *Hesperotestudo* have been found from North America to Central America.

Two metal sculptures are located on the east side of Galleta Parkway at the junction of Stagecoach Way.

FT-3: Merriam's Tapir—*Tapirus merriami*

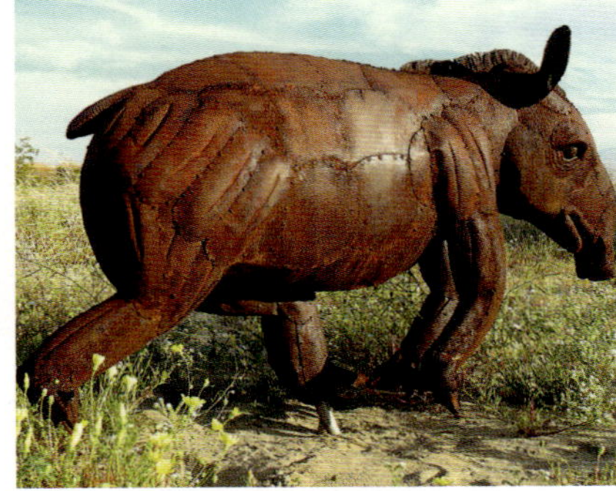

Members of the Tapiridae family are perissodactyls (see FT-1) who have changed very little evolutionarily since they first appeared some 40 to 30 million years ago. The minor changes that have occurred include a general increase in size, premolar teeth becoming more molar-like, and refinement of the proboscis. Both the North American Plio-Pleistocene fossil tapirs and the extant relatives all belong to the same genus, *Tapirus.* Plio-Pleistocene tapirs came in two sizes—large and small. In the Southwest, *Tapirus merriami* was the larger form, and its fossil remains in Anza-Borrego date from a little more than 2 million years ago. The most complete fossil specimen of this species was found in Anza-Borrego. Their closest relatives are the odd-toed ungulates—horses and rhinoceroses.

Seven Sky Art tapir sculptures are found on the east side of Galleta Parkway inside of Indian Head Ranch, midway between the entrance gate and Stagecoach Way.

FT-4: Gracile Sabertooth Cat—*Smilodon gracilis*

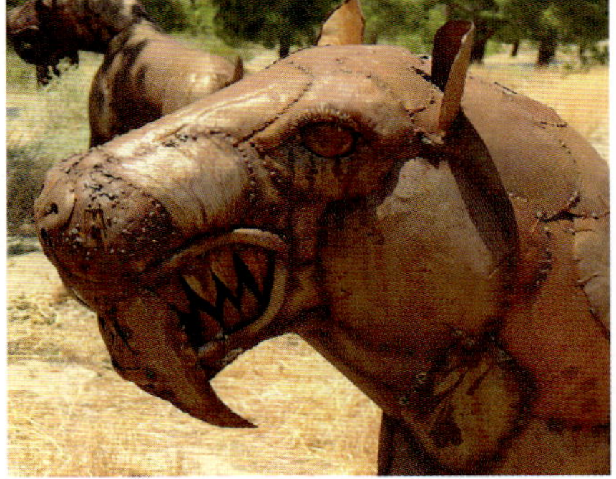

The felids are the most represented fossils of large carnivores found in Anza-Borrego. They fall into the following subfamilies—the extinct Machairodontinae (the sabertooth cat), the Pantherinae (the jaguar), and the Felinae (cheetah-like cat). Of the three, the most commonly recovered species is *Smilodon gracilis,* the gracile sabertooth cat. Anza-Borrego holds the only fossil record for this species in western North America, and it dates from 2.1 million to less than 1 million years ago. It is the smallest of the *Smilodon* species and is a direct ancestor to the larger *Smilodon fatalis*, the California state fossil. Powerful legs and a short tail indicate that the gracile sabertooth cat used stealth and ambush rather than speed to capture its prey. It could open its mouth 120 degrees, as compared to a lion, which can open its mouth 65 degrees. In size, they were comparable to the extant jaguar. They were forest adapted.

The Sky Art metal sculptures are found just within the entrance gate to Indian Head Ranch on the east side on Galleta Parkway.

FT-5: Giant Tortoise—*Hesperotestudo* sp.

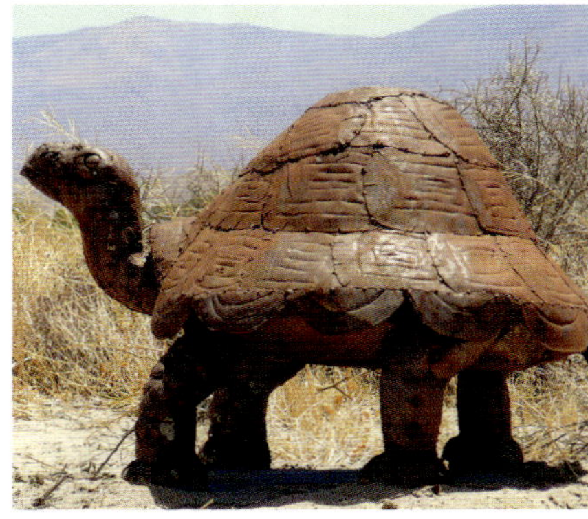

See FT-2 for a description. There are five giant tortoise sculptures positioned on the south side of Henderson Canyon Road across from the entrance gate to Indian Head Ranch and one to the west of the entrance on the north side of the road.

FT-6: African Elephant—*Loxodonta africana*

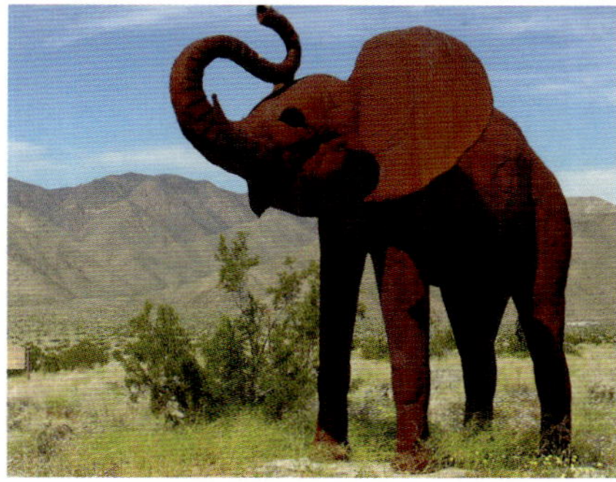

The name of the order Proboscidea refers to the elongated nose or proboscis (trunk) of family members that include the mastodons, gomphotheres, and elephants. This order arose out of Africa. The elephant family includes mammoths, the African elephant, and the Asian elephant. The African or savanna elephant was not found in North America. It is the largest land mammal in the world, weighing about 10,000 pounds. Fossil remains of proboscideans found in Anza-Borrego include gomphotheres and mammoths. Mastodon fossils have not yet been found here. See FT-10 for a discussion on gomphotheres and FT-14 for information about the Columbian mammoth.

Two African elephant metal sculptures are found on the east side of Borrego Springs Road, north of Santa Rosa, at the Galleta Meadows Estate sign. Also at the same location is a metal plaque commemorating the Anza expeditions to Alta California.

FT-7: Camelids—*Hemiauchenia* sp. and *Camelops* sp.

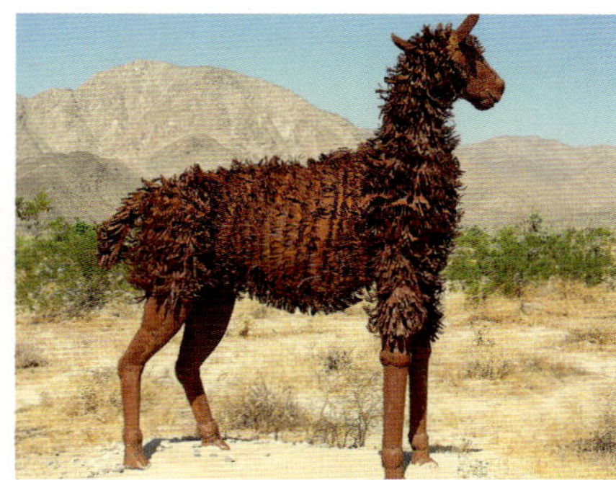

The family Camelidae originated in North America about 44 million years ago. The two subfamilies include Tribe Lamini, represented today by llamas and alpacas of South America, and Tribe Camelini, represented today by the bactrians of Asia and the dromedaries of Africa. *Hemiauchenia* sp. and *Camelops* sp. are in the Tribe Lamini. No Sky Art sculpture represents Tribe Camelini, although fossil remains of one genus—*Gigantocamelus*—have been found in Anza-Borrego. Fossils of the Camelid family are the second most commonly found fossils of Anza-Borrego after horses. They are, however, first in diversity of species. The various

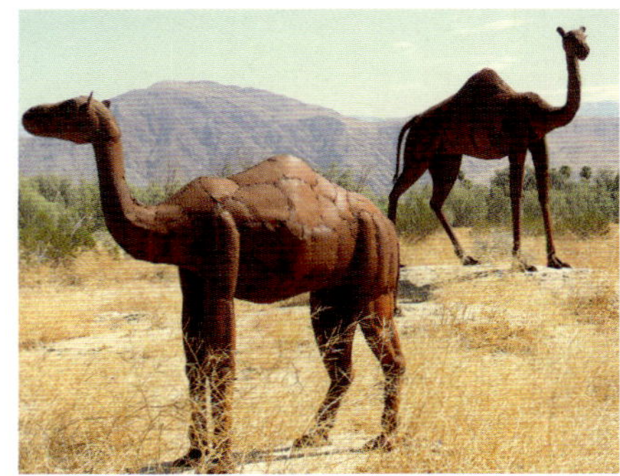

species of camel are found in deposits that date from 5 to 0.5 million years ago. Camelids are distinguished by ipsilateral limb pairs, that is, the fore and hind limbs on the same side move forward and back at the same time. They also have very distinct foot bones—the four foot toes were reduced to two—which allowed them to thrive in open country and later dryer lands.

Hemiauchenia is the typical llama whose ancestral version was found in Anza-Borrego. It was an open-plains animal that fed on grasses. Although *Camelops* closely resembled modern day camels, morphologically they were closer to llamas. The largest *Camelops* sp. was seven feet tall, almost twenty percent larger than today's dromedary camels.

The Sky Art Camelids found at the southeast corner of Catarina Drive and San Ysidro Drive depict three *Hemiauchenia* sp. and two *Camelops* sp.

FT-8: Harlan's Ground Sloth and Camelid—*Paramylodon harlani* and *Camelops* sp.

Animals in the order Xenarthra are unusual for their dentition, which is bony, and for the presence of extra articulations between the vertebrae of the lower back. This order evolved in South America and dispersed into North America in three "invasions" in the late Cenozoic. Included in this order are anteaters and armadillos,

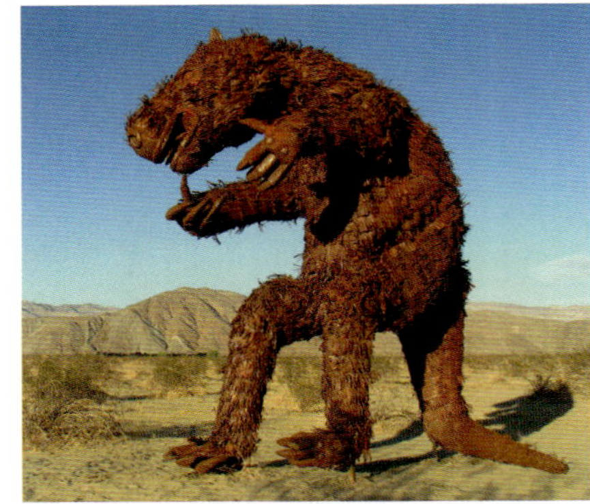

which are still living, and ground sloths, which are extinct. Fossil finds of ground sloths in Anza-Borrego are from all three invasions, which are represented by different sloths, each of which utilized different types of habitats. The earliest xenarthrans entered North America in the late Miocene, about 9 million years ago, while the last ones arrived during the Pleistocene.

Paramylodon harlani arrived in North America during the second invasion and first appears in the fossil records in Anza-Borrego about 2.3 million years ago. It was the largest of the Anza-Borrego ground sloths. The muzzle of this ground sloth is much wider than that of the Shasta ground sloth. Harlan's ground sloth is thought to have been a mixed feeder that lived in a more open countryside, such as a savanna. The skin contained dermal ossicles—pieces of imbedded bone—which are not found in the other ground sloth species. These bony nodules on the back of the animal provided protection from preying animals. They also had very strong forearms and curved claws that suggest they could dig.

A large upright 800-pound metal Harlan's ground sloth is found on the east side of Borrego Springs Road north of Big Horn Road. It stands seventeen feet tall. Just to the south of this sloth is another with a baby on its back.

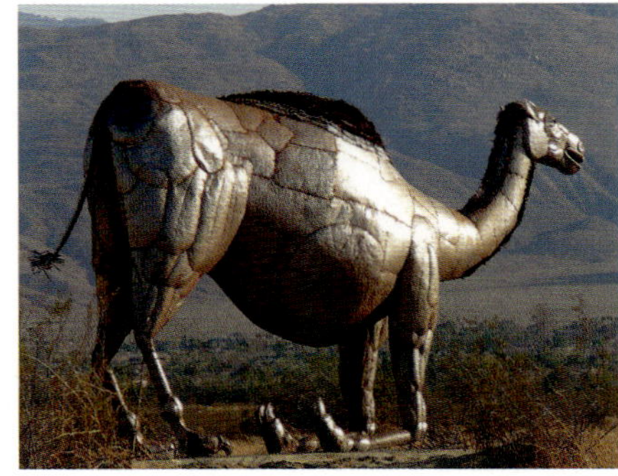

Two large *Camelops* sp. are found to the south of the ground sloths. The unique toe structure of these animals, well adapted to long-distance travel across soft sand, is clearly visible. See FT-7 for a description.

FT-9: Shasta Ground Sloth—*Nothrotheriops shastensis*

See FT-8 for evolutionary history of ground sloths. *Nothrotheriops shastensis* arrived during the last invasion and was the smallest of the North American ground sloths, said to be about the size of a small calf. The skull of the Shasta ground sloth is longer and narrower than that of the other sloth species. It may have been a browser that was better adapted to arid desert conditions

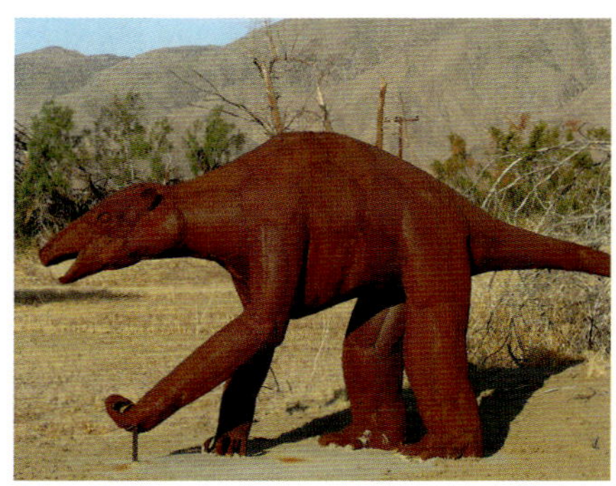

than the other ground sloths. The earliest fossils of the Shasta ground sloth found in Anza-Borrego date from 2 million years ago.

The two metal sculptures of the Shasta ground sloth are found on the north side of Big Horn Road, midway between Borrego Springs Road and Di Giorgio Road.

FT-10: Gomphothere and Camelid—*Gomphotherium* and *Camelops* sp.

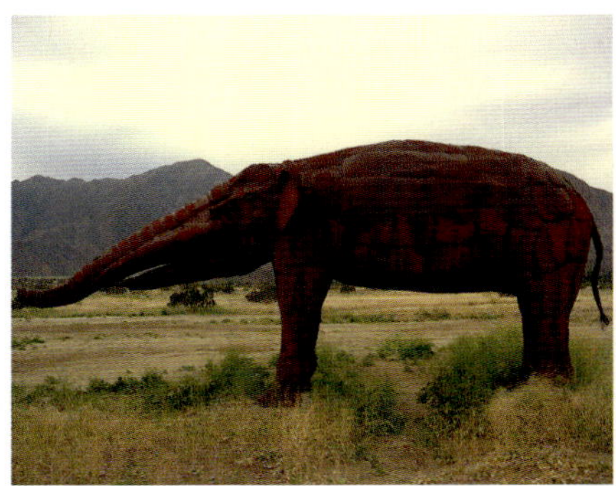

The gomphotheres are one of the distinct families in the order Proboscidea. See FT-6. Gomphotheres differed from elephants in their tooth structure and tusks. Two members of this family are found in Anza-Borrego—*Gomphotherium* and *Stegomastodon. Gomphotherium* crossed the Bering Land Bridge to North America about 15 million years ago. It was a hippopotamus-size animal with short legs and four tusks. A distinguishing characteristic was its elongated chin that caused the tips of the lower tusks to extend almost to the tips of the larger upper tusks. *Gomphotherium* lived in marshy areas. The oldest *Gomphotherium* fossils found in the Anza-Borrego area date back 9 million years.

The *Gomphotherium* Sky Art sculptures found at the southeast corner of Borrego Springs Road and Big Horn Road depict a family. The larger pieces weigh 1,000 pounds and stand twelve feet tall. They are twenty feet long. Oddly enough, the Greek translation for *Gomphotherium* is "welded beast." Directly to the north of the three sculptures are a mother *Camelops* and its calf. See FT-7 for a description of *Camelops.*

FT-11: Gracile Sabertooth Cat and Extinct Horse—*Smilodon gracilis* and *Equus* sp.

See FT-4 for a description of the gracile sabertooth cat. The six sabertooth cats are located on the south side of Highway S-3, 3.8 miles south of Christmas Circle. They are variously posed in active stance, attacking prey, lying in ambush, and fighting.

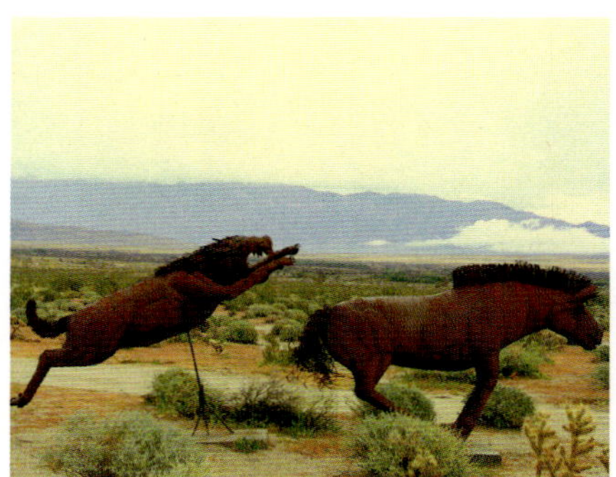

Horses are perissodactyls (see FT-1 and FT-3) or odd-toed ungulates that generally bear hooves. In the case of the horse, this is extreme, whereby the central toe (digit) is huge and the other lateral toes have become accessory splint bones—an evolutionary adaptation to running. They are members of the family Equidae, which includes true horses, zebras, and asses. Equine horses originated in North America about 57 million years ago. There were several successful emigrations to the Old World, crossing the Bering Land Bridge, throughout their history. They became extinct in the Pleistocene Epoch in North America about 11,000 years ago. They were later reintroduced to North America when the Spaniards conquered Mexico.

Fossil remains in Anza-Borrego capture the more recent evolutionary history of the horse. These horses were adapted to eating coarse, gritty plants rather than leaves. Dental patterns are often used in identifying horse species. The first fossil record for the modern domestic horse may have been

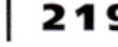

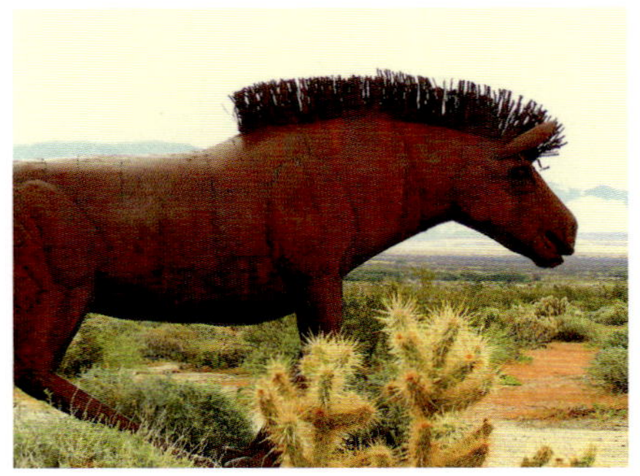

recorded in Anza-Borrego. It is still not conclusive. The oldest fossils are from the ancestors of *Equus* and date to just over 4 million years ago, and possibly they may be the youngest occurrence of *Dinohippus* in North America.

Four Sky Art sculptures depict the extinct horse as it is being pursued by hunting carnivores—chased, attacked, and stalked by the gracile sabertooth cats.

FT-12: Incredible Wind God Bird—*Aiolornis incredibilis* in Its Nest

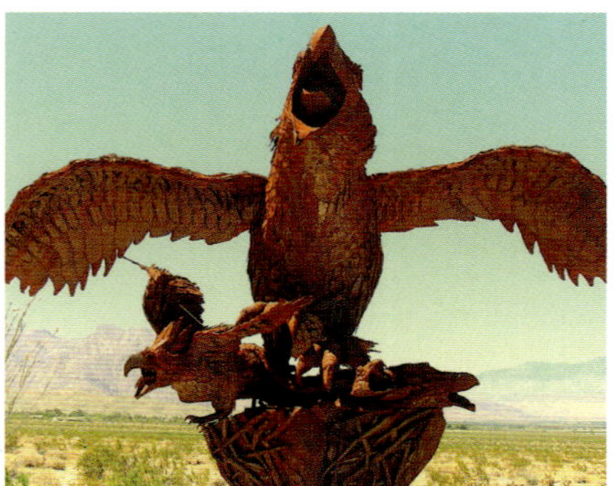

The largest flight-capable bird in North America was the *Aiolornis incredibilis,* with a wingspan of sixteen to seventeen feet. It stood about four feet tall. Only six specimens of this four-foot-tall bird have been found, and three of those come from Anza-Borrego, with the oldest fossil specimens dating to about 3.5 million years ago and the most recent about 0.5 million years ago. The fossil specimens help to establish a reflection of the climatic setting of the time, which indicate a much different area with streams, lakes, and ponds. The name *Aiolornis* translates from Greek as "incredible wind god bird." It had previously been called *Teratornis incredibilis* when it was thought that this bird was a scavenger, like condors and vultures. It is now assumed that this bird was a predator more closely related to Old World storks.

The metal sculpture located to the north of Highway S-3, almost four miles south of Christmas Circle, depicts *Aiolornis incredibilis* in its nest with two fledglings who have been presented a snake for their dinner. The entire sculpture weighs more than 1,400 pounds.

FT-13: Extinct Horse—*Equus* sp.

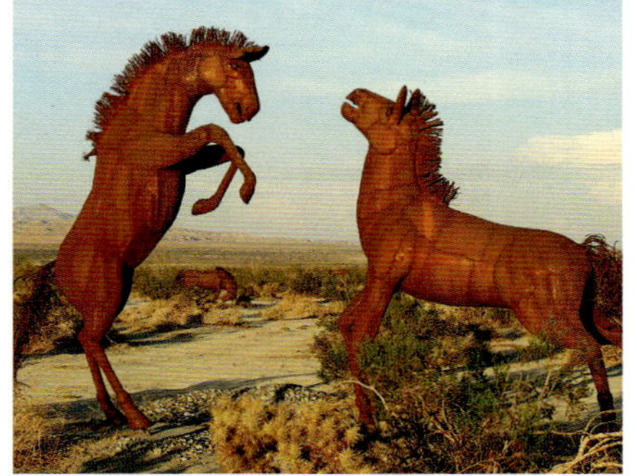

See FT-11, FT-3, and FT-1 for information about horses and perissodactyls. The nine Sky Art sculptures of *Equus* sp. found on the north side of Highway S-3 between the *Aiolornis* and the mammoths are found in various poses as they might have appeared in Anza-Borrego during the Pleistocene.

FT-14: Columbian Mammoth—*Mammuthus columbi*

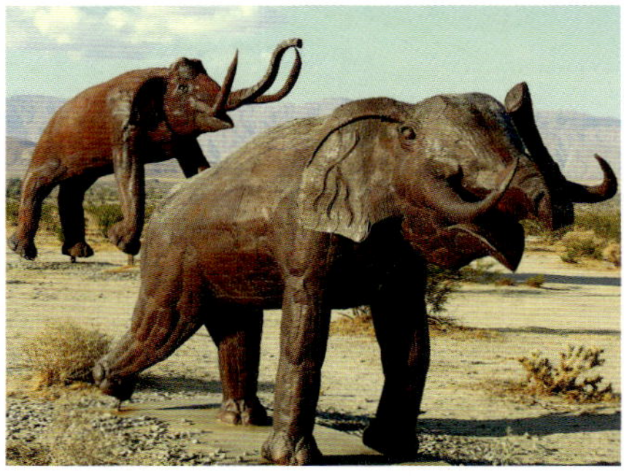

Mammoths (*Mammuthus*) are medium- to large-size elephants that originated in southern and eastern Africa about 4 million years ago, subsequently spreading through Europe, Asia, and North America. Four species of mammoth originally crossed the Bering Land Bridge to North America, and only two of the species are found in Anza-Borrego—the southern mammoth and the Columbian mammoth. The southern mammoth was a medium-size elephant that was here at least 1.4 million years ago. The Columbian mammoth was the largest North American elephant and its skeletal remains date from 1.1 million years ago. For a long time the imperial mammoth was thought to have been a separate species, but it is now considered an early evolutionary stage of the Columbian mammoth. All of the Columbian mammoth species found in Anza-Borrego belong to this early evolutionary stage. A specimen from a later evolutionary stage was found east of the state park near the Salton Sea.

Sky Art metal sculptures of a *Mammuthus columbi* family are found on the north side of Highway S-3, northwest of Anzio Drive.

FT-15: Incredible Wind God Bird with Prey—*Aiolornis incredibilis* with *Platygonus* sp.

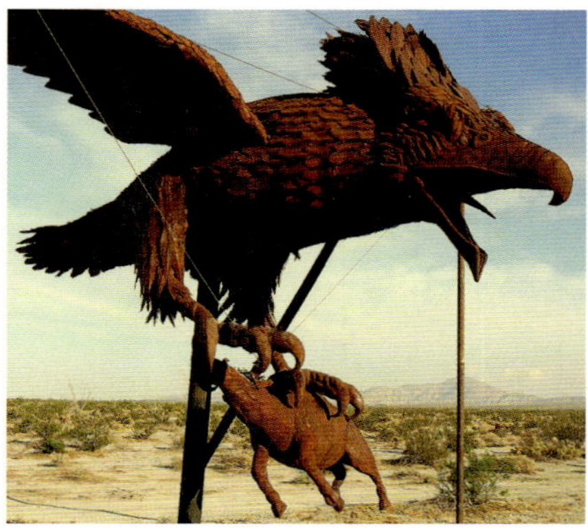

The 1,400-pound metal sculpture found on the west side of Anzio Drive, south of Highway S-3, depicts *Aiolornis incredibilis* as it has just captured a *Platygonus* sp. The sculpture is seventeen feet long from beak to tail and thirty feet wide from wing tip to wing tip. This is almost twice the size of the actual fossil bird whose wing span was sixteen to seventeen feet. See FT-12 for information about *Aiolornis incredibilis* and FT-1 for a description of the *Platygonus* sp.

HN: SKY ART INSPIRED BY HISTORICAL EVENTS AND NATURAL FEATURES OF THE ANZA-BORREGO DESERT

The Sky Art sculptures are numerically listed as they are generally found in a north to south order.

HN-1: (1) Peninsular Bighorn Sheep—*Ovis canadensis cremnobates*

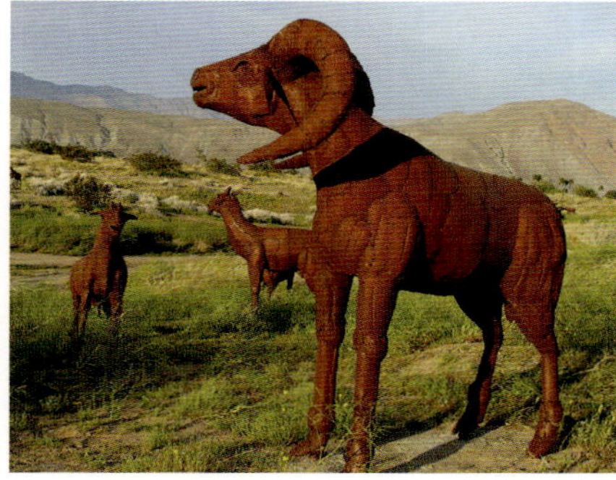

One of the last refuges of the endangered Peninsular bighorn sheep, *Ovis canadensis cremnobates*, is Anza-Borrego Desert State Park. The sheep's special relationship to this preserve is seen in the park's name—*borrego* is Spanish for lamb or sheep. The very survival of this animal is dependent on having open wilderness areas in which it can roam. Anza-Borrego Desert State Park contains ninety percent of California's designated wilderness areas. "Peninsular" refers to the Peninsular Mountain Ranges (in turn, named for the peninsula of Baja California) where this subspecies lives. Peninsular bighorn sheep are currently designated as endangered only north of the Mexican border. They were added to the federal list of endangered species in March 1998. They are fully protected by law, and it is illegal to hunt them. Drought, disease, and mountain lion and coyote predation are a threat to their existence. The Peninsular bighorn is also San Diego County's official animal.

Bighorn sheep are very elusive and difficult to see. The Sky Art sculptures make it possible for all to see the sheep in their native habitat. The sculptures are found on the south side of Stagecoach Way, 0.2 miles west of Galleta Parkway in Indian Head Ranch.

HN-1: (2) Gold Miner and His Mule

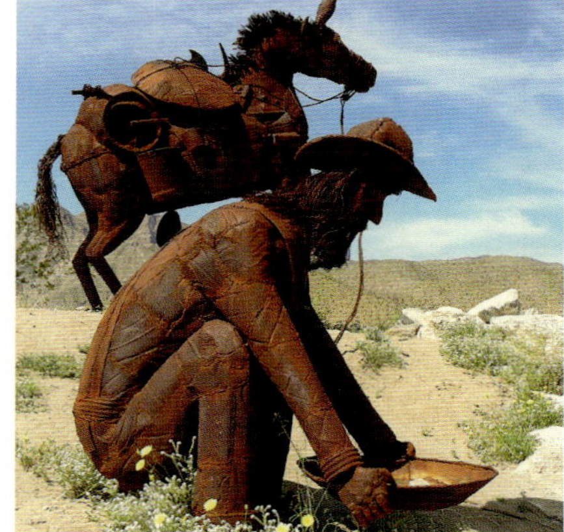

It was the alluring call of gold that first brought emigrants to California after James W. Marshall's discovery in 1848.

The rush was on, and the Southern Emigrant Trail, which crosses through the southern portion of the Anza-Borrego desert, became the all-weather route whereby thousands of emigrants passed en route to the goldfields of the Sierra Nevada.

The earliest claim for actually finding gold in the Anza-Borrego area goes to mountain man Thomas Long "Pegleg" Smith, who spread tales about his 1829 discovery in San Francisco bars, years after California's Gold Rush. His stories, combined with the actual discovery of gold in the Julian area, were enough to keep prospectors looking for gold in the Anza-Borrego area for years to come. The many stories eventually led to the creation of the Pegleg Smith Liar's Contest in 1948, an annual event celebrated at Pegleg Smith Monument on Highway S-22 (at mile 25.5) the first Saturday night in April.

Gold was discovered in Julian in 1869 and then in Banner and Chariot canyons. The only significant gold mine in the park was the Oriflamme Mine. Primarily worked from 1870 to 1885, it yielded less than $25,000. There were other diggings in Mine Canyon, Grapevine Canyon, Blair Valley, and the Santa Rosa Mountains.

The Sky Art sculptures of the gold miner and his mule are found on Stagecoach Way, 0.2 miles west of Galleta Parkway in Indian Head Ranch.

HN-2: Indian Head—Representing Sebastián Tarabal and/or Salvador Palma

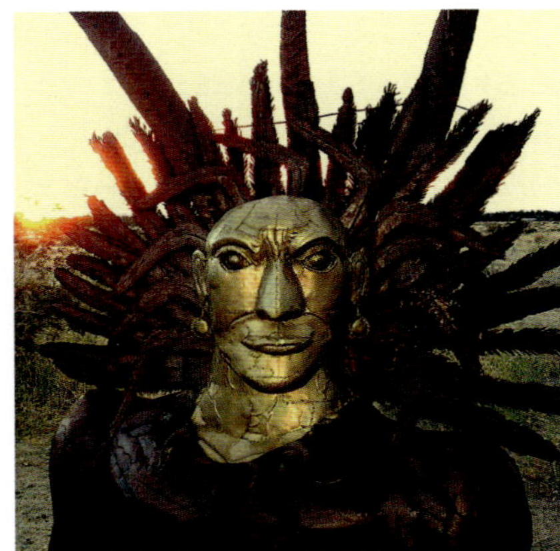

The Indian head (and upper torso), located appropriately across from the entrance gate to Indian Head Ranch on Henderson Canyon Road, faces toward the sculpture of the padre and the entrance to Coyote Canyon. The sculpture represents the two Indians who played a significant role in the Anza expeditions. Or it could represent just one of them.

Sebastián Tarabal

Sebastián Tarabal was a Cochimí Indian born at Mission Santa Gertrudis, north of San Ignacio, in Baja California. He was recruited to accompany Captain Gaspar de Portolá and Fr. Junípero Serra on the overland expedition to establish the first mission in what was then known as Alta California in 1769. Tarabal and his wife later became residents of San Gabriel Mission.

In the fall of 1773, Tarabal, his wife, and a companion fled from the virtual enslavement suffered by all Mission Indians and attempted to cross the desert to Arizona. Only Tarabal survived the rigors of the crossing. He arrived at Tubac in January 1774, just as Juan Bautista de Anza was ready to leave on his first exploratory expedition to find a route to California. Immediately, Anza recruited him as a guide to lead them to San Gabriel Mission. Anza named the campsite near the marsh at San Sebastian for Tarabal.

Salvador Palma

Olleyquotequiebe, whose name meant "wheezy one" and who may have been asthmatic, was chief of the Yuma (Quechan) Indians when Juan Bautista de Anza arrived at the Colorado River in 1774 while exploring for a road to California. Anza named him Chief Salvador Carlos Antonio Palma. The crossing of the Colorado River was a vital link for a road to California. Knowing this, Anza viewed friendship with Chief Palma as indispensable. Palma was treated with every courtesy and was presented a medal in the likeness of the Spanish king. The Yumas, in turn, offered protection and a base of operations for crossing the river. It was also Palma who brought Sebastián Tarabal to Anza as he was readying himself to begin the first expedition to find the road to the San Gabriel Mission.

HN-3: (1) Spanish Padre—Representing Fr. Francisco Garcés and/or Fr. Pedro Font

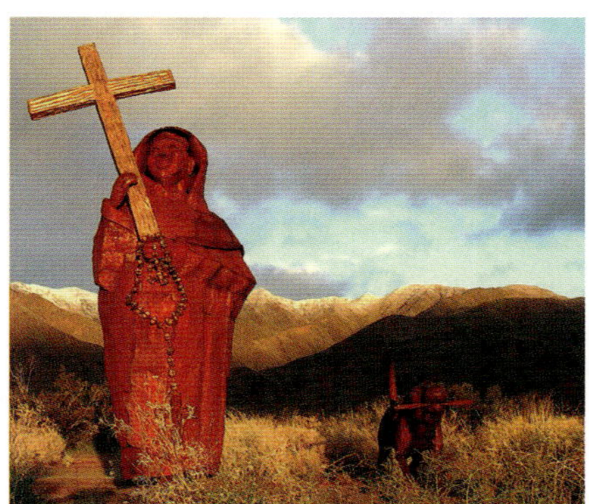

The first Anza expedition of 1774 opened the overland road to California while the second expedition in 1775–1776 brought the first colonists to California. The padre represents one or the other or both of the padres who accompanied the Anza expeditions. The padre is located north beyond the pavement of Borrego Springs Road, west of the entrance to Indian Head Ranch.

Fr. Francisco Garcés

Franciscan missionary Francisco Hermenegildo Garcés served as the padre on the first Anza expedition. He was born in Aragon, Spain, and after he was ordained, he was assigned to Mission San Javier del Bac, near present-day Tucson, Arizona. He was known as the "wandering priest" because of his explorations of the southwest. In 1771 he explored west down the Gila River to the Colorado River and then he explored west to within sight of Signal Mountain. Looking across the Anza-Borrego desert, he saw a break in the Peninsular Ranges at Coyote Canyon that suggested a pass or a river course through the mountains that might lead to the coast and the California settlements. He shared this information with Juan Bautista de Anza, presidial captain at Tubac, and was later recruited as guide and spiritual advisor on Anza's first expedition to California in 1774.

Fr. Pedro Font

Franciscan friar Pedro Font was the chaplain and navigator on the second Anza expedition to California in 1775–1776. Font had the training and ability to determine latitudes. He was chosen as diarist and spiritual guide for the expedition, while his other skills would prove valuable for navigation.

Font is remembered for his negative comments on the expedition. He was sick most of the time and found fault with almost everything that Anza did. He did not approve of celebrations that Anza allowed on the expedition involving drinking, singing, and dancing. He could see no beauty in Coyote Canyon and saw it only as a worthless wasteland. His comments about the Indians are degrading. And yet he is honored in name for one of the most picturesque areas of the park—Fonts Point. Font was, however, very observant. He was the first to correctly surmise about the origin and antiquity of the marine fossils that he saw en route, and he was also the first to make note of the wild bighorn sheep of the area.

HN-3: (2) Saguaro

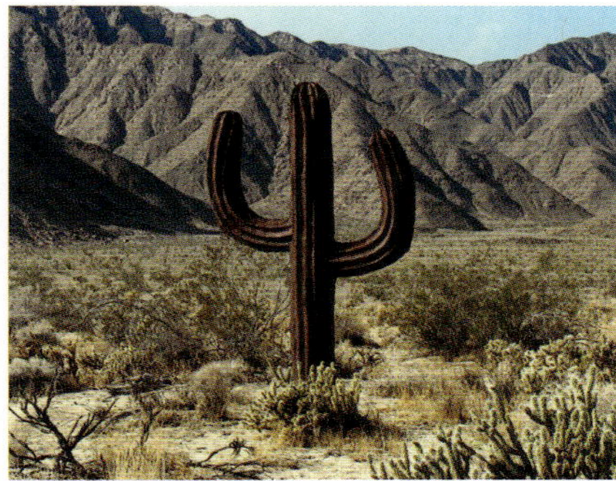

The saguaro Sky Art sculpture found to the west of the padre does not represent a plant found in this desert. It is a native of the Sonoran Desert found to the east of the Colorado River and is found in the Tubac/Tucson area, where Anza launched his expeditions.

HN-4: 1946 Willys Jeep (CJ-3A)

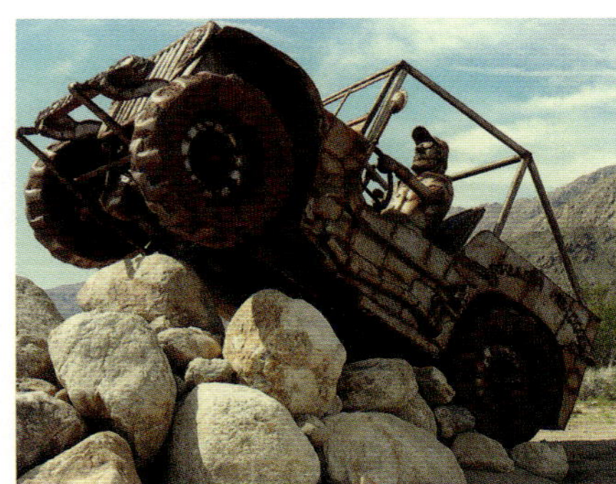

The iconic World War II military Jeep, manufactured from 1941 to 1945, was a small four-wheel-drive utility vehicle. Willys-Overland took its Jeep public with its first full production of the civilian version—the CJ series—beginning in 1945. The classic CJ-3A had improvements over the first CJ, and 132,000 were produced between 1946 and 1953. (The author's first Jeep was one of these.)

After WWII, surplus military Jeeps also became available to the public. The Jeep literally opened up desert exploration and forever changed access to this state park (then known as Anza Desert State Park). It created a crisis in park management that was not resolved until 1976, when the 14,000-acre Ocotillo Wells State Vehicular Recreation Area (OWSVRA) was created. The conflict had to do with conservation vs. preservation. Today the off-road area is more than 80,000 acres in size—the second largest unit within the California State Park system after Anza-Borrego Desert State Park. Intrusions by off-roaders who do not obey state park regulations continue to be a problem for the park, especially in areas bordering the off-road area.

This "ode to the off-roaders," as Dennis calls it, was inspired by a group of responsible off-roaders who enjoy "poking around the desert" at their own pace. This informal group calls itself The Herd of Turtles, and they emphasize that they are "careful to leave everything" as they find it and to stay on designated park trails.

The sculpture is found west of the Indian head on Borrego Springs Road.

HN-5: Farm Workers in Di Giorgio Fruit Corporation Grape Fields

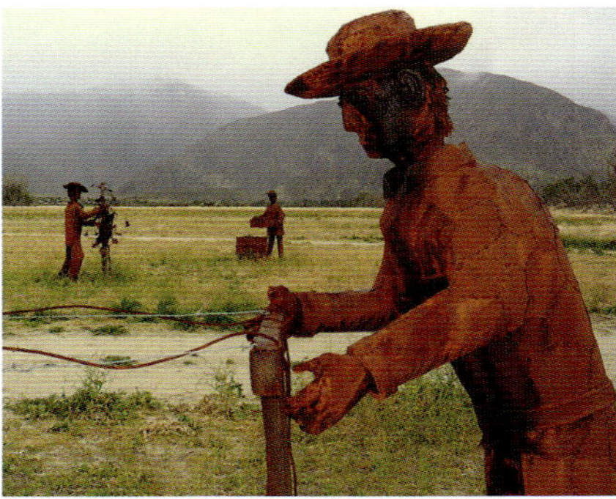

The sculptures on the southwest corner of Di Giorgio Road and Big Horn Road are a reminder of the role that migrant farm workers played in the harvesting of grapes grown by the Di Giorgio Fruit Corporation in Borrego Valley beginning in 1948. The Di Giorgio Fruit Corporation was one of the companies targeted by the United Farm Workers union (UFW) during the five-year grape strike and national grape boycott from 1965 to 1970 that drew attention to the plight of farm workers and the unfair business practices of growers.

One incident in Borrego Valley on June 29, 1966, later became an issue in a suit brought against the Di Giorgio Fruit Corporation by the UFW. On that day key leaders were arrested and inhumanely treated at the Di Giorgio Ranch in Borrego Valley. Those arrested included César Chávez, president of the UFW, Rev. Wayne Hartmire Jr., head of the California Migrant Ministry, and Fr. Victor Salandini. The three had been asked to peacefully accompany ten field workers who had walked off their job that day and were afraid to go back to the labor camp on the ranch to pick up their checks and their personal belongings because of past harassments.

As soon as the group entered ranch property, they—including the minister and the priest—were arrested for trespassing, stripped naked, and chained together in groups of three by sheriff's deputies and transported to the San Diego County jail. The next day they were released on bail and returned to Borrego Springs, where the strike was still in progress. All of the 279 farm workers, of which one third were women, voted to strike and left their $1.20-per-hour jobs.

The various strikes and heated court battles that followed eventually brought the resolution that the UFW sought. It also brought to a close the twenty-year history of harvesting grapes in the Borrego Valley.

HN-6: Capt. Juan Bautista de Anza on His Horse

Juan Bautista Agustín de Anza, for whom the state park is named, was an Indian fighter, soldier, explorer, colonizer, and an administrator. He was a presidial captain at Tubac, the

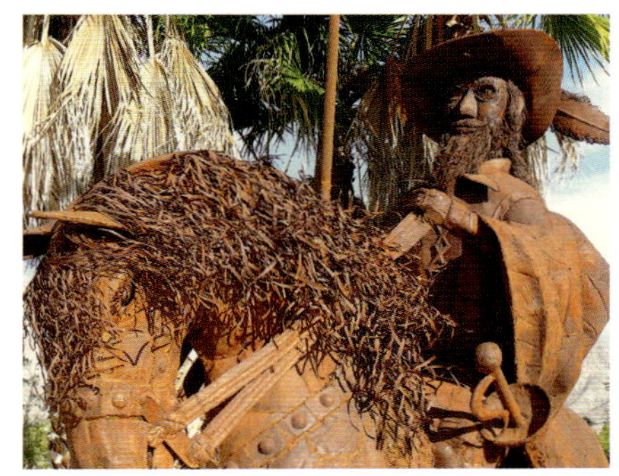

northernmost frontier outpost of Mexico, outside of California. When a need developed to find a land route to California, Anza submitted a request to do so and was granted permission in 1774. The success of the first exploratory expedition led to his promotion to lieutenant colonel and his orders to recruit settlers and lead a second expedition of colonists to California to establish a presidio, mission, and village on San Francisco Bay. A new promotion followed the second expedition. He was appointed the political and military governor of the Province of New Mexico and held this post until his death on December 19, 1788.

The Sky Art sculpture of Anza sits prominently in front of the Borrego Springs Chamber of Commerce on the northwest corner of Palm Canyon Drive and Stirrup Road.

WF: SKY ART INSPIRED BY THE WHIM AND FANTASY

No dinosaur ("terrifying or powerful lizard") fossils have been found in the Anza-Borrego area. Their initial inclusion in Sky Art was pure whim based on the artist's interest in dinosaurs, stimulated by the *Jurassic Park* films. The later addition of the serpent was transforming whim to fantasy to create a new imaginary creature. The Sky Art sculptures in this category are numerically listed as they are generally found in a north to south and east to west order.

WF-1: *VELOCIRAPTOR*—Found in Mongolia

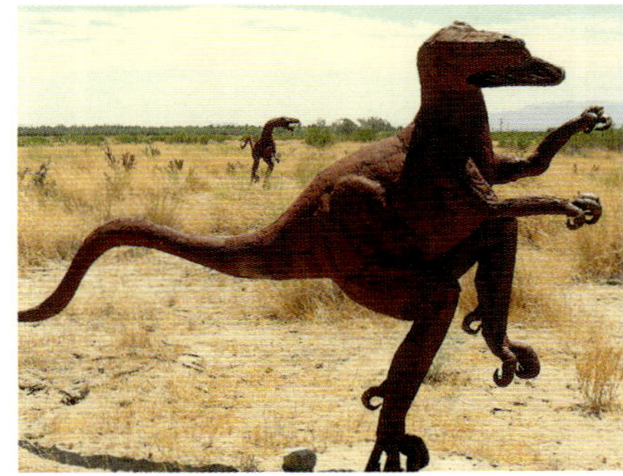

The "Speedy Raider" was a dromaeosaurid ("running or swift lizard"), which was a small to medium-size, carnivorous, birdlike theropod dinosaur with feathers, commonly referred to as a raptor. The *Velociraptor* was the smartest of the dromaeosaurids and was equipped with a large sickle-shaped foot claw and forelimbs with digits that had three strongly curved claws. It had slender legs and an S-shaped neck and spine. The *Velociraptor* stood two to three feet tall, weighed fifteen to thirty pounds, and was about five or six feet long. *Velociraptors* lived during the late Cretaceous period, about 85 to 80 million years ago. Several fossil specimens have been found in Mongolia, where Anza-Borrego has a sister park. They may have run up to forty miles per hour and also may have hunted in packs.

When the movie *Jurassic Park* was made, the actual size of the *Velociraptors* was exaggerated for dramatic purposes. At that time, no dromaeosaurid was thought to have existed that was so large. However, soon after the film was released, the first *Utahraptor* specimen was found and it more than matched the size of that portrayed in the film. See WF-5.

The *Velociraptor* was the first Sky Art dinosaur installation. It is located on the east side of Galleta Parkway in Indian Head Ranch, south of Stagecoach Way and the giant tortoises.

WF-2: SERPENT—Pure Imagination

The Borrego Valley serpent combines a real reptile with mythological and legendary creatures to make its own fantastical being. A rattlesnake tail

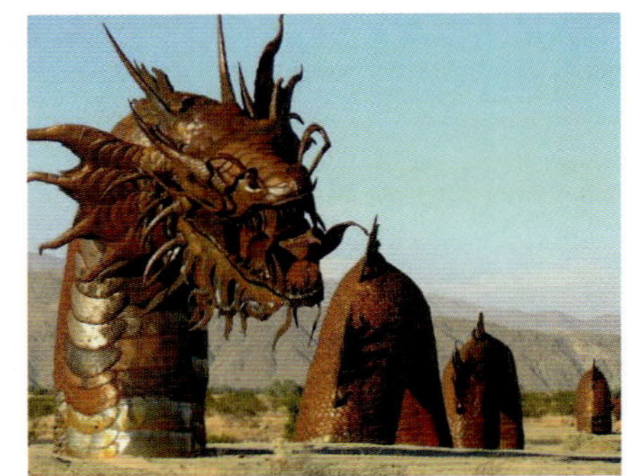

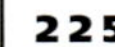

is on the body of a sea serpent that is topped with the head of a dragon. Whether or not one would symbolically associate this creature with certain attributes or powers linked to dragons is up to individual and cultural interpretation. Does it represent a primal force of nature or possess some form of magic? Or is it just for fun?

The 350-foot-long serpent is located south of San Ysidro Road straddling Borrego Springs Road.

WF-3: *Spinosaurus*—Found in Egypt and Morocco

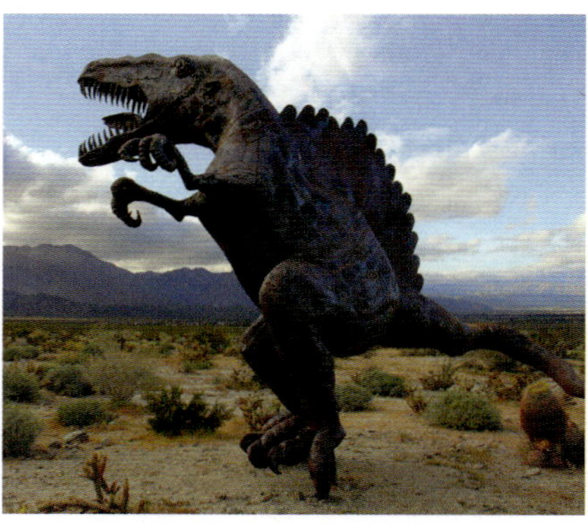

The "Spiny Lizard" was a carnivorous theropod that lived in Africa during the late Cretaceous period, about 98 to 95 million years ago, and had a six-foot-long sail-like structure protruding from its back vertebrae that may have had some use in thermoregulation, defense or display threat, or sexual attraction. It weighed more than four tons and was forty to fifty feet long. It had a large crocodile-like skull and jaws with long sharp teeth. Only incomplete fossils have been found, including the neural spines.

A Sky Art sculpture of a *Spinosaurus* with three juveniles is found by following a dirt road south 0.5 miles past the end of the pavement of Anzio Drive, and then turning west and proceeding 0.1 miles. They are found on the north side of the road.

WF-4: Fighting Dinosaurs

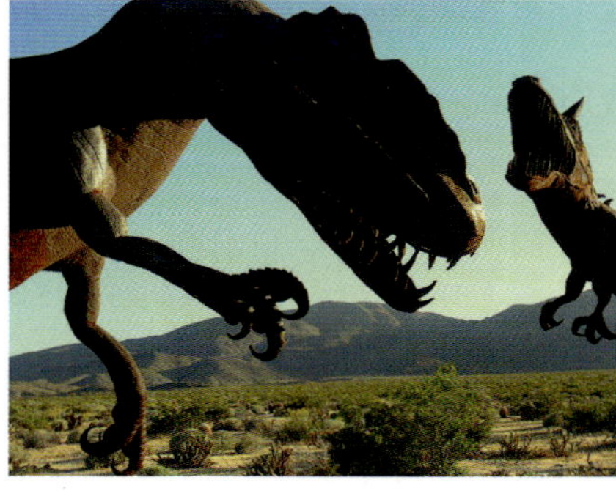

The Sky Art "fighting" dinosaurs are found by following a dirt road south 0.5 miles past the end of the pavement of Anzio Drive and then turning west and proceeding 0.2 miles. They are found on the south side of the road. The sculptures weigh about 1,000 pounds each.

Carnotaurus—Found in Argentina

This "Flesh-Eating Bull" from Argentina lived in the Cretaceous period about 113 to 91 million years ago and had two hornlike protrusions above its eyebrows. Its forelimbs were even smaller than those of *Tyrannosaurus rex*, and the digits were fused and immobile, and lacked claws. It weighed about one ton, stood about six feet tall, and was about twenty-five feet long. Only a single fossil specimen has been found, in Patagonia. It had a long neck, a small head, and a slender lower jaw. Its eyes were close together and it may have had binocular vision, which was unusual for a dinosaur. It had a row of bumps along the spine that became larger toward the tail.

Allosaurus—Found in North America

The "Different Lizard" had vertebrae that were lighter in weight than those of other dinosaurs. This huge carnivorous theropod weighed about two or three tons, stood ten to fifteen feet tall, and was about thirty to forty feet long. It lived during the late Jurassic period, about 150 to 140 million years ago. Fossils have been found in North America, Europe, Africa, and Australia. *Allosaurus* had a large head with sharp serrated teeth, short limbs, and claws with three digits. It was at the top of the food chain and may have demonstrated some cooperative behavior.

WF-5: *Utahraptor*—Found in the United States

"Utah's Raider" was a carnivorous theropod that lived in the early Cretaceous period, about 125 million years ago, and was in the same family as the *Velociraptor*. It has been found only in

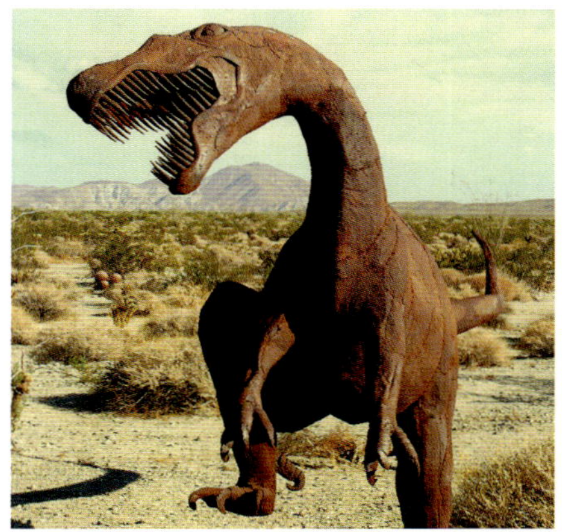

the United States. It was the largest member of the dromaeosaurids, standing six feet tall. It was twenty-three feet long and weighed 1 ton. It resembled a giant roadrunner with about a nine-inch-long middle-toe claw and three digits with large curved claws. It was a light, fast, agile, birdlike dinosaur that was highly intelligent with large, sharp, serrated teeth, powerful jaws, and a long, stiff, rodlike tail that allowed it to keep its balance. Like other dromaeosaurids, it may have hunted in packs. See WF-1.

The two *Utahraptor* metal sculptures and nest are found by following a dirt road south 0.5 miles past the end of the pavement of Anzio Drive and then turning west and proceeding 0.3 miles. They are found on the south side of the road.

WF-6: *Tyrannosaurus rex*—Found in North America

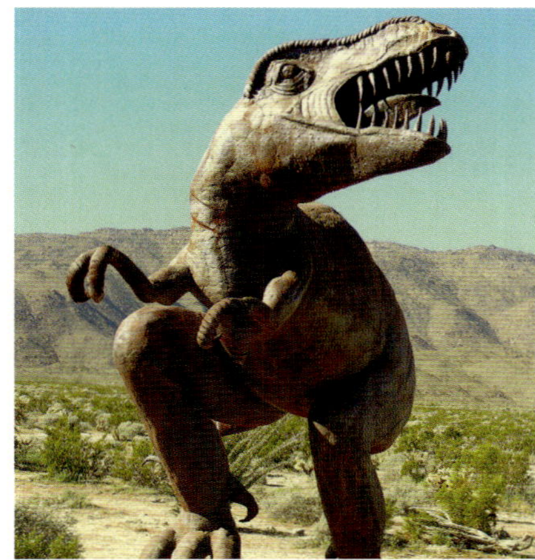

The "Tyrant Lizard King" was a massive carnivorous theropod that lived during the late Cretaceous period, about 85 to 65 million years ago. It stood about thirteen feet tall, weighed up to 7 tons, and was about forty feet long. It was a smart and fast-running predator with hollow bones and small forelimbs about three feet long. Its jaw was larger than its forelimb at about four feet, and it had about fifty to sixty long, conical teeth that were serrated and continually replaced. It could consume hundreds of pounds of meat in one bite. *Tyrannosaurus* had a stiff, pointed tail that acted as a counterbalance for its enormous head. Fossilized skin specimens show that the skin was similar to that of an alligator. It was one of the last nonavian dinosaurs to exist before the Cretaceous-Tertiary extinction about 65 million years ago. About thirty incomplete fossils have been found in North America as well as Mongolia.

The Sky Art *Tyrannosaurus rex* and her four juveniles are found by following a dirt road south 0.5 miles past the end of the pavement of Anzio Drive and then turning west and proceeding 0.3 miles. They are found on the north side of the road. The large thirteen-foot sculpture weighs about 1,000 pounds.

For more information regarding the entries above, see *Geology and Lore of Northern Anza-Borrego Desert Region* published by the South Coast Geological Society and the San Diego Association of Geologists.

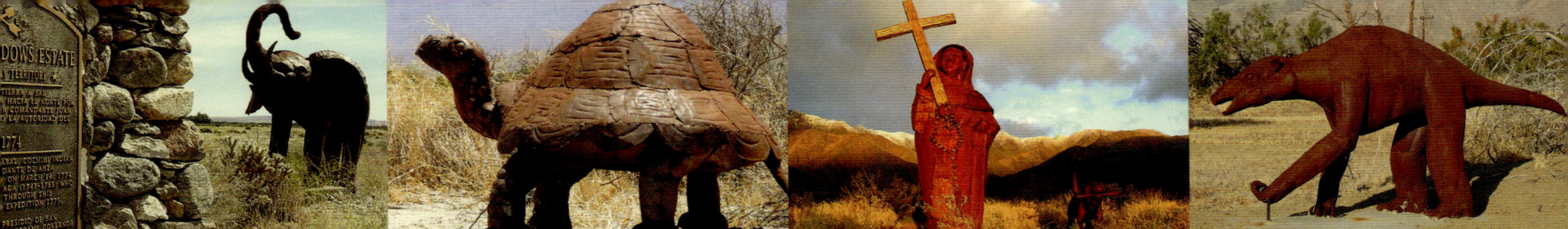

GALLETA MEADOWS SKY ART SITES

MAP LEGEND

FT Sky Art Inspired by *Fossil Treasures of the Anza-Borrego Desert*
HN Sky Art Inspired by the History and Nature of the Anza-Borrego Desert
WF Sky Art Inspired by Whim and Fantasy

FT-1: Peccary–*Platygonus* sp.
FT-2: Giant Tortoise–*Hesperotestudo* sp.
FT-3: Merriam's Tapir–*Tapirus merriami*
FT-4: Gracile Sabertooth Cat–*Smilodon gracilis*
FT-5: Giant Tortoise–*Hesperotestudo* sp.
FT-6: African Elephant–*Loxodonta africana*
FT-7: Camelids–(Llamas) *Hemiauchenia* sp. and (Camelops) *Camelops* sp.
FT-8: Harlan's Ground Sloth–*Paramylodon harlani* and (Camelops) *Camelops* sp.
FT-9: Shasta Ground Sloth–*Nothrotheriops shastensis*
FT-10: Gomphothere–*Gomphotherium* and (Camelops) *Camelops* sp.
FT-11: Gracile Sabertooth Cat–*Smilodon gracilis* and Extinct Horse–*Equus* sp.
FT-12: Incredible Wind God Bird–*Aiolornis incredibilis* in Its Nest
FT-13: Extinct Horse–*Equus* sp.
FT-14: Columbian Mammoth–*Mammuthus columbi*
FT-15: Incredible Wind God Bird–*Aiolornis incredibilis* with Prey –*Platygonus* sp.

HN-1: Peninsular Bighorn Sheep–*Ovis canadensis cremnobates* Gold Miner and His Mule
HN-2: Indian Head–Representing Sebastián Tarabal and/or Salvador Palma
HN-3: Spanish Padre–Representing Fr. Francisco Garcés and/or Fr. Pedro Font with an Arizona Sonoran Desert Saguaro
HN-4: 1946 Willys Jeep (CJ-3A)
HN-5: Farm Workers in Di Giorgio Fruit Corporation Grape Fields
HN-6: Capt. Juan Bautista de Anza on His Horse

WF-1: *Velociraptor*–Found in Mongolia
WF-2: Serpent–Pure Imagination
WF-3: *Spinosaurus*–Found in Egypt and Morocco
WF-4: *Carnotaurus*–Found in Argentina *Allosaurus*–Found in North America
WF-5: *Utahraptor*–Found in the United States
WF-6: *Tyrannosaurus rex*–Found in North America

ENLARGED AREA AT RIGHT

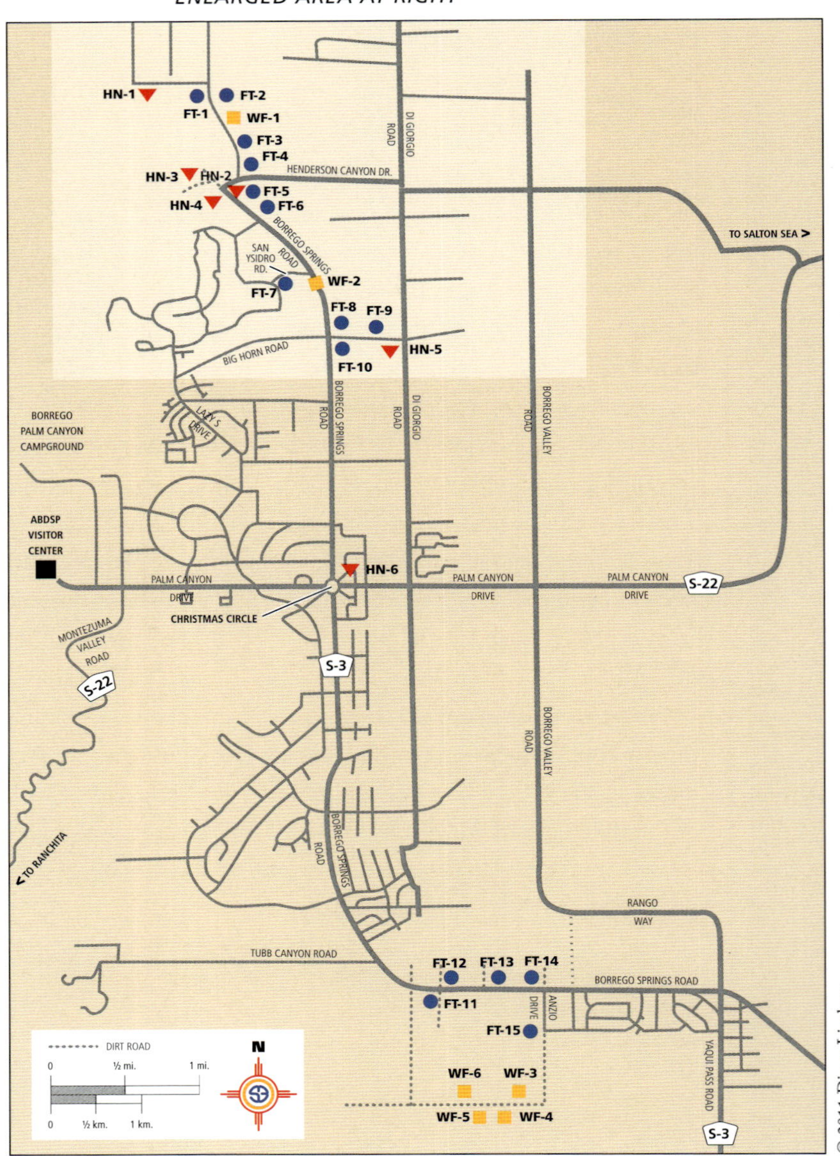

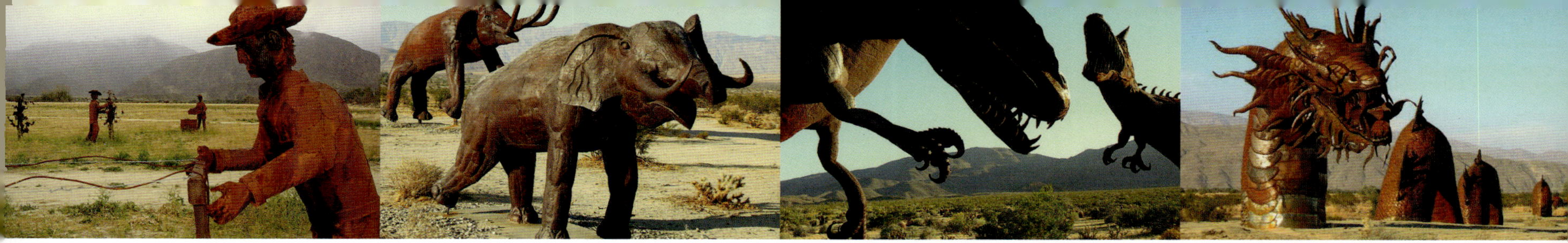

ENLARGED AREA

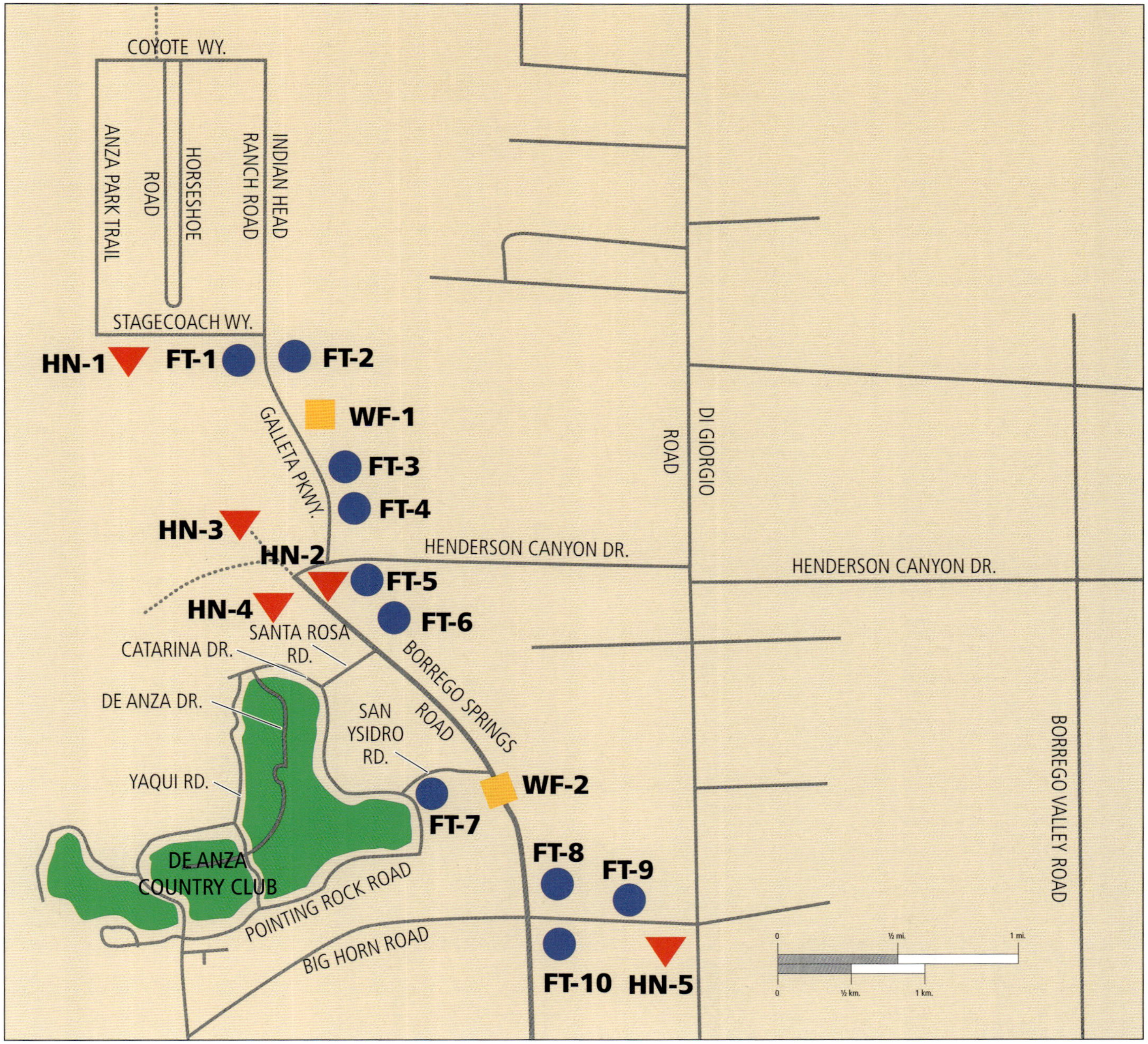

COYOTE WY.
ANZA PARK TRAIL
HORSESHOE ROAD
INDIAN HEAD RANCH ROAD
STAGECOACH WY.
HN-1
FT-1
FT-2
WF-1
GALLETA PKWY.
FT-3
FT-4
HN-3
HN-2
HENDERSON CANYON DR.
FT-5
HN-4
FT-6
SANTA ROSA RD.
CATARINA DR.
BORREGO SPRINGS ROAD
DE ANZA DR.
SAN YSIDRO RD.
YAQUI RD.
WF-2
FT-7
DE ANZA COUNTRY CLUB
POINTING ROCK ROAD
FT-8
FT-9
BIG HORN ROAD
FT-10
HN-5
DI GIORGIO ROAD
HENDERSON CANYON DR.
BORREGO VALLEY ROAD
0 ½ mi. 1 mi.
0 ½ km. 1 km.

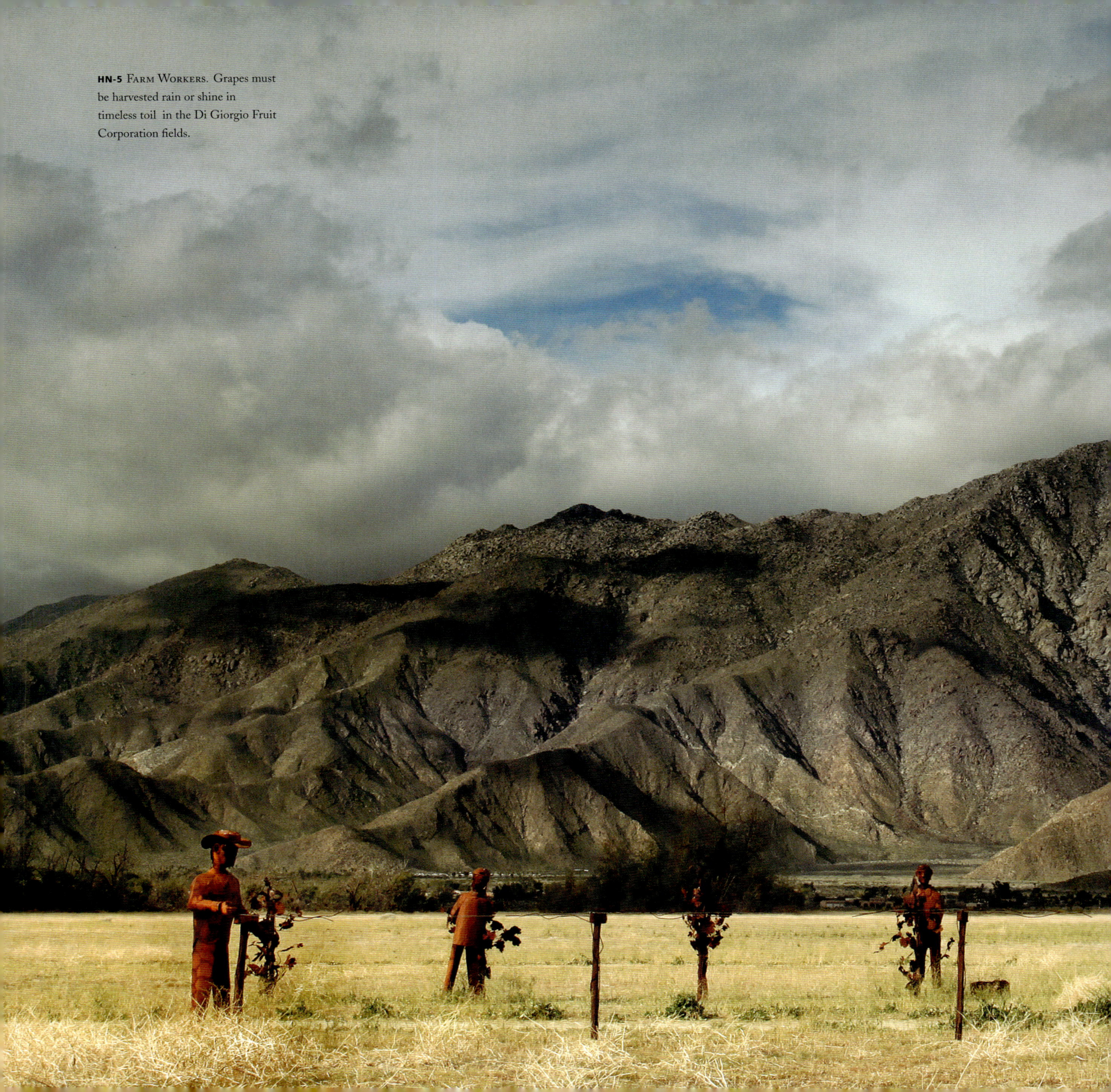

HN-5 Farm Workers. Grapes must be harvested rain or shine in timeless toil in the Di Giorgio Fruit Corporation fields.

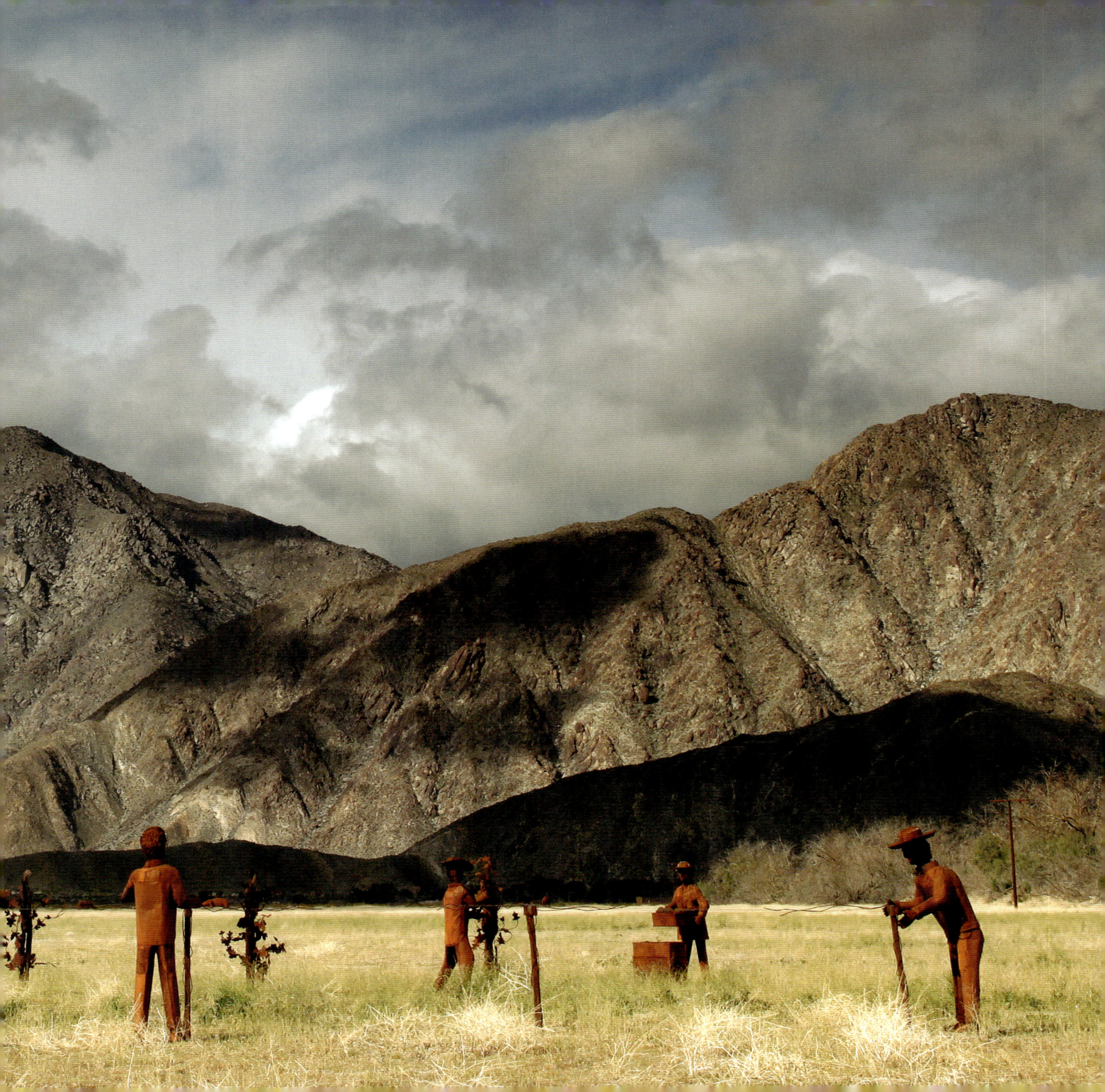

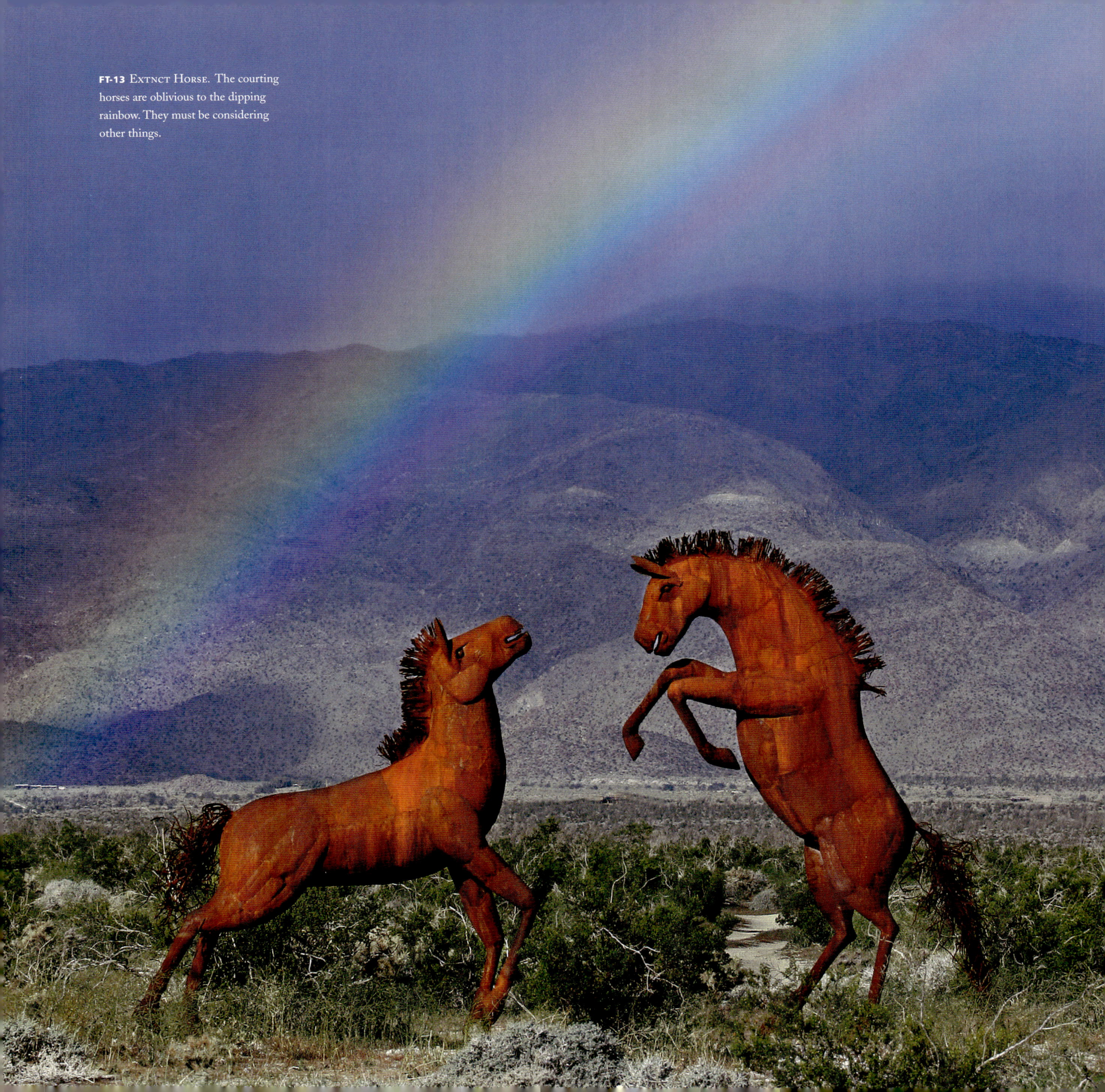

FT-13 Extnct Horse. The courting horses are oblivious to the dipping rainbow. They must be considering other things.

ACKNOWLEDGMENTS AND CREDITS

Like raising a child, a book takes a village of people to make it right. It is not just the author and the photographers.

I am grateful to the e-wizards who invented the Internet, Google Maps, and YouTube. These tools vastly simplified my research for towns where Ricardo grew up and helped me to frame much more specific questions for answers I needed.

I could not have been as systematic in my research had it not been for early strict training in research methodology under the distinguished historian Dr. David Weber who was my thesis chairman at San Diego State University and later the founding director of the William P. Clements Center for Southwest Studies at Southern Methodist University.

I would not have been able to tackle this challenge without the complete support of my lifetime colleague Lowell Lindsay and our staff at Sunbelt Publications who saw little of me during this time period.

This project would never have been launched were it not for Monte Murbach, then president of the South Coast Geological Society, who encouraged me to write a paper for a cooperative publication with the San Diego Association of Geologists in the fall of 2010. Their joint trip to the northern Anza-Borrego desert area included my paper analyzing Sky Art and how it was inspired by science, history, nature, and whim. A major portion of that work is found in the appendix of this book.

Barbara Nickerson, executive director of the Borrego Art Institute, was very helpful in providing information about the Fifth Annual Plein Air Invitational and in encouraging the board of the institute to include a day when artists could use the Sky Art sculptures as subjects for their paintings.

The Borrego Springs Chamber of Commerce, including their executive director, Linda Haddock, and president, Pat Havens, provided information regarding the impact that Ricardo's art has had in the community. Linda also graciously included me in the photo shoot for professional motorcycle stunt driver Robbie Maddison when he jumped over the gomphothere sculptures.

Martha Deichler, the principal of the Borrego Springs Elementary School, came to my rescue when I needed a group of children for photographs. I really appreciated the vanload of local students for an outing with Ricardo at the sculptures.

Gerald Gamble, assistant to Dr. Hannis L. Stoddard III, provided dates and information regarding the installation of Ricardo's sculptures at AVID MicroChip Company in Norco, while Dr. Stoddard gave us permission to use the AVID logo.

Paleontologist George T. Jefferson gave generously of his time and expertise to enhance and correct my presentation of the rich fossil record of the Anza-Borrego region. Colorado Desert District Paleontologist Lyndon K. Murray gave us permission to use illustrations by John Francis and Pat Ortega that originally appeared in *Fossil Treasures of the Anza-Borrego Desert*.

When I put out a call for photographs for this book, I had many willing responses. I am most grateful to Sam Webb, who made the extra effort to show up with camera in hand at special photo shoots such as Maddison's gomphothere jump and the Borrego Valley Elementary School outing. Sam's photo from that shoot graces the front cover of this book. Sam also did some Photoshop wizardry to improve some photos that needed work.

John Wilson provided photos from the Galleta Meadows website, and the Arroyo Breceda family provided other much-needed photographs. A complete list of contributors whose works appear in this book is listed below.

Multilingual Kaare Kjos accompanied me on my first trip to Perris Jurassic Park to assess how I could best work with Ricardo. Thanks also to Judy Botello for the excellent translation of La Opinión. That newspaper article was very valuable in piecing together the early history of Perris Jurassic Park.

The trip to Durango would not have been so successful had it not been for Ricardo's gracious family, who tolerated nonstop questions and demands for family photographs that they later entrusted to me. They also never complained when I got my camera out and just started shooting pictures of them informally.

Ricardo's Rosarito Beach crew endured hours of photographing them as they worked, and afterward, Porfirio and the crew answered all my questions when I knew they were tired and hungry. Thanks to them for accommodating me, as did Lianna when she gave me an afternoon of her time for a taped interview. Their candid responses to my questions were appreciated.

It is the editor who makes sure the author is really communicating with the reader. Thanks to Barbara Villaseñor and Myra Westphall of First Reads for cleaning up my words. Then it goes to the designer who receives all the parts and puts them together to make it a stunning book. Thanks to Barbara Balch for creating an eye-catching design. For overall management of this project, I am grateful to Debi Young who brings valuable years of publishing experience to Sunbelt.

I am humbled to have Victor Villaseñor write the foreword for this book. His books have done so much to help understand the challenge for a Mexican to be accepted in our society while retaining pride in his Mexican culture and heritage.

Most of all, I am indebted to Dennis Avery for having faith in my ability to pull all of this together in the specified time. It has been a true delight working with him to see the birth of this book.

And, above all else, it was a real pleasure working with Ricardo Breceda. He really is an artistic genius, and I love his twinkling eyes, his love of life, his family, and his mischievousness, even though it probably cost me a few gray hairs! *¡Gracias, amigo!*

—Diana Lindsay

PHOTO AND ILLUSTRATION CREDITS: Les Anderson, ii-iii; Thomas Antel, 33; Arroyo Breceda Family, 10 (left), 10 (right), 11 (right), 36 (left); Dennis Avery, 155 (right bottom); AVID, 137 (right); Don Barrie, iv-v; Germar Bernhard, 55 (right), 218 (middle column); Mike Bigelow, 149; Ricardo Breceda, 76 (left), 117 (top), 156; John Francis, 21 (right), 28 (left); Sayard Gaglio, 190 (botom); Linda Gilbert, 151 (right); Jim Goodrich, 63 (left); Maria Groschup-Black, 104-105, 121, 171; Mike Hart, 93; Paul Johnson, 60-61, 197, 230-231, 232; Jeanne Johnstone, 150 (left), 150 (right); Sandra Keeley, 151 (left); Deborah Knapp, 165, 166, 226 (left column); Sonja Lane, 69, 83, 96; Lowell Lindsay, 190 (right top); Dennis Mammana, 67; Lisa McNatt, 170; Joerg Mitter, 188-189, 190 (top right); Monte Murbach, 162 (left); Pat Ortega, 53 (right), 54 (left), 59 (right), 91 (right), 97 (right); Grace Rickard, 124-125, 138 (left), 141 (right), 191 (left top); Jim Rickard, 162 (right); John Ruddley, 242; Sunbelt Publications © 2006 California State Parks, 225 (middle column); Ward Thompson, 186-187; Laura Webb, 79, 81; Sam Webb, front cover (top), front cover (bottom), 16-17, 116, 154-155 (top), 175 (right), 208, 223 (right column top); John Wilson, 26, 48, 49, 50, 62, 94-95, 157, 207.

SELECTED BIBLIOGRAPHY

Books and Articles

Allen, Karie. 2003. "Dino might: Motorists are startled by a hobbyist's metal monsters along Interstate 215." *The Press Enterprise*, 24 November.

Borrego Sun. 2008–2011.

De Wyze, Jeannette. 2010. "Ricardo Loves Dinosaurs." *San Diego Reader*, 5 May. Accessed at http://www.sandiegoreader.com/news/2010/may/05/feature-ricardo-loves-dinosaurs/

Jefferson, George T. and Lowell Lindsay, eds. 2006. *Fossil Treasures of the Anza-Borrego Desert*. San Diego: Sunbelt Publications.

Jones, J. Harry. 2008. "Beauty and the beasts." *Sign on San Diego*, 26 April. Accessed at http://legacy.signonsandiego.com/news/northcounty/20080426-9999-1m26beasts.html

Lindsay, Diana. 1973. *Our Historic Desert: The Story of the Anza-Borrego Desert—The Largest State Park in the United States of America*. San Diego: Copley Books.

———. 2001. *Anza-Borrego A to Z: People, Places, and Things*. San Diego: Sunbelt Publications.

———. 2010. "Galleta Meadows Sky Art Inspired by Science, History, Nature, and Whim." In *Geology and Lore of Northern Anza-Borrego Desert Region*, eds. Charles E. Houser and Monte L. Murbach, 114-136. San Diego: San Diego Association of Geologists.

McKinnon, Julissa. 2008. "Perris sculptor populates Anza-Borrego 'creature desert' with dinosaurs, extinct mammals, more." *The Press Enterprise*, 30 June. Accessed at http://www.pe.com/localnews/rivcounty/stories/PE_News_Local_S_dinosaur30.4310b60.html

Monita, Ashlyn. 2010. "A Marvelous Metal Zoo Resurrects Prehistoric Desert Creatures in Anza- Borrego." *Borderzine*, 25 May. Accessed at http://borderzine.com/2010/05

Morales, Miguel Angel. 2003. "Perris Jurassic Park." *La Opinión*, 1 December.

Interviews and Correspondence

Arroyo, Lianna. 2011. Recorded interview, 22 February.

Arroyo Breceda family. 2011. Recorded interviews in Durango, Mexico, 27–29 March.

Arroyo Breceda, Ricardo. 2011. Recorded interviews, January–April.

Avery, Dennis. 2008–2011. E-mail correspondence with the author.

Gamble, Gerald. 2011. Recorded interview, 23 March.

Havens, Pat. 2011. E-mail correspondence with the author, 5 April.

Nickerson, Barbara. 2011. E-mail correspondence with the author, 15 April.

Sandoval Sanchez, "Porfirio" Edgar Omar. 2011. Recorded interview, 7 April.

Websites

www.borregoartinstitute.org

www.borregospringschamber.com

www.galletameadows.com

www.perrisjurassicpark.com

www.ricardobreceda.com

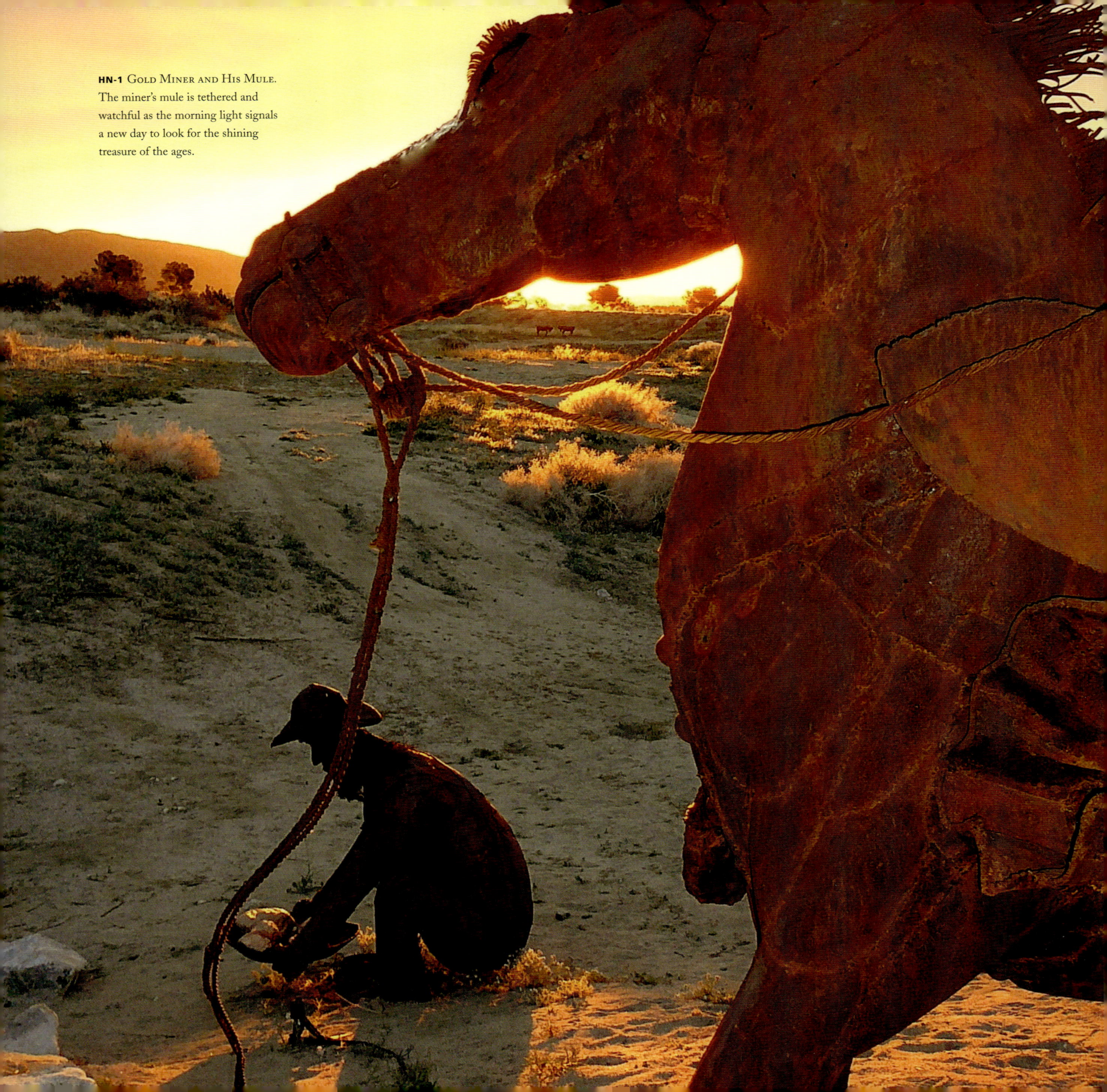

HN-1 Gold Miner and His Mule. The miner's mule is tethered and watchful as the morning light signals a new day to look for the shining treasure of the ages.

INDEX

Note: **Bold page references** indicate photographs or illustrations.

A

B

A NOTE ABOUT THE FRONT COVER: Photographer Sam Webb ties the past to the present with these two photos. The top photograph shows the ancestral lands where elephant-like gomphotheres once roamed through these lands millions of years ago. Their fossil remains were discovered by paleontologists in the badlands where the Santa Rosa Mountains merge into the desert floor. The bottom photograph captures artist Ricardo Breceda telling first-grade students how he made the gomphotheres. Ricardo is speaking in Spanish to students enrolled in a Dual Language Program at Borrego Springs Elementary School. This very progressive and research-based Dual Language Program for kindergarten through fifth-grade students partners both English speaking and English language learners in classes. By the fifth grade, these students are bilingual and biliterate in English and Spanish.

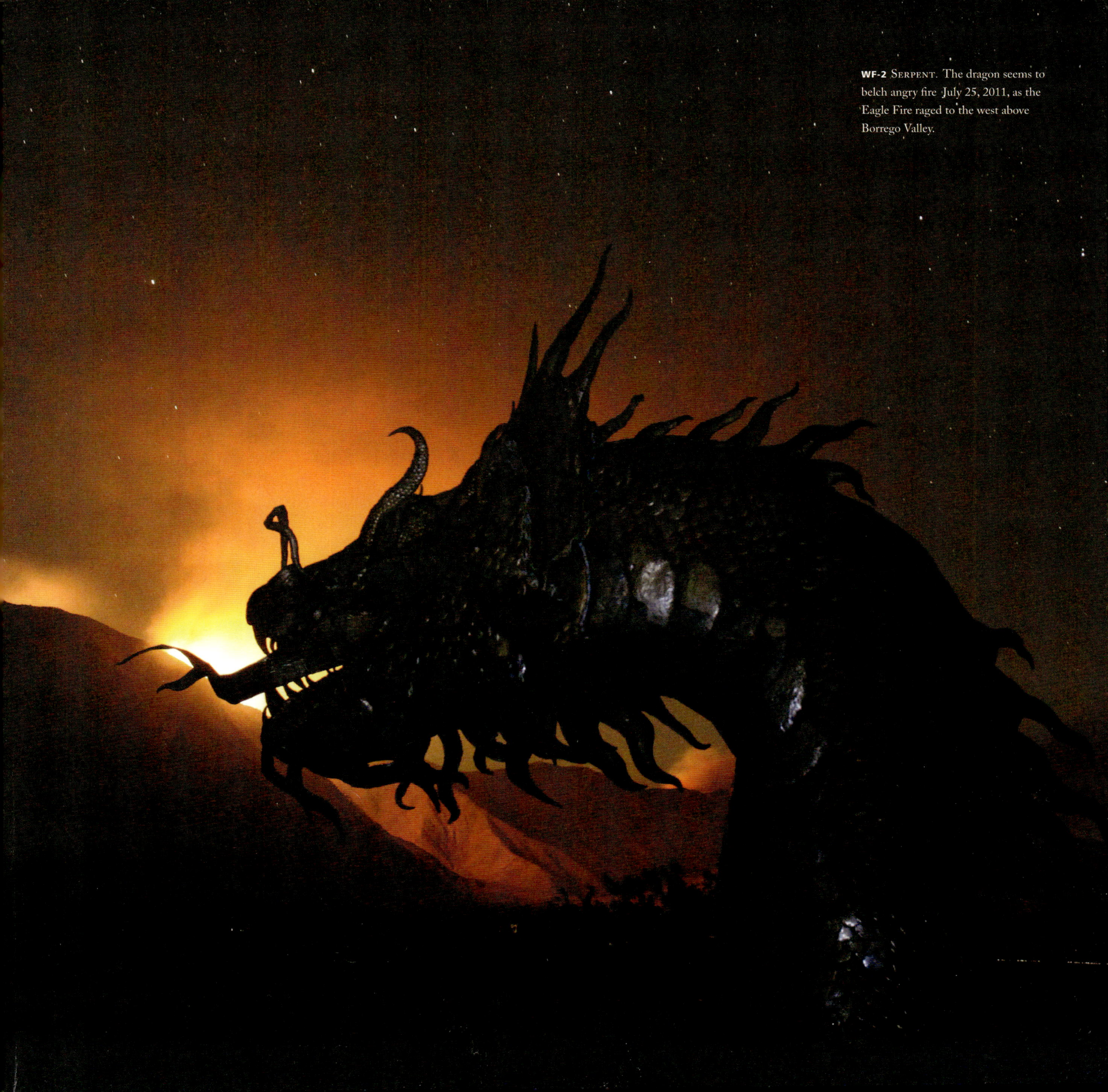

WF-2 Serpent. The dragon seems to belch angry fire July 25, 2011, as the Eagle Fire raged to the west above Borrego Valley.

SUNBELT'S DESERT BOOKSHELF

Anza-Borrego: A Photographic Journey
Ernie Cowan
This coffee table book exhibits striking full-color photography of Anza-Borrego Desert State Park, featuring ecosystems from mile-high mountains to sea level in this largest state park in the contiguous United States.

Anza-Borrego A to Z: People, Places, and Things
Diana Lindsay
An encyclopedic reference to the history and place names of the region, this is a companion to *The Anza-Borrego Desert Region*. Includes listings on famed Spanish explorers such as Fages, Anza, Portolá, and Serra.

Anza-Borrego Desert Region (Wilderness Press)
Diana Lindsay, Lowell Lindsay
A complete guide to the Anza-Borrego area including the state park, surrounding BLM lands, Ocotillo Wells State Vehicular Recreation Area, and other nearby open spaces. Map included.

Cave Paintings of Baja California: Discovering the Great Murals of an Unknown People
Harry W. Crosby
This full-color account of the great murals of a forgotten people depicts the author's discovery and documentation of a world-class archaeological region in remote central Baja California.

Fossil Treasures of the Anza-Borrego Desert
George T. Jefferson, Lowell Lindsay, Eds.
A richly illustrated volume by 23 leading scientists and specialists that reveals North America's most continuous fossil record for the last 7 million years. Includes camels, giant sloths, mammoths, and sabertooth cats.

Geology and Lore of the Anza-Borrego Region (SDAG)
Monte L. Murbach, Charles E. Houser, Eds.
A wide-ranging earth science tour including the self-guiding roadlog from the 2010 SCGS-SDAG joint field trip. Topics range from mines, history, groundwater, and faulting, to the "Sky Art" of Borrego Valley.

Geology of Anza-Borrego: Edge of Creation
Paul Remeika, Lowell Lindsay
This non-technical guide introduces the Southern California desert enthusiast to one of the most active geologic and seismic regions in North America. Eight field trips journey through deep time in the desert.

Marshal South and the Ghost Mountain Chronicles
Diana Lindsay, Ed.
A complete collection of Marshal South's *Desert Magazine* articles that chronicle his family's controversial primitive lifestyle on Ghost Mountain. Includes never-before-published photos of the family.

Palm Springs Oasis: A Photographic Essay
Greg Lawson
An elegant display of beautiful Palm Springs and the Coachella Valley with breathtaking sights of enchanting, spring-fed canyons and brilliant desert flowers. Text is in English, Spanish, French, and German.

Ricardo Breceda: Accidental Artist
Diana Lindsay
The story of Ricardo Breceda, the unlikely metal sculptor dubbed "Picasso of Steel." A detailed map plots each sculpture in Borrego Valley where over 120 of his creations decorate the landscape. Full-color photos throughout.

Spanish Lingo for the Savvy Gringo
Elizabeth Reid
Focusing on the Spanish that is spoken in Mexico, and most frequently in the United States, this book teaches the language and provides insights into Mexican culture and its customs.